The Theological Interpretation of Scripture

BLACKWELL
READINGS IN
MODERN
THEOLOGY

General Editors: L. Gregory Jones and James J. Buckley
Duke University, North Carolina; Loyola College, Maryland

Blackwell Readings in Modern Theology is a series of constructive anthologies on important topics in modern theology. Each volume brings together both classic and newly commissioned essays on a particular theme. These essays will provide students and teachers in colleges, universities, and seminaries with a critical entry to key debates.

For a full contents listing or for more information visit our web site at http://www.blackwellpublishing.com/religion

Published works

The Theological Interpretation of Scripture
Classic and Contemporary Readings
Edited by Stephen E. Fowl

The Postmodern God
A Theological Reader
Edited by Graham Ward

Inquiring After God
Classic and Contemporary Readings
Edited by Ellen T. Charry

Theology After Liberalism
A Reader
Edited by John Webster and George Schner

Theology and Sexuality
Classic and Contemporary Readings
Edited by Eugene F. Rogers, Jr.

_The

THEOLOGICAL INTERPRETATION OF SCRIPTURE

CLASSIC AND CONTEMPORARY READINGS

Edited by

Stephen
E. Fowl

Loyola College, Maryland

Blackwell
Publishing

© 1997 by Blackwell Publishing Ltd

350 Main Street, Malden, MA 02148-5020, USA
108 Cowley Road, Oxford OX4 1JF, UK
550 Swanston Street, Carlton, Victoria 3053, Australia

First published 1997
Reprinted 1997, 1998, 2000, 2001, 2003, 2005

Tranferred to digital print 2007

Library of Congress Cataloging-in-Publication Data

The theological interpretation of Scripture: classic and contemporary
readings / edited by Stephen E. Fowl
    p. cm.
Blackwell readings in modern theology
Includes bibliographical references and index.
ISBN 1-55786-834-4 (hbk: alk. paper) — ISBN 1-55786-835-2 (pbk: alk. paper)
1. Bible—Theology. I. Fowl, Stephen E.
BS543.T48   1997
203—dc21   96-19722
                                                    CIP

A catalogue record for this title is available from the British Library.

Set in 10.5 on 12 pt Ehrhardt
by Ace Filmsetting Ltd, Frome, Somerset

For further information on
Blackwell Publishing, visit our website:
http://www.blackwellpublishing.com

Contents

Acknowledgements

A reader such as this one obviously combines the work of a great many people. The most obvious are those who agreed to contribute their work to this volume. I am particularly grateful to them and especially pleased to present their work here. Several people, who for various reasons were not able to contribute essays to this volume, did offer valuable advice along the way. Mark Brett and Luke Johnson in particular offered helpful pieces of advice at particularly crucial times. Alison Mudditt at Blackwell Publishers has done a great deal of hard work in moving this volume from an idea to a book. My friends and colleagues Greg Jones and Jim Buckley have worked closely with me throughout the various stages in the life of this volume. I am especially thankful for their willingness to co-mingle the pleasures of friendship with the rigors of hard work.

This volume is dedicated to Brendan and Liam, who never cease to remind me that there is more to life than interpretation.

Stephen E. Fowl
Easter 1996

The authors and publishers gratefully acknowledge the following for permission to reproduce copyright material:

Selections from Henri de Lubac's *The Sources of Revelation* trans. J. O'Neill (New York: Herder and Herder, 1968). Used by permission.
David C. Steinmetz, "The Superiority of the Pre-Critical Exegesis," *Theology*

Today, vol. 37, no. 1 (1980), pp. 27–38. © Theology Today. Used by permission.

George Lindbeck, "The Story-Shaped Church," reprinted from *Scriptural Authority and Narrative Interpretation*, edited by Garrett Green, copyright 1987 Fortress Press. Used by permission of Augsburg Fortress.

Claudia V. Camp, "Feminist Theological Hermeneutics: Canon and Christian Identity," pp. 154–71, from *Searching the Scriptures, Volume One: A Feminist Introduction*, edited by Elizabeth Schüssler Fiorenza. Used by permission of the Crossroad Publishing Company, New York.

Vincent Wimbush, "The Bible and African Americans" is reprinted by permission from *Stony the Road We Trod* edited by Cain Hope Felder, copyright © 1991 Augsburg Fortress.

David Yeago, "The New Testament and Nicene Dogma" is a revision of an essay published under the same title in *Pro Ecclesia* 3:2 (1993), pp. 152–64. Used by permission.

Tod Linafelt, "Speech and Silence in the Servant Passages: Towards a Final Form Reading of the Book of Isaiah," *Koinonia* 2, 1993, pp. 174–90, reproduced with permission of the author.

Selections from David J. A. Clines, *I, He, We, They* (Sheffield: JSOT Press, 1976) used by permission of Sheffield Academic Press.

Luther's Works, Volume 21: Commentary on the Sermon on the Mount; copyright Concordia Publishing House. Used by permission.

Selections from *The Cost of Discipleship*, 2nd edition by Dietrich Bonhoeffer, translated from the German by R. H. Fuller with some revision by Irmagard Booth. Copyright 1959 by SCM Press Ltd. Reprinted with permission of Simon & Schuster.

Richard Lischer, "The Sermon on the Mount as Radical Pastoral Care" *Interpretation* 41 (April 1987), pp. 157–69. Used by permission.

Selections from *Augustine on the Romans: Propositions from the Epistle to the Romans*, trans. Paula Fredriksen Landes, Society of Biblical Literature Texts and Translations 23, Scholars Press, 1982.

Selections from *Augustine: Earlier Writings*, trans. John Burleigh (Library of Christian Classics). Used by permission of Westminster/John Knox Press.

Paul W. Meyer, "Romans 10:4 and the End of the Law" in *The Divine Helmsman*, edited by J. Crenshaw and S. Sandmel, KATAV Publishing House, pp. 59–78. Used by permission.

The publishers apologize for any errors or omissions in the above list and would be grateful to be notified of any corrections that should be incorporated in the next edition or reprint of this book.

List of Contributors

Stephen Fowl
Associate Professor of Theology, Loyola College in Maryland

Henri de Lubac, S. J. (1896–1991)
French Jesuit theologian

David C. Steinmetz
Professor of Church History, The Divinity School, Duke University

George Lindbeck
Pitkin Professor of Historical Theology (emeritus), Yale University

Claudia V. Camp
Associate Professor of Old Testament, Texas Christian University

Vincent L. Wimbush
Professor of New Testament and Christian Origins, Union Theological
Seminary in New York

David S. Yeago
Michael C. Peeler Associate Professor of Systematic Theology, Lutheran
Theological Southern Seminary

Joseph W. Trigg
Rector, Christ Church, Port Tobacco Parish, La Plata, Maryland

Corrine Patton
Assistant Professor of Theology, University of St Thomas

Terence C. Fretheim
Professor of Old Testament, Luther Northwestern Theological Seminary

Walter Brueggeman
Professor of Old Testament, Columbia Theological Seminary

Angela Russell Christman
Assistant Professor of Theology, Loyola College in Maryland

Kathryn Greene-McCreight
Visiting Lecturer, Yale College

Tod Linafelt
Assistant Professor of Biblical Studies, Georgetown University

David J. A. Clines
Professor of Biblical Studies, University of Sheffield

Beverly J. Stratton
Associate Professor of Religion, Augsburg College

Robin Darling Young
Associate Professor of Theology, The Catholic University of America

Mark S. Burrows
Associate Professor of Church History, Andover Newton Theological School

Brian K. Blount
Assistant Professor of New Testament, Princeton Theological Seminary

Dietrich Bonhoeffer (1906-45)
Theologian, Pastor in the Confessing Church in Germany, Martyr

Richard Lischer
Professor of Homiletics, The Divinity School, Duke University

Peter Gorday
Staff Counselor, Georgia Association for Pastoral Care

Eugene F. Rogers Jr.
Assistant Professor of Religion, University of Virginia

Paul W. Meyer
Helen H. P. Manson Professor of New Testament Literature and Exegesis
(emeritus), Princeton Theological Seminary

E. Elizabeth Johnson
Associate Professor of New Testament, New Brunswick Theological Seminary

Neil Elliott
Associate Professor of Theology, The College of St Katherine

Introduction

Stephen Fowl

I have tried to take seriously the notion that this volume is to be a reader. By that I understand that the chief aim of this volume is to provide a sampling of work in a particular area. In providing such a sampling I have a variety of aims. First I want to introduce students to a set of issues and concerns that, in part, comprise a specific field of inquiry. In addition, by providing concrete examples of a particular set of intellectual and theological practices I hope to engage students in such a way that they might begin to learn how to perform these practices themselves. Further, such a sampler needs to try to strike a balance between representing the vast diversity of views on this subject in a way that paralyzes a student on the one hand, and being so selective in what one presents as to give a false picture of unity on the other. With this in mind, this reader will introduce some of the important issues and debates about how and in what way theological concerns might be brought to bear on the interpretation of scripture. There seem to be an increasing openness and interest among some theologians and some biblical scholars in bridging the chasms that often separate the two disciplines. I hope this reader can provide some material for that bridge. Moreover, like those readers our teachers used when we were first learning how to read, I hope that this reader will provide a basic building block for those English-speaking students who are starting out on the process of learning how to bring theological concerns to bear on the interpretation of scripture.

Even with these concerns in place, there still seem to be several possible ways to organize a reader in the theological interpretation of scripture. It is not exactly clear what theological interpretation of scripture is or ought to be. There are a variety of ways of construing the subject matter of this reader and I cannot claim that mine is the only way to do this. Indeed, the authors of the various components of this volume might disagree sharply with my proposals. Nevertheless, in both commissioning and selecting pieces for this reader I have tried to allow for a fairly expansive definition of "theological interpretation." Hence, the selections in this reader will not all conform to a single account of what theological interpretation of scripture is or ought to be. In this introduction I would like to give a slightly fuller account of what I take such an interpretation to be.[1] I will explain how the selections presented here contribute to a fuller account of theological interpretation. Along the way I will also comment on some things that are not in this reader and why I left them out.

In brief, I take the theological interpretation of scripture to be that practice whereby theological concerns and interests inform and are informed by a reading of scripture. In this respect, throughout Christian history it has been the norm for Christians to read their scripture theologically. That is, Christians have generally read their scripture to guide, correct, and edify their faith, worship, and practice as part of their ongoing struggle to live faithfully before the triune God. Indeed, until relatively recently it would have been unusual to suggest that scripture might be read for other purposes.

I do not mean to say that there was ever a time when there was only one way of interpreting the Bible. Christians developed a wide range of interpreative techniques in their attempts to read scripture theologically. In addition, people usually recognized rough and ready distinctions between various theological tasks. For example, Thomas Aquinas as well as his contemporaries would have recognized that in writing his commentary on John's Gospel he was engaged in a different sort of task than his *Summa Theologiae*. Thomas and his contemporaries, however, would have been puzzled by the notion that in writing one he was acting as a biblical scholar and in writing the other he was working as a systematic theologian. These tasks, however, were all seen as part of a more or less unified theological program of articulating, shaping and embodying convictions about God, humanity, and the world.

With the rise of modernity, however, it is possible to detect a whole new range of interests which in effect, if not in intent, helped to fragment this theological program within which scriptural interpretation had clear, if multivalent, roles. First, a variety of critical questions and practices which came to be known as "historical criticism" began to dominate scholarly study of the Bible. One of the long-term results of historical critical methods of reading was to separate the practice of reading the Bible in a manner geared toward historical reconstruction from the practice of developing a theologically significant reading.[2] By the time it came to dominate scholarly biblical study in America, historical criticism had largely become separated from the theological ends it was initially meant to serve.[3] While most biblical scholars of both Testaments still continue to identify themselves as Christians, they generally are required to check their theological convictions at the door when they enter the profession of biblical studies.[4]

Second, theology itself as an academic discipline has tended to fragment into a variety of discrete activities. These activities are largely carried out in isolation from one another and often for very different ends. As a result, the work of professional biblical scholars is often seen by professional theologians as both too technical and irrelevant for their own interests. Further, professional biblical scholars tend to find the interests of, for example, systematic theologians abstract and ill-suited to their professional interests in the Bible.

Another, often overlooked, factor underwriting the separations between biblical study and theology has been the professionalization of both disciplines within the structure of the modern university.[5] To be counted as a professional within each field, one has to master such a diverse body of knowledge particular to each field that it is rare to find a scholar in one of these fields whose work is read and used by those in the other. This professionalization even influences seminaries and small liberal arts colleges insofar as they draw their faculties from graduate programs at research universities. Further, such faculties often have professional allegiances to scholarly societies whose interests and agendas are largely shaped by the concerns of the university.

Professionalization has had several important effects that are reflected more or less directly in the way the Bible is taught and read. First, it institutionalized the separation between biblical study and theology. Because there is a strong temptation in most universities to treat the work of professional scholars as commodities that can be exchanged for various professional rewards (e.g. tenure, promotion, and the like), there is little incentive to take the time needed to engage seriously with the work of those outside one's own field. In fact the commodification of scholarship works to specialize and fragment disciplines rather than to encourage the breaking down of disciplinary boundaries.[6]

This even tends to happen in institutions like seminaries. Although seminaries should have a clear interest in overcoming divisions like those between professional biblical study and theology, their faculties are, by and large, trained in research universities, where disciplinary divisions are strictly maintained if not jealously guarded. This leaves many seminary faculties ill-equipped to overcome the fragmentation within their own disciplines much less across the theological disciplines as a whole.

Despite the fragmenting processes of modernity, it is not the case that theological interpretation of scripture ever ceased. Christians have always had to read scripture theologically. The Church's identity and mission have always depended on Chrstians' abilities to interpret scripture theologically, to engage in debate over both how to interpret scripture and how to embody such interpretations in specific contexts, and to form members of the body of Christ to be wise readers of scripture. What does seem to be the case is that over the past 250 years the aims and desires which shape and are shaped by theological interpretation of scripture became increasingly irrelevant to professional biblical scholars. At least within an American context, as historical criticism came to dominate professional biblical scholarship within universities that were at the same time self-consciously loosening their ties to various denominations and churches, theological interpretation of scripture became increasingly marginalized.[7] Of course, in almost equal measure, Christians within most congregations have little connection with, access to, or interest in the work of biblical scholars and theologians.

To the extent that theological concerns became marginal to scriptural interpretation in Germany, this phenomenon can be read more as an ironic, unintended consequence of a variety of social, theological, philosophical, and political factors. Because the factors shaping the German scene are very different from those at work in America and because one needs a great deal of time and expertise to work oneself into this discussion, I am not including any representatives of German-speaking biblical scholarship. There are, however, several very good volumes in English to which students might turn to begin to work themselves into this discussion.[8]

While the fragmenting pressures of professionalization continue within most universities, over the past 15 to 20 years, historical critical ways of reading the Bible have come under increasing attack from a variety of scholarly circles. It is impossible to characterize the diffuse types and aims of these attacks as a single movement. There is, however, a growing dissatisfaction with both historical criticism's interests and its results. This in many ways mirrors a more general dissatisfaction with the various intellectual projects which came to characterize modernity.[9] For the purposes of this volume there seems little point in trumpeting the total eclipse of either historical criticism or modernity more generally. I have no particular interest in predicting the future for historical criticism. My point is simply that this disatisfaction with historical critical ways of reading has opened spaces in which different critical approaches are being brought to bear on the biblical texts. It is clearly the case that the interpretative interests and aims of biblical scholars have become irreducibly pluralistic. Further, the disciplinary boundaries that characterized the modern university are (at least in theory) much more permeable than even a generation ago. In another context, it would be interesting to argue about the shape of this pluralism and its consequences for professional biblical scholars.[10] Here, however, I simply want to point out some of the ways a notion of theological interpretation of scripture might fit into the current state of biblical studies.

The fissures appearing in the various intellectual projects of modernity and the appearance of non-modern alternatives allow me to point out a distinction between the discipline of biblical theology and the type of theological interpretation I am trying to introduce here. Biblical theology in its strictest sense is a discipline that is most comfortable within the structures of the modern university. Indeed, if one takes J. P. Gabler's inaugural address in 1787 at the University of Altdorf, "On the Proper Distinction between Biblical and Dogmatic Theology and the Specific Objectives of Each,"[11] as the formal beginning of biblical theology, then one of the earliest aims of this movement was to secure for itself a place as a discipline within the modern university, a discipline which would interact with other newly disciplined modes of inquiry (particularly philosophy and theology), but one which would also have its own particular integrity.[12] Hence, biblical theology was "born" in the process of the disciplinary fragmentation that theological interpretation wants to resist. The effects of this desire for disciplinary integrity have led to two sorts of emphases in works of biblical theology.[13] On the one hand, those who followed Gabler tend to produce readings of the Bible that are decisively shaped (if not driven) by strong commitments to particular philosophical systems.[14] On the other, and more commonly, those who followed Wilhelm Wrede (who considered his own project to be a more consistent working out of Gabler's proposals) and the History of Religions School tend to see biblical theology as a historical report on the religion of the Israelites or the first Christians.[15] Clearly, there are many people producing work that goes under the title biblical theology who do not fit these patterns. Further, in making this distinction between biblical theology and theological interpretation I do not mean to disparage any particular work of biblical theology. There is and will continue to be much that any biblical interpreter can learn from works that situate themselves within this disicpline. Nevertheless, biblical theology is, in large part, a child of modernity and subject to the limits modernity attempted to set on intellectual activity more generally and theology in particular.[16]

Unlike biblical theology, theological interpretation of scripture will be nonmodern in several respects. First, it will be interested in premodern biblical interpretation. Second, it will shape and be shaped by the concerns of Christian communities seeking to live faithfully before the triune God rather than by the concerns of a discipline whose primary allegiance is to the academy. Third, theological interpretation of scripture will try to reject and resist the fragmentation of theology into a set of discrete disciplines that was the result of the conceptual aims of modernity and the practical result of professionalization. Finally, theological interpretation of scripture will be pluralistic in its interpretative methods; it will even use the interpretative methods of modernity to its own ends.

The Importance of Premodern Biblical Interpretation

With a few notable exceptions, modern biblical scholars have paid little attention to premodern biblical interpretation.[17] Such work was within the purview of historical theology. To the extent biblical scholars addressed premodern interpretation at all, it was generally to treat it as a form of error, as a series of failed attempts to uncover the meaning of the biblical text.

Currently, however, a great number of biblical scholars have abandoned, or at least loosened, their commitment to the notion that texts have unitary meanings, a meaning uncovered by the proper application of the methods of historical criticism. The pluralism characteristic of contemporary biblical scholarship reflects this view that texts, biblical texts included, should not be viewed as containers into which a single, stable meaning has been poured (usually by the author) and which can be extracted by means of the appropriate method. It is the case, however, that while the profession of biblical scholarship is *de facto* pluralistic, many individual biblical scholars are not. To the extent that individual biblical scholars have recognized methodological pluralism, they have been relatively slow to recognize that the theoretical arguments which underwrite interpretative pluralism also undermine the arguments against seriously attending to pre-modern biblical interpretation. One cannot treat premodern biblical interpretation as a failed attempt to uncover the single meaning of a biblical text if one has already abandoned the modern quest for a single, eternally stable meaning. This is not to say that all premodern exegesis is equally worthy of attention. Further, one need not excuse, for example, the heavily anti-Jewish elements that pervade certain premodern interpretations. Such interpretations and the practices they underwrote must always be criticised.

For the purposes of theological interpretation, there are other important reasons for attending to premodern interpretation. First, contemporary Christians should not presume that they are the first to struggle to read scripture in order to live faithfully before the triune God. Rather, Christians must see themselves as part of an ongoing tradition extending down to the present. This is at least in part what is entailed when Christians regularly confess their belief in the communion of saints and the catholicity of the Church. This should not lead Christians to simply repeat the results of premodern interpreters.[18] Rather, premodern scriptural interpretation should be seen as a conversation partner providing insights and resources for reading scripture theologically in the present.[19]

In addition, premodern exegetes would not have acknowledged the disciplinary fragmentation of theology which has come to be characteristic of modernity. They would have seen their scriptural interpretation as an integral part of their overall theological work. If contemporary theological interpretation of scripture depends on resisting the disciplinary fragmentation of modernity, the practices of premodern interpreters may help show a way forward.[20]

For these reasons I have included two pieces which argue that contemporary interpreters should pay attention to premodern interpretation. "The Superiority of Pre-Critical Exegesis," by David Steinmetz is relatively well known. The central thrust of this essay is that the medieval theory of levels of meaning was able both to generate and accommodate a (not unlimited) plurality of meanings in a manner that is far superior to modern biblical scholarship's devotion to a single, stable meaning. The other selection comes from Henri de Lubac, S. J. While many Protestant biblical scholars may be unfamiliar with de Lubac's work, he is arguably the twentieth century's most important commentator on premodern biblical interpretation. Lamentably, little of his work in this area is translated into English. In regard to the theological interpretation of scripture, the most significant of de Lubac's works (he wrote more than 40 books) are *Histoire et Esprit* (1950), which is a study of Origen's exegesis, and the four-volume *Exégèse Médiévale* (1959–64). De Lubac was also a co-editor of *Sources chrétiennes*, which provided critical editions and translations of patristic texts.[21] The piece which is reprinted here is from an English translation of the final chapter of *Histoire et Esprit*.[22] I have decided to focus on de Lubac's account of "spiritual understanding." It is probably this aspect of premodern biblical interpretation that seems most fanciful and mystifying to modern critical sensibilities. What de Lubac's account of "spiritual understanding" is able to do is to situate it within a larger theological framework so that spiritual understanding comes to be seen as the practice of reading scripture in ways that transform one's life as part of an ongoing process of conversion.[23]

In addition to these two secondary accounts of premodern interpretation I have included selections from a variety of premodern interpreters in the sections of this reader that address specific biblical texts. Each of the texts discussed – Exodus 3; Isaiah 52–53; Matthew 5–7; Romans 9–11 includes selections from patristic commentators as well as selections from medieval/ reformation commentators. The inclusion of these texts shows both the continuities and discontinuities between premodern and contemporary approaches to theological interpretation. Further, these texts provide exemplars from the past that might aid in teaching students how one might (and might not) interpret scripture theologically. I will say more about the content of each of these selections in due course.

The Importance of Context

By defining a theological interpretation of scripture as a reading aimed at shaping and being shaped by a community's faith and practice, I have at the same time indicated a location where such reading will be most at home. That is, theological interpretation of scripture will take place primarily within the context of the church and synagogue, those communities that seek to order their common life in accord with their interpretation of scripture.

This is not to deny the obvious fact that many professional biblical scholars are also believing Christians and Jews. Neither is it a claim that the church or synagogue should have nothing to do with the academy. Rather, it is the case that the concerns of a theological reading of scripture presuppose a setting within Christian or Jewish communities. This setting provides both the direction for theological interpretations and the standards against which such readings can be judged. This means that a whole range of factors and considerations will come into play in evaluating theological interpretations of scripture that do not normally constitute part of the discourse of professional biblical studies. These factors have to do with how the church or synagogue is guided by its reading of scripture and how the political constitution of these communities can shape their reading of scripture. There are a variety of essays which address these issues.[24] In this volume I have included an essay by George Lindbeck, "The Story-Shaped Church: Critical Exegesis and Theological Interpretation." This essay was originally part of the *Festschrift* for Hans Frei, hence comments about Frei's work frame both the beginning and ending of the essay. Lindbeck aims to bring historical–critical concerns and premodern ways of reading scripture into a conversation that will shape and be shaped by ecclesiology. "Both historical criticism and classical narrational interpretation are piecemeal procedures, and the revisionary force of combining them varies from topic to topic. Thus all that this essay claims is that in some areas, of which ecclesiology is one, a renewed focus on narrative meanings, together with critical awareness of how they functioned, provides scriptural authorization (but not directives) for major changes in theological interpretations" (see chapter 3, p. 40).

Within the guild of professional biblical critics one of the most important results of current dissatisfaction with the dominant practices of historical criticism is the recognition that all interpretation, biblical or otherwise, comes out of a particular context. In America this concern with context is most clearly represented in the work of feminist and African–American biblical scholars. It would be a mistake, however, to assume that all feminist scholars or all African–American scholars share a similar set of concerns. Moreover, these concerns have been well represented in a variety of recently published volumes to which a student should turn to get a more detailed picture of the current state of scholarship.[25] To present a sampling of this work I have included an essay by Claudia Camp, "Feminist Theological Hermeneutics: Canon and Christian Identity," and one by Vincent Wimbush, "The Bible and African Americans: An Outline of an Interpretative History."

As Claudia Camp's essay indicates, one of the crucial issues for feminist theological interpretation of scripture is the notion of authority in all of its guises. In the course of her essay she is able to chart and organize a variety of feminist responses to questions of authority. This makes her contribution particularly helpful for beginning students who wish to organize their own thinking and future reading on this subject. African-American biblical interpreters draw on a long and rich tradition of interpretative practices shaped by the Black Church. Vincent Wimbush's essay provides an outline of his attempt to "relate and then interpret that history [of African Americans] through attention to the various ways in which the Bible has been engaged by African Americans" (see chapter 5, p. 71).

Both feminist and African-American interpretative practices can be characterized as part of a larger set of movements most often known as liberation theology. American students in particular should be aware that a large amount of theological interpretation of the Bible is being carried out in a variety of contexts around the globe. Africa, Asia, and Latin America are generating a wealth of theological interpretation of scripture from their own particular contexts. Much of this is unpublished or not available in English. Nevertheless, there is an increasing number of books and articles which open up these worlds to English-speaking students.[26] While the social and political contexts in which much liberation theology takes place are not the contexts of most of the people who will use this volume, these theologians have a claim on the attention of those who are both believers and participants in the social and material cultures of the so-called First World.

Doctrine and Interpretation

I have also included an essay of a more methodological nature in Part I. "The New Testament and Nicene Dogma," by David Yeago, is a work of particular importance for biblical scholars who tend to view the development of the doctrines such as the Trinity as discontinuous with the concerns of the New Testament. Under the influence of historical-critical concerns the Trinity and other classical doctrines have "come to seem a superstructure overlaid on the texts by theological speculation, at best a time-conditioned expression of spiritual experience somehow distantly responsive to the scriptural witness, at worst the token of the 'Hellenized' Church's cultural alienation from that witness" (see chapter 6, p. 87). The great strength of Yeago's essay is the argument that "the Nicene *homoousion* is neither imposed *on* the New Testament texts, nor distantly deduced *from* the texts, but rather, describes a pattern of judgements present *in* the texts, in the texture of scriptural discourse concerning Jesus and the God of Israel" (Ibid.).

Readings

In many respects the most important elements of this volume are the varied examples of theological interpretation that appear. Given that one of the aims of this volume is to help students begin to learn how to read scripture theologically, it seems important to have exemplars of such reading. Whereas, in this introduction, I have tried to present a more or less unified conception of theological interpretation, it will be clear that in actual exegetical practice there is a rich variety of views about what constitutes theological interpretation. I have focused these examples around four specific texts: Exodus 3; Isaiah 52–53, Matthew 5–7, and Romans 9–11. For each of these texts I have included an example of patristic interpretation, an example of medieval or reformation interpretation, and then three contemporary pieces. Each of the patristic and medieval selections is accompanied by a short introduction by a contemporary scholar which aims to point out the central interpretative concerns of each writer. In some cases that scholar has provided a new translation of the texts under consideration. While I will say something about each of these pieces I have tried to offer more extensive comments on the less familiar pieces.

Exodus 3

This text relates the call and commissioning of Moses. In addition, through the dialogue between Moses and God we have both a poignant display of divine/ human interaction and a revealing insight into God's character.

The patristic text for this passage comes from Gregory of Nyssa's *Life of Moses*. In many respects this selection will seem most alien to modern readers. Gregory's allegorical approach to the life of Moses allows him to present Moses as an exemplar of the life of virtue which is to characterize all Christians. Gregory's approach to the Old Testament was marked by the (deutero) Pauline view that all of Scripture is "useful for rebuke, correction and training in righteousnes" (2 Tim. 3:16). For Gregory (and for Origen) "the Old Testament, read in the light of the Word incarnate, Jesus Christ, actually becomes a gospel, an embodiment of the Logos. With such an understanding of the function of the Old Testament, Gregory considered a life of Moses an appropriate response to a request from an anonymous correspondent for 'advice in the perfect life' [Life of Moses 1.2] (see chapter 7, p. 105).

The selection from Nicholas of Lyra should introduce students to one of the most influential commentators in the history of biblical interpretation. Lyra's importance for subsequent interpreters primarily lies in his commitment to the "literal sense" of the biblical text. For Lyra, the literal sense is the foundation on which subsequent interpretations must be built. In addition, Lyra was one of the few Christian commentators of his day capable of working with the Hebrew text of scripture as well as Jewish interpretative traditions.

The three contemporary essays show the diverse ways one can theologically interpret this rich text. Terence Fretheim focuses on the divine speech and activity in this chapter as a way of revealing aspects of God's character. Walter Brueggemann sees in Exodus 3 the convergence of two narrative lines of development, the history of Yahweh as related in Genesis and the history of the Egyptian empire which begins in Genesis 47. Thus, in Exodus 3 these two narratives converge to begin the "narrative of Israel's revolutionary existence." Peter Ochs's essay represents the only Jewish contribution to this reader. There are several reasons why there are not more Jewish contributions, most of them are logistical. In addition, however, Christian readers need to understand that, within Judiasm, the practices of theological scriptural interpretation never really suffered from the effects of modernity that worked to eclipse Christian theological interpretation.[27] Ochs's essay demonstrates from a Jewish perspective the variety of interpretative interests and theological questions that a text like Exodus 3 is able to engage without at any time lapsing into a vicious relativism. Finally, Ochs's essay demonstrates how many of the post-critical philosophical impulses to which I have previously alluded bear on the interpretation of a specific biblical text.[28]

Isaiah 52–53

This text contains both the fourth of the so-called "servant songs,"[29] which runs from 52:13 to 53:12, as well as a reflection on Zion and its future (52:1–12). Early on Christians read the "servant song" christologically. That is, they saw this text prefiguring the person and work of Christ. While modern interpreters have rejected this reading as being incompatible with the original author's intentions, they still are primarily interested in the identity of the servant.

The selection from Theodoret of Cyrus's commentary on Isaiah shows that, as was generally the case in this period, he saw the servant song as prefiguring the life and death of Jesus. As Angela Christman mentions in her introduction, Theodoret tries to strike a balance in his interpretation between extensive allegorizing and an interpretation which woodenly maps historical events in the world onto this text. In addition to his christological and apologetic interests in this text, Theodoret also read this passage in the light of the christological controversies of his own day to combat both the Arians and the monophysites.

The selection from Calvin's sermons shows how the servant songs have been read christologically. "While it would not be entirely accurate to say that Calvin believed that Isaiah predicted Christ in any detail, he clearly did understand Isaiah to preach the gospel about Jesus in advance" (see chapter 13, p. 187). In doing so, Calvin does not ignore the point that Isaiah is speaking to Israel about Israel's own condition before God. As Kathryn Greene-McCreight argues in her introduction, "Calvin hears the prophet to be speaking to Isaiah's time and to his own time with the same voice" (ibid., p. 187).

The selection from David Clines's *I, He, We, They* is less obviously theological. Its great strength lies in its attempt to rescue Isaiah 53 from historical critical scholarship which has tended to view this poetic text as a code to be cracked. Clines's "rhetorical" rendering of the text is designed to restore its integrity as a poem. Beverly Stratton's essay studies the metaphors of Zion and the servant of Yahweh in this passage. This allows her to raise and begin to address important issues about suffering and God's relationship to human suffering. Tod Linafelt's essay traces the themes of speech and silence throughout all four servant songs as a way of showing how the servant passages cohere within the final form of Isaiah.

Matthew 5–7

Almost from the beginning Christians have struggled to deal with the radical shape of discipleship found in the Sermon on the Mount. In many respects one might say that the history of interpretation of this passage is a history of how to avoid the life-changing demands of this text. The selections here, however, do not engage the Sermon in that way.

The first selection comes from John Chrysostom's homilies on Matthew. Chrysostom's 90 homilies on Matthew, preached throughout the year 390 in Antioch, represent the first systematic commentary on Matthew's Gospel. Like other "Antiochene" exegetes (including Theodoret of Cyrus, included in this volume) Chrysostom avoided the allegorical interpretations favored by Origen and the Alexandrian school (see also the selection from Gregory of Nyssa in this volume), favoring a more historical approach. As Robin Darling Young points out in her introduction, however, it would be a mistake to see Chrysostom as a proto-historical critic. Chrysostom's commitment to the "historical" sense of scripture stems from his conviction that the spirit can clearly speak through such interpretations to the hearts of those listening to his sermons.

The selection from Luther, along with Mark Burrows's introduction, should bring students into contact with the great reformer's interpretative practice. As

Burrows shows, Luther shares with his patristic and medieval predecessors the commitment to reading scripture as a unity. Luther, however, also shares the more modern commitment to the "literal sense" of scripture as the foundation for all interpretation. Unlike Enlightenment interpreters, however, understanding of the "literal sense", for Luther, could not be carried out without a set of theological convictions about scripture.

I have also included a selection from one of Luther's modern successors, Dietrich Bonhoeffer. The selection reprinted here is from Bonhoeffer's extended meditations on the Sermon on the Mount, *The Cost of Discipleship*. Bonhoeffer wrote the *The Cost of Discipleship* when he was in charge of the Confessing Church's seminary at Finkenwalde, Germany in 1937. Bonhoeffer's task was to prepare clergy to serve churches that would be capable of resisting the claims of Hitler. This task demanded a revitalization of discipleship learned and lived in Christian community. Even before taking on this task Bonhoeffer had been turning to the Sermon on the Mount as a sort of charter for discipleship. The needs of Finkenwalde and Bonhoeffer's long-standing interest in the Sermon on the Mount come together in *The Cost of Discipleship*. In the text presented here Bonhoeffer is commenting on Matthew 6:5–15. In his discussion of Matthew 5 Bonhoeffer lays out the a life of discipleship that results in a public, visible form of life. In Matthew 6 Jesus's focus shifts to an account of the hiddenness of the Christian life. "There is a pointed contrast between chapters 5 and 6. That which is visible must also be hidden. . . . We have to take heed that we do not take heed of our own righteousness" (see chapter 20, p. 287). The discussion of prayer and the exposition on the Lord's Prayer presented here are shaped by this concern with hiddenness.

Brian Blount's essay brings the interests of socio-linguistics to bear on the Sermon to indicate how the Matthean community read and interpreted the material we have come to know as the Sermon on the Mount. He argues that Matthew's community was shaped by its conflict with the synagogue. It was "a community without a real social home, it remained a community under fire" (see chapter 19, p. 275). For these believers the Sermon would have presented a "spirituality for transformation." Blount concludes with some very suggestive comments about how such a spirituality might be embodied within African-American Christian communities to bring about social and cultural transformation. "Doing the imperatives of the sermon becomes a performative strategy, a conjure act, which induces, summons, and conjures the divine for the realization of an emancipatory future" (ibid., p. 278).

Richard Lischer's "The Sermon on the Mount as Radical Pastoral Care" addresses the communal and eschatological focus of the Sermon. That eschatological focus, and the Beatitudes in particular, provide Christian communities with a vision of their promised destiny. Lischer argues that it is only within this context that the demands of the Sermon might actually be life-giving. "Our only hope of living as the community of the Sermon is to acknowledge that we do not retaliate, hate, curse, lust, divorce, swear, brag, preen, worry, or backbite because it is not in the nature of our God or our destination that we should be such people" (see chapter 21, p. 298). Lischer then goes on to show how taking the communal and eschatological nature of the Sermon seriously would radically transform our notions of pastoral care and pastoral ministry.

Romans 9–11

Over the past 25 years scholarly work on Paul has dramatically shifted its focus. The so-called new view of Paul attempts to shift the focus of Pauline studies away from a picture of Paul as a man overcome with his own sinfulness and his inability to find forgiveness within Judaism. Instead, the new view of Paul recognizes that from his birth to his death Paul considered himself a Jew. In the course of his life, however, he came to reconceive his Judaism in the light of his convictions about the life, death, and resurrection of Jesus, the Messiah of Israel. Given these considerations, it is easy to see the importance of a text like Romans 9–11. This text, however, never really lost its importance for theological interpretation.

One of the common moves that has accompanied this new view of Paul is to denigrate a series of exegetical positions that are attributed to Luther and Augustine. While the new view of Paul is generally quite compelling, it is less so when it comes to its rather cavalier dismissal of Augustine. As the selections from Augustine, along with Peter Gorday's introduction, show, Augustine paid relentless attention to the logic of Paul's argument in Romans in order to transform the less rigorous exegetical tradition to which he was heir. It is also clear, however, that Augustine's exegesis was driven by interests very different from those of contemporary biblical scholars. Augustine read Paul with an eye towards addressing pressing theological issues of his own day: "how could one make a convincing case for the reality of a rational, benign divine governance of the world and at the same time continue to believe in human responsibility for the outcome of historical events? . . . In order to answer [this question] Augustine sought for a rational principle in the actions of God, as these are evidenced in scripture, and for a way to affirm human free will in the face of the fatalism and determinism offered by his Manichean opponents and then, somewhat later, in the face of the legalism represented in the teachings of the Donatist sect" (see chapter 22, p. 308).

For Protestant readers, Thomas Aquinas may be best known as a systematic theologian. As Eugene Rogers's introduction argues, however, Aquinas must be understood first as a biblical theologian, who, in fact, only gave lectures on scripture. Even his systematic writings should be seen as arising from commentary on scripture. The selection from Aquinas demonstrates how deeply concerned Aquinas was with issues of election and the relationships between the Church and Israel. Aquinas takes very seriously Paul's claim that all Israel will be saved even to the extent of claiming that the sacraments of penance and baptism will be unnecessary for Jews.

Paul Meyer's essay addresses that perplexing text, "Christ is the end of the Law," in Romans 10:4 in ways that reflect the concerns of the so-called new view of Paul. "Thus what we meet in Romans 9:30–10:4 is not an apostate Jew accusing his kinsmen of disobeying God because they have not been won over to his new interpretation of God's righteousness, or of persisting in an anachronism because they cannot accept God's putative termination of his Torah, or of being so attached to Moses that they have been unable to follow the living God in his new revelations of himself in unexpected ways. Rather, we encounter a Jewish Christian whose new religious identity depends on continuity with his old; who must, for his own sake and the sake of those who have made the move with him, as well as for the sake of the right understanding of his gospel on the part of Gentile Christians (11:13), undertake such a review" (see chapter 24, p. 349).

E. Elizabeth Johnson's contribution addresses two issues in contemporary scholarship on these chapters. She addresses both the claim that Paul's argument is incoherent, and the tendency of commentators to treat chapter 11 as simply a restatement of the positions laid out in chapters 9 and 10. She clearly and systematically shows that the inner logic and coherence of all three chapters lie in their persistent attention to the sovereign God's plan for the salvation of the world. Neil Elliott's essay builds on Johnson's arguing that, "If – in contrast to the traditional Christian appropriation of Paul – Romans is recognized as 'the very antithesis of all Christian triumphalism and imperialism,' it may flower in a genuine theology of liberation . . ." (p. 385).

It is my hope that, despite the diversity of these essays, students will begin to get a feel for how theological concerns might shape and be shaped by the interpretation of scripture. Working through this volume will not make the novice an expert. It should, however, contribute to an ongoing process whereby students develop their own proficiency in interpreting scripture theologically. Of course, Christians have always recognized that such proficiency is not simply reflected in increased intellectual capacities. Rather, for Christians, proficiency in reading scripture theologically is ultimately reflected in a life that is transformed to conform more nearly to the image of Christ.

Notes

1 See also my essay, "The New Testament, Theology and Ethics," in *Hearing the New Testament*, ed. Joel B. Green (Grand Rapids: Eerdmans, 1995), pp. 394–410; and the book I authored with L. G. Jones, *Reading in Communion: Scripture and Ethics in Christian Life* (Grand Rapids: Eerdmans, 1991).

2 When one looks, for example, at Gabler's (1787) proposal for "pure" biblical theology, it becomes clear that he intended his historical interests to further his particular vision of theology. That things very quickly moved in other directions may have more to do with conflicts over the place of theology in the university and with modernity's persistent interest in policing theology. For an insightful account of the way biblical theology as an academic discipline developed from Gabler, see Ben C. Ollenburger, "Biblical Theology: Situating the Discipline," in *Understanding the Word*, ed. J. T. Butler, E. Conrad and B. Ollenburger (Sheffield: JSOT, 1985), pp. 37–62. I am not convinced that Ollenburger's situating of Brevard Childs as the only real heir of Gabler is correct, but I am persuaded by his situating of Gabler in relation to both Kant and Wrede.

3 For now I would like to leave open the question of whether historical criticism could ever have served anything but the theological ends of modernity. Regardless of this issue, Robert Morgan is surely right when he states, "Histories of biblical scholarship are accordingly sometimes presented as the progressive elimination of religious influence." (See Robert Morgan with John Barton, *Biblical Interpretation* (Oxford: OUP, 1989), p. 27.) For an example of this sentiment see Werner Georg Kümmel's comment, "It is impossible to speak of a scientific view of the New Testament until the New Testament became the object of investigation as an independent body of literature with historical interest, as a collection of writings that could be considered apart from the Old Testament and without dogmatic or creedal bias." (*The New Testament: The History of the Investigation of its Problems*, tr. S. M. Gilmour and H. C. Kee (London: SCM, 1972), p. 13.)

4 The alternative, which may happen more often than not, is that biblical scholars tend to adopt to greater or lesser degrees the theological convictions best suited to historical criticism – liberal Protestantism or its Catholic correlatives.

5 For a stimulating discussion of the fragmenting effects of professionalization in American higher education, see Burton Bledstein, *The Culture of Professionalism* (New York: W. W. Norton, 1976). Largely due to the policies of the Conservative government in Britain during the mid to late 1980s, one can see similar patterns emerging in British universities.

6 This phenomenon is particularly clear in American academic life; it seems to be increasingly the case in Britain as well. In the German context, the relationships between state, Church, and university mean that the situation is and has been quite different. In developing countries a whole different range of pressures shapes the interests of academics.

7 See George Marsden, *The Soul of the American University* (Oxford: Oxford University Press, 1994). Also J. T. Burtchaell, "The Decline and Fall of the Christian College (parts 1 and 2)" *First Things* 12 and 13 (1991), pp. 16–29 and 30–8 and P. Gleason, *Contending with Modernity* (Oxford: Oxford University Press, 1995).

8 In addition to Robert Morgan's *Biblical Interpretation*, see his *The Nature of New Testament Theology* (London: SCM, 1973); see also a variety of works by John Rogerson,

especially, *Old Testament Criticism in the Nineteenth Century: England and Germany* (London: SPCK, 1984) and his biography of DeWette; also Hans Frei, *The Eclipse of Biblical Narrative* (New Haven: Yale University Press, 1974) and especially the appendicies to *Types of Christian Theology* ed. George Hunsinger and William Placher (New Haven: Yale University Press, 1992); and A. C. Thiselton's illuminating essay, "New Testament Interpretation in Historical Perspective," in *Hearing the New Testament* ed. Joel B. Green (Grand Rapids: Eerdmans, 1995), pp. 10–36. What makes these works particularly good on this topic is that they situate the characters and issues under discussion into their wider social, political, and philosophical environments.

9 For a useful introduction to the political and philosophical issues of modernity and postmodernity in their relation to biblical studies, see A. K. M. Adam, *What is Postmodern Biblical Criticism?* (Minneapolis: Fortress, 1995).

10 For two competing attempts to situate theological interpretation of scripture within professional biblical studies, see Francis Watson, *Text, Church, World* (Grand Rapids: Eerdmans, 1994) and Philip R. Davies, *Whose Bible is it Anyway?* (Sheffield: Sheffield Academic Press, 1995). While many of my proposals are much closer to Watson's than Davies's, on this particular issue I would like to split the difference between them. Unlike Watson, I do not think that theological interests should be the only ones biblical scholars pursue. Unlike Davies, I think it is not too difficult to articulate theological interests in the Bible that even he would have to admit into his account of the discipline of biblical studies.

11 For a translation from the Latin original, see J. Sandys-Wunsch and L. Eldredge, "J. P. Gabler and the Distinction Between Biblical and dogmatic Theology: Translation, commentary and Discussion of His Originality," *Scottish Journal of Theology* 33 (1980): 133–58.

12 See ibid., pp. 136–8 and in particular Ollenburger's discussion of Gabler in relation to Kant, "Biblical Theology," pp. 44–6.

13 Of course, both of these emphases can be found in the same works.

14 While I agree with Ollenburger's characterization of the way things developed, I am not convinced that Childs's work stand in methodological continuity with Gabler. Clearly, there is an aspect of Bultmann's *Theology of the New Testament*, 2 vols, tr. K. Grobel (London: SCM, 1971) which bears the heavy stamp of his commitments to existentialism. On the other hand Bultmann also worked within the thoroughly historical paradigm set forth by W. Wrede. In regard to the Old Testament one can find the influence of Hegel's work in a variety of nineteenth century OT theologies, particularly W. Vatke's. For a nuanced account of Vatke's Hegelianism see John Rogerson, *Old Testament Criticism*, pp. 69–78.

15 See Robert Morgan's translation of Wrede's "The Tasks and Methods of New Testament Theology," in *The Nature of New Testament Theology*, pp. 68–116.

16 For a proposal which tries to stake out the contours of a New Testament theology that is not constructed by the concerns of modernity, see A. K. M. Adam, *Making Sense of New Testament Theology* (Macon, GA: Mercer University Press, 1995).

17 The most prominent American exception to this is Brevard Childs. Even here, however, when one compares Childs's commentary on Exodus (Philadelphia: Westminster, 1974) with those works following the *Introduction to the Old Testament as Scripture* (Philadelphia: Westminster 1979), his work seems to demonstrate a decreasing interest in premodern biblical interpretation.

18 See Nicholas Lash's argument against the very possibility of such repetition in "What Authority Has Our Past?" in *Theology on the Way to Emmaus* (London: SCM, 1986), pp. 54–5.

19 George Lindbeck has recently argued that a theologically oriented history of Christian scriptural interpretation "is the theologically most crucial of all historical fields, including biblical studies, for those who think . . . that the church's future depends on its postcritical reappropriation of precritical hermeneutical strategies" (from his review of *Biblical Hermeneutics in Historical Perspective: Studies in Honor of Karlfried Froehlich on his Sixtieth Birthday*, ed. Mark Burrows and Paul Rorem (Grand Rapids: Eerdmans, 1991), *Modern Theology* 10 (1994): 101–6).

20 For an example of someone trying to use pre-critical theologians as a way of combatting the disciplinary fragmentation of contemporary theology, see Ellen Charry's essay, "The Case for Concern: Athanasian Christology in Pastoral Perspective," *Modern Theology* 9 (1993):265–84.

21 For a good brief introduction to the thought of de Lubac see Hans Urs von Balthasar, *The Theology of Henri de Lubac*, tr. J. Fessio, S. J. (San Francisco: Ignatius Press, 1991). See also J. A. Komonchak, "Theology and Culture at Mid-Century: The Example of Henri de Lubac," *Theological Studies* 51 (1990): 579–602.

22 This is translated in the volume entitled *The Sources of Revelation*, tr. Luke O'Neill (New York: Herder and Herder, 1968). In addition to the portion reprinted here, this volume contains chapters from *Exégèse Médiévale*.

23 "The Word of God, a living and effective word, acquires true fulfillment and total significance only by the transformation which it effects in the one who receives it. This is why the expression 'passing on to spiritual understanding' is equivalent to 'turning to Christ' – a conversion which can never be said to have been fully achieved" (see chap. 1, p. 13).

24 If space had permitted I would have liked to include essays on these issues from both a radical reformation and a Roman Catholic perspective. See, for example, John Howard Yoder's "A Hermeneutics of Peoplehood," in *The Priestly Kingdom* (Notre Dame: U. of Notre Dame Press, 1984), pp. 15–45; and Joseph Cardinal Ratzinger, "The Spiritual Basis and Ecclesial Identity of Theology," in *The Nature and Mission of Theology*, tr. Adrian Walker (San Francisco: Ignatius Press, 1995), pp. 45–72.

25 For feminist biblical interpretation, see the two volumes of *Searching the Scriptures* ed. Elizabeth Schüssler Fiorenza (New York: Crossroad, 1993, 1994). For a more basic introduction see the volume edited by Letty Russell, *Feminist Interpretation of the Bible* (Oxford: Blackwell, 1985). On African-American biblical interpretation see the essays in *Stony the Road We Trod* ed. Cain Hope Felder (Minneapolis: Fortress, 1991) and Felder's own book, *Troubling Biblical Waters* (Maryknoll: Orbis, 1989). See also the incisive essay by Michael Cartwright, "Ideology and the Interpretation of the Bible in the African American Christian Tradition," *Modern Theology* 9 (1993): 141–58.

26 See, for example, the work of Gerald West, especially *Biblical Hermeneutics of Liberation* (Pietermaritzburg: Cluster Publications, 1991), and "Reading the Bible and Doing Theology in the New South Africa," in *The Bible and Human Society*, ed. D. Carroll, D. Clines and P. Davies (Sheffield: Sheffield Academic Press, 1995), pp. 445–58. Also *Voices from the Margin: Interpreting the Bible in the Third World*, ed. R. S. Sugirtharajah (Maryknoll: Orbis, 1991), and Jon Levison and Priscilla Pope-Levision, "Global

Perspectives on New Testament Interpretation," in *Hearing the New Testament*, ed. Joel B. Green (Grand Rapids: Eerdmans, 1995), pp. 329–48.

27 To understand the effects of modernity on Jewish biblical scholarship see Jon Levenson's *The Hebrew Bible, the Old Testament and Historical Criticism* (Louisville: WJKP, 1993), especially chs 2, 3, and 4.

28 This has been one of Ochs's long-running concerns. See the volume he edited entitled *The Return to Scripture in Judaism and Christianity* (New York: Paulist, 1993) and "Scriptual Logic: Diagrams for a Postcritical Metaphysic," in *Rethinking Metaphysics* ed. L. G. Jones and S. E. Fowl (Oxford: Blackwell, 1995), pp. 65–94.

29 I have used this terminology because it is so deeply ingrained in the discourse of biblical scholarship. For a very brief but convincing argument against viewing the "servant songs" as separate parts of Isaiah see Hans Barstadt's "The Future of the 'Servant Songs': Some Reflections on the Relationship of Biblical Scholarship to its own Tradition," in *Language, Theology and the Bible*, ed. S. Ballentine and J. Barton (Oxford: Clarendon Press, 1994), pp. 261–70.

PART

I

The Contexts of Theological Interpretation

Spiritual Understanding

Henri de Lubac, S.J.

Translated by Luke O'Neill

1 Introduction

An archeologist might lovingly labor to make Minoan civilization live again in our mind's eye, or he might derive intense delight from reconstructing the religious life of the cities of Upper Asia during the era of the great Buddhist pilgrims. Yet he has probably no real desire to take us back either to the mores of Minos or to the beliefs of the Monks of Khotan. Even so, he is convinced that his motivation is something other than idle curiosity. Surely no one can doubt that such investigations into man's past are fruitful; they enrich the human spirit and bestow upon it a new fertility. Research becomes a kind of rich and bountiful humus. As man explores and increases his appreciation of the varied creations of the human genius, he acquires greater insight into his own potential. Each sounding into ancient cultures seems to tap another spring which nourishes his own culture.

Could it be, though, that what we so readily acknowledge when we are dealing with distant eras or far-off societies should be questioned when we are dealing with the rather fragile forms which the Christian genius has elaborated? While it is certain that not everything about these forms possesses the permanent value which flows from truth, we cannot say that even their ephemeral aspects should be without interest for us; *a fortiori*, that we can ignore their earlier importance without falling into error. Actually, we must in all seriousness beware of an inability to appreciate the human significance of precisely those things which are most mingled with illusion. Faced with the exegetical constructs of the Fathers of the Church, we can easily be tempted to object: This was, of course,

3

a great and lovely dream, but critical research has long since discredited it – and faith can get along perfectly well without it. Even though the historian lavishes his professional admiration on it, today's Christian has no need of it. This kind of reaction, though at least in part disputable, is readily understandable. "When we say that Greek tragedy is a thing of the past, this does not impair in the least its immortal beauty."[1] But if we were to say: "There is nothing great, nothing really new in the Christian past – those early happenings were just an aberration and are quite undeserving of an historian's sympathetic curiosity or of any effort to rediscover their essence," we would be making a false historical judgement, and this would be detrimental to the preservation and to the renewal of Christian culture.

We would be just as mistaken – and, here again, we are overstating the case, without suggesting that the opinion can actually be supported – if we admired the ancient constructs so much that we longed to make them our permanent dwelling; or if we canonized such doctrines so as to become unconscious of their weak or outdated aspects; or if we believed that fidelity to an author meant that we had to copy him or imitate him slavishly. In doing so, we would be abandoning the present without being able to find refuge in the past. Today's "primitives" simply do not give us an accurate notion of the true character of primitive humanity, which was brimming with creative energy and an openness to further and unforeseeable developments. Nor can a modern "figurist" reproduce for us the spirit of the great founders of spiritual exegesis. If the desire for servile imitation were to be accompanied by a contempt, even though only on the practical side, for the scientific methods which, painstakingly applied, have renewed our historical understanding of the sacred books, then our infidelity to the spirit of an Origen, a Jerome, or even an Augustine, would be still more evident. There is no point in wondering what one of the ancients would do if he were alive today, in totally different conditions, and discovered all sorts of curious things unknown in his own day, enjoyed a more advanced stage of scientific development, could use the new tools of scholarship, was enlightened by an experience of the world whose very orientation could not have been foreseen by him. There is simply no answer to such questions. Still in all, the clearest history adequately demonstrates Origen's high regard for science, and his ardor and trail-blazing zeal in research. Consequently, we cannot, at least in this area, question Origen's authority, nor can we fault him with even the slightest negligence. It remains true, however, that his brand of Alexandrian Platonism created a rather dangerous climate of thought, where neither the world of natures nor the world of history possessed any real solidity. This lies behind the hasty flight, from the one as from the other, towards spiritual significance, and accounts for the tendency to pause over literal exegesis no longer than one would in the natural sciences. Thus, historical data are frequently given short shrift, and serve as springboards rather than as terms for thought. This can be observed in Augustinianism as well as in Origenism, but it obviously did not prevent St Augustine – whose openness to scientific problems was not as great as Origen's – from having, like Origen, a profoundly historical view of life. Furthermore, as we glance over the history of Christian exegesis during the last few centuries, we see that the persistent obstacle – it was still with us, only yesterday – to critical research was not (a few significant exceptions aside) spiritual interpretation at all. It was false science; it was a pernicious literalism, "which took everything literally, out of a desire to follow the literal meaning alone";[2] it was a mania for harmonization, and false notions of biblical inerrancy or tradition. The marvelous thing is that the mind is freed from this sort of approach by regular recourse to our ancient authors.

A still more subtle misconception is possible. This concedes the tribute of admiration to the "allegorism" of the Fathers, but considers it basically as a game. The criticism may well be deserved by some of the later authors.[3] Such a case could even be made against an Origen, at least *prima facie*. Origen's thought developed with such a profusion and wealth of symbols that a note of the gratuitous appears. He discovers a role for classical aesthetics in expressing the Christian history of salvation. Yet these findings, however important they might be in themselves, should not mask what is essential. Critical effort would be at fault if it stopped at them. Origen is consistently sober and respectful towards the text he has chosen to comment upon. Of course it is possible to play with scripture as one would with a toy, or to play on "spiritual meanings." But if we are looking for this kind of amusement, we shall have to knock on another door than Origen's. For Origen, as for his equals, scripture is always the Word of God, and not merely in general but here and now. In the hands of these commentators (or, rather, in the divine hands), scripture is the arm of battle against the enemy powers, the sword whose sharpened point reaches to the division of soul and spirit.

Moreover, their exegesis answered to the needs of a Christianity which was still being born. We find it difficult today to appreciate this sufficiently. It is not because it was unimportant that the role of this exegesis escapes us, but because the need for it has been perfectly satisfied. We who are in peaceful possession and enjoyment of its permanent achievements can no longer imagine the situation which made it necessary. The mystical interpretation of scripture, Möhler has written, "stands as one of the most remarkable phenomena of the early Church; it has never been appreciated as much as it deserves, nor has it ever been fully understood. It would be impossible to calculate the amount of good accomplished by this method in the spread of Christianity among pagans and Jews. This mystical interpretation is also, and by its very essence, tied in with the birth of a very pure conception of the Christian life."[4] During his brief career, Möhler clearly established his penetrating grasp of the spirit of Christianity, and his observations are accurate and undeniably significant. Even so, we think they are inadequate. We are dealing with something which not only is of capital importance for our understanding of primitive Christianity but also touches upon the permanent foundation of Christian thought, as Möhler himself seems to suggest at the end of the passage quoted. So we have good reason to rejoice that it has reappeared in our own day, although naturally in quite new forms, as one of the prime concerns of exegesis and theology. The process has been accompanied by much trial and error, by many obscure arguments, indeed by many mistakes. But who can be surprised by this? We shall now make an effort to see just what is at issue here – without in the least undertaking the development of all the viewpoints which can be held on a subject of such extraordinary complexity, a subject which is notoriously difficult to grasp at its vital center.[5]

For a long time now, each new generation has received from its predecessors in the faith a Christianity which, objectively, was "ready-made," from the most elementary dogmatic formulation to the most sophisticated expression of spirituality. Somehow the task seems to have been done once for all, and to have won for us this universe of perfect expressions. Without troubling ourselves about the tree, we have only to gather the fruits. For this reason, among others, we can behave like pure literalists in our exegesis without any great harm. We find it perfectly natural to view purely as historians – and, in doing this, we have incomparably richer resources at our disposal than our predecessors did – everything which is to be found in the books of the Old Testament. Its figurative substance has, so to speak, already been extracted and put at our disposal.[6] But at the very beginning, and even two or three centuries afterwards, we could not have afforded the luxury of a disinterestedness of this sort. The very reading of the holy books then put into question, and in a very immediate way, the whole idea of the new faith. During that period, the spiritual interpretation of the Bible was in no sense a practice of supererogation. And it was certainly not a game. Before it was acknowledged as something well established, it had first made a contribution to the very establishment of the faith, or at least to the translating of it. It did not constitute what might be called a surplus *vis-à-vis* an already existent religious capital. Rather, it entered into the constitution of that very capital, and as an essential part of it. In other words, it played an indispensable role in getting Christianity out of its diapers without breaking it off from its roots. Christianity had to acquire complete self-awareness and it had to be assured of its independence of Judaism, while still being preserved from the crude interpretations by which it was also menaced by the pagan spirit. Still more importantly, the objective expression of Christianity had to be hammered out. And while with Christ everything – absolutely everything – had, of course, been already given, the very fact of Christ still had to be expressed.

Let us give some careful thought to the question. Christian truth did not burst upon empty minds, nor was it interpreted from a purely neutral point of view. It received its embodiment and its capacity to be grasped principally from biblical realities. Indeed, we can say that the formulation of Christian truth was a prolongation of those realities. Thanks to the dual law of analogy and contrast, studious reflection on the Old Testament in the light of Christ made possible a better grasp of the New Testament and also a better appreciation of its newness. While this reflection served the exposition of the faith, its primary fruit was an increased understanding, even perception, of the object of faith.

In this way, the former economy's traditional pedagogic role was carried on at the very heart of the new economy and, in a fashion unique in religious history, the former economy lived on in a mysterious way. The Christian mystery, because of the magnificent providential economy which embraces both Testaments and links them together, has not been handed down to us as a collection of timeless definitions, unrelated to any historical situation and demanding only to be clothed, according to our fancy, with biblical images as with just so many illustrations. The intimate links between the two Testaments are of quite another kind. Within the very consciousness of Jesus – if we may cast a human glance into that sanctuary – the Old Testament was seen as the matrix of the New or as the instrument of its creation.[7] This meant something much more than extrinsic preparation. Even the categories used by Jesus to tell us about himself are ancient biblical categories. Jesus causes them to burst forth or, if you prefer, sublimates them and unifies them by making them converge upon himself.[8] But he somehow needs them. Furthermore, in this new employment, they are neither abstract categories nor accidental images. They retain all of their original value and flavor as allusions to precise facts, unique realities. These realities, in the context of which Jesus places himself and which he thereby transforms, are sown all through the history of Israel and constitute the very object of Israel's expectation. We could make the same kind of statement about everything, or almost everything, which his first witnesses teach us about his person and his work. Thus, "biblical images," and the concrete facts behind them, furnish the thread, both historical and noetic, from which is woven the Christian mystery in all its newness and transcendence.

"Although it is always profitable," as Père Spicq points out, "to illuminate the New Testament teachings on baptism, for example, through recourse to the typology of the Red Sea, much more fruit can be obtained from a biblical theology which is derived from a study of St Paul and St John according to the literal meaning. The fulfillment of revelation affords more clarity than do its beginnings; in point of fact, the beginnings are illuminated by their fulfillment."[9] There can be no argument about the last statement, which is expressive of a reality always useful to recall. The real question, however, is to determine whether the beginning of revelation played a role, and perhaps a significant one, in the final formulation of revelation itself. Put in another way, may not the New Testament teaching be formulated and, in its literal meaning, become intelligible through some spiritual signification bestowed by Christ upon the facts of the Old Law? In the example considered here, it seems clear that "the typology of the Red Sea" or that of the Cloud is not merely a comparison which is added on to the Pauline theology: it is an explicit part of it.[10] There can be no doubt that the Apostle viewed the comparison as something more than a means of illuminating from without a doctrine on baptism which had already been put in final form. The comparison was more than a casual spiritual fruit.

It has very rightly been said that "our fathers in the faith knew of the first Adam only in relation to the Second; of Melchisedech only in relation to the Eucharist; of the tree of paradise in relation to the tree of the Cross; of the passage through the Red Sea in relation to baptism; of the Psalms of David in relation to Christ; and of the temple in relation to the Church."[11] But even that must be considered as the other side of a truth which, in all essential aspects, has first to be stated in inverse terms.[12] Baptism, Eucharist, Church, and so forth, were first thought of, at least when they were seriously reflected upon, only as "functions of" Melchisedech, the Pasch under the Law, the passage through the Red Sea, the manna, the Assembly in the desert, the Temple at Jerusalem. All the basic biblical themes: Covenant, Election, People of God, Word, Messiah, Kingdom, Day of the Lord, and so forth, enter into the Christian idea of salvation. The mystery of the Redemption, purifying us and tearing us away from servitude to sin, occupies the central role in our faith. But the truth is that if it obtained admittance into the minds of the first generations of believers, it did so by reason of a transposition, prepared for by the Prophets, of the Law's ideas of sacrifice and expiation as well as by reason of the stories about the two captivities (in Egypt and Babylon) and about the double liberation of his people which the God of Israel effected through a ransom.[13] And did not the entire New Covenant appear to be sealed by the blood of Christ just as the Old Covenant had been sealed by the blood of victims?[14] Thus "the rock of Golgotha was intelligible to humanity because it stood out against the background of ancient Judaism, its beliefs, its aspirations, its worship."[15] The Jewish people prefigured the Church while preparing for it, and prepared for it while prefiguring it, and the earthly kingdom which seemed promised to them was the image of the kingdom of heaven which Jesus was to announce. Ultimately, "the most specifically new themes of the Gospel: adoption by the Father, gift of the Spirit, as well as revelation of the Son, take on all their meaning, and actually possess meaning, only when they are seen as the common ground of the great themes of the prophetic Word."[16] Furthermore, is it not sufficient to read with a little attention the stories which make up our "New Testament" to see that, regardless of the special genius of individual authors or of the diversity of genres, all are basically presented as a perpetual

8

interpretation of the scriptures, that is to say, of what we know as the "Old Testament?"[17] In the majority of cases, this interpretation is a spiritual transposition and, as such, is effected through a symbolic utilization. But, again, in the majority of cases, whether the interpretation is immediate or reflective, it must not be compared to some tacked-on embroidery; it lies within the very texture of the fabric. Were we to view Christianity as a body of doctrine, the interpretation would not be a garment thrown over it after the event but a part of the body itself, whose unifying spirit is the present reality of the Saviour.[18]

2 "Spiritual Meaning"

The word which was first used by St Paul, and which was generally used thereafter in the Latin tradition, to express this symbolic transposition was *allegory*.[19] For a long time, allegory was taken by theology to mean, and often in the broadest sense, the mysteries of Christ and of the Church as they appeared in scripture. Hence, the allegorical meaning was the dogmatic meaning *par excellence*, and it was firmly rooted in history.[20] Far from compromising the historical foundations of the faith, it actually insured for all Christian thought the essentially historical character which is so perfectly in keeping with the Christian faith, but which has so often been disturbingly blurred. The word lost favor, however, for reasons which are readily understandable. The word's etymology suggests that allegory is a meaning *other* than the letter, or auxiliary to it, lacking organic relationship with it. Its modern usage contrasts it either to ontological sign or to parable, but in both instances this is false to the ancient acceptation: actually, it evokes the idea of an analogy which is artificial, elaborately detailed, or the idea of an exploitation of image to develop an idea which is already formed.[21] Such an evocation corresponds only too well to what has in fact become the usage of scriptural "allegory." It can even suggest certain fatal negations.[22] Moreover, even among the ancients themselves, the banner of Christian allegory often flew over foreign wares, and this accounts for the ambivalences and the variations in acceptance and rejection which can be found in the work of a single author. As a consequence, there has been a preference for other terms in modern times.

Certain writers, noting that the early Fathers sought "the deep Christian significance of the Scriptures in the hollow of the literal meaning," propose to restrict themselves to an expression of that meaning. As they see it, this sort of expression adequately delimits – provided it is "perceived by faith" in all its fullness – "the one true meaning of the Bible." In approaching the matter in this way, they show an admirable concern for unity, while at the same time avoiding the confusion of the authentic exegesis of the Fathers, which "consists in drawing forth the profound and objective significance of a text, in the light of the entire economy of salvation,"[23] with an "allegorizing exegesis," in the manner of Philo or of the Greeks. They properly desire to get rid of the "allegorizing stucco" which is thrown over "the living architecture of the Bible."[24]

Now it is true that everything *is*, in some sense, contained within the letter, for that which lacks foundation in the letter must be something which has been added to the text, and is therefore arbitrary. "We must never seek the spiritual meaning behind the letter, but always within it, just as we do not find the Father behind the Son but in him and through him."[25] Even so, it seems to us that this terminology,[26] though it might have the advantage of simplicity, is just too much at odds with universal usage to be fully acceptable. It also conflicts with the traditional distinction according to which the inspired scriptures are set apart from other books, in that the things signified by its words possess a signification willed by God, a signification which relates to salvation. How is it possible for the meaning of the thing to be, without more, the meaning of the letter, thus of the word, since the proper function of the word, thus of the letter, is to signify that thing? Whatever is true of the practice we find the distinction in unity well expressed in a formula of St Gregory the Great: "*Aliquando in historia litteram suscipiunt, aliquando vero per significationem litterae spiritum requirunt*" (We sometimes receive the letter in history, but sometimes we also seek the spirit through the meaning of the letter).[27] For the letter is "the sacrament of the spirit."[28] Moreover, the terminology which we are discussing does not seem to be particularly precise; just because something is within the letter, or under the letter, it does not follow that it is literal.[29] Finally, though the terminology might avoid one kind of confusion, does it not court another by implying that the entire meaning of scripture should be reduced to what the sacred writer could explicitly perceive of it?[30]

Thus it is that we are more likely today to speak of *typology*. The word is a neologism and has been barely a century in use.[31] But it was very happily coined. Since the time of St Paul, traditional exegesis has always been concerned with "types," figures, and we can occasionally find "typical meaning" used synonymously with mystical or allegorical meaning, or even with figurative meaning, as in Pascal.[32] "Typology" also has the virtue of doing away, at least in intention, with all the old straw in the grain of Christian exegesis, something which could not be accomplished by the word "allegory" alone. But it has the drawback of referring solely to a result, without alluding to the spirit or basic thrust of the process which produces that result. Its connotations may also be too narrow, for, strictly speaking, it corresponds solely to the first of the three meanings spelled out in the classical division after the literal sense, "history." Typology thus puts narrow limitations on its object. In any event, it does not include within its scope the most properly spiritual explanations. This is a serious shortcoming, and it is perfectly possible that it may sometimes be

10

intended. Although "typology" as an original suggestion was on solid ground, it was much too circumscribed. We should not place exclusive dependence upon it unless we are prepared to reduce the bold and pregnant teaching of a St Paul to a game of figures, no matter how completely they may be authenticated.

In the final analysis, is it not preferable to revert to the most traditional[33] and the most general expression of all, and – without ruling out other terms or later refinements – to speak once again, quite simply of "spiritual meaning," "spiritual understanding"? Some find the word intimidating, and it can, of course, lend itself to abuse.[34] But the mere possibility of abuse should not force us to "dim the flame." It should not rob us of one of the essential words in the Christian language, a word which scripture formally countenances. There is no good reason for brushing it aside. Actually, we cannot do without it if we are to obtain a relatively complete view of the reality described by it. With unique forcefulness, it expresses a characteristic note of the whole new Economy, in which the ancient people of Israel become, in the Church, Israel according to the spirit. The Old Law in its entirety becomes the Law of the spirit. As St Augustine teaches, the sole aim of all the pedagogy, both historical and prophetic, in the Old Testament is to lead us to perceive the spiritual realities which, no longer past or future, eternally perdure.[35] And is there not a consistently spiritualizing quality about the typology of the liturgy? And is this not also true of the biblical symbolism of early Christian art?[36]

Now this spiritualization is simultaneously an interiorization: in saying "spiritual," we are also saying "interior."[37] The New Law is no longer engraved on tablets of stone, but on hearts, and the visible bonds which unite Christians in the "Body of Christ" simply express or minister to bonds in the mystical order. What we have here is a dual transposition, a dual passage (something which cannot be finally achieved in any one of us as long as the present age has not achieved its course) from the first Testament to the second. The fruit of the interpretation of scripture which takes account of this dual passage is, therefore, appropriately called "spiritual meaning."[38]

The expression proves its appropriateness in other ways as well. In the language of Christian tradition, "spirit" is naturally allied with "truth," taken in the vigorous, substantial sense possessed by that word when expressing the reality of Christ as contrasted with the shadows and figures which had gone before. From another point of view, it also allows us to exploit the Pauline antithesis of letter, or flesh, and spirit. Obviously, we must remember that the letter is by no means equivalent to the literal meaning, and the flesh still less. It is a sort of sterilized literal meaning, stripped of the spiritual potencies which lie, like seeds, within it; a materialized meaning, rigid, exclusive, and thereby falsified; as such, it is in opposition, now that the fullness of time has arrived, to the dual passage we have just spoken of. As Origen pointed out, it is a figure which, unwilling to acknowledge itself as such, refuses to yield to the reality.

11

This was the temptation of the beneficiaries of the Old Covenant, once the message of Christ was proclaimed. But let us not delude ourselves that all analogous temptations have disappeared from within Christianity itself. The Lord must constantly renew the changing of water into wine, lest we fall back into "Judaic" interpretations. The latter were to be detected even in an apparently totally Christian "typology." Nor have the strong warnings of St Paul lost their timeliness – nor will they ever lose it. To give but one example, mild enough to begin with and much too old to offend anyone, can anyone seriously doubt that the great Bossuet's *Politique tirée de l'Ecriture sainte* would have been quite different if he had pondered over them more deeply?

Besides, why should we resist calling the meaning which comes in a special way from the Holy Spirit the "spiritual meaning?"[39] This, most probably, is far too obvious to need elaboration. It cannot be doubted that the literal meaning also comes from the Holy Spirit; every true scriptural meaning is inspired, and inspiration is unique. Still in all, we have not completely perceived the intention of the Spirit as long as we have failed to penetrate to the deepest level. And if we deliberately stop short of that intention, we have been unfaithful to it. Thus we see that the spiritual meaning bears a special relationship to the Spirit, and this is further evidence that it is well named. Since the spiritual meaning, as the meaning of things, is not bestowed upon them by the human author of a book, it stems totally from the Spirit. In it we find the *Spiritus Sancti sacramenta*.[40] Through it we enjoy the *Spiritus Sancti consortium*.[41] Furthermore – and is this not its essential characteristic? – it is the meaning of the New Testament,[42] that is to say, the meaning taught by the Spirit of Truth[43] who is the Spirit of Christ. There is no resource of the human mind, no method, no scientific procedure which will ever be enough to make us hear "the music written on the silent pages of the Holy Books."[44] Finally, and to put it still more simply, it is the meaning which is related to Christ, to the Lord: now "the Lord is the Spirit," precisely the Spirit of the scriptures.[45]

Even the ambiguity of the word "spiritual" can add to its value. The word "allegory," on the other hand, could be dangerously ambiguous, and there surely is an interest in carefully distinguishing the imaginative literal meanings from the mystical or "typical" meanings, which were often badly confounded by many of the ancients. To approach the subject from another viewpoint, we see that there are excellent reasons for continuing the use of the single expression, "spiritual understanding," for the activity which leads to both of these meanings. In spite of objective diversity, the same basic movement of the spirit is present, under the influence of the same Spirit[46] and towards the same penetration of the spirit of the text, whether our purpose be to discover an advance indication of Christ, to abandon the seemingly carnal meaning of certain prophecies, to understand a parable, or to obtain greater penetration into the teachings of Jesus in the Sermon on the Mount. And there is the constant goal of arriving at the *scientia spiritualis* and the *purus sensus* which, according to St Caesarius of Arles, are conferred upon the Church.[47]

Finally – and here again we have an important point – the spiritual meaning, understood as figurative or mystical meaning, is the meaning which, objectively, leads us to the realities of the spiritual life and which, subjectively, can only be the fruit of a spiritual life. That is where it leads; for to the extent that we have not arrived at it, we have not drawn a totally Christian interpretation from the Scriptures. It is certain that the Christian mystery is not something to be curiously contemplated like a pure object of science, but is something which must be interiorized and lived. It finds its own fullness in being fulfilled within souls.[48] *Ad haec etiam omnis Testamenti Veteris historia pertinet, quae carnaliter gesta ita denuntiat, ut in eis spiritualis vitae intelligentiam exquirendam edoceat* (The whole history of the Old Testament is also concerned with the facts reported as having physically taken place, but in such a way as to teach us to seek in them the understanding of the spiritual life).[49] But the converse is just as true: the spiritual meaning of a mystery is the meaning we discover – or, rather, into which we penetrate – by living that mystery. Still more fundamentally, the entire process of spiritual understanding is, in its principle, identical to the process of conversion. It is its luminous aspect. *Intellectus spiritualis credentem salvum facit*, (Spiritual understanding saves the believer).[50] The Word of God, a living and effective word, aquires true fulfillment and total significance only by the transformation which it effects in the one who receives it. This is why the expression "passing on to spiritual understanding" is equivalent to "turning to Christ" – a conversion which can never be said to have been fully achieved. Reciprocal causality also exists between this conversion to Christ, or this "passage to Christ," and the understanding of the scriptures.[51] *Cum autem conversus fuerit ad Dominum, auferetur velamen* (But when a man turns to the Lord the veil is removed).[52]

If we want to get to the root of the problem of spiritual understanding, which is being more and more widely discussed today, it seems advisable to refer to the act of conversion. We should look into the Church's conversion to her Lord, the Church viewed especially as made up of the first generations of the faithful. Nothing is better calculated to make us aware of the *seriousness* of a problem like this, the same sort of seriousness which we found so impressive in an Origen, for example, but which may well be masked from us by exuberance of image or subtlety of analysis. All scripture is perceived in a new light by the soul which is open to the gospel and adheres to Christ. All scripture is transfigured by Christ. *Accedite ad eum, et illuminamini* (Come to him, and you will be enlightened). As can be seen, a unique activity is involved, and it implies a global interpretation which remains indeterminate as to many points, just as it is obscure to many individuals (each one of us is not the whole Church, in whose faith and understanding and hope of glory we participate only as members of the whole body). A unique movement is involved; beginning with initial incredulity, it ascends by faith to the very summits of a spiritual life which does not have its term here below.[53] Its unfolding is coextensive with the gift of the Spirit, with the progress of charity.[54] All Christian experience, in all its phases, is, in principle, comprehended therein. Newness of understanding is correlative with "newness of life." To pass on to spiritual understanding[55] is, therefore, to pass on to the "new man," who never ceases to be renewed *de claritate in claritatem*.

This amounts to saying that this understanding cannot lead to results which are completely controllable by a particular method for which are apt to be gathered together into a definitive canon. It amounts to saying that it can never be made completely objective. It always envelops and transcends what has been grasped, and is, at the same time, enveloped and transcended by what it has as yet been unable to grasp: *dicta igitur sacri eloquii, cum legentium spiritu excrescunt* (the utterances of sacred language thus grow with the spirit of those who read it).[56] For, "to penetrate into the spirit of scripture means, in the final analysis, to learn to recognize the inner nature of God, to appropriate to oneself God's thoughts about the world."[57] But is it possible to conceive that we can ever have learned this? The dialectic is endless, analogous to that of mysticism and mystery. We can really speak of it only in the singular, as single act. We would never be able to understand it if we tried to judge it from a purely objective viewpoint, or to reduce it to a scientific discipline.[58] On this point, some of its partisans are in agreement with some of its adversaries. The practice of spiritual understanding, once it is no longer carried forward by the movement which initiated it, soon becomes nothing but idle fancy, barely respectful of the divine Word – unless, in its desire for perfect objectivity, it limits itself to the recording of a series of symbols, whose respective values are determined by the dual criterion of greater or lesser resemblence to the object signified and frequency of affirmation in tradition. A good dictionary could dispose of the problem once for all. Furthermore, even though there be a legitimate interest in them, it is inevitably a limited one. Then too we can see that the two criteria do not belong to the same order nor do they always overlap: certain symbolisms, very well supported in tradition, still have about them an air of the artificial or the tenuous. It remains an open question whether we can aim for something else today, whether we even have the right to do so. But, limiting ourselves for the moment solely to the historical aspect, we must approach matters in greater depth and with greater freedom if we hope to recapture anything of the spiritual interpretation of scripture as it existed during the first centuries of the Church. We must, above all else, reproduce a spiritual movement, often through completely different methods, while avoiding a retreat into the archaic or into slavish imitation. And this is the struggle of Jacob with the Angel of God, a struggle which we must begin again and again.[59]

But there is another misunderstanding which must also be eliminated. We sometimes demand of the "spiritual meaning" something which it cannot give us. And sometimes we reject it as lacking importance or even as detrimental to the true understanding of the Bible, because we have misunderstood both its nature and its proper sphere of influence. The misunderstanding is, moreover, enhanced by a number of faulty distinctions which are to be found throughout the history of exegesis, the most ancient as well as the most recent. At the risk of somewhat overstating the case, we can sum it all up antithetically by saying that we must make a careful distinction between the spiritual meaning of scripture, as it has been understood by an unbroken tradition, and the religious meaning of the Bible.[60]

The acceptations which we shall distinguish are mutually exclusive and do not have the same ends. They can hardly be compared without being contrasted. The religious meaning of the Bible is also a historical meaning. We can study the history of religion – including the religion of Israel – like any other collection of facts, but we cannot do it in any serious fashion without carefully educing, by means of an effort which goes further than mere critical erudition, the religious meaning of the texts which express it. In doing this, the historian somehow becomes contemporary with the facts he must describe and explain. Intent upon avoiding both an overestimation of the texts and a superficial interpretation of them, he seeks to reconstruct the religious consciousness of men in the biblical past, just as he would do for any other past. He studies carefully the spirit of an Abraham, a Moses, a David; the spirit of an Elijah, an Isaiah, a Jeremiah. He strives to understand the religious institutions of the people of Israel precisely as understood by them, not only in general but also in particular. He restructures his own view of the universe, and he discovers in ancient documents the wellsprings for his own prayer. He certainly does not deny himself the advantages which are his by reason of his having been born in a later generation and of his ability to encompass a long series of events in a single glance. While preserving himself from the facile ultimate explanations and the extremely arbitrary views sheltered under the name of "philosophy of history," he is skilled in sorting out the interplay of causality and influence, and in discovering what promise existed, even though unknown to its subject, in a particular institution, a particular light, a particular new attitude. For, in the history of the human mind, whether religious or secular thought is involved, certain moments possess a special density, a special fertility, and these can be properly evaluated only by taking account of their antecedents, their "sources," and especially the progression originating in them. Even the least profound ' religious experience, however crude its first expression, contains spiritual seeds which will only bear fruit in the tradition issuing from it. The "inevitable refraction" stemming from the glance backwards created by perspective thus becomes a legitimate and illuminating "elaboration."[61]

Nevertheless, the historian will always be attentive to differences in historical situations. He will, for example, highlight the abyss which separates "the religious level of Yahweh's Covenant with a few tribes of looting nomads whose only aim is to assure themselves of the conquest of a long-coveted territory and the transcendent level on which the Spirit of Jesus consecrates the love-union of the elect with the father for eternal life in his Son."[62] All his attention is directed towards reconstituting the past. This is not devoid of interest for the believer, not by any means. Since we are dealing with a unique history, it is important that the historian who recounts that history do so as a believer – but he will still be a believer.

The "spiritual meaning" strikes us as quite another thing altogether, particularly when it is considered in the pure form usually found in tradition. It does not derive from any backward-oriented curiosity. Even though it is, in its own way, or at least in one respect, an interpretation of the Jewish past, it interprets the Jewish past solely from the viewpoint of the Christian present. It is the Old Testament understood in the spirit of the New. Far from having to be wary of an ultimate view, it presupposes such a view, and this is completely legitimate since the ultimate view is based on a definitive event,[63] which in certain respects is already "the end of history." But this ultimate view is of necessity a view in faith. The meaning which stems from it is only perceived in the light of Christ[64] and under the action of his Spirit, within his Church. One who takes up the study of the history of Israel's religion in this fashion gives all its historical importance to it, because he understands it as the salvation history of the Church. Strictly speaking, though, he does not study this salvation history as a historian, whose goal is to see the spectacle of events unfold before him; he meditates on it as a believer – and not as a Jewish believer, but as a Christian believer – in order to live by it. This is his own history, from which he cannot remove himself. This history interests him personally. It is a mystery which is also his own mystery, identically. Consequently, he does not question the Bible as he would any other document or series of documents about the past, but he "searches the Scriptures" to discover God's thoughts and designs on him. He is not attracted by the psychology of the Old Testament believers. Besides, he knows that they could not have been explicitly aware of everything which he discovers in their writings; the seals of the Book had to be broken by the Lion of the Tribe of Judah.[65]

The antithesis which we have set out is, to be sure, a formal one. We can even admit that it is somewhat artificial. Its precise importance can be measured by what will follow. Concretely, the spiritual meaning of scripture and the religious meaning of the Bible coincide at many points. The ideal is for them to continue each other and interpenetrate. They somehow need each other: the former must have a permanent basis, and the latter must not be truncated. We might express this fact by saying that, before we can undertake any spiritual interpretation of the Old Testament through the New, we must first have historically understood the New Testament through the Old. It is of equally great importance – and the formula itself indicates it – that we avoid confusing the disciplines.[66] Their union is desirable, and even necessary, but it is a delicate one. Spiritual interpretation, even though it is, in an eminent way, historical interpretation, must not imprudently or prematurely interfere with historical study. Still more certainly, it should not be confused with history, even religious history, or be substituted for it. Left to its own devices, it would be somewhat hostile to history. Its use, even in the most authentic tradition, while it might be easily complemented by historical criticism, is not always in line with the religious understanding of the ancient texts. The more religiously beautiful and powerful a text is, the more is it stripped of its beauty and power by too ready or rigid an attempt to find a "spiritual meaning" in it. Yet if we were to combine the dual exclusivism of the critical and the allegorical methods, the process would be just as sterilizing. We must, therefore, reject too all-embracing or too automatic a practice of spiritual interpretation, so as to preserve the religious value of the Old Testament, considered both literally and in its historical situations.[67]

This is not to say that there is no tendency to disparage the Jewish scriptures in the doctrine of the spiritual meaning (not as it can be reconstructed in idea, but as historically given, as apparent from traditional usage). Generally speaking, the *modus judaicus intelligendi* is referred to in the doctrine only to be rejected with disdain. Let us not forget its Pauline origins.[68] It results, principally, from the Apostle's polemic stance. Paul pits one Testament against the other. He pits the letter which kills against the Spirit which gives life.[69] He pits vain shadows against the fullness of Christ. He argues against Jewish law. The danger in following him would, therefore, be that we would underestimate historical fact, not that we would overestimate it by going beyond the letter.

The danger can, however, be rather easily avoided. We must not take the Pauline opposition solely from the historical point of view. It was not set up between two different ways of evaluating Israel's ancient religion. When Paul looked towards the past, he magnified the privileges of his race and exalted the religion of his ancestors.[70] The entire point of his polemic was directed against "Israel according to the flesh," with its pretensions about perpetuating itself after its rejection of the Messiah, or against unstable Christians who still placed their hope in abrogated practices. It was not the Old Covenant as such which was the object of his scorn, but the Old Covenant as superannuated, the Old Covenant become aged, the Covenant whose role in history had come to an end. He holds no brief against "Jewish antiquities," only against Jewish decay – and

17

this implies, in tacit antithesis, the Christian newness.[71] Paul takes aim at "the letter," not at the literal meaning.

After Paul, we shall again see this opposition concentrated exclusively on the law of Moses. St Augustine, for example, will speak of those Judaizers who, *"exstinguentes prophetiae spiritum vivum, ad carnalia opera sine vita, hoc est, sine intellectu spirituali remanserant"* (killers of the living spirit of prophecy, abide in the works of the flesh without life, that is, without spiritual understanding).[72] From this standpoint, it is a legal system, a cult, and not a history which is at the core of the problem. And in the later tradition spiritual interpretation will almost always find its chosen ground in the Pentateuch. It is, in fact, on the most thoroughly material data of Mosaism that it prefers to dwell. In any event, it will always be the search for the meaning of *things*. Spiritual interpretation will, therefore, offer us an analysis of extrinsic facts and objective institutions rather than an elucidation of feelings or thought, and, generally speaking, will not undertake to fill the gap between the primary meaning of those institutions or facts, as understood and lived by the majority of ancient Jews, and the Christian meaning received, in sign, by them.[73]

Notes

Citations to Clement and Origen are principally to the editions of the Leipzig-Berlin Corpus: *Die Griechischen Christlichen Schriftsteller der ersten drei Jahrhunderte*; in such instances, the citation is to the page of the volume containing the cited work. Some Latin authors are quoted according to the Vienna Corpus: *Corpus scriptorum ecclesiasticorum latinorum*. The letters of Jerome, numbers 1 to 120, are quoted from the edition of the *Lettres* by J. Labourt (Paris, 1949–58). In addition, the following abbreviations are used:

ET	English translation
ETL	*Ephemerides Theologicae Lovanienses*
NRT	*Nouvelle Revue Théologique*
PG	Migne, *Patrologia Graeca*
PL	Migne, *Patrologia Latina*
R. bibl.	*Revue biblique*
RevScPhTh	*Revue des sciences philosophiques et théologiques*
RSR	*Recherches de science religieuse*

1 M. J. Lagrange, *Eclaircissements sur la méthode historique*, p. 91.
2 M. J. Lagrange, *La Méthode historique* (2nd edn), p. 120.
3 See Henri Davenson, in *Esprit*, June 1936, p. 457: "Allegorical exegesis . . . was not only a weapon in the hands of the theologians. It was also a noble game for literate Christians in early antiquity, a game which their parents had taught them to practise on Homer and Virgil." See also H. I. Marrou, *Saint Augustin et la fin de la culture antique*, II: *Retractatio* (1949), pp. 646–51.

4 *L'unité dans l'Eglise*, App. VII (French tr., collection "Unam Sanctam," 1939, pp. 260–1).

5 Thus we shall not explicitly consider the relationship of spiritual understanding with the idea of tradition, even though this is one of the problem's principal aspects. And we shall have nothing to say on the subject of biblical symbolism.

6 We are not referring to Old Testament teachings or laws which can be found as such in the New Testament. This is self-evident. See, for example, Ambrose's distinction between the *mystica legis* and the *moralia probitatis*: *In Lucam*, 1. 8, n. 2 (*PL*, 15, 1792D). Or Augustine's distinction of *sacramenta, promissa, praecepta* in the Law: *In Psalmum 73*, n. 2 (*PL*, 36, 930). On the precepts of the Law which must still be accomplished literally: Origen, *Num.*, h. 11, 1 (p. 75). See Irenaeus, *Adv. Haereses*, 4, 12–13 (*PG*, 7, 1004–1010).

7 Consider the example suggested by Père Augustin George: "Did not the old story of Moriah help him to think about his death? The Fathers, in their later comparisons between the sacrifice of Abraham and that of Jesus, frequently emphasize purely accidental analogies, but they are basically correct in seeing the profound kinship of the two sacrifices." *Le sacrifice d'Abraham, essai sur les diverses intentions de ses narrateurs* in *Etudes de critique et d'histoire religieuse* (Lyon, 1948), p. 109.

8 See the word of which Origen was so fond: αὐτοβασιλεία. Similarly, Pseudo-Barnabas, ch. 6, and Hippolytus. *The Apostolic Tradition*, ch. 23, likened the Promised Land to the flesh of Jesus, and so forth.

9 C. Spicq, *RevScPhTh*, 1948, p. 90.

10 1 Cor. 10:1–3. The same can be said of the deluge, 1 Pet. 3:20–1.

11 Dom Olivier Rousseau. *Histoire du mouvement liturgique*; ET *The Progress of the Liturgy* (Westminster, 1951), pp. 146–7.

12 It may be that the mental operations of the New Testament authors transcend any such duality: simultaneously, they express the New Testament by the Old and spiritualize the Old by the New. As we reflect on an already constituted New Testament, we, in our historical exegesis, must comment on the New Testament through the Old, and then on the Old through the New. Our operation is a dual one, as is our movement – we are conscious of a rhythm whose alternating beats become distinguishable only in terms of one another.

13 See Jacques Guillet, "Le Thème de la marche au désert dans l'Ancien Testament," in *RSR*, 1948. St Augustine, following St Paul, will say, for example: *"Qui eduxi te de terra Aegypti. Non illi tantum populo dicitur. Omnes enim educti sumus de terra Aegypti, omnes per mare rubrum transivimus, inimici nostri persequentes nos in aqua perierunt."* (*In Psalmum 80*, 15 (*PL*, 37, 1042). St Irenaeus had written in like vein (*Adv. Haereses*, 1. 4, 30, 4): *"Universa enim quae ex Aegypto profectio fiebat populi, a Deo typus et imago fuit profectionis Ecclesiae, quae erat futura de Gentibus"* (*PG*, 7, 1067C). See Deut. 7:10 and Isa. 41:14.

14 1 Cor. 11:25 and Exod. 24:8, and so forth. Bernard, *In Octava Paschae*, sermo 1, n. 5 (*PL*, 183, 294C).

15 Jean Levie, S.J., "La crise de l'Ancien Testament," *NRT*, 1929, p. 835. See Louis Bouyer, "La première Eucharistie dans la dernière Cène," *La Maison-Dieu*, 18, p. 47: "It is only through the avenues which were opened up to the mind and heart of man by the events of the Exodus, the passage of the Red Sea, the settling in Palestine that we shall ever be able to understand our deliverance from the Evil One, our passage, by baptism, 'from the kingdom of darkness into the kingdom of the Son.'"

16 Augustine, *De vera religione*, c. 27, n. 50: "... *series populi uni Deo dediti ..., cujus historia Vetus Testamentum vocatur, quasi terrenum pollicens regnum; quae tota nihil aliud est quam imago novi populi, et Novi Testamenti pollicentis regnum caelorum*" (*PL*, 34, 144). *In Psalmum 75*, n. 1: "Judaea vera, Christi Ecclesia" (*PL*, 36, 958). Louis Bouyer, in *La Vie spirituelle*, vol. 80 (1949), p. 580.

17 See Jean Levie, S.J., "Les limites de la preuve d'Ecriture sainte," in *NRT*, 1949, pp. 1012–13: The dogmatic efforts of St Paul are "efforts to express as well as possible, using yesterday's words, using old formulas inherited from the Old Testament, the new revelation which was made to humanity, or to the Apostle in particular, about Christ. To speak about Christ and about the dramatic newness of his message, he has nothing at his disposal but traditional Jewish concepts and words, which he took, just as they were, from his environment and education, and which formed the point of departure for his thought; and yet this new reality, communicated by God, is infinitely richer than traditional concepts and words; nonetheless, it must be understood with those concepts as a starting point, ... "; see also p. 1028.

18 These remarks could probably be made more general. In order to be actualized, every thought requires an expression which, by analogy or contrast, relates it to some previously expressed thought. Thus allusion is essential to it. This is even more strictly true for the period when the particular thought is being formed, prior to being transmitted, for the period of invention and creation, when something new must fill man's mind so as to transform him, "open" him to some area which was unexplored, unsuspected, until then. Thus it is true in the highest degree when the mind must humanly translate the Object of divine revelation, so as to acquire a reflective awareness of it and somehow "grasp" it. Thus there will be still more reason, in this second logical moment, to speak of invention and creation, inasmuch as revelation, and thereby welcome and reception, is so much more basically involved. Consequently, there will be more room for symbolism. We might add that, even when a thought can readily be formulated in the abstract, without any need for explicit recourse to an earlier thought which serves as impulse or symbol, such recourse can still be useful, and even necessary for all practical purposes, if we are to take better account of it and to grasp it in a more living way. In this case, the operation will be less spontaneous and will have less independent ontological significance: thus "thought comments upon itself" (J. Baruzi). A third logical moment could be found in the pedagogical use of the image or system of images.

19 There are a hundred examples. Here are a few: Gregory, *In Ezechielem*, 1. 2, hom. 3, n. 18: "*Scriptura ... in litteram dividitur et allegoriam*" (*PL*, 76, 968); 1. 1, hom. 3, n. 4 (*PL* 807C). Jerome, *In Amos*, 1. 2, c. 4: "*allegoriam, id est, intelligentiam spiritualem*" (*PL*, 25, 1027D). Thomas, *Ia*, q. 1, a. 10.

20 See "Sur un vieux distique, La doctrine du 'quadruple sens,' " in *Mélanges Cavallera* (1948), pp. 347–66.

21 One of the best explanations of the difference between symbol and allegory in their structure and noetic importance is given by Jean Baruzi in *Saint Jean de la Croix et le problème de l'expérience mystique* (2nd edn), pp. 323–9. It would be wrong to speak uniformly ill of allegory, even where it seems to be at its most artificial, for in certain cases it can be the vehicle in which a great and authentic symbolism is itself symbolized in a hundred different ways. We sometimes find in certain authors, and generally among

20

the Fathers, a hint of the allegorical which should not throw us off, lest we thereby forfeit the opportunity of penetrating its spirit. But we also must be wary of indulging in an "atomistic" exegesis of the writings of the Fathers, no less than of Scripture itself.

22 See Spinoza, *Epist. 25: "Christi passionem, mortem et sepulturam tecum litteraliter accipio, ejus autem resurrectionem allegorice."* In his Latin commentary on the Song of Songs, Luis de Leon well distinguished the two acceptations of the word: *"Tota hujus libri oratio figurata est et allegorica. Allegoricam dico, non ea allegoria quam, sancto Paulo auctore, inducunt Theologi, cum in sacris Litteris a litterae, quem vocant, sensu allegoricum sensum distinguunt; sed quam tradunt rhetores effici ex perpetua metaphora"* (*Opera*, vol. II, Salamanca, n.d., p. 15). According to Oscar Cullmann, "for allegorical exegesis, history is only a symbol behind which something else is to be sought"; this exegesis takes as point of departure "a completely formulated idea so as to find it again in the text at any price." *La nécessité et la fonction de l'exégèse philologique et historique de la Bible*, in *Verbum Caro*, vol. III, 1949, p. 6. For Abbé Jean Vilnet, the allegorical meaning "consists in using facts or words from the Bible, which have a literal value, as pure symbols of other realities to which they appear to be totally unconnected" (*Bible et mystique chez saint Jean de la Croix*, 1949, p. 84, n.) This, however, is not the true traditional acceptation, which is all we are concerned with here.

23 See Dom Célestin Charlier in a fine study, filled with traditional vigor and packed with excellent suggestions, *La lecture sapientielle de la Bible*, in *La Maison-Dieu*; ET *The Christian Approach to the Bible* (Westminster, 1958), pp. 255–63. See Charlier's "Exégèse partistique et exégèse scientifique," in *Esprit et Vie*, 1949, p. 62.

24 "Typologie ou Evolution. Problèmes d'exégèse spirituelle," in *Esprit et Vie*, 1949, p. 594.

25 Hans Urs von Balthasar, "Die Schrift als Gottes Wort," in *Schweizer Rundschau*, 1949, p. 10. See Maurice Pontet, *L'exégèse de saint Augustin prédicateur*, 1946, p. 586.

26 As a matter of fact, this is the terminology which was proposed by the great Arnauld, "Remarques sur 'l'ancienne nouveauté de l'Ecriture sainte'," (*Oeuvres*, vol. V, p. 346): "We must remain in agreement that the true literal meaning of Scripture is the meaning which the Holy Spirit intended to point out to us ... Thus we are interpreting the Prophets very literally when we apply what God promised the Jews at the time of the Messiah to Christians throughout the history of the Church; the other interpretations, however, are not literal but Judaic." It is true that Arnauld, as can be seen, applies his principle only to prophecies properly so called. He also adds that those who understand them in another fashion deserve to be told: *"Nescitis cujus spiritus estis*, you do not know what the spirit of Christianity is."

27 *In Ezechielem*, 1. 1, h. 3, n. 4 (*PL*, 76, 807C).

28 Dom Charlier, *La lecture sapentielle*, p. 279. See Jerome, *In Amos*, 1. 2, c. 5: *"medulla spiritus"* (*PL*, 25, 1036B). Gregory, *In Ezechielem*, 1. 2, h. 10, n. 2: *"latens in littera spiritualis medulla"* (*PL*, 76, 1058). Hesychius, *In Leviticum* (*PG*, 93, 780B). It is also true that, taking the terms very precisely, it is not scripture as text, but sacred history as contained in scripture, which offers a spiritual meaning, since spiritual meaning is not the meaning of words but the meaning of things: it is διὰ τύπου προφητεία because διὰ πραγμάτων προφητεία; see John Chrysostom, *De Paenitentia*, h. 6, n. 4 (*PG*, 49, 320); 1. 17, c. 5, n. 2 (*PL*, 41, 313). The paradox which is here the object of our faith makes it impossible, as in every analogous case, for us to express it in language which is perfectly adequate and coherent.

29 Similarly, if it is true that "there is no divine content in the Bible outside of its historical signification" (Charlier, in *Esprit et Vie*, 1949, p. 590), we should beware of the inference that there is no divine meaning in the Bible other than the historical meaning.

30 *Règles pour l'intelligence des saintes Ecritures* (1716), p. 10: "I call the first the immediate meaning, and the second the prophetic . . . The second is almost always more literal than the first because it is the meaning which the prophet had principally in mind." On the other hand, as Thomas says, *IIaIIae*, q. 173, a. 4, the sacred writer is an *instrumentum deficiens* in the hands of God, and he never sees what he is writing about except *cum aliquo cognitionis defectu*; also, *etiam veri prophetae non omnia cognoscunt quae in eorum visis et verbis aut etiam factis Spiritus sanctus intendit*. See F. Ogara, "De typica apud Chrysostomum prophetia," in *Gregorianum*, 1943, p. 71: "(*Spiritus Sanctus*) *Veteris rudibus saepe figuris Novi mysteria significare voluit, quidquid tandem de illis mysteriis futuris scriptor humanus intellexerit*." Newman also thought that "the sacred authors did not always know or even suspect the spiritual and profound meaning" of what they wrote. J. Seynaeve, "La doctrine de Newman sur l'inspiration," in *ETL*, 1949, p. 366.

31 The word seems to be of Lutheran origin, but this is certainly no reason to find it objectionable, any more than we object to the words "patristic" or "patrology."

32 But even if we use the term "typological exegesis," we shall be careful to avoid using "typological meaning": the latter is pure jargon, for which there is neither need nor excuse. See Thomas, *Quodl. 7*, q. 6, a. 15: "*allegoricus sensus vel typicus*." On the words "type," "figure," "mystery," and "mystical meaning" as used in Christian antiquity, see our *Corpus mysticum* (2nd edn), 1949, chs. 2 and 3.

33 Thomas, *Quodl. 7*, q. 6, a. 15: "*Sensus iste qui ex figuris accipitur, spiritualis vocatur*."

34 It was against the pretense of a completely "spiritual" (that is to say, falsely spiritual) Christianity that Newman delivered at Littlemore his two sermons: "The Christian Church, a Continuation of the Jewish," and "The Principle of Continuity between the Jewish and Christian Churches," collected in *Sermons Bearing on Subjects of the Day* (new edn), 1879, pp. 181–217. In these sermons, he stresses the literal and not merely "spiritual" fulfillment of the prophecies.

35 *De vera religione*, c. 7, n. 13 (*PL*, 34, 128). See *Epist. 196*: It is by reason of "the spiritual and apostolic understanding" of the Old Testament that the Christian can be called "a Jew according to the spirit," a son of Abraham according to the spirit (*PL*, 33, 891–9). Florus of Lyons, *In Epistulam ad Romanos* (*PL*, 119, 294A.).

36 The sacrifice of Isaac, for example, signifies not merely the exterior fact of Christ's death, but also man's salvation by Jesus. Jonah, vomited out by the whale, is not only Jesus leaving the tomb, but the Christian being reborn to eternal life. See A. Pérate, *L'archéologie chrétienne*, (Paris, 1892), pp. 69, 74, 102, 112; O. Marucchi, *Manual of Christian Archeology* (Paterson, 1935), pp. 302–8. P. Perdrizet, who refers to these examples in his *Etude sur le speculum humanae salvationis* (Paris, 1908), p. 114, wrongly concludes that this symbolism is "purely moral."

37 See Thomas, *In Joannem*, c. 6, lect. 4, n. 8: "*Quanto aliquid est magis spirituale, tanto magis est intrinsecum*."

38 See Alcuin, *In Joannem*: "*interiorem intelligentiam spiritualis sensus*" (*PL*, 100, 821C). Bernard, *Sermo 67 de diversis* (*PL*, 183, 690A–B).

39 See Bernard, *In Cantica*, sermo 45, n. 7: "*Sed attende Spiritum loqui, et spiritualiter oportere intelligi quae dicuntur*" (*PL*, 183, 1002D). Rupert of Deutz, *In Nahum*, 1. 2 (*PL*, 168,

555B). Thomassin, *Dogmata Theologica*, vol. III, tr. 1, c. 8, n. 6: "*Scripturae non litteram tantum sed Spiritum maxime sugere insuescant, cum ille Spiritus sanctus sit, qui has nobis Scripturas modulatus est.*" Scheeben, *Dogmatik*, 237: "The divine origin of Scripture implies besides that its words do not only have the literal meaning intended by the human authors . . . they also have . . . a spiritual meaning proper to the Holy Spirit."

40 Jerome, *In Ezechielem*, 1. 1, c. 1 (*PL*, 25, 26D).

41 Ibid., 1. 12, c. 41 (*PL*, 25, 399D).

42 See *In Apocalypsin expositio, visio tertia: "Spiritualis intelligentia in Veteri Testamento, nihil est aliud, quam Novum Testamentum"* (*PL*, 17, 807D).

43 Didymus, *Liber de Spiritu Sancto*, n. 33 (*PG*, 39, 1063C).

44 Louis Massignon, "L'expérience mystique et les modes de stylisation littéraire," in *Le Roseau d'or*, no. 20 (1927), *Chroniques*.

45 2 Cor. 3:17. See the commentary of Père Allo, *in loc.*, p. 95 and p. 107. The meaning of this expression of St Paul is by no means exhausted by this presentation. See J. Lebreton, *Histoire du dogme de la Trinité*, vol. I, (6th edn), pp. 611–15.

46 Gregory, *In Ezechielem*, 1. 1, hom. 3, n. 19 (*PL*, 76, 814C).

47 *Expositio in Apocalypsin: "In zona aurea accincta pectori, potest etiam scientia spiritualis ac purus sensus datus Ecclesiae intellegi"* (*Opera Omnia*, Morin ed., vol. II, p. 212). See Augustine, *In Psalmum 67*, n. 9 (*PL*, 36, 817). It is also legitimate to say that the figures of David or Joshua, like the characters in the Song of Songs, have a spiritual signification. On the "spiritual" meaning of St John of the Cross, see Jean Vilnet, *Bible et mystique chez saint Jean de la Croix* (1949), pp. 85–6, 91, 184–7.

48 For one example, see Jean Daniélou, "Les repas de la Bible et leur signification," in *La Maison-Dieu*, 18, pp. 28–30; ET "The Banquet of the Poor" in *The Lord of History* (Chicago, 1958), pp. 235–238, with reference to the Passover meal. See Hilary, *Tractatus Mysteriorum*, I, 22: "*Numquid non corporaliter gestis spiritualiter gerenda succedunt?*"; 2, 9 (Brisson ed.), pp. 112, 144. Gregory, *In Ezechielem*, 1. 1, hom. 7, nn. 16–17, commenting on "*spiritus vitae erat in rotis*" (*PL*, 76, 848).

49 Othloh of St Emmeran, *Dialogus de tribus quaestionibus*, c. 33 (*PL*, 146, 102).

50 Augustine, *In Psalmum 33*, sermo 1, n. 7 (*PL*, 36, 305).

51 See Augustine, *Contra adversarium Legis et Prophetarum*, 1. 2, c. 7, n. 29 (*PL*, 42, 655). Gregory of Nyssa, *Contra Eunomium*, 1. 7 (*PG*, 45, 741–5). This is true of the perception of prophetic signs, in the most narrow sense of the word prophetic (*prophetia in verbis*). But spiritual understanding only expands within that faith which has already been received. This is also one of the sources (the other is liturgical) of the idea of "understanding in faith." See *Evagrii altercatio legis inter Simonem Judaeum et Theophilum Christianum*, 1. 2; answer of Theophilus to Simon's quotations of texts from Deuteronomy and Isaiah: "*Sacratissima Christi vox est quam, si tu volueris cognoscere, oportet te primum credere. Tunc demum poteris intelligere. Esaias enim redarguit te dicens: nisi credideritis, non intelligetis*" (Bratke ed., p. 3).

52 2 Cor. 3:16; see Exod. 34:34. Augustine, *In Psalmum 64*, n. 6 (*PL*, 36, 778). Here we are taking St Paul's words in the sense which tradition has regularly given them (a meaning which is, moreover, completely in line with Pauline thought). For the immediate meaning of the text, see Dom Jacques Dupont, "Le Chrétien, miroir de la gloire divine," in *R. bibl.*, 1949, p. 399. See also the beautiful passage in Clement of Alexandria, *Stromata*, 6, c. 12 (Stählin ed.), vol. II, p. 484. See Othloh of St Emmeran,

once again applying the symbolism of the miracle of Cana to our subject (*PL*, 146, 212C, 213A).

53 In other words, God who reveals himself in scripture always remains "*magis significatus quam demonstratus.*" Augustine, *Contra Maximinum arianum*, 1. 2, c. 10 (*PL*, 42, 811).

54 Augustine, *De catechizandis rudibus*, n. 35 (*PL*, 40, 336).

55 See Bernard, *In Epiphania Domini sermo 2*, n. 2 (*PL*, 183, 148B).

56 Gregory, *In Ezechielem*, 1. 1, hom. 7, n. 10 (*PL*, 76, 846A); see no. 9 (844C). See Stanislas Fumet, *L'impatience des limites* (Fribourg, 1942), pp. 106–107: "Advancing like the figure of Ezekiel with those four animals, each moving forward in all directions, it [scripture] goes beyond all things." The thought is analogous also to that of St Gregory in Paul Claudel's *Les cinq premières plaies d'Égypte*: "The word of God is not like a projector designed to throw light in advance on particular points but is like a hand-held torch, shedding light around us as we move forward."

57 Hans Urs von Balthasar, "Die Schrift," p. 11. Thus we must say about the understanding of scripture what St Augustine said about the knowledge of God: "*Si finisti, Deus non est*" (sermo 53, n. 12 (*PL*, 38, 370)). Also, "*Si quasi comprehendere potuisti, cognitione tua te decepisti; hoc ergo non est, si comprehendisti; si autem hoc est, non comprehendisti*" (sermo 52, n. 16 (*PL*, 38, 360)).

58 Assuredly, this is not to say that there are some explanations with objective validity and others which are solely derived from individual fancy. As for the reasons for believing: only those which are valid make of the act of faith a reasonable act. But it should be added that the more these reasons approach the character of a personal sign, the less capable they are of being directly universalized. This, *mutatis mutandis*, is what happens here, where the role of personal opinion can be legitimate – always, of course, within the "analogy of faith."

59 Rupert of Deutz, *De Trinitate et operibus ejus, In Genesim*, 1. 8, c. 9 (*PL*, 167, 498).

60 This "equivocation" has been attacked by Père Spicq in *RevScPhTh*, 1948, pp. 90–91.

61 These expressions are to be found in H. I. Marrou, *Saint Augustin et la fin de la culture antique*, *Retractatio* (1949), p. 644, n. 12. See the study, cited above, by Louis Massignon, "L'Expérience mystique et les modes de stylisation littéraire." These remarks have greater significance where the Bible is concerned, because "the Hebrew mind, unlike the Greek mind, never cultivated the tendency to give precise definition to notions. Its mode of thought was dynamic; it uses terms and concepts more for the purpose of suggesting that it transcends them than for the purpose of signifying that it stops at them; all the elements of vocabuluary are somehow reflective of the tendency to become symbolic and thereby acquire a 'plusvalue'." J. Coppens, *Les harmonies des deux Testaments*, p. 53, summarizing J. DeZwaan, *Hermeneutical Plus-Value, in Conjectanea Neotestamentica in honorem A. Fridrichsen* (1947), pp. 242–50. This is basically what Massignon finds to be true of all Semitic languages. A similar observation can be found as early as Luis de Leon: "The Hebrew language, in which this book [The Song of Songs] was written, is, in its constitution and even in its particulars, a language of a few words and short expressions, and the latter are filled with a multitude of meanings" (quoted by Alain Guy, *La pensée de Fray Luis de Leon*, p. 270).

62 Dom Célestin Charlier, "Les Thèmes bibliques et leurs transpositions successives," in *Esprit et Vie*, 1948, p. 153.

63 On the incomplete character of history outside of this perspective, see Origen, *Jos.* 4, 8, 4 (pp. 339–340); h. 16, 3 (pp. 395–6).

64 See the extremely profound words of St Augustine, *In Psalmum 47*, n. 1: "... *ut intelligas Deum fecisse lucem, cum Christus a mortuis resurrexit*" (*PL*, 36, 532). Only the Christian knows this spiritual meaning, because he has received from the Lord τὴν ἀκριβαστάτην ἐκ καταβολῆς κόσμυ εἰς τέλος ἀλήθειαν (Clement, *Stromata*, 6, 9; vol. II, p. 470).

65 See Jerome, *In Isaiam* (*PL*, 24, 332). Gregory, *In Ezechielem*, 1. 2, hom. 4, n. 19 (*PL*, 76, 983–984). Caesarius of Arles, *Expositio in Apocalypsin* (*Opera Omnia*, vol. II, pp. 221–2).

66 Père Lagrange suggested an analogous distinction, which stemmed from the same concern, when he distinguished in prophecy a "literal meaning considered under its religious aspect" from a "spiritual meaning." "Pascal et les prophéties messianiques," in *R. bibl.*, vol. 15 (1906), p. 541. Here, however, we think that the two meanings tend to come together.

67 Abbé Jean Steinmann is perfectly correct when he writes: "The allegorists are mistaken in pretending, through their game of facile appearances, to draw the true religious meaning from the inspired text"; he is also correct in thinking that "the historian's entire effort should allow him to become an intimate of God's witness, to know his particular language, the style which expresses his soul, to know his habits and his interior life, the rites which he observed, his tastes, and the flavor of his meditation." And yet we are still inclined to believe that, properly understood and properly limited, the spiritual understanding of scripture is immune to his criticism and fails to bear out his fears. See "Apologie du Littéralisme," in *La Vie intellectuelle*, May 1948.

68 They are quite Johannine as well, and perhaps more so. But we do find in St Paul a number of strongly phrased theoretical formulas which had a decisive influence on Christian tradition.

69 2 Cor. 3:6 See, on this text, P. Benoît, "La Loi et la Croix d'après saint Paul," in *R. bibl.*, 1938, p. 491. It is commonly acknowledged that the Apostle's thought is often punctuated by antithesis: see Jean Nelis, "Les antithèses littéraires dans les épîtres de saint Paul," in *NRT*, vol. 70 (1948).

70 See Rom. 3:21; 9:4–5. But Paul exalts it precisely as the religion of the Promise, and to the extent that it must end in Christ.

71 We can find this expressed in Père Merlin, for example, in his *Dissertations sur la nature de la Loi de Moïse*, First Part, appealing to the authority of St Paul: "You may be wondering where all these arguments of St Paul are leading. They are leading to the proclamation to the Jews that, if they refuse to answer the call of Jesus Christ, they can never again hope to share in grace and in justification, which they could until then have received by an outpouring of the riches of the Gospel on the ages which preceded ..." (*PL*, 47, 1058–9).

72 Sermo 10, n. 3 (*PL*, 38, 94).

73 See Eusebius, *Ecclesiastical History*, 1. 1, c. 3, n. 4, on the συμβολικὴ λατρεία established by Moses. This would be no less true of a St John of the Cross, for example, whose primary interest was in the soul of Prophet or Psalmist and who discovers all his own experience in theirs: See J. Vilnet, *Bible et mystique*, pp. 130, 138–43, 161. It is not possible to reduce to a single formula everything which Christian tradition has actually incorporated into its understanding of scripture.

The Superiority of
Pre-Critical Exegesis

David C. Steinmetz

The medieval theory of levels of meaning in the biblical text, with all its undoubted defects, flourished because it is true, while the modern theory of a single meaning with all its demonstrable virtues, is false. Until the historical-critical method becomes critical of its own theoretical foundations and develops a hermeneutical theory adequate to the nature of the text which it is interpreting it will remain restricted – as it deserves to be – to the guild and the academy, where the question of truth can endlessly be deferred.

In 1859 Benjamin Jowett, then Regius Professor of Greek in the University of Oxford, published a justly famous essay on the interpretation of scripture.[1] Jowett argued that "Scripture has one meaning – the meaning which it had in the mind of the Prophet or Evangelist who first uttered or wrote, to the hearers or readers who first received it."[2] Scripture should be interpreted like any other book and the later accretions and venerated traditions surrounding its interpretation should, for the most part, either be brushed aside or severely discounted. "The true use of interpretation is to get rid of interpretation, and leave us alone in company with the author."[3]

Jowett did not foresee great difficulties in the way of the recovery of the original meaning of the text. Proper interpretation requires imagination, the ability to put onself into an alien cultural situation, and knowledge of the language and history of the ancient people whose literature one sets out to interpret. In the case of the Bible, one has also to bear in mind the progressive nature of revelation and the superiority of certain later religious insights to certain earlier ones. But the intepreter, armed with the proper linguistic tools, will find that "universal truth easily breaks through the accidents of time and place"[4] and that such truth still speaks to the condition of the unchanging human heart.

Of course, critical biblical studies have made enormous strides since the time of Jowett. No reputable biblical scholar would agree today with Jowett's reconstruction of the gospels in which Jesus appears as a "teacher . . . speaking to a group of serious, but not highly educated, working men, attempting to inculcate in them a loftier and sweeter morality."[5] Still, the quarrel between modern biblical scholarship and Benjamin Jowett is less a quarrel over his hermeneutical theory than it is a disagreement with him over the application of that theory in his exegetical practice. Biblical scholarship still hopes to recover the original intention of the author of a biblical text and still regards the pre-critical exegetical tradition as an obstacle to the proper understanding of the true meaning of that text. The most primitive meaning of the text is its only valid meaning, and the historical–critical method is the only key which can unlock it.

But is that hermeneutical theory true?

I think it is demonstrably false. In what follows I want to examine the pre-critical exegetical tradition at exactly the point at which Jowett regarded it to be most vulnerable – namely, in its refusal to bind the meaning of any pericope to the intention, whether explicit or merely half-formed, of its human author. Medieval theologians defended the proposition, so alien to modern biblical studies, that the meaning of scripture in the mind of the prophet who first uttered it is only one of its possible meanings and may not, in certain circumstances, even be its primary or, most important meaning. I want to show that this theory (in at least that respect) was superior to the theories which replaced it. When biblical scholarship shifted from the hermeneutical position of Origen to the hermeneutical position of Jowett, it gained something important and valuable. But it lost something as well, and it is the painful duty of critical scholarship to assess its losses as well as its gains.

I

Medieval hermeneutical theory took as its point of departure the words of St Paul: "The letter kills but the spirit makes alive" (2 Cor. 3:6). Augustine suggested that this text could be understood in either one of two ways. On the one hand, the distinction between letter and spirit could be a distinction between law and gospel, between demand and grace. The letter kills because it demands an obedience of the sinner which the sinner is powerless to render. The Spirit makes alive because it infuses the forgiven sinner with new power to meet the rigorous requirements of the law.

But Paul could also have in mind a distinction between what William Tyndale later called the "story-book" or narrative level of the Bible and the deeper theological meaning or spiritual signifiance implicit within it. This distinction was important for at least three reasons. Origen stated the first reason with unforgettable clarity:

> Now what man of intelligence will believe that the first and the second and the third day, and the evening and the morning existed without the sun and moon and stars? And that the first day, if we may so call it, was even without a heaven? And who is so silly as to believe that God, after the manner of a farmer, "planted a paradise eastward in Eden," and set in it a visible and palpable "tree of life," of such a sort that anyone who tasted its fruit with his bodily teeth would gain life; and again that one could partake of "good and evil" by masticating the fruit taken from the tree of that name? And when God is said to "walk in the paradise in the cool of the day" and Adam to hide himself behind a tree, I do not think anyone will doubt that these are figurative expressions which indicate certain mysteries through a semblance of history and not through actual event.[6]

Simply because a story purports to be a straightforward historical narrative does not mean that it is in fact what it claims to be. What appears to be history may be metaphor or figure instead and the interpreter who confuses metaphor with literal fact is an intepreter who is simply incompetent. Every biblical story means something, even if the narrative taken at face value contains absurdities or contradictions. The interpreter must demythologize the text in order to grasp the sacred mystery cloaked in the language of actual events.

The second reason for distinguishing between letter and spirit was the thorny question of the relationship between Israel and the Church, between the Greek Testament and the Hebrew Bible. The Church regarded itself as both continuous and discontinuous with ancient Israel. Because it claimed to be continuous, it felt an unavoidable obligation to interpret the Torah, the prophets, and the writings. But it was precisely this claim of continuity, absolutely essential to Christian identity, which created fresh hermeneutical problems for the Church.

How was a French parish priest in 1150 to understand Psalm 137, which bemoans captivity in Babylon, makes rude remarks about Edomites, expresses an ineradicable longing for a glimpse of Jerusalem, and pronounces a blessing on anyone who avenges the destruction of the Temple by dashing Babylonian children against a rock? The priest lives in Concale, not Babylon, has no personal quarrel with Edomites, cherishes no ambitions to visit Jerusalem (though he might fancy a holiday in Paris), and is expressly forbidden by Jesus to avenge himself on his enemies. Unless Psalm 137 has more than one possible meaning, it cannot be used as a prayer by the Church and must be rejected as a lament belonging exclusively to the piety of ancient Israel.

A third reason for distinguishing letter from spirit was the conviction, expressed by Augustine, that while all scripture was given for the edification of the Church and the nurture of the three theological virtues of faith, hope, and love, not all the stories in the Bible are edifying as they stand. What is the spiritual point of the story of the drunkenness of Noah, the murder of Sisera, or the oxgoad of Shamgar, son of Anath? If it cannot be found on the level of narrative, then it must be found on the level of allegory, metaphor, and type.

That is not to say that patristic and medieval interpreters approved of arbitrary and undisciplined exegesis, which gave free rein to the imagination of the exegete. Augustine argued, for example, that the more obscure parts of scripture should be interpreted in the light of its less difficult sections and that no allegorical interpretation could be accepted which was not supported by the "manifest testimonies" of other less ambiguous portions of the Bible. The literal sense of scripture is basic to the spiritual and limits the range of possible allegorical meanings in those instances in which the literal meaning of a particular passage is absurd, undercuts the living relationship of the church to the Old Testament, or is spiritually barren.

II

From the time of John Cassian, the Church subscribed to a theory of the fourfold sense of scripture.[7] The literal sense of scripture could and usually did nurture the three theological virtues, but when it did not, the exegete could appeal to three additional spiritual senses, each sense corresponding to one of the virtues. The allegorical sense taught about the Church and what it should believe, and so it corresponded to the virtue of faith. The tropological sense taught about individuals and what they should do, and so it corresponded to the virtue of love. The anagogical sense pointed to the future and wakened expectation, and so it corresponded to the virtue of hope. In the fourteenth century Nicholas of Lyra summarized this hermeneutical theory in a much quoted little rhyme:

> Littera gesta docet,
> Quid credas allegoria,
> Moralis quid agas,
> Quo tendas anagogia.

This hermeneutical device made it possible for the Church to pray directly and without qualification even a troubling Psalm like 137. After all, Jerusalem was not merely a city in the Middle East; it was, according to the allegorical sense, the Church; according to the tropological sense, the faithful soul; and according to the anagogical sense, the center of God's new creation. The Psalm became a lament of those who long for the establishment of God's future kingdom and who are trapped in this disordered and troubled world, which with all its delights is still not their home. They seek an abiding city elsewhere. The imprecations against the Edomites and the Babylonians are transmuted into condemnations of the world, the flesh, and the devil. If you grant the fourfold sense of scripture, David sings like a Christian.

III

Thomas Aquinas wanted to ground the spiritual sense of scripture even more securely in the literal sense than it had been grounded in Patristic thought. Returning to the distinction between "things" and "signs" made by Augustine in *De doctrina christiana* (though Thomas preferred to use the Aristotelian terminology of "things" and "words"), Thomas argued that while words are the signs of things, things designated by words can themselves be the signs of other things. In all merely human sciences, words alone have a sign-character. But in Holy Scripture, the things designated by words can themselves have the character of a sign. The literal sense of scripture has to do with the sign-character of words; the spiritual sense of scripture has to do with the sign-character of things. By arguing this way, Thomas was able to show that the spiritual sense of scripture is always based on the literal sense and derived from it.

Thomas also redefined the literal sense of scripture as "the meaning of the text which the author intends." Lest Thomas be confused with Jowett, I should hasten to point out that for Thomas the author was God, not the human prophet or apostle. In the fourteenth century, Nicholas of Lyra, a Franciscan exegete and one of the most impressive biblical scholars produced by the Christian Church, built a new hermeneutical argument on the aphorism of Thomas. If the literal sense of scripture is the meaning which the author intended (presupposing that the author whose intention finally matters is God), then is it possible to argue that scripture contains a double literal sense? Is there a literal-historical sense (the original meaning of the words as spoken in their first historical setting) which includes and implies a literal-prophetic sense (the larger meaning of the words as perceived in later and changed circumstances)?

Nicholas not only embraced a theory of the double literal sense of scripture, but he was even willing to argue that in certain contexts the literal-prophetic sense takes precedence over the literal-historical. Commenting on Psalm 117, Lyra wrote: "The literal sense in this Psalm concerns Christ; for the literal sense is the sense primarily intended by the author." Of the promise to Solomon in 1 Chronicles 17:13, Lyra observed: "The aforementioned authority was literally fulfilled in Solomon; however, it was fulfilled less perfectly, because Solomon was a son of God only by grace; but it was fulfilled more perfectly in Christ, who is the Son of God by nature."

For most exegetes, the theory of Nicholas of Lyra bound the interpreter to the dual task of explaining the historical meaning of a text while elucidating its larger and later spiritual significance. The great French humanist, Jacques Lefevre d'Etaples, however, pushed the theory to absurd limits. He argued that the only possible meaning of a text was its literal-prophetic sense and that the literal-historical sense was a product of human fancy and idle imagination. The literal-historical sense is the "letter which kills." It is advocated as the true meaning of scripture only by carnal persons who have not been regenerated by the life-giving Spirit of God. The problem of the proper exegesis of scripture is, when all is said and done, the problem of the regeneration of its interpreters.

IV

In this brief survey of medieval hermeneutical theory, there are certain dominant themes which recur with dogged persistence. Medieval exegetes admit that the words of scripture had a meaning in the historical situation in which they were first uttered or written, but they deny that the meaning of those words is restricted to what the human author thought he said or what his first audience thought they heard. The stories and sayings of scripture bear an implicit meaning only understood by a later audience. In some cases that implicit meaning is far more important than the restricted meaning intended by the author in his particular cultural setting.

Yet the text cannot mean anything a later audience wants it to mean. The language of the Bible opens up a field of possible meanings. Any interpretation which falls within that field is valid exegesis of the text, even though that interpretation was not intended by the author. Any interpretation which falls outside the limits of that field of possible meanings is probably eisegesis and should be rejected as unacceptable. Only by confessing the multiple sense of scripture is it possible for the Church to make use of the Hebrew Bible at all or to recapture the various levels of significance in the unfolding story of creation and redemption. The notion that scripture has only one meaning is a fantastic idea and is certainly not advocated by the biblical writers themselves.

V

Having elucidated medieval hermeneutical theory, I should like to take some time to look at medieval exegetical practice. One could get the impression from Jowett that because medieval exegetes rejected the theory of the single meaning of scripture so dear to Jowett's heart, they let their exegetical imaginations run amok and exercised no discipline at all in clarifying the field of possible meanings opened by the biblical text. In fact, medieval interpreters, once you grant the presuppositions on which they operate, are as conservative and restrained in their approach to the Bible as any comparable group of modern scholars.

In order to test medieval exegetical practice I have chosen a terribly difficult passage from the Gospel of Matthew, the parable of the Good Employer or, as it is more frequently known, the parable of the Workers in the Vineyard (Matt. 20:1–16). The story is a familiar one. An employer hired day laborers to work in his vineyard at dawn and promised them the standard wage of a denarius. Because he needed more workers, he returned to the marketplace at nine, noon, three, and five o'clock and hired any laborers he could find. He promised to pay the workers hired at nine, noon, and three what was fair. But the workers hired at the eleventh hour or five o'clock were sent into the vineyard without any particular promise concerning remuneration. The employer instructed his foreman to pay off the workers beginning with the laborers hired at five o'clock. These workers expected only one-twelfth of a denarius, but were given the full day's wage instead. Indeed, all the workers who had worked part of the day were given one denarius. The workers who had been in the vineyard since dawn accordingly expected a bonus beyond the denarius, but they were disappointed to receive the same wage which had been given to the other, less deserving workers. When they grumbled, they were told by the employer that they had not been defrauded but had been paid according to an agreed contract. If the employer chose to be generous to the workers who had only worked part of the day, that was, in effect, none of their business. They should collect the denarius that was due them and go home like good fellows.

Jesus said the kingdom of God was like this story. What on earth could he have meant?

VI

The Church has puzzled over this parable ever since it was included in Matthew's Gospel. St Thomas Aquinas in his *Lectura super Evangelium Sancti Matthaei* offered two interpretations of the parable, one going back in its lineage to Irenaeus and the other to Origen. The "day" mentioned in the parable can either refer to the life-span of an individual (the tradition of Origen), in which case the parable is a comment on the various ages at which one may be converted to Christ, or it is a reference to the history of salvation (the tradition of Irenaeus), in which case it is a comment on the relationship of Jew and Gentile.

If the story refers to the life-span of a man or woman, then it is intended as an encouragement to people who are converted to Christ late in life. The workers in the story who begin at dawn are people who have served Christ and have devoted themselves to the love of God and neighbor since childhood. The other hours mentioned by Jesus refer to the various stages of human development from youth to old age. Whether one has served Christ for a long time or for a brief moment, one will still receive the gift of eternal life. Thomas qualifies this somewhat in order to allow for proportional rewards and a hierarchy in heaven. But he does not surrender the main point: eternal life is given to late converts with the same generosity it is given to early converts.

On the other hand, the story may refer to the history of salvation. Quite frankly, this is the interpretation which interests Thomas most. The hours mentioned in the parable are not stages in individual human development but epochs in the history of the world from Adam to Noah, from Noah to Abraham, from Abraham to David, and from David to Christ. The owner of a vineyard is the whole Trinity, the foreman is Christ, and the moment of reckoning is the resurrection from the dead. The workers who are hired at the eleventh hour are the Gentiles, whose complaint that no one has offered them work can be interpreted to mean that they had no prophets as the Jews have had. The workers who have borne the heat of the day are the Jews, who grumble about the favoritism shown to latecomers, but who are still given the denarius of eternal life. As a comment on the history of salvation, the parable means that the generosity of God undercuts any advantage which the Jews might have had over the Gentiles with respect to participation in the gifts and graces of God.

Not everyone read the text as a gloss on Jewish – Christian relations or as a discussion of late conversion. In the fourteenth century the anonymous author of the *Pearl*, an elegy on the death of a young girl, applied the parable to infancy rather than to old age. What is important about the parable is not the chronological age at which one enters the vineyard, but the fact that some workers are only in the vineyard for the briefest possible moment. A child who dies at the age of two years is, in a sense, a worker who arrives at the eleventh hour. The parable is intended as a consolation for bereaved parents. A parent who has lost a small child can be comforted by the knowledge that God, who does not despise the service of persons converted in extreme old age, does not withhold his mercy from boys and girls whose eleventh hour came at dawn.

Probably the most original interpretation of the parable was offered by John Pupper of Goch, a Flemish theologian of the fifteenth century, who used the parable to attack the doctrine of proportionality, particularly as that doctrine had been stated and defended by Thomas Aquinas. No one had ever argued that God gives rewards which match in exact quantity the weight of the good works done by a Christian. That is arithmetic equality and is simply not applicable to a relationship in which people perform temporal acts and receive eternal rewards. But most theologians did hold to a doctrine of proportionality; while there is a disproportion between the good works which Christians do and the rewards which they receive, there is a proportion as well. The reward is always much larger than the work which is rewarded, but the greater the work, the greater the reward.

As far as Goch is concerned, that doctrine is sheer nonsense. No one can take the message of the parable of the vineyard seriously and still hold to the doctrine of proportionality. Indeed, the only people in the vineyard who hold to the doctrine of proportionality are the first workers in the vineyard. They argue that twelve times the work should receive twelve times the payment. All they receive for their argument is a rebuke and a curt dismissal.

Martin Luther, in an early sermon preached before the Reformation in 1517, agreed with Goch that God gives equal reward for great and small works. It is not by the Herculean size of our exertions but by the goodness of God that we receive any reward at all.

But Luther, unfortunately, spoiled his point by elaborating a thoroughly unconvincing argument in which he tried to show that the last workers in the vineyard were more humble than the first and therefore that one hour of their service was worth twelve hours of the mercenary service of the grumblers.

The parable, however, seems to make exactly the opposite point. The workers who began early were not more slothful or more selfish than the workers who began later in the day. Indeed, they were fairly representative of the kind of worker to be found hanging around the marketplace at any hour. They were angry, not because they had shirked their responsibilities, but because they had discharged them conscientiously.

In 1525 Luther offered a fresh interpretation of the parable, which attacked it from a slightly different angle. The parable has essentially one point: to celebrate the goodness of God which makes nonsense of a religion based on law-keeping and good works. God pays no attention to the proportionately greater efforts of the first workers in the vineyard, but to their consternation, God puts them on exactly the same level as the last and least productive workers. The parable shows that everyone in the vineyard is unworthy, though not always for the same reason. The workers who arrive after nine o'clock are unworthy because they are paid a salary incommensurate with their achievement in picking grapes. The workers who spent the entire day in the vineyard are unworthy because they are dissatisfied with what God has promised, think that their efforts deserve special consideration, and are jealous of their employer's goodness to workers who accomplished less than they did. The parable teaches that salvation is not grounded in human merit and that there is no system of bookkeeping which can keep track of the relationship between God and humanity. Salvation depends utterly and absolutely on the goodness of God.

VII

The four medieval theologians I have mentioned – Thomas Aquinas, the author of the *Pearl*, the Flemish chaplain Goch, and the young Martin Luther – did not exhaust in their writings all the possible interpretations of the parable of the Workers in the Vineyard. But they did see with considerable clarity that the parable is an assertion of God's generosity and mercy to people who do not deserve it. It is only against the background of the generosity of God that one can understand the relationship of Jew and Gentile, the problem of late conversion, the meaning of the death of a young child, the question of proportional rewards, even the very definition of grace itself. Every question is qualified by the severe mercy of God, by the strange generosity of the owner of the vineyard who pays the non-productive latecomer the same wage as his oldest and most productive employees.

If you were to ask me which of these interpretations is valid, I should have to respond that they all are. They all fall within the field of possible meanings created by the story itself. How many of those meanings were in the conscious intention of Jesus or of the author of the Gospel of Matthew, I do not profess to know. I am inclined to agree with C. S. Lewis, who commented on his own book, *Till We Have Faces*: "An author doesn't necessarily understand the meaning of his own story better than anyone else."[8] The act of creation confers no special privileges on authors when it comes to the distinctly different, if lesser task of interpretation. Wordsworth the critic is not in the same league with Wordsworth the poet, while Samuel Johnson the critic towers over Johnson the creative artist. Authors obviously have something in mind when they write, but a work of historical or theological or aesthetic imagination has a life of its own.

VIII

Which brings us back to Benjamin Jowett. Jowett rejected medieval exegesis and insisted that the Bible should be read like any other book.[9] I agree with Jowett that the Bible should be read like any other book. The question is: how does one read other books?

Take, for example, my own field of Reformation studies. Almost no historian that I know would answer the question of the meaning of the writings of Martin Luther by focusing solely on Luther's explicit and conscious intention. Marxist intepreters of Luther from Friedrich Engels to Max Steinmetz have been interested in Luther's writings as an expression of class interests, while psychological interpreters from Grisar to Erikson have focused on the theological writings as clues to the inner psychic tensions in the personality of Martin Luther. Even historians who reject Marxist and psychological interpretations of Luther find themselves asking how Luther was understood in the free imperial cities, by the German knights, by the landed aristocracy, by the various subgroups of German peasants, by the Catholic hierarchy, by lawyers, by university faculties – to name only a few of the more obvious groups who responded to Luther and left a written record of their response. Meaning involves a listener as well as a speaker, and when one asks the question of the relationship of Luther to his various audiences in early modern Europe, it becomes clear that there was not one Luther in the sixteenth century, but a battalion of Luthers.

Nor can the question of the meaning of Luther's writings be answered by focusing solely on Luther's contemporaries. Luther's works were read and pondered in a variety of historical and cultural settings from his death in 1546 to the present. Those readings of Luther have had measurable historical effects on succeeding generations, whose particular situation in time and space could scarcely have been anticipated by Luther. Yet the social, political, economic, cultural, and religious history of those people belongs intrinsically and inseparably to the question of the meaning of the theology of Martin Luther. The meaning of historical texts cannot be separated from the complex problem of their reception and the notion that a text means only what its author intends it to mean is historically naive. Even to talk of the original setting in which words were spoken and heard is to talk of meanings rather than meaning. To attempt to understand those original meanings is the first step in the exegetical process, not the last and final step.

Modern literary criticism has challenged the notion that a text means only what its author intends it to mean far more radically than medieval exegetes ever dreamed of doing. Indeed, contemporary debunking of the author and the author's explicit intentions has proceeded at such a pace that it seems at times as if literary criticism has become a jolly game of ripping out an author's shirt-tail and setting fire to it. The reader and the literary work to the exclusion of the author have become the central preoccupation of the literary critic. Literary relativists of a fairly moderate sort insist that every generation has its own Shakespeare and Milton, and extreme relativists loudly proclaim that no reader reads the same work twice. Every change in the reader, however slight, is a change in the meaning of the text. Imagine what Thomas Aquinas or Nicholas of Lyra would have made of the famous statement of Northrop Frye:

> It has been said of Boehme that his books are like a picnic to which the author brings the words and the reader the meaning. The remark may have been intended as a sneer at Boehme, but it is an exact description of all works of literary art without exception.[10]

Medieval exegetes held to the sober middle way, the position that the text (any literary text, but especially the Bible) contains both letter and spirit. The text is not all letter, as Jowett with others maintained, or all spirit, as the rather more enthusiastic literary critics in our own time are apt to argue. The original text as spoken and heard limits a field of possible meanings. Those possible meanings are not dragged by the hair, willy-nilly, into the text, but belong to the life of the Bible in the encounter between author and reader as they belong to the life of any act of the human imagination. Such a hermeneutical theory is capable of sober and disciplined application and avoids the Scylla of extreme subjectivism, on the one hand, and the Charybdis of historical positivism, on the other. To be sure, medieval exegetes made bad mistakes in the application of their theory, but they also scored notable and brilliant triumphs. Even at their worst they recognized that the intention of the author is only one element – and not always the most important element at that – in the complex phenomenon of the meaning of a text.

IX

The defenders of the single meaning theory usually concede that the medieval approach to the Bible met the religious needs of the Christian community, but that it did so at the unacceptable price of doing violence to the biblical text. The fact that the historical-critical method after two hundred years is still struggling for more than a precarious foothold in that same religious community is generally blamed on the ignorance and conservatism of the Christian laity and the sloth or moral cowardice of its pastors.

I should like to suggest an alternative hypothesis. The medieval theory of levels of meaning in the biblical text, with all its undoubted defects, flourished because it is true, while the modern theory of a single meaning, with all its demonstrable virtues, is false. Until the historical-critical method becomes critical of its own theoretical foundations and develops a hermeneutical theory adequate to the nature of the text which it is interpreting, it will remain restricted – as it deserves to be – to the guild and the academy, where the question of truth can endlessly be deferred.

Notes

1 Benjamin Jowett, "On the Interpretation of Scripture," *Essays and Reviews*, 7th edn. (London: Longman, Green, Longman and Roberts, 1861), pp. 330–433.
2 Ibid., p. 378.

3 Ibid., p. 384.

4 Ibid., p. 412

5 Helen Gardner, *The Business of Criticism* (London: Oxford University Press, 1959), p. 83.

6 Origen, *On First Principles*, ed. G. W. Butterworth (New York: Harper and Row, 1966), p. 288.

7 For a brief survey of medieval hermeneutical theory which takes into account recent historical research see James S. Preus, *From Shadow to Promise* (Cambridge, Mass.: Harvard University Press, 1969), pp. 9–149; see also the useful bibliography, pp. 287–93.

8 W. H. Lewis, ed., *Letters of C. S. Lewis* (New York: Harcourt, Brace and World, Inc., 1966), p. 273.

9 Jowett, "Interpretation," p. 377.

10 This quotation is cited by E. D. Hirsch, Jr., *Validity in Interpretation* (New Haven: Yale University Press, 1967), p. 1, at the beginning of a chapter which sets out to elaborate an alternative theory.

The Story-Shaped Church: Critical Exegesis and Theological Interpretation

George Lindbeck

For many of Hans Frei's readers, his greatest contribution has been to make possible the restoration of the christologically centered narrative sense of scripture to its traditional primacy. His *Eclipse of Biblical Narrative*, they believe, has shown how the confusion in the last two centuries of biblical studies, between the narrative and historical (i.e. "factual") senses, has resulted in gross misunderstandings of premodern interpretation as this was generally practiced up through the Reformation. On their view, the opposition between historical-critical and premodern exegesis is as misconceived as that between evolution and Genesis. They are inclined to think that Frei's work marks the beginning of a change in biblical interpretation as decisive – though in a different direction – as that occasioned by Albert Schweitzer's *Quest of the Historical Jesus*.

This essay assumes this assessment and turns to further questions. Granting the compatibility of premodern narrative interpretation and modern historical-critical study, what more can be said about their relation? Are they logically independent, or does historical criticism make a difference to narrative meaning?

I shall discuss this issue in reference to the topic of the Church.[1] The conclusion will be that classical narrative reading, in combination with historical-critical awareness, makes the Church as the New Testament presents it look more like Israel, including Israel *post Christum*, than Christians have customarily supposed. This change occurs only when the two approaches are conjoined: when pursued independently, no such result need follow. The importance of their interaction in this instance, however, cannot be generalized.

39

Both historical criticism and classical narrational interpretation are piecemeal procedures, and the revisionary force of combining them varies from topic to topic. Thus all that this essay claims is that in some areas, of which ecclesiology is one, a renewed focus on narrative meanings, together with critical awareness of how they functioned, provides scriptural authorization (but not directives) for major changes in theological interpretations.

The task of supporting this claim is both the exegetical-historical one of determining what the text meant and the theological one of interpreting what it means. (This is an inadequate way of stating the contrast between exegesis and theology for many purposes, but not, I think, for our present ones.) We shall in the first two sections stipulate what for our purposes are the crucial differences between historical and theological interpretation, comment on the relation between classical narrative hermeneutics and other approaches, and in view of both these points, sketch an exegetical account of biblical narrative ecclesiology. This will provide the basis for a discussion in the third section of later distortions of this ecclesiology, and the possibilities of its reappropriation in a critically corrected form.

History, Theology, and Narrative Meaning

History interprets what the text meant, and theology what it means. More fully, historians, insofar as their work is theologically relevant, describe the religiously significant functioning of a text in its original setting, and theologians make proposals about how the text should be understood and used so that its present meaning may be faithful to its original one. In stipulating this distinction, I simply assume what I take to be the contemporary commonplace that, for example, the stories that expressed and molded the communal self-understanding of early Christians need to be retold and reinterpreted if they are to function appropriately in later periods. In brief, what the Bible properly means theologically is the right application of what it meant historically.

The notion of right application, it should be noted, includes the possibility of no application at all. The biblical tolerance of slavery, for example, is now almost universally regarded by Christians as totally and permanently inapplicable. Conceivably the same holds for what scripture meant by the Church. Perhaps faithfulness to the central meaning of scripture, to Christ, requires that Christians now substitute some quite different way of thinking about Christian community. I shall later have more to say about that. For the moment I shall simply posit that part of the practice of reading a text as authoritative, even in the minimal sense of "classic," is that what it meant does have present relevance unless there are good reasons for supposing the contrary. The burden of proof is on those who deny applicability. Paul himself recognized this, for otherwise he would not have accepted the burden of arguing at length that the scriptural requirement of circumcision no longer held, at least for Gentiles.

Exegetical and theological interpretation interact. If a certain kind of meaning seems important for understanding what a sacred text meant, the inclination is to think it theologically important also, and vice versa. One powerful post-Reformation tendency has been to give factual meanings both exegetical and theological primacy. The extreme conservative version of this outlook holds that everything depends on the complete reportorial and scientific accuracy of scripture; for the liberal version, the critical reconstruction of, most notably, the historical Jesus is crucial. In contrast, there are also other outlooks, invariably susceptible to both liberal and conservative uses, for which doctrinal, or moral, or existential, or symbolic, or narrational meanings were or are religiously more important. From these perspectives, Enlightenment-spawned debates over factuality are of secondary interest even historically. For example, if one focuses on symbolic meaning, questions regarding the import of patriarchal images of God may seem historically as well as theologically more significant than the issue of whether the whale swallowed Jonah or whether claims about the resurrection are empirically meaningful in the sense, for example, of falsifiable. The decision between these orientations is not usually a historical-critical matter. It rather depends, as David Kelsey has argued, on an unformalizable global assessment (discrimen) of what once was or now is the religiously most intelligible, efficacious, and faithful way of reading the text.[2]

Perhaps, however, there is a partial exception to this. The claim to primacy of the narrative meaning of the stories about Jesus for scripture as a whole is embedded in the way these stories are told in the gospels and is sometimes explicit as well as implicit in other New Testament writings. This is a historical judgement, not simply a critically unassessable discrimen. The stories in their narrative function unsubstitutably identify and characterize a particular person as the summation of Israel's history and as the unsurpassable and irreplaceable clue to who and what the God of Israel and the universe is. They interpret the Hebrew Bible in terms of christological anticipations, preparations, and promissory types. Jesus' story fulfills and transforms the overall biblical narratives of creation, election, and redemption, and thereby specifies the meanings of such concepts and images as Messiahship, Suffering Servanthood, Logos, and divine Sonship. He is the subject, everything else is predication. Some New Testament writings may not clearly exhibit this pattern (Luther would cite James), but insofar as they are treated as parts of a narrationally and christologically unified canon, they are submitted to the same hermeneutical rule. If one characterizes the literal sense as that which a community of readers takes to be the plain, primary, and controlling signification of a text (a less problematic move than appealing to authorial intention or to some property ingredient in the text), then, as Frei has suggested,[3] the narrative meaning of the stories about Jesus was the uniquely privileged *sensus literalis* of the whole of scripture for the groups by and for whom those stories were composed. It continued to be so for the later generations who added the New Testament canon to the Old, and it remained the dominant view, if Frei's *Eclipse* is right, until the post-Reformation era, when primacy began to be accorded to rationalistically doctrinal, pietistically experiential, and empiricistically factual meanings. Thus there are historical-critical grounds for reading the Christian Bible in chiefly (though not, of course, exclusively) narrational terms if one wants to know what it originally meant.

This, as we have indicated, does not settle the question of what the Bible means – of how what it meant historically should now be theologically applied. But before we turn in the third section to that issue, we must ask about what it meant. Detailed exegesis, needless to say, is out of the question. I shall simply comment on the tacit rules or principles (perhaps we could even say "grammar" or "doctrines")[4] that structured the biblical pattern of thinking about the Church.

Exegesis and the Biblical Story of the Church

The first and, in a narrative approach, tautological rule for reading is that the Church is fundamentally identified and characterized by its story. Images such as "body of Christ," or the traditional marks of "unity, holiness, catholicity, and apostolicity," cannot be first defined and then used to specify what is and what is not the Church. The story is logically prior. It determines the meaning of images, concepts, doctrines, and theories of the Church rather than being determined by them. Just as the story of the Quakers is more fundamental than descriptions such as "church of the poor" or "church of the wealthy" (for they have been both), and the story of the French is more fundamental than "monarchy" or "republic" (for France has been both), so also in the case of the Church.

A corollary of this priority of story is that "Church" ordinarily refers to concrete groups of people, not to something transempirical. An invisible Church is as biblically odd as an invisible Israel. Stories of the biblical realistic-narrative type can only be told of agents and communities of agents acting and being acted upon in a space – time world of contingent, unpredictable happenings. The primacy of narrative thus implies that exalted concepts and images such as "holy" and "bride of Christ" usually refer to empirical Churches in all their actual or potential messiness.

For the early Christians, in the second place, Israel's history was their only history. They did not yet have the New Testament or later Church history as sources. Thus for the writings they produced, the Hebrew scriptures (usually in the Septuagint form) were the sole ecclesiological text. This is the second rule for reading what they say about the Church.

A third rule is an extension of this second one. Not only was Israel's story their only story, but it was the whole of that story which they appropriated. It was not only the favorable parts, the Old Testament histories of faithful remnants, that they applied to themselves. All the wickedness of the Israelites in the wilderness could be theirs. They might rebel as did Korah (Num. 16), or perish for fornication as did three and twenty thousand in the desert (Num. 25). These happenings, Paul tells his readers, are types (*tupoi*) written for our admonition (1 Cor. 10:5–11). As of old, judgement continues to begin in the house of the Lord (1 Pet. 4:17), and the unfaithful Church can be severed from the root no less than the unbelieving synagogue (Rom. 11:21). There is nothing in the logic of this hermeneutic to deny that the bride of Christ, like the betrothed of Yahweh (Ezek. 16 and 23), can be a whore worse than the heathen. The typological transfer is not actually made,[5] but then, the responsible narrative exegete will note, situations as extreme as the one Ezekiel confronted did not develop until later in Church history.

Thus, despite most later exegesis, the relation of Israel's history to that of the church in the New Testament is not one of shadow to reality, or promise to fulfillment, or type to antitype.[6] Rather, the kingdom already present in Christ alone is the antitype, and both Israel and the Church are types. The people of God existing in both the old and new ages are typologically related to Jesus Christ, and through Christ, Israel is prototypical for the Church in much the same way that the exodus story, for example, is seen as prototypical for all later Israelite history by such prophets as Ezekiel. Christ is depicted as the embodiment of Israel (e.g., "Out of Egypt have I called my son"; Matt. 2:15), and the Church is the body of Christ. Thus, in being shaped by the story of Christ, the Church shares (rather than fulfills) the story of Israel. The communal fulfillment will take place in God's kingdom which, though already actualized in the crucified, resurrected, and ascended Lord, is only anticipated in the communities that witness to him before and after his first coming. Something like this is the pattern structuring much, at least, of the New Testament Churches' appropriation of what for them were the only extant scriptural stories of God's people.

From this it follows, fourth, that Israel and the Church were one people for at least many early Christians. There was no breach in continuity. A new age had begun, but the story remained the same, and therefore also the people it identified. The French remain French after the revolution, the Quakers remain Quakers after becoming wealthy, and Israel remains Israel even when transformed by the arrival of the eschaton in Christ. The Church is simply Israel in the time between the times. The continuity of the story and the identity of the people are not broken.

Discontinuity and nonidentity are problems in the New Testament, not for the church *per se* but for unbelieving Jews, on the one hand, and gentile Christians, on the other. The apostle Paul says of the first group in Romans 11 that they have been cut off, but that this can happen does not differentiate them from Christians. Christians also, as we have already noted, can be severed from the root. They can, in the even more vigorous language of Revelation, be spewed forth, expectorated (3:16). Yet when this occurs, it does not alter the identity of the people of the promise. "The gifts and the call of God are irrevocable" (Rom. 11:29). The identity of the chosen people in the new age as in the old depends utterly on God's election, not at all on its own faithfulness or unfaithfulness. For the one New Testament writing in which the problem is directly addressed, Judaism after Christ is as inalienably embraced as the Church in the continuous overarching story of the single people consisting of faithful remnants and unfaithful masses which stretches from the patriarchal period to the last days. Unbelieving Jewry will ultimately be restored.

So strong was this sense of uninterrupted peoplehood that the only available way to think of gentile Christians was, in Krister Stendahl's phrase, as "honorary Jews."[7] The uncircumcised, "alienated from the commonwealth of Israel," have become "fellow citizens of the household of God," "fellow heirs, fellow members of the body, fellow partakers of the promise" (Eph. 2:11, 19; 3:16). This inclusion of the Gentiles is represented in Ephesians as the most wondrous aspect of the work of Christ. Where there were two, there is now one, the new man in Christ (2:11–3:11). Thus has begun the inclusion of all humankind in God's people, the promised ascent of the nations to worship in Zion, the crowding of the Gentiles into the heavenly Jerusalem. But Zion does not change identity: the gates of the new Jerusalem are marked with the names of the twelve tribes (Rev. 21:12). The inclusion through Christ of the uncircumcised in the one eternal covenant constituted, for the early Christians, not the formation of a new people but the enlargement of the old.

This enlarged people, to be sure, is also said to be Spirit-filled. For many later Christians, ranging from papalists to anti-institutional spiritualists, this has been the major reason for thinking of the Church as discontinuous with Israel.

When one looks at the function of the New Testament references to the Holy Spirit, however, one discovers that they often serve to distinguish the believing Church from the unbelieving synagogue in the new age.[8] This age is indeed the epoch in which the words of Joel come true, in which the Spirit is poured forth on all flesh, and sons and daughters prophesy (Acts 2:17ff.). The faithful are Spirit-filled as they were not before, and it is therefore this gift that now most sharply differentiates them from the unfaithful. But the Spirit also spoke through prophets before Christ, and it departs from the faithless in the present as it did in the past. Faithful Israel *ante Christum* is more Spirit-filled than the faithless Church, and the same can be true of the synagogue *post Christum*. There are strands of thought in the New Testament suggesting this, even though there are no explicit claims. First, those who have not heard the message live theologically in the time before Christ, incapable of either acceptance or rejection (Rom. 10). Second, if one adds, as later history testifies, that Jews for the most part do not and cannot hear because of Christian persecution, it follows that Judaism, living theologically before Christ, can on occasion be more Spirit-filled than Christianity. Whether or not this reasoning holds,[9] it is clear that the Spirit-wrought holiness of the Church is a relational attribute referring to what God is making and will make of it, not to an inherent property. Pentecost marks the beginning of the age of unheard-of possibilities, gifts, and callings, not the formation of a new people.

Narrative interpretation, it will be observed, presses the exegete toward finding the same basic understanding of the Church in all the New Testament literature. The variations from book to book can be construed as arising from changes in circumstance and application. When Paul was preoccupied by the persecution of the Church in Thessalonica (1 Thess. 2:14-6), for example, he seemed to contradict what, as we have noted, he later wrote about unbelieving Israel in Romans. But even if in fact he changed his mind, it is misleading, on a narrative approach, to describe this as a change in his ecclesiology (or "Israelology," as it could just as well be called). The normative story remained exactly the same (for that, in Paul's thinking, was to be found in scripture, not in his head), as did also the procedures for applying it. But situations alter, and the faithful use of the ancient tales to shape the unfolding story of the nascent Church required new and surprising twists and turns. It is of the very nature of narratives to subsume variations that outside their narrational context are contradictions. Desert wanderers settle in the promised land, and those liberated from Egypt are repeatedly enslaved. This compatibility of contrary descriptions does not imply harmonization: the differences are real. Further, some differences, such as the "sectarianism" of the Johannine communities and the "Platonism" of Hebrews, may under some circumstances be Church-dividing. Only those exegetes, however, who focus on theological ideas, such as Ernst Käsemann, will risk judgements that they must always be so.[10] Those for whom narrative meaning is primary and who try to understand this in the context of social history will be more cautious. Even if one reads the New Testament writings as discrete literary units rather than in their canonical unity, their ecclesiological agreement from the perspective we have outlined is considerable.

It is hard to see how it could have been otherwise. Early Christians were a variegated Jewish sect, no more (and perhaps less) remote from the thought world of "normative Judaism" (if there was such a thing) than the Essenes, the Qumran community, or at the other extreme, intellectual Hellenists like Philo.

They adhered to a crucified and resurrected Messiah who authorized them, some of them believed, to welcome the uncircumcised into their fellowship, but they were also deeply committed to maintaining their legitimacy as Jews. All the categories they possessed for communal self-understanding were derived from their only scriptures, the Hebrew Bible, and they interpreted this as Jews. It was natural that they should understand their communities as *ecclesia*, as *qahal*, the assembly of Israel in the new age. (For once, philology and etymology cohere with broader historical considerations.)[11] Thus the story of Israel was their story, and they had good reason for construing it in terms of the principles of the continuity of the narrative, the unity of the people, and the possibility of churchly unfaithfulness which we have described.

The historical-critical contribution to this description is basically the negative one of removing interpretative prejudices and making it believable that these principles did indeed guide the New Testament uses of Israel's story. There is nothing novel in the details of the interpretation I have offered. These are for the most part commonplaces of New Testament scholarship. What is different is the significance the details acquire for understanding biblical ecclesiology when narrative meaning is taken as primary. Then something like the reading suggested in this section is both the plain and critical account of what the Church meant in the early Christian writings.

Theological Interpretation

The question of what the Church means in these same writings is quite different from, and for the most part only indirectly related to, what was meant (even, in some cases, to what the interpreter thinks was meant). It is this bearing of critical exegetical findings on theological interpretation which will concern us in this last section in reference, first, to principles; second, to past ecclesiologies; and last, to present and future possibilities.

As has already been emphasized, what the Bible means does not necessarily correspond imitatively to what it meant; or to put this same point in uncompromisingly theological language, what God said in scripture is not necessarily what he now says, The proper theological interpretation is one that is intelligible, efficacious, and scripturally faithful, but the conditions for intelligibility and efficaciousness change, and faithfulness is not equivalent to reiteration. Departures from the story-shaped understanding of the Church may thus at times be desirable even for those who hold to the primacy of narrative meanings.

This is so because on a narrative construal, it will be recalled, the controlling *sensus literalis* is the narrative meaning of the stories about Jesus. Meanings contrary to this sense must be excluded. Thus when the biblical narrational understanding of the Church engenders meanings inconsistent with the Jesus story, the narrative must be altered or abandoned. A nonbiblical way of describing the Church may in changed circumstances better accord with the christological center.

The history of ecclesiological reflection in its entirety can be invoked to illustrate these principles. Modifications of the biblical story of the Church started in the very first generations. The hardening of the opposition between synagogue and Church led even Jewish Christians, as such documents as the *Letter of Barnabas* testify, to reject the notion that unbelieving Jews remained part of God's people. Faithfulness became the mark of election, and election, conversely, became conditional on faithfulness. The doctrines of predestination and salvation *sola gratia*, insofar as they persisted, tended to be applied only to individuals and not to communities. Heretical groups were more and more regarded as not really the Church at all. They were not seen after the fashion of the ancient prophets as the adulterous spouse whom the Lord may cast out for a time but never divorce.

A second development was that the Church quickly became wholly gentile, and the New Testament awareness of the Church as, sociologically speaking, a Jewish sect disappeared. It became intellectually and practically difficult for gentile Christians to think of themselves as naturalized citizens in the continuous, uninterrupted commonwealth of Israel. Thus not only was the synagogue excluded but the one people of God was broken into two peoples, the old and new. This created the problem of how to relate them, and the solution was to read the scriptures as if Israel were the type no longer simply of the coming kingdom and of its instantiation in the person of Christ but also of the Church, which thus became the antitype, the fulfillment. The more unsavory aspects of the history of Israel were no longer genuinely portions of the history of the Church but were projected exclusively on the synagogue.

These modifications, it will be observed, are quite explicitly changes in the canonically unified and authorized narrative pattern[12] rather than simply new applications. Yet despite the monstrous offspring they ultimately engendered, they cannot be flatly condemned as simply unfaithful. They were the historically (i.e. contingently) necessary conditions for the Church's appropriation of Israel's story. Without that appropriation, we may plausibly speculate, Gnosticism would have wholly triumphed, the Marcionite rejection of Israel's scriptures and Israel's God would have become universal among Christians, and the Nazi heresy that Jesus was not a Jew would have become orthodoxy from the second century on. Because the modifications were the only available alternative to utter subversion of the christological center, they can be regarded, despite their magnitude and consequences, as scripturally faithful interpretations of the story of the Church.

Such excuses become increasingly inapplicable, however, after the empire was converted and persecuted Christians became the persecutors. Anti-Semitism was the paradigmatic problem, but it needs to be seen as an acute manifestation of a more general disease. The dissonance between antitypical claims to fulfillment and empirical reality was the central difficulty. The Church was now a *corpus mixtum* composed overwhelmingly of visible sinners rather than visible saints. The pressure was great to refer its high claims not to the overall pattern of communal life but to segregated aspects: to pure (ultimately infallible) doctrines, to uniquely (and in vulgar understanding, magically) efficacious sacraments, and to divinely established institutions. Even these developments, to be sure, did not always function antiscripturally. They might be compared, perhaps, to the Israelite monarchy, to which God consented *contre coeur* (1 Sam. 8), and yet which he also mightily used to preserve his people and prepare for the Messiah (Jesus sprang from the Davidic line). In somewhat similar fashion, one could argue, the imperial Church preserved the faith amid barbarian chaos, converted Europe, and was the cradle of the first civilization to become worldwide (whether there is anything messianic about Western-spawned modernity is another question). The antitypical pretensions of Western ecclesiastical establishments (from which Reformation Churches were by no means wholly exempt) could not help evoking sectarian reactions (which, incidentally, have not been so strong in the East, where Caesaropapism, whatever its faults, muted churchly arrogance).

The sectarian solutions to the Church's dilemma have on the whole been less biblical, but not uniformly less faithful to scripture, than the earlier catholic ones. They have been less biblical because for the most part they have no longer understood God's people in terms of Israel's story but have rather modeled themselves after New Testament depictions of fervent first-generation communities, especially as found in Acts. Yet however unbiblical one may think the ecclesiology of, for example, the Quakers, it is hard to deny that such groups have at times been faithful remnants amid the faithless masses. Insofar as they are protest movements against Constantinian Churches, the sects are in general scripturally justified, but they are also deeply problematic. The intense effort to make the empirical reality of Christian communities conform visibly to images of antitypical fulfillment can have consequences in some ways worse than institutional triumphalism. The arrogant self-righteousness of the company of the visibly holy may on occasion compare ill with the concern for publicans and sinners sometimes found in Churches that conceive of themselves as arks of salvation, as hospitals for sick souls.

The difficulties in traditional ecclesiologies, whether Catholic, Reformation, or sectarian, have led in recent centuries to new ways of thinking about the Church that depart even further from biblical patterns but that, once again, can have scriptural authenticity. Not only is Israel's story abandoned but also the referential primacy of empirical communities. Something other than these communities is really the Church, is really the subject of the claims to antitypical fulfillment, with the result that ecclesial arrogance of either the catholic or sectarian types is no longer theologically legitimate.

For example, the Church is characterized denotatively (not simply connotatively, or predicatively, or in some promissory or other illocutionary mode) as event, or mission, or liberating action, or the new being in Christ, or the fellowship of the Spirit, or the communion of Christ's justifying grace which works in anonymously as well as explicitly Christian ways. For the most part, any suggestion that the Church is invisible is stoutly resisted. Rather, it necessarily takes visible form, and in some interpretations, referential primacy is accorded to what is empirically or experientially identifiable (e.g., event, mission, or liberating action). Nevertheless, however observable or experienceable the main referent may be, it is not first of all a people. It is not empirical Churches in all their crass concreteness. These latter are rather imperfect manifestations, realizations, participations, or thematizations of the Church's true, eschatological reality.

Thus in terms of our earlier exegesis, what for the Bible are predicates are in these modern approaches turned into subject terms. The reference of these terms is not an agent or community of agents of the kind whose identity is rendered by realistic narratives, and it must therefore be described in some other way than by telling its story. Systematic ecclesiology replaces the narrational variety. This is what has happened in our day in almost all major theological outlooks, whether Catholic or Protestant.[13]

Yet, to return to the starting point, these unbiblical ways of thinking about the Church are not, for all that, unfaithful. They eliminate occasions for anti-Semitism and ecclesial arrogance by making the antitypical Church something other than the empirical Churches. In this and other respects they may be more genuinely Christian than their predecessors. It would be artificial but not impossible to write a history of ecclesiology in which increasing departures from the Bible were correlated with increasing closeness to Christ. In this area, whatever might be true of others, neither conservatives nor progressives mean by the Church what scripture meant, and the re-recognition of the original narrative pattern (assuming that that is what we have described) does not by itself mandate a return. The Bible may for our times be no more adequate concerning the Church than concerning slavery.

Yet the exegetical findings do make a difference. For one thing, they block eisegesis. Possibilities that were once excluded because of theologically biased readings of what scripture meant once again become options. As we earlier put it, the burden of proof is on those who think that what scripture meant is now inapplicable. Perhaps it is, but this needs to be shown, and in trying to show it, if that is what theologians try to do, they will find themselves struggling with a way of thinking about the Church that has been unknown and unimaginable for nearly two thousand years.

They may even begin wondering whether what "Church" once meant it can now mean again. In some respects, the present situation is more similar to the first century than to the intervening periods. Christendom is passing and Christians are becoming a diaspora. The antagonism of the Church to the synagogue has been unmasked (we hope definitively) for the horror it always was. Christian pretensions to fulfillment have become obnoxious to vast numbers of Catholics and Protestants alike. Some of the reasons for distorting the story are disappearing, and perhaps its original version is again applicable.

Certainly there are reasons for wanting to apply it. The empirical Churches are losing the loyalty and devotion of their members. Special-interest enclaves are replacing comprehensive communities as the locus of whatever shreds of communal identity the isolated individuals of our society retain. The conviction that the Churches even in their crass concreteness have a place in God's plans has weakened. All these considerations call for a return to Israel's story as the template by which the Church shapes its own history. It needs to understand itself as a witness that God has irrevocably chosen to testify to his glory in both its faithfulness and unfaithfulness, in both God's mercy and God's judgement. It needs to acknowledge that its election despite unfaithfulness is the source of its identity. Such convictions have made of Jews the great exception to the sociological and historical generalizations that apply to other nations, and have enabled them, despite their dispersion and small numbers, to be a major force in history (not least, it should be recalled, when they were wholly in the Diaspora). History shows that Israel's story has unique ability to confer communally significant meaning on whatever happens: it has, one might say, unrivaled power to encode successfully the vicissitudes and contradictions of history. Christianity, it can be argued, has urgent need to make greater use of that same tale if it is to be comparably tenacious and flexible in maintaining its identity as a people irresistibly called (and ineluctably failing) to witness by selfless service of all humankind to the universal yet thoroughly particular God of Abraham, Isaac, Jacob, and Jesus.

It must be added, however, that there are as yet few signs that this is happening. On the right, apocalyptic conservatism is on the rise, but this, despite its often ardent support for the Israeli state, not only thinks of Christianity as the replacement of Judaism but also restricts the Church to the company of the datably converted. On the political left, liberationists selectively appropriate episodes from Israel's history, especially the exodus, but use these as legitimating precedents for their own campaigns, not as shapers of a comprehensive community of sinners and saints, oppressors and oppressed, tyrants and liberators. More generally, despite such dubious phenomena as Jews for Jesus, Christianity continues for the most part to be as gentile in its self-understanding as ever, and few Christians are in the least inclined to think of themselves as even remotely analogous to a Jewish sect or honorary Jews. As long as this is the situation, a biblically Israel-like understanding of the Church will not be intelligible, efficacious, or scripturally appropriate.

Frei's metahistorical critique of biblical criticism helps free the exegete to find the biblical meaning of the Church in the story of Israel as appropriated by the early Christians. This recovery of what was meant creates the permanent possibility of an ecclesiological revolution, but whether the possibility will be exploited is a question beyond the scope of this essay. In the meantime, whether Frei knows it or not, and whether we thank him or not, his work is a challenge to all those concerned with what Christian community is and should be.

Notes

1 Frei's sole *ex professo* comments on the doctrine of the Church (in *The Identity of Jesus Christ: The Hermeneutical Bases of Dogmatic Theology* (Philadelphia: Fortress Press, 1975), pp. 157–64) are only tangentially related to the present essay but are, I believe, consistent with it.

2 David H. Kelsey, *The Uses of Scripture in Recent Theology* (Philadelphia: Fortress Press, 1975).

3 "The 'Literal Reading' of Biblical Narrative in the Christian Tradition: Does It Stretch or Will It Break?" in *The Bible and the Narrative Tradition*, ed. Frank McConnell (New York: Oxford Univ. Press, 1986), pp. 36–77.

4 See George A. Lindbeck, *The Nature of Doctrine: Religion and Theology in a Postliberal Age* (Philadelphia: Westminster Press, 1984), esp. chaps. 1, 4, and 5, for discussions of the similarities of doctrines and grammatical rules.

5 To be sure, 2 Cor. 11:1–4 explicitly evokes the possibility of the Church betrothed to Christ becoming a whore; and gross actual or potential unfaithfulness is also in view in Galatians, in Hebrews, and as we shall later note, in Revelation (see esp. 2:4, 20–3; 3:15–19). (I am indebted to Richard B. Hays for suggesting this note as well as for help at other points in this essay.)

6 The kind of work that James Samuel Preus has done in his *From Shadow to Promise: Old Testament Interpretation from Augustine to the Young Luther* (Cambridge: Belknap Press of Harvard University Press, 1969) needs to be extended more fully to specifically ecclesiological themes. It is noteworthy that even as recently as the Second Vatican Council the relation of Israel and the Church was said to be that of type and antitype.

7 Krister Stendahl, *Paul among Jews and Gentiles, and Other Essays* (Philadelphia: Fortress Press, 1976), p. 37.

8 Jacob Jervell, "Das Volk des Geistes," in *God's Christ and His People: Studies in Honour of Nils Alstrup Dahl*, ed. Jacob Jervell and Wayne A. Meeks (Oslo: Universitetsforlaget, 1977), pp. 87–106. Jervell's argument amply supports the statement in the text that the references to the Holy Spirit "often" function in this way, but perhaps not his much stronger claim that they almost always do so indirectly even if not directly.

51

9 Given the dependence of this reasoning on a hypothesis about how the New Testament texts apply in a situation of Christian persecution of Jews that was wholly outside the purview of the early Church, it is more properly characterized as theological than exegetical interpretation (as Richard Hays has pointed out to me), but in an exploratory essay such as the present one the untidiness of making this theological point in an exegetical discussion is perhaps excusable.

10 Ernst Käsemann, "The Canon of the New Testament and the Unity of the Church," in *Essays on New Testament Themes* (Naperville, Ill.: Alec R. Allenson, 1964), pp. 95–107, is often cited in this context. Those who disagree with Käsemann about the contradictions of New Testament ecclesiologies – such as the Roman Catholic scholar Raymond Brown – nevertheless in the absence of a narrative approach fail to find much unity. From the perspective of this essay they confuse disparateness of situations and applications with an ununifiable disparateness of views of the Church.

11 Krister Stendahl's summary of the philological and exegetical evidence in *Die Religion in Geschichte und Gegenwart*, 3rd edn, 3:1297–1304, is a gem of concise exposition.

12 One can, to be sure, proof-text later Christian understandings of the relation of Israel and Church, as Richard Hays has reminded me in a written memorandum: "See, e.g., Matthew's distinctive 'moral of the story' to the parable of the vineyard-tenants (21:43) and his version of the parable of the marriage feast (22:1–10)." Giving hermeneutical priority to such passages, however, makes a canonically unified reading impossible. If e.g., Matt. 21:43 is the last word on Israel and the Church, then Romans 9–11 makes no sense; but if the passage from Romans is taken as the interpretative key, then the verse from Matthew retains its force as the description of a temporary situation.

13 Karl Barth, despite popularizing the nature of the Church as event, is in large part an exception to this generalization. The story-shaped people of God, embracing both Christians and Jews, is usually referentially primary in the later volumes of the *Church Dogmatics*. It is well to observe in this connection, however, that the popularity of the designation "people of God" in recent ecclesiology (manifesting itself not least in the second chapter of Vatican II's *Constitution on the Church*) does not necessarily indicate a return either to narrative or to denotative concreteness. Often "people of God" is treated as an attributive rather than denotative term. Thus, e.g., Paul Minear discusses it as an "image" of the Church logically comparable to others such as "body" or "bride" of Christ (*Images of the Church in the New Testament* (Philadelphia: Westminster Press, 1960), pp. 66–104). In such an approach, "people of God" becomes competitive with other attributions, and warnings against overemphasis may seem appropriate (as in fact happens in Raymond E. Brown, *The Churches the Apostles Left Behind* (New York: Paulist Press, 1984), pp. 60, 83). Nils A. Dahl (*Das Volk Gottes: Eine Untersuchung zum Kirchenbewusstsein des Urchristentums*, 2nd edn (Darmstadt: Wissenschaftliche Buchgesellschaft, 1963) is one author who in practice recognizes that "people of God" in the Bible, like "America" in ordinary usage, is usually a denotative term, and that when the biblical phrase is employed in this way, it makes no more sense to inveigh against overuse than in the case where "America" or "church" is employed referentially in discourse.

Feminist Theological Hermeneutics: Canon and Christian Identity

Claudia V. Camp

The title of this essay already contains five terms – feminist, theological, hermeneutics, canon, and Christian identity – each of which could be, and has been, the subject of volumes of contentious discussion. Moreover, even the most cursory attempt to deal with them generates at least three more terms – authority, Christ, and Church – that are equally problematic. I would suggest, in fact, that the question of authority is the central question of this whole complex of ideas.

Let me begin by offering (at least) minimal definitions of the title's terminology or, in certain cases, by raising questions that prevent me from offering even a minimal definition. By "feminist" I mean (at least) an approach to culture that understands and analyzes gender relations in structural terms, with particular attention to the structural disempowerment of women. By "theological" I mean (at least) reflection that is determined by the assumed experience of self-transcendence. Thus, by definition, theology must address those areas of life that are not discernible or testable by standards of objectivity. By "hermeneutics" I mean (at least) the process of conscious reflection on how interpretation is done and who does it. The major difficulty with respect to these three terms lies not so much in defining them individually as in determining their relationship to one another. Is all interpretation hermeneutical? Is all hermeneutics theological? Must all theology be feminist?

The terms "canon" and "Christian identity" are less easy to specify briefly. Within Protestantism (and in most current popular usage) "canon" has referred to the sacred writings of Christianity, the Bible with its two Testaments. The word "canon" has, however, a more general meaning – "rule" – and has been so used within Catholicism ("canon law"). While feminists agree with the need for a canon, in the sense of standards of judgement, the question of where that rule is to be located remains open. We may thus ask: How will a feminist theological hermeneutics define "canon"?

To ask about *identity* is to ask: Who authorizes, who authors our lives? To say that one's identity is "Christian" has generally meant counting as important at least three things: Christ, the Church, and the Bible. But it is precisely the authority of Christ, Church, and Bible that is called into question when a person identifies herself also as "feminist." What is the nature of biblical authority in the life of a feminist? Is the notion of the authority of an androcentric text relevant at all to what Elisabeth Schüssler Fiorenza calls a "self-identified woman"? The question, however, is not only one of how a feminist relates to the Bible, but further of how a feminist relates to other Christian women who also claim a place in the Church, and who are willing to accept more traditional understandings of "biblical authority." That is to say, can a feminist hermeneutics be both critical *and* inclusive?[1] Our investigation must consider, then, both the general issue of women's relationship to the Bible and the more specific, critical concerns of feminist scholarship, as well as how these arenas interrelate.

Feminism, Theology, and Hermeneutics

The questions raised above about the relationship of interpretation, hermeneutics, and theology only become problematic in the context of modern historical scholarship. In an earlier era, it was taken for granted that interpretation was done to serve the needs of the Church of that day and that it would be done by men of faith for whom the world of the text was transparently their own world. It was only with the rise of historical methods and questions in the last two hundred years that consciousness arose of the distance between the text and the contemporary world. With the awareness of distance came as well two other, competing demands. One was the imperative of historical science for objectivity, seeking the facts of the past untainted by beliefs and attitudes of the present. The other was the concomitant need for people of the Church to overcome this distance, in order that the Bible might remain relevant to the present.

The struggles and unconscious compromises of imagined objectivity entailed by these competing imperatives have been well elaborated by Schüssler Fiorenza, as has a programmatic alternative which rests in a new view of history, not as "that which happened" but rather as "that which is remembered."[2] Endemic here, not secondary, is the act of interpretation. This perspective abandons the illusion of objectivity in favor of the realization that all interpretation is constrained by the questions of the contemporary interpreter. Granting this perspective, then, indeed, all interpretation necessarily involves a hermeneutics: even that sort of interpretation that purportedly seeks only "the facts of the past" will have access to those "facts" only in the form that fits the question asked. The better part of intellectual credibility is to acknowledge at the outset the factors motivating one's questions.

Even more to the point, from the perspective of feminist liberation theology, is the acknowledgement that the work of interpretation is always engaged either for or against the struggle of the oppressed for liberation. Schüssler Fiorenza presses this issue a step further. In challenging biblical scholarship to become more critical of "its own professed objectivism and value-free stance," feminist theology

> also challenges biblical scholarship to become more theological in the precise sense of the word. If Christians understand the Bible as divine revelation, then biblical interpretation is a theological task in the strictest sense. Insofar as the Bible as Holy Scripture speaks about God, biblical scholarship must develop a critical method and hermeneutics that does not "render God" as a God of patriarchal oppression.[3]

Thus, while the biblical scholar *is* engaged in a hermeneutical process that is aware of the inevitable interaction between "what the text meant" and "what the text means," Schüssler Fiorenza does not envision a simple consensual circle of text and interpretation engaging in mutual self-correction. A patriarchal text read in a patriarchal culture will never self-correct! The role of biblical scholars must, then, be more like that of "culture critics who subject both the historical-critical interpretations of their colleagues and of 'ordinary' believers and preachers to a critical evaluation and hermeneutics of liberation."[4]

Defining Canon: Critical Perspective and Inclusivity in Feminist Hermeneutics

An Inclusive Perspective

One of the most inclusive understandings of feminist theological hermeneutics is the five-part typology of Carolyn Osiek. She poses the following question:

> When women today in Christian communities become aware of their situation within a patriarchal religious institution and, moreover, when they recognize that the Bible is a major implement for maintaining the oppression of patriarchal structure, what are the ways in which they respond and adjust to that situation?[5]

The five ways she identifies are rejectionist, loyalist, revisionist, sublimationist, and liberationist. Certain feminists, from Elizabeth Cady Stanton to Mary Daly, have lived out the *rejectionist* model, finding not only the Bible itself but the whole of both Judaism and Christianity to be so corrupted by patriarchalism as to be irredeemable. Fully counter to this is the *loyalist* mode. Osiek's definition here is both subtle and important. In defining loyalists as feminists, she is *not* referring to those women who simply accept the traditionally understood biblical mandate of female inferiority and submission. Although their argumentation varies, feminist loyalists assert both the reality of the Bible as divine revelation, the Word of God, *and* the validity of the notion that God wills women and men to live in "true happiness and mutual respect."[6] The third model, the *revisionist* hermeneutic, represents a midpoint between the first two, holding that "the patriarchal mold in which the Judeo–Christian tradition has been cast is historically but not theologically determined."[7] This mode looks to reform from within by reading the Bible for positive role models for women and by depatriarchalizing the interpretation of texts. The work of Phyllis Trible is often cited as a classic example of this mode. A fourth alternative, the *sublimationist* hermeneutic, posits an essential distinction between the masculine and the feminine. Rather than denigrating the feminine, however, as androcentric interpretation would do, it exalts what it takes to be female traits as equal to or higher than the male. This mode tends to focus on the world of symbols, and is not typical of biblical scholars: even feminist biblical scholars usually maintain some allegiance to their textual and historical training. *Liberationist* feminism, the fifth mode identified by Osiek, defines salvation as liberation in this world. It consciously adopts an advocacy position, using the struggle of women against oppression as its hermeneutical key, and thus striving toward a "transformation of the social order."[8]

Part of the value of Osiek's approach, aside from the usefulness of its typology, is the fact that she too works from an admitted "advocacy position," one that might be defined as advocacy of inclusivism. She believes that these five positions are all "truly alternatives, that is, within the limits imposed on us by our experience and human conditioning, we really are free to choose our own hermeneutical direction."[9] The urge to include a wide range of women's interpretative experiences must confront, however, the challenge of critical rigor, both in an intellectual and in a political sense. Are all these positions equally capable of coherent argumentation? Do all of them deal equally well with the sources of oppression (including classism and racism, as well as sexism), and do they all provide equally adequate means to combat such oppression? Such critical questions are posed most forcefully in the work of Elisabeth Schüssler Fiorenza, whose work on feminist theological hermeneutics, because of both its quantity and its sophistication, has virtually defined the field.

A Critical Perspective

Schüssler Fiorenza is identified by Osiek as one of several liberationist feminists, but Osiek's discussion elides the fact that Schüssler Fiorenza has directed serious criticism at fellow liberationists Letty Russell and Rosemary Radford Ruether, categorizing both as neo–orthodox![10] These three feminists share a commitment to "women-church," a woman-centered Christian praxis oriented toward transforming the structures of both Church and world. What distinguishes Schüssler Fiorenza from the others is precisely her approach to the use of scripture. Both Russell and Ruether, she argues, search for "a critical universal principle or normative tradition from particular historical texts and specific cultural situations."[11] Ruether identifies in the Bible what she calls its "liberating-prophetic critique." Russell cites the biblical witness to "God's liberating action on behalf of God's creation."[12] According to Schüssler Fiorenza, however, a feminist theological hermeneutics that relates to the Bible in these ways is problematic because it "still adheres to the archetypal biblical paradigm that establishes universal principles and normative patterns" and does not "seriously take into account the androcentric character of biblical language on the one hand and the patriarchal stamp of all biblical traditions on the other hand."[13] The hermeneutics of Russell and Ruether – because they distinguish language from content, patriarchal expression from liberating tradition, and androcentric text from feminist "witness" – "seems to rely on an untenable linguistic-philosophical position that divides form and content, linguistic expression and revelatory truth."[14]

In a move indicative of her Roman Catholic heritage, Schüssler Fiorenza alters the typical Protestant understanding of canon, shifting from the sense of canon as written scripture to canon as definitive measurement: feminist critical hermeneutics will follow "Augustine, Thomas, and the Second Vatican Council in formulating a criterion or canon that limits inspired truth and revelation to matters pertaining to the salvation, freedom, and liberation of all, especially women."[15] The source of this canon, moreover, is not scripture but rather the community, specifically, the community of women struggling against oppression. Feminist theological hermeneutics is, then, a *critical* hermeneutics, which does not regard the Bible as a mythical archetype (the critique lodged against Ruether and Russell, as well as against more traditional interpreters), but as a "historical prototype, or as a formative root-model of biblical faith and life." As against the ideal and unchanging form of an archetype, a prototype is understood to be open to the possibility of transformation. The vision of liberation and salvation in this hermeneutics "is *informed* by the biblical prototype but is not *derived from it. It places biblical texts under the authority of feminist experience* insofar as it maintains that revelation is ongoing and takes place 'for the sake of our salvation.'"[16]

On occasion, Schüssler Fiorenza slips into the more conventional usage of canon-as-scripture,[17] but these are exceptions that prove the rule. Scripture is canon in the sense of being a "root-model," and what is modeled is precisely a "multiform" understanding of Christian Church and life. The fact that the Bible includes many interpretations of faith does not, however, mean that all are equally valid today. Christian *teaching* must preserve all traditions, precisely to preserve the multiformity of the written canon. Christian *preaching*, however, must discern between oppressive texts and liberating ones: only the latter deserve a place in proclamation.[18]

The work of Schüssler Fiorenza challenges the critical adequacy of much of what Carolyn Osiek would call feminist hermeneutics. In practice, a good bit of the enterprise to which Schüssler Fiorenza exhorts feminists is not unlike that of the "neo-orthodox" revisionists and liberationists she criticizes. It involves searching for the "lost coin" of "traditions and visions of liberation among [our] inheritance of androcentric biblical texts and their interpretations."[19] We recover maternal God-language; we restore the elided history of women's leadership in ancient communities; we identify the people of God according to the Bible's own inclusive norm in beginning with creation and ending with the new creation. What makes Schüssler Fiorenza different, and it is an important difference, is her insistence on the authority of women over the Bible. We must understand the background of this assertion not simply in terms of the desire of feminism to advance the cause of women but also in terms of a critical theory that refuses to validate its claims by appeal to a "transcendent other." If there are biblical texts that support women's struggle against oppression, they do so because women claim them in this struggle, not because God (or any other transcendent, de-historicized ideal) says so.

Tension and compromise

In my own wrestling with the ways, means, and effects of biblical interpretation, I have come to a position in full accord with Schüssler Fiorenza's critical stance, perhaps in some measure even more critical: I find it hard to speak at all of "revelation," for example. On the other hand, I partake of both a past experience and a present context that lead me to ask further questions and to imagine the activity of feminist theological hermeneutics in some different, though complementary, ways.

The past experience to which I refer is that of having been led in part *by scripture* to my current critical faith, which holds so much against this same scripture. I have had the experience of relating to Hebrew scripture in a way that feels "personal" and, indeed, to some extent personifies the text, an intellectual sin of which Schüssler Fiorenza finds Phyllis Trible, for example, guilty.[20] This sense of "relationship" was part of the beginning of the raising of my feminist consciousness. I cannot say that scripture alone made me a feminist: I was studying the Bible in an academic context that was influenced by feminism, and that raised this agenda in conversation with the Bible. Yet the Bible did also provide an energy and a motivation for pursuing feminist concerns. It did so by means of another interpretative model criticized by Schüssler Fiorenza, namely, Ruether's idea of the prophetic principle of justice. Like Ruether, I saw this principle as applicable to women today, in spite of the prophets' own tendency to submerge it in sexism.

Today, on the one hand, I assent to Schüssler Fiorenza's critique of these positions: they are indeed apologies for scripture. Yet they are not only that. Such apologias derive from a commitment (even if an insufficiently critical one) to the cause of women. To embrace them is to embrace critical compromise. It may also be to embrace effective pedagogy, beginning where the learner is, and thus to claim a source of power in educating Christian Churches toward a theological feminism. My past experience poses for me the question of the relationship between a feminist hermeneutics that holds itself accountable to rigorous critical standards and a feminist pedagogy that finds value in the art of compromise.

In my present context, moreover, I find that an analogous tension between critical rigor and efficacious compromise also exists in the conversation between feminist hermeneutics and feminist politics. I am a member of a congregation of the Christian Church (Disciples of Christ), a reputedly "liberal" congregation with, nonetheless, a strong resistance to facing feminist issues directly. This congregation, though almost entirely middle economic bracket Caucasian, participates in a countywide grassroots political organizing group that crosses racial, economic, and denominational lines. Although the member congregations show varying degrees of resistance to practicing gender equality within their churches, the organization itself provides an unparalleled context for women (as well as men) to receive leadership training, acquire political power, and make an identifiable difference in their communities' quality of life.

Both my immediate and my community-wide church contexts reinforce my sense of the necessity of hermeneutical compromise, not because all versions of feminist hermeneutics are equally valid, as Osiek seems to suggest, but because the facts of religious-political life in the twentieth-century West are what they are. For most Christians with whom I come in contact, the Bible simply *is* authoritative. For change to come in my congregation, critical hermeneutics has to be adapted for conversation to take place with women who still interpret their lives in traditional ways. The same is true, for different reasons, within my political organizing group. There the Bible functions as a source of empowerment for political action. Although it is indeed used against women on one level, it also motivates women and men together to become agents of social change. In the area of the country in which I live, I know of

59

no more effective movement toward improving the actual lives of women, especially poor women, than this one in which I participate, even though it is woefully inadequate in terms of feminist hermeneutics or rhetoric.

What is at issue here, I believe, is the need for reconceptualizations of biblical authority, re-visions that embrace Schüssler Fiorenza's focus on the authority of biblical *people* but also take into fuller account the work of the Bible in defining those people. Assuming Schüssler Fiorenza's model of scripture as historical prototype, I offer here three complementary models for scriptural authority that expand on and nuance her work.

Three Models of Biblical Authority in Feminist Hermeneutics

The Dialogical Authority Model

The first model begins with the experience, still formative for many women, of the fundamentally "nonintellectual commitment to scripture as somehow determinative for the personal and communal identity of Christians."[21] The model envisions an educational effort to clarify the nature of *authority* in this commitment, and especially to distinguish authority from *coercion*, on the one hand, and from *influence*, on the other. To experience scripture as *coercive* is to experience it as threatening one with its inherent ability to carry out its warnings and promises. Fundamentalists who construe scripture as the literal word of God may experience it as having such coercive power. The experience of scriptural *influence*, on the other hand, is one of its persuasive potential, the sense that it provides information about our environment and may help in the decision-making process, but that it has no more inherent value in such a process than any other worthwhile source of information or guidance. Susan Brooks Thistlethwaite correlates these perspectives with the "conservative" and "liberal" views on authority in general: "The conservative view is that authority is always exercised through coercion and therefore that an authoritarian order must be hierarchical. The liberal view has been that authority is vested in an order of persuasion by reason and therefore must be egalitarian."[22]

In distinction from coercion and influence, *authority* is defined here as a free surrendering to the jurisdiction of scripture. What it means to live within the jurisdiction of scripture will vary from person to person. What is constant is that an uncoerced acknowledgement of this authority has been made. Once authority is granted, one attempts to live in alignment with its source without need of threat, promise, or argumentation. Thus, obedience to true authority involves no loss of freedom.

But what induces such granting of authority and, most importantly, what keeps such an orientation from becoming mindless obedience? Political theorist David V. J. Bell suggests that the answer lies in a shared set of values or beliefs held by both the one who gives and the one who takes authority.[23] Such "credenda" authenticate authority. Thus, one might ask, what credenda might women looking toward the beginning of the twenty-first century hold in common with an ancient and androcentric text? I offer these reflections.

Within scripture itself, the authority of text is always understood in relation to the authority *of persons*. Whether in Moses or Huldah, in David or Esther, in Solomon or Woman Wisdom of Proverbs, the authority of the text is always an embodied authority: persons must authorize the text, even as it authorizes them. Thus, true authority has a *dialogical* quality. Paradoxically, in order to grant authority to someone or something else, one must first *have* the authority to do so. Legitimate and uncoerced granting occurs from a position of strength, not of weakness. This granting is, moreover, reciprocal. For a text to have this dialogical authority, it must continually create new persons to participate in this ongoing interaction. In other words, a truly authoritative text will have a generative, life-giving quality.

Many Christian women, including feminist women, whose lives and vocations have been shaped by scripture, have been "created" by the text in this way. The life-giving quality of scripture provides a powerful, experiential point of departure to encourage others to participate in this dialogical exchange of authority. The act of interpretation becomes the bringing together of the biblical traditions with present circumstances to create life for the present and future, a process that Schüssler Fiorenza envisions in her discussion of the hermeneutics of remembrance and of creative actualization.[24]

Precisely this celebrative identification with scripture may prepare the ground for the more painful aspects of remembrance and also for what Schüssler Fiorenza calls the hermeneutics of suspicion and of proclamation, the recognition that the Bible's patriarchal, androcentric character must be named and condemned.[25] For sometimes the authority of scripture that is embodied in persons will call for the destruction of the existing, coercive institutions that have usurped authority. In fact, the first example of such a call occurs the very first time anyone is reported to have interpreted scripture, and that interpreter was a woman. In 2 Kings 22, the prophet Huldah proclaims the message of the newly found book of the covenant to be the destruction of Judah. Working from her example, we can imagine further that the process of dialogical authority entails that the woman whom scripture authorizes will sometimes have occasion to de-authorize scripture itself. Thus, *the authority of women over scripture becomes a primary credendum of scriptural authority*.

This model of biblical authority suggests one way of transcending the polarity of the critical versus the inclusive in feminist theological hermeneutics. It presupposes both that persons are created by their traditions, and that individuals may take up liberated subject positions in a generally oppressive discourse, presuppositions that are supported by a poststructuralist feminist theory that resists idealization of a unified conception of women's (or even feminist) "experience."[26] This model potentially withholds – or at least delays – a thoroughgoing critique of the tradition, but it does so in the interest of remaining in conversation with women who may yet be empowered to make a fuller acknowledgement of their own biblically grounded authority with respect to the Bible, the Church, and society.[27]

The metaphor model

In three books, theologian Sallie McFague has elaborated the structure of a metaphorical theology. The purpose of this theological model is to carve a third way between religious language that is idolatrous, regarded by its users as having the capacity to refer literally to God, and language that is irrelevant, so skeptical of making valid claims about God that it seems meaningless. Over against these alternatives, metaphor perceives similarity in dissimilarity, sees "this *as* that," without confusing "this *for* that." A metaphorical theology, then, will be one that sees connections between God and the world, but sees them as "tensive, discontinuous and surprising," one that "insists on the dialectic of the positive and the negative, on the 'is *and* the is not.' "[28]

Although McFague's project as a whole involves a constructive theological task, a significant part of her argument has to do with the authority and use of scripture. There is no language more likely either to become idolatrous or seem irrelevant than that of the Bible! McFague's proposal to transcend these two undesirable possibilities is to view the Bible as a "poetic classic" and a "classic model" for Christianity.[29] The word "classic" in each phrase points to the Bible's proven ability, across many times and places, to make itself relevant as a discloser of reality. Its "classic" quality points to its intrinsic authority. The word "classic" also, however, indicates the Bible's conservative character. It requires qualification by the terms "poetic" and "model," which suggest its "reforming and revolutionary power."[30] "As model, the distance between the Bible and the reality it is attempting to express is always maintained. A model or metaphor is . . . never identifiable with its object; the Bible as model can never *be* the word of God."[31] By the same token, as a poetic text, the Bible's greatness is defined by its ability to say many things, its intrinsic demand to be interpreted always anew. The multivocal rhetoric of poetry and the is/is not conceptuality of the model are aligned in metaphorical thinking. Precisely because of the Bible's metaphorical characteristics, "tension, dialectic, openness, change, growth and relativity must be intrinsic to a proper understanding of its authority"; further, the Bible calls *inherently* for a questioning of its linguistic distortions and false consciousness.[32]

62

McFague's construal of the Bible as a classic model/poetic classic provides, in one sense, an elaboration on Schüssler Fiorenza's concept of the Bible as historical prototype or root-model (see above). McFague's focus on language, however, as well as her orientation to a larger constructive theology, also provides a different, though complementary, set of possibilities for actualizing a feminist hermeneutics. Work by McFague and others has contributed numerous examples of metaphors whose affective depth and structural power often derive from their classic source in scriptural traditions, but whose authority is grounded in their capacity to generate new and liberating structures in the contemporary world. McFague regards "the kingdom of God" as the root metaphor of Christianity. As a root metaphor, it is both "supported and fed by many extended metaphors, the various parables," which leave its meaning "ambiguous, multileveled [and] imagistic"; it also generates "translation languages" into more conceptual discourses, which lend it "precision and consistency."[33] McFague's emphasis here on *parable*, a form of extended, narrative metaphor, is characteristic of her work and is evident also in her discussion of the life and death of Jesus as a "parable of God":

> In order to understand the ways of God with us – something unfamiliar and unknown to us, about which we do not know how to think or talk – we look at that life as a metaphor of God. What we see through that "grid" or "screen" is at one level an ordinary, secular story of a human being, but also a story shot through with surprise, unconventionality and incongruities which not only upset our conventional expectations (for instance, of what a "savior" is and who gets "saved"), but also involve a judgment on our part – "Surely this man is the Christ."[34]

This metaphorical perspective on classic theological loci – kingdom and Christ – in the biblical tradition is complemented in McFague's work by attention to other, more peripheral images by means of which she seeks to open and augment theological discourse – for example, the universe as God's body, and God as lover, mother, and friend.[35] The present author has followed McFague's lead in analyzing a Hebrew Bible metaphor, Wisdom as Woman in the book of Proverbs, as a theological root metaphor.[36] In the context of feminist theology, the metaphor of Woman Wisdom affirms the priority of human experience, especially women's experience, in the development of theology, as well as articulating a human relationship with God as Goddess. Woman Wisdom, furthermore, both reinforces and undercuts the concept of an authoritative scripture, defining this authority as personal, relational, and liminal. One final example of the fruitfulness of metaphorical theology can be found in Susan Brooks Thistlethwaite's *Metaphors for the Contemporary Church*.[37] Thistlethwaite proposes that what we see the Church "as," how we metaphorize it, is crucial to the kind of Church it will be. She commends the metaphors "Body of Christ" and "the Poor" as appropriate metaphors for the North American context.

The concept of metaphor, then, can provide both a theoretical perspective on the nature of scriptural authority itself and also a methodological tool for allowing liberating seeds of the tradition, heretofore scattered and fallow, to blossom forth with possibilities for new structures of reality. In this process, the metaphor model serves two other purposes for a feminist hermeneutics. First, by emphasizing the poetic, it taps into the power of imagination, a crucial source of energy and vision for creating a new future. Second, by emphasizing interpretation, it allows us to experience both our distance from the past, as we seek to understand a given metaphor's function in ancient times, and our connection with that past, as we meditate on the metaphor's meaning and power today. The written canon will be one, though not the only, source for such seeds. The authority of the metaphor will derive, moreover, not only from its source but also from its capacity to empower the transformation of individuals and society toward wholeness and inclusivity.

The Trickster Model

A third model for a feminist theological hermeneutics is more radical than the first two, yet still remains in touch with the experience of empowerment through conversation with the text. I shall call this hermeneutical stance that of "reading as a trickster" or, to use an image at home in the Bible itself, "reading as a strange woman."[38] In the folklore of many traditional cultures, the trickster is a "liminal" figure, that is, one who stands at the margins of authority, who embodies ambiguity and chaos, and who reminds the established orders that such forces of indeterminacy are inescapably present in their midst. The last point is crucial: different cultural worldviews may attempt to "explain" disorder in any number of ways, but they cannot ultimately deny its presence. The trickster figure, by embodying chaos in the guise of humor, allows for its acknowledgement and its embrace within the bounds of order. This embrace of chaos, in turn, imbues a potentially static, deadly order with liveliness and flexibility.

Distinctive yet similar, the biblical image of the "strange woman" may provide a hermeneutical key for the difficult attraction of Christian women and androcentric text. In the book of Proverbs, the Strange Woman is a highly condensed symbol of evil, an evil defined by the chaos of all that lies outside the acceptable system: the foreigner, the adulterer, the prostitute, the ritually impure. Remarkably, the Proverbs texts also develop an equally powerful symbol of all that is good, Wisdom personified as a woman. Though they are evaluated as moral opposites, similarity in vocabulary and imagery links these two figures to a considerable degree: both appear in the public sphere of streets and market; both invite listeners to their houses; both are to be grasped and embraced. This bonding of female-identified good and evil creates a dynamic not unlike that of folklore's trickster, the experience of ambiguity and potential chaos invading orderly oppositions. The tricksterlike ambiguity of the Strange Woman may also be seen in other biblical narratives about foreign women. Tamar (Gen. 38), Ruth, and Delilah, for example, are all figures who render the distinction between good and evil ambiguous by posing the possibility that good – indeed, the will of God – can come from (women's) evil.

To read, then, as a trickster or a strange woman involves, first, claiming identity with those at the margins and, second, willingness to read against the text, to read subversively. Tricksters and strange women recognize that, although the editor of Proverbs united the figures of Woman Wisdom and Woman Stranger by means of female imagery, his intent was to compel his male readers to tell the difference: to embrace Wisdom and avoid the Stranger. A hermeneutics of strangeness teaches us to tell the sameness, to undercut the apparently absolute opposition between good and evil; to illuminate instead their paradoxical, but experientially validated, unity; to affirm the disorder that energizes our struggle against unjust order.

It oppresses women to classify us as ideal wife or evil temptress. Although the Bible is, on one level, androcentric throughout, blatantly sexist passages such as these in Proverbs confront modern readers with unavoidable choices that may be masked elsewhere. It would seem at first glance that the choice is an either – or. Either we choose to accept the text's sexist ideology or, from out of our modern historical consciousness, we argue that such ideas are the product of a prior age, not relevant to us, worthy only of being ignored. But if we will listen only to those parts of the Bible we agree with, where then is its challenge to faith, its ability to make us see the log in our own eye, as we rub at the speck we find in Israel's?

To read subversively, to read as a strange woman, is to take seriously this saying from Proverbs 18:21:

> Death and life are in the power of the tongue,
> and those who love her shall eat of her fruits.

We are bound, in our humanity, to be lovers of language. The proverb reminds us of the inescapable duality that results, the encounter with both death and life. Every word contains its opposite. Meaning is not just multiple, but always ambiguous, indeterminate. The responsibility is thus ceded to us to find life as well as death in the power of the word and, with the responsibility, also the authority.

Subversive reading goes beyond even this recognition of responsibility in the face of indeterminacy. In a spirit of serious play, it leads us to revalue the oppressive absolutes of the past and the present by re-creating the very terms

65

in which those absolutes are expressed. We thank the tradition which attempted to cast out its strange women for helping us find our name, and thereby reassert our place in that tradition. As one further example of how one might read as a strange woman, I offer this reflection on one of the Bible's most misogynistic comments. Ben Sira, author of the deuterocanonical book Christians call Ecclesiasticus, opines (Sir. 25:24):

> From woman is the beginning of sin
> and because of her all die.

What would happen if tricky readers were daring enough to embrace rather than reject this statement? If we said, yes, human reality does include evil and death? And woman encompasses them, just as she encompasses goodness and life. Woman does indeed represent *all* of human reality. To turn the text's seemingly ultimate condemnation to the cause of a caricatured ultimate empowerment is to take a stand in the tradition with a sense of both humor and justice, the defining traits of the trickster. It replicates, moreover, the courage of our forebears in claiming the name "Christian," initially a derogatory term used against them by the Romans.

Finally, the hermeneutical model of the strange woman, the trickster, may contribute to mediating the tension between inclusiveness and critical perspective that runs through feminist hermeneutics. To read the Bible as a strange woman is to read through it to see the continuing paradox that persists in the lives of women and men today. In Proverbs, we are met first by the strong, exalted, almost deified figure of Woman Wisdom, surely the apex of biblical female imagery. It is good, we nod to ourselves. But then we confront her opposite, the Strange Woman, and begin to fear that once again women are being used by male authors to support their own place of power in the social structure, and the view of reality that supports it. Reading as a strange woman opens yet a third possibility: a positive valuation of women's power as antistructural, regenerative because of its liminality. But again we face paradox: What structures are being regenerated by this liminality? Is it all too convenient for the beneficiaries of an unjust power structure to give liminality its due in order to draw on its power for themselves?

The reality is that all of these conflicting forces are at work in the mix of human life, which is one reason why feminists have no choice but to acknowledge varied courses of resistance to the patriarchal system, the sum of which may finally generate real change. Some choose to separate themselves, to live on the margins of patriarchy. Women and men turn their backs on biblical faith, developing spiritualities that reflect their lives and serve their needs as persons who condemn the ways of those who own the center. Christians cannot ignore the challenge of those who have moved to the margins, though there is danger in this choice. For in removing liminality from the center of the world, one abdicates the power to transform the world. But perhaps a new world is possible. Others choose to work within the system, to become pastors and lay leaders of churches, to teach in seminaries, sculpting a new reality within the old. This again is a valid choice, but only paradoxically so: the power that might transform the world also helps to support its present form. But perhaps the gain will outweigh the loss. In either case, there is an energy for change that comes when strange women seize the paradox of our existence, draw on the power of our liminality for ourselves, read the Bible as tricksters, and teach others to do so also.

Notes

1 For earlier formulations of this question, see Dorothy Bass, "Women's Studies and Biblical Studies: An Historical Perspective," *JSOT* 22 (1982): 6–12; and Katharine Doob Sakenfeld, "Feminist Uses of Biblical Materials," in *Feminist Interpretation of the Bible*, ed. L. Russell (Philadelphia: Westminster, 1985), pp. 55–64.

2 Elisabeth Schüssler Fiorenza, *Bread Not Stone: The Challenge of Feminist Biblical Interpretations* (Boston: Beacon Press, 1984), pp. 93–115.

3 Ibid., p. 118.

4 Ibid., p. 135.

5 Carolyn Osiek, "The Feminist and the Bible: Hermeneutical Alternatives," in *Feminist Perspectives on Biblical Scholarship*, ed. A. Y. Collins (Chico, CA: Scholars Press, 1985), p. 97.

6 Ibid., p. 99.

7 Ibid., p. 100.

8 Ibid., p. 103.

9 Ibid., p. 104.

10 Elisabeth Schüssler Fiorenza, *In Memory of Her: A Feminist Theological Reconstruction of Christian Origins* (New York: Crossroad, 1983), pp. 14–19; eadem, *Bread Not Stone*, pp. 12–13.

11 Schüssler Fiorenza, *Bread Not Stone*, p. 13.

12 Letty Russell, "Feminist Critique: Opportunity for Cooperation," *JSOT* 22 (1982): 68.

13 Schüssler Fiorenza, *Bread Not Stone*, p. 13.

14 Ibid.

15 Ibid., p. 14.

16 Ibid. (emphasis added).

17 Ibid., p. 36.

18 Ibid., p. 37.

19 Ibid., p. 16.

20 Phyllis Trible, *God and the Rhetoric of Sexuality* (Philadelphia: Fortress, 1978); Schüssler Fiorenza, *In Memory of Her*, pp. 19–21.

21 Claudia V. Camp, "Female Voice, Written Word: Women and Authority in Hebrew Scripture," in *Embodied Love: Sensuality and Relationship as Feminist Values*, ed. P. Cooey, S. Farmer, and M. E. Ross (San Francisco: Harper & Row, 1987), p. 97.
22 Susan Brooks Thistlethwaite, *Metaphors for the Contemporary Church* (New York: Pilgrim, 1983), p. 155.
23 David V. J. Bell, *Power, Influence and Authority* (New York: Oxford University Press, 1975).
24 Schüssler Fiorenza, *Bread Not Stone*, pp. 19–22.
25 Ibid., pp. 15–19.
26 See Chris Weedon, *Feminist Praxis and Poststructuralist Theory* (Oxford: Basil Blackwell, 1987).
27 See Schüssler Fiorenza, *Bread Not Stone*, p. 84.
28 Sallie McFague, *Metaphorical Theology: Models of God in Religious Language* (Philadelphia: Fortress, 1982).
29 Ibid., pp. 54–66.
30 Ibid., p. 63.
31 Ibid., p. 62.
32 Ibid., pp. 64–5.
33 Ibid., pp. 26–7.
34 Ibid., p. 18.
35 Ibid., pp. 182–92; eadem, *Models of God: Theology for an Ecological, Nuclear* (Philadelphia: Fortress, 1987).
36 Claudia V. Camp, "Woman Wisdom as Root Metaphor: A Theological Consideration," in *The Listening Heart: Essays in Wisdom and the Psalms in Honor of R. E. Murphy* ed. K. Hoglund et al. (Sheffield: JSOT Press, 1987).
37 See n. 22.
38 See Camp, "Wise and Strange: An Interpretation of the Female Imagery in Proverbs in Light of Trickster Mythology," *Semeia* 42 (1988).

Recommended reading

Bass, Dorothy. "Women's Studies and Biblical Studies: An Historical Perspective." *JSOT* 22 (1982): 6–12.
Camp, Claudia V. "Female Voice, Written Word: Women and Authority in Hebrew Scripture." In *Embodied Love: Sensuality and Relationship as Feminist Values*, edited by P. Cooey, S. Farmer, and M. E. Ross, pp. 97–114. San Francisco: Harper & Row, 1987.
——"Wise and Strange: An Interpretation of the Female Imagery in Proverbs in Light of Trickster Mythology." *Semeia* 42 (1988): 14–36.
——Woman Wisdom as Root Metaphor: A Theological Consideration." In *The Listening Heart: Essays in Wisdom and the Psalms in Honor of R. E. Murphy*, edited by K. Hoglund et al., pp. 45–76. Sheffield: JSOT Press, 1987.
Cannon, Katie Geneva, and Elisabeth Schüssler Fiorenza, eds. *Interpretation for Liberation. Semeia* 47. Atlanta: Scholars Press, 1989.

Chopp, Rebecca. *The Power to Speak: Feminism, Language, God.* New York: Crossroad, 1989.

Duck, Ruth C. *Gender and the Name of God: The Trinitarian Baptismal Formula.* New York: Pilgrim Press, 1991.

McFague, Sallie. *Metaphorical Theology: Models of God in Religious Language.* Philadelphia: Fortress, 1982.

———*Models of God: Theology for an Ecological, Nuclear Age.* Philadephia: Fortress, 1987.

Osiek, Carolyn. "The Feminist and the Bible: Hermeneutical Alternatives." In *Feminist Perspectives on Biblical Scholarship,* edited by A. Y. Collins, pp.93–106. Biblical Scholarship in North America 10. Chico, CA: Scholars Press, 1985.

Russell, Letty. "Feminist Critique: Opportunity for Cooperation." *JSOT* 22 (1982): 67–71.

———ed. *Feminist Interpretation of the Bible.* Philadelphia: Westminster, 1985.

Sakenfeld, Katharine Doob. "Feminist Uses of Biblical Materials." In *Feminist Interpretation of the Bible,* edited by L. Russell, pp. 55–64. Philadelphia: Westminster, 1985.

Schüssler Fiorenza, Elisabeth. *Bread Not Stone: The Challenge of Feminist Biblical Interpretation.* Boston: Beacon Press, 1984.

Thistlethwaite, Susan Brooks. *Metaphors for the Contemporary Church.* New York: Pilgrim, 1983.

Tolbert, Mary Ann. "Defining the Problem: The Bible and Feminist Hermeneutics." *Semeia* 28 (1983): 113–26.

Trible, Phyllis. *God and the Rhetoric of Sexuality.* Philadelphia: Fortress, 1978.

Weems, Renita. "Reading Her Way through the Struggle." In *Story the Road We Trod: African-American Biblical Interpretation,* edited by Cain Hope Felder, pp. 57–80. Minneapolis: Fortress, 1991.

Williams, Delores S. *Sisters in the Wilderness: The Challenge of Womanist God Talk.* Maryknoll, NY: Orbis.

The Bible and African Americans: An Outline of an Interpretative History

Vincent L. Wimbush

Introduction: The Bible as Language-World

There has been no lack of efforts in the last decade or so to make sense of the religious traditions of African Americans. Such traditions have been interpreted, for example, as institutional or denominational history,[1] as a liberation movement,[2] as part of a history-of-religions paradigm for aboriginal America,[3] as sociological phenomena,[4] and as historical manifestations of the African world view and piety in a particular context among the "dispersed."[5] I have learned much about African Americans from these and other studies. But I have been left dissatisfied with what appears in far too many of these studies to be either a total neglect or a superficial treatment of the role of the Bible in the religious traditions of African Americans. The argument here for attention to the Bible among African Americans has less to do with any assumed valorization – "authority," "inspiration," among other concepts now current in religious circles – of the Bible in some timeless, abstract manner, than with concern about an understanding of the range of its functions in the history of African Americans. My suspicions and theses are that greater clarity about the role that the Bible has played in the history of African Americans can shed light on the different responses African Americans have made to the socio–political and economic situations in which they have found themselves. Since every reading of important texts, especially mythic or religious texts, reflects a "reading" or assessment of one's world, and since the Bible has from the founding of the nation served as an icon,[6] a history of African Americans' historical readings of the Bible is likely to reflect their historical self-understandings – as Africans in America.

One useful way of beginning to clarify the issues involved in thinking about the function of the Bible among African Americans is to think of the Bible as a language, even language-world. The experience of being uprooted from their African homeland and forced to labor in a strange place produced in the first African slaves what has been termed a type of disorientation.[7] This disorientation, obviously contrived by the white slavers because of its advantages for them, was most evident in language or powers of communication. Part of the Europeans' and Americans' justification for the enslavement of Africans was the "strangeness" of the latter – their physical attributes and their culture, especially their languages.[8] Of course, many of the Europeans and their counterparts in the "New World" deemed the Africans' physical features and cultures inferior – Africans were considered to be hideous in their looks and barbaric in their ways. Certainly, part of what it meant to be fully enslaved was to be cut off from one's cultural roots.

Although groups of the Africans who were captured and enslaved could have communicated with one another without problem, the slavers took steps to frustrate communication. So being deprived initially of a language with which meaningful communication could be realized, the first African slaves experienced a type of "social death,"[9] cut off from their roots, including their languages and religious heritage. This is what slavery was supposed to mean in the eyes of many.

But this state of affairs did not always obtain even for the African slaves. A great many of the slaves did adopt – as part of the complex phenomenon of acquiring a number of new skills, symbols, and languages for survival – the Bible as a "language" through which they negotiated both the strange new world that was called America and the slave existence. With this "language" they began to wax eloquent not only with the white slavers and not only among themselves, but also about themselves, about the ways in which they understood their situation in America – as slaves, as freed persons, as disenfranchised persons, as a people. For the great majority of African Americans the Bible has historically functioned not merely to reflect and legitimize piety (narrowly understood), but as a language-world full of stories – of heroes and heroines, of heroic peoples and their pathos and victory, sorrow and joy, sojourn and fulfillment. In short, the Bible became a "world" into which African Americans could retreat, a "world" they could identify with, draw strength from, and in fact manipulate for self-affirmation.

Nearly all interpreters have acknowledged that the Bible has played an important role in the history of African Americans. What remains is a comprehensive effort to relate and then interpret that history through attention to the various ways in which the Bible has been engaged by African Americans. This essay is an attempt to provide only a working outline of such a history. Its importance lies in its suggestiveness, or heuristic value, not its comprehen-

71

siveness. It is no more than an outline of what I have isolated as the major types of readings of the Bible among African Americans from the beginning of their introduction to it in the period of slavery up to the modern period. The types of readings actually correspond to different historical periods and are meant to reflect different responses to historical (socio–political–economic) situations and (collective) self-understandings.

Other initial clarifying statements are in order. First, each "reading" is assumed to be public, or communal, not private, or individualistic. Second, each "reading" is assumed to have emerged out of particular life-settings, and to have been more or less manifested and preserved in different types of sources – e.g., songs, sermons, testimonies, addresses. The "more or less" is significant: The sources are not absolutely mutually exclusive of different types of readings. Third, each type of reading is assumed not to be in evidence solely in terms of the direct quotation of certain biblical passages – although the occurrence of certain clusters of biblical materials over and over again would obviously be significant, especially in terms of the development of a "canon" (see the discussion below). Again, emphasis will be placed upon the discernment of the range of *functions* of the Bible in African-American communities. Fourth, although the discussion to follow is divided according to types of readings, the predominant orientation and method are historical, and are best understood in this way. The ultimate goal is an *interpretative history* of African Americans based on their readings of the Bible.

Having said this, it is important for me to note that even as each type of reading represents a period in the history of African Americans, the types of readings are not strictly chronologically successive – no one reading completely disappears when another begins. There is much overlap of readings in different historical periods. One period differs from another for the most part in terms of emphases. So given the nature of the historical inquiry that this essay represents, strict chronological perimeters or dates to correspond to the different types of readings would not be helpful; they could in fact serve only to frustrate the thesis that will govern the essay – that there is much overlap of readings between periods. Nevertheless, some general dating perimeters will be referenced throughout the essay.

First "Reading": Rejection, Suspicion, and Awe of "Book Religion" (Beginning of African Experience in the New World)

What the Africans faced in the New World was what the European settlers had also to face – strangeness. The latter, however, set out from the beginning to conquer the strangeness and bend it to their will and ethos. They conquered native peoples and declared that European customs, languages, and traditions were the law. The Europeans' embrace of the Bible helped to lend this process legitimacy. Since many of them through their reading of and reference to the Bible had already defined themselves as dissenters from the dominant social, political, and religious traditions in their native countries, they found it a rather natural resource in the context of the New World. The Bible functioned as a cultural image-reflector, as a road map to nation-building. It provided the Europeans justification to think of themselves as a "biblical nation," as God's people called to conquer and convert the New World to God's way as they interpreted it.[10]

The Africans could not and did not fail to notice the powerful influence of the Bible upon the Europeans' self-image, culture, and orientation. Their first reaction, as far as evidence allows, to the Europeans and to the Europeans' understanding of themselves can be seen – and, I think, more clearly explicated – in their response to the Bible, referred to by Europeans as "Holy Scripture" or the "Holy Book." For the great majority of the first African slaves the first reaction was an admixture of rejection, suspicion, and awe. On the one hand, they seemed to reject or be suspicious of any notion of "Book Religion." As is the case with most nonliterate peoples with well-established and elaborate oral traditions, the Africans found the notion of piety and world view circumscribed by a book to be absurd.[11] On the other hand, the fact that those who had enslaved them and were conquering the New World were "Bible Christians" was not at all lost on the Africans: It did not take them long to associate the Book of "Book Religion" with power.[12]

Even before the Africans were able to manipulate the Bible in a self-interested, affirming manner, their early capacity and willingness to engage "the Book" were significant, for they demonstrated the Africans' ability to adapt themselves to different understandings of reality. That capacity and willingness also reflected their will to survive, to accommodate themselves to the New World, even as they understood it to be dominated by the European slavers. What form and meaning this "accommodation" would assume would be debated in times – and reflected in "readings" of the Bible – to come.

Second "Reading": Transformation of "Book Religion" into Religion of Slave Experience (Beginning of Mass Conversions in the Eighteenth Century)

It was not until the revival movements – in the North and South – of the eighteenth century that Africans began to convert to Christianity in significant numbers, significant enough to justify labeling this period as the beginning of a type of African-American religious ethos. They responded to the Europeans' evangelical preaching and piety, especially the emphasis on conversion experience as the sign of God's acceptance of the worth of the individual, and the often spontaneous formation of communities of the converted for fellowship and mutual affirmation. Because testimony regarding personal experience with God was the single most important criterion – relativizing, though not obliterating, social status and racial identification – for entry into the evangelical communities, and because that criterion held the promise of a degree of egalitarianism and affirmation, it was no wonder that the Africans began to respond in great numbers to the white Methodists and Baptists.[13]

The sacralization of the Bible among white evangelical Protestants, North and South, could hardly have been ignored by the Africans. The young nation officially defined itself as a "biblical nation"; indeed, popular culture was also thoroughly biblical.[14] It would have been difficult not to take note of the diversity of views that reading the Bible could inspire, not only between North and South as cultural, political readings, but also among evangelical communities – Baptist, Methodist, Presbyterian. The lesson that the Africans learned from these evangelicals was not only that faith was to be interpreted in light of the reading of the Bible, but also that each person had freedom of interpretation of the Bible. Given differences between individuals and different religious groups, the Africans learned that they, too, could read "the Book" freely. They could read certain parts and ignore others. They could and did articulate their interpretations in their own way – in song, prayers, sermons, testimonies, and addresses. By the end of the century "the Book" had come to represent a virtual language-world that they, too, could enter and manipulate in light of their social experiences. After all, everyone could approach the Bible under the guidance of the Spirit, that is, in his or her own way.[15]

And interpret they did. They were attracted primarily to the narratives of the Hebrew Bible dealing with the adventures of the Hebrews in bondage and escaping from bondage, to the oracles of the eighth-century prophets and their denunciations of social injustice and visions of social justice, and to the New Testament texts concerning the compassion, passion, and resurrection of Jesus. With these and other texts, the African-American Christians laid the foundations for what can be seen as an emerging "canon." In their spirituals and in their sermons and testimonies African Americans interpreted the Bible in light of their experiences. Faith became identification with the heroes and heroines of the Hebrew Bible and with the long-suffering but ultimately victorious Jesus. As the people of God in the Hebrew Bible were once delivered from enslavement, so, the Africans sang and shouted, would they be delivered. As Jesus suffered unjustly but was raised from the dead to new life, so, they sang, would they be "raised" from their "social death" to new life. So went the songs, sermons, and testimonies.

In his classic collection and interpretation of the spirituals James Weldon

Johnson captures well the importance of the Bible in the imaginations of the earliest African Americans:

> At the psychic moment there was at hand the precise religion for the condition in which [the African] found himself thrust. Far from ... his native land and customs, despised by those among whom he lived, experiencing the pang of separation of loved ones on the auction block ... [the African] seized Christianity, ... the religion which implied the hope that in the next world there would be a reversal of conditions. ... The result was a body of songs voicing all the cardinal virtues of Christianity. ... through a modified form of primitive African music. ... [The African] took complete refuge in Christianity, and the Spirituals were literally forged in the heat of religious fervor. ... It is not possible to estimate the sustaining influence that the story of the Jews as related in the Old Testament exerted upon the Negro. This story at once caught and fired the imaginations of the Negro bards, and they sang, sang their hungry listeners into a firm faith.[16]

Of course, Johnson's interpretation of the function of "other-worldly" religion among oppressed peoples has been significantly modified and corrected by current research in the sociology of religion in general,[17] as well as by studies on African-American religion in particular.[18] But very few interpreters of African Americans, from whatever methodological perspective, have captured and articulated so well the importance of the Bible in the imagination of African Americans.

The spirituals reflect the process of the transformation of the Book Religion of the dominant peoples into the religion reflective of the socio-political and economic status of African slaves.

> Go down, Moses
> 'Way down in Egypt land,
> Tell ole Pharaoh, Let my people go.
>
> Dey crucified my Lord,
> An' He never said a mumblin' word.
> Dey crucified my Lord,
> An' He never said a mumblin' word,
> Not a word – not a word – not a word.
>
> Dey nailed Him to de tree,
> An' He never said a mumblin' word.
> Dey nailed Him to de tree,
> An' He never said a mumblin' word,
> Not a word – not a word – not a word.
>
> Dey pierced Him in de side,
> An' He never said a mumblin' word,

Dey pierced Him in de side,
An' He never said a mumblin' word,
Not a word – not a word – not a word.

Sometimes I feel like a motherless child,
Sometimes I feel like a motherless child,
Sometimes I feel like a motherless child,
A long ways from home.

These and other songs, as well as numerous sermons, addresses, and exhortations,[19] reflect a hermeneutic characterized by a looseness, even playfulness, *vis-à-vis* the biblical texts themselves. The interpretation was not controlled by the literal words of the texts, but by social experience. The texts were heard more than read; they were engaged as stories that seized and freed the imagination. Interpretation was therefore controlled by the freeing of the collective consciousness and imagination of the African slaves as they heard the biblical stories and retold them to reflect their actual social situation, as well as their visions for something different. Many of the biblical stories, themselves the product of cultures with well-established oral traditions, functioned sometimes as allegory, as parable, or as veiled social criticism. Such stories well served the African slaves, not only on account of their well-established oral traditions, but also because their situation dictated veiled or indirect social criticism – "hitting a straight lick with a crooked stick."[20]

That the songs and sermons reflect a type of indirect or veiled commentary on the social situation that the African slaves faced has been noted by most interpreters.[21] But more careful attention to the manner in which the images and language of the Bible were used can shed more light on the question of the oppositional character of African-American religion.[22] I would argue that study of both the selection of biblical texts/stories and their redaction by these early African Americans can force entirely different and more illuminating categories upon the discussion. Attention to both biblical story and African-American redaction will more likely bring to focus the major emphases and concerns of the African Americans who sang, prayed, and testified in the language of the Bible. Detailed exegetical treatments of the raw materials of the African experience of this period are in order. More specifically, comparative, or redaction-critical studies of biblical text/stories in relation to African-American stories drawn from the Bible are in order.

I would also argue that this reading of the Bible on the part of African Americans was foundational: All other readings to come would in some sense be built upon and judged against it. This reading is in fact the classical reading of the biblical text for African Americans; it reflects the classical period in the history of African Americans (the eighteenth century). It reflects what arguably has been so basic to the orientation of the majority of African Americans that all subsequent debates about orientation, world view, and strategies for survival and/or liberation have begun with this period and what it represents. In sum, it represents Africans' pragmatic, relative accommodation to existence in America. "Pragmatic" because it attempts to come to grips with what opportunities were at hand for survival and amelioration of social status; "relative" because it never assumed that persons of African descent could ever be fully integrated into American society. This response, therefore, is at base hermeneutically and socially critical. It reflects the fact that the Bible, understood as the "white folk's" book, was accepted but not interpreted in the way that white Christians and the dominant culture in general interpreted it. So America's biblical culture was accepted by the Africans, but not in the way white Americans accepted it or in the way the whites preferred that others accept it.

My thesis about the general function of the Bible among African Americans makes all the more important the need for the detailed study of African-American songs and sermons alongside of the appropriate biblical texts. Such studies should confirm or disconfirm the general thesis.

Third "Reading": Establishment of Canon and Hermeneutical Principle (Beginning of Independent Church Movements in the Nineteenth Century)

In the pre-Civil War northern states, Africans were only slightly less enslaved than their southern counterparts. A few were "allowed" some opportunities to educate themselves both formally and informally. A few were "allowed" access to important public forums – especially those forums dedicated to debating the issue of the morality, social utility, and politics of slavery. And some received good formal education in spite of many frustrations and stumbling blocks. In this climate Africans of the northern states led the way toward the third collective reading of the Bible among African Americans. This reading corresponded to and illuminates the self-understanding of a significant number of African Americans of the period.

In this period, the independent congregations and local and regional denominational bodies developed among African Americans.[23] This development symbolized the oppositional (that is, primarily antiracist) civil rights agenda and character of African-American religion.[24] Attention to the nature of the reading of the Bible among the African-American churches during this period will shed more light on the nature of the oppositional character of the independent church movements.

Sermon after sermon and oration after oration crafted by slaves and freed persons reflected concern about the social lot of Africans in America. What for

77

our purposes is striking is that both the explanation for the social situation of the Africans and the solution to their problems were cast in biblical language. Black freedom-fighters waxed biblical about the kinship of humanity under the sovereignty of the one God, about slavery as a base evil in opposition to the will of God, about the imperatives of the teachings of Jesus to make all nations a part of God's reign, and about the judgement that is to be leveled against all those who frustrate God's will on earth.[25]

During this period African Americans seemed anxious to institutionalize as an ethical and moral principle one of the rare New Testament passages they found attractive and even identified as a *locus classicus* for Christian social teaching – "There is neither Jew nor Greek, there is neither slave nor free, there is neither male nor female; for you are all one in Christ Jesus" (Gal. 3:28). Ironically, this biblical verse stressing the principle of Christian unity was embraced and referred to over and over again as the separate church movements got under way. This and other passages were used to level prophetic judgement against a society that thought of itself as biblical in its foundation and ethic.

In a social situation in which the Bible figured prominently in debates about a number of public policy issues, including slavery, African Americans joined the debate with their own reading of the Bible. Since colonial days white Americans had been familiar with reading the Bible from a nationalist perspective. The story of the Hebrews' long struggle to come into possession of the Promised Land was a paradigm for the Europeans' struggles to come into possession of the American "Promised Land." In the nineteenth century African Americans began to hold forth against such typological claims of white Americans (Protestants, for the most part). African Americans pointed out that their own experience in the New World was an antitype of the ancient Hebrews' experience with respect to Palestine.[26] This they did by applying their favorite biblical passages to an array of social issues – in sermons, prayers, official denominational addresses, creeds, and mottos.

This reading of the Bible among African Americans extends at least from the nineteenth century up to the present. It has historically reflected and shaped the ethos and thinking of the majority of African Americans. If the period of enslavement (certainly eighteenth century through emancipation) represents the classical period, the nineteenth century represents the period of self-conscious articulation, consolidation, and institutionalization. Frederick Douglass and David Walker stand as eloquent examples of nineteenth-century biblical interpreters who took the hermeneutical principle of the kinship of humanity under the sovereignty of God and applied it to the emancipation agenda. These two, among many others, were eloquent in their excoriations of "Christian" and "biblical" America. So Douglass in 1845:

The Christianity of America is a Christianity, of whose votaries it may be truly said, as it was of the ancient scribes and Pharisees, "They bind heavy burdens, and grievous to be borne, and lay them on men's shoulders, but they themselves will not move them with one of their fingers. All their works they do for to be seen of men." . . . Dark and terrible as is this picture, I hold it to be strictly true of the overwhelming mass of professed Christians of America. . . . They would be shocked at the proposition of fellowshipping a sheep-stealer; and at the same time they hug to their communion a man-stealer, and brand me an infidel, if I find fault with them for it. They attend with Pharisaical strictness to the outward forms of religion, and at the same time neglect the weightier matters of law, judgment, mercy, and faith.[27]

So also David Walker in 1829:

Have not the Americans the Bible in their hands? Do they believe it? Surely they do not. See how they treat us in open violation of the Bible! . . . Our divine Lord and Master said "all things whatsoever ye would that men should do unto you, do ye even so unto them." But an American minister, with the Bible in his hand, holds us and our children in the most abject slavery and wretchedness. . . . I tell you Americans! that unless you speedily alter your course, you and your country are gone!!!! Will not that very remarkable passage of Scripture be fulfilled on Christian Americans? Hear it Americans!! "He that is unjust, let him be unjust still: – and he that is filthy, let him be filthy still; and he that is righteous, let him be righteous still; and he that is holy, let him be holy still."[28]

From the nineteenth century into the present, the ideal of the kinship and unity of all humanity under the sovereignty of God has been important to a great number of African Americans, and the official mottos and pronouncements of the independent denominations have reflected that. Two examples will help to demonstrate this.

At the twentieth quadrennial session of the General Conference of the African Methodist Church, in May 1896, the saying of Bishop Daniel Payne, "God our Father; Christ our Redeemer; Man our Brother," became the official motto of the denomination:

This is the official motto of the A.M.E. Church, and her mission in the commonwealth of Christianity is to bring all denominations and races to acknowledge and practice the sentiments contained therein. When these sentiments are universal in theory and practice, then the mission of the distinctive colored organizations will cease.[29]

In his presidential address before the forty-second annual session of the National Baptist Convention, in December 1922, Dr E. C. Morris specified how Afro-Baptists understood and justified their separate existence:

We early imbibed the religion of the white man; we believed in it; we believe in it now. . . . But if that religion does not mean what it says, if God did not make of one blood all nations of men to dwell on the face of the earth, and if we are not to be counted as part of that generation, by those who handed the oracle down to us, the sooner we abandon them or it, the sooner we will find our place in a religious sect in the world.[30]

The reading of the Bible in evidence here can be characterized as prophetic apology. By this term I mean to refer to African Americans' use of the Bible in order to make self-assertive claims against a racist America that claimed to be a biblical nation. The clamor from African Americans was for the realization of the principles of inclusion, equality, and kinship that they understood the Bible to mandate. In the nineteenth century we see among African Americans the beginnings of more consistent and systematic attempts to make use of the Bible in order to force "biblical" America to honor the biblical principles. The very fact that the Bible was so read revealed African Americans' orientation and collective self-understanding – they desired to be integrated into American society. Their critical, polemical, and race- and culture-conscious reading of the Bible reflected the desire to enter the mainstream of American society. The Bible itself had apparently come to represent American society. So a critical reading of it was a critical reading of American society. That the Bible – and the whole of the tradition of which it was a signal part – was engaged at all signified relative acceptance of American society.

Irony must be seen in the fact that it was from the situation of institutional separatism that the prophetic call went out for the realization of the biblical principles of universalism, equality, and the kinship of all humanity. Perhaps African Americans had begun to see the inevitability of the irony in America: the call for oneness could be made only apart from others, lest particularity be lost; but since particularity in America often meant being left out or discriminated against, an apology for the inclusion was made.

Fourth "Reading": Esoteric and Elitist Hermeneutical Principles and Texts (Early Twentieth Century to the Present)

This reading has its origins in the early twentieth century; it continues to have great influence in the present, especially in large urban areas of the North and South. Included here are a number of different groups with little or no formal ties to one another. What they have in common, however, is a tendency to develop esoteric knowledge or principles of interpretation of the (Protestant and/or Catholic) Bible; to lay claim to the absolute legitimacy of that knowledge and those principles; to claim exclusive possession and knowledge of other holy books, or previously apocryphal parts of the Bible; and to practice bibliomancy (the reading of holy books for the purpose of solving personal problems or in order to effect some wonder from which one can benefit). These are to be seen only as tendencies; not all tendencies would be in evidence among all groups included in this category.

The groups included in this period have often been labeled sects. All African-American religious communities have been so labeled by many social-scientific researchers of American religions, since the former were understood to have been founded in response to, and continue to exist on account of, tensions with the dominant society. However, it should be clear at this point that this essay is in part a response to the inadequacy of such labeling of African-American religious communities, past and present. What is required is a typology that can more accurately register the religious diversity among African Americans.

In terms of groups that predominate and characterize readings and periods in the religious history of African Americans, the Baptists and Methodists should certainly be placed in the earlier periods and identified with the corresponding readings. They dominated both the classical and institution-building periods and can be classified as a type of mainstream among African-American religious communities. But in this fourth reading and in the corresponding historical period, the groups that emerge and predominate are different. Among these groups are the Black Muslims, the Black Jews, the African Orthodox, the Garvey movement, the Holiness/Pentecostal Churches, and the Reverend Ike's United Church and Science of Living Institute.[31]

With a more critical perspective of the world and of American society and its biblical self-understanding, these groups are different from the worldly and mainstream Baptists and Methodists, among others. They share a more fundamental disdain for and mistrust of American society. They are less concerned about "cashing the check" on America's promise of democracy, equality, and freedom of opportunity. They tend to be less concerned about holding America to its responsibilities as a biblical nation because they generally do not believe any of America's claims about itself to be true. In sum, such groups can be characterized by their consistent rejection of both American society in general and the older established African-American religious communities. The former is rejected on account of its racism; the latter are rejected on account of their accommodationism.

It is their reading of the Bible, or religious texts in general, that more poignantly reflects these groups' difference from the others. Their claims to esoteric knowledge and principles of interpretation of holy books correspond to their rejection of the boundaries that the dominant society and the accommodationist minority communities agree upon for dialogue and debate about key issues. Outright rejection of the canon itself, or additions to the canon, or esoteric principles of interpretation of whatever canon – these tendencies evidence the radical psychic stance of these groups *vis-à-vis* the dominant society. It should be noted, however, that the irony in this period lies in the fact that the separatism of the groups in this period notwithstanding, many of the groups often called for, and saw partially realized in their boundaries, the integration that yet eludes mainstream religious communities – black and white. And it is the engagement of biblical and other religious texts that clearly reflects this phenomenon. The syncretistic teaching of many of these groups implies a universalism that intends to transcend the limiting historical reality. In other words, through the esoteric books and esoteric knowledge about such books, a new, egalitarian, cosmopolitan community-world is envisioned.[32] Rabbi Matthew, an early twentieth-century leader of the Black Jews of Harlem who taught a variant of Ethiopianism, serves as an important example of this type of reading of the Bible and other religious texts:

> I must treat briefly the history of the sons of men, from Adam, of whom it is only necessary to say that when God decided on the necessity of man's existence, He did not choose to make a black man, or a white man: He simply decided to make man – not white nor black – from the dust of the earth, in whom He encased the reproductive power of all colors, all species, all shades of all races and eventual nationalities. From Adam to Noah, there were only two classes of men, known as the sons of God, and sons of men: a Godly and an ungodly group. . . .
>
> The two classes eventually met in Noah and his wife: Noah was a son of the Godly (a son of God), he chose a wife from the daughters of men (the carnal-minded), and to the time of the flood he had three sons: Shem, Ham, and Japheth. After the flood Ham took the lead. . . .
>
> As Cush rose in power, Africa, the entire continent, including Egypt, became the center of the world's cultural and religious education, and thus Ham secured for himself and his posterity for all time, a name – Pioneers of the World's Civilization.[33]

Fifth "Reading": Fundamentalism (Late Twentieth Century)

The fifth and most recent type of African-American readings of the Bible has to do with fundamentalism and an attraction to white fundamentalist communities. Not unlike the catalysts for the rise of fundamentalist piety among whites in the early decades of this century, the rise of such piety among African Americans in *significant numbers* in the last few decades signifies a crisis – of thinking, of security.

White America at the end of the nineteenth century and in the first few decades of the twentieth century was faced with the onslaught of change in every facet of life – the scientific revolution, inventions, a world war and the new awesome weapons it introduced, new questions about reality, and new methods of inquiry designed to address these questions in the universities that were becoming more comprehensive and research-oriented. The cumulative change was so great, so radical, that it has been termed a virtual revolution, a "paradigm shift of consciousness."[34]

The shift took different shapes in different contexts at different times. In religious circles, in theological seminaries, to be more precise, it began early to surface in the adoption of new methods of interpretation of the Bible. Among many biblical scholars it was no longer assumed that the confessional traditions or the literal rendering of the text was enough to get at meaning. Historical consciousness required the historical-critical reading of the Bible as an ancient document, written in different social contexts and different times by different human authors. Many reacted violently to this new scholarship, branding it as heresy, as an attempt to undermine the authority of the scriptures and take them away from common folk. The fundamentalist movement was born in reaction. It had felt the old, comforting, simple world slipping away. It deemed that it was necessary to provide a way for common folk to read the Bible that would keep the old world intact, and at the same time speak to some of the difficulties that the new breed of scholars had pointed out. An inductive reading of the texts and a dispensationalist hermeneutic were devised and promoted among the new "Bible-believing" churches, associations, denominations, and academies founded at this time. This response was intended to secure the "fundamentals" of the faith drawn up by the movement against "modernism."[35]

African Americans were not a significant part of the beginnings of the fundamentalist movement in America.[36] Only in recent decades have significant numbers come to embrace in a self-conscious manner fundamentalist ideology and white fundamentalist communities. This phenomenon seems to reflect a rejection of – or at least a relativizing of the importance of – racialist or culturalist perspectives insofar as they are associated with the African-American heritage. The intentional attempt to embrace Christian traditions, specifically the attempt to interpret the Bible, without respect for the historical experiences of persons of African descent in this country radically marks this reading and this period from others.

The growth of fundamentalism among African Americans is evident both in the different orientations of African-American churches and in the increase in the number of African Americans who actually join white fundamentalist churches, and send their children to white fundamentalist academies. Those African Americans who actually join white fundamentalist communities find themselves for the most part having to relativize race and culture as factors in religious faith and piety, and having to argue for the universal nature of the fundamentalist perspective. At the seventeenth annual meeting of the National

83

Black Evangelical Association in 1980 controversy broke out over resignations in leadership provoked by differences of opinion about the theological perspective that should characterize the organization. Although this organization has the reputation for being relatively moderate on theological, social, and political issues, it could not escape having to address the tension between race and culture, on the one hand, and "pure" doctrine, on the other hand. Two divergent views emerged: one maintained that covenant theology, understood as emphasizing God's work in the black community through history, should be embraced by the association; the other maintained that a strict premillennial and dispensationalist stance was essential. A spokesperson for the second position argued that the association "must rest on the Word, be unified in theology, not culture, color, or history."[37]

Perhaps, very much like the whites who in earlier decades had experienced a crisis situation with the onslaught of modernism, some African Americans have embraced fundamentalism because they are experiencing a crisis. Their crisis has to do with their perception of the inadequacy of culturalist religion – African-American religion – to vouchsafe, or guarantee, the traditions that are "Christian." Buttressing this perception is the assumption that anything distinctively black is inadequate in the dominant white world. Of course, this latter assumption has always been held by some African Americans. In the last few decades, however, many events – especially the failures of the African-American leadership itself – have confirmed the assumption in the eyes of many. That this is the case even in the churches, traditionally the place where black self-confidence and pride were concentrated, is most significant. This lack of confidence is leading some African Americans to abandon their churches, to attempt to transform them into fundamentalist camps, and even to consider debating the question whether culture and color should inform a reading of the Bible or the quest to know God.

Summary

This essay has sought to provide only an outline of an interpretative history of African Americans as they have spoken about themselves and the worlds in which they have lived through their readings of the Bible. It is hoped that sufficient problems have been posed, questions raised, and arguments provoked to justify serious discussion and further research. The story is still being told because the Bible is still being read "in divers places and at sundry times."

Notes

1 James M. Washington, *Frustrated Fellowship: The Black Baptist Quest for Social Power* (Macon, Ga.: Mercer University Press, 1986).

2 In the modern period beginning with the watershed book of James H. Cone, *Black Theology and Black Power* (New York: Seabury Press, 1969). For a bibliography on the development of black theology see especially James H. Cone and Gayraud S. Wilmore, eds., *Black Theology: A Documentary History, 1966–1979* (Maryknoll, N.Y.: Orbis Books, 1979).

3 Charles H. Long, *Significations: Signs, Symbols, and Images in the Interpretation of Religion* (Philadelphia: Fortress Press, 1986).

4 C. Eric Lincoln, *Race, Religion, and the Continuing American Dilemma* (New York: Hill and Wang, 1984); and Harold D. Trulear, "Sociology of Afro-American Religion: An Appraisal of C. Eric Lincoln's Contributions," *Journal of Religious Thought* 42, no. 2 (Fall – Winter 1986): 44–55.

5 See Albert J. Raboteau, *Slave Religion: The "Invisible Institution" in the Antebellum South* (New York: Oxford University Press, 1978); and George E. Simpson, *Black Religions in the New World* (New York: Columbia University Press, 1978).

6 Martin E. Marty, *Religion and Republic: The American Circumstance* (Boston: Beacon, 1987), pp. 140–67.

7 Long, *Significations*, pp. 97–113, 158–84.

8 Donald G. Matthews, *Religion in the Old South* (Chicago: University of Chicago Press, 1977), pp. 136 ff.

9 Orlando Patterson, *Slavery and Social Death: A Comparative Study* (Cambridge: Harvard University Press, 1982).

10 Sydney Ahlstrom, *A Religious History of the American People* (New Haven: Yale University Press, 1972), pt. 2.

11 Raboteau, *Slave Religion*, p. 242; and Samuel D. Gill, *Beyond "The Primitive": The Religions of Nonliterate Peoples* (Englewood Cliffs, N.J.: Prentice-Hall, 1982).

12 Harold W. Turner, *Religious Innovation in Africa: Collected Essays on New Religious Movements* (Boston: G. K. Hall, 1979), 271–88; and Gill, ibid. pp. 226–8.

13 Matthews, *Religion in the Old South*, pp. 198ff; and Lawrence W, Levine, *Black Culture and Black Consciousness* (New York: Oxford University Press, 1977), pp. 136ff.

14 Mark A. Noll, "The Image of the United States as a Biblical Nation, 1776–1865," in N. O. Hatch and Mark A. Noll, eds, *The Bible in America* (New York: Oxford University Press, 1982), pp. 39–40; and N. O. Hatch, "Sola Scriptura and Novus Ordo Seclorum," in ibid., pp. 74–5.

15 Raboteau, *Slave Religion*, pp. 239ff; and Matthews, *Religion in the Old South*, pp. 212–36.

16 See James Weldon Johnson, ed., *The Book of American Negro Spirituals* (New York: Viking Press, 1925), pp. 20, 21; Howard Thurman, *Deep River and the Negro Spiritual Speaks of Life and Death* (Richmond, Ind.: Friends Press, 1975); and Benjamin E. Mays, *The Negro's God as Reflected in His Literature* (New York: Atheneum, 1969), pp. 19–96.

17 Bryan R. Wilson, *Magic and the Millennium: A Sociological Study of Religious Movements of Protest among Tribal and Third World Peoples* (New York: Harper and Row, 1973).

18 See Trulear, "Sociology of Afro-American Religion."
19 See Mays, *The Negro's God*; and Milton C. Sernett, ed., *Afro-American Religious History: A Documentary Witness* (Durham, N.C.: Duke University Press, 1985).
20 Raboteau, *Slave Religion*, p. 250.
21 See Johnson, ed., *The Book of American Negro Spirituals*; Thurman, *Deep River*; Mays, *The Negro's God*; Cone, *Black Theology and Black Power*; Raboteau, *Slave Religion*; and Cone and Wilmore, eds., *Black Theology*.
22 Cone and Wilmore, eds., *Black Theology*, pp. 227ff.
23 Sernett, ed., *Afro-American Religious History*, chaps. 2, 3; see Washington, *Frustrated Fellowship*; and Cone and Wilmore, eds, *Black Theology*.
24 Thomas R. Frazier, "Historians and Afro-American Religion," *Journal of the Interdenominational Theological Center* (Fall 1985): pp. 3–4.
25 Peter J. Paris, *The Social Teaching of the Black Churches* (Philadelphia: Fortress Press, 1985); and Sernett, ed., *Afro-American Religious History*, pp. 188–226.
26 Marty, *Religion and Republic*, pp. 140–65; and see Noll, "The Image of the United States as a Biblical Nation."
27 Sernett, ed., *Afro-American Religious History*, pp. 105–6.
28 Ibid., pp. 191–2.
29 Cited in Paris, *The Social Teaching*, p. 13.
30 Cited in ibid., pp. 51.
31 Hans Baer, *The Black Spiritual Movement: Religious Response to Racism* (Knoxville: University of Tennessee Press, 1984), pp. 8–9.
32 Turner, *Religious Innovation in Africa*, pp. 280–1; Baer, *The Black Spiritual Movement*, p. 133; and Cone and Wilmore, eds, *Black Theology*, pp. 145–66.
33 Sernett, ed., *Afro-American Religious History*, pp. 399–400.
34 Timothy P. Weber, "The Two-Edged Sword: The Fundamentalist Use of the Bible," in Hatch and Noll, eds, *The Bible in America*, pp. 101–20.
35 Ibid., pp. 113–14.
36 George M. Marsden, *Fundamentalism and American Culture: The Shaping of Twentieth Century Evangelicalism: 1870–1925* (New York: Oxford University Press, 1980), p. 228.
37 Anthony T. Evans, quoted in Jimmy Locklear, "Theology – Culture Rift Surfaces among Black Evangelicals," *Christianity Today* 24 (May 23, 1980): 44.

The New Testament and the Nicene Dogma: A Contribution to the Recovery of Theological Exegesis

David S. Yeago

Introduction

One of the consequences of the Western Church's two centuries of fumbling with the implications of the historical-critical method is a loss of any sense of the connection between the classical doctrines of the Church and the text of scripture. It is assumed that a truly scholarly interpretation of the scriptural texts methodologically excludes any reference to Christian doctrine as a hermeneutical touchstone, and as a matter of historical fact, though not of logical necessity, the historical-critical enterprise has often been understood as the liberation of rational intelligence and religious experience from the dead hand of dogma. The doctrines, in such a context, come to seem a superstructure overlaid on the texts by theological speculation, at best a time-conditioned expression of spiritual experience somehow distantly responsive to the scriptural witness, at worst the token of the "Hellenized" Church's cultural alienation from that witness.

By contrast, one has only to look at the sermons, commentaries, and treatises of the Fathers, Aquinas, or Luther to see how seriously they took, for example, the Trinitarian and Christological doctrines as analyses of the logic of the scriptural discourse, formal descriptions of the apprehension of God *in* the texts, which then serve as guides to a faithful and attentive reading *of* the texts.[1] Where this conviction is no longer intelligible, the classical doctrines come to seem, in one way and another, superfluous to the life of faith and of the believing

87

community, venerable baggage perhaps invoked from time to time out of respect for the ancients (a commodity in short supply just lately!) but scarcely objects of zealous and painstaking study. No theory of the development of doctrine which attempts to save the classical doctrines without accounting for the unanimous conviction of the Christian tradition that they are *the teaching of scripture* can overcome the marginalization of the doctrines which is so evident in the contemporary Western Church and theology.[2]

In this essay I shall make a contribution to an argument that the ancient theologians were right to hold that the Nicene *homoousion* is neither imposed *on* the New Testament texts, nor distantly deduced *from* the texts, but, rather, describes a pattern of judgements present *in* the texts, in the texture of scriptural discourse concerning Jesus and the God of Israel. I shall go on to argue on the basis of this example that the exegesis underlying classical Christian doctrines is in certain crucial respects methodologically superior to the "critical" exegesis which has claimed to invalidate it.

Obviously, the exegetical aspect of this discussion could be ramified indefinitely; to substantiate the thesis of this essay fully would require an exegetical-theological study on the scale of Athanasius's *Orations* against the Arians, Gregory of Nyssa's *Against Eunomius*, or Cyril of Alexandria's *Dialogue*. What is offered here is no more than an example in aid of an argument. It will succeed in its purpose if it sends its readers back to the great Patristic treatises prepared to take seriously their claim to be engaged in exegesis of the scriptures.

Jesus and the God of Israel: Paul and Nicæa

The New Testament does not contain a formally articulated "doctrine of God" of the same kind as the later Nicene dogma. What it does contain is a pattern of implicit and explicit judgements concerning the God of Israel and his relationship to the crucified and risen Jesus of Nazareth. The dogma is the Church's attempt to take account articulately of this more basic state of affairs: in both the preaching and the worship of the Church, according to the witness of the New Testament, God is inescapably *apprehended and identified as the* Triune *God*. This Trinitarian apprehension of God arises at the juncture of two contexts which are central to the Church's identity, and which were also the primary points of reference for the New Testament writers themselves: the distinctive practices of Christian worship, and the scriptures of Israel.

The God of Israel, the God in whose name Jesus of Nazareth claimed to speak, has raised him from the dead and exalted him as Lord. This is the founding Christian affirmation. The interpretation of this founding affirmation takes place, for the New Testament writers, at the intersection of two authoritative contexts: the worship of the Church in the Spirit, which is the concrete locus of the Church's present relationship to the risen *kurios*, and the prophetic witness of the scriptures of Israel, also the work of the Spirit who thus "testified in advance to the sufferings destined for Messiah and to the subsequent glory" (1 Pet. 1:11).

The Trinitarian faith was embraced in the *practice* of the Church already in the very earliest days of the Christian movement, when Christians, and Jewish Christians at that, began to *call on the name of Jesus in worship* – an astonishing thing for *any* group of Jews to do. There is every reason to believe that the earliest Christians were vigorous Jewish monotheists determined to worship no God but YHWH. Nevertheless, they began to focus their worship of the God of Israel on the figure of Jesus from a very early date – indeed, so far as anyone can tell, from the very beginning.[3] They solemnly invoked Jesus' name, addressed praise and petition and acclamation to him, and appealed to him as *mareh* or *kurios*, thus associating him with the holy name of YHWH.[4]

According to the message of the apostles, reflected in the worship practices of the early communities, in the resurrection and exaltation, the God of Israel has *identified* himself with the particular human being, Jesus of Nazareth. God has not, in exalting Jesus as Lord, merely affirmed that he was right, nor only identified himself with Jesus' "cause" or teaching. In his exaltation, Jesus' *person*, Jesus himself, has been definitively identified with God. The particular human being Jesus is thus addressed as one who sits at God's "right hand" and rules with God's own authority. And so the Church likewise awaits the appearance of this same Jesus to judge the world on YHWH's behalf.

So, for example, as Paul says in Philippians 2:9, possibly citing early Christian liturgy, the exaltation means that Jesus has been given "the name that is above every name."[5] There can be little doubt what name *that* is, in the context of any communal life nurtured on the Psalms. The "name above every name" is the majestic name, the name in which the oppressed take refuge, and to which the people of God make music, the name of YHWH.[6]

Paul (or his source) continues: this name has been bestowed "so that at the name of Jesus, every knee should bend, in heaven and on earth and under the earth, and every tongue confess that Jesus Christ is Lord, to the glory of God the Father" (Phil. 1:10–11). This is, of course, a direct allusion to Isaiah 45:21–24:

> There is no other god except me,
> no saving God, no Saviour except me!
> Turn to me and you will be saved,
> all you ends of the earth,
> for I am God, and there is no other.
> By my own self I swear it;
> what comes from my mouth is saving justice,
> it is an irrevocable word:

all shall bend the knee to me,
by me every tongue shall swear,
saying, "In YHWH alone
are saving justice and strength,"
until all who used to rage at him
come to him in shame.

The text from Philippians *identifies* the prophesied turning of all the earth to
YHWH as the only God with the universal acclamation of Jesus as Lord; that
Jesus is acclaimed as *kurios* "to the glory of God the Father" implies that
YHWH comes to his rightful, exclusive sovereignty over the whole creation,
proclaimed in Isaiah, precisely *through* creation's acknowledgement of the
lordship of the particular person Jesus. Within the thought-world of Israel's
scriptures, no stronger affirmation of the bond between the risen Jesus and the
God of Israel is possible.

This remarkable identification reflects the inner logic of the worship of the
Church in the Spirit. Whether the text from Philippians is an actual fragment
of early Christian liturgy, or a free composition of Paul, its background is clearly
the liturgical acclamation of Jesus (cf. Rom. 10:9–13; 1 Cor. 12:1–3). In the
resurrection, as the Church confesses it in worship, God has so utterly
identified himself with Jesus, and Jesus has been so inextricably associated with
God, that *it is not possible to turn to the God of Israel without at the same time
turning to Jesus.* In the Church's celebration of the resurrection and exaltation
of Jesus, the God of Israel and Jesus of Nazareth are apprehended as united
inseparably in a unique relationship which definitively identifies and characterizes them both.

It is perfectly consistent with this that the early communities came to speak
by preference of the God of Israel as Jesus' *Father* and of Jesus as God's unique
Son, in a relationship definitive for the identity of each.[7] The point of this
language (as St Athanasius saw) is that each title asserts an identity to which
relationship is intrinsic. One can be "Father" only by virtue of a relationship
to another, to some particular offspring. One can likewise be "Son" only by
virtue of a relationship to another, to some particular progenitor. When YHWH
and Jesus are identified as Father and Son, then their mutual relationship is
inscribed constitutively into the identity of each. The language of Father and
Son precisely articulates the apprehension of the relation of YHWH and Jesus
implicit in the worship of the *ekklēsia*.

But the invocation of Isaiah 45 in Philippians 2:10–11 also brings us up
against the New Testament's other normative reference point, the scriptures
of Israel. And it is the intersection of this context with the context of early
Christian worship that generates the New Testament's Trinitarian apprehension of God.

The text from Isaiah proclaims the coming vindication precisely of the *unique* and *incomparable* deity of YHWH: "I am God, and there is no other." And in so doing it reiterates the deepest theme of Israel's faith: only YHWH, the particular one who brought the people out of Israel, is *elohim*, "god."[8] What is so profoundly odd about Philippians 2:10–11 is that it identifies the prophesied universal acknowledgement of the *unique* deity of YHWH with the universal cultic acclamation of an apparent "other," Jesus of Nazareth. The difficulty is palpable: if "there is no other" how can the bending of knees and the loosing of tongues at the name of some other be compatible, much less identified, with the recognition of the "glory" of the God of Israel?

The eagerness of many modern scholars to distance the New Testament as much as possible from the later development of dogma has needlessly obscured the simple fact that the conceptual possibilities in the face of this question are not infinite. N. T. Wright has summed them up concisely:

> For consider: if the God who will not share his glory with another has now shared it with Jesus (the position asserted in 2:9ff), then there are only three possible conclusions that can be drawn. It might be the case that there are now two Gods. Or Jesus – who up until then had been a man and nothing but a man – might now have been totally absorbed into the one God without remainder (so to speak). Or there might be a sense – requiring fuller investigation, exploration, and clarification, no doubt – in which Jesus, in being exalted to the rank described in 2:9ff, is receiving no more that that which was always, from before the beginning of time, his by right.[9]

That is to say, *either* Philippians 2:9ff is proclaiming the mythical divinization of the human being Jesus, in what would then have to be read as a rather violent subversion and repudiation of Isaiah 45:21–24, *or else* it must be confessed that Jesus is *not* "other" than YHWH in the relevant sense. The relationship between YHWH and Jesus which the Church hymns in her worship must *always have been* intrinsic to YHWH's identity.

It is, of course, easy enough to admit that the resurrection is not the beginning of the relationship between Jesus and the God of Israel. It is, rather, the *vindication*, the victorious *assertion*, of a relationship which already existed, but was denied and unrecognized. Here the Church's confession of the resurrection and her memory of Jesus interpreted each other. Already before the resurrection, Jesus had claimed unique intimacy with the God of Israel. Already before the resurrection, Jesus had spoken of the God of Israel as uniquely his Father. Already before the resurrection, Jesus had implicitly claimed God's authority in a way that provoked hostility and rejection. The resurrection is the vindication and verification of an *already existing* relationship between Jesus and YHWH. With the resurrection, that relationship enters into a new phase, begins to be lived out in a new mode, but it did not come into being at that moment.

But the logic of the theological situation we are considering requires a further step. If relationship to Jesus of Nazareth is *intrinsic* to the identity of YHWH, if Jesus is not "other" than YHWH in the sense of Isaiah 45, then it is impossible to fix *any* moment as the moment when that relationship began. For that moment would then be the moment when the creature Jesus became divine. If "there was when he was not" (Arianism) or if any moment can be identified as the beginning of his relationship with YHWH (Adoptionism), then his association with YHWH would amount to the enthronement of a "second god" alongside the Lord God of Israel. And we are forbidden to think *that* by the deepest logic of Israel's faith: there is only one God, YHWH, incomparable and unique.

The affirmation that *this* God has so radically identified himself with Jesus can rhyme with Israel's confession of the singularity and incomparability of God *if and only if* their relationship is *eternal*. There is only one God, YHWH, and relationship to Jesus of Nazareth is somehow intrinsic to this God's identity from everlasting. There is only one God, but the one God is never without his only-begotten Son.

The Church's acclamation of Jesus and the witness of the scriptures of Israel can therefore be rhymed only if the exaltation of Jesus implies, not that the one God shares his glory with another, but that the glory of the one God is *manifested* in the exaltation of his Son, who belongs intrinsically to the reality of the one God. The exaltation of Jesus does not *add* to God's being; it vindicates and manifests the glory of God's being, to which relationship to Jesus of Nazareth is essential. Only if the exaltation manifests a relationship intrinsic to God's being from everlasting, does the exaltation not imply that there are now two gods, Jesus and YHWH, but, rather, makes known that Jesus was always included in the glory of the one God, even before the foundations of the world were laid (John 17).

This step has already been taken in Philippians 2: according to verse 6 the one who has been exalted and given the name above every name began his way in the "form of God" and as "equal" to God. The force of these predicates is that the one who humbled himself and was exalted was full sharer in whatever reality is ascribed to YHWH.[10] The affirmation of the text is that one who shared fully in the singular reality of the God of Israel has *chosen* to share in the reality of human beings.

That the primary points of reference for the confession of Jesus' equality with God are the Church's worship of the exalted Jesus and the Old Testament's proclamation of the singularity of God was quite clear, it should be noted, to the Fathers who formulated the church-doctrine of the Trinity in the fourth century. Thus, for example, St Gregory of Nyssa:

> God commands us by the prophet not to regard as God any new god, nor to
> worship any alien god (Ps. 81:9; Exod. 34:13). Now it is clear that what is not

from eternity is called "new" and, on the contrary, that which is not new is called "eternal." Thus whoever does not believe that the Only-begotten God is from the Father eternally does not deny that he is new, for that which is not eternal is necessarily new. Now anything which is new is not God, as scripture says, "There shall be no new god among you." Therefore whoever says that the Son "once was not" denies his deity. Again, when God says, "You shall not worship an alien god" (Exod. 20:3), he forbids us to worship an alien god; and an "alien god" is so called in contradistinction to our own God. Who, then, is our own God? Clearly, the true God. And who is the alien god? Necessarily, one who is alien from the nature of the true God. So if our own God is the true God, and if, as the heretics say, the only-begotten God is not of the nature of the true God, then he is an alien god, and not our God. . . . Then what will they do, who say that he is a creature? Do they worship that same creature as God, or not? If they do not worship him, they follow the Jews in denying the worship of Christ: and if they do worship him, they are idolaters, for they worship one alien to the true God. Now, it is equally ungodly not to worship the Son, and to worship an alien god. Therefore it is necessary to call him the true Son of the true Father, so that we may both worship him, and avoid being condemned as worshippers of an alien god.[11]

Judgements and Concepts: The Logic of Theological Exegesis

To suggest so immediate a relationship between the Nicene theology of Gregory of Nyssa and the theology of Paul runs afoul of a great chorus of biblical scholars which has insisted for two centuries that Paul's "equality with God" is "not the same" as the *homoousion* of Nicæa. But those who press this point rarely seem to have any clear notion of what it means for two assertions to be "the same."

It is essential, in this context, to distinguish between *judgements* and the *conceptual terms* in which those judgements are rendered. We cannot concretely perform an act of judgement without employing some particular, contingent verbal and conceptual resources; judgement-making *is* an operation performed with words and concepts. At the same time, however, the same judgement can be rendered in variety of conceptual terms, all of which may be informative about a particular judgement's force and implications. The possibility of valid alternative verbal/conceptual renderings of the identical judgement accounts for the fact that we ourselves often do not realize the full implications of the judgements we pass: only *some* of their implications are ever unpacked in the particular renderings we have given them.[12]

This point is especially important when we ask about the relationship between the New Testament and later Church teaching. Unity in teaching must be sought at the level of judgements and not at the level of concepts, for discourse only *teaches*, makes claims that can be accepted or rejected, insofar as it passes and urges judgements. An inquiry which remains at the level of concepts, cataloging and tracing the history of the diverse conceptual resources employed in the New Testament texts and the theology of the Fathers, will never succeed even in properly *raising the question* of the relation between New Testament and later Church teaching.

Information about the history of the concepts is helpful only if we are attentive to the particular ways in which the concepts are *employed* in affirmation and denial within a body of discourse. When we compare judgements, we must ask (1) about the logical subjects of which predicates are affirmed and denied, (2) about the logical type of the particular predicates affirmed or denied within the conceptual idioms they employ, and (3) about the *point* or function of their affirmations or denials within their respective contexts of discourse.

Thus if one concluded that one's psychiatrist friend and one's elderly relative were indeed talking about the same individual, that the clinical description offered by the former and the latter's "a most disturbing young man" were predicates of the same type within their respective idioms, and that the point of both statements was to give warning, one would say that both of them had "said the same thing" about the person in question. Nor would we be inclined to revise this conclusion on the basis of a learned account of the Freudian background of the terms used by the psychiatrist, accompanied by an exhaustive demonstration that one's uncle had never studied Freud.

When the question is considered in these terms, a strong, and in my view conclusive, case can be made that the judgement about Jesus and God made in the Nicene Creed – the judgement that they are "of one substance" or "one reality" – is indeed "the same," in a basically ordinary and unmysterious way, as that made in a New Testament text such as Philippians 2:6ff:

1   The logical subjects in each case are identical: the crucified and exalted *kurios* Jesus of Nazareth and the God of Israel. The Creed employs narrative markers to secure the identity of the "Jesus" it talks about with the one to whom the New Testament bears witness, and likewise makes clear that it is the specific God of Israel to which it makes reference; no other putative deity could be meant by "one God . . . ruler of all, maker of heaven and earth."

2   Each text predicates of these two subjects the most intimate possible bond, using the strongest terms available within the conceptual idiom of each. *Homoousion tô Patri* and the complex of terms employed in the Philippians text – *en morphê theou*, "equal to God," "name above every name," and the whole set of associations arising from the evocation of Isaiah 45 – are in this

respect logically equivalent, playing the same role within their respective contexts, and to that extent of the same type, despite their differences in historical background.

3   The point of the two affirmations is substantially the same: to articulate the judgements implicit in distinctive Christian proclamation and practices of worship (as well as the Christian mission to the nations).

Thus Philippians 2:6ff and the Nicene *homoousion* meet all our ordinary criteria of "sameness": despite the conventional wisdom of the critics, it is not at all odd or naive to claim that they "say the same thing" about Jesus and the Father.[13]

The results of ignoring the distinction between judgements and concepts can be seen in James D. G. Dunn's *Christology in the Making*,[14] a disappointing book by an immensely learned and deservedly influential exegete which exemplifies the logical confusion in which a great deal of contemporary biblical scholarship is mired.

Although Dunn's study is subtitled "A New Testament Inquiry into the Origins of the Doctrine of the Incarnation," his real subject matter is not a *doctrine* at all, that is, a teaching which urges certain judgements, but, rather, the *concept* of incarnation. Indeed, Dunn uses the terms "doctrine" and "concept" more or less interchangeably. That is to say, Dunn believes that he can account for the Christology of the New Testament simply by recounting the history of its conceptualities; the question of the judgements which the texts make concerning Jesus of Nazareth is never clearly posed.

The outcome, in Dunn's case, is that in practice he identifies "the doctrine of the incarnation" in a rather wooden fashion with the conceptual apparatus of the Johannine prologue: a text contains a "doctrine of the incarnation" if and only if its conceptual idiom is identical with that of the first 14 verses of John. Thus his inquiry devolves into a long and surely unnecessary demonstration that the prologue to John is conceptually singular within the New Testament canon.

Moreover, not only his overall strategy, but also his exegesis of particular texts, is vitiated by his assumption that one understands the "doctrine" of a text, not by attending to what it says and implies, but by speculating about its conceptual and terminological background. This enables him to pursue a curiously perverse policy of minimalizing the content of the non-Johannine Christological traditions in the New Testament often in clear contradiction of what the old exegetes called the *circumstantia litterarum*, "the way the words go."[15]

Thus, for example, he argues that because Philippians 2:6ff reflects the conceptual background of an "Adam-Christology," it is wrong to find in it any affirmation of the pre-existence of Christ, despite what seems its obvious sense, because "pre-existence" is not part of the "Adam-Christology."[16] We may pass by the point that the "Adam-Christology" is a scholarly construct, so that Dunn is in effect overriding the "way the words go" in Philippians 2:6ff by reference to a fictional entity. Even if we had available for reference a copy of a first-century textbook, *Principles of the Adam-Christology*, with Paul's name on the flyleaf, Dunn's procedure would be confused, because it does not respect the distinction, and therefore the proper ordering, of judgements and concepts.

In general, judgements are not instrumental to concepts but concepts to judgements; we cannot infer in any but the most general and open-ended way from the structure of a concept, or the history of its previous employment, the range of possible uses to which it may yet be put in the rendering of judgements. The only way to uncover the judgements made in a text is to pay close attention to what is said and implied, to the specific, contingent ways in which its conceptual resources are deployed: to attend, in short, to the *circumstantia litterarum*.[17] Thus the most precise and detailed history of the "Adam-Christology" would not, by itself, settle any questions whatsoever about what is asserted or implied in Philippians 2:6ff.

The reasons for the long dominance of this sort of confusion in modern biblical study would have to be sought in the historic coupling of historical criticism with a "project of enlightenment" aimed at liberating mind and heart from the shackles of ecclesiastical tradition. In the modern context, claims to "enlightenment" must be backed up with the claim to have achieved a proper *method*, capable of producing real knowledge to replace the pre-critical confusion and arbitrariness of tradition. To this must be added the pervasive contempt for logic which Humanism, some streams of the Reformation, and Pietism bequeathed to both theology and the humanities in modern times.[18]

All these factors have coalesced in a firmly institutionalized self-image of the discipline of biblical criticism which affects the work even of scholars who are not personally hostile to traditional doctrine. The notion that the task of biblical exegesis is to get at the true meaning of the biblical texts through historical research seems too obvious to be questioned.

But if "biblical exegesis," in its fullest dimensions, is taken to be an inquiry into the content and unity of biblical teaching, and not simply a historical examination of the terms and concepts employed in the biblical texts, then there is and can be no *distinctively* "historical critical" discipline of "biblical exegesis." The only possible way of investigating the content and unity of biblical *teaching* is to inquire attentively into what the texts say and how they say it, in search of unifying common judgements which may be rendered in very diverse ways, attempting to redescribe or re-render those judgements so as to do justice to the significance of their various articulations across the range of the canon.

This is not to say that historical research contributes nothing to the enterprise of Biblical exegesis so defined. Study of the history of the conceptualities employed in the texts can provide significant material for comparison, so that the distinctive employment of these conceptualities in the rendering of judgements in the biblical texts stands out more sharply.[19] Another extremely important service of historical research is to bring to light the context of communal *practices* presupposed in the biblical writings, for practices are a crucial clue to judgements, as our discussion of the significance of early Christian worship for the New Testament apprehension of God suggests.[20]

But in all this, historical research is propaedeutic to the real theological-exegetical task. If "biblical theology" is anything coherent at all, it is just "theology," an engagement with the biblical texts no different in principle from that undertaken in the theological exegesis of St Athanasius, St Basil, St Thomas, Martin Luther, and Karl Barth, and it will not fare well if it is not pursued by the means proper to theological reflection. Those means are chiefly those of close reading and conceptual analysis, attention (in St Athanasius's terms) to the *skopos* and *akolouthia*, the tenor and coherence of the judgements rendered in the texts.

The Prospects for Theological Exegesis

A final word needs to be said about the prospects for a renewal of theological exegesis. Such a project presupposes that we have reasons to *care* about the judgements rendered in the biblical writings. The Fathers, scholastics, and reformers had such reasons: they believed that when we conform our thinking to the pattern of judgements imbedded in the prophetic and apostolic scriptures, our understanding is illumined by a divine light (Ps. 36:9) and so we come to share the *nous Christou*, the mind of Christ (1 Cor. 2:16).[21]

It is not at all clear that much of contemporary Western Christianity shares any longer in this motivation. Mainline theology has failed to replace the untenable early-modern doctrines of propositional revelation and verbal inspiration with any account of scripture's role in the purposes of God which provides reasons for a passionate and attentive engagement with the texts. Indeed, such engagement would only hinder many contemporary theological and ecclesiastical projects; institutional interests of all sorts are best served by an instinctive polemical tarring of any attempt to commend a posture of deference towards the scriptural texts with the dreaded fundamentalist brush. Anti-fundamentalism has become a powerful ideological tool in the mainline Western Churches which almost guarantees the marginalization of any call to "biblical seriousness," however clear its actual differences from fundamentalism.

In such a situation, subversion is perhaps a more hopeful strategy than frontal attack. That is to say, the future of theological exegesis may depend on those who quietly go about learning how to do theological exegesis from the tradition and the clearest-headed contemporary sources, and then actually let the voice of the texts be heard in their preaching and theologizing. And this may simply mean that we are forced back into a posture which is itself biblically normative, modeled for the Church in the self-presentation of the Apostle Paul:

> My speech and my proclamation were not with plausible words of wisdom, but with a demonstration of the Spirit and of power, so that your faith might rest not on human wisdom but on the power of God (1 Cor. 2:4).

Notes

1 Cf. the fine description of this in the review by J. A. DiNoia, O.P., of John Meier's *A Marginal Jew*, *Pro Ecclesia* II/1, 122–125. DiNoia's discussion of historical criticism is also relevant to this essay.

2 And perhaps especially evident in contemporary theological education.

3 "The hymn to Christ grew out of the early services of the community after Easter, i.e., it is as old as the community itself." Martin Hengel, "Hymns and Christology," in *Between Jesus and Paul: Studies in the Earliest History of Christianity* (Philadelphia: Fortress, 1983), p. 93.

4 On all this, see the excellent historical study by Larry Hurtado, *One God, One Lord: Early Christian Devotion and Ancient Christian Monotheism* (Philadelphia: Fortress, 1988). On *mareh*, cf. p. 107. Notice how Paul equates "calling on the Name of the Lord" and confessing Jesus in Romans 10:9–13.

5 In what follows, I am much indebted to N. T. Wright, *The Climax of the Covenant: Christ and the Law in Pauline Theology* (Minneapolis: Fortress 1991), chap. 4.

6 Cf. Pss. 8:1; 54:1; 113:1–3; 130:1–4.

7 I leave to one side for the moment the question of the extent to which this language originates in Jesus' own self-presentation.

8 Israel's faith appropriates the *general concept* of *elohim* or "god" to the *particular* one identified by the story of the Patriarchs and the Exodus. Only *this* one is rightly and properly referred to as *elohim*. Where the term *elohim* is not so conclusively appropriated to YHWH as to be used as a proper name, it seems to mean something like, "a higher power which must be reckoned with," as in Exodus 7:2: "Look, I have made you as a god for Pharaoh, and your brother Aaron is to be your prophet." The scriptures of Israel are not at every stage *theoretically* monotheistic, but they do insist that whatever powers may exist, only YHWH has the right to be considered *elohim*; even if there are other "gods," other "higher powers," YHWH is nonetheless the god with whom the gods themselves must reckon. On the logic of "YHWH is God," cf. Gregory of Nyssa's discussion of the logical status of the predicate *theos* in "On the Holy Trinity, and of the Godhead of the Holy Spirit, to Eustathius," *Nicene and Post-Nicene Fathers*, series

2, vol. 7, 328–9; cf. also K. H. Miskotte, *When the Gods Are Silent*, trans. by J. W. Doberstein (New York: Harper and Row, 1967).

9 Wright, *The Climax of the Covenant*, p. 94. Strictly speaking, however, the second option is *not* a real possibility, at least as an interpretation of Philippians 2:9ff, for in that case, there would be no referent left for the "name of Jesus." I will therefore disregard it in the subsequent discussion.

10 Denials that this is in fact what is affirmed here can, in my judgement, only be carried out by hermeneutical sleight-of-hand. Cf. Wright, ibid., pp. 90–8.

11 Gregory of Nyssa, "On the Faith, to Simplicius," my trans. Cf. *Nicene and Post- Nicene Fathers*, series 2, vol. V, p. 337.

12 So when we are trying to get someone to see the implications of his or her judgements, we often restate them in other terms which bring out the relevant consequences: "Aren't you really saying such and such? And doesn't that imply this?"

13 In a full-dress hermeneutical discussion, which cannot be offered here, it would be important to consider also the significance of the fact that the scriptural texts do nonetheless render such judgements *differently* from later dogmatic statements, and the consequent possibility of always returning *from* the dogmas *to* the scriptures to be instructed anew.

14 Westminster, 1980.

15 On this notion, cf. Bruce Marshall, "Absorbing the World: Christianity and the Universe of Truths," in Marshall, ed., *Theology and Dialogue: Essays in Conversation with George Lindbeck* (Notre Dame, 1990), pp. 69–102; esp. 90–7.

16 See *Christology in the Making*, pp. 114–21. "*Phil 2.6–11* certainly seems on the face of it to be a straightforward statement contrasting Christ's pre-existent glory and post-crucifixion exaltation with his earthly humiliation" (p. 114). The discussion that follows is an extended attempt to do an end-run around this acknowledged character of the *circumstantia litterarum*.

17 In this respect, I suspect that the importance of St Athanasius in the history of biblical hermeneutics has been underestimated. His achievement, one might suggest, was to have worked out for the first time the principles of a "doctrinal" exegesis of scripture, as distinguished from (but not necessarily opposed to) the "edifying" or "spiritual" exegesis most common in the earlier tradition. One might say that he first gave attention in its own right to the hermeneutics of the "literal sense," which was rather taken for granted by the earlier tradition. Cf. Thomas Torrance, "The Logic and Analogic of Biblical and Theological Statements in the Greek Fathers," *Theology in Reconstruction* (SCM, 1965), for some suggestive reflections on Patristic theological exegesis.

18 The scholastic "logic-chopping" of which early moderns complained was in fact the most sophisticated logical organon ever developed; prior to the work of Frege, classical modernity was dependent on logical resources which were *primitive* in comparison to those available in the middle ages. On this, cf. Graham White, "Luther and Logic," *Modern Theology* 4 (1987): 17–34.

19 It was a weakness of the "biblical theology" movement that it often sought the distinctiveness of biblical faith in distinctive concepts (a claim that could not stand under historical analysis) rather than in the distinctive ways in which concepts are employed in the biblical witness.

20 Much of the work of Martin Hengel acquires its acute theological relevance in this way.

The degree to which Patristic exegesis profits from being located in a communal continuum of practice with the New Testament communities should not be underestimated, as the text cited from Gregory of Nyssa suggests.

21 To be sure, conformity of the intellect to the judgements embedded in the texts was not all that the Christian tradition aimed at in its engagement with scripture. There was also a formation of the imagination and the affections which was likewise understood as issuing in conformity to God.

PART

Theological Interpretations of Select Biblical Texts

Selections from Gregory of Nyssa's *Life of Moses*

Translated and introduced by Joseph W. Trigg

Only in our time has Gregory of Nyssa (*c*.337 to *c*.395) emerged from the shadow of the other two Cappadocian Fathers, his brother, Basil of Caesarea (referred to as "the Great"), and his friend, Gregory of Nazianzus (uniquely referred to as "the Theologian"). Although he lacked the opportunities they had to study rhetoric and philosophy at Athens and never achieved their eminence as ecclesiastical leaders, Gregory is now recognized as more profound and original than either. Educated at home by Basil and their sister Macrina, Gregory became deeply learned in philosophy and theology as well as an able rhetorician. His work exhibits a command of Greek philosophy, particularly Plato and his followers including, most likely, Plotinus; of the principal theologians in the Christian tradition, particularly Origen; and of the works of Philo. Basil enlisted him, along with Gregory of Nazianzus, in the struggle which eventuated in the definitive promulgation of the doctrine of the Trinity at the Council of Constantinople in 375. For all of them the chief adversary was the gifted theologian Eunomius, who made a compelling case for the rejection of the Nicene formula that the Son is "of the same being" (*homoousios*) with the Father. Eunomius argued that God's being (*ousia*) is best characterized as ingenerate, making it necessary to conclude that the Son, admittedly begotten or generated by the Father, is unlike the Father with respect to being. In opposition to this theology, all three Cappadocians argued that God's being is fundamentally incomprehensible, an argument which derives its power from their ability to evoke an awed reverence before the divine mystery. Initially repelled by asceticism, Gregory of Nyssa later came to embrace it as a necessary element in the quest for God. This was the topic of his treatise *On Virginity*, the one work he composed before Basil's death in 374. In this connection, Gregory exhibits the influence of the experiential ascetic piety known as Messalianism and preserved in the Pseudo-Macarian writings.

Basil's death seems to have liberated Gregory as an author. Two of his works were major theological treatises. He ably continued his brother's literary struggle against the theology of Eunomius in a major theological treatise, *Against Eunomius*. He also composed the *Great Catechetical oration*, a masterful summary of Christian theology. Gregory gradually found his own distinctive approach to exegesis. Basil, in his *Homilies on the Hexæmeron*, had made a self-conscious attempt to present the biblical creation story of Genesis 1 as literally true, rejecting the interpretations of Philo and Origen which treated it as mythical. Gregory, by contrast, while avoiding the word "allegory" – he refers to figurative interpretation as *theôria*, "contemplation" or "insight" – did not hesitate to point out the impossibility of literal readings. This already enabled him, in *On the Creation of Man*, his first exegetical work written under Basil's influence, to make connections between the biblical text and understandings arising out of philosophical anthropology. Gregory's later exegetical works included homilies which constituted commentaries on Ecclesiastes, the Song of Songs, and the Beatitudes. The preface to his *Homilies on the Song of Songs* includes a classic defense of the allegorical interpretation he practices in that work.

The *Life of Moses* is exegetical, following the narrative portions of Exodus in the Septuagint, but it is not a commentary. It is, rather, a *bios*, a well-defined classical genre, best known today in the *Parallel Lives* of Plutarch, which characteristically held up the life of its subject as a moral example. This form evidently appealed to Gregory, who also wrote a *Life of Macrina*, his sister, and composed an oration which is, in effect, the *Life of Gregory Thaumaturgus*. Gregory Thaumaturgus ("the Wonderworker") was the bishop and theologian, most likely a student of Origen, who brought Christianity to Gregory's native region, Pontus, and to his own family. Philo, whose *Life of Moses* was also in two books, provided a model which Gregory of Nyssa freely adapted to his own needs and concerns. Philo treated Moses' life in Book I and his legislation in Book II. Gregory, by contrast is entirely concerned with Moses' spiritual development. The difference stems, to a large extent, from the purposes each author envisaged; Philo wrote to justify Judaism to pagans and to educated Jews, Gregory wrote to assist Christian ascetics in their quest for perfection.[1] His brief Book I retells the narrative (*historia*) of Moses' life and his fuller Book II deals with its deeper meaning in contemplation (*theôria*). Both Philo and Gregory are selective in their use of the biblical narrative. Thus, in dealing with the Exodus

3–4, Philo deals with God's giving Moses the power to turn water into blood and his attempt to refuse his commission, which Gregory omits, while Gregory makes much of menacing encounter with an angel, which Philo omits. Their interpretations of the burning bush make apparent their characteristically Jewish and Christian concerns. Philo interpreted the bush as a symbol of Israel, seemingly weak, especially as it languished under Egyptian oppression, but in fact extraordinarily resilient. For Gregory, as we shall see, it symbolizes the mystery of the virgin birth.

Today such interpretations may seem fanciful and arbitrary, so much so that it is hard to take Philo or Gregory seriously as theologians and exegetes. We can gain a sympathetic appreciation of Gregory if we realize that for him the Bible, as received in the Septuagint version, was the Church's book, a book whose primary function was to assist the believer to progress in understanding and virtue. *Mutatis mutandis*, Philo works with similar presuppositions. We find the classic expression of this principle in 2 Timothy 3:16: "all scripture is divinely inspired and useful [*ôphelimos*] for teaching, for rebuke, for correction, and for education in righteousness." While the formulation is probably deutero-pauline, it accurately characterizes the Apostle's use of the Old Testament. Paul seems to assume such a principle when he justifies using the punishments inflicted on the Israelites in the wilderness as a lesson for the Corinthians: "These things occurred to them as an example [*typikôs*], but they were written as an admonition for us" (1 Cor. 10:11).[2] Manlio Simonetti has shown how Origen makes "usefulness" (*ôpheleia*) a fundamental principle of biblical interpretation and it is this, above all, which Gregory shares with him.[3] For Origen the Old Testament, read in the light of the Word incarnate, Jesus Christ, actually becomes a gospel, an embodiment of the Logos.[4] With such an understanding of the function of the Old Testament, Gregory considered a life of Moses an appropriate response to a request from an anonymous correspondent for "advice in the perfect life."[5] He justifies using a great figure from the Old Testament as a model of virtue by appeal to Isaiah 51:2: "Look to Abraham your father and Sarah who endured birth-pangs for you." Such towering figures function like a distant beacon to souls who might otherwise be lost in the sea of life.[6] In the *Life of Moses* the vision at the burning bush marks Moses' transition from a life of solitary contemplation to a life of service, the second and third of four phases Gregory recognized in Moses' life. Here also, as he explained in his *Homilies on the Song of Songs*,[7] the vision at the burning bush is the first of three theophanies which procure for Moses successively fuller knowledge of God. In keeping with Gregory's negative theology, this revelation in light is but a preliminary to the two theophanies on Sinai, first as cloud and then as darkness.

The modern interpreter may also find it difficult to take Gregory's exegesis seriously because it is done on the basis of the Septuagint text, which, in this particular case, gives a highly misleading impression of the sense of the original Hebrew. Here the Septuagint text translated Exodus 3:14, where God responds to Moses' question about his name, as *egô eimi ho ôn*, "I am the one who is." As Esther Starobinski-Safran notes in a penetrating discussion of Philo's treatment of the text, this is a significant modification of the Hebrew *ehyeh asher ehyeh*: "The Greek designates a stable reality, expressed by the present, even though the Hebrew indicates an unfinished realization which continues in time, a permanent becoming."[8] Gregory, like all pre-modern Christian exegetes, works with the Exodus text as received in the Church. Even Origen, who was aware of the original Hebrew and must have known that its translation was questionable, takes the Septuagint translation for granted in his extant works dealing with this text. This translation provided an opening between the biblical text and Platonic philosophy which is already apparent in Philo's interpretation:

> But he, not being unaware that his own people as well as all others would disbelieve his words, said: "If, then, they ask, 'what is the name of the one who sent you?' and I am unable to tell them, will they not consider me a deceiver?" But God said: "First say to them 'I am the one who is,' so that they may learn the difference between being and non-being and that they may learn the additional lesson that, strictly speaking, no name at all can be applied to me, to whom alone being appertains.[9]

Philo, however, effects a genuine synthesis of Platonism with the Bible. Moses' two lessons are expressed in a philosophical vocabulary but have at least as much to do with the first two of the Ten Commandments as they do with Plato. "The difference between being and non-being" thus links the First Commandment insistence on worshipping only one God, a god who "is" in contrast to the gods of polytheism which do not exist, with the Platonic distinction between being (*to on*, with the present participle of *eimi*, "to be" in a neuter form rather than the masculine of the Septuagint text) and becoming as set forth in *Timaeus* 27d–28e:

> We must make a distinction and ask, What is that which always is and has no becoming [*to on aei, genesin de ouk ekhon*], and what is that which is always becoming and never is? That which is apprehended by intelligence and reason is always in the same state, but that which is conceived by opinion with the help of sensation and without reason is always in the process of becoming and perishing and never really is [*ontôs de oudepote on*].[10]

The second lesson in Philo's interpretation, that no name at all applies to God, also links the second commandment's refusal of any image to God, arguably the original negative theology, with Plato's insistence, in *Timaeus* and in *Letter VII*, that God is ineffable.[11] Both of these themes, the distinction between being and becoming, and the namelessness of God, became all the more prominent in the later Platonic tradition. Ironically, this passage, which seems to have functioned in the E tradition as the place where God revealed his proper name, Yahweh, is taken to show that God has, strictly speaking, no name. Before Gregory's time, Philo's assimilation of the Bible to Platonism had already shaped Origen and his presumed mentor, Clement of Alexandria, whose favorite term for God, echoing both Plato and the Septuagint, is "the one who really exists" (*ho ontôs ôn*).

Philo's interpretation becomes part of the common currency of the Christian tradition: God cannot, properly speaking, be named at all, but may be referred to as the source of all being in the term, "he who is." This negative moment in the exegetical tradition appealed to the Cappadocians in their struggle with Eunomius. In this connection Gregory of Nazianzus, whose interpretation of Moses may have influenced his younger namesake, spoke in his *Theological Orations* of "he who is" as one name of God which refers to God in himself, without reference to anything else.[12] About five years later, in a Christmas sermon, Gregory of Nazianzus made much the same point in a magnificent, lyrical passage:

> God always was, is, and will be. Rather, he always "is." For "was" and "will be" are divisions of our time and of fluctuating nature. But he always is, and that is how he names himself in speaking oracularly to Moses on the mountain. Gathering all things in himself, he has being, neither starting nor stopping, like an ocean of being, infinite and boundless, surpassing every notion of time or nature, appearing as a silhouette to the mind alone, and even then obscurely and incompletely, not being based on God himself but on the things around him, the representation being collected from here and there so as to form an image of the truth, one which flees before it can be controlled and escapes before it can be understood, illumining our governing faculty – once, that is, we have been purified – as brief as a bolt of lightning which flashes before our eyes without pausing.[13]

This passage, which Gregory of Nyssa probably knew, seems to allude to Moses' vision, understood, as it is in our passage, as a sudden, brilliant illumination. Gregory of Nyssa himself referred to Exodus 3:14 in other works. In his *Against Eunomius* he argued that "he who is" applies to the common divine being shared by the Father and the Son, not, as his adversary claimed, to the Father alone.[14] Like Gregory of Nazianzus, he carefully excludes inferring, as Jean-Luc Marion points out, "that this name, *ho ôn*, might define the essence of God himself."[15]

Gregory's concern here is not, however, to draw out the philosophical implications of the text, even though he is well aware of them, but to seek its implications for persons straining for perfection. For Gregory, Moses' encounter with God in the burning bush foreshadows our encounter with God in the Incarnate Word. Although the initiative is with God, the encounter entails an appropriate human response. Just as, after seeing the light, Moses must remove his shoes before understanding the meaning of the theophany as a revelation of what really is, so the believer seeking perfection, having seen the light of the Incarnate Word, must put away sinful inclinations before arriving at a full apprehension of the truth. Like Moses, who received at the burning bush the commission to liberate his people, the believer who has come to know God in this way can now proceed to help liberate others from their bondage to sin. In this effort they are assisted by the divine Word, whose coming to humanity in the Incarnation is symbolized by the miracles God enables Moses to perform. The encounter with an angel who seeks to kill Moses as he is on his way to Egypt and is appeased by the circumcision of Moses' son seems to be integral to Gregory's interpretation of the burning bush. Although philosophy, symbolized by Moses' Ethiopian wife, is a useful adjunct in progress toward perfection, it can also expose the believer to danger if the ideas which it engenders are not purified of their errors. Arguably, Gregory chose to emphasize this event in the narrative, which Philo passed over in his *Life*, precisely because he was aware of using the platonic distinction between being and becoming to interpret the burning bush. In telling the story of the encounter with the angel he vindicates his use of philosophy while affirming that he approaches it critically.

The translation below is from Grégoire de Nysse, *La vie de Moïse*, edited and translated by Jean Daniélou, 4th edition (Paris: Éditions du Cerf, 1987), in *Sources chrétiennes* 1bis, pp. 60–2 and 116–30.

Book I, Narrative, 20–2

20. After some time had elapsed in this sort of life [as a shepherd], the narrative states that an awe-inspiring theophany occurred to him. At high noon a light brighter than the sun's light flashed upon him, astonished by the strangeness of the sight, he lifted his eyes to the mountain and saw a bush from which fiery splendor blazed. While the branches of the bush remained fresh in the fire as if it were dew, he said to himself: "Let me step forward and see this great sight," but he had scarcely said this when the marvelous light ceased to affect his eyes only, but, what is most extraordinary of all, the splendor of the rays began to irradiate his hearing, for the grace of the light was divided between the two senses, it illuminated the eyes with the flashing of its rays and it enlightened the hearing with pure doctrines. Thus the voice of that light forbade Moses to approach the mountain weighed down with dead sandals, but, when he had loosed the sandals from his feet, he could touch the earth that was illuminated by the divine light.

21.   After this (for it is necessary, I suppose, for the account to avoid dwelling on the details of the narrative about the man, so that it may keep to the matters proposed), empowered by the theophany which he had seen, he was ordered to deliver his race from slavery to the Egyptians. And so that he might better learn the power God had conferred on him, he tested it at God's command with what he had in his hands. This was the test. A rod, falling from his hand, was turned into a living animal, but when he picked it back up with his hand, it became what it was before its transformation. Then the appearance of his hand, when he took it out of his breast, took on the whiteness of snow, but, when he put it back, it regained its natural condition.

22.   As Moses was going down into Egypt, accompanied by a spouse of another race and the children she had borne, an angel was said to have encountered him, threatening him with death, whom his wife appeased with the blood of the son's circumcision. There ensued his meeting with Aaron, who himself had been prompted to the encounter by God.

Book II, Contemplation, 19–41

19.   Just as we are luxuriating in a manner of life that is peaceful and devoid of conflict, truth will enlighten, dazzling the eyes of the soul with its flashes. But God is the truth, appearing to Moses through that unspeakable illumination.   20. If, also, the flame, by which the soul of the prophet was illumined, was kindled from some thorny bush, this detail will not be irrelevant to our investigation. If God is truth, and truth is light (these are among the exalted and divine terms with which the Evangelist's voice testifies to God appearing to us through flesh) it follows that virtuous conduct will lead us to the knowledge of that light which has descended to human nature, not shining from one of the stellar luminaries, in such a way as to lead us to ascribe its radiance the matter by which it is constituted, but from an earthly bush whose radiance outshines the heavenly luminaries.   21. By this we are taught as well the mystery of the Virgin, for in her the light of divinity manifested through birth in a human life left unscathed the bush in which it was kindled, when the blossom of virginity was not marred in giving birth.

22.   By this light we are taught what to do in order to stand within the rays of the true light, namely that one cannot to run with bound feet up to that height where the true light has appeared without removing the dead and earthly covering of skins from our soul's feet, the skins which

originally became fastened to our nature when, by disobeying the divine will, we were stripped bare. There will thus follow, once this has happened to us, the knowledge of the truth, the truth manifesting itself, for the recognition of that which is becomes a purification of our assumptions about what is not. 23. In my opinion the definition of truth is "not to be deceived in the perception of what is." Falsehood is a fantasy present to the mind respecting what is not, giving a specious impression of what exists, but truth is the accurate perception of what really is. Thus even someone tranquilly engaged in philosophical study of such exalted concerns for a long time will barely perceive what being truly is (that, namely, which has being by its own nature) and what is non being, which exists only in appearance, having by itself a nonexistent nature.

24. It seems to me that the great Moses had been instructed by the theophany to know that none of the things that are grasped by sensation or those that are contemplated by the mind have really existed, except for most exalted essence and cause of the universe from which everything depends. 25. Even if the mind sees among beings something else, reason contemplates in no other being a complete independence, enabling it to exist without participation in being. But that which always remains the same, that which can be neither augmented nor diminished, no less unchangeable either for better or for worse (since it is opposite to the worse and there is nothing better), that which has no requirement for anything else, that which alone is desirable, that which is participated in by everything and in the participation is not abridged by those things which participate in it, that is truly the really existent and its apprehension is knowledge of the truth.

26. This, accordingly, is what occurs, either to him then or now to everyone who removes his earthly covering as he did and also looks at the light of the bush, namely the ray enlightening us through this thorny flesh, which is, in the words of the Gospel, the genuine light and the truth. Such a person is then able to assist others to salvation, delivering into freedom all who are oppressed by wicked servitude. The alteration of the right hand and the transformation of the rod into a serpent are the first instances of miracles. 27. This seems to me to intimate enigmatically the mystery of the divinity's appearance to men through the Lord's flesh, which brings about the overthrow of the tyrant and the liberation of those oppressed by him. 28. Testimonies from both testaments lead me to this interpretation. The Prophet says: "That is the alteration of the right hand of the Most High" (Ps. 76:11), indicating that, even though the divine nature is contemplated in immutability, it has been altered to our form and image by condescending to the weakness of human nature. 29. The legislator's hand, when he took it from his bosom, was altered to an

unnatural color, but when he put it back into his bosom it resumed its own natural grace. The only-begotten God, who was in the bosom of the Father, is the right hand of the Most High. 30. When he appeared to us from the bosom, he was altered to resemble us, when he had healed our infirmity he returned to his bosom the hand which had taken on our coloration in coming to us (the Father is the bosom of the right hand), his impassible nature had not been altered so as to become passible, instead the nature which is changeable and passible had been transformed by its connection with the impassible.

31. Do not let the rod's transformation into a serpent disturb those who love Christ, as if we were comparing the mystery of the Word to an inappropriate animal. The Truth himself, speaking in the Gospel, does not repudiate such an image when he says: "Just as Moses lifted up the serpent in the wilderness, so must the Son of Man be lifted up" (John 3:14). 32. The Word is clear. For if the father of sin is named a serpent by Holy Scripture, it does not follow that sin is synonymous with the one who begot it. But indeed the apostolic word testifies that the Lord became sin for us (see 2 Cor. 5:21) by assuming our sinful nature. 33. Therefore the enigma is reasonably applied to the Lord. If sin is a serpent, but the Lord became sin, it evidently follows that by becoming sin he became a serpent, which is nothing else but sin. But for our sake he became a serpent, in order to devour and consume the Egyptian serpents brought to life by magicians. 34. Once this had happened, he was transformed back into a rod. By it those who sin are chastised and those who are mounting the difficult upward path of virtue are assisted, relying through good hopes on the rod of faith, for faith is the substance of things hoped for (see Heb. 11:1).

35. One who has an awareness of these things has become a god in contrast with those who have resisted the truth, who have had their attention diverted toward materiality and insubstantial fraud while they disdain to listen to him who is as if it were inconsequential to do so. For Pharaoh said "Who is he, that I should listen to his voice? I do not know the Lord" (Exod. 5:2). He considered worthwhile only material and fleshly things corresponding to the irrational senses. 36. If then he has been empowered to such an extent by the illumination of the light and had received such great power and authority against the enemies, then, just as an athlete who has sufficiently trained in athletic excellence in the presence of his trainer, he has become bold and confident, holding his rod, the word of faith, by which he intended to vanquish the Egyptian serpents.

37. His foreign spouse will also accompany him. For there is something in secular education which cannot be disdained when it comes

to wedding ourselves to the engenderment of virtue. For moral and natural philosophy could somehow be a spouse, friend, and companion to the highest life only if those things brought to birth from her retain no foreign pollution. 38. Because this has not been circumcised and removed, to cleanse him of anything harmful and impure, the angel who encounters him will threaten him with death. His consort propitiated this angel when she demonstrated her offspring was pure, since she has removed that property by which he would be recognized as foreign. 39. I suppose that for him who has been initiated into the implications of the narrative, the connection to advancement in virtue which the discourse discloses will be evident. For there is something fleshly and uncircumcised in the doctrines engendered by philosophy. When it is removed, what is left is noble Israelite breeding. 40. The foreign philosophy even says that the soul is immortal; this is its pious offspring. But it also teaches the transmigration of souls from body to body and that the soul can be transformed from a rational nature into an irrational one; this is fleshly and foreign uncircumcision. There are many other such things. It says that God exists, but it supposes him to be material. It confesses that he is the Creator, but thinks that matter is necessary for creation. It attributes to him goodness and power, but supposes him to constrained in many things by the requirements of destiny. 41. And why should one elaborate in detail how the good things among the teachings of secular philosophy are corrupted by absurd additions, but when these are removed, the angel of God will favourably attend us, rejoicing at the legitimate offspring of such doctrines.

Notes

1 On the relationship of these two works, see David T. Runia, *Philo in Early Christian Literature: a Survey* (Assen: Van Gorcum and Minneapolis: Fortress, 1993) pp. 256–61.
2 Other examples are 1 Corinthians 10:8–12a, where the commandment in Deuteronomy 25:4 not to muzzle an ox treading out grain was "written for our sake" to justify remuneration for missionaries, and 2 Corinthians 3:7–18, where the Israelites' inability to look on Moses in Exodus 34:29–35 anticipates the inability of the Jews to see Christ in the Old Testament.
3 Manlio Simonetti, *Lettera e/o allegoria: un contributo alla storia dell'esegesi patristica* (Rome: Institutum Patristicum *Augustinianum*, 1985), pp. 79 and 147.
4 See Origen, *Commentary on John* 1. 6. 32–6.
5 Gregory of Nyssa, *Life of Moses* 1.2.
6 Ibid., 1.11.
7 Gregory of Nyssa, *Homilies on the Song of Songs* 11.1000–01

8 Esther Starobinski-Safran, "Ex. 3, 14 chez Philon" in Paul Vignauz, ed., *Dieu et l'Être: Exégèses d'Exode 3, 14 et de Coran 20, 11-24* (Paris: Études Augustiniennes, 1978), p. 48. Translations are by the author unless otherwise indicated.
9 Philo, *Life of Moses* I: 74-5.
10 Plato, *Timaeus* 27d-28a, tr. by Benjamin Jowett in Plato, *The Collected Dialogues*, ed. by Edith Hamilton and Huntington Cairns (Princeton: Princeton University Press, 1963), p. 1161.
11 See *Timaeus* 28c and *Letter VII* 341c.
12 Gregory of Nazianzus, *Theological Oration* 4 (*Oration* 30) 18. See Marguerite Harl, "Exode 3, 14 chez les Pères Grecs" in Vignaux, *Dieu et l'Être*, pp. 87-108.
13 Gregory of Nazianzus, *Oration* 38.7.
14 Gregory of Nyssa, *Against Eunomius* 1.8.
15 Jean-Luc Marion, *God Without Being*, tr. by Thomas A. Carlson (Chicago: University of Chicago Press, 1991), pp. 73-4.

Further reading

Gregory of Nyssa, *The Life of Moses*, translated and introduced by A. J. Malherebe and E. Ferguson, New York: Paulist Press, 1978.
Trigg, Joseph W. *Biblical Interpretation*. Message of the Fathers of the Church, vol. 9, Wilmington, DE: Michael Glazier, 1988.
Young, Robin Darling, "Gregory of Nyssa's Use of Theology and Science in Constructing Theological Anthropology" *Pro Ecclesia* 2:3 (1993) 345-63.

Selections from Nicholas of Lyra's *Commentary on Exodus*

Translated and introduced by Corrine Patton

Nicholas of Lyra (*c*.1270–1349) was one of the most influential biblical exegetes in the late Middle Ages. A French Franciscan, Lyra was most known for his literal approach to biblical interpretation and his extensive use of Jewish interpretation. While the approach itself was not new, Lyra's work provided later exegetes with what amounted to an encyclopedia of literal meaning. Using every source available to him, Lyra's work was thorough, logical, balanced. He stood firmly within Catholic interpretative traditions, showing obvious reliance on Jerome, Augustine, Gregory the Great, Bede, Hugh and Andrew of St Victor, Peter Lombard, Abelard, and Aquinas, to name only a few. His knowledge of Hebrew allowed him to read both the Hebrew Bible and Jewish interpreters directly and critically, balancing one opinion against another, in order to arrive at the one he deemed most literal within the confines of Christian exegetical principles. Such an even approach led him to be used widely throughout Europe, and guaranteed his lasting influence on such scholars as Luther and Calvin.

Not much is known with certainty about Nicholas's life.[1] He was certainly born in Lyre, Normandy around the year 1270. He joined the Friars Minor at Verneuile (*c*.1300) and received his doctorate at the University of Paris in 1309. He became the Franciscan provincial of Burgundy twice, first in 1314 and again in 1325. He was a noted lecturer at the Sorbonne, and a prominent member of the faculty. His name appears on a few transactions in Paris, the latest of which in 1349 provides an approximate date for his death. Lyra was most certainly a Christian by birth, although after his death stories circulated that he was a converted Jew. Such stories, however, are not substantiated by any public record of conversion, or any mention in Lyra's writings.

Lyra's work exhibits influence from the major intellectual traditions of his day, especially from the scholastic tradition. His philosophical interpretations often align with those of Aquinas, while his exegetical principles closely follow the Victorine school. From references in his work, he was familiar with classical authors including Aristotle, Ovid, and Boethius. In addition, the use of early critical philological and biblical tools within the universities is readily apparent in his work.

By far Lyra's most important work was the *Postilla litteralis super totam Bibliam*, a running literal commentary on the whole Bible, fully in line with scholastic methodology. Lyra produced his commentary to address a wide range of issues in literal interpretation: textual, factual, as well as semantic. In support of this, Lyra used the Hebrew text of the Old Testament as his base. Lyra's expressed purpose was to determine the one literal sense of the text, without which no theological or spiritual interpretation could be drawn. Without the proper base in the literal sense, according to Lyra, the whole exegesis collapses like a building without a solid foundation.[2] Therefore, any theological or spiritual meaning of the text must work from, and not contradict, the established literal sense.

Lyra utilized not only the Hebrew text itself, but also Hebrew works of Jewish scholarship, in particular Rashi.[3] Although Lyra was later criticized for over-utilization of Jewish interpretation, Lyra himself did not automatically prefer conclusions by Jewish exegetes, but judged their conclusions by the same criteria he used for Christian exegetes. In fact, Lyra most often rejects Jewish interpretations when they are not deemed close to the "literal" sense. He uses Jewish exegesis for philological and semantic information primarily, but also for any elucidation of the "plain sense" of the text, whether that be the plot line (*res gestae*), the internal coherence of the story at hand, or the meaning intended by the author, whether human or divine.

The influence of Lyra's work over the following two centuries cannot be exaggerated. His was the first commentary to be printed and, as such, it enjoyed a very wide distribution. There are over seven hundred extant manuscripts of his biblical commentary dating between 1350 and 1450 in European libraries alone,[4] as well as more than a hundred editions of this commentary printed between 1471 and 1641.[5] By 1500, parts of the work had been translated into French, German, and Italian.[6] It became the standard commentary in the university, often printed with both the complete Vulgate text and the Glossa Ordinaria on the same page. Wood argues that the practical effect of Lyra's commentary on Luther's biblical interpretation was to provide a literal sense of the text which Luther could assume would match that of his audience.[7] In addition to his influence among biblical exegetes, evidence of his influence has been found on figures as wide-ranging as Chaucer[8] and Michelangelo.[9]

His work did not avoid criticism, however. Paul of Burgos found it necessary to defend Lyra's methodology against its critics, while at the same time publishing extensive addenda to correct comments he felt were not faithful to the "saints and scholars."[10] Jean Gerson rejected Lyra's literal interpretation because it opposed the tradition.[11] Erasmus considered Lyra a theologian who "dares to tutor Jerome and to tear apart many things hallowed by the consent of so many centuries on the basis of Jewish books."[12] Luther felt Lyra was too literal and overly reliant on Jewish interpretation.[13]

Lyra's sustaining popularity, however, rested on his ability to crystallize the rising sensitivity to history, philology, and the *sensus litteralis*, while demonstrating a successful independence of thought within biblical studies. By placing effective limits on "over-Judaizing" by tempering the acceptance of interpretations by a "plain reading" of text, as well as by fighting "over-allegorization" in the same manner, he showed in practical terms that "new" or even non-Christian interpretations are not inherently theologically destructive. His care to remain solidly within Christian tradition and his consistent demonstration of the value of the biblical text in its historical context effectively insured the success of his endeavor.

The Commentary on Exodus 3 in the Context of Christian Exegesis

One of the first things that strikes a reader familiar with Lyra's work is that nowhere within the commentary on this chapter of Exodus does he refer to any prior exegete or scholar by name, except "blessed Gregory." Yet, a close reading of the text reveals obvious reliance on both Christian and Jewish interpretative traditions. The text of Exodus 3 presented many controversial issues for the medieval biblical theologian, issues Lyra does not fail to address. From the nature of the divine name to the morality of God's command to plunder the Egyptians, the chapter provided fodder for the exegete who had to utilize a wide variety of approaches to the text.

Perhaps the most significant issue raised in the biblical text is the revelation of God's name (Exod. 3:14). While this verse remains a difficult philological problem for modern exegetes, for pre-critical exegetes, both Jewish and Christian, the name itself was seen as a key to understanding the nature of God. Within Jewish tradition, the varieties of divine names employed by the biblical text, from Yahweh[14] to God (*Elohim*) to Lord of Hosts (*Yhwh saba'ot*), revealed different manifestations or modalities of God. For instance, Lord of Hosts referred to God's activity in war, while God or *Elohim* referred to God's acts of judgement. The tetragrammaton revealed in Exodus 3 represented God's mercy and compassion toward Israel. Therefore one exegetical tradition within Judaism understood that this name was revealed at this point in the text to express God's promise to accompany Israel throughout the subsequent events in the exodus and wilderness periods.

More prominent, however, within both Judaism and Christianity is a philosophical or metaphysical interpretation of the name. It would be impossible in such a short space to catalogue the scholars who fall within this tradition. From very early texts within ancient Judaism and Christianity, the name was understood to connote God's nature as eternal. The nature of the Hebrew verbal system encouraged such an interpretation, since the verbal form used when God says "I am who I am" is essentially tenseless, connoting continuous action either past, present, or future. This connotation lent itself to understanding the God of the Old Testament as eternal. Later scholastic tradition stressed further the connection of God as the source of all that exists, i.e. that God is Being itself. Lyra sums up this approach when he states that God is the only thing whose essence is existence itself. Lyra, however, does not have to defend or prove such a conclusion; he can merely provide an outline of the argument as support for the conclusion.

A second exegetical problem present in the text is the nature of the sign that God offers Moses as proof that God will be with him (Exod. 3:12). A plain reading of the verse implies that the proof that God will be with Moses is that the mission will eventually succeed, hardly an effective sign for a person such as Moses who is unsure of assuming the mantle of responsibility. Why would God offer such a nonsensical sign? A variety of answers to this problem was offered by both Jewish and Christian exegetes, many of which Lyra lists in his comment. Several Jewish interpreters, including Rashi, suggested that the sign was the phenomenon of the burning bush itself,[15] while most Christian scholars preferred to see the verse as a prophetic oracle of the future reception of the law on Mount Sinai. For both Hugh and Andrew of St Victor, however, the exodus itself was the sign that God was with Moses.[16]

A third major issue commonly addressed is the significance of God's appearance in a bush that burns but is not consumed. While this text presents no grammatical or historical problems *per se*, all exegetes, Christian and Jewish, assume that the choice of such a phenomenon must have had significance in and of itself. Why would God choose a bush, say, rather than a majestic tree? Why is the bush on fire, and what is the relationship between the angel who appears in the bush and the subsequent divine speech said to be the words of God, not the angel? This attention to the detail of the text, this conviction that every word, every image has a purpose, and that it is the exegete's job to uncover this meaning, not only characterizes medieval biblical interpretation, but is perhaps its most important contribution to the field of biblical interpretation.

The most common Jewish interpretation, as noted by Lyra, sees the bush as Israel, the thorns of the bush as Israel's many troubles, and the fire as their persecution in Egypt that could not consume them. This Jewish interpretation, voiced in Rashi, is noted by Christians as early as Bede.[17] Lyra also repeats the conclusions of Andrew of St Victor and Bede, who note that wood of a bush cannot be carved into an idolatrous image, thus explaining why God did not appear in a tree. However, other common Christian interpretations listed by Augustine,[18] Gregory,[19] and Bede are tacitly ignored by Lyra. These include the rather disparaging view that the bush was Israel, the thorns their sins and the fire the law which was unable to eradicate the sinfulness of Israel. In addition, Lyra does not reproduce a common allegorical interpretation of the figure, perhaps best expressed by Bede, that sees the bush as the Church on fire from persecution, not consumed, because it is the site for God's voice to be heard in the world. Lyra's concentration on the literal meaning of the text and sensitivity to the historical context of the passage effectively eliminated both of these interpretations.

Finally, the text presents a moral problem in the plundering of the Egyptians. When God commands the Israelites to take their neighbors' jewels, God is essentially commanding the Israelites to steal. Jews and Christians alike address the moral problem inherent in the text. Most exegetes use the text as an opportunity to discuss the relationship between justice and a divine command. Among Christian scholars, such as Augustine and Aquinas, a moral distinction is made between what is just in the human realm, and God's sovereignty over all creation. God's commands cannot be unjust because all belongs to God. In fact, as Augustine notes, to disobey the command would be unjust. Lyra tries to salvage God's decision, however, by noting that since the Hebrews had not been paid during their years of slavery and servitude, these goods rightly belonged to them as recompense. By this command God pronounces judgement on Egypt and rights the prior injustice. Finally, a common Jewish interpretation, noted by Christian scholars such as Hugh of St Victor, focuses on the word "favor" in the text, and claims that the Egyptians would recognize that the Hebrews were graced or favored by God, and thus hand over their goods voluntarily.

Tracing Lyra's primary sources for the chapter remains problematic. The ubiquitousness of many of the interpretations he shares hinders positing any direct reliance on a single exegete. For example, Lyra's discussion of the divine name reflects that of Augustine, Aquinas, and even Rashi. It is more probable that he is presenting "current opinion" on the subject. His mention of Gregory demonstrates that he is reading his works, yet Gregory's moral interpretations of many elements in Exodus 3, found throughout his works, do not factor into the commentary. Jerome wrote very little on Exodus 3, and no comment in Lyra shows direct dependence on any of Jerome's statements. Augustine's comments are also scattered throughout his work and, outside of the *Quaestiones in Exodum*, primarily focus on the nature of God revealed by the divine name; it is Augustine's work in the *Quaestiones*, however, with which Lyra's commentary shows most affinities. Bede made abundant use of Exodus 3, but most of his interpretations are allegorical, and, again, go unremarked in Lyra's work. Among Christian scholars, Lyra seems to draw most often on the works of Hugh and Andrew of St Victor.[20] Every place the Victorines note that "the Hebrews say," Lyra repeats the information, showing clear reliance on their work.

Lyra's use of Jewish interpretation in this section is complex, since every place where he asserts "The Hebrews say" can be found in earlier Christian texts and do not represent an independent, direct reading of the Jewish sources. Bede and Andrew note two Jewish interpretations of the bush, Hugh cites their interpretation of the plundering of the Egyptians, and Andrew states their interpretation of the absence of the Girgashites, as well as their custom for removing shoes on holy ground. This suggests that Lyra's use of independent Jewish sources in this chapter is rather limited. However, occasionally he voices conclusions apparently found only in Jewish sources, without, however, attributing them as such.[21] These include the reason Moses was shepherding in the wilderness, and the dual promise of God to the Israelites. In particular, reliance on Rashi and Nachmanides seems clear.[22] Less obvious is whether he read the Midrash on Exodus (*Exodus Rabbah*) independently.

Finally, when Lyra is read in the context of a rich Christian interpretative tradition, what he fails to mention is also notable. For instance, the appearance of the angel in the bush was a common source for the proof of the existence of the Trinity in the Old Testament, but Lyra not only does not advance such a view but fails to even mention it. In fact, his whole avoidance of any semblance of allegorical interpretation contrasts sharply with that of an Augustine or a Bede. He also does not mention at this point the use of this chapter in Acts 7. His focus remains on the meaning of this text as a historical document reflecting the events and circumstances of the actual exodus.[23] His goal is to reconstruct what actually happened, and what motivated the historical Moses. The theological meaning of the text for Lyra is in the historical events themselves, and not what they tell us about the later Church or even the ancient or modern Jewish community. In this way he lets the text speak for itself, assuming continuity between the Israelites who came out of Egypt and the present believing community. This history is the Church's history, and these acts of salvation, redeeming for the Church itself.

The translation here is based on Nicolaus de Lyra, *Postilla super totam Bibliam*, Strassburg, 1492, available in reprint by Minirva GmbH., Frankfurt, 1971.

Commentary on Exodus 3

Moses, however [3:1].[24] Next, the mission of Moses to liberate the people is described.[25] First his commission is described, and second, the expansion of the commission in chapter 4 below when it says, "Moses left, etc." [4:18]. Up to that point the appearance of the divinity is first described, second, Moses' commission, where it says, "To whom the Lord said" [3:4], third the instruction concerning what must be done, where it says, "And Moses said" [3:13].[26] Concerning the first point, the place of the apparition is noted when it says:

When he had led the flock further into the wilderness [3:1], both because the pastures were better there, and partly to remove himself far from cultivated land, so that the flocks would not feed on another person's harvest.[27]

He came to Horeb, the mountain of God [3:1]. This is mount Sinai, which is foreshadowed as "the mountain of God" with respect to the future, because God would give the law there.[28] Also the manner of appearance is described when it says:

And the Lord appeared to him [3:2]. In Hebrew it has, "The angel of the Lord appeared to him." Although this angel appeared, it spoke in the person of God.[29] Therefore, sometimes an angel is called "Lord" following the same principle which Blessed Gregory notes concerning Isaiah 6: the angel who cleansed Isaiah's lips with a burning coal is called a *seraphim* because of the act of burning, although it would not have been from the seraphic order.[30]

In a flame of fire from the middle of the bush [3:2], for the people of Israel were prone to idolatry. Therefore, the one who cannot be fashioned into an image appeared in a flame and in a bush without thorns, as it says in Hebrew, because an image can not be made from such things.[31] This was in order that the people of Israel, who were about to come to that place because of the aforementioned apparition, would not make anything related to idolatry.

He saw that the bush burned but was not consumed [3:2], because the flame engulfing the verdant bush was not diminishing, as it would with combustible material. Through this is signified that the humiliating servitude, which is designated by the fire, would neither consume nor destroy the children of Israel, in whom there was mortal weakness, but, rather, they would be wonderfully freed.[32] The Lord appeared to Moses in order to act through Moses for this purpose. Therefore, the apparition was constructed as such because of its suitability to the matter at hand, just as any apparition is constructed according to how fitting it is to people.

Moses, Moses [3:4]. This duplication signifies election,[33] and elicits the attention of the one called.

Do not approach here [3:5]. It is as if it said that human fragility should not presume to inquire about the secrets of God out of mere curiosity, as in Proverbs 25, "The one who searches out grandeur will be crushed by glory."[34]

Take off your shoes [3:5], because it was the custom of the ancients, especially of the Hebrews, not to proceed into a sacred space with shoes on their feet. It is from this that the Saracens do not dare to enter a place of prayer unless unshod.[35]

The ground is holy [3:5], because of the appearance of the divinity there.[36]

Moses hid his face [3:6] out of reverence for the divine.

The Lord said further [3:7]. Next is described the commission of Moses, carried out in order to liberate the people, when it says:

I have seen the affliction of my people [3:7] with an eye of compassion for this very liberation. In this the Lord uncovered to Moses the meaning of the wonderful vision previously mentioned, for, although divine matters must not be sought presumptuously, nevertheless, through divine revelation they are humbly acknowledged. Therefore, when Moses did not proceed out of curiosity, but humbly hid his own face, then the Lord revealed to him that he hides such things "from the wise and the prudent," but he reveals them "to infants," as is maintained in Matthew 11.[37]

I have come down [3:8], that is, through his effects, since he cannot come down in and of himself.[38]

Into a good land [3:8] which is shown when it adds:

Flowing with milk and honey, as if to say it produces great yield with small effort.[39]

Spacious [3:8], which is obvious from this text because many groups lived there,[40] which is stated when it adds:

To the places of the Canaanites and the Hittites [3:8]. Here the text is silent about the Girgashites, although they appear in many other places where the others are named. This is because, as the Hebrews say, they did not oppose the children of Israel through war like the others, but they retreated from the land before the immigrations of the children of Israel.[41]

Therefore, the cry [3:9] because of the killing of innocent people, and the unjust affliction of the laborers. For the killing of the innocents is said "to cry to God" in Genesis 4, "Behold the sound of the blood of your brother, Abel, cries to me from the earth,"[42] or, similarly, the harassment or swindling of the laborers in James, "Their cry is in the ears of the Lord of hosts, etc."[43]

But come, I will send you [3:10]. For although God was powerfully in Moses' presence, nevertheless he said "come," signifying through this that Moses ought to be quick to accept the command of God with mind and will, although he was bodily present.

And Moses said [3:11]. Next is described the training and confirmation of Moses himself, which are required in order to take up such an office. First he is prepared and strengthened by words, second by associates joined (to him), where it says, "you and the elders will proceed," third, from the miraculous signs in the beginning of chapter 4. Concerning the first, the senselessness of Moses' speech is set forth.

Who am I? [3:11] as if he would say, "I am altogether unsuitable for such negotiations." Therefore the Lord consoles him, saying:

I will be with you [3:12], I who am sufficient and powerful enough to protect and guide you.[44]

And you will have a sign that I have sent you [3:12]. According to the Hebrews this refers to what precedes as if it would say, "The vision of the bush which I have shown you is the sign to you that I am sending you."[45] According to the Catholics it refers to the following words when it says, "When you have led out my people from Egypt, you will worship God on this very mountain," as if it says, "I am foretelling to you that after leading my people out, you will worship God on this very mountain; when this happens to you it will be a sure sign to you that I had been with you leading the people out of Egypt."[46] It will even be a sign for the future, because the Lord had said two things to Moses:[47] just as he led the people out of Egypt, he would lead them into a land flowing with milk and honey. Therefore, just as the worship had been foretold as a sign with respect to events in the past, namely his miraculously freeing them from servitude in Egypt, so it would be a sign with respect to the future, since he would lead everyone into the Promised Land.[48]

If they say to me what is his name, what will I say to them? [3:13]. For in this Moses has asked him to express the name of the one sending him, and, tacitly, to express something about that one's nature.[49] The Lord responds first to the second query about the nature of the one sending him, saying:

I am who I am [3:14]. In Hebrew it has, "I will be who I will be." Nevertheless the same thing is signified by both phrases, which is the eternal and immutable necessity of Being in every way,[50] a condition appropriate and unique to God himself.[51] For everything else, which is from nothing, has its beginning from God himself for it to exist, and has the potential to be turned back into nothing, since by taking away the divine hands sustaining them, they fall into non-being. Therefore non-being is more suitable for such things as much as this state alone stems from themselves, but they have being from God according to which it is said in Isaiah 41, "Behold, you are from nothing, and your work is from that which does not exist."[52]

Thus say to the children of Israel [3:14], as if he says, "If they ask you who sent you, you will answer:"

I who am sent me [3:14], that is, he who has the necessity and fullness of being from himself without any restriction or determination.

And God said to Moses, etc. [3:15]. As if he said, "If they ask next for the name of the one sending you, you will answer, 'The Lord God of your fathers, the God of Abraham, etc.' This is my name, etc." It follows:

Go, gather the elders of Israel [3:16]. By this, the text does not mean all the elders of the people. Since there were six hundred thousand pedestrians that comprised this people, as is maintained below in chapter 12,[53] all of the elders of the people could not be gathered easily. But the word "elders" means the judges, who held rule over the people.[54]

I have surely given heed to them [3:16]. This is used in a manner of speaking because Joseph, when he was dying, thus foretold, "After my death God will pay you heed and make you go up from this land," as it has in Genesis chapter 50.[55]

And they will listen to your voice [3:18]. For they were prudent men, knowing the promise made to Abraham in Genesis chapter 15, where it says, "They will return here in the fourth generation."[56] Therefore they would believe in the words of Moses before the sign would occur. It talks about this in the following chapter.

And you will proceed [3:18]. Here is placed the instruction of Moses, as well as the alleviation of his burdens by the group that was joined to him in order to speak to the king, when it says, "You will proceed, you and the elders of Israel," etc.

Let us go on a journey of three days [3:18]. It does not say of one or two days, because this would not be sufficiently far enough away from the Egyptians, who would stone them if they knew they were sacrificing animals which they worshipped as gods. Nor does it say six or eight days, so that it would not seem that they were not seeking to sacrifice to God, but rather to flee. Therefore, it says three days, not more, in order to express that to whatever degree the request is reasonable, to that degree the king of Egypt would be more inexcusable for disobedience to God. For the Lord knew that he would not heed this petition, so that he would deserve to be scourged by God. In this way, although unwilling, the king concedes even more things, such as the exit of the totality of the population, and indeed not only concedes to their exiting from the land, but compels them, as it says below in chapter 12.[57] It adds:

But I know that he will not send you away just by my command expressed simply by a word. Therefore it adds:

Unless through a mighty hand [3:19], that is, through my power grievously afflicting him as well as his own people, just as will be apparent in the following.

And I will give you favor [3:21]. The Hebrews say that when the people left Egypt, the Lord gave them such favor that the Egyptians freely offered to give them precious jewels.[58] But this does not seem to agree with the literal meaning of the following when it says "A woman will demand from her neighbor" [3:22]. Even afterwards it adds:

And you will plunder Egypt, which does not seem true if the Egyptians had given those things to them. It must be said that they took hold of them from the Egyptians by borrowing them, and thus they took them with them. The Egyptians were eager to bury their dead, because "there was no Egyptian home in which death had not fallen," as is maintained below in chapter 12.[59] Thus they were uninterested in attacking again. The Hebrews did not then practice robbery either, because they did this by the will and authority of the Lord, as is clear since he is the Lord of all things. Therefore, he can carry off by his own power whatever he will without injury or injustice, and give it to others as he wills.[60] It must even be contemplated that this very ordinance of God was reasonable, stemming from a consideration of this people, since the Hebrews were slaves to the Egyptians in many exceedingly grave ways. They had not had improvement or recompense either for their labors, or for the violence done to them, or for the drowning of their own people. Therefore the Egyptians were held accountable to them for many things, as is clearly the literal meaning for these words.

Notes

1 The most thorough and accessible sources for Lyra's biography are a series of articles by H. Labrosse in *Études franciscaines* (16 (1906): 383–404; 17 (1907): 488–505, 593–608; 19 (1908): 41–52, 153–75, 368–79; and 35 (1923): 171–87, 400–32) and C. V. Langlois, "Nicolas de Lyre, Frère Mineur," *Histoire littéraire de la France* 36 (1927). These are neatly summarized by A. S. Wood, "Nicolas of Lyra," *EvQ* 33 (1961): 196–206.

2 See the second prologue to the *Postilla litteralis*.

3 This aspect of Lyra's exegesis has drawn considerable attention. See, among others, H. Hailperin, "Nicholas de Lyra and Rashi: The Minor Prophets," *Rashi Anniversary Volume* (Texts and Studies, 1; Philadelphia: Jewish Publication Society, 1941), pp. 115–47; *Rashi and the Christian Scholars* (Pittsburgh: University of Pittsburgh Press, 1963); and J. Cohen *The Friars and the Jews: The Evolution of Medieval Anti-Judaism* (Ithaca: Cornell University press, 1982), pp. 170–95. [There are also a series of dated articles that trace Lyra's use of Rashi in Hectateuch: C. Siegfried "Raschi's Einfluss auf Nicolaus von Lira und Luther in der Auslegung der Genesis," *Archiv für wissenschaftliche Erforschung des Alten Testamentes* 1 (1869): 428–56; F. Maschkowski, "Rashi's Einfluss auf Nikolaus von Lyra in der Auslegung des Exodus: Ein Beitrag zur Geschichte der Exegese des Alten Testamentes," *ZAW* 11 (1891): 268–316; A.J.Michalski, "Rashis Einfluss auf Nicolaus von Lyra in der Auslegung der Bücher Leviticus Numeri und Deuteronomium," *ZAW* 35 (1915): 218–45; 36 (1916): 29–63; "Rashis Einfluss auf Nicolaus von Lyra in der Auslegung des Buches Josua," *ZAW* 39 (1921): 300–7.]

4 R. Wood, "Nicholas of Lyra and Lutheran Views on Ecclesiastical Office," *JEH* 29 (1978): 451.

5 Labrosse, *Etudes* (1906): 383. See also E. Gosselin, "A Listing of the Printed Editions of Nicholaus de Lyra," *Traditio* 26 (1970): 399–426.

6 R. Wood, "Lutheran Views on Ecclesiastical Office," p. 451.

7 Ibid., p. 452.

8 D. Wurtele, "Chaucer's *Canterbury Tales* and Nicholas of Lyre's *Postilla litteralis et moralis super totam bibliam*," in *Chaucer and Scriptural Tradition*, ed. D. L. Jeffrey (Ottawa: University of Ottawa Press, 1984), pp. 84–107.

9 H. B. Gutman, "Nicholas of Lyra and Michelangelo's Ancestors of Christ," *Franciscan Studies* 4 (1944): 223–8.

10 H. de Lubac, *Exégèse médiévale: Les quatre sens de l'écriture* (Paris: Aubier, 1959), pp. 355–9.

11 J. S. Preuss, *From Shadow to Promise: Old Testament Interpretation from Augustine to the Young Luther* (Cambridge, Mass.: Harvard University Press, 1969), pp. 79–84.

12 Quoted in H. A. Obermann, *Forerunners of the Reformation: The Shape of Medieval Thought Illustrated by Key Documents* (Philadelphia: Fortress, 1966), pp. 311–12.

13 See G. Rupp, *The Righteousness of God: Luther Studies* (London: Hodder and Stoughton, 1953), p. 133.

14 I use the standard vocalization here, although within Jewish tradition the name is never pronounced.

15 It must be noted, however, that Rashi lists this interpretation along with others, including the giving of the law and the exodus itself.

16 I am drawing on Hugh's exegetical work in the *Adnotationes Elucidatoriae in Pentateuchon* (PL CLXXV, 62). Andrew's exegetical work on Exodus is part of his *Expositio super heptateuchum* (Corpus Christianorum, Continuatio Mediaeualis, 53).

17 Unless otherwise noted, all comments from Bede are from his *In Pentateuchum Commentarii* (PL XCI, 293–5). He discusses Exodus 3 in a variety of places, but references to the work outside of the commentary either merely mimic the commentary or provide an allegorical interpretation which Lyra ignores.

18 All opinions cited from Augustine are from the *Quaestiones in Exodum*, unless otherwise noted.

19 *Homiliae in Hiezechihelem prophetam*, hom. VII, lines 185–93.

20 It is often unclear whether Lyra is reading Hugh or Andrew, since wherever the two overlap, Andrew follows Hugh extremely closely.

21 It must be noted that the use of *"Hebraei dicunt"* in this section is uncharacteristic for Lyra. As noted, he uses it only for Jewish opinions gleaned from other Christian authors, and he avoids it when he apparently has independent knowledge of Jewish interpretation. In other sections of the *Postilla*, he is not at all hesitant to attribute his conclusions to a reading of Rashi, Josephus, or other Jewish writers. This suggests to me that either this section is simply less well documented than others, or that in fact all of the comments he includes he has found in Christian texts, and none represents independent knowledge of Jewish sources here. For further study, a detailed comparison of Raymond Martin's *Pugio Fidei* with the *Postilla* could be useful. See Cohen, *The Friars and the Jews*, pp. 265–6 for one such attempt.

22 These will be noted in the commentary.

23 P. Krey nicely summarizes three elements that characterize Lyra's historiography: his avoidance of anachronisms and wrong chronology, the attention to detail, and the importance of social and historical context ("Nicholas of Lyra: Apocalypse Commentary as Historiography" (Ph.D. diss., University of Chicago, 1990), p. 196). All of these elements are present in his commentary on Exodus 3.

24 Lyra first cites a lema or short form of the verse upon which he is commenting, and then provides the interpretation. I have provided chapter and verse numbers based on the NRSV throughout the translation.

25 This first section is the prologue which Lyra provides for each chapter. In the prologue he outlines the contents of the chapter, while often highlighting major points he will cover in the detailed commentary. The divisions of the text are characteristic of a scholastic approach to the Bible.

26 Within the commentary, however, Lyra notes the beginning of Moses' instruction at 3:18.

27 Rashi says much the same thing: Moses takes the flock out into the wilderness "to keep them from robbing by grazing on others' fields."

28 While Rashi states that the phrase refers to the future, the word he uses has an eschatological connotation, and does not refer to the giving of the law.

29 This verse was often discussed within Christian tradition because it raises the problem of the identification of the angel with God implied in the text. Augustine suggests that the angel refers to a tangible appearance of the divine realm that should not be identified with God. Within Jewish tradition, while Nahmanides claims the angel is Michael who is accompanied by God's glory, Rashbam and Ibn Ezra say that it is merely an angel who

speaks in God's name (see F. Maschkowski, "Raschi's Einfluss auf Nikolaus von Lyra in der Auslegung des Exodus," *ZAW* 11 (1891) 278). Among Christian exegetes, Hilary says much the same thing in *De Trinitate*, book 4, chap. 32. Augustine, on the other hand, uses the text as an opportunity to prove the existence of the Trinity in the Old Testament (see both *Sermones*, sermon 7 (Corpus Christianorum, Series Latina, p. 41), and *Quaestiones in Exodum* on this verse).

30 He discusses the differences between cherubim and seraphim in *XL Homiliarum in Evangelia Libri Duo*, book 2, homily 39, chap. 12.

31 See both Bede and Andrew of St Victor for similar statements.

32 Bede includes this interpretation among those he lists for this verse.

33 The *Midrash Rabbah* for this verse states that one of the options for the significance of the duplication of the name is that it demonstrates God's "love and encouragement" of Moses. The word Lyra uses here, *dilectio*, can mean either love or election.

34 Here Lyra clearly follows the Vulgate of Proverbs 25:27, rather than the Hebrew text, which contains a textual error.

35 Many Jewish exegetes, such as the *Exodus Rabbah* and Nahmanides, make the observation that the priests serving in the Tabernacle work unshod, but I have found no other place where this is connected to contemporary Muslim practice.

36 Bede, Hugh, Andrew, and Nahmanides all note this as well.

37 Verse 25.

38 This is a typical observation characteristic of scholasticism.

39 While Augustine states that this statement about the later land of Israel is patently untrue, and therefore must be interpreted allegorically (*Quaestiones in Exodum*), Nahmanides states that the two items refer to a high yield in both livestock (milk) and produce (honey).

40 The same statement can be found in Andrew of St Victor.

41 While this is noted in various Jewish exegetical works, including both Rashi and Nahmanides, Andrew introduces the same comment with the phrase "Hebraei aiunt."

42 Genesis 4:10.

43 James 5:4.

44 Andrew also notes God's protection of Moses.

45 This can be found in Rashi; Andrew also notes this interpretation, but does not relate it to Jewish interpretation. Bede includes it as one of two Hebrew interpretations of the text.

46 Rashi, however, also notes this interpretation, as does Andrew, who, like Hugh, prefers to understand the sign as the exodus itself.

47 This statement makes better sense in Nahmanides. He states that God promises two things here: first that the people will be led out of Egypt (see Hugh and Andrew of St Victor), and that they would be led into Canaan. He goes on to say that the Israelites knew how difficult the conquest of the land would be, which is why they would be reluctant to follow Moses. The future sign on Mount Sinai then is not to convince them that God has really sent Moses, but to show them that God will remain with them during the conquest, thus guaranteeing its success.

48 What Lyra tries to say here is that when they get to Mount Sinai and see that the first part of God's promise had come to pass, they will be assured that the second part of the promise will also come true. It is in this way that the worship of God on Mount Sinai truly functions as a proper sign.

49 The text implies that the people did not know God. This seemed impossible to both Christian and Jewish exegetes. Within Judaism, the revelation of the name expressed the nature or aspect under which God acts here, not in the absolute sense, but rather as that characteristic of God which is manifested by the name. However, when Lyra states that Moses is seeking God's nature, he means it in the philosophical, absolute sense, quite a different matter from what one sees in, say, Nahmanides.

50 The eternity of God is noted in almost every Jewish and Christian exegete. Christian exegetes also tend to stress God's immutability here as well. The extension of this to God's essence equaling existence itself takes prominence among scholastics such as the Victorines and Aquinas (see, in particular, *Summa Theologica* pars I, ques. 13, art. 11 on the name of God). For further reading see B. Childs *The Book of Exodus: A Critical, Theological Commentary* (Old Testament Library; Philadelphia: Westminster, 1974), pp. 84–6.

51 I use masculine pronouns, following Lyra's usage.

52 Verse 24.

53 Verse 37.

54 Rashi states that the elders include only those who comprise a "council," since all of the elders would be too large of a group for this purpose.

55 Genesis 50:25 is commonly cited by Jewish exegetes such as the *Exodus Rabbah*, Rashi, and Nahmanides, as a parallel to this one in Exodus. However, they cite it because of the grammatical construction in Hebrew of the infinitive absolute alongside of a finite Hebrew verb. Lyra seems to misunderstand the reason for the quotation, even though he preserves it here. He compares the content of the two verses, rather than their grammatical constructions.

56 Verse 16.

57 This refers to 12:35–6 which relates the actual "plundering" of the Egyptians.

58 This Hebrew tradition, found in *Exodus Rabbah*, is noted in Hugh and Andrew of St Victor.

59 Verse 30.

60 This interpretation of the justice of the divine command can be seen in Augustine (*Quaestiones in Exodum*) and Aquinas (see, for instance, *Summa Theologica* pars I–II, ques. 100, art. 8, ad. 3, as well as pars I–II, ques. 94. art. 5, ad. 2).

Further reading

Cohen, J., *The Friars and the Jews: The Evolution of Medieval Anti-Judaism*, Ithaca: Cornell University Press, 1982.

Gosselin, E. A., "A Listing of the Printed Editions of Nicholaus de Lyra," *Traditio* 26 (1970), pp. 399–426.

Preus, J. S., *From Shadow to Promise: Old Testament Interpretation from Augustine to the Young Luther*, Cambridge: Harvard University Press, 1969.

Skevington-Wood, A., "Nicolas of Lyra," *Evangelical Quarterly* 33 (1961), pp. 196–206.

Three Postcritical Encounters with the Burning Bush*

In memory of Emmanuel Levinas z"l [may his memory be
for a blessing] (died December 25, 1995)

Peter Ochs

*The Israelites were groaning under the bondage and cried out . . . God heard
their moaning . . . and God took notice of them (Exod. 2). Now Moses, tending
the flock of his father-in-law . . . drove the flock into the wilderness, and came
to Horeb, the mountain of God. An angel of the Lord appeared to him in a
blazing fire out of a bush. He gazed, and there was a bush all aflame, yet the
bush was not consumed. Moses said "I must turn aside to look at this marvelous
sight; why doesn't the bush burn up?". . . And the Lord continued, "I have
come down to rescue [My people] . . . Come, therefore, I will send you to
Pharoah. (Exod. 3)*[1]

The following reflections are composed at the end of the first month of mourning
for Emmanuel Levinas, z"l, the world's most influential Jewish philosopher.
With other Jewish philosophers, I am preoccupied now with thoughts about his
legacy as a scriptural reader. In the tradition of Hermann Cohen, Levinas
mastered a dominant Western philosophic method (in his case, phenomenology),
and became his nation's (France's) most beloved teacher of that method, but in
so doing also showed how this method's most profound contribution lies beyond
philosophy as defined up to now: it is to further the end of human ethics, as
articulated in the biblical-rabbinic injunction to love one's neighbor or, in
Levinas's terms, to see the face of one's neighbor as a face of the Other. Turning

* This essay revisits reflections on Exodus 3 and its rabbinic readers that I offered in "Scriptural
Logic: Diagrams for a Postcritical Metaphysics," *Modern Theology* 11:1 (Jan. 1995): 65–92. There,
I read these texts in light of an imagined dialogue between Lindbeck and the philosopher Charles
Peirce. Here, the dialogue is with Levinas.

to the text of Moses' encounter with these images of Levinas on my mind, I find myself imagining Levinas in Moses' stead – Moses tending his flock on the mountain plain, preoccupied with concerns about his people's suffering, about his new family and his conflict with Pharaoh. A fire-flash interrupts him, and he turns to consider the marvel. In his stead, Levinas would be preoccupied with concerns about the agony of modern Europe and the incapacity of modern philosophy to do much about it. In place of the bush, the biblical text would burn, words aflame but the text not consumed, and Levinas would turn and hear these words as substitutes for philosophic rhetoric. At this point in the image, Levinas resembles Hans Frei, of blessed memory, and George Lindbeck, offering additional ways of interrupting what Frei called "mediating theology": the self-preoccupation of modern reading, as it puts concept before word and the logic of the ego before the grammar of the text. But then, interrogating the text the way Moses interrogates God, Levinas would seem to remain philosopher after all, no longer like Frei and Lindbeck. The image is complicated by God's retorts: God invents some strange names, and then Moses gets God angry. Levinas is at least unlike any modern philosopher. But his specific identity gets as hazy as God's. And his relation to Frei's and Lindbeck's postcritical project?

In memory of Levinas and in honor of a dialogue I would like to have heard among Levinas, Frei, and Lindbeck, I offer here three different musings on the text of Exodus 3, presented as three different postcritical encounters with the burning bush.

Encounter 1: The Fire Burns the West; the Text Absorbs the World

In the first encounter, Moses' preoccupations prefigure Frei's and Lindbeck's, as understood by a first wave of "postcritical" Christian theologians. Here, bondage in Egypt prefigures bondage to the reductive practices of modern Western biblical scholarship: interpreting the words of scripture *either* as signs that refer, behind the text, to some historically situated events that took place on the soils of the ancient Near East; *or* as signs that instantiate some collection of *a priori* principles that hover above the text but may also be disclosed directly in human reasoning. In the first case, the meaning of the Bible is interpreted exclusively by groups of historical-critical inquirers for whom the biblical text is what semioticians call an *indexical* sign of an antecedent historical reality. In the second case, it is interpreted exclusively by conceptual analysts – philosophers, theologians, or structuralists – for whom the text is an *icon* of a self-disclosing logos. The two general types of inquiry generate a dialectic of contrary readings of scripture, and there is no *tertium quid* through which the contraries are resolved.

In this first encounter, Moses' *turning* to look at the burning bush prefigures the postcritical inquirers *turning* from matters outside the text to gaze again at whatever lies within. For this encounter, the biblical text itself descends like fire into the preoccupations of modern scholarship. This is not, however, like the fires that ascend from the earth, consuming material things the way abstractive ideas replace the experiences that have given rise to them. This is a descending fire that envelops material things without changing their materiality, the way proper names envelop people with identities that do not augment or diminish their bodily characteristics. For the postcritical inquirer, the Bible descends whole into modernity, "aborbing the world" in Lindbeck's words, but not consuming, negating, or overthrowing it:

> For those who are steeped in [the authoritative texts that are the canonical writings of religious communities], no world is more real than the ones they create. A scriptural world is thus able to absorb the universe. It supplies the interpretive framework within which believers seek to live their lives and understand reality.[2]

According to Frei, the Reformers anticipated this approach to intratextuality:

> The Protestant Reformers had said that the Bible is self-interpreting, the literal sense of its words being their true meaning, its more obscure passages to be read in the light of those that are clear. This tradition was expressed typically in Luther's oft-quoted remark that scripture is "through itself most certain . . ., interpreting itself . . ., judging all the words of all men."[3]

The postcritical alternative to modern scholarship has its Jewish antecedents as well. There is the Talmudic image of the Torah text as "black fire on white fire" (*TB Shekalim* 41d) – heavenly fire that, according to the Midrash on Exodus 3 "burns but does not consume, and is black in color; whereas fire used here below . . . is red and consumes but does not burn" (*Shemoth Rabbah* II.5). Or the Talmudic commentary on Exodus 24:7 – where, after receiving the Tablets the first time, Moses "took the record of the covenant and read it aloud to the people. And they said, 'All that the Lord has spoken we will faithfully do' [*naaseh v'nishmah*]." The Talmudic sages interpreted the phrase *naaseh v'nishmah* to mean that the Israelites "committed themselves to *doing* before *hearing* – which is the very "secret that the angels make use of," as it is written, "Bless the Lord, Oh, His angels, you mighty ones, who do His word, hearkening to the voice of His word" (*TB Shabbat* 88a–b). In his earliest collection of Talmudic lectures, Levinas contrasts this angelic state of obedience with "the condition of Western" humanity, which is to subordinate "any act to the knowledge that one may have of that act." Levinas calls this "the temptation of temptation," which is to be eager to try everything, to experience everything. . . . What tempts . . . is not pleasure but the ambiguity of a situation in which pleasure is still possible but in respect to which the Ego keeps its liberty, has not yet given up its security. . . . The temptation of temptation is philosophy, in contrast to a wisdom which knows everything without experiencing it. . . . For experiencing itself is already committing oneself, choosing, living, limiting onself. We want to know before we do. But we want a knowledge completely tested through our own evidence.[4]

Like Lindbeck and Frei, Levinas offers a scriptural response to the modern West. This is not simply to "act" before doing – such innocence, he writes, would be "contemptuous of the information with which the European is tempted by temptation" – but to consent, by way of first reading the scriptural word, to a revelation that conditions humanity's very freedom to act as well as to understand. It is to "accept the Torah before one knows it," not through blind belief, or any belief at all, but through accepting responsibility *to* the God who has spoken this Torah *for* the creatures on behalf of which it has been spoken.

For the first postcritical encounter, therefore, the text of scripture stands over-against modernity the way a Midrash says Mount Sinai hung over the heads of the Israelites: "if they accept the Torah, all is well, if not . . ."[5] In Levinas's first collection of commentaries, this is the encounter between the cultural options he calls "Greek" and "Hebrew." In Robert Gibbs's reading, Levinas's "deeply critical view of 'Greek' is obvious" in 'his philosophic work of the late 1950s and 1960s."[6] Here, 'Levinas identifies 'Greek' as the politics of the universal [that] subordinates individuals and their various moral codes under one, anonymous rule"; in place of the 'Greek," "is a universalism that for Levinas is Messianism proper, that is bound to my unique responsibility for the other unique person. 'Hebrew' universalism is intrinsically tied to particularism."[7]

Encounter 2: Modernity Resists the Fiery Voice; Postcritical Inquiry Divides within Itself

In this encounter, it is not Moses' *turning* that summons the reader's attention, but, rather, Moses' challenging dialogue with the voice that emanates from the burning bush (Exod. 3:11–4:15)

Who am I that I should go to Pharaoh? . . .
I will be with you [*ehyeh imach*] . . .
When the Israelites ask me "What is His name [*mah shmo*]?" what shall I say?. . .
Vayomer elohim el moshe, ehyeh-asher-ehyeh. God said, I will be what I will be . . .
Thus shall you say to the Israelites, *ehyeh* sent me to you.
What if they do not believe me? . . .

What is that in your hand? . . . Cast it on the ground . . .
But . . . I am slow of speech! . . .
Who gives man speech? . . .
Make someone else Your agent . . .
The Lord became angry with Moses . . . You shall speak to [Aaron] and put the
words in his mouth.

Against the angelic image of Israel's doing first what God bids at Moont Sinai
and asking about it only later,[8] Moses challenges God's commands *before*
carrying them out. This Moses no longer prefigures postcritical *obedience* before
a text that absorbs the world; his challenges prefigure, instead, recent
postcritical challenges to earlier postcritical doctrines of intratextuality. The
dramatis personae have also changed. Participants in the first encounter were
pioneers in postcritical inquiry who struggled head-on against recalcitrant
colleagues to win even a modest place for intratextual study of the Bible. As
students of the pioneers, participants in the second encounter face the less
combative tasks of enacting the Bible reading and of evaluating how that reading
may actually reshape academic inquiry and public practice. The biblical text
spoke to the pioneers in the voice of their ancestors' God, calling them to return
to the faith of "Abraham, Isaac, and Jacob," *over-against* the practices of their
Westernized contemporaries. This voice commanded them to choose, clearly,
between the Hebrew Bible and Greek philosophy, one or other. Having already
accepted their teachers' choice, the first generation of postcritical students now
asks its primary questions of the biblical text rather than of the West: *who* are
we that we should attempt to refashion Western biblical inquiry? *Whom* shall
we say has sent us to do this? What if our colleagues do not believe us?

In a recent issue of *The Postmodern Jewish Philosophy Network*,[9] Roger
Badham and Ola Sigurdson ask questions that illustrate the struggles of this
"second postcritical encounter." Introducing a section on "Postcritical Christian philosophy," they write:

> Lindbeck . . . appears to insist (with Barth) that the reader submit to the text and
> come without any "forestructures," or "prejudices" that affect the reading. [But,]
> both Heidegger and Gadamer have demonstrated that understanding demands
> these forestructures. . . . No greater example . . . can be offered than the early
> church's Hellenistic readings of the Hebrew texts. Two worlds collided, the
> intratextual world of Christian biblical reading and the intratextual world of
> Platonic, Aristotelian and Stoic philosophies. . . . The transformative synthesis
> of these worlds led to the creation of many of the doctrines which Lindbeck seeks
> to describe as the rules of grammar for [Christian] thinking. . . . While Lindbeck
> calls for us, as readers, to be thoroughly "steeped in" the canonical writings, it
> is naive to think that we read without extrabiblical structures at work, however
> . . . much we attempt to submit ourselves to the text. . . . That is what it means
> to be formed culturally and linguistically in Geertz's broader sense.

Challenges like these interrupt this generation's efforts to repair Western reasoning through Bible reading. If arguing from outside the text, however, these challengers appear to stand nevertheless with Lindbeck, inside a shared circle of postcritical inquiry. In this way, the relationships that typify the second postcritical encounter differ from those of the first encounter. According to the pioneers, modern scholarship took its stance outside the biblical tradition; measure for measure, they therefore took their stance *outside* modernity. The pattern of relationship here was oppositional. But the postcritical students offer their challenges in dialogue with the pioneers, who, in the image of God's dialogue with Moses, respond in kind to them. In place of a polemic of Hebrew versus Greek, we therefore have a dialectic of what we might label the theological and philosophic poles of postcritical inquiry. The exchange might sound like this:

T (postcritical theologian): Our response to modernity draws on Wittgenstein's philosophic argument that any reading has meaning only within some particular "language-game." Yet we do not, as you fear, identify this language-game with the text by itself, but with the practices ("customs," *Gepflogenheiten*, in Wittgenstein's usage) of the community of Bible readers for whom the Bible means what it means: the "plain sense" of scripture, or its life in the customs of the Church.

P (postcritical philosopher): Your model accounts for the way languages are learned when those languages come to the learner ready-made. In this sense you might speak of the Bible's "absorbing the world": meaning that learning the Bible is *just* like learning a language that already exists. Learning the Bible, however, is not just like learning a language that already exists. Learning the Bible requires a degree of linguistic literacy, but that literacy is not *sufficient*. It does not account for the *transformational* dimension of Bible learning, which entails the Bible's implicating the reader in its reading – the reader, that is, in her particularity, which means in her place somewhere outside the Bible as well as in it. As also outside it, she is not asked merely to come to the Bible; the Bible also comes to her: this is the dialogically performative–and thus transformative – dimension of biblical language. This dimension cannot be reduced to the terms of a finite language-game, because it brings any such game into question.

T: That is why I assume that I always come naked to the Bible, as it were, as someone who will learn something he did not know before.

P: You are not speaking of literal language-learning, are you: learning the Hebrew letters and philology?

T: No, I mean that only as a means to learning the plain sense itself.

P: If this plain sense is transformative in the way we both seem to assume, then to be "naked" must mean to have one's prior learning laid bare and questioned. This means that what one brings from outside the Bible will be central to biblical learning: not as the condition of learning, but as what in particular we must *transform* in the process of reading the Biblical text.

T: But the transformation is a consequence of the new learning. First we practice this new reading, then we understand what we misunderstood before.

P: You seem to assume that this initial "reading" does not also *involve* the activity of questioning one's prior assumptions. Isn't this the reason Moses must challenge God before obeying? Like us, Moses is no angel who learns automatically, but a human who learns each command only in the way it challenges the specific beliefs or habits he has at the time.

T: You are speaking of *application* not *acquisition*. I have claimed only that the language of scripture is self-disclosing; you are describing how the person goes about changing in order to receive this self-disclosure.

P: But you are imagining that "the language of scripture" is a *something* already formed prior to this particular act of reception.

T: God spoke first to Moses.

P: But what God said is precisely what Moses questions.

T: And those questions elicit God's self-disclosure.

P: Is God's name a *self*-disclosure, or the way God says something to someone for some reason? What this disclosure means remains in question.

This dialectic between P and T would appear to continue interminably. If so, it has a prototype in the medieval Jewish thinkers' interminable arguments about the meaning of God's response to Moses. Moses Maimonides typifies those who argue that God's name is self-disclosing. Maimonides says that Moses' question was not about a name to be pronounced, but about a proof of who it is who spoke.

> God made known to [Moses] the knowledge . . . through which [the Israelites] would acquire a true notion of the existence of God: this knowledge being: *I am that I am*. This is a name deriving from the verb *to be* [*hayah*], which signifies existence, for *hayah* indicates the notion: he was. . . . The whole secret consists in the repetition in a predicative position of the very word indicative of existence . . . accordingly Scripture makes, as it were, a clear statement that the subject is identical with the predicate. . . . This is what demonstration necessarily leads to: . . . there is a necessarily existent thing that has never been, or ever will be, nonexistent.[10]

God's name thus appears to be the essential attribute of necessary being or

135

substance. Moses Nahmanides's critique of this reading is prototypical of medieval Judaism's contextualist alternative. Nahmanides argues that Maimonides's reading violates the narrative context of our passage, since the Israelites would hardly be of a mind to consider proofs of something they did not already recognize. Moses needed no rational proofs, since

> the very mention of the [divine] Name to [the elders of Israel] [would] be the proof, sign and token on the matter. . . . Instead, . . . Moses asked only by what divine attribute he was being sent: by *El-Shaddai* as known to the patriarchs, or by the higher attribute of Mercy "with which You will perform signs and wonders that will be new phenomena in creation." God told him he was being sent "with the attribute of justice, which is within the attribute of mercy" [as unified in the one Name].[11]

God's name is thus an *act* of naming. Moses has dramatized the Israelites' insecurity; this naming is God's way of offering reassurance: *ehyeh imach,* I will-be with-you. The medieval debate appears, once again, to be interminable.

Self-consciously separating his "Greek" and "Hebrew" writings, Levinas appears to have offered up his entire corpus as an arena for this interminable dialectic. Addressing philosophers, he wrote vast phenomenological studies that, while offered on behalf of "Hebrew" as opposed to "Greek" thinking, exclude biblical or Talmudic text study; addressing Westernized Jewish thinkers, he composed Talmudic commentaries that, while promoting a philosophic reading of the Bible, exclude Western philosophic rhetoric. While characteristic of all Levinas's work, the dialectic appears more rigid in his earlier Talmudic commentaries and more dialogic in the later ones. In between, the dialectic seems to divide even against itself, as if it too could be defined by either its "Greek" or "Hebrew" pole.

A case in point is Levinas's commentary on *TB Menahot* 99b–100a, "Model of the West." Here, the Talmud itself ponders the legitimacy of Greek wisdom.

> R. Johanan said in the name of R. Simeon b. Yohai, Even though a man but reads the *Shema* morning and evening, he has thereby fulfilled the precept of "(*This book of the law*) shall not depart." It is forbidden, however, to say this in the presence of *am ha-aretz* [an uncultured man]. But Raba said, It is a meritorious act [a mitzvah] to say it in the presence of *am ha-aretz.* – Ben Damah the son of R. Ishmael's sister once asked R. Ishmael, May one such as I who have studied the whole of the Torah learn Greek wisdom? He [R. Ishmael] therefore read to him the following verse, *This book of the law shall not depart out of thy mouth, but thou shalt meditate therein day and night* (Joshua 1:8). Go then and find a time that is neither day nor night and learn then Greek wisdom.

Levinas asks:

Does this mean that such an hour does not exist, and that Greek wisdom is being excluded from the Jewish universe?. . . Is it, on the contrary, an allusion to the hours of dusk, neither day nor night, hours of uncertainties where recourse to Greek wisdom would be possible, perhaps even necessary? An opinion to be considered. . . . [Greek wisdom] is excluded only from the hours where Israel is either master of its difficult wisdom, or blindly subjected to its tradition. It would be necessary in the hours of hesitation, capable as it is of reducing multidimensional questions to the disjunction of yes or no. And does not the seduction exercised on a whole epic of Jewish history by this rationalism of yes and no measure the degree of our Jewish uncertainties?[12]

In his earlier commentary on the Israelites who declared "*we do and then we understand*," Levinas found proof-texts for his clear-cut preference for "Hebrew" doing over "Greek" understanding. In this commentary, however, Levinas locates antecedents for the present "hour of hesitation," when "Greek" wisdom may have some value. As Gibbs suggests, "I cannot but think that Levinas had to rediscover a positive "Greek" to justify writing so much in 'Greek'."[13] But what is "Greek"? Collecting references to "Greek wisdom" as opposed to "Greek language" in several Talmudic sources, Levinas concludes that the rabbis flatly reject only the former, while tolerating or in specific contexts even praising the latter.

Greek wisdom . . . is an opening, but it is also the possibility of speaking through signs which are not universally understood and . . . thus have the power to betray. Greek wisdom, in as much it is enveloped by ambiguity in a certain language, is thus a weapon of ruse and domination. In philosophy, it is the fact that it is open to sophistry; in science, that it places itself in the service of strength and politics.[14]

Greek language, or literature, may be an opening to what is noble and beautiful; "Greek wisdom" is the misuse of that language for the sake of deceiving and dominating. When Levinas seeks to "translate" the wisdom of Torah into "Greek," it is into a language that can deliver "Hebrew" wisdom to the West, but not into any competing "wisdom" of the West.

But the logic and ethics of translation remain ambiguous. "Greek" language remains, itself, outside the biblical text. To translate is to speak to a context outside the text. This is a challenge, like Moses', or the postcritical students'; and the response is not yet clear.

Encounter 3: The Text Interrupts Itself; Postcritical
Inquiry Returns to the World . . .

Moses protests his inability to speak publicly; God offers him Aaron: a mouthpiece who speaks through his actions on behalf of a people that, in its various ways, would also be included in these encounters. Postcritical scholars, pioneers and students, have begun to realize that their dialogue belongs to a broader community that has need of both of them. It is Israel's suffering, after all, that prompted God to burn the bush in the first place. The suffering now takes center stage again, prompting God to send Moses off to his work and interrupting any further inquiry into God's identity. The biblical text ushers itself back out into the world, where everything is outside the text and everything is absorbed into the text.

The third encounter is thus the *telos* of a movement from the single modern thinker's turning to text in the first encounter, to the dialectic of contrary postcritical readings in the second, toward a dialogue among distinct yet complementary voices: illustratively the faithful theologian, the challenging philosopher, and now the one who brings the biblical text into the everyday life of the people – the Aaronite priest or, after the Destruction, the rabbi, jurist, or teacher.

The relatively late collection of rabbinic *midrashim*, *Exodus Rabbah*, redacts together the following readings of Exodus 3:

> *When I come and say the God of your fathers has sent me (Ex. 3:13)* Moses thereupon desired to be enlightened with regard to his future course, afraid that they might ask him, "What is His name?". . . R. Abba b. Mammel said: God said to Moses, "You want to know My name? Well, I am called according to My work . . . When I am judging created beings, I am called *elohim* (God). . . . When I suspend judgment for someone's sins, I am called *el shaddai* (Almighty God) . . . and when I am merciful towards my world, I am called *yod-he-vov-he*, which refers to the Attribute of Mercy, as it is said in Ex. 34:6: The Lord, the Lord, God, merciful and gracious. Thus, *EHYEH ASHER EHYEH* in virtue of my deeds."
>
> R. Isaac said: God said to Moses: "Tell them that I am now what I always was and always will be, for this reason the word *ehyeh* is written three times."
>
> Another explanation of *EHYEH ASHER EHYEH* is offered by R Jacob b. Abina in the name of R. Huna of Sepphoris: God said to Moses: "Tell them that I will be with them in this servitude, and in servitude will they always continue, but I will be with them!" Whereupon Moses said to God: "Shall I tell them this? Is the evil of the hour not sufficient?" God replied," *NO, thus shall you say to the Children of Israel: I am has sent me to you.* To you only do I reveal this (suffering), but not to them."[15]

The three readings differ, but as distinct yet complementary voices. Anticipating Nahmanides's concern, and the students' challenge, the third reading says that the name communicates God's particular message of comfort to these people at this moment. Anticipating Maimonides's concern, and the pioneer's faith, the second says that the name reveals God's constancy. Joining one to the other, the first reading says that the name names the fact that God constantly acts in response to the varying needs of the moment and is known and named only by these actions. This "name of names," we may assume, is excluded from this last list, since it is not uttered by any human on the occasion of any of God's acts, but is uttered only by God, to Moses, and only on the occasion of Moses' *interrupting* God's acts. The name of names belongs, therefore, only to the third encounter, as the unfolding narrative of those who have witnessed God's redemptive actions, have interrogated those actions critically, and now trace the meaning of those actions in the obligation of the interrogator, him or herself, to act. The name of names ends the story, accompanying the transformation of listener into agent of action, reader into a knowing doer.

In one of his later lectures, "The Name of God According to a Few Talmudic Texts," Levinas identifies this transformation with "the transcendence of the Name of God," which is also "effacement." The source text, from *TB Shevuoth* 35a,

> teaches us first that in copying the names of God one must on no account efface them. It lists those names that are proper names . . ., among which figure names like *EL* or *Eloha*, which are usually translated, however, as "God." It lists the names that may be effaced, such as the names made up of substantival attributes: the Great, the Mighty . . . the One Abounding in Kindness. . . . In the final section of the extract that concerns us, the text wonders whether all the names of God mentioned in Scripture fall under the rules that have just been expressed. . . . It is obvious that behind the practical problem of "which names may be erased?" the text deals with the question of the dignity of the various names and, ultimately, the very meaning of the relation to God.[16]

Anticipating the telos of his struggle between "Greek" thought and "Hebrew" action, Levinas's commentary also provides a philosophic theology for the third postcritical encounter. I conclude with some commentaries on Levinas's commentary.[17]

> The name of God is always said to be a proper name in the Scriptures. The [generic] word God would be absent from the Hebrew language! . . . The word designating the divinity is precisely the word Name, a generic term in relation to which the different names of God are individuals.[18]

There is no description of God; like the divine fire that surrounds but does not enter into the burning bush, the names accompany God's mundane actions without describing any inner life. "The names express relations not essence."[19] "But revelation by the proper Name is not solely the corollary of the unicity of a being; it leads us further. Perhaps beyond being."[20] The nearer the names get to the divine being, the less they reveal of it: as if the holiness of God – literally "separateness" in the Hebrew, *kedushah* – *confers* absence on those who know God. The point is extended in a commentary in Tractate *TB Temurah* 4a on Deuteronomy 6:13, "you shall fear the Lord your God and serve Him."

> Added to the obligation not to efface is the obligation . . . not to "utter for no purpose". . . . A new gradation is established; this time, among the names not to be effaced. The Tetragrammaton . . . is privileged [by] . . . having never to be pronounced. . . . The name is revealed and is hidden. Whatever comes in the context of meaning must also always be anchoretic or holy.[21]

Receiving the text as theologian, Levinas becomes philosopher/interrogator again in the encounter with this most intimate absence: "But what is the positive meaning of the withdrawal of this God who says only his names and his orders?"[22] As if with relief, he answers, "This withdrawal does not cancel out revelation."

Without making the absent present, the name *performs* an assurance that "I will be with you," *ehyeh*, says God, means *ehyeh imach*. But *through what performance do we receive this assurance?*

> [This withdrawal] is not purely and simply a non-knowledge. It is precisely man's [the human's] obligation toward all other men [humans].[23]

The absence is known *as* an obligation for human action. That is, the absence is itself *imitable in the human's effacing himself or herself for the sake of the human other*.

"The transcendence of God is his actual effacement."[24] This is "the Revelation that becomes ethics," because it reveals how we have been created:

> The human soul is obligated before all commitment. It is not only practical reason, the source of its obligations for others, but responsibility in the forgetting of self.[25]

"A responsibility preceding freedom, . . . preceding intentionality!"[26] Created in the image of this absent God, we live effaced toward the other before we are turned toward ourselves; in fact, we turn toward ourselves as to another for whom we are also responsible. We are thus engaged in an activity that is prior to the very distinction before *doing* (for others) and *hearing* (for ourselves): the activity of being in relation to the other. This relation is our intimacy with an absence that is palpably present. Thus, "the Transcendent . . . cannot enter into relation with the soul without beginning within it; but by doing so it ceases to justify its transcendence."[27] It does not speak of itself, that is, but simply becomes what it is becoming. The text breaks off. "*And Moses . . . went out,*" back to the same human concerns he had before the encounter, but no longer facing them alone.

Other encounters will follow, of course. As postcritical scholars turn more to social, political, and economic affairs, Aaron's encounters may become more suggestive, and Tzipporah's, and David's.

Notes

1 English translation from *Tanakh* (Philadelphia: The Jewish Publication Society, 1985).

2 George Lindbeck, "Toward a Postliberal Theology," in P. Ochs, ed., *The Return to Scripture in Judaism and Christianity* (New York: Paulist Press, 1993), p. 90.

3 Hans Frei, *The Eclipse of Biblical Narrative* (New Haven: Yale University Press, 1974), pp. 18–19; citing Luther, "*Assertio omnium articulorum,*" *Werke* (Weimar: Böhlau, 1883), vol. 7, pp. 96ff.

4 *Nine Talmudic Readings by Emmanuel Levinas*, trans. Annette Aronowicz (Bloomington: Indiana University, 1990), pp. 32–4.

5 *TB Shabbat* 88a cited in ibid.

6 Robert Gibbs, *Correlations in Rosenzweig and Levinas* (Princeton: Princeton University Press, 1992), p. 158.

7 Ibid., pp. 159–60.

8 *Naaseh v'nishmah*: "we will do and then we will understand," Exod. 24:3, as cited in B. Talmud *Shabbat* 88a.

9 Now in its sixth year of electronic publication, *The Postmodern Jewish Philosophy Network* (c/o *pochs@drew.edu*) offers a forum for Jewish and Christian reflection on the postcritical turn to "Hebrew" sources. Of related interest is the journal *Modern Theology*, which, under former editor Stephen Fowl, and current editors Gregory Jones and James Buckley, gives voice regularly to this generation of Christian and Jewish postcritical inquirers. Several recent collections have done the same: for example, Garrett Green's *Scriptural Authority and Narrative Interpretation* (Philadelphia: Fortress, 1987) collects essays that explore the implications of Frei's studies of biblical narrative. Bruce Marshall's *Theology and Dialogue* (Notre Dame: University of Notre Dame, 1990) offers postcritical *Essays in Conversation with George Lindbeck*, examining Lindbeck's dialogical theology in particular. This author's *The Return to Scripture in Judaism and Christianity* (New York: Paulist, 1993) collects *Essays in Postcritical Scriptural Interpretation*, examining hermeneutical strategies shared by Jewish and Christian postcritical thinkers. Steven Kepnes's *Interpreting Judaism in a Postmodern Age* (New York: New York University, 1996) collects essays by Jewish students of postcritical inquiry.

10 Moses Maimonides, *The Guide of the Perplexed* I. 63, trans. Shlomo Pines (Chicago: University of Chicago Press, 1963), pp. 153–6.

11 Moses ben Nahman, Commentary on Exodus 3:13.

12 Emmanuel Levinas, *Beyond the Verse, Talmudic Readings and Lectures*, trans. Gary D. Mole (Bloomington: Indiana University Press, 1994), p. 26.

13 Gibbs, *Correlations*, p. 163.

14 Levinas, *Beyond the Verse*, p. 28.

15 Trans. S.M. Lehrman, in *Midrash Rabbah* III: (London: The Soncino Press, 1961).

16 Levinas, *Beyond the Verse*, pp. 118–19.

17 Taking a rhetorical cue from the commentary form Gibbs' uses in ch. 9 of *Correlations*.

18 Levinas, *Beyond the Verse*, p. 119.

19 Ibid.

20 Ibid., p. 120.

21 Ibid., pp. 121–2.

22 Ibid., p. 123.

23 Ibid.

24 Ibid., p. 125.

25 Ibid.

26 Ibid., p. 127.

27 Ibid.

Exodus 3:
A Theological Interpretation

Terence E. Fretheim

This essay offers a theological interpretation of Exodus 3. I begin with some reflections on the task.

One issue concerns the word "theology," which is sometimes used to specify only post-biblical formulations of a "systematic" or "confessional" sort. Inasmuch as Exodus (or any biblical book) is neither, reflections of a theological nature are often adjudged to be external impositions on the text. "Theology," however, has a more wide-ranging reference; it appropriately describes the content of texts which have to do with God. In such cases, we have to do with a theology that is "in" the text.[1] Rendtorff says it well:

> The Hebrew Bible is itself a theological book. That means that the Bible does not only *become* theological through interpretation by a later-elaborated theology, be it rabbinic or Christian; rather, it is possible and necessary to find the theological ideas and messages of the biblical texts themselves. At the same time, this implies that the authors of the biblical texts themselves should be deemed to be in a certain sense theologians, who had theological ideas and purposes in mind when they spoke or wrote their texts, and even when they assembled the texts into larger units or books.[2]

Hence, biblical studies need not only scholars with historical or literary skills but also those with theological expertise to unfold what the text presents.

From another angle, the word "theology" has been suspect because it is thought to introduce subjective factors into an "objective" enterprise. But, in the last third of the twentieth century in particular, we have come to see that every person who works with the text, from whatever angle, introduces subjective factors, whether admitted or not. Theological analysis is not innately any more subjective than, say, literary study. Even more, given the theology in these texts, every scholar's work with this content will inevitably include theological dimensions. Indeed, some of the most traditional theology in biblical studies is transmitted, often uncritically, by those with no special theological interests.[3]

The theology "in" the text never surfaces on its own or in some "naked" form. The making of meaning, including theological meaning, is a product of the interaction of text and reader. Hence, any restatement or elucidation of a text's theology is a combination of the theology of the text and that of the reader. My theological work in this essay, for example, will inevitably be informed by the fact that I am a Christian and a Lutheran, and read the works of certain systematic theologians but not others. Yet, this is not to claim that any theological interpretation of the text will do; the text cannot mean anything just because it can mean many things. Certain constraining factors are at work, including the text itself, historical background information, and the communities within which the text and readers with their interpretations function.

Exodus 3 is a classic text. It has had a major place, not only in Exodus commentary[4] but in Old Testament studies more generally. One need only cite the story of the burning bush, the commissioning of Moses, the divine agenda regarding the oppressed Israelites, and the revelation of the divine name, Yahweh. More specifically, chapter 3 cannot be separated out from the continuation of the God–Moses dialogue in 4:1–17, the assertions regarding the divine name in 6:2–3, and the restatement of Moses' commission in 6:1–13 and 6:28–7:7. Indeed, chapter 3 and its pervasive theological interests undergird the rest of the book of Exodus.[5]

Most pointedly, Exodus 3 is integral to a proper theological interpretation of the deliverance from Egypt. In speaking about God's revelation to Israel, scholars have commonly centered on the exodus event itself: Israel drew inferences from what happened regarding, say, the nature of God. This may be so, but from the perspective of the text as it presently stands, Exodus 3 insists on a more comprehensive formulation. Israel was able to see something more in the event because of God's prior word to Moses. That is, God gave Moses the interpretative clue regarding the meaning of that future event: the deliverance of Israel from Egypt is on God's agenda. While participation in the event no doubt enabled a fuller development of that meaning, the basic revelatory event was God's encounter with Moses in chapter 3. The key revelation was thus more a private and internal matter than a public and external one; it was more a personal word from God than a speechless deed. This view enhances the role of Moses as a recipient of divine revelation and understands his various words and deeds as richly informed by a direct divine encounter.

Exodus 3 is a preeminent theological text because God plays such a prominent role therein. We lay out the balance of this essay primarily in terms of its divine speech and action.

1 God Appears to Moses

Exodus 3 initially follows the pattern of a prophetic call narrative (cf. Jer. 1:4–9), with these elements: divine appearance (3:1–4a); introductory word (3:4b–9); divine commission (3:10); Moses' objection (3:11); divine reassurance (3:12a); sign (3:12b). The continuing conversation between God and Moses expands upon this basic form (3:13–4:17). Like the prophets, Moses is called to be a messenger of the word of God (Deut. 18:15; 34:10).

God takes the initiative in calling Moses (vv. 1–6). Moses does not seek the encounter, and the place has no religious connections at this point. The divine strategy in this initiative is worth remarking. God does not coerce Moses or frighten him with a display of divine power and glory. Rather, God sets up an unusual situation that piques Moses' curiosity, seeking to draw him into an encounter. God's strategy is effective; Moses turns aside to see this bush that burns but is not consumed. Only when God sees (v. 4) that Moses has moved to satisfy his curiosity does God call to him.

This divine move may betray God's knowledge of Moses and what might attract him. This would relate well to the sketches of Moses in 2:11–22. In these vignettes Moses exhibits a sense of justice that transcends boundaries of nationality, gender, and kinship. He demonstrates a courage and a concern for life, especially the life of the weaker members of the society, and an intolerance for abuse inflicted by the strong. These sympathies for those less fortunate and his risky response on their behalf anticipates God's own deeds (14:13, 30; 15:1–2) and words (22:21–7). The Moses that God chooses is a known entity, a person with gifts well suited for the kind of activity that God has in mind. The giftedness that Moses brings to this moment, a testimony to the creative work of God in his life up to this point, is not negated (see 14:31).

The bush functions as an attention-getting device, but its importance moves at several levels. The word for bush (*seneh*) is a verbal link to Mount Sinai and, with the fire, anticipates God's appearance there to Moses "in fire" (19:18; Deut. 4:12). That 'the angel of Yahweh" appears "in" a flame of fire and speaks as God (vv. 2, 4) anticipates God's leading Israel "in" a pillar of fire (13:21), speaking "in" a cloud (19:5; 34:5; cf. Lev. 16:2), and delivering them at the sea in the form of an "angel" "in" a pillar of cloud and fire (cf. 14:19 with 14:24). The angel/messenger of Yahweh is a way of speaking of God's appearing in human form (see Gen. 18:1–2, 16; 19:1). The flame of fire is not the form of God's self-manifestation but the veil or envelope for the human form of the divine appearance (cf. The combination of fire and human form

145

in Ezek. 1:26–8). The narrator, having apprised the reader that the angel who appears "from a bush" (v. 2) is Yahweh who speaks "from the bush" (v. 4; cf. 14:19, 24), has God inform Moses that this is the God of his ancestors (v. 6). Moses does not have an ecstatic vision here; nor is it simply an inward sight. As with other theophanies, God uses created realities, including the human form, as vehicles for "clothing" the divine.[6] To use more modern language: the finite is capable of the infinite.

In some fashion, one must speak of a God who assumes human form in order to encounter Moses. The word is spoken by one who is embodied in the world; the word has both oral and visible/tangible components. It is often claimed that the word spoken is the focus of the theophany. Probably so, but the sight is not simply an accessory, the human form is not incidental. Both word and appearance are important for Moses (words for seeing occur ten times in 3:1–9). When God asks Moses to report his encounter with God to the elders of Israel (3:16), it is deemed important to say not only that God spoke, but that God appeared. Appearance in human form makes a difference to words; it renders the personal element in the divine address more apparent and makes for a greater intensity and directness in the words spoken, with greater potential effectiveness. Moreover, such "visible words" affirm that the word of God is not simply for minds and spirits. Moses' response was not simply to believe or to speak; Moses is called to act, to reembody the word in the world.

The appearance of God makes the ground holy (3:5), both because of the holiness of the one who appears (though this language is not explicitly used for God) and the purpose for which this place is chosen. No holiness inheres in the place itself; it becomes holy by virtue of being set part for special use by God, namely, the events of Sinai/Horeb in chapters 19–24. These events, though communal, are specifically anticipated in the "come no closer" (19:12–24) and in the sign given Moses in 3:12. As noted below, such holiness does not reduce Moses to passivity or timidity or fear.

As noted, appearance alone is insufficient for the divine purpose; the word from God is crucial for Moses. The word spoken names the one speaking, names the situation being addressed, makes articulate the divine agenda in this situation, commissions Moses as a co-deliverer of the Israelites, reassures Moses with a promise of presence, and sketches a scenario for the future. We will consider several components of the divine word.

2 God Commissions Moses to a Task and Interacts with Him

Characteristic of chapter 3, indeed much of the narrative through 7:7, is a continuing dialogue between God and Moses (cf. chapters 32–4; Num. 11–16).

Over the course of this conversation Moses voices repeated objections to the divine commission, eight in all (3:11, 13; 4:1, 10, 13; 5:22–3; 6:12, 30). While prophetic (and other) figures also raise objections to divine commissions (cf. Gideon in Judg. 6:13–15), the extent of Moses' interaction is unparalleled. This dialogue is theologically significant.

Moses' recognition of holiness (3:6) does not render him mute or passive in the presence of God. Moreover, the word of the holy God now spoken (vv. 7–10) bespeaks not distance but closeness. Moses' exchange with God moves from worshipful deference to animated dialogue. God's holiness is of such a character that it invites rather than repels human response.[7] Disagreement, argument, and even challenge play an important role. God does not demand a self-effacing Moses but draws him out and works with him. The oft-noted speech disability of Moses adds an ironic twist to this point. It is not only a human being who challenges God; an inarticulate one does so, and holds his own!

Indeed, it is Moses' persistence that occasions a greater fullness in the divine revelation. Human questions find an openness in God that leads to fuller knowledge. Simple deference in the presence of God would have closed down the revelatory possibilities. God thus reveals himself, not simply at the divine initiative, but in interaction with a questioning human party. Even more, God treats the dialogue with integrity and honors Moses' insights as important ingredients for the shaping of the task that lies ahead. God has so entered into relationship with him that God is not the only one who has something important to say. God will move with Moses, even adapting original divine plans in view of Moses' considerations (the choice of Aaron in 4:10–17). In other words, human response can contribute in a genuine way to the shaping of the future of both God and Israel.[8]

From another perspective, this dialogue bears witness to God's initial lack of success in persuading Moses to take up his calling. God's persuasive powers are brought to bear on Moses and he remains unconvinced for some time. God's efforts do not meet with instant success; God's will is resistible. Hence, in 4:10–17, in the face of Moses' resistance, God resorts to Plan B, calling Aaron to be Moses' voice. God is not delighted with this option; in fact, God is angry (4:14). But God goes with what is possible; using Aaron is now the best option available to God. God always aims for the best in every situation, but God often has to work with options that are less than the best (witness Aaron's failure in chapter 32). God does not perfect people before deciding to work in and through them, and hence one must not necessarily confer a fully positive value on the results.[9]

This dialogue reveals that God's way into the future is not dictated solely by the divine word and will (cf. 32:9–14). God places this commission into the hands of Moses to do with what he will. That is for God a risky venture, fraught with negative possibilities. God will now have to work in and through Moses' frailties as well as his strengths. This will mean something less than what would have been possible had God acted alone; God is not in total control of the ensuing events.

3 The Situation Being Addressed and God's Response to It

Verses 7–10, God's first words in Exodus, repeat the essence of the narrator's report about God's activity in 2:23–5. As such, these words are programmatic; they set all that follows into motion and reveal the kind of God who acts.

God takes the initiative calling Moses, but this divine move was provoked by the cries of oppressed Israelites (2:23).[10] For the narrator, the divine actions of hearing, remembering, seeing, and knowing (2:24–5) have been prompted by the voices of those who are not God. The cries have given God a new point of view regarding the situation; human groaning moves God to act. God acknowledges this to be so, repeating three of these verbs in 3:7 (two in 6:5). Though it is not stated that Israel's cries were directed to God, God is responsive nevertheless. At the same time, it is important to note that this divine response is grounded in a prior divine initiative. God responds to these cries in view of the covenant with the Israelites' ancestors (2:24; 6:5; Gen. 17:4–8), wherein God has committed the divine self to be their God. God is now bound to so respond if God would be faithful to the covenant. God's entering into the covenant entails a limitation regarding the divine options – some loss of freedom – with respect to Abraham's descendants. God has exercised freedom in making the covenant in the first place, but thereafter God's freedom is truly limited by those promises. God will be faithful to God's own promises.

This pattern of distress, lament, and divine word/deed is characteristic of many Old Testament texts (e.g. lament psalms). Typical of this structure is that God's deeds are not undertaken in independence from the specifics of the human situation. The acts of God on Israel's behalf are not isolated from human experience. Particular needs have been expressed to which God responds quite directly. Hence, God does not respond to oppression of a socio–political sort by ignoring these realities in the shape which Israel's salvation takes. God's saving acts directly respond to expressed creaturely need.

What does it mean that God hears, sees, and knows (3:7–10)? Basically, such verbs mean that God receives the world into the divine self. This divine experience of the world is not superficial; God takes it in, in as real a way as people who hear and see and know. Actually, in a way that is more real, for God takes it *all* in (see Jer. 32:19). This is emphasized by using the verb "to see" with the infinitive absolute in 3:7 (God *truly* sees) and repeating the verb in 3:9. Moreover, these words are marked by a sixfold use of the first person singular, making it sharply clear that this word is deeply personal, coming directly from God's own heart and will. That verses 7–10 open and close with the phrase "my people" reinforces the personal dimensions of God's relationship with Israel.

The use of the object "sufferings" with the verb "know" in 3:7 (unlike 2:25) reflects the intensity of this divine experience of the world. This verb, as often in the Old Testament (cf. its use for sexual intercourse), does not focus on the reception of information (which, presumably, God already has). To know is to so share an experience with another that the other's experience can be called one's own. Such a phrase speaks of God entering into Israel's sufferings at a deeply personal level, feeling within the divine self what Israel is having to endure. This "inside knowledge" is reinforced by repeated references to Israel's cries and sufferings, including a fivefold reference to Egypt and its taskmasters. God has here chosen not to remain removed and secure in some heavenly abode, untouched by human sorrows. God is not portrayed as a typical monarch dealing with the issue through subordinates. Unlike Pharaoh, whose heart is hardened, Israel's God is not an unmoved mover.[11]

One might conclude from this language that the God of the text is not the immutable God of classical theism. God is truly affected by the divine experience of the world; indeed, in a subsequent text the book of Exodus will not back away from using the language of change for God (see 32:14). But, to be true to the texts, such language must be qualified by the above-noted testimony to divine faithfulness to promises made. To bring these themes together, one might speak of a God who is both mutable and immutable; God will change in interaction with the world in order to remain faithful to promises and steadfast in love. Moreover, while God suffers with the people, God is not thereby rendered powerless in the face of adversity. However much God's work may be complicated by such realities, the actual situation does not define what is possible for God. God is never stymied or immobilized by the engagement with the world. God does find a way to move into Israel's situation in such a way that the people are delivered from oppression.

4 God's Promise of Presence

In response to Moses' expression of inadequacy ("Who am I?"), God reassures him with a promise of divine presence: "I will be with you" (v. 12). Donald Gowan gathers the import of this common phrase: it is not a statement of general divine presence among the people, but a particular promise for one facing risk and danger, pledging that God will be at his side through thick and thin.[12] Indeed, of the eight divine responses to Moses' objections, this is the force of most of them. Moses' "I" will be accompanied by the divine "I"; his

"Who am I?" will be undergirded by the God who is certain of the divine identity, a sign of which is the giving of the personal name.

But such a promise is necessary not only for Moses' sake, but also for the sake of the word spoken. The God who gives the word does not leave the word to do its own work. Word of God and presence of God must remain together; in fact, word depends finally on presence. The word of God does not assume an autonomous existence and go forth to do its work independent of the God who speaks it.[13] If the word is to accomplish the divinely intended aim, God must continually be at work in the world, matching words with deeds. God does not leave a word and retreat or lie back and simply watch it work. The power of the word depends finally on God's ongoing work on its behalf (see Isa. 48:3). And so, in the chapters to come, God will accompany this word of Israel's deliverance with specific activity at every step along the way.

But, while God continues to work on behalf of the word, it is now not only in God's hands. The word is now in the world. It has been received by human beings who can join God in working on its behalf or can misuse the word and twist it toward ends not consonant with God's purposes (one thinks of 32:1–6). After much dialogue, divine anger at his reluctance (4:14), and a false start with Pharaoh (5:1–23), Moses becomes co-participant with God on behalf of the word. Moses joins God in bringing Israel out of Egypt (14:31), just as God's commission had stipulated (3:10).

The latter text (3:10) affords an excellent example of how source-critical decisions are informed by theological considerations. Verses 7–8 and 9–10 are commonly considered to be a composite of two sources, reflecting different perspectives. But these verses are coherent; indeed they function together as a proper theological assessment of the divinely announced exodus. Neither God (v. 8) nor Moses (v. 10) acts alone in bringing Israel out of Egypt. God acts in and through the agency of Moses (as well as various non-human agents). The activity of both is crucial for what is to happen (as 14:31 recognizes). God takes the initiative, calls Moses, and sets the agenda, but God enlists Moses as an instrument through whom to work toward this objective. God chooses to be dependent on that which is not God. The emphasis in v. 9 on the crux of the matter, namely, God's seeing of the oppression of Israel, is repeated from verse 7 as an introduction to the specific charge to Moses. Because I, God, have seen, you, Moses are sent to do this task. God's seeing leads directly to Moses' sending; but it was important for Moses to see as well.

5 The Revelation of the Divine Name

God initially identifies himself in 3:6, "I am the God of your [Moses'] father, the God of Abraham, the God of Isaac, and the God of Jacob." God thereby ties into the faith of Moses' own family, demonstrating a continuity *in God* between Moses and his ancestors. This is God's story as well as that of Moses, and the promising part of that story now begins to take the shape of fulfillment in the word to Moses (see 2:24). This identification will also occur in the narrative that follows, probably to stress the continuity of the divine promise with these events (3:15–16; 4:5; 6:3–8).

The narrator identifies this God with Yahweh by using the not-yet-revealed name in 3:2, 4, 7 (the first usage in Exodus). This clarifies for the reader that the name about to be revealed is to be identified with the God of Moses' own family. The same link is made to Moses himself in 3:15–16. In 6:2–3, God seems to claim that God had not made himself known by the name Yahweh to Moses' ancestors. But, if so, how is one to explain its use in Genesis (e.g. 15:2)? Scholars have often concluded that this is evidence for separate sources; one source (J) used Yahweh from Genesis 2:4 on; the other sources (E in 3:14–15; P in 6:2–3) believed that this name was first revealed to Moses. While this may be historically accurate (though uncertainties abound; Yahweh may be an old name with no special distinctiveness), the present composite text makes another, theological claim: Yahweh is the same God who was active among the ancestors though known by another name.[14]

Moses continues the conversation with a question. His Who am I? becomes a Who are you? Moses' question is effective; it draws forth God's own name from God. God responds to what Moses believes he needs to know in order to do what he is called to do. Both God and Moses recognize that God is not demystified through further understanding. Indeed, the more one understands God, the more mysterious God becomes. God is the supreme exemplification of the old adage: the more you know, the more you know you don't know.

Why is not the name revealed in 3:6 sufficient for Moses? The assumption seems to be that, if Moses has been commissioned to bring the people out of Egypt, Moses should have a divine name commensurate with this new development in *God's* relationship with Israel. This name is to be given to the people (3:15).

Exodus 3:14 is one of the most puzzled-over verses in the Hebrew Bible.[15] The name given, *'ehyeh 'aser 'ehyeh*, consists of the repeated verb "to be" (*hāyāh*) in the first person singular plus the relative particle (actually, Yahweh is a third person form). The most common translation is that given in the NRSV, "I AM WHO I AM." Other translations include: "I will be what [who] I will be'; "I will cause to be what I will cause to be"; "I will be who I am/ I am who I will be." The last-noted seems to be the best option, in essence: I will be God for you. The force is not simply that God is or that God is present, but will be faithfully God for them.

The use of the same verbal form in 3:12; 4:12, 15 (cf. 6:7; 29:45) reinforces this. Yahweh will be God with and for the people at all times and places. Yahweh can be counted on to be who God is; Yahweh will be faithful to self and this entails faithfulness to promises. This name now gives a special shape to Israel's story, and the story as it proceeds will give further texture to the name. At the same time, there are now new stakes in this for God; God has to live up to the name.[16]

Some scholars suggest that God's response is a refusal to give the name, out of a belief that knowing the name gives some control over the one named. Yet, that the name Yahweh is immediately used in apposition to the God of your fathers (vv. 15–16), and that it is used as a personal name throughout the Old Testament, suggests a more positive meaning. There is a lack of final definition in the name Yahweh, of course. But, as with all names, this is simply to recognize the limits of drawing inferences from a name regarding the nature of the one who bears it. Names are never fully revealing of nature; to know the divine name does not demystify God.

What does this divine name-giving mean for Israel? Though not fully revealing, the name gives some insight into God; the giving of the name is a revelatory act. Naming entails distinctiveness; it sets the one named off from others who have names, including gods. Even more, to link this name to the ancestral God ties this God to a certain history (see above). That this is to be God's name for "all generations" speaks of a divine commitment to participate in the history of the people who use this name. Moreover, giving the name entails a certain kind of relationship. A relationship without a name would mean some distance; naming the name entails closeness, it makes true encounter and communication possible. There now can be genuine address on the part of both parties, say, in prayer. But this will mean vulnerability for God. In becoming so available to Israel, God is to some degree at the disposal of those who can name the name. God's name can be misused and abused (see Exod. 20:7; 23:13) as well as honored.

Finally, it might be noted that Israel is not to keep this name for itself. Moses is to speak in the name of this God (5:23). The driving force of God's activity in Exodus is captured in 9:16, "that my name may be declared through all the earth." The call of Moses is in the service of this divine mission.

6 God's Promised Future for Israel

Name moves to promise (3:17, detailed in vv. 18–22). We have noted above that the ancestral promises undergird this chapter (2:24; 6:3–8). It is *from within* those promises that God makes this promise to deliver Israel, that is, this promise is in the service of the overarching ancestral promises. God "declares" the promise that Moses is to repeat to the people. Moses is to be the bearer of new possibilities in what would appear to be an impossible situation (carried out in 4:30–31). God promises Israel a future free of oppression; God will deliver Israel from the Egyptians.

At the same time, God will not leave the people destitute; they will gain favor in the eyes of the Egyptians and will collect valuables on their way out of the land, a kind of just reward for their labor. Even more, God will not leave the Israelites in a halfway house, with no place to call their own. God will give Israel a land, but not just any land; God will give Israel a "good and broad land, a land flowing with milk and honey," capable of supporting all the people mentioned (3:8, 17). These are the gifts of God's good creation to the newly redeemed people. God's historical work of redemption is not an end in itself; its objective is a new creation.[17]

Notes

1 On this formulation, see Terence Fretheim, *Exodus* (Louisville: John Knox, 1991), pp. 10–12; see also Donald Gowan, *Theology in Exodus: Biblical Theology in the Form of a Commentary* (Louisville: John Knox, 1994), pp. ix–xviii.

2 Rolf Rendtorff, *Canon and Theology: Overtures to an Old Testament Theology* (Minneapolis: Fortress, 1993), pp. 40–1.

3 An example would be Meir Sternberg, *The Poetics of Biblical Narrative* (Bloomington: Indiana University Press, 1985). One instance may be cited (p. 101): the Bible "not only assumes or deploys but also inculcates a model of reality where God exercises absolute sway on the universe (nature, culture, history) in conspicuous isolation and transcendence." This is certainly not the God of Exodus 3.

4 For example, some 40 percent of Gowan's book (fn. 1) is devoted to Exodus 3–4. In comparing Gowan's theological treatment of these chapters with my own, I am struck with how little overlap there is, even when addressing the same topic. This may be rooted in confessional issues. In his imaging of God, images of sovereignty are dominant (e.g., the irresistibility of the divine will, p. 126) and his formulations have a greater continuity with traditional God-talk. For me, images of sovereignty are qualified by images of affectability and a genuine divine engagement with the world. This perspective gives more attention to images of God that have been neglected in the tradition. On this issue, see my "Suffering God and Sovereign God in Exodus," *Horizons in Biblical Theology* 11 (1989): 31–56.

5 The following interpretation follows the reflections in my *Exodus*, esp. pp. 51–67.

6 For further texts and argumentation, see Fretheim, *The Suffering of God* (Minneapolis: Fortress, 1984), pp. 93–7.

7 This dimension of the text (and its sense of divine holiness) is neglected in D. Gowan's extensive chapter on the numinous (*Theology in Exodus*, pp. 25–53); his fascination with this theme is heavily dependent on the categories of Rudolph Otto's *The Idea of the Holy*, and deals in a selective way with Old Testament theophanies. See the distinction drawn

between theophanies of God as warrior and God as bearer of the word in J. Jeremias, "Theophany in the Old Testament," *IDBSup* (Nashville: Abingdon, 1976), s.v.

8 I find this statement of M. Greenberg very helpful: "Those who are brought close to God retain their integrity even in moments of closest contact. They are not merely passive recipients, but active, even opposing respondents. There is true address and response, genuine give and take. The human partner has a way in shaping the direction and outcome of events." *Understanding Exodus* (New York: Behrman House, 1969), p. 94. For a development of this understanding of the God–Israel relationship with reference to prayer, see S. Balentine, *Prayer in the Hebrew Bible: The Drama of the Divine–Human Dialogue* (Minneapolis: Fortress, 1993).

9 On the implications for a claim that God's knowledge of the future is not absolute, see the discussion of divine foreknowledge in Fretheim, *The Suffering of God*, pp. 45–59.

10 See W. Brueggemann, "The Book of Exodus," *The New Interpreter's Bible* (Nashville: Abingdon, 1994), p. 707.

11 On issues of divine affectibility, see Fretheim, *The Suffering of God*, esp. pp. 45–59, 107–48.

12 Gowan, *Theology in Exodus*, pp. 54–75.

13 See Anthony Thiselton, "The Supposed Power of Words in the Biblical Writings," *JTS* 25 (1974): 283–99.

14 See R. W. L. Moberly, *The Old Testament of the Old Testament: Patriarchal Narratives and Mosaic Yahwism* (Minneapolis: Fortress, 1992).

15 For a thorough discussion of the issues, see B. S. Childs, *The Book of Exodus: a Critical, Theological Commentary* (Philadelphia: Westminster, 1974), pp. 60–70.

16 See J. G. Janzen, "What's in a Name? 'Yahweh' in Exodus 3 and the Wider Biblical Context," *Interpretation* 33 (1979): 235.

17 For this theme in Exodus, see T. Fretheim, "The Reclamation of Creation: Redemption and Law in Exodus," *Interpretation* 45 (1991): 354–65.

Exodus 3: Summons to Holy Transformation

Walter Brueggemann

Exodus 3 is the decisive moment in which the narrative of Israel's revolutionary existence begins. It enacts a beginning for which we (and the Israelites) were ill-prepared. This dramatic moment of beginning, however, is not without antecedent or context. We may suggest, as our starting point, that the eruption which here begins Israel is made possible by the convergence of two lines of narrative development which heretofore had no contact with each other.

I

The first of these antecedent narratives is the history of Yahweh, the God of Israel, in the book of Genesis. The narrators and liturgists in the book of Genesis offer no explanation for the character Yahweh. This God is simply there at the outset, to dominate the narrative which is given us in two parts. The first part is the tale of creation in Genesis 1:1–2:4a, with its unfolding in Genesis 2:4b–11:32. At the beginning of that tale, God has decreed to the first human beings, "Be fruitful and multiply" (1:28).[1] God had offered permission to the human family to reproduce and flourish, and God had provided the generative power to enable this to happen. God had invested creation with the force of generativity, a force that continued with the family of Abraham and Sarah, who are to be blessed with many descendants (15:5; 22:17; 32:12). Abraham and his family emerge as the carriers of the blessing given in Genesis 1.

The second line of narrative development takes place in the heart of the

Egyptian empire. For a variety of political, bureaucratic, and technological reasons, Egypt had established a monopoly of food supplies, in an environment much vexed with famine (cf. Gen. 12:10–20). Our particular interest in this situation of famine and food begins in Genesis 47. Joseph, great grandson of Abraham, mostly now remote from that family of promise, had learned well the lessons of bureaucratic finesse. He had advanced through the layers of imperial power and intrigue, until he was second only to Pharaoh (Gen. 41:40). In his eager service to the Crown, he had managed to confiscate all the available food and brought it under royal administration, to be used as a political tool (41:46–9). The outcome was the creation of a servile workforce for the empire (Gen. 47:13–26). Slavery, we are told, came about as a response to famine, midst the bureaucratic cunning of the empire.

The upshot of these two stories, one of blessing and the other of food monopoly and slavery, is visible in Exodus 1–2. The story of the God who decreed "be fruitful and multiply" is hidden here and quite modest. We are told only that Israel had indeed "multiplied and grew exceedingly strong" (Exod. 1:7). Thus the initial decree of Genesis 1:28 is operative, even in this bondaged community. The midwives, Shiprah and Puah (Exod. 1:15), found that the "Hebrew women are not like the Egyptian women; for they are vigorous" (1:19), so that the people Israel "multiplied and became very strong" (1:20). The discerning listener will notice that the story of powerful blessing persists even in this unlikely place, and even in this surreptitious manner.

But the second tale, from Genesis 47, the tale of wretchedness, is underway even more powerfully among these slaves. There was a "new king" (1:8) who was ruthless and gave them hard service (1:13–14), until he had reduced them to helplessness and hopelessness. The Hebrews became simply fatigued cogs in the imperial production machinery. Into this helpless, hopeless community (which knew nothing of the book of Genesis) came this uncredentialed Moses.[2] He was born illegally in hiding, in order to evade the murderous decree of the king (2:2), and he lived afloat the river Nile, the very river the obsessed Pharaoh had turned into a channel of death (1:22). This nobody of a Moses, in his early adulthood, one day acted precipitately in his rage and passion, and killed an abusive Egyptian taskmaster (2:11–12). And then he fled for his life, a homeless fugitive from the empire (2:13–15).

The context presents us two tales, each of which features its lead character. There is the tale of blessing, featuring Yahweh, who causes birth and well-being, who creates new futures where none seemed possible. And there is the tale of bondaged wretchedness, whose main character is Moses, a desperate man, passionate, but now *persona non grata* in the empire. The remarkable assumption in Exodus 1–2 is that these two stories proceed close to each other, but without contact or mutual acknowledgement. The community in Egypt knows nothing of Genesis or the God of blessing. The Lord of blessing as yet pays no heed to that abused community of slaves. It is possible for the two stories to exist apart from each other: God does not notice the wretchedness, and Israel, with Moses, is fully enwrapped in its trouble.

We arrive at an emergency in the slave narrative in Exodus 2:23–5. The brutalizing Pharaoh dies, and things become unglued. Long-silenced slaves groan out loud. Hopeless people find risky voice. They cry in their anguish. They cry to no one in particular. They cry out, addressing no one, for they know none to address, not having read the book of Genesis. Oddly, inexplicably, their cry of wretchedness "rose up to God." We do not know why. We are not told. In that moment, in any case, the two narratives make contact with each other. The cry of wretchedness makes contact with the God of new futures. The slaves had to take the initiative in making this contact possible. But the God of Genesis promptly evidences a peculiar receptivity to hurt: "God heard, God remembered [Genesis], God looked, God took notice." It takes these two stories, and the two main characters, together to generate the text we now take up in Exodus 3.

II

It is as though these two narratives, one of futuring and one of wretchedness, and their two central characters, Yahweh and Moses, had been waiting for this moment of contact. Our text begins with a meeting (vv. 1–6). It is a meeting completely inexplicable, which our narrative takes no pains to justify. Scholars call this narrative report a "theophany," but the term helps very little.[3] The narrative tells of a meeting that is direct, momentous, defining, inscrutable. It is the sort of meeting that happens only rarely in the Bible, or anywhere else. We are told of a direct, voice-to-voice encounter between the Lord of blessing and the chief of wretchedness. Moses is sheep-herding. The scene is not idyllic or peaceable. Moses is a fugitive. He is a member of this community of groaning.

But he is "visited." He is confronted by an awesomeness from which he does not shrink. He is addressed, called by name. The speaker is not yet "the angel." It is "the Lord" who speaks directly to Moses, in a sovereign way, calling his name twice (v. 4). The address has the same cadence with which Abraham is addressed in his testing (Gen. 22:11), with which the boy Samuel was pressed into dangerous service in the midst of a revolution (1 Sam. 3:10). Moses must answer, and he does so with great deference.

The thrust of the meeting is in the hands of Yahweh. Moses only presents himself, and is acted upon. This is not a meeting between equals. The meeting is not, first of all, for planning or promising. Its first function is to reposition Moses into the story of Yahweh, to relocate the community of the wretched into God's tale of blessing. The meeting permits the lordly voice of Yahweh

157

two utterances. First, there is a warning to Moses (v. 5). Face to face these two are not equals. Yahweh yields nothing to Moses, but retains all the initiative. Second, Yehweh intrudes the buoyant book of Genesis into the misery of the book of Exodus (v. 6). The God now present to Moses and to the slave community is the one who has made awesome promises to Abraham and Sarah, who has visited barren women with children, who has guarded Jacob in his devious behavior, and who has kept Joseph in his risky ascent to power. A new character is present in the slave tale for the first time, and that new character decisively alters the slave tale. That is all that happens in the meeting proper, in verses 1–6. The lead characters now know each other and must come to terms with each other. The tale of Moses and slaves is now decisively transformed, and will never again be the same. For the groans heard are different groans, now marked by hope. And need is different now, for it has been noticed. Israel, behind and before, now will live its future in the presence of and at the behest of the God who gives blessings and makes promises.

III

Formally, the encounter at the bush continues through 4:17, until "Moses went back to his father-in-law" (4:18). The narrative, however, pays no more attention to the mood or circumstance of the genre of theophany, and moves on promptly to other genres. The narrative, moreover, pays no attention to the locus of the bush. As is characteristic in Israel, the encounter eventuates in a speech, and it is the speech which now commands our attention (vv. 7–9). These verses are a self-pronouncement of Yahweh, who now picks up on the exodus deliverance themes signalled in 2:24–5. It is as though the narrative leaps over 3:1–6, except that we now know that the speaker of the exodus assurances is the God of the ancestors in the book of Genesis. In this speech, Yahweh's self-announcement characterizes Yahweh in terms of attentiveness to the slave community.

In 2:24–5, four verbs are used to characterize the ways in which Yahweh is attentive to the slaves: hear, remember, see, know. In 3:7, three of these verbs – see, hear, know – are repeated. The fourth verb, "remember," has dropped out, and the Genesis connection is not reiterated. These three repeated verbs, however, are intensified in two ways. First, the verb "see" is stated with an infinitive absolute, thus, "I have really seen." Second, the objects of the verbs are more concrete: "See the affliction of *my people*, hear their cry *on account of their task masters*, and know *their sufferings*." The actual situation of wretchedness had been mentioned in 2:24, but now it is much more fully acknowledged. And, almost in passing, Yahweh has referred to this needy people as "my people," thus entering into or acknowledging a solidarity which from now on is definitional for both parties. God has fully engaged the wretchedness of Moses and of his community.

This recital of three verbs in verse 7 now advances with two verbs in v. 8 which have no counterpart in 2:24–5, and which portray Yahweh as prepared to act decisively upon what has now been acknowledged as Israel's untenable circumstance: "I will come down to deliver." The God of all creation now enters into the slave camp, submits to their circumstance. The purpose is to rescue (*nṣl*) the slave community, and to oppose their adversary, "the Egyptians," the quintessential oppressor. Yahweh commits Yahweh's very self in a struggle for the future of Israel.

The verb "come down" (*yrd*) (to deliver) is matched by a second verb, "to cause to come up" (*lh*) to bring up) to an alternative land. It is evident, as von Rad had seen most clearly, that the core story of Israel revolves around these two actions, these two verbs and their cognates.[4] Israel's memory and identity are shaped by "going out" and "coming in," from bondage to well-being, all accomplished by the power and resolve of Yahweh, who will do for Israel what Israel cannot do for itself.

In this promise of God stated in these two verbs, it is striking that the exodus verb is handled tersely, whereas the verb pertaining to the new land receives a relatively long exposition. The land to which Israel is to be delivered is characterized three times in three different ways: (1) it is a good and broad land; (2) it flows with milk and honey; and (3) it is already occupied by the stereotypical seven nations, a recognition that forecasts violence at the core of Israel's life and self-understanding. The promise is overloaded with land. In this utterance, Yahweh has in purview all that is to follow for Israel. Yahweh resolves a complete reversal of the fortunes of the slave community. The tale is aimed at land, which assured the political materiality of this community, and which anticipates peaceable well-being as its outcome. The deliverance is not an isolated act; it is a starting point for a tale which culminates in a rightly ordered land, ordered by the God who will override the nations, their practices, and their gods. There is something enormously reassuring and something provocatively totalitarian in this primal utterance of the new tale of the slaves.

Verse 9, the culmination of this speech of self-disclosure on the part of Yahweh, is something of a reprise, looking back to 2:24–5 and 3:7. This defining acknowledgement juxtaposes Israel and Egypt, and defines their relation, an Israelite *cry* and Egyptian *oppression*. Yahweh inserts Yahweh's own self into this drama of Israelite and Egyptian, into the transaction of cry and oppression. There is nothing in this self-assertion of Yahweh that is escapist or spiritualizing. This lordly utterance is now no longer hidden in a bush, but is inserted into public affairs with high stakes and hurting people.

In this utterance, the story of Israel's life and future is shaped by the God who will "deliver." And the life of Yahweh is recharacterized by this resolve.

This text does not say so explicitly, but invites us to notice the oddness of Yahweh. The cry of 2:23, on the part of the slaves, was aimed at no one in particular. It was too elemental to take the form of a specific address. Nevertheless, it "rose up to God." It comes up to this God, and to no other. We must notice this oddity in order to understand the story. Does this God have a predisposition to hear cries and to notice wretchedness? Or was this "my people" even before they knew their status? Did the cry establish their role as "my people"? None of that is articulated by the narrator and we are left to ponder. But we cannot ponder very long, for the narrator moves us along abruptly to the next odd turn in the narrative.

IV

Neither we nor Moses is prepared for the odd and unexpected turn of verse 10, in which God issues to Moses an assignment. In the self-disclosure of verses 7–9, Yahweh had uttered first-person verbs: "I will come down. I will come down to deliver. I will come down to bring them up." Yahweh is filled with resolve, and asserts that Yahweh alone is the subject of the action and of the verbs. We would expect that. We expect decisive action by Yahweh. First, because Yahweh is a God from whom we have learned in Genesis to expect action. And second, we expect such action because we already know the slave community to be helpless to act for itself.

Verse 10, however, surprises us. Now all Yahweh will do is "send." Yahweh will send Moses. It is Moses, not Yahweh, who will go to Pharaoh. It is Moses who will provide the confrontation with Egyptian political power, and who will carry on the dangerous negotiations to follow. It is Moses who will be the exposed point man of Israel's dangerous departure, while Yahweh remains in the background, as the powerful legitimator.

There is in verse 10 a second exodus verb, the first being "deliver" (*nṣl*) in verse 8. Here the verb is "bring out" (*yṣ'*). The conventional reading, following the Greek, is "You Moses" shall bring Israel out. The Hebrew lacks the second person suffix, so it is a third-person verb, "He [Pharaoh] will bring Israel out." The NRSV successfully skirts the grammatical problem by rendering it as an infinitive. In any of these readings, it is clearly Moses who must trigger the action, regardless of how the following verb is to be understood.

In this verse, we are at the center of the drama of our chapter. Yahweh's self-disclosure and resolve issue in human vocation. Yahweh's resolve for the liberation of Israel issues in a dangerous summons to Moses to run risks and speak liberating truth to oppressive power. In current conversation about the Exodus narrative as a model liberation narrative, this matter is a crucial one. There is no doubt that in contemporary Central American liberation theology, liberation is a revolutionary human activity, undertaken in the political-economic-military arena. There is a propensity on the part of some to suggest that whereas contemporary liberation theology bespeaks a human enterprise, the Exodus narrative, free of Marxian categories, sees liberation as a work wrought by Yahweh, and not by human agents. Thus Jon Levenson, in his polemic against Georg Pixley, can write: "Such a construal projects Marxist and kindred egalitarian ideas into texts that had a very different view of the matter."[5]

The caesura between verses 9 and 10, however, gives us pause with such an assertion as that of Levenson. Indeed, if we follow the course of the Exodus narrative, it is clear that Moses (sometimes accompanied by Aaron) is a human agent, and must engage in sustained, courageous acts of defiance wrought with great cunning. To be sure, "the plagues" are events of mighty upheaval beyond any human operation, but in any case, these upheavals are triggered by and depend upon the intentional instigation of Moses, the human agent. They do not happen until Moses has announced them. And indeed, in the perspective of the narrative, they would have no force for the liberation of the slaves until they had been announced, anticipated, and identified by Moses.

I suggest, then, given the juxtaposition of verses 7–9 and v. 10, that the attempt to assign exodus liberation to Yahweh alone, so as to screen out human agency, or the complementary attempt to omit Yahweh and make liberation only a human, revolutionary activity, is to misconstrue the way this text works. It is precisely the convergence of the tale of Yahweh and the tale of Moses which is the subject of Exodus 3. And while the claim of verses 7–9 and the summons of verse 10 are rhetorically quite distinct, in the subsequent narrative of the plagues the enterprise is profoundly synergistic.

The liberation of Israel traces the inscrutable working of the Lord of creation.[6] But the liberation would not have happened without the insistence, rage, and cunning of Moses, who conducts political theater. Read in one dimension, the exodus is a struggle among the gods, Yahweh versus the Egyptian gods (cf. Exod. 12:12). At the same time, however, Israel's tale of future possibility is saturated with human courage and calculation. The story does not begin in verse 10 with the action of Moses. Behind Moses, and endlessly with him, there is this cosmic legitimacy, regularly expressed in the familiar formula, "Thus says the Lord."[7] The work Moses has to do is the work of the one who sends him – but it is his work (cf. John 5:17). And he must do it.[8] The work which Moses must do, as verse 10 concludes, is *vis-à-vis* the Egyptians. There is no easy place for revolutionary obedience. And it is for "my people." Moses has work to do. It is human agency in the service of Yahweh's solidarity with Israel.

IV

The summons to Moses in verse 10 is indeed a dangerous one for him. Moses immediately recognizes the danger, and so he resists.[9] The resistance of Moses to the summons of Yahweh now generates an extensive exchange between Yahweh and Moses (3:11–4:17). Formally we are still at the scene of the bush, but the substance of what now follows concerns five protests on the part of Moses and five lordly refutations of the protests on the part of Yahweh:

1   Protest of Moses (3:11)   Response of Yahweh (3:12)
2   Protest of Moses (3:13)   Response of Yahweh (3:14–22)
3   Protest of Moses (4:1)   Response of Yahweh (4:2–9)
4   Protest of Moses (4:10)   Response of Yahweh (4:11–12)
5   Protest of Moses (4:13)   Response of Yahweh (4:14–17).

This exchange, which is extremely nervy on the part of Moses, builds to increasing exasperation on the part of Yahweh. The full power of the exchange is only available by considering the entire drama. For our purposes in this discussion, however, we will consider only the first two protests that fall within the scope of chapter 3.

The first protest of Moses indicates that he has well understood Yahweh's summons in verse 10; both the magnitude and the danger of the assignment given to him by Yahweh. Moses' prompt response to Yahweh is a rhetorical question which asserts his own insignificance and his lack of the qualities which would make such an assignment possible. (See the same self-diminishment in the response of Gideon to the call of Yahweh: Judg. 6:15.) Moses acknowledges himself to be an uncredentialed nobody. His lack of social standing is ludicrous, when juxtaposed to the might of Pharaoh. Yahweh has in mind a massive mismatch between mighty Egypt, mighty theologically and mighty politically and militarily, and this nobody of a shepherd. Moreover, Moses understands the mission. Now, in contrast to verse 10, there is no ambiguity about the verb of deliverance, $yṣ'$, as there was in verse 10. Moses is unambiguously and unmistakably the subject of the verb, and his work is nothing less than the emancipation of the slave labor force of the empire. Yahweh intends to extricate "my people" from the empire, and Moses is to effect that extrication. Moses is being summoned to be "the subject of his own history," the agent who gives to his people a genuine liberated future. Moses declines! But of course that is what characteristically happens to those who have long been denied voice and power. The refusal to become the subject of one's own history, to engage in self-assertion and in an act of risky power, is not difficult to understand.

Moses' word of refusal, of course, is not the last word, or our narrative would end here. The last word in this exchange belongs to Yahweh. Yahweh answers the protest of Moses immediately and decisively. Yahweh does not bother to refute Moses' statement of self-diminishment. Apparently that point is conceded by Yahweh, for Moses is indeed a nobody. The response of Yahweh is not a comment upon Moses, except indirectly. The direct comment is upon Yahweh: "I will be with you" (v. 12). Yahweh's own self is invested in the confrontation with Pharaoh. Moses is not alone, and the success of the mission does not depend upon Moses' capacity. Moses is an agent, but it is Yahweh who will act. Thus, later on, it is Yahweh who issues the imperative of liberation which is to be in the mouth of Moses: "Let my people go." The resolve is that of Yahweh, not of Moses.

But, like Moses, we should not regard this assurance as too persuasive. Here we run into the elemental problem of this theological character engaged in public action. We are accustomed to a profound dualism in all our thinking about God and public affairs. Yahweh is essentially a religious phenomenon, and the mission of Moses is to be a political one. The question raised is a fair one: how does a religious "phenomenon" engage in a political confrontation? We must shun our habituated dualism.

And yet in the very utterance, Yahweh concedes the problem. Yahweh will be with Moses. But it takes a "sign" to verify. There is no direct evidence, and a sign is a cubit removed from the reality of Yahweh's own self. Moreover, the sign that is to come is no sign. The sign offered is post-confrontation. The verification that this is Yahweh's mission will be enacted after the fact, when liberated Israel worships at Sinai. Or put more cynically, Moses will know Yahweh is with him – if the mission works and there is liberation. If there is no liberation and no subsequent worship at Sinai, Moses can be sure that Yahweh was not with him.

But, then, the capacity to become the subject of one's own history, and the readiness to generate an alternative future for one's people, are always a high-risk venture. One never knows and cannot know ahead of time if there is sufficient support and legitimacy for the venture. If there were no risk, others would already have done it. But this is the first attempt about which we know anything, in all the history of the world, to give slaves their own historical identity and possibility, apart from the operation of the empire. Moses is summoned now to go – theologically, politically – where none has ever been. He is being called and sent, on the basis of a promise of accompaniment, in order to challenge the political-economic practice of Pharaoh. And with it, he is sent to undermine the theological legitimacy claimed by Pharaoh from his imperial gods. It is no wonder that the first protest of Moses, scarcely answered by Yahweh, issues immediately in a second protest.

V

The second protest of Moses ups the ante (v. 13). In the first protest, Moses had expressed uncertainty about himself and his own role. Now, however, he expresses uncertainty about Yahweh. Yahweh is not known by name in Israel. Yahweh has not given that much of self away to Moses. To be sure, the narrator knows the name; but Moses knows nothing of Genesis or of that old history of blessing. The God of the bush has come *de novo* into the life of the slave community, alluding in 3:6 to the ancestors. But the formulation of God with reference to the ancestors is something less than God's own name. This is indeed a "new God" (cf. Judg. 5:8) who invites a new public possibility. This is a God not enmeshed in Egyptian reality, inviting Israel and Moses out beyond Egyptian reality.

Now, because the second protest directly concerns the identity of God, Yahweh must give a much fuller answer than Yahweh gave to the first protest (vv. 14–22). This answer to Moses on God's part is in fact an exposition of the first answer in verse 12, "I will be with you." But who is this one who will be with? In this rather complex response to Moses, we may identify six elements, which together make a formidable, but not very clear assurance.

First, Yahweh had said in verse 12, "I will be (*'hyh*) with you." Now in verse 14, enigmatic as it is, is a play on the verb, "I will be" from verse 12. God gives to Moses God's name, but it resolves nothing. The phrase "I will be" seems to derive the proper name YHWH from the verb "to be" (*hwh*) but the proper name itself is not used. The elusive quality of this response is evident in the richness of scholarly debate over what it means.[10] It may be that we do not understand the idiom that is employed in Yahweh's self-disclosure. More likely, Yahweh's response is intentionally elusive. It is enough that Moses will be accompanied by this one who in active, faithful ways is whom God's own mouth is said to be. The last part of verse 14, " 'I am' has sent you," indicates that Moses is to let his people know he is not alone, and that their alternative future is not his own initiative.

Second, beyond that enigmatic and unhelpful response, Yahweh promptly gives a second response (v. 15). Now Yahweh returns to the ancestral formula already employed in 2:24 and 3:6. The narrative is determined to link this crisis to the book of Genesis. The God announcing this liberation is the God who makes durable promises. Beyond that, however, now for the first time in Moses' hearing, the name is uttered: YHWH. The God who undertakes the exodus is the God of faithful presence and generative power. This is the God who governs the processes of life, now facing Pharaoh who administers only the powers of death (1:22). In this second response, Moses has received a direct answer to his question in verse 13, an answer linking Exodus to Genesis, deliverance to promise, but also giving finally Yahweh's proper, freighted, enigmatic name. Now Moses knows.

Third, however, Yahweh's response to the protest of Moses is not content to remain with talk about God's character and identity. Rather, Yahweh issues an oath of Yahweh's intended transformative actions (vv. 11–17). In these verses, Yahweh recites Israel's classic credo we have already heard in verse 17. Yahweh's intended action, characteristically, is in two parts: emancipation from Egyptian bondage, and (no verb!) to the good land of milk and honey. The *exit* from Egypt is matched by an *entrance* which voices the core transaction in Israel's life, from slavery to milk and honey, from misery to well-being, from death to life. The resolve of God puts a decisive terminus upon Egyptian oppression and abuse. It cannot last. Moreover, this awesome God has "heeded" Israel's plight. Indeed, the Hebrew is stronger. With the use of an absolute infinitive, "I have really paid attention. I know the crisis and the need of the slaves."

Fourth, Moses is joined by the "elders," the responsible leadership in the slave community, those daring to receive an alternative future (vv. 18–19). The elders will participate with Moses in the awesome challenge to Egyptian power.

The larger exodus narrative is filled with twists and turns of delay and negotiation, some of which seem designed for artistic effect and some of which seem politically credible. Indeed, the narrator tells us in 10:1–2 that the delays are choreographed by Yahweh, in order to produce a more engaging narrative for the grandchildren! In chapter 3, verses 18–19 bespeak such an artistic delay. Moses and the elders will go to Pharaoh. But Pharaoh will not give freedom for the slaves to leave. Pharaoh will refuse, and will resist Yahweh's mighty imperative. Indeed the larger narrative is an account of how Pharaoh's resistance to Yahweh is slowly, methodically overcome.[11] Here, however, the resistance of Pharaoh is flat and without dramatic nuance. Thus the assurance of verse 18 is cancelled by the resistance of verse 19. Entrenched evil does not yield easily, not even to the summons of Yahweh.

It is necessary then, Yahweh already knows, to the conflict (v. 20). Thus the fifth element in Yahweh's refutation of Moses' protest is the assurance that Yahweh is fully prepared to raise the stakes, and to confront Pharaoh with more compelling force. Yahweh and Pharaoh are to engage in an "arms race." The operational word is "wonder" (*npl*). In the context of the exodus narrative, this word usage is a harbinger of the plague cycle which is to come, acts of inscrutable power which will compel Pharaoh to act against his own greedy interest, in order to conform to Yahweh's will. Pharaoh will be brought by force to obey Yahweh's imperative.

The term "wonder," however, is not confined to the Exodus narrative.[12] Indeed this word is one of Israel's most characteristic terms to bear witness to the inscrutable, inexplicable, irresistible deeds of power, whereby Yahweh's sovereign will override the habits and interests of earthly power. We conventionally term these acts "miracles." The term is correct, except that "miracle" tends to be sweet, and plays to the modern notion of "natural law." There is something ominous about this "wonder" that destabilizes and delegitimates resistance to Yahweh. Yahweh operates in ruthless, raw power in order to accomplish liberation. Yahweh will do whatever is necessary to enact the larger exodus narrative, the full promise of the credo.

At the end of this long speech, sixth, Yahweh seems to engage in something of an afterthought (vv. 21–2). When Israel leaves Egyptian slavery, as it surely will, it will not go empty-handed and excessively vulnerable. It will take enough material goods in order to have some economic staying power (cf. 11:2; 12:35). David Daube opines that this narrative notice is made with reference to the legal provision of Deuteronomy 15:7–11.[13] Slaves released, according to that law, are to be given enough wherewithal to reenter the economy with dignity and viability. On a very large scale, then, this provision at the end of Yahweh's speech is to assure Israel's economic viability in the world of nations, when it departs from slavery and begins to operate freely.

It may be, however, that this concluding note is not so "noble" or rooted in legal tradition as that. It may be a humorous notice designed to embolden Israel and to humiliate Egypt. "Take their silverware!" The entire exodus is, so to speak, an illegal action, or action in the service of a law which Pharaoh does not acknowledge. The disadvantaged might in the end think they are owed such a special "gift," because of long, miserable servitude. But since the silver and gold will not be readily given, perhaps it must be "appropriated."

Here Yahweh's second answer to Moses ends. Moses will continue his resistant protest in 4:1, 10 and 13. But Yahweh is unyielding (4:2–9, 11–12, 14–17). In the end, Yahweh loses patience with Moses, is angry and forecloses the discussion. The long exchange of 3:11–4:17 is for nought. We are in fact pushed back to 3:10 and the summons to Moses. Soon, in 5:1, Moses (with Aaron) is at his new, dangerous task. He says directly and tersely to Egyptian power, on behalf of Yahweh: "Send my people." Pharaoh refuses Yahweh's imperative (5:2, 4). Pharaoh will refuse for a long time – but not finally!

VI

It is no wonder that this chapter, which sets in motion the larger drama of Exodus 3–15, regularly propels the imagination of those inside and outside this community of faith. It is this articulation, in all the world of texts, which joins the holy power of God to the risky, demanding work of public, political, historical emancipation. We may identify four concentric circles of liberated imagination, whereby this narrative text has seeded revolutionary energy in the world.

1   It is of enduring importance that it is this exodus narrative that provides the script for Jewish Passover.[14] Of all of the remembering, ritual activities in the life and faith of Judaism, it is this one that most drives communal imagination. And because the text is taken up liturgically, it is inescapable that the exodus is not simply some ancient historical event. It is, rather, an available, palpable possibility in the current imagination and contemporary life of the Jewish community. The Exodus liturgy is a refusal to accept the givenness of the status quo – most often repressive and oppressive – and an affirmation that the juices of transformation are alive in the world in ways that finally cannot be resisted.

2   It is unmistakably clear that the New Testament community which bore witness to Jesus had its imagination fed and decisively shaped by the exodus narrative. Thus, for example, Matthew must begin his gospel narrative by retelling the tale of the exodus, as the story which Jesus is about to reenact (Matt. 2:13–15). And Luke, at the pivotal moment of Jesus's "transfiguration," cannot avoid taking up the word "exodus," indicating that this entire grid of narrative imagination is operative in his gospel (Luke 9:31).[15]

But more importantly, it is clear that the story of Jesus's life is to be understood as a tale of liberation, whereby Jesus confronts oppressive power and engages in daring gestures of solidarity with the unfree. Such a way of reading begins in concrete acts: "the blind receive their sight, the lame walk, the lepers are cleansed, the deaf hear, the dead are raised, the poor have good news brought to them" (Luke 7:22). Jesus's engagement with the exodus theme culminates in his final confrontation with established power in his trial before Pilate (John 18:28–19:16).[16] And then in more lyrical language, he is said to deal even with the last oppressor, death (1 Cor. 15:26). I do not imagine that Christians have any warrant for preempting the exodus story, which is resolutely Jewish. It is evident nonetheless that, belatedly, Christians delight in retelling that story with reference to Jesus. In the telling, however, nothing important in the plot is changed. The main character is still the Holy One who envisions transformation, and this main character conscripts this Agent who becomes "the subject of our history."

3   This peculiarly Jewish narrative construal of the historical process, in contrast to that of the "Rulers of this Age" who want to deny and repress, moves into wider circles, even in contemporary society. Thus it is out of this narrative that Central American Roman Catholic bishops could arrive at the formula, "God's Preferential Option for the Poor."[17] This formula asserts that God is not the even-handed maintainer of equality who treats all the same. The God of the exodus is a partisan advocate whose lot is thrown in with the weak, poor, and helpless, so that the terrible, unjust imbalance in worldly power and goods may be forcibly redressed. That redress of course does not happen in a supernatural redistribution. It happens now, as it did in the first telling of this

narrative, by liturgical acts of empowerment, by which human, historical agents are invited and authorized to imagine the world differently, and then to act in bold, concrete ways out of that imagination.

One notes that in the contemporary formula of the preferential option for the poor, the preference of God is no longer simply for Hebrews/Israelites/Jews, but for all of the poor. Thus the ethnic specificity of the narrative has disappeared. We are bound to note, for example, Jon Levenson, who polemically resists the notion that this Jewish story can be wrenched from its Jewishness into a more generic account of reality.[18] Levenson's concern about supersessionism is well grounded, for the exodus story is indeed relentlessly Jewish. And yet, in the end, even Levenson agrees that the story functions paradigmatically for liberation in many quarters well beyond Jewish confines.[19]

The exodus narrative, on its face is Jewish. It cannot, however, be contained there, but has its own say well beyond Jewish boundaries. It is inescapable, in my judgement, that serious interpreters of Jesus, such as the Roman Catholic bishops in Central America, finally must come to see that the God who moved Moses against Pharaoh is the God who in many times, places, and circumstances moved the historical process toward transformation and freedom. Thus the affirmation of Amos 9:7 is finally a most telling one, that the God of Israel is the very God who works exoduses in many other places as well. The narrative surely has a particular Jewish focus, but in the end, the story is about this God who works in the same way among many peoples.

4   The narrative of Exodus 3 has turned loose its imaginative power in many directions. Its first aim is the children of the passover, and only after them has it reached those who gathered around Jesus. When the text comes to the person of Jesus, it was not a daring step to imagine that Jesus was the one sent by God to speak truth to power. Even more belatedly, moreover, did this text recruit for its purposes the bishops at Meddallin, and this bold assertion of the preferential option of God. These specific points of contact between text and human courage for transformation, however, are only among the most visible in a long line of contacts between text and human transformation.

Michael Walzer in broad strokes has suggested the ways in which this text has persistently loomed powerfully in the midst of human power and human possibility.[20] Everywhere this text has been voiced, energy and courage and freedom for historical possibility have been released. Sometimes the text has been heard as a mandate from Yahweh, the legitimator, to go meet Pharaoh. Sometimes however, the mandate to go meet Pharaoh has been accepted, without the legitimating dispatch of Yahweh. Sometimes the revolutionary risk has been understood theologically as grounded in God's holiness. Sometimes, on the contrary, it is the political confrontational residue of the narrative, without the theological grounding, which has been enough. Thus Walzer shows how in Marxian and in more conventional non-Marxian ways, this text has stirred the public process of newness.

The yield of this text is the conviction that entrenched power, with all of its self-justifying ideology, does not need to be accepted as a given. What is said to be a given is only a posture. And if the posture moves in contradiction to the holy purposes of God for humanity, it will not and cannot endure. Thus behind modern and contemporary options for revolutionary social transformation stands this Jew Moses and this Jewish Yahweh, one sent, the other sending, the two together not shunning the violence that produced many "Egyptians dead on the seashore" (Exod. 14:30).

The starting point of this world-defining enterprise of social transformation is given us in the text. The Holy One, the one who decreed "fruitful and multiply," the one who blessed the barren, bereft ancestors, stays concealed in a bush. But this is no ordinary bush. It is a bush from which comes a revolutionary voice of assurance and mandate. It is that voice which continues to be heard in the human process, a voice that commands the wretched bold and challenges the arrogant.

The end point of this text has not yet been reached, or even known. It touched down (we say decisively) in Jesus. But it also touched down in Mao and Mandela and Havel and Arafat and Adams, some noble and celebrated, some ignoble and finally not celebrated.[21] The end of the reach of this text will not come, until the last man or women enacts courage and possibility. A voice from a bush is a flaming warrant for "truth to power." It has often been found adequate and in the end irresistible. Each time the text is heard, the one who provisionally "turns aside" (cf. Exod. 3:3) must decide again if this haunting, demanding voice is an adequate ground for an alternative, risky history. Those in the train of Moses are never certain. But those in the hard procession of Pharaoh have been and continue to be on notice.

Notes

1 Phyllis Trible, *God and the Rhetoric of Sexuality* (OBT; Philadelphia: Fortress, 1978), pp. 76–82, refers to the first human beings as "the earth creatures." The phrase is suggestive of the expansive scope of the decree for fruitfulness, which in Exodus will be assigned to the slave community.

2 The vexed question of the relation between the Genesis stories and the Exodus tradition has been admirably explored by R. W. L. Moberly, *The Old Testament of the Old Testament: Patriarchal Narratives and Mosaic Yahwism* (OBT; Minneapolis: Fortress, 1992).

3 On the genre of theophany, see Jörg Jeremias, *Theophanie: Die Geschichte einer alttestamentlichen Gattung* (WMANT 10; Neukirchen-Vluyn: Neukirchener Verlag, 1965) and J. Kenneth Kuntz, *The Self-Revelation of God* (Philadelphia: Westminster, 1967). It is worth noting that Jeremias does not consider our passage an exemplar of the genre. Nonetheless, it has enough marks to be regarded as a case of the use of that genre.

4 Gerhard von Rad, *The Problem of the Hexateuch and Other Essays* (London: Oliver and Boyd, 1966), pp. 3–8. The pairing of these two terms and these two traditions of course dominates much of von Rad's interpretation of Old Testament theology.

5 Jon D. Levenson, "Exodus and Liberation," *The Hebrew Bible, the Old Testament and Historical Criticism: Jews and Christians in Biblical Studies* (Louisville: Westminster/John Knox, 1993), p. 133.

6 Terence E. Fretheim, "The Plagues as Ecological Signs of Historical Disaster," *JBL* 110 (1991): 285–96.

7 On the "messenger formula," see W. Eugene March, "Prophecy," in *Old Testament Form Criticism* ed. by John H. Hayes (San Antonio: Trinity University Press, 1974), pp. 146–57. Special attention should be paid to the work of Claus Westermann.

8 In anticipation of the later Christian Christological formula, perhaps one can say that here we see "two agents in one narrative," thus anticipating the formula, "Two natures in one person."

9 Norman Habel, "The Form and Significance of the Call Narrative," *ZAW* 36 (1965): 297–323, has considered the Moses narrative as a clear example of a firmly established literary genre of "call narrative." Among other things, Habel has shown that resistance to call is a recurring and predictable element in the genre.

10 See the balanced judgement of Dennis J. McCarthy, "Exod. 3:14: History, Philosophy and Theology," *CBQ* 40 (1978): 311–22.

11 I have traced this narrative strategy in my commentary, "Exodus," *The New Interpreter's Bible* I (Nashville: Abingdon Press, 1994). Most important are the texts Exod. 8:25–8; 10:8–11, 24–6.

12 See Judg. 6:13, Jer. 21:2, Mic. 7:15, Pss. 119:18, 136:4, 145:5.

13 David Daube, *The Exodus Pattern in the Bible* (London, 1963).

14 On the liturgic casting and origin of the Exodus tradition, see Johannes Pedersen, *Israel: Its Life and Culture III–IV* (Copenhagen: Branner, 1940), pp. 728–37.

15 More generally, see Sharon H. Ringe, *Jesus, Liberation, and the Biblical Jubilee* (OBT; Philadelphia: Fortress Press, 1985).

16 The narrative presentation of Jesus before the authorities surely contains echoes of Moses before Pharaoh. For a shrewd and sensitive reading of the trial of Jesus in the Fourth Gospel, see Paul Lehmann, *The Transfiguration of Politics* (London: SCM Press, 1975), pp. 48–70.

17 On the formula and its historical, theological significance, see Gustavo Gutierrez, *A Theology of Liberation: History, Politics, and Salvation* (London: SCM Press, 1974).

18 Levenson, *The Hebrew Bible*, pp. 155–8 and passim.

19 Ibid., p. 159.

20 Michael Walzer, *Exodus and Revolution* (New York: Basic Books, 1986).

21 The claim of this text does not depend upon being able to cite contemporary enactments of its claim. Nonetheless, it is remarkable that we live in a moment of world history when established, oppressive givens are yielding to social revolution, much of which is rooted

in the biblical tradition. This remarkable convergence of revolutionary changes might include the collapse of Soviet hegemony in Eastern Europe, the transformation of South Africa, and perhaps the possibility of newness in Israel with the Palestinians and among Roman Catholics and Protestants in Northern Ireland. Of course each and all of these events can be understood in ways other than through the claims of this text. But no doubt the ancient emancipation of Hebrew slaves also could have been alternatively understood.

Selections from Theodoret of Cyrus's *Commentary on Isaiah*

Translated and introduced by
Angela Russell Christman

In the annals of the Church's history Theodoret, Bishop of Cyrus[1] in the first half of the fifth century, is perhaps best known for his role in defending Nestorius and Antiochene christology against the 12 anathemas of Cyril of Alexandria. However, Theodoret was also a prolific biblical exegete, and the corpus of his biblical commentaries is one of the largest extant among patristic authors. It includes both "Questions and Answers" on the Octateuch and the historical books of the Septuagint and verse-by-verse commentaries on the prophetic books, the Psalter, and the 14 Pauline epistles.

Unfortunately, we have little direct evidence as to the setting and date of Theodoret's commentaries. However, scattered comments in Theodoret's writings (both the epistles and the commentaries) in conjunction with significant changes in the christological language used in his exegesis seem to indicate that he wrote the commentaries between CE 435 and 447.[2] Moreover, in several works, Theodoret lays out the order in which he wrote his commentaries, indicating that the *Commentary on Isaiah* was written just before his last commentary, the *Commentary on Jeremiah*. Thus, although the *Commentary on Isaiah* cannot be dated precisely, it was probably written not too long before 447. Evidence for the setting of Theodoret's commentaries is even scarcer than that for dating. However, the commentaries' length, references to both hearers and readers, as well as the parenetic material and concluding doxologies found at the end of each major division of the commentaries all combine to suggest that Theodoret's commentaries were probably first delivered as lectures (perhaps to educated clergy and lay people in Antioch), taken down by stenographers, and then revised by Theodoret later for publication and dissemination to a wider audience.[3]

As a biblical commentator, Theodoret was conscious of being an inheritor of the interpretative tradition which began with the first disciples and continued in the Church's life. Preserving and furthering this tradition was, in his view, one of the main tasks of the Christian exegete. His understanding of himself as standing within this interpretative tradition can be seen clearly in references he makes to his indebtedness to "the blessed Fathers" who are "the luminaries of the world."[4] He considers himself, he explains, to be like a gnat buzzing among the bees which hum in "the apostolic meadows."[5] However, Theodoret's awareness of being indebted to earlier exegetes should not mislead us into assuming either that Theodoret was merely a compiler of others' interpretations or that he lacked originality. While Theodoret intentionally draws upon, and thus preserves, parts of the interpretative tradition, he also expresses the desire to add his own contribution to the edifice of the Church's interpretation.[6] Moreover, recent studies have demonstrated that although Theodoret borrowed from exegetes – both Antiochene and Alexandrian – who preceded him, he also did not shrink from originality in his interpretation, especially where the theological controversies of his day demanded.[7]

Perhaps the two most noteworthy characteristics of Theodoret's exegesis are its brevity and its christological orientation. Theodoret sought to keep his exposition of a passage brief because he realized that conciseness could lure potential readers: "I know that conciseness encourages even those who live idly to read," he wrote in the preface to his commentary on the Pauline epistles.[8] The purpose of his exegesis was, as he understood it, to nurture the life of the Church; reaching the widest possible audience was essential.

Theodoret shared the concern, characteristic of Antiochene exegetes, for the historical referent of the biblical text. However, he was equally concerned to guard the text's christological, and in some cases ecclesiological, fulfillment. Theodoret was troubled by those Christian exegetes who interpreted certain Septuagint texts as being fulfilled in the history of the people of Israel before the coming of Christ and denied these texts' fulfillment in the life of Christ or in the Church. Such strictly historical readings were objectionable to Theodoret because he feared that Christian interpretations of the Septuagint which place the text's fulfillment in the history of the Jewish people would undermine the Christian claim that Jesus Christ fulfills the messianic prophecies. In the prologue to his *Commentary on the Psalms*, Theodoret explained that interpretations which "find fulfillment of the prophecy in certain historical events" are "an advocate for the Jews, rather than for the children of faith."[9] In his exegesis Theodoret sought to steer a middle course between such a strictly historical reading of the text and what he considered excessive allegorizing. As a result, the content of Theodoret's biblical interpretation – especially of Septuagint texts – often has more in common with Alexandrian exegetes (e.g. Origen, Eusebius of Caesarea, Cyril of Alexandria) than with other Antiochene exegetes (e.g. Theodore of Mopsuestia, John Chrysostom).

Theodoret's desire to balance historical exegesis with christological and ecclesiological interpretation is clearly manifest in his exegesis of Isaiah 52. With the exception of a brief discussion of the earthly Jerusalem and the heavenly Sion in the exposition of 52:1, Theodoret interprets Isaiah 52:1–6 with reference to the people's exile in Babylon. Most of his comments are terse and seem geared primarily to elucidating the prophet's train of thought. The focus moves from the history of Israel to the life of the Church, however, beginning with the exegesis of 52:7[10] which Theodoret understands as being fulfilled primarily in the apostles as they traversed the earth by foot, preaching the gospel. In the exposition of 52:7 and the following verses he does not entirely eliminate the historical referent but, rather, makes it clear that the biblical text finds its most fitting fulfillment in the Church's life. Theodoret's exegesis of Isaiah 52:1–12 is part of Book 16 of the entire commentary, and he brings the book to a close with a short exhortation to follow Jesus faithfully and a trinitarian doxology.[11]

Turning to the servant song of Isaiah 52:13–53:12 in Book 17 of his commentary, Theodoret observes that in this passage the prophet accurately predicts Christ's passion. Here Theodoret draws upon a well-established interpretative tradition. From the earliest days of the Church Isaiah 52:13–53:12 was a biblical text of paramount significance for Christians because it helped them to understand the meaning of not only Jesus' life and ministry but also the ignoble death Jesus had endured on the cross.[12] Moreover, because the humiliating nature of Jesus' death was at the heart of both Jewish and pagan objections to the Church's assertion of Jesus' messiahship, this text had a central place in Christian apologetic and the development of soteriology.[13] Like those before him, Theodoret highlights the congruences between Isaiah's prophecy and the accounts of Jesus' passion and death. Throughout his exposition Theodoret also emphasizes the Gentiles' acceptance of the gospel and the Jews' refusal to recognize Christ as the Messiah.[14] Moreover, in Isaiah 53:2 ("a root in parched earth") Theodoret finds confirmation for Christian interpretation of Isaiah 7:14 as a prophecy of Christ's birth from a virgin, a point of contention between Jews and Christians.[15] In this section of the commentary Theodoret's discussion of Christ's passion not only sounds apologetic notes, but also stresses general soteriological principles: the depth of human sin which required the Incarnation, the salvific benefits of Christ's suffering, and the remarkable and unexpected way in which God brings about human redemption.

Although Isaiah 52:13–53:12 was a mainstay in Christian apologetic and soteriology, as is clearly reflected in Theodoret's interpretation, the bishop of Cyrus brought another theological question to this text, indeed to the entire book of Isaiah: the relationship between the human and divine in the person of Christ. Throughout the christological controversies of the first half of the fifth century, Theodoret insisted that the two natures of Christ were not mixed. To give up this claim would, for Theodoret, inevitably lead either to the subordinationism of the Arians or to the monophysite christology of Apollinaris of Laodicea.[16] Theodoret read Isaiah 52:13–53:12 with this concern very much in mind. In expounding the servant song, he understood the prophet to refer to Christ's human nature (e.g. Isa. 52:13), his divine nature (e.g. Isa. 53:8, "Who can describe his generation?"), and the relationship between the human and divine in Christ (e.g. 53:3, 7b–8a). Thus in his interpretation of this servant song Theodoret attempted to defend his dyophysite Christology by showing that its foundation is found in the very words of scripture.

The text below is translated from *Théodoret de Cyr: Commentaire sur Isaïe*, 3 vols, ed. and trans. J-N Guinot (Paris: Les Éditions du Cerf, 1980–4).

Book 16

Wake up, wake up, Sion. Put on your strength Sion, and you, Jerusalem, holy city, put on your glory. No longer will the uncircumcised and the unclean continue to go through you. He calls the city below Jerusalem and the city above Sion. But both cities came to their fulfillment in one city. So, for example, he promises the renewal to both; and since the foreign nations roamed through the city fearlessly after the inhabitants became captives, he promises their release. *Shake off the dirt, arise, sit down, Jerusalem.* He promises these things either because she has been destroyed or because she laments and has been trampled down with her head in the dirt. *Loose the chain from your neck, captive daughter of Sion.* The chains are part of captivity. Therefore, he reveals beforehand the freedom through the release from the chains.

Thus says the Lord, "You were sold for nothing and you shall be ransomed without silver." They were sold because of their sins, but they obtained their deliverance by God's love for humankind. *Thus says the Lord, "My people went down at first into Egypt to dwell there, and among the Assyrians,"* but *by force*, after having enslaved them, they carried them away. *And now, why are you thus?* By the question he shows the reason for what happened, and that it was unexpected. Did you not go out of Egypt? How then did you return?

Thus says the Lord, "Because my people were taken for nothing, you are amazed and you cry aloud. "You are astounded, he says, when you lament over the exile because, although you are called my people, you have endured these things. Do not be amazed, but rather consider that, *on account of you, my name is blasphemed continuously among the nations.* Thus, it is not distressing that you suffer these things justly, because I am blasphemed on account of you and the nations think that you endured these things because of my weakness. *Because of this my people will know my name in that day, they will know that I am, that I am the one who says, "Here I am."* He calls "day" the time of their restoration to the land of Israel. You will obtain this, not because of your worthiness, but because of the nations' blasphemy. I will free you from slavery because I wish to show them my power. I will do this at once, and I will bring about the word's fulfillment.

How beautiful on the mountains are the feet of the one who proclaims tidings of peace, who proclaims good things. This received fulfillment figuratively when the release of the captives was announced to those who dwelt in Jerusalem. But truly and fittingly the prophecy refers to the holy apostles. For their feet are beautiful, the feet which the master's hands washed[17] and made strong to run through the entire world, to carry the good news of God's peace, and to reveal the enjoyment of the good things which had been promised. *Because I shall make your salvation heard, when I say to Sion, "Your God shall be your king."* And in a similar way, these things refer more fittingly to the holy apostles, for it was through them that the kingdom of God and of our Savior was preached abroad. Before the apostles' time,[18] the earthly Sion did not wish to be ruled by God.

The voice of your watchmen was lifted up. And with that voice, at the same time, they will rejoice because they shall see with eyes upon eyes when the Lord has mercy upon Sion. These are they who preach the gospel, guard it, and secure its joy. For they were eyewitnesses to the Savior, when he became incarnate and revealed himself to Sion. Thus also the blessed David says, "Out of Sion, the dignity of his beauty,"[19] and, "The Lord will send you the scepter of power out of Sion."[20] *Break forth in joy all together, you desert places of Jerusalem, because the Lord had mercy upon his people and ransomed Jerusalem.* Again he promises joy to the desert places of Jerusalem which are – as he said in an earlier passage[21] – situated in the west and which he said were compared to God's garden.

He teaches how these things will come about: *The Lord will reveal his holy arm before all the nations and all the mountain tops of the earth shall see the salvation of our God.* The God of the universe, he says, will show his power to all the nations – for "arm" means power – and all peoples will know the one who bestows salvation.

Stand apart, stand apart, go out thence, and do not touch anything unclean, go out from the midst of her. The prophetic passage exhorts those who have believed to separate themselves from unbelievers. *Set yourselves apart, you who bear the Lord's vessels.* "Vessels" means those who are deemed worthy of election. He spoke about the blessed Paul in this way, for he says to Ananias, "Go, for he is a chosen vessel of mine to carry my name before nations and kings and the sons of Israel."[22] And the divine apostle himself says, "If any one purifies himself from what is ignoble, then he will be a vessel for noble use, consecrated and useful to the master of the house, ready for any good work."[23] *Because you shall not go out with confusion, nor shall you go in flight, for the Lord, the God of Israel, will go before you and gather you together.* When the Romans were about to march against Jerusalem, all who had received the proclamation of the gospel traveled to other cities, for they had learned of the misfortunes that were to befall her. The Lord himself ordered them to do this: "When" he says, "you see Jerusalem surrounded by armies, then know that its desolation has come near"[24] and again, "Then let those who are in Judea flee to the mountains; let him who is on the housetop not go down to take what is in his house."[25] Since they knew of these events beforehand, they withdrew and departed from the misfortunes of the siege. The Savior himself guided their way, leading them to the nations and gathering the Church from the nations.

Since we too have learned these things, let us flee unfaithfulness, let us cleave to the faith, let us guard the divine commandments, and let us travel the straight road with the Lord Jesus as the guide for our journey. Glory to the Father, in union with him, with the all holy Spirit, now and always, to the ages of ages. Amen.

Book 17

Behold, my servant understands and he will be exalted, glorified, and lifted up very high. Now Isaiah foretells the Master's passion in a more accurate way. He showed, in order, all of Christ's human aspects: the wisdom, the working of miracles, the awe of all who saw him. For the phrase, "My servant understands" is like that well-known passage in the gospel, "Jesus advanced in age and wisdom."[26] The phrase, "He will be exalted, glorified, and lifted up very high," signifies the astonishment of those who saw the miracles. For according to the gospel narrative, when they wished to make him king they cried, "Hosanna to the son of David, hosanna in the highest."[27]

But after the miracles, there is the Passion. It is surely because of this that the prophet arranged the prediction in this way. He says, *As many will be astonished at you, so that your form will be held in no esteem among mortals and your glory among the sons of mortals.* He was nailed to the cross, they placed thorns about his head, and when they beat him with a reed, they said, "Prophesy to us Christ, who is it that struck you?"[28]

Then, after this dishonor, the prophet predicts the world's amazement: *Thus many nations shall marvel at him.* For not all believed, but those who have believed admired beyond measure "the mystery of piety."[29] *And kings will shut their mouths.* When they clearly see his power, those who long ago persecuted him and had the effrontery to blaspheme him will put away their language of abuse. Therefore the prophet says more clearly: *Because those who did not receive the prophecy about him will see, and those who did not hear will understand.* Those who did not receive the prophetic announcements but were worshipping idols will see – through those who preach the truth – the strength of the one who is proclaimed, and they will know his power.

Thus he foretold these things concerning the nations, and he predicted the Jews' unbelief: *Lord, who has believed our report? And to whom was the Lord's arm revealed?* The nations, Isaiah says, who had heard nothing beforehand about him from us, the prophets, received the proclamation of the gospel with zeal. But although the Jews had heard us [the prophets] often and had experienced his power, they continued to be unbelieving and disputatious.

We announced before him, that is, before this people which now is disputatious. What did you announce? *Like a child, like a root in parched earth.* According to Aquila[30] the prophet says, "like a root from untrodden earth." We predicted, the prophet says, the birth from a virgin: he called her "untrodden" and "parched" since she in no way received a man's footprint or the rain of marriage. And we announced this, that *He has no form or glory.* This was at the time of the Passion, for great was the dishonor and wanton violence. *And we saw him, and he had no form or beauty, but his form was dishonored, his form was wanting in comparison with the sons of mortals.* Very great is the activity of the all holy Spirit, for in this way the Spirit showed the holy prophets beforehand the things which happened many generations later, so that they do not say, "we have heard," but rather, "we have seen."

The prophet next teaches the forms of dishonor and disgrace: *He was a man wounded.* He showed the nature which received the Passion. For the body was nailed to the cross, but the divinity made the Passion its own. *And he knew how to bear weakness.* This also is said about his humanity. For to endure patiently and to live like a philosopher are appropriate not to divine nature, but to human. *Because his face turned away, he was dishonored and considered of no account.* The Three translated the passage in this way: "And as his face was concealed from himself, he was treated with contempt and considered of no account." That is, he concealed his divine power, since he accepted the Passion knowingly and did not defend himself against those who had crucified him, for while he was being crucified he said, "Father forgive them, for they know not what they do."[31]

Isaiah teaches the reasons for the Passion: *This one bears our weaknesses and suffers for our sake.* Symmachus translates it in this way: "Truly, he took upon himself our maladies and patiently bore our sufferings." Since we were liable to death for the sins we had committed, and for this reason had received this judgement of death, he consented to death on our behalf. And since we were subject to the curses on account of the trangression of the law, "he became a curse for us. For it is written, 'Cursed is everyone who hangs on a tree.' "[32] *And we considered that it was by God's doing that he was in suffering, sorrow, and distress.* The prophet appropriated for himself the people's ignorance, and says he supposed him [the servant, Christ] to suffer these things on account of his own sins.

But he was wounded on account of our iniquities and made weak on account of our sins. Since we had sinned, we were subject to punishments; but he, although free of sins, was subjected to punishments for our sake. *Upon him is the punishment which brings us peace.* Since we had sinned, we were enemies of God, and it was necessary that we be punished in order to obtain peace. But he, by taking the punishment on himself, made us worthy of peace. *And by his bruise we are healed.* This is a way of healing that is new and unexpected: the physician underwent the operation, and the sickly patient obtained the healing.

All we like sheep have gone astray, each has wandered on his own way. The trespasses of all were not equal, nor was the sort of impiety the same, for the Egyptians, the Phoenicians, the Greeks, and the Scythians each worshipped different idols. But still, even if the forms of error were different, all of us alike had abandoned the true God and were like sheep, wandering and exposed to wolves. *And the Lord delivered him up for our sins.* The prophet says that he was offered on behalf of the whole human race.

And while being afflicted, he does not open his mouth. The narrative of the holy gospels teaches this: although before the Passion he conversed with the people night and day and offered his beneficial teaching, during his Passion, he was silent. *Like a sheep that is led to slaughter, and a lamb silent before its shearer, thus he does not open his mouth during his humiliation.* He showed clearly that he was silent at the time of his passion; for in his time of humiliation he was like a sheep that is shorn and slaughtered and is silent. Yet he showed two things through what was said: the passibility of the human nature and the impassibility of the divine, for he calls the Passion not only a slaying but also a shearing. The human nature was slaughtered, but the divine nature seems in some way to be shorn from the fleece of his humanity. While not being separated from his humanity – even at the time of the Passion – his divinity did not itself receive the Passion.

His judgement was taken away. Symmachus translates the verse in this way: "And he was taken far from a tribunal." The others translate it this way also. For the unlawful tribunal of the Jews produced this decree against him.

Who can describe his generation? The divine nature is incomprehensible. Since the prophet said many things concerning the human nature, of necessity he also gave a glimpse of the divine magnificence. *Because his life was taken up from the land.* He did not remain in the tomb, but he rose and was taken up into the heavens. *By the lawlessness of my people he has come to death.* The one who bears the name "my people," who habitually transgresses the law, undertook these things against him.

Then he foretells the things that will happen to them again: *And I shall give the evil ones for his tomb and the rich for his death.* The Three said "he will give" rather than "I shall give," for he who suffers these things will hand them over in the war with the Romans. And he called the Pharisees, Scribes, and the High Priests "rich," and similarly "evil," for they took for themselves the possessions of all others. When he was teaching, the Lord said, "Woe to you, Scribes and Pharisees, because you devour widows' houses."[33] *Because he had committed no transgression, and there was no deceit in his mouth.* He did not sin, in either word or deed, but he preserved his human nature undefiled and free from sins. But they nailed him to the tree like a criminal. *And the Lord wishes to cleanse him from his wound.* That is, to show he was innocent and not subject to death. So the blessed Peter also said, "This Jesus God raised up, having loosed the pangs of death, because it was not possible for him to be held by it."[34]

Thus, after the prophet foretold the people's transgression, he presents them with the exhortation to repentence – for he foresaw those among them who would believe after these events. Among these was the most godly Paul, among these the three thousand and the many thousands[35] – and he says, *If you offer a sacrifice for sins, your soul will see long-lived offspring.* If you confess your impiety and seek salvation, you will obtain everlasting life, for this is what he means by "long-lived."

And the Lord wishes by his hand to take away his soul's suffering, to show him light, and to shape his understanding, to justify the righteous one who serves many well. He showed the deliverance from death which came to pass through the Lord himself, for it was "by his hand," that is, by the hand of the one who suffered. He loosed the pain of death, showed the light of the resurrection, and molded, as it were, a new form incorruptible and immortal, and he justified not the sinful one, but the righteous, that is the one innocent of sins. The phrase "who serves many well" corresponds to the passage in the gospel, for the Lord himself said, "Even as the Son of Man came not to be served but to serve, and to give his life as a ransom for many."[36] Therefore "he girded himself with a towel" and he washed "the disciples' feet."[37] *And he himself will bear their sins.* Aquila put "he will lift up" in place of "he will bear," and Theodotian put "he bore." For, according to that holy man John, he was "the lamb of God who takes away the sins of the world."[38]

Therefore he will inherit many, that is, all the nations. For thus, on behalf of God the Father, the blessed David said, "Ask of me, and I will give the nations to you as your inheritance and the ends of the earth as your possession."[39] *And he will divide the spoils of the mighty.* He calls the demons "mighty" and human beings "spoils." The weapons of those who have been killed are called "spoils." In the past humans were the weapons of demons, for they made war against us in our own members.[40] But after the Master, Christ, destroyed them, he distributed their spoils to the apostles when he appointed them the teachers of the Romans, the Egyptians, and the Indians.

For the sake of which, his soul was delivered up to death. That which is considered the very dishonor of the Passion will bring reverence from all of them. *And he was reckoned among criminals.* Not only did he submit to the punishment which had been assigned to transgressors, but he also was crucified with thieves. The evangelist [Mark] also quoted this passage. After he said that they crucified two thieves with him, he said the scripture was fulfilled which said, "And he was reckoned among criminals."[41] *He took upon himself the sins of many and he was delivered up on account of their transgressions.* Symmachus translated this, "he took upon himself[42] the sins of many and he opposed those who rejected him." The rest [i.e., Aquila, Theodotian] translate this in the same way. He says that they put him together with lawless thieves. But when he took upon himself the sins of all, he endured the passion and opposed the demons who had rejected him.

Notes

1 Cyrus, a town in ancient Syria, is approximately 60 miles northwest of Antioch. Although Theodoret wrote in Greek, he also knew this area's native language, Syriac.

2 That is, after the Council of Ephesus in 431 and before the Robber Council of Ephesus in 449 which deposed and exiled him. See Jean-Noël Guinot, trans. and ed., *Théodoret de Cyr: Commentaire sur Isaïe*, 3 vols. (Paris: Les Éditions du Cerf, 1980–4), vol. 1, pp. 16–18. My translation of Theodoret's exegesis of Isaiah 52–3 is based upon this edition. The text printed in Migne's *Patrologia Graeca*, vol. 81 is unsatisfactory because it has numerous gaps. Unfortunately, critical editions of Theodoret's other commentaries have not yet been produced; when citing them I refer to the text in the *Patrologia Graeca* (hereafter *PG*).

3 P. M. Parvis argues persuasively for this setting in *Theodoret's Commentary on the Epistles of St Paul: Historical Setting and Exegetical Practice* (Unpublished doctoral dissertation, Oxford University, 1975), pp. 253–70. Although Parvis's primary focus is Theodoret's exegesis of the Pauline epistles, he draws upon all of Theodoret's commentaries, and his conclusions about the setting of the commentaries are not limited to the Pauline commentaries.

4 *PG* 82.37ab.

5 *PG* 82.37a.

6 See Guinot's discussion, *Commentaire*, vol.1, p. 33.

7 The most important of these is the work of Parvis cited above. See also Guinot, ibid, pp. 19–33, and D. Trakatellis, "Theodoret's Commentary on Isaiah: A Synthesis of Exegetical Traditions," in Bradley Nassif, ed., *New Perspectives on Historical Theology: Essays in Memory of John Meyendorff* (Grand Rapids, Michigan: William B. Eerdmans, 1996), pp. 311–42.

8 *PG* 82.37b; quoted from Parvis, *Historical Setting*, p. 67.

9 *PG* 80.860c. In criticizing strictly historical exegesis, Theodoret is almost surely referring to the work of Theodore of Mopsestia. For an excellent discussion of the way in which Theodoret sought to counter Theodore's historical exegesis with christological exegesis, see Jean-Noël Guinot, "La cristallisation d'un différend: Zorababel dans l'exégèse de Théodore de Mopsueste et de Théodoret de Cyr," *Augustinianum* (24); 527–47.

10 "How beautiful on the mountains are the feet of the one who proclaims tidings of peace, who proclaims good things."

11 Each book in the commentary may represent what was originally one lecture delivered orally, see Parvis, *Historical Setting*.

12 In the New Testament, this can be seen most clearly in Acts 8:26–40 where the text which the Ethiopian eunuch is reading when Philip encounters him is Isa. 53:7–8. Other direct quotations from this Servant Song occur in Luke 22:37, Matt. 8:17, and 1 Pet. 2:22–5; also, throughout the New Testament there are numerous allusions to Isa. 52:13–53:12.

13 See, e.g., Justin Martyr's *Dialogue with Trypho*, chap. 50. Similarly, Origen quotes the entire servant song when responding to Celsus' objection about Jesus' death (*Contra Celsum*, 1.54). In this section of the *Contra Celsum*, Origen answers objections which Celsus has placed on the lips of a Jewish interlocutor. Athanasius also quotes the song when responding to Jewish objections in *On the Incarnation*, 34, 37. For a discussion of Christian writers' attempts to refute Judaism's claims on this issue, see Marcel Simon, *Verus Israel: A study of the relations between Christians and Jews in the Roman Empire (AD 135–425)* (Oxford: Oxford University Press, 1986), pp. 156–78.

14 See, e.g., his exposition of Isa. 53:1 ("Lord, who has believed our report? And to whom

was the Lord's arm revealed?"). Theodoret's interpretation of Isa. 52:1–12 is also tinged with anti-Jewish polemic; see, e.g., his comments on Isa. 52:7b.

15 See Simon, *Verus Israel*, pp. 159–60.

16 In *Ep.* 21, Theodoret explains that if the two natures of Christ are not kept distinct, the result is subordination of the Son (Yvan Azéma, ed. and trans., Théodoret de Cyr, *Correspondance* 3 vols. (Paris: Les Éditions du Cerf, 1964–82), vol. 2, pp. 75–7). In his summary of the second dialogue of his *Eranistes*, Theodoret explains his theological objections to monophysite christology: "Those who believe that one nature resulted from the union of the divinity and the humanity destroy by this teaching the individual properties of both natures; and the destruction of these [properties] results in a denial of both natures. For mixing the realities that were united prevents us from considering flesh as flesh, and God as God. But if there was a clear difference between the realities united even after the union, there was no mixture; a union without mixture took place. If one admits this, then Christ the Lord is not one nature, but one Son, who shows both natures without mixture" (*Eran. suppl.*; quoted from Gerard H. Ettlinger, ed., Theodoret of Cyrus, *Eranistes* (Oxford: Clarendon Press, 1975), pp. 6–7).

For a more complete discussion of Theodoret's dyophysite christology, see A. Grillmeier, *Christ in Christian Tradition*, vol. 1: *From the Apostolic Age to Chalcedon (451)* (Atlanta: John Knox Press, 1975), pp. 488–95; F. Young, *From Nicaea to Chalcedon* (Philadelphia: Fortress Press, 1983), pp. 265–89. Guinot, *Commentaire*, gives a detailed account of how Theodoret's christological concerns are brought to bear throughout the *Commentary on Isaiah* (vol. 1, pp. 89–103).

17 John 13:4–5.

18 Literally, "Before their time."

19 Ps. 49:2 (LXX).

20 Ps. 109:2 (LXX)

21 Isa. 51:3.

22 Acts 9:15.

23 2 Tim. 2:21.

24 Luke 21:20.

25 Matt. 24:16–17.

26 Luke 2:52.

27 Cf. John 6:15, Matt. 21:9.

28 Matt. 26:68.

29 1 Tim. 3:16.

30 Although Theodoret's biblical text is based on the Lucianic version of the Septuagint, he had access to Origen's *Hexapla* which included the translations of Symmachus, Theodotian, and Aquila. Theodoret referred to these translations often, singly or as a group, describing them as "the Three." After quoting one, he will sometimes refer to the other two as "the others."

31 Luke 23:34.

32 Cf. Gal. 3:13.

33 Matt. 23:14; this verse is found only in certain manuscripts and most modern translations put it in critical notes.

34 Acts 2:32, 24.

35 Acts 2:41; 21:20.

36 Matt. 20:28.
37 John 13:4–5.
38 John 1:29.
39 Ps. 2:8.
40 Cf. Rom. 7:23.
41 Mark 15:28; this verse is found only in certain manuscripts and most modern translations put it in critical notes.
42 The Septuagint text which Theodoret quotes has ἀνήνεγκε where Symmachus has ἀνέλαβε.

Further reading

Guinot, Jean-Noël, trans. and ed. *Théodoret de Cyr: Commentaire sur Isaïe*, 3 vols. Paris: Les Éditions du Cerf, 1980–4.

Parvis, P. M. *Theodoret's Commentary on the Epistles of St Paul: Historical Setting and Exegetical Practice*. Unpublished doctoral dissertation, Oxford University, 1975.

Simonetti, Manlio. *Biblical Interpretation in the Early Church: An Historical Introduction to Patristic Exegesis*. Edinburgh: T & T Clark, 1994.

Trakatellis, D. "Theodoret's Commentary on Isaiah: A Synthesis of Exegetical Traditions," in Bradley Nassif, ed., *New Perspectives on Historical Theology: Essays in Memory of John Meyendorff*. Grand Rapids, Michigan: William B. Eerdmans, 1996, pp. 311–42.

Trigg, Joseph Wilson. *Biblical Interpretation*. Message of the Fathers of the Church, vol. 9. Wilmington, Delaware: Michael Glazier, 1988.

Selections from John Calvin's Sermons on Isaiah

Translated and introduced by
Kathryn Greene-McCreight

Of all of John Calvin's works, his sermons are probably the least read and most often overlooked examples of his theological method. This could be in part because translations of his sermons are harder to find than translations of his other works, and possibly because Calvin is generally regarded as a theologian rather than a preacher and biblical interpreter. This is unfortunate, for if one is not familiar with Calvin's sermons, one does not know either Calvin the biblical interpreter or Calvin the theologian.

Calvin was a prolific preacher, at some points in his career preaching as often as six times per week. Usually, five out of these six sermons were on texts from the Old Testament. His sermons display his ability as a linguist and biblical scholar: he preached in French, reading the biblical text in Hebrew or Greek, possibly in Latin as well, and would simultaneously translate the passage he was expositing.[1] He probably also quoted scripture from memory while preaching, for his biblical quotations are quite fluid even within any single sermon and do not consistently follow any of the French Bibles to which Calvin would have had access. Not only was he able to read biblical languages with ease, Calvin had a concordance-like familiarity with the biblical text. This makes it almost impossible to extricate from his sermons the biblical references and allusions, for they are so tightly woven into the fabric of the sermon and he rarely points out when he is using other biblical texts to address the passage at hand. His comments on Isaiah 53 refer and allude to texts from all areas of the canon. Indeed, extended sections of his sermon on Isaiah 53:11 appear to be more of an exposition of the argument of Romans than of Isaiah 53:11. Calvin should not be understood in this to be harmonizing biblical texts or engaging in eisegesis; rather, this practice of using one biblical text to illuminate another follows from Calvin's view of scripture as self-interpreting, as speaking prophetically in all parts and always of the reality of the crucified and risen Messiah of Israel and Savior of the world. This theological claim about scripture which Calvin inherits from the Church Fathers precedes his biblical interpretation rather than emerging *de novo* from it.

Calvin's Christology is informed in large measure by Isaiah 53 and Philippians 2, particularly in the motif of the debasement and exaltation of Christ; those interested in Calvin's Christology therefore cannot afford to pass up his commentaries and sermons on these texts in particular.[2] The centrality of the atoning death and resurrection of Jesus in Calvin's theology is perhaps nowhere clearer than in his mini-series of sermons on what we now often refer to as the "Suffering Servant." Calvin unabashedly reads Isaiah's prophecies of the servant-figure's vicarious suffering to speak of the atoning work of Jesus Christ, not in a mystical or allegorical sense, but clearly and plainly. Indeed, according to Calvin, Isaiah speaks not only of the atoning death of Jesus, but also of his descent into hell and resurrection.[3] While it would not be entirely accurate to say that Calvin believed that Isaiah predicted Christ in any detail, he clearly did understand Isaiah to preach the gospel about Jesus in advance. The difference, while subtle, is hermeneutically and theologically profound, and often disregarded by those attempting to follow in Calvin's footsteps.

Despite Calvin's own humanist interest in texts and philology, he does affirm traditional understandings of scripture which require that it not be read "like any other book." While Calvin does apply in his reading of the Bible the methods of interpretation which he would apply to any other text, sacred or secular, he affirms traditional constraints on reading the Bible, which in effect set limits on the results of any methodology.[4] He hesitates to "twist" the plain sense of the text in order to hear the prophetic element, but he is so drawn by the strength of the morphological fit between Isaiah's servant figure and the New Testament portrayal of Christ that he cannot but understand the plain sense of the prophet to be christological.[5] Not surprisingly, therefore, most of Calvin's scriptural allusions and references which explicate Isaiah 53 in these sermons are drawn from the New Testament.

This is not to say that Calvin does not acknowledge the "historical" placement of the prophet as messenger to the Jews at the time of their exile.[6] Calvin hears the prophet to be speaking to Isaiah's time and to his own with the same voice. He sees the prophet's description of the servant as despised and rejected to be necessary for Isaiah's Jewish audience, for their expectations of the Messiah had to be reshaped before they could accept this crucified and risen one.[7] But Isaiah's words are not for them alone; they are also for Calvin's contemporary audience and, presumably Calvin would add, also for us at the end of the twentieth century, "for this stumbling block has remained since the resurrection of our Lord Jesus Christ . . . Even more for us is it necessary to hold on to this teaching, that the Son of God would be thus without form or beauty, that He would have nothing to admire in Him, according to human opinion" (*CR*, p. 617). Indeed, the prophet speaks directly to Calvin's contemporary audience: "This is why the Prophet calls here to each of us and says 'You poor people, look at what you are until God declared his mercy to you in our Lord Jesus Christ His Son. For we all have erred, you all are lost animals.' This is his intention. And he says 'We all' because he numbers himself among them" (*CR*, p. 631). This, then, is what it means for Calvin to read scripture as prophecy: it has a multivalent quality through which all ages and times are addressed and told of the one reality through which they find salvation. This is the hermeneutical correlate of Calvin's statement that the two covenants are identical in substance while different in dispensation.[8]

The extent to which he hears Isaiah speaking to the sixteenth-century Church becomes clear, for example, in Calvin's typical Reformation polemic. For Calvin, Isaiah is the quintessential Reformation prophet who speaks against Rome, insofar as he taught of justification by grace alone.[9] Calvin slings mud not only at the Papists but also the "libertines," and regarding Servetus's claim that Isaiah's prophecy refers not to Jesus Christ but to Cyrus the Persian, Calvin withholds no venom.[10] Not only does Calvin seek to correct the errors of the Papists and the heretics, but according to Calvin Isaiah does as well.

The following text consists of excerpts from Calvin's sermon on Isaiah 53:4–6, the third of a series of seven sermons Calvin preached in June 1558 on Isaiah 52:13–53:12.[11] This series can be found in two modern English translations: *The Gospel According to Isaiah: Seven Sermons on Isaiah 53 Concerning the Passion and Death of Christ, by John Calvin*, translated by LeRoy Nixon (Grand Rapids: Eerdmans, 1953); *Sermons on Isaiah's Prophecy of the Death and Passion of Christ, by John Calvin*, translated and edited by T. H. L. Parker (London: James Clark and Co., 1956). A modern French translation by Pierre Marcel appears in *La Revue Réformée*, 1951, vols. 1 and 2.[12] It is to state the obvious to say that sermons are an oral medium, and even more so for Calvin who never stepped into the pulpit with a written manuscript or even notes.[13] As he preached, his sermons were simultaneously transcribed by a secretary, and even though the transcription would later pass Calvin's approval, the oral nature of Calvin's sermons cannot be overlooked. Translation of his sermons should therefore follow slightly different criteria than translation of his tightly composed written works such as *The Institutes*. In the following translation of the *Corpus Reformatorum* text, I have tried to capture the oral quality of the sermon, to inclusivize language where the task of translation would not be violated, and to point out as many scriptural allusions as my ear was able to catch. I am sure

Calvin would have pointed out more if he had written and annotated his sermons himself.

When we contemplate the works of God in all the world, they tell us that He should be praised for His greatness and grandeur; but when we come to the person of our Lord Jesus Christ, we must learn to glorify God in His lowliness. [. . .] [W]e should always have this goal, that instead of the unbelievers who are shocked when they see that Jesus Christ was afflicted this way by the hand of God His Father,[14] and who take the opportunity of scandal to distance themselves from him, we ought to be all the more spurred on to seek Him. And we should be completely swept away by His love, for he did not spare Himself[15] but wanted to take on all of our burdens so that we might be relieved of them.[16] So when we see that our Lord Jesus Christ made such an exchange on our behalf, and wanted to pay off entirely all of our debts so that we would be cleared of them, that he wanted to be condemned in our name, and as if in our person so that we might be absolved, this is what should draw us to Him. [. . .]

Now, it is stated point-blank that "He was afflicted by the Hand of God," and that this was for our iniquities. For if we have no regard for the judgement of God, the death and passion of our Lord Jesus Christ will be useless, and we will receive no benefit from it. [. . .] And this is why He is called the Lamb without blemish.[17] He is called Lamb for He was offered up in sacrifice. He was without blemish to show that He bore all of our burdens. And this is why it is also said that His blood is our cleansing: for we are filthy and full of impurity until the blood of our Lord Jesus Christ cleanses us. So it is not without cause that the Prophet brings us back to God's Judgement, saying that Jesus Christ was afflicted because it was necessary for Him to bear our condemnation. In short, each time and whenever we think of how the death and passion of our Lord Jesus Christ benefitted us, let each and every one of us stand before the judgement seat of God. There we will find that we are all outlaws. Now, how severe is the judgement of God? How terrible is his vengeance? Enough to swallow us up and throw us down into the abyss. But insofar as our Lord Jesus Christ was not spared,[18] but, rather, as God executed the severity of His judgment on Him, and as He was there in our name as a pledge for us, so now we can rest assured that God will no longer pursue us, will no longer bring charge against us,[19] will no longer punish us according to our failings and offenses. But why? Because our Lord Jesus has cleared us of them.[20] [. . .]

This is then how we should take the words of the Prophet when he says that Jesus Christ was not only crucified by human hands, but that He was presented before the judgement seat of God, that there He answered on our behalf, that there He yielded to take up the burden which we deserved. And this is also why he adds in particular that "He bore our sins and transgressions," just as St Peter also speaks of this and expresses this with "cross" or "tree," to show that this kind of death that the Son of God suffered was a visible and clear witness that our iniquities were placed on Him.[21] For it is said in the Law: "Cursed be the one who hangs from a tree."[22] Jesus Christ was hung there so that we might know that He was as though accursed in our place, as Saint Paul says in Galatians.[23] For he suggests that in this we should consider the wonderful goodness of God, and the infinite love of our Lord Jesus Christ which He bears for us, for He wanted not only to die for us but also to suffer such an accursed death so that we might be blessed by God. And although our own iniquities terrify us (and although we cannot be but terrified before the judgement of God when we see what is contained there, to see that we are abominable when we offend against our God, and that our conscience gives us remorse) let us not fail to rest assured that He will pardon our sins and will accept us as His well-loved children, just and blameless since our curse was abolished on that tree on which our Lord Jesus Christ was hung. This is what the Prophet intended to add for greater expression.

Now, he adds that He was afflicted because the correction or the chastisement of our peace was on him. He adds nothing new here, but declares to himself in his own manner to show how this must be understood: that our Lord Jesus was beaten and struck by the hand of God so that we might be acquitted. He thus carries the correction that is due us, and what a correction of peace! It is true that some understand that our Lord Jesus Christ had to be punished in this way on our part because we were so thick that none would think to humble himself before God and that we were blinded in our wrongs. But we see the natural sense of the Prophet is such that to have peace with God we had to be reconciled by some other means. [. . .] If God pardoned us without Jesus interceding for us and standing as pledge on our behalf, we would not even think twice. We each would wipe the egg off our face and seize the opportunity to take greater liberties. But when we see that God did not even spare His only Son[24] but treated him with such extreme severity that he suffered bodily all the agony that was possible to suffer, and that even in his soul he was afflicted to the bitter end, crying out "My God, My God, why have you deserted me?"[25] When we hear these things it is impossible for us, without being harder than stone, not to shudder in fear and astonishment to the point of complete disorientation, without our offenses and iniquities being absolutely detestable to us since they so provoke God's wrath against us. [. . .]

. . . "By his wounds we have healing." It is true that we do not even see our vices because hypocrisy has blindfolded us and pride rules us. So people deceive themselves and make themselves believe that God is still indebted to them, or they are so deadened that they do not even come to think about it at all. Now, the Prophet shows that without the wounds of our Lord Jesus Christ, there is nothing in us but Death, and that we must seek our healing in Him. So when we wish to feel the benefits which the death and passion of Our Lord Jesus Christ bring us, let us discern that the vices rooted in our being are all sorts of mortal wounds and diseases, even though they may not be evident. I ask you, if someone gets an abscess inside the body, say in the stomach or intestines, wouldn't it be much worse like this than if one could see the abscess and lance it? Anyone who imagines he is healthy simply because an illness is not visible is crazy. Our maladies are all the more lethal when they are secret. And besides our vices we carry whose roots are hidden in us, the wrongs that we commit each day show that our being is perverse and accursed and that we are completely twisted. Since there is nothing in us but spiritual infection and leprosy, and since we are rotten in our iniquities, what should we do? What is the remedy? Should we go in search of the Angels of paradise? Alas, they are of no use. Instead we should come to our Lord Jesus Christ, who was willing to be disfigured from the crown of his head to the soles of his feet, covered in wounds, whipped time and again, who bore the crown of thorns, who was nailed up on the cross, whose side was pierced. This is how we are healed; this is our true medicine with which we must be content and to which we must lend our affection, knowing that never in any other way can we find rest, but that we would be tormented and tortured to hell if Jesus Christ did not console us and appease the wrath of God toward us. When we are certain of that, we are given opportunity to sing His praise instead of groaning in our disorientation. This in a nutshell is what we have to hold on to from the words of the Prophet.

Now, St Matthew in the eighth chapter refers to this passage when he narrates how our Lord Jesus healed all sorts of illnesses, how he gave sight to the blind, and made the lame to walk, and restored hearing to the deaf, raised up the half-dead and paralytics, cast out demons. St Matthew says this shows that the Prophet Isaiah had good reason to say that He bore our infirmities and carried our weaknesses. Surely the Prophet does not speak here of bodily illness. It seems then that the Evangelist poorly applied this passage. Rather, he declares that our Lord Jesus, in healing the evident illnesses, wanted to lead us further, to make us contemplate is in a figure why He came into the world. When we hear that our Lord Jesus Christ raised the paralytics and even resurrected the dead, that he also heals all illnesses, we should know that He declared visibly on account of our crude weakness that He is our spiritual Doctor, and that we might learn as I already have said that the vices to which we are inclined are, rather, corruptions of the soul. In short, when we join what St Matthew proposes with what the Prophet Isaiah wanted to declare, we should know that on our part we are full of corruption and villainy, and that there is not a drop of health in us, that our souls are full of deadly vices, but that our Lord Jesus delivered us from all that, and that when we come to him, we will find healing. When, I say, we join one with the other, we discover that unless we have our refuge in this Redeemer, we must stagnate and rot in our vices and miseries. [. . .]

This is why the Prophet calls here to each of us and says, "You poor people, look at what you are until God declared his mercy to you in our Lord Jesus Christ His Son. For we all have erred, you all are lost animals." This is his intention. And he says "We all" because he numbers himself among them. Already we have seen that it was necessary for the Jews to be shut up in this general condemnation of humanity because it would seem to them otherwise that they should be exempt. For they always had this crazed outrageous confidence that since God had adopted and chosen them they thought themselves to be more worthy than the rest. But the Prophet here envelops them in eternal death until they search out the remedy of their deliverance in Jesus Christ. We are then all of us shut up in this condemnation. And he uses the word "all" to rule out all exception as if he said "None should boast, not one among you, to be justified before God, to be able to pass by this remedy which I now declare to you, for the most perfect, and the one who has the greatest sanctity in the opinion of others, will be culpable before God."[26]

So now we see the Prophet's intention, but still he does not content himself there. He says, "each one has turned to his own way." And why does he repeat this, going from "all" to "each"? Because when he condemns us in general, we still are not moved with such liveliness as is required. It is true that we must acknowledge the condemnation when he says that among people there is none just. In another passage of the Psalm it is said that God looked but could not find a single individual who was not rotten in wickedness.[27] The virtuous are also referred to here, and those who have the greatest reputation as well as the most debased. It is said that they all turned aside and down to the last one none was found who was not totally corrupt before God. Holy Scripture is full of this teaching, and St Paul demonstrates it often in the third chapter of Romans when he strings together all the passages from both the Psalms and Prophets, where it is said that all are depraved and that there is nothing in them except malice and betrayal, that they are full of cruelty, that there is nothing but venom and violence, fraud and theft, and that their throat is a tomb.[28] When all these things are said there, St Paul adds that all are included without exception, until God has changed them and renewed them by His Holy Spirit. Now when this doctrine is preached, we should all bow our heads, for we will be ashamed and horrified at replying before God. And in fact, what would we gain in all of our disputes? In spite of ourselves, we have to feel that it is not in vain that we are condemned since God is our Judge. But even still, each of us will return home without being moved, and what is said will barely touch us. We will say, "Sure, we are all sinners, and there is none who is not guilty before God." Yet will we feel our wickedness to the point of being displeased, to the point of being spurred on to seek grace from our Lord Jesus Christ and renouncing ourselves? Not in the least: it is enough for us to have conceded that we are all sinners. Even worse, we will often see those who take cover and strength when accused of their faults and they see themselves convicted, saying, "Surely, it is true, we are all sinners." A wicked individual will have blasphemed the name of God, or will have committed some enormously abominable deed, and if reprimanded, will deny it at first. Never will an individual come to confess unless by constraint. So, do they really see themselves to be convicted? "It is true, we are all sinners," they will say. In other words, you are an evil hypocrite who mocks God. So we see that under this generalizing many will seek some excuse so that their turpitude is not acknowledged for what it is. For this reason, the Prophet after having said "All have erred" adds "each one, each one," as if to say "Pay no attention to general human nature, but each look inside and there you will consider and face what you really are." For then we are touched by God's judgement, and we are led into true humility when we feel our evil so as to be led to repentance and when each will have thus examined the self in secret. So now we see the intention of the Prophet.

As for the rest, by saying that each has turned his own way, he shows in the first place how individuals conduct themselves by their own appetites, and according to their own reason and wisdom. And this is again a point we should note, because we will see some who are so crazy that no one can ever convince them that they are throwing themselves away into perdition when they do whatever seems good to them, and others who are so stupefied by their own desires that they do not even recognize that they are deliberately diving headfirst into deepest hell unless God pulls them back up. These days we see the Papists, when one overcomes them by the Word of God and they see themselves convicted, they say, "Very well, leave me alone, I will go my own way no matter what." "Then you can go to hell because that is where you are going when you go your way." "But look, my devotion is so great; is it really possible that God would reject it?" "Yes, but the Prophet Isaiah speaks here as well about the devotion of each individual, and do you think that the Holy Spirit who spoke by his mouth at that time didn't know well enough that you would be a bigot, you monk, you nun, full of pride and venom? That you would conduct yourself according to your own whim, that you would forge the worship of God in your ecclesiastical tasks, that you would adore idols, and think it was good to do so, that you would have in these things your devotion? Didn't the Holy Spirit well know such villainies? Look what he states: 'each one to his own way,' which is to say that each went to hell, each thrown into perdition, when he followed his own course."

Such are the ways of mortals. So we are taught by this passage to rid ourselves of all crazed arrogance and recognize that doing anything that seems proper to us and which we judge to be indeed reasonable is as if we were conspiring with Satan, throwing ourselves into his snares. This teaching should correct our every presumption so that we might suffer alone to be governed by the Spirit of God and by His Word, and equally that we should take to heart these words declared by the Prophet Isaiah that although we might recognize the good we will not stop being addicted to evil. And why is that? Because all of our desires rebel against God: although we see that evil must be swept aside, we will not stop being swept away by it, not by force but by a voluntary malice which is so hidden in us that only the fruits betray the root. Thus we know in the first place that there is no logic in us to walk the straight and narrow, but that there is only one road which God approves of and which will lead us to salvation.[29] That is to acknowledge that our Lord Jesus Christ will take us under his charge and that we will be the sheep of his flock, and that will follow him as our Shepherd.[30] Even more let us learn that all of our desires are corrupt and that we will look for evil in place of the good until our Lord Jesus Christ corrects and reforms us and until he has placed in us the proper desire to obey Him. This is what the Prophet wished to state.

Now we have only to conclude that all who circle about here and there turn away from our Lord Jesus Christ. For the Prophet declares that there was not one, neither among Patriarchs nor Prophets nor all the holy Fathers nor Martyrs, who did not need to be reconciled to God by the death and passion of our Lord Jesus Christ. If Abraham father of the faithful, if David mirror of all justice, if the others like them, such as Job and Daniel, who are named as mirrors of all holiness and perfection, if even these, I say, were poor sheep, astray and lost until they were rescued by our Lord Jesus Christ, alas! what about us? So when we go seeking them as our mediators and imagine escaping the perdition we are in by means of them, do we not show ourselves to be incredibly ungrateful to our Lord Jesus Christ? Yet we are so deprived of our senses that we go begging among those who themselves need to have recourse to the death and passion of our Lord Jesus Christ. For if necessity constrains us to search out a remedy, we must go to Him in whom the Faithful of all times have had their refuge, since there is neither a Holy Father nor St Peter, nor St Paul, nor the Virgin Mary, nor anyone else, who is exempt. So let us learn to come to the source and spring to draw the water there which we need.[31] For our Lord Jesus has enough to quench us all, and there is never need to worry that the fullness of His grace might run dry. He will give to each of us our portion when we come seeking it.

So let us come boldly to our Lord Jesus Christ, and He will be enough for us all. Whoever turns away here or there cannot access the remedy which God offers, but, rather, rejects it in doing so. This ingratitude prevents such a one from enjoying the grace offered. And we are all the more inexcusable since this is proclaimed to us daily. For God is not content to have sent His Son once for all and to have exposed him to death and to have struck Him in His wrath even though God loved him as His only Son (for although He wanted to cast Him down and used all severity against him, He was indeed the well-beloved Son as we have said, but all this was so that we might be absolved), no, He is not content with that. No, every day He offers us this treasure so that was might rejoice in it. He declares that Jesus Christ who was pierced in the side today opens His heart to us so that we might be certain of the love He bears for us. And that Jesus Christ who had His arms fixed to the cross now extends them to draw us to Him. And He wants all of these things to benefit us: just as He once spilled His blood, today He wants for us to be plunged into it. When God invites us so gently and when Jesus Christ offers us the fruit of his death and passion and shows that His blood is always fresh (as the Apostle says in the letter to the Hebrews) and that it is not blood which runs dry or trickles slowly but, sanctified by His heavenly power, is always new blood (as also the Apostle used this word). Let us know then that His power is not diminished and that it always carries full and entire effect, as always from the beginning, such that we may all come to gather before Jesus Christ. And after having confessed our poverty and disorientation let us not doubt that it will suffice to give us such a remedy that we will be able to conclude that we are received and recognized by God as His own children and that He counts us as though righteous and perfect instead of impure before him. See then how we should hold this teaching. Today, seeing some jest and mock and others rise up in pride and presumptuousness imagining their righteousness to satisfy God, let us renounce such blasphemy and in true faith and repentance let us seek out our Lord Jesus Christ and let all our desire be to come and gather about Him, when we feel as if we are laden with this unbearable burden. Now let us bow down before the Majesty of our good God, acknowledging our faults, praying to Him . . .

Notes

1 T. H. L. Parker, trans. and ed., *Sermons on Isaiah's Prophecy of the Death and Passion of Christ, by John Calvin* (London: James Clarke and Co., 1956), p. 12.

2 For the claim about the influence of Isaiah 53 and Philippians 2 on Calvin's Christology, see Max Dominicé, *L'humanité de Jésus Christ d'après Calvin* (Paris, 1933), p. 122.

3 "Thus the Prophet spoke of the fruit which we get out of the death and passion of our Lord Jesus Christ, and now he adds that He will be raised by the power of God His Father." (*Corpus Reformatorum*, vol. 63, p. 639; hereafter abbreviated *CR*.) "Now, it was certainly necessary for our Lord Jesus to descend to the Abyss before being exalted in the glory of the heavens" (*CR*, p. 641). NB: Calvin's translation of Isaiah 53:8 reads: "He was raised from anguish [Calvin adds "from prison", p. 638] and judgement [Calvin changes this to "condemnation", p. 641], and who will speak of his age? He was cut off from the land of the living and pp. suffered the wounds which were due my people." See also *CR*, pp. 656, 665 for instances where Calvin may be referring to the descent into Hell.

4 For further comments on these additional constraints, see my unpublished dissertation, "Ad Litteram: Understandings of the Plain Sense of Scripture in the Exegesis of Augustine, Calvin and Barth on Genesis 1–3," Yale University, 1994.

5 For example, in speaking of "He shall sprinkle," Calvin says ". . . the natural sense of the Prophet is that Jesus Christ will sprinkle all nations, that although He is a dry and sterile trunk, even so the whole world will be watered by His power" (*CR*, p. 603).

6 ". . . the Prophet already shows here that in awaiting their Redeemer, the Jews must shut their eyes to all that they have been accustomed to look for, and must give way to faith in order to remain certain of God's goodness, no matter how repulsive it may appear to them. And this means not only the person of our Lord Jesus Christ, but the entire course of His gospel and the order with which He maintains and governs the faithful" (*CR*, p. 599), and again "[The Prophet] shows that . . . the Jews should not expect some human means but that they should hope that God would surpass all that mortals could imagine" (*CR*, p. 603).

7 ". . . first because they had always awaited an earthly Kingdom . . . Thus God had to warn them that the Redeemer would be . . . rejected by the world" (*CR*, p. 616).

8 E.g., "Although this sentence of the prophet Joel was said before Jesus Christ appeared, certainly the faithful at the time of the Law practiced it that we should ourselves by their example be confirmed and assured now, (we I say, who have perfection and fulfillment of all that was figured under the Law) that when we come to pray and invoke our God in the name of Him whom He established as our advocate, we should feel in truth that He intercedes still for us, so that we will be heard in all our requests" (*CR*, p. 688).

9 E.g., "Today the Papists try to slander falsely the doctrine which we preach, that we must be saved by the gracious goodness of God and that we must find our refuge in Jesus Christ, knowing that there we have all perfection and righteousness. 'Yes', they say, 'and each will live according to his or her own desire and will have no scruples against offending God.' Now it is true that these dogs can bark on like this because they have never tasted the remission of sins. For these hypocrites openly mock God and all piety and never have grasped what it is to have transgressed the law of God. And we see how they think to acquit themselves: if they have sung mass and mumbled prayers, if they have fooled around and performed absurdities, God must be appeased like a baby with a rattle. See then how these mockers of God are able to blaspheme against the Gospel" (*CR*, pp. 644–5). Examples of this abound in Calvin, and while his polemic is certainly not as biting as is that of Luther, for example, the statement that Calvin "refuses to enter into debate with opponents" is Calvinist hagiographical apologetic. *Pace* Richard Gamble, "Brevitas et Facilitas: Toward an understanding of Calvin's Hermeneutic," *WTJ* 47 (1985): 3.

10 E.g., "This is a terrible falsification of this beautiful prophesy, and in fact the sense that this unfortunate dreamed up was never before thought of by a human creature. For although many heretics set out to pervert the teaching of Holy Scripture, they never went this far" (*CR*, p. 656). It should be noted that this is just one of the instances where Calvin disallows a "historical" reading of a biblical text in favor of the traditional reading.

11 Calvin would preach continuously through a whole book of the Bible from beginning to end, and he preached through Isaiah from the summer of 1556 until the summer of 1559.

12 Parker's translation is based on a collation of a microfilm copy of the 1558 edition and the version in vol. 63 of the *Corpus Reformatorum* published in 1887. When one examines carefully the list of errata Parker finds in the *CR* edition which he includes as an appendix to his translation, one is struck by the relative insignificance of any difference in translation which actually results from the collation, especially when keeping in mind the orality of the medium and the fact that the sermons are transcribed.

13 T. H. L. Parker, *Calvin's Preaching* (Louisville: Westminster John Knox, 1992).

14 1 Cor. 1:18.

15 Rom. 8:32.

16 Gal. 6:2.

17 1 Pet. 1:19; Heb. 9:12–14; John 1:29; Jer. 11:19; Rev. 5:6–12.

18 Rom. 8:32.

19 Rom. 8:33.

20 Rom. 8:34.

21 1 Pet. 2:4.

22 Deut. 21:23.

23 Gal. 3:13.

24 Rom. 8:32.

25 Matt. 27:46, Ps. 22:1.

26 Rom. 3:10, 27.

27 Pss. 14:1, 3; 53:1.

28 Matt. 23:27; Ps. 5:9.

29 John 14:6.

30 John 10; Luke 15/Matt. 18; Isa. 40:11; Ezek. 34; Ps. 23.
31 John 4:14.

Further reading

Calvin's sermons
The Deity of Christ and Other Sermons, trans. Leroy Nixon. Grand Rapids: Eerdmans, 1950.
   Especially useful for following up the sermons on Isaiah 53, this collection includes
   sermons on New Testament texts on the passion, ascension, and second coming of Jesus,
   and on Pentecost, following and expanding on apparently unbeknownst to the translator
   the collection published by Conrad Badius in 1558.
A Selection of the Most Celebrated Sermons of John Calvin. New York: S. & D. A. Forbes,
   1830. Includes sermons on the Pastoral Epistles.
Sermons on Deuteronomy. Edinburgh: Banner of Truth, 1987.
Sermons on the Epistle to the Ephesians. London: Banner of Truth Trust, 1973.
Sermons on Jeremiah, trans. Blair Reynolds. Lewiston, N.Y.: E. Mellen Press, 1990.
Sermons on Job, trans. Arthur Golding. Edinburgh: Banner of Truth, 1993.
Sermons on Micah, trans. Blair Reynolds. Lewiston, N.Y.: E. Mellen Press, 1990.
Sermons on Second Samuel, chs. 1–13. Carlisle, PA: Banner of Truth Trust, 1992.
Secondary literature
Parker, T. H. L. *Calvin's New Testament Commentaries*. Grand Rapids: Eerdmans, 1971.
——*Calvin's Old Testament Commentaries*. Edinburgh: T & T Clark, 1986.
——*Calvin's Preaching*. Louisville: Westminster/John Knox Press, 1992.
Puckett, David L. *John Calvin's Exegesis of the Old Testament*. Louisville: Westminster/John
   Knox Press, 1995.
Torrance, T. F. *The Hermeneutics of John Calvin*. Edinburgh: Scottish Academic Press, 1988.

Speech and Silence in the Servant Passages: Towards a Final-Form Reading of the Book of Isaiah

Tod Linafelt

The growth of scholarly interest in the final form of the Book of Isaiah reflects a significant trend in much of contemporary biblical scholarship. Such interest with regard to Isaiah was no doubt largely precipitated by Brevard Child's programmatic treatment of the book in his *Introduction to the Old Testament as Scripture*.[1] In that treatment, Childs attempted to move beyond historical-critical questions, which had been determined by the strict division of the book into a First Isaiah (chapters 1–39, dated to the eighth century) and a Second Isaiah (chapters 40–66, dated to the Babylonian exile).[2] Childs did not, of course, question the judgement that the material in chapters 40–66 reflects a much later historical context than chapters 1–39, but he did argue that "the theological context completely overshadows the historical."[3] A number of important studies have followed that of Childs and have discerned significant literary and theological connections between First and Second Isaiah.[4]

Also of interest for the study of Isaiah is the question of the servant figure. Prominently circumscribed from the rest of the book of Isaiah by Bernhard Duhm in 1892,[5] the "servant passages" (42:1–4; 49:1–6; 50:4–9; 52:13–53:12) have received enormous scholarly attention. The main point of contention has been the identity of the servant figure. The servant has been variously understood as (1) an anonymous contemporary of Second Isaiah; (2) Second Isaiah himself; (3) a group of people (i.e. Israel as a nation or a remnant); (4) the expected Davidic messiah; and (5) the city of Zion as a representative of Israel.[6]

In the present study, I will bring together these two interpretative trajectories and focus on the theme of "convenantal discourse." I borrow the phrase "covenantal discourse" from Harold Fisch,[7] who uses it to characterize the dialogue which, on the one hand, binds Israel to God and, on the other hand, provides the language, symbols, and modes of speech that make Israel's communal life possible.[8] More specifically, by tracing the themes of speech and silence through the four servant passages, I will make a proposal concerning not only the identity of the servant but also how the servant passages cohere within the final form of Isaiah.

The Servant Figure as Speaking Subject

What is striking about the servant passages, when read in light of an emphasis on speech, is the disparity in the nature of the servant figure as a speaking subject. In the first and last passages (42:1–4 and 52:13–53:12), for example, the servant is presented as one who characteristically does not speak. We may note in particular the following verses:[9]

> He will not cry or lift up his voice.
>   or make it heard in the street. (42:2)

> He was oppressed and he was afflicted,
>   yet he opened not his mouth;
> like a lamb that is led to the slaughter,
>   and like a sheep that is dumb,
>   so he opened not his mouth. (53:7)

The absence of speech portrayed here reinforces, in concrete terms, the more general sense of the servant figure's powerlessness conveyed by the passages.

In the middle two servant passages (49:1–6 and 50:4–9), however, we find that the servant does not remain silent:

> Listen to me, O coastlands, and hearken, you peoples from afar.
> The Lord called me from the womb, from the body of my mother he named my name.
> He made my mouth like a sharp sword . . . (49:1–2)

> The Lord God has given me the tongue of those who are taught,
>   that I may know how to sustain with a word, him that is weary. (50:4)

In short, there seems to be a vast difference between the silent servant of the first and last passages, and the servant of the middle passages who commands attention as a speaking subject.

If we are to adjudicate these differences, we may begin by referring to the proposal of Wilcox and Paton-Williams[10] that there is a shift in the identity of the servant at the point of the second servant passage. Following Westermann,[11] they posit a transition in "the oracles of Deutero-Isaiah" at the midpoint of chapter 49. In chapters 40–48 there are seven explicit references to Israel as the servant (41:8; 44:1, 2, 21 (twice); 45:4; 48:20). Only in chapter 49 do we run into difficulty identifying the servant as Israel, for here the servant is described both as *identical with* Israel (49:3) and as *having a mission to* Israel (49:5). Wilcox and Paton-Williams suggest that here the identification of the servant as Israel shifts to an identification of the servant as the prophet. The declaration of 49:3, "you are my servant Israel," becomes – according to this reading – the recommissioning of the *prophet* as the *"new* Israel." Their positing of this shift in the character of the servant is supported by the evidence that nowhere in chapters 49–55 is Israel referred to as the servant, in contrast with the seven times in chapters 40–48 cited above.

My own discussion of the servant figure will assume such a shift in identification, though I will argue for the shift at 49:4 rather than 49:1. I will consider the shift in identification in conjunction with the patterns of speech and silence we have identified in the servant passages – and will examine more closely the relationship of the servant passages to their surrounding literary contexts. I will first look at each servant passage in light of these considerations individually and then conclude with a consideration of what our results contribute to the study of the book as a whole.

The First Servant Passage: 42:1–4

One aspect of the book of Isaiah's concern for what I have called covenantal discourse is Israel's ability to hear the speech of YHWH. This concern may be seen most dramatically in Second Isaiah's frequent repetition of the command to "hear" or "listen." Consider the following texts, for example:

Listen to me in silence, O coastlands;
  let the peoples renew their strength. (41:1)

Who among you will give ear to this,
  will attend and listen for the time to come? (42:23)

But now hear, O Jacob my servant,
  Israel whom I have chosen! (44:1)

Hearken to me, O house of Jacob,
  all the remnant of the house of Israel. (46:3)

> Hearken to me, you stubborn of heart,
>   you who are far from deliverance. (46:12)

> Hear this, O house of Jacob,
>   who are called by name of Israel. (48:1)

> Assemble all of you and hear!
>   Who among them has declared these things? (48:14)

> Hearken to me, you who pursue deliverance,
>   you who seek the Lord. (51:1)

> Listen to me, my people,
>   and give ear to me, my nation. (51:4)

There is evidence of this concern that Israel hear in First and Third Isaiah as well. For example, in 30:9 Israel is called a "rebellious people . . . who will not hear the instruction of the Lord." Again, in 66:4 the reason given by YHWH for the rejection of the people's sacrifices is as follows:

> because, when I called, no one answered,
>   when I spoke they did not listen.

A second aspect of covenantal discourse in Isaiah is that of speaking rightly about God. Thus, in 40:9 Israel is admonished to declare the "good tidings" of YHWH:

> Get you up to a high mountain,
>   O Zion, herald of good tidings;
> lift up your voice with strength,
>   O Jerusalem, herald of good tidings,
>   lift it up, fear not;
> Say to the cities of Judah,
>   "Behold your God!"

Again, this same theme is also found in texts from First and Third Isaiah. In 30:19 we read:

> Yea, O people in Zion who dwell in Jerusalem;
> you shall weep no more. He will surely be
> gracious to you at the sound of your cry;
> when he hears it he will answer you.

And in 65:1 YHWH says:

I was ready to be sought by those who did not ask for me;
I was ready to be found by those who did not seek me.
I said, "Here am I, here am I," to a nation that did not call on my name.

As this last passage indicates, Israel seems unable to speak rightly about God. Either Israel remains conspicuously mute or, in the few instances where Israel's speech is described (but never voiced in the first person), Israel speaks wrongly (cf. 5:20; 30:10ff; 40:27).

It should come as no surprise, then, that we find the servant Israel in chapter 42 silent. The nation has yet to assume its role as the one who speaks rightly about YHWH. That the servant is not *meant* to remain silent is made clear in 42:10, where YHWH admonishes Israel to:

Sing to the Lord a new song,
his praise from the end of the earth!

This is also hinted at in the contrast in chapter 41 between the servant of YHWH and "the false gods" who are incapable of speech. YHWH dares them to "set forth their case" (41:21) and to "tell us what is to come hereafter" (41:23). However, the false gods can only remain silent: "there was none who declared it, none who proclaimed . . . who, when I ask, gives an answer?" (41:28). The false gods and "the nations" cannot answer. Israel, however, as YHWH's partner in covenantal discourse, should be able to give witness to YHWH's deeds. But at this point in the book, Israel remains a broken people. Wilcox and Paton-Williams note that, "captive and discouraged, Israel is only fit for a passive role in the new thing that YHWH is doing."[12] Or, in terms more congenial to my argument, Israel has yet to claim its proper role as speaking subject.

The Second Servant Passage: 49:1–6

It is this passage that has constituted the primary dilemma in identifying the servant, for here the servant is explicitly *called* Israel (v. 3) and at the same time said to have a mission *to* Israel (v. 5). It also presents a problem in terms of our analysis of the power of speech, for we saw that in chapter 42 the servant was described as silent. Yet here the servant is presented as one who speaks in the first person, who commands the attention of the "coastlands" and "peoples from afar," and who refers to the servant's own mouth as "like a sharp sword" (v. 2).

As indicated above, Wilcox and Paton-Williams have offered the intriguing notion that in chapter 49 the identity of the servant shifts from the nation Israel to the person of the prophet. Israel has failed to fulfill its mission as servant, and so the prophet is given that mission (to the nations), as well as his previous mission to Israel itself. This proposal does indeed deal quite nicely with the traditional problems raised in identifying the servant. Moreover, it accords well with our previous analysis of the servant figure of chapter 42 as failing to fulfill its role. In my judgement, however, the prophet is not given the role of servant until 49:4, rather than 49:1, as suggested by Wilcox and Paton-Williams.

My argument is that 49:1–3 is much more closely connected with the passage immediately preceding it than has previously been recognized. If we look back to 48:20, we find (as in so many other sections of the book) the command for Israel to speak rightly about YHWH:

> Go forth from Babylon, flee from Chaldea,
> declare this with a shout of joy, proclaim it,
> send it forth to the end of the earth;
> say, "The Lord has redeemed his servant Jacob!"

Instead of closing the quote after this one phrase, however, I submit that we are to understand the quote to extend down through 49:3. The first section of this servant passage, then, is part of what the servant Israel is supposed to "declare" and "proclaim," as commanded in 48:20. It is not the servant speaking in the first person after all but, rather, YHWH describing what the speech of Israel should be! The Book of Isaiah has not yet presented the people of Israel as speaking correctly; there is no indication that the situation has suddenly changed.

There *are* ample instances of YHWH coaxing the community to speak rightly, however, and it is this that we find here. That Israel has not yet claimed its role as servant may be seen in the chapters that follow, where YHWH continues in the role of comforter with a series of "Thus says the Lord . . ." statements (49:7, 8, 22, 25; 50:1). Each of these statements functions to assure the broken, dejected, and speechless Israel that YHWH is still actively working on its behalf.

To support our contention that Israel still has not responded to God's urgings, we may cite 49:14, the first time that Israel explicitly speaks:

> But Zion said, "The Lord has forsaken me,
> my Lord has forgotten me."

Here, while Israel does indeed finally engage in speech, we find none of the confidence which the servant of 49:1–3 is portrayed as having. Instead, we have only a despairing refrain that must have been repeated over and over by the disheartened exilic community. And so it is here that we find the change of plans; it is here that YHWH commissions the prophet to be the new servant.

According to my reading, 49:4 is the voice of the prophet, lamenting that his oracles have had no effect on the people of Israel. That is, they seem no closer than before to engaging YHWH in dialogue. Yet, as the second half of verse 4 indicates, the prophet knows the creative power of YHWH's word. If he has indeed been proclaiming the word of YHWH and not his own whim, then there must be some result.[13]

In 49:5, then, we find the shift in identity posited by Wilcox and Paton-Williams. As Westermann has observed,[14] the poem is constructed so that the "*waw*-consecutive" sets off both verse 4 and verse 5, respectively. According to my reading, verse 4 is set off because it is the change in voice from YHWH to the prophet, who wonders over the failure of YHWH's word to fulfill its purpose. Verse 5 is set off because it is the point at which the new identification of the *prophet* as servant is made. This shift also makes sense in terms of the use here of *'attâ* ("now"), which is, according to Knight, "Deutero-Isaiah's choice of technical term for the contemporary moment."[15] Because Israel has failed to assume the role of servant and to speak rightly, as called to do in 48:17–49:4, the prophet is "now" given the task of witnessing to "the nations" (49:6) in addition to his previous task of bringing back Israel (49:5–6).

The Third Servant Passage: 50:4–9

Having established that the identity of the servant has shifted from Israel to the prophet, the interpretation of the third servant passage is more straightforward than the others. In terms of the power of speech, the prophet-as-servant is presented as the one who both hears the word of YHWH (vv. 4b, 5a), and who speaks rightly about God (v. 4a). In particular we see the contrast with the failure of Israel-as-servant in 50:5:

> The Lord God has opened my ear,
>> but I was not rebellious.

Here again we find the *waw*-consecutive, "*but* I was not rebellious." Westermann[16] speculates that the *waw* refers back to the implied persecutions of the servant. In my judgement, however, the *waw* refers back to 48:8:

> from of old your ear has not been opened,
>> . . . from birth you were called a rebel.

The prophet-as-servant, who hears the word of YHWH and is not rebellious, is contrasted with Israel-as-servant, who did not hear the word of YHWH and was rebellious.

In the third servant passage, then, the prophet is given as the exemplar for what Israel's role as servant should be. The servant is one who willingly speaks rightly about God and invites others (i.e. the nations) "to contend" (v. 8).

The Fourth Servant Passage: 52:13–53:12

Thus far we have seen a movement in the servant passages from a silent Israel-as-servant in the first passage to the ideal of what Israel *should* be saying in the second passage and to the prophet as exemplar of what Israel should be in the third passage. Now, finally, we come to the silent prophet-as-servant in the fourth passage. But the silence of the prophet in this passage is qualitatively different from the silence of the community in chapter 42. While the silence in chapter 42 was presented as the result of Israel's inability to hear and respond to YHWH, here the silence of the prophet is presented as obedience in the face of persecution (53:7)[17]

Silence is certainly still understood as a sign of the powerlessness of the servant. However, in an ironic twist, it is this silent servant who will "be exalted" (53:13) "and make many to be accounted righteous" (53:11). In a particularly sardonic reversal we read that "the kings shall shut their mouths because of him" (52:15). The ones who are most powerful and whose speech is most grandiose will themselves become powerless and incapable of speech on account of the servant.

The reversal will not be complete, however, until Israel, the powerless nation, finally speaks. The ultimate goal of the suffering and silent servant is to mobilize the speech of Israel, as shown in the imperative of 54:1:

> Sing, O barren one, who did not bear;
> Break forth into singing and cry aloud,
> you who have not been in travail.

Israel is again called to "fear not . . ." (54:4), for "you shall confute every tongue that arises against you in judgement" (54:17). The vicarious silence and suffering of the prophet-as-servant is meant as the final step in convincing Israel to claim its voice.[18] Indeed, within the servant passage itself, we see the beginnings of the return of Israel's speech as the community ruminates on the persecution (and possibly the death) of the servant in 53:1–10.

The Servant Passages and the Final Form of the Book

We may now turn to the question of what this analysis might contribute to the current conversation on the final form of the book of Isaiah. Our consideration of each of the servant passages has shown that there is a movement from a silent community in the first passage to a community beginning to regain its power for speech in the final passage. I submit that this reflects the larger movement in the book of Isaiah from a community that does not speak or hear in the beginning to a community that engages in covenantal discourse at the end.

We find this larger movement foreshadowed by the royal narratives of chapter 7 and chapters 36–9, in the stories of Ahaz (a king who does not hear or speak) and Hezekiah (a king who engages in covenantal discourse)[19] In Isaiah 7, we find that when Ahaz hears the words "Syria is in league with Ephraim," he and the people become afraid. When the word of the Lord comes to Ahaz (via Isaiah) he will not listen (vv. 3–9), and when he is commanded to speak he refuses (vv. 11–12). As a result, the narrative ends with a threat concerning the King of Assyria.

In a parallel situation, Hezekiah hears disturbing words from the Rabshekah sent by Sennacherib (36:13–22). Hezekiah responds in the proper mode, however, by addressing God (via Isaiah; cf. 37:1–4) and he is assured that the words of the Rabshekah are no reason to fear. When Hezekiah is threatened again by the words of the Rabshekah (37:8–13), he goes directly to YHWH in a prayer that admonishes YHWH to "hear" (v. 17) and to "save us" (v. 20). As a result of Hezekiah's adherence to the covenantal discourse, the word of YHWH returns against Sennacherib (vv. 22–35), thereby sealing his fate. It is significant that the mistake of Sennacherib is presented as "raising your voice . . . against the Holy One of Israel" (v. 23) and "mocking the Lord" (v. 24). Sennacherib, having no concept of the covenantal discourse, has no answer to YHWH's question, "Have you not heard that I determined it long ago?" (v. 26). For this reason YHWH says "your arrogance has come to my ears" (v. 29). The final verdict of YHWH concerning Sennacherib is given in 37:33–5 and it is then immediately fulfilled in vv. 36–8.

The royal narrative of chapters 36–9 does not end on a wholly positive note, however, as we see in 39:5–8. Here, I submit, Hezekiah fails to speak rightly in response to the word of YHWH in verse 5. Instead of responding with lament at the announcement of the coming exile, Hezekiah selfishly thinks, "there will be peace in my days" (v. 8). By saying that this is "good" Hezekiah becomes, essentially, "one who calls evil good and good evil" (cf. 5:20). The covenantal discourse is broken down; for the people at this point are silent, relying on the speech of the King (see 36:21). With Hezekiah speaking wrongly, Israel fails to fulfill its side of the covenantal discourse.

The book of Isaiah is finally less concerned with Ahaz or Hezekiah, however, than it is with the larger community of Israel. The silence of Ahaz and the wrong speech of Hezekiah serve to accent the importance of the speech of the community. It is for this reason that YHWH coaxes and threatens and allows the prophet to suffer vicariously for Israel. After such a long scroll of silence, Israel finally regains its voice in 63:1, asking the all-important question:

> Who is this that comes from Edom,
>   in crimson garments from Borzah,
> he that is glorious in his apparel,
>   marching in the greatness of his strength?

YHWH replies:

> It is I, announcing vindication,
>   mighty to save.

So begin the final chapters of Isaiah, in which the back and forth dialogue between YHWH and Israel assures us that the covenantal discourse has been restored. It is significant that in these final chapters we find sections of both praise (63:7–14) and lament (63:15–64:12), the two primary poles of speech available to Israel.[20] Even the lament is a welcome sound, for what is important is that the community has regained its voice; the movement of the book is complete.

Our focus on the function of speech in the servant passages has pointed to the connectedness of these passages with the rest of the Book of Isaiah, mirroring the movement of the book as a whole from a silent community in the beginning to a community that speaks in the end. Israel's first step toward regaining its power for speech does not happen, of course, until the prophet-as-servant suffers vicariously on behalf of the community, and the prophet is himself made silent. The poignant and paradoxical image of a God who is able to work even through a silent prophet is thus used to show the power of YHWH to speak even the most desolated exilic community back into existence.

Notes

1 Philadelphia: Westminster, 1979, pp. 311–38.
2 Following Bernhard Duhm, *Das Buch Jesaia*, 4th edn (Göttingen: Vandenhoeck and Ruprecht, 1922), some scholars posit a Third Isaiah (chapters 56–66, dated to the Persian period). While there is less of a consensus on this proposal, the distinction between chapters 1–39 and 40–66 has functioned as a virtual given.
3 *Introduction*, p. 326.
4 See, in particular, the studies of Roland E. Clements, "The Unity of the Book of Isaiah," *Interpretation* 36 (1982): 117–29; Walter Brueggemann, "Unity and Dynamic in the Isaiah Tradition," *JSOT* 29 (1984): 89–107; Christopher R. Seitz, "Isaiah 1–66: Making Sense of the Whole," in his (ed.) *Reading and Preaching the Book of Isaiah* (Philadelphia: Fortress, 1988), pp. 105–26; and Edgar W. Conrad, *Reading Isaiah*. Overtures to Biblical Theology (Minneapolis: Fortress, 1991).

5 *Das Buch Jesaia.*

6 For a summary and bibliography of relevant material see David J. A. Clines, *I, He, We, and They* (Sheffield: JSOTS, 1976), pp. 25–6.

7 *Poetry with a Purpose* (Bloomington: Indiana University Press, 1988), p. 118.

8 Fisch uses the term "covenant" in a somewhat broad sense, without specific reference to its political dimension in the ancient Near East. Though the scope of this study precludes an in-depth theoretical treatment of "discourse," I am largely convinced by Berger's and Luckmann's notion of the "social construction of reality." According to this notion, "the most important vehicle for reality-maintenance is conversation": *The Social Construction of Reality: A Treatise in the Sociology of Knowledge* (Garden City: Doubleday and Co., 1966), p. 152. With regard to *covenantal* discourse, see Brueggemann, *Abiding Astonishment: Psalms, Modernity, and the Making of History.* Literary Currents in Biblical Interpretation (Louisville: Westminster/John Knox Press, 1991), p. 27, who writes that for Israel, "when speaking and hearing are stopped, history comes to an end."

9 Unless otherwise noted all biblical quotes are from the Revised Standard Version.

10 "The Servant Songs in Deutero-Isaiah," *JSOT* 42 (1988): 79–102.

11 *Isaiah 40–66: A Commentary* (Philadelphia: Westminster, 1969).

12 "The Servant Songs," p. 88.

13 For a wonderful (albeit somewhat tongue-in-cheek) discussion of how prophetic oracles function as "performative utterances," see T. Eagleton, "J. L. Austin and the Book of Jonah," in *The Book and the Text: The Bible and Literary Theory*, ed. Regina Schwartz (Oxford: Basil Blackwell, 1990), pp. 231–6.

14 *Isaiah 40–66: A Commentary*, p. 207.

15 *Isaiah 40–66: Servant Theology* (Grand Rapids: Eerdman's Press, 1984), p. 120.

16 *Isaiah 40–66: A Commentary*, pp. 229–30.

17 Dunn writes of the distinction "between the silence of primordial chaos, which is simply confused, and the silence experienced at the end of a Waiting for Godot, which is stark and clear": "Speech and Silence in Job," *Semeia* 19(1981): 99–103, p. 102. I find the reference to the silence of "primordial chaos" particularly suggestive for our discussion, since the book of Isaiah draws heavily on creation language. Just as God was able to create out of the "silence of the primordial chaos," so is God now able to create out of the silence of "exilic chaos."

18 For a consideration of how the suffering and death of an individual can be considered both "despised" (53:3) and "healing" (53:5), see R. Girard, *Violence and the Sacred* (Baltimore: Johns Hopkins Press, 1977).

19 Conrad, *Reading Isaiah*. Overtures to Biblical Theology. (Minneapolis: Fortress, 1991), pp. 46–9, also notes this foreshadowing, but his reading of the royal narratives differs in important ways from my own and he gives very little attention to the servant passages.

20 See Westermann, *Isaiah 40–66: A Commentary*, pp. 18ff, for a discussion of praise and lament as modes of speech in Israel. In a recent article (Linafelt, "Psalm 138: Thanksgiving and the Relentless Imagination of Israel," *Paradigms* 8(2) (1993): 1–9), I accept Westermann's basic categories but suggest that "thanksgiving" is perhaps a more appropriate mode of speech in opposition to "lament."

Selections from *I, He, We, They: A Literary Approach to Isaiah 53*

David J. A. Clines

Done by Saying: Language as Event

Our study suggests that some approach to Isaiah 53 other than that of conventional historical criticism will be appropriate. Not only has the historical-critical method failed to provide acceptable solutions for the enigmas of the poem, but also our close reading of the poem's rhetoric has ruled out any merely objectivist approach to its meaning.

The outlook of the "new hermeneutic" school provides, I suggest, a framework within which some kind of justice may be done to the character and quality of this poem. A brief sketch of some aspects of the new hermeneutic particularly appropriate for our study thus seems to be called for.[1]

1 The new hermeneutic stresses that language can become event; that is, that language need not be mere talk *about* something, but that it can itself *do* something. E. Fuchs therefore commonly uses the term *Sprachereignis* ("language event") for this understanding of language.[2] And G. Ebeling remarks: "We do not get at the nature of words by asking what they contain, but by asking what they effect, what they set going."[3]

2 This notion of language as *doing* – which goes against the conventional contrast between speech and action, between logos and praxis – is parallel, as Robert W. Funk has pointed out,[4] to the concept developed by J. L. Austin of "performative utterances," in which "the issuing of the utterance is the performing of an action."[5] Some well-known examples mentioned by Austin are: "I name this ship the *Queen Elizabeth*," "I give my watch to my brother"

(in a will), "I bet you sixpence it will rain tomorrow."[6] Fuchs similarly points out that to name a man "brother" performatively is thereby to admit him into a brotherly relationship.[7] Austin of course is interested primarily in performative utterances in ordinary language, Fuchs and Ebeling in "speech-events" in kerygmatic language, especially in the language of Jesus and in particular within his parabolic utterances, while I am interested in this functional aspect of literary language in general, and of high poetry in particular.

3   The next question concerns the *way* in which the language of parable or poem can be event. Here Austin's interest must of course drop out of sight, since he has established simply that one conventional use of language is as deed, thus providing the basic and irrefutable foundation for the more sophisticated superstructure of hermeneutical theory.

The *way* in which language is event is by its creating of an alternative *world* and thereby destroying the universal validity of the conventional "world." Thus Fuchs speaks of language as "world-forming and world-destroying."[8] "World" can be defined as "the total set of perception and participation in which we exist, the locus of historical being."[9] A literary text creates an alternative "world," another set of principles, values, relationships, and perceptions, which then confronts the reader. The result is a conflict between two worlds, two ways of seeing things, which puts the ball into the reader's court.

4   The world thus created invites the reader to enter it. It is not a world that can be viewed objectively, from the outside, as a spectator. One needs to be a participant in it, to experience it, in order to understand it. This is the way to more than mere knowledge (*Erkenntnis*), as H.-G. Gadamer points out;[10] it leads to "understanding" (*Verstehen*), which is reached through "modes of experience in which truth comes to light" (*Erfahrungsweisen*) as one is taken hold of by creative language or art. Unless one "enters" the alternative world created by language one cannot be gripped by its reality, but is condemned to remain a spectator. Gadamer is thinking of the analogy of a game, whose *reality* is experienced only by the players, and not by the spectators – however much they may know about its theory.

5   The process of moving from the one "world" to the other has been strikingly termed by Gadamer a "merging of horizons" (*Horizontverschmelzung*).[11] One cannot abandon overnight one's original world, because it is only in that world that one has one's bearings and knows therefore one's own identity at the intersection of a three-dimensional grid of space and time and personal relationships. But also the "other" world may not sometimes be anything more than another perspective on the original world.

Hence the significance of the simile of "horizons." A. C. Thiselton has expressed Gadamer's concept of horizons thus:

When language brings a new "world" into existence, the hearer who enters this world becomes aware of new horizons of meaning. But these necessarily differ from the horizons of understanding which have hitherto marked the extent of his own world. Thus, to begin with, two different worlds stand over against each other, each with its own horizon. Yet the peculiarity of horizons is that their positions are variable, in accordance with the position from which they are viewed. Hence adjustments can be made in the hearer's own understanding until the two horizons come to merge into one. A new comprehensive horizon now appears, which serves as the boundary of an enlarged world of integrated understanding.[12]

6   When the text is seen as creating a world which the reader is invited to "enter,"[13] it becomes obvious that the conventional model of the relation between a text and its interpreter has been made obsolete. No longer can it be said of a text such as poem or parable (though it may still properly be said of a legal document or technical manual or business letter) that it is the "object" of scrutiny by the "subject" (the interpreter) – the familiar Cartesian distinction – but that the text as language–event, world–creating and world–destroying, has the primacy over the interpreter. As James M. Robinson has put it:

> The flow of the traditional relation between subject and object, in which the subject interrogates the object, and, if he masters it, obtains from it his answer, has been significantly reversed. For it is now the object – which should henceforth be called the subject matter – that puts the subject [the interpreter] in question.[14]

It is significant that it is precisely in relation to art (the plastic or literary work of art) that it becomes clear that the categories of subject and object must be transcended. As Heidegger argued, if the dualist subject–object perspective is adopted, either art is reduced to the realm of the purely sensual, in which case it cannot be said to reveal truth; or else it is elevated into the realm of intellectual concepts, in which case it becomes reduced to the level of aesthetics.[15] Literary critics have, indeed, often recognized the primacy of the work of art, which interprets the critic rather than being interpreted *by* the critic, as the following remark shows: "The first demand any work of any art makes upon us is surrender. Look. Listen. Receive. Get yourself out of the way."[16]

7   Another way of putting the relationship of the world of the text and the interpreter is for the interpreter to "actively assume one of the concrete roles which it offers him." The interpreter is then "carried forward by a kind of inner logic of consequences which the chosen role brings with it."[17]

Said and Doing: Isaiah 53 as Language-Event

The relevance of the foregoing sketch for our understanding of Isaiah 53 is doubtless already obvious; nevertheless, some points of contact should perhaps be spelled out.

1   The impasse of historical-critical scholarship in the face of the enigmas of the poem can function heuristically in directing our attention away from a sense of "the poem as problem" to the poem as language-event.

It is remarkable that Old Testament scholarship has never made such a step, but has almost without exception taken an apparently masochistic delight in the intractability of the "problems" of the poem, as if it were primarily a brain-teaser, a puzzle for the most advanced students. Only Claus Westermann has recognized the insensitivity of such an approach, and has vigorously denied that quests for "identification" – i.e. problem-solving inquiries – are appropriate.[18] The language of the servant songs, he says, "at once reveals and conceals the servant."

> The veiled manner of speaking is intentional . . . Exegesis must then be conscious of the limit thus imposed, and be careful to call a halt at those places where the distinctive nature of the songs demands this . . . On principle, their exegesis must not be controlled by the question, "Who is this servant of God?" . . . Precisely this is what they neither tell nor intend to tell us. The questions which should control exegesis are: "What do the texts make known about what transpires, or is to transpire, between God, the servant, and those to whom his task pertains?"[19]

Westermann thus bars the way to a false path, but his suggestion of another direction in which exegesis should strike out is still too fixated by the concept of the text as information.

2   Once it is recognised that the text does not exist as a carrier of information, but has a life of its own, it becomes impossible to talk of *the* meaning of a text, as if it had only *one* proper meaning. Recognition of the hermeneutical circle, in which meaning is seen to reside not in the text but in what the text becomes for the reader, also leads to the legitimacy of *multiple* meanings.[20]

A similar conclusion is reached, quite independently of the "new hermeneutic" school, by literary critics who stress, to one degree or another, the "autonomy of the work of art." While it is too extreme, I believe, to regard a literary work of art as totally autonomous of its author, and consequently to be understood independently of the circumstances of its origin,[21] there is truth in L. Alonso-Schökel's remark that when an author produces a work the umbilical cord has

213

to be cut and the work must go forth into the world on its own. Thus the original author's meaning, which is what is generally meant by *the* meaning of the text,[22] is by no means the only meaning a text may legitimately have (or, rather, create). We cannot even be sure that a literary text (or any work of art) "originally" – whenever that was – meant one thing and one thing only to its author; even the author may have had multiple meanings in mind.

We may therefore prepare ourselves to recognize various meanings that our text, Isaiah 53, can create. When, for example, Philip the evangelist "begins" at that scripture and preaches Christ to the Ethiopian eunuch, we should not think so much of a *reapplication* of the prophetic text which once meant something quite different, but of one of the vast variety of meanings the text itself can create. The text creates a world in which participants in the world of the text get to know their way around, and come to be able to say, like Wittgenstein, "Now I can go on."

Similarly we may reconcile ourselves to *not wishing* to identify the persons or groups of the fifth century BC to which the text may have alluded. Of course, if, for example, the "servant" is a code-name for Deutero-Isaiah, and his deliverance from "death" is a poetic expression for release from a Babylonian prison, and so on, all other interpretations of the poem are *quite* wrong. On the understanding advanced here, it is not a matter of being quite wrong or even quite right: there are only more and less appropriate interpretations, no doubt, according to how well the world of the poem comes to expression in the new situation.

3   The poem is free to do its work by its very lack of specificity, its openness to a multiplicity of readings.

Of course, that lack of specificity, the enigmatic quality of the poem *could* perhaps be simply a historical accident. It *could* be that once there was a key to the enigmas of the poem, and that that key has been lost, so that *we* can never know what the poem means precisely and exactly – and, on this view, truly. Perhaps a line has dropped out at the beginning of chapter 53 which made clear who the "we" were;[23] perhaps it was "obvious" to the "original audience" (to use the language familiar to an unliterary historical-critical scholarship) who the servant was; perhaps in that case it was equally plain what the nature of his sufferings was, and whether he underwent death or not. Perhaps too it was clear whether his mission extended to the Gentiles or only to Israelites of the dispersion.

May it not be, however – and does not this approach respect the integrity of the text rather more than a circle of cautious "perhapses"? – that the enigmas are part of what the poem must be in order to be itself? That is, that it exists to create another world, a world indeed that is recognizably our own, with brutality and suffering and God and a coming-to-see on the part of some, but not a world that simply once existed and is gone for good. The poem's very lack of specificity refuses to let it be tied down to one spot on the globe, or frozen at one point in history: it opens up the possibility that the poem can become true in a variety of circumstances – that is its work.

4   The world which the poem creates is a topsy-turvy world when judged by ordinary human standards.[24]

It is a world where a servant (*or* slave) is elevated above kings, to the consternation of conventional wisdom; compare Proverbs 19:10: "It is not fitting for a fool to live in luxury, much less for a servant to rule over princes." It is a world where *one* achieves what the *many* cannot, and where the "intercession" of one avails for the many (53:12). It is a world where, so the poem makes out, the man God designates as his servant and as a hero is an object of loathing, so disfigured that he looks subhuman (*mošḥat mē' īš mar' ēhû*, 52:14).[25] In this world, it is assumed with none too delicate irony, a man who serves God by "practising non-violence and never speaking dishonestly" (53:9) inevitably finds himself in the condemned cell (note the force of *al* in 53:9b). Here too it is taken for granted in a mere half verse that the suffering of a righteous man is the will of God (53:10a), a breach with conventional theology so drastic that elsewhere a whole book (Job) is devoted to its ramifications. So the social order, the strength of numbers, good taste, ordinary human decency, and the justice of God are all in turn called into question by this topsy-turvy, not to say shocking, poem.

This is the world that the reader is bidden to give his assent to – or, rather, to enter. It is not an obviously appealing invitation. To allow the horizon of the poem to "merge" with any conventional horizon would almost seem to call for standing on one's head. But this is a poem precisely about horizons: it concerns perspectives, the way one *sees*, as we have noted above. It sets forth a vision of the world which is radically different from our prior expectations; it is a new "world" in that its scale of values differ from the conventional.

5   The means by which the reader of the poem is able to enter the world of the poem is by identification with the *personae* of the poem, that is, by an assumption of one of the roles presented in the poem.

If one identifies with the "they," who find the history of the servant unbelievable and his aspect revolting, one is still on the edge of the poem's world, an observer looking in on it but not committed to it. Yet the "they" are at least aware of the servant; they "see" and "ponder" the servant's fate. Though repelled, they are at the same time fascinated by the servant, so they have made the first step towards the way of the servant. What is more, those who identify with the "they" of the poem find, by the time they reach 53:11ff, that the servant proves in their presence (*lārabbîm*) to be innocent and to have borne punishment on behalf of them, the many (*ḥēṭ ' rabbîm nāśā'*).

If one accepts that the suffering of the innocent is in any way because of, for the sake of, or on behalf of, oneself who deserves to suffer, then one has joined the ranks of the "we." They are the group who once felt like the "they" but have had their eyes opened to the true relationship between themselves and the servant: "he was pierced because of our rebelliousness" (53:5). Identification with the "we" puts one entirely within the world of the poem; it involves a recognition that things are not what they seem and that one can have been dreadfully mistaken about the identity and nature of the true servant of the Lord. It requires also a questioning in order to discover who and where is the servant of Yahweh for oneself. No one can enter the world of the poem without becoming a participant in that world; no one truly understands who the "we" are and what they mean to say unless one has shared their experience of revulsion towards and rejection of the servant and their experience of "conversion," i.e. their recognition of being mistaken, their assurance that the servant is for them the significant other and not an insignificant being, despised and rejected.

There is yet another role in the poem which the reader is invited to assume: that of the servant himself. Naturally, if the servant *is* Deutero-Isaiah or some other historical figure, one may empathize with the servant; but I am arguing that the poems' lack of specificity about the servant's identity enables a relationship between the servant and the reader that is deeper than empathy to come into being. It is not simply that the reader may, by exercise of a vivid imagination, put himself in the servant's shoes, and empathetically share the servant's experience. It is, rather, that the figure of the servant presented by the poem has the potency to reach out from the confines of a historical past and from the poem itself and to "seize" the reader and bend him to a new understanding of himself and of the direction of his life. The reader can, in the presence of this, the central *persona* of the poem, cease to be the active subject interrogating the text, and become the one who is questioned and changed by the text. It is the same case if the servant is not a historical personage but an ideal figure. Here again, the force of the poem is not simply to invite the reader to approximate his behavior and life-style to that of the servant as best he can; it is, rather, that the figure of the servant seizes, imposes itself upon, a reader – with or without the reader's assent (so this is not the same thing as empathy) – and insists upon interpreting the reader rather than being interpreted by the reader. The assumption of the servant's role becomes not the voluntary act of a dramatic role-playing, but a compulsion by the figure of the servant. The language becomes more than a tool for the conveyance of information or even emotion; it creates an event: it destroys a world and replaces it by a new one which it brings into being.

6   Cannot something more specific be said about the nature of this figure of the servant?

It can, but not perhaps in the style of an academic paper; perhaps only the language of testimony or confession, which the "we" of the poem find themselves using, can properly express what the servant is, for that means: what the servant is _for me_. Others are questioned and changed by different facets of the servant figure, but for me what is most compelling is that the servant of Yahweh in Isaiah 53 _does nothing and says nothing but lets everything happen to him._ In looking at the verbal pattern of the poem, the servant is acted upon more often than he acts. Even his "actions" are by turns negative ("he did not open his mouth") or passive ("he bore the punishment"). There is, as we saw, no concrete action done by the servant; he suffers. Even his "intervention" (_yapgîa'_, 53:12) for the rebellious, and his "carrying" of punishment (_nāśâ, sābal_, 53:4, 11, 12), his "exposing" himself to death (_he'râ_, 53:12), are nothing more than his suffering; they are not the acts of a Superman intervening at the critical moment, of an Atlas carrying the world-guilt on his shoulders, of a hero of the trenches exposing himself to enemy fire. They are: his letting everything happen to him.

And, he says nothing: he does not open his mouth. What kind of silence that is I do not well know, for it is so rare in our world. It is not Stoic silence or insolent silence; it is not dumb brutish silence or dumbfounded amazed silence; it is not heroic silence, for he has no one to betray by his speech, but neither is it the silence of ignorance, for he knows what he is doing. It can only be the silence of suffering, his speech and his action mysteriously but deliberately absent.

In a religious culture such as our own, where commitment is measured almost quantitatively by speech and action, the servant of the Lord of Isaiah 53 is ill at ease, for his commitment to the "purposes of Yahweh" (53:10) lies entirely in his silent and unresisting suffering. No one wants to claim that there are no other servants of the Lord except this one of Isaiah 53, that this poemparable is the only glimpse we have of the reality of servanthood. But this servant still walks among us, wordlessly calling in question our images of servanthood and with his suffering reproaching our easy activisms.

Notes

1 I am much indebted to my colleague A. C. Thiselton for stimulating my interest in this approach to biblical interpretation and for clarifying many issues. Of special value have been his papers, "The New Hermeneutic," in _New Testament Interpretation_, ed. I. H. Marshall (Exeter: Paternoster, 1976), and "The Parables as Language Event: Some Comments on Fuchs's Hermeneutics in the Light of Linguistic Philosophy," _SJT_ 23 (1970) 437–68.

2 E. Fuchs, _Hermeneutik_, 4th edn (Tubingen: Mohr, 1970), p. 131; cf. R. W. Funk, _Language, Hermeneutic, and Word of God_ (New York: Harper and Row, 1966), p. 51.

3 G. Ebeling, _The Nature of Faith_ (London: Collins, 1961), p. 137.

4 *Language, Hermeneutic, and Word of God*, pp. 26ff.

5 *How to do Things with Words*, 2nd edn, ed. J. O. Urmson and M. Sbisà (Oxford: Clarendon Press, 1975).

6 Ibid., p. 5.

7 *Studies of the Historical Jesus* (London: SCM, 1964), p. 209.

8 Quoted by W. G. Doty, *Contemporary New Testament Interpretation* (Englewood Cliffs, N.J.: Prentice-Hall, 1972), p. 42. C. S. Lewis speaks of the "unmaking of your mind" in a similar connection (*An Experiment in Criticism* (Cambridge: Cambridge University Press, 1961), p. 39).

9 Doty, ibid., p. 37.

10 H.-G. Gadamer, *Truth and Method* (New York: Seabury, 1975). See also Thiselton, "Parables as Language Event," pp. 443ff, and cf. Lewis, *Experiment in Criticism*, p. 139.

11 Gadamer, ibid., pp. 269–73.

12 Thiselton, "Parables as Language Event," p. 445.

13 C. S. Lewis speaks of "cross[ing] the frontier into a new region" in the same connection (*Experiment in Criticism*).

14 *The New Hermeneutic*, ed. J. M. Robinson and J. B. Cobb (New Frontiers in Theology, 2; New York: Harper and Row, 1964), pp. 23ff.

15 A. C. Thiselton kindly drew my attention to this point. Heidegger's essay "The Origin of the Work of Art" is translated in *Philosophies of Art and Beauty*, ed. A. Hofstadter and R. Kuhns (New York: Random House, 1964).

16 Lewis, *Experiment in Criticism*, p. 19.

17 Thiselton, "Parables as Language Event," p. 441.

18 *Isaiah 40–66: A Commentary* (Philadelphia: Westminster, 1969), p. 20.

19 Ibid., p. 93.

20 Cf. T. S. Eliot's remark that the meaning of a poem is "what the poem means to different sensitive readers" ("The Frontiers of Criticism,") in *On Poetry and Poets* (London: Faber and Faber, 1957), p. 113.

21 See, for example, E. Staiger, *Die Kunst der Interpretation*, 4th edn (Zurich: Atlantis, 1963); M. Weiss, "Wege der neuen Dichtungswissenschaft in ihrer Auswendung auf die Psalmenforschung," *Bib* 42 (1961): 255–302, p. 259; R. E. Palmer, *Hermeneutics* (Evanston: Northwestern University Press, 1969), pp. 246ff. For criticism of this approach, see for example Helen Gardner, *The Business of Criticism* (Oxford: Clarendon Press, 1959) pp. 17–23.

22 See, for example, E. D. Hirsch, *Validity in Interpretation* (New Haven: Yale University Press, 1967).

23 So, for example, O. C. Whitehouse, *Isaiah XL–LXVI* (Edinburgh: T. & T. Clark, 1908), p. 199.

24 This is made clear within the poem itself, which speaks of its own message as "something never heard before" (52:15).

25 The figure of Achilles, "bloom of the heroes, who grew up like a sprouting shoot, nourished like a plant in the luxuriant earth" (*Iliad* 18:437ff) is a convenient point of reference in the "real" world. Still closer to hand is Krt, "the beautiful one, servant of El" (*nˁ mn ǵlm 'el*).

Engaging Metaphors: Suffering with Zion and the Servant in Isaiah 52–53

Beverly J. Stratton

For centuries the haunting poem of Isaiah 52:13–53:12 has captured its listeners.[1] Many commentators, often reading Duhm's four servant poems in isolation from the rest of Deutero-Isaiah, have focused historically on the identity of the servant.[2] Recently scholars have begun considering the poem in relation to its literary context in the Book of Isaiah, but they often pay little attention to the role of Zion in the surrounding chapters. In reading these chapters theologically, I consider Zion and the servant in Isaiah 52–53 with both ancient and modern audiences in mind. These poems were written for and exemplify some of the torture and pain of battered and beleaguered Israel. They continue to be read as scripture today by victims, perpetrators, and survivors of abuse. Thus feminist scholarship on abuse and its relation to female metaphors in the prophets informs my work. Zion and the servant in Isaiah 52–53 are engaging metaphors, moving both God and the people to new understandings and relationship. In this essay I consider Zion and the servant separately before addressing their rhetorical function together.

Zion as Woman

A theological reading of Isaiah 52–53 must address Zion, personified as a woman,[3] and her relationship with Yhwh. The speaker in Isaiah 52:1–2 calls on Zion to arise from the dust and to put on her beautiful garments. Readers may wonder why Zion is sitting in the dust and inappropriately clad. Two options present themselves from the biblical prophetic literature generally and from the context in Isaiah: (1) Zion is in mourning, and (2) Zion has been debased, perhaps abused and sexually defiled.

Mourning mothers are a recurring image in prophetic literature. Perhaps most familiar, Rachel weeps for her children in Jeremiah 31:15. Mothers wail in Zion for their children in Jeremiah 9:17–22, and in Isaiah 3:26 the gates of Zion herself lament and mourn.[4] Similarly, in Lamentations 2:18–20, the walls of Zion weep and cry out for her children because their mothers have eaten them. The city as woman may even charge Yhwh with being her enemy and murdering her children (cf. Lam. 2:22).[5] In her role as mourning mother, Jerusalem gives voice to the people's suffering, grief, and loss. A poem may move from describing the city's destruction and desolation, to addressing her, and finally to adopting her *persona* as a speaker.[6] Rhetorically, Barbara Kaiser argues that the poet's adoption of a female voice in this way intensifies the participant's anguish when the poem is used in worship.[7]

Alternatively, Zion's dusty situation in Isaiah 52:2 may reflect her punishment. The prophets recognize Zion or Jerusalem as an adulterous woman (Isa. 1:21; Jer. 4:30–1; 30:14–17; and Ezek. 16, 23). The debased woman as metaphor for Israel appears prominently elsewhere in the prophets (Hos. 1–3 and Jer. 2–3).[8] Feminist interpreters often note the sexual nature of the city-woman's punishment, particularly outside Isaiah.[9] For example, in Ezekiel 16:37–40 Jerusalem is exposed before her lovers, stripped and hacked to pieces at their hands. Similarly, in Micah 4:11 Zion is profaned as the nations gaze on her. Feminists raise questions about whether such graphic portrayal of a metaphorical woman's debasement at the hands of her male suitors and in view of male Israel (the prophet's audience) is pornographic,[10] and they consider the role of actual and metaphoric rape in relation to war.[11]

Zion as woman and the related metaphor of Israel as a prostitute or promiscuous wife may have been effective in ancient Israel because it played on male fears of or disdain for female sexuality. Ancient Near Eastern treaty-curses threatened men with rape or soldiers with becoming prostitutes for failure to keep the covenant.[12] The metaphor may function in Hosea, then, analogously with Nathan's parable to David: telling male Israel, who would be disgusted with the metaphorical woman's fornicating behavior, that "You are the woman."[13]

Moreover, feminist interpreters note that the woman's chastisement comes with the approval or at the hands of her husband Yhwh.[14] Particularly striking in the case of Hosea 2 is how the pattern of restriction, punishment, and loving reconciliation mirrors the three phases of the domestic abuse cycle as it is understood today by those who counsel women who have been in battering relationships: tension-building phase, acute battering incident, and kindness and contrite, loving behavior.[15] Such parallels prompt some feminist interpreters to challenge whether such biblical texts can continue to function authoritatively in faith communities.[16]

Perhaps because the allusions to Zion as woman are more dispersed in Isaiah or because she seems to be the object of more comforting than abuse, feminist scholars have not focused as much attention on the city-as-woman metaphors in Isaiah. Below, I consider Zion's portrayal in the whole book, with particular attention to her laments in Second Isaiah.[17]

Zion's Portrayal in Isaiah

Zion is God's special place. The name of the Lord of Hosts abides there (Isa. 18:7). The city was established by the Lord so that the afflicted may find shelter in it (14:32). As a city of kings, God promises to protect and save Zion for the sake of David (37:35) and in response to Hezekiah's prayer (38:5–6).

But the city has sinned. Like the people of Israel in other prophetic books, Zion is portrayed in Isaiah as a promiscuous woman. The overture to the book charges that the faithful city has become a harlot: the city's crime, referring to those of its inhabitants, is its failure to judge rightly the cases of orphan and widow (1:21–3). Because of its sins the city is destroyed. Daughter Zion is left "like a city beleaguered" (1:8, JPS). Emptied, she sits on the ground (3:26). Zion becomes a desert, Jerusalem a desolation, and the temple is consumed by fire (64:10; E 64:11). The city is ruined by famine and sword (51:19).

This destruction occurs at the hands of God. God purposes to do in Jerusalem what God did to Samaria (10:11–12). God removes the protective hedge so the vineyard can be ravaged, trampled, and dry (5:5); god hews off tree-crowns near Mount Zion (10:33). God washes filth from the daughters of Zion, rinsing and purging through judgement (4:4). God turns the city into a stone heap (25:2), laying siege against it (29:3). Both the city and her sons (inhabitants) drink the cup of God's wrath/rebuke to the dregs (51:17, 20–1). God will make war against Zion (31:4), vowing "I will harass Ariel" till it only whispers from dust (29:2, 4).

In Second Isaiah God admits to having defiled his heritage (47:6). The defilement may be that Jerusalem was entered by the "uncircumcised and unclean" as 52:1 suggests. But what kind of entry does the metaphor of Zion as woman suggest? Spoken here in the context of the dethronement, stripping, and abasement of fair maiden Babylon, these words about defilement may allude to Zion's own rape and exposure. Indeed, God vowed in 3:17 to lay bare "their opening" (פּתְהֵן). As F. Rachel Magdalene points out, this "opening," typically translated "secret parts," is a wordplay for the gate/opening of the city: "Nowhere in the Hebrew Bible is the military metaphor of the ravaged city as ravished female seen more clearly."[18]

But even in the midst of destruction, God promises eventual restoration. Zion will again be called "City of Righteousness, Faithful City" when God restores judges from of old (1:26). God will found in Zion a firm tower so that those who trust need not fear (28:16). God promises to respond as soon as God hears the people in Zion/Jerusalem (30:19), and God does. The restoration is grand. The redeemed return, coming with singing to Zion (35:10). The city is again inhabited by folk whose sin has been forgiven (33:24). Though she had lost her children, the redeemed Zion eventually gives birth painlessly (66:7–8). The city both consoles her children at her bosom (66:11) and suckles herself at royal breasts (60:16).

Like the destruction, the restoration also occurs through God's intimate involvement with the city. God comes as a redeemer to Zion (59:20) and fills Zion with justice and righteousness (33:5). The Holy One again dwells in the midst of Zion (12:6), making the city secure (33:20). God protects the city with a cloud by day and a flaming fire by night (4:5; cf. God's protection of the returning exiles both before and behind in 52:12), and Zion is again called "City of the Lord" (60:14). Having been forsaken and desolate, Zion is renamed "I delight in her" and "espoused" (62:4); she is now "Sought Out, A City Not Forsaken" (62:12). Both her sons and God rejoice over the city as a bride (62:5), one whom God has clothed with garments of salvation (61:10). God creates Jerusalem as a joy, her people as a delight (65:18); God makes Zion God's pride and joy (60:15).

Zion's Lament

Perhaps most poignant in Second Isaiah is not the city's wrenching story but the pathos with which the poet here renders Zion's broken and healing relationship to Yhwh – the city and her God engage in dialogue: lament and response. The major speeches occur in 49:14–23; 49:24–50:3, 51:9–52:6, and 54:1–17, but attention to Zion begins in 40:1–2, 9 with God seeking a mediator to speak comfort to Jerusalem and to announce God's presence. In spite of much speech to Jacob/Israel as God's servant, in chapters 40–48 Zion is both silent and seemingly ignored. (She appears briefly in 46:13.) Unlike the servant who speaks anonymously in 49:1–6 (and perhaps in 48:16b), in 49:14 the poet credits Zion with her words, announcing: "Zion speaks." Though perhaps reduced to whispering (29:2), Zion not only speaks, but she speaks to God, lamenting her fate: Yhwh has forsaken her, *adonai* has forgotten her. Through God's response in 49:15–23 we learn more of woman-Zion's situation. The city is bereaved and barren, yet she will be readorned and filled with children. Even better than mother-Zion, God describes himself as a mother who does *not* forget her children. (Zion did not mention hers in her complaint of 49:14.) God will not forget Zion; he has engraved her on his palms. God promises that Zion will know that he is the Lord and that those who trust him will not be shamed.

Zion (we may infer) questions God in 49:24, suggesting that she may not yet be ready to trust God.[19] To her question about whether spoil and captives (the missing children, presumably) can be retrieved from a warrior (their Babylonian captors), God insists that "yes" God will contend with Zion's adversaries, turning them into cannibals, so that all people will know that God is Zion's savior and redeemer (49:25–6).

Then God takes the offensive, questioning Zion and her offspring in 50:1–2. God's rhetorical question in 50:1 seems to imply that God did not divorce Zion. The children were sold off for their sins and their mother, Zion, dismissed for her children's crimes. Still, in 50:2 God seems genuinely puzzled or miffed that no one responded when he came (home?) or called, and God's manhood seems to be threatened by his family's lack of confidence in him: "is my arm, then, too short to rescue?" After an interlude where the servant speaks, God resumes his plea in 51:1–8, calling on the people to listen and hearken to him and reminding his people that even the coastlands look to his arm (51:5).

Unconvinced, Zion resumes her lament in 51:9–11, attempting to rouse God's "arm." With a double imperative that echoes the overture's call to "comfort, comfort my people" (40:1), Zion calls on God's arm to "awake, awake!" Zion links creation out of chaos language (hacking Rahab, piercing the Dragon) with creation of a people images (drying up the sea so that the redeemed could walk) in order to persuade God to let the ransomed return to Zion. God's response in 51:12–52:2 reverses Zion's complaints. While Zion laments, God claims to provide comfort and wonders at her fear of mere mortals. Though Zion accused the deity of forgetting her (49:14) and reminded him of creation (51:9), God says that *Zion* is the one who forgot *her* maker (51:13). Zion recalled to God his drying up of the sea (51:10), but God reminds Zion that he *stirs up* the sea (51:15). While Zion would awaken the arm of the Lord (51:9), God tells her to rouse *herself* (again with a double imperative in both 51:17 and 52:1). Whereas Zion called on God to clothe his arm with splendor (51:9), God comforts Zion with the command that she clothe *herself* in splendor (52:1). Zion's watchers bear witness on God's behalf, confirming that God does comfort, redeem, and bare his arm in victory in the sight of all the nations (52:9–10). What is most striking in these speeches is that God attends closely to Zion's fears and concerns: God listens and takes up Zion's language in the deity's responses.[20] Zion's speech is effective, causing God to muse in 52:3–6 about the people's situation and persuading God to take action so that he will be known to the people as one who utters the trustworthy and faithful response: "Here I am" (52:6; cf. 65:1).

Zion's lament does not end with a vow of praise. Instead, after the servant poem in 52:12–53:13, God resumes the conversation in 54:1–17, offering endearing words and lavish promises. God himself here speaks tenderly to Jerusalem.[21] Zion is silent. God encourages Zion to shout for joy, noting that she will have many children.[22] The image of Zion spreading out her tents to accommodate them (54:2–3) may remind listeners of a pregnant woman. While Zion is silent, God's words of comfort suggest that she may continue to fear, to cringe, and to remember her disgrace, reproach, and shame (54:4). Though God had implied earlier (50:1) that he had not divorced Zion, his song to her here confesses that indeed he had cast her off, hidden his face from her, and forsaken her for a little while in a surge of anger (54:6–8). But now he will redeem and espouse her (54:5), calling her and bringing her back with deep compassion (רחם) and everlasting kindness (חסד; 54:6–8). God's promises to Zion that he will never again be angry with her are as sure as the covenant with Noah that God would never again flood the earth; they are sturdier than the potentially quaking mountains (54:9–10).[23] When Zion remains unhappy, storm-tossed, and uncomforted, the deity offers jewels (financial security?), happy children, safety, and absence of fear – what any abused mother might treasure (54:11–14).

Yet God's poem to Zion continues with divine assurances that may also seem to be implicit threats: "no harm can be done without my consent" (54:15) and "it is I who create the instruments of havoc" (54:16). With the recently angry deity in control, can Zion be confident that she will defeat anyone who contends with her at law or who forms a weapon against her (54:17)? Is the silence in chapter 54 of she who courageously spoke so recently a sign of Zion's continued distress or of her secure comfort at last? Zion's laments moved God to act, but will Zion only cherish the brief respite of the contrition phase of what continues to be an abusive marital relationship before the tension-building phase resumes, or has her brave speaking out and God's solicitous response led to the possibility of sincere and enduring reconciliation for the couple? The question of God's potential abuse of woman-Zion is unanswered. The lack of resolution in the couple's relationship at this point in Isaiah leaves readers open to the prophet's continuing rhetoric in chapters 55–66.

The Offense of the Servant's Actual Suffering

If feminists are concerned about the potential abuse of women perpetuated in part due to the marriage metaphors in the prophets, including the scattered comments and allusions in Isaiah, they are even more troubled by the role suffering may seem to play in the servant poem of 52:13–53:12.[24] Joanne Carlson Brown and Rebecca Parker explore the implications for suffering in prominent Christian atonement theories, charging that traditional understandings of the atonement amount to understanding God as guilty of "divine child abuse".[25] It is tempting, following Brown and Parker, to explore the Isaiah 53 passage, analyzing it using ancient Israel's or the early Church's understandings of atonement. One might also rail against the text, following Brown and Parker's complaints and warnings about the dangers of a God who is a divine child abuser and of suffering being seen as an example to be emulated.

The point of the passage, however, seems to be precisely to give offense – to portray an image of human suffering so revolting that one's response can only be to cringe in horror.[26] And perhaps, if one thinks of God as a God of retribution, to reflect on one's own sin and deserving of suffering. This may be what the speaking "we" has done. Their assumption that the servant was struck down by God (53:4) shows that they do (or did) think of God in this way. But their position changes. In the next verse they recognize (because of God's vindication of the servant?) that they have been made whole through the suffering of this one (53:5). We need not assume substitutionary atonement – the Hebrew text avoids the preposition "instead of" (תחת).[27] By its vivid portrayal of suffering and rejection and use of an anonymous "we," spoken by its readers and listeners, the poem invites our participation in experiencing the horror, the offense.

The poem is likewise decidedly ambiguous about who caused the servant's suffering. One might, with my suggestion below about a eunuch providing a model for the physical horror and rejection of the servant, assign the blame to the Babylonians acting on their own initiative (though Isaiah's prophecy to Hezekiah in 39:7 haunts). This notion gets God off the hook as causing the suffering in this instance, but it does not shield God from accusations elsewhere of inflicting suffering on God's people.[28] The book of Isaiah as a whole, the prophetic literature more broadly, and responses (such as Lamentations) to the events announced by the prophets affirm that Israel sometimes understood God as inflicting suffering on God's people.[29]

The point in the poem, however, is not whether God is responsible for this particular suffering, but God's claim of vindicating the servant from a suffering that is recognized as actual, real, present. God has been trying throughout the Book of Isaiah, to be recognized by his people, to be known by them as their God (as well as being known by the nations as the God of Israel),[30] to be trusted or even to be turned to in complaint.[31] Though the personified city Zion does cry out to God in lament, asking for vindication, she serves as a foil for a people who remain resolutely silent, accepting beatings at God's hand, turning to their gods of wood and stone instead of to the Holy One of Israel, to God their redeemer. By means of the actual suffering in the poem, the people recognize that God is the ultimate source of their wholeness (53:5). While they do not here speak directly to God in confession of sins or out of their own pain, they do recognize God's involvement in suffering because of their sins. God's vindication of the servant enables the speaking "we" to acknowledge that their wholeness and healing come from God. The point of the poem is not the nature of the suffering, though this is described in graphic detail. The point of the poem is its effect – its achieving atonement in the present for its hearers.

Atonement and Example

Brown and Parker are right in insisting that none of the classical Christian atonement theories they discuss will do – they make God out to be a "divine child abuser."[32] Similarly, while it is undoubtedly true that God suffers with us and that suffering is often part of a liberation process,[33] simply understanding God or suffering in these ways does not reconcile us with God. Suffering understood as an image of horror to be rejected may move in the right direction, but it is incomplete as an understanding of atonement. Suffering only becomes atonement when it works – when God is able, in this case through the suffering of a servant who actually experiences the alienation caused by sin (53:8), to be God to us in the way that God would be God. When God creates faith in us so that we recognize God as merciful, electing, and present and we place our trust in God, then atonement happens *for us*. This is how atonement happens in the servant poem: God finally gets through to an alienated people, to us. The message to Zion alone was insufficient (52:1–2, 7–10), the people need to *see*[34] – not only the despised, rejected, suffering servant, but also God's exaltation and rewarding of him.[35]

Changed Yet Somewhat Predictable God

The exaltation of the suffering servant is not so much a reward for his suffering as an indication of a change in God. God has been the Holy One, a God of wrath, absent, hiding God's face from the people. But Zion's loud laments and the servant's visible but silent suffering have moved God. Jack Miles sees the servant's suffering as having a profound impact upon God: "God did not realize that once they [Assyria and Babylon] had inflicted his punishment for him, his feelings, rather than only those of a vindicated suzerain, would also be those of a grieving husband for a battered wife."[36]

While perhaps still frightening to women who have been abused, because of the control that husband God retains and threats he may still subtly pose, Isaiah 54 reveals God as a God of deep love. God here makes a covenant with the people as God did in the days of Noah. While God, after the deluge, recognized the people's continued wickedness and made a covenant never again to destroy the whole world by flood, God in Isaiah 54 unilaterally promises God's people that God will never again be angry and rebuke them (54:9–10). The suffering of Zion and the servant was too much. Zion and Israel received at God's hands double for their sins (40:1). God is changed. The God who is slow to anger and abounding in steadfast love restrained his wrath against his people (48:9), but God now forsakes his wrath, rather than forsaking his people, forever.

Renita Weems claims that the marriage metaphor is particularly appropriate for God's relationship to Israel not only because of the implied hierarchy in the relationship but also because of its unpredictability.[37] It is the abuser's unpredictability, his too easy shift from contrite and loving to furious and lashing out, that frightens and paralyzes so many battered women. If God's change in Isaiah 54 is only as temporary as that of an abusive husband, not only woman-Zion but all Israel and readers today are in perpetual danger. Trust is destroyed.

But God in Isaiah is not unpredictable in this way. Second Isaiah proclaims the God of history, the God who foretold the former things (41:22; 42:9; 43:9; 48:3) as well as the God who announces the new things (42:9; 43:19; 48:6). God is clearly powerful and in charge, but God will be *known* to Israel. God may bring destruction because of the people's sins or to somehow get their attention, but God, through the prophets, proclaims this to Israel in advance, so that they may know why their fate befalls them (40:21; 41:22; 43:9–10). They are not subject to the whims of an abusive God. They can rely, instead, on God's word fulfilling its purpose (40:8; 55:11). Yet the God who tells the former things also does the new things. God can change. If God promises never again to be angry and rebuke Zion, the people can count on God being faithful to that promise because God has been faithful in fulfilling God's word – even God's earlier words of destruction. Zion's and the servant's suffering is final. God's love is everlasting.

If Zion's and the servant's suffering is final and God's love is everlasting, then how do we explain or understand or live with suffering today? Women are still raped, in wars and in bedrooms by acquaintances. As the Holocaust demonstrates, suffering is real and actual. Its horror knows that peoples are still crushed, cut off from the land of the living, their generations extinguished. Many of us continue to experience God's wrath in our lives, in events of suffering or in loneliness and despair. What do the Zion and servant poems offer for our ongoing experience and observation of suffering in relation to God?[38]

Envisioning the Servant

The servant poem in Isaiah 52:13–53:12 functions as a vision. A people who will not listen to a message of good tidings (40:9), who will *not hear* that their God is king (52:7), that God will comfort his people (52:9), that the God of Israel is their protector – their leader and rear guard (52:12) – are invited instead to *see* (52:13). They will see the Lord's return to Zion (52:8) and the victory of their God in the baring of his holy arm (52:10). It is this vision of the suffering servant that brings onlookers to speech in the poem. The graphic portrayal of the servant's misery, the heaping up of terms for his anguish eventually moves those who see him to a new understanding both of what they had heard and of their own sins. Belief that had been unlikely now becomes possible because the servant's plight requires reflection. Relationship with Yhwh may yet be restored. Unlike the city Zion who cries out to God in lament, the people in the servant poem still only speak *about* God, not to God. Though they do not yet address Yhwh, the speakers are at least reflecting now on their guilt and on God's relationship to the servant's suffering and to their wholeness. The poem suggests that they may eventually come to believe (53:1). What they did not or would not hear, they will see and understand (52:15).

I would like to suggest one potential historical vision of the identity of the servant – not to settle the question, but in order to stimulate our imaginations about contemporary sufferers and outcasts.[39] Imagine the servant as an exiled Israelite who had become a eunuch in the Babylonian court. The proposal is not beyond the realm of possibility;[40] it may even explain the Ethiopian eunuch's fascination with this Isaiah poem in Acts 8. It also helps make sense out of some aspects of the poem's context in Isaiah. In an unusual word to Hezekiah, Isaiah prophesies that some of Hezekiah's own sons "will be taken away, and they will become eunuchs in the palace of the king of Babylon" (Isa. 39:7). No biblical text specifically records the fulfillment of this prophecy and some scholars see it simply as a metaphor for exile, but Isaiah does take up the matter of eunuchs again in 56:3–5, where their complaints are recognized and God opens a place for them (and foreigners) in the covenant community. (Eunuchs had been excluded from the worshipping community in Israel. See Deut. 23:2; E Deut. 23:1.)

The language of the eunuchs' complaints in this Isaiah passage is particularly striking. Is the eunuch who in 56:3 is not to say "I am a withered tree" (עץ יבש) like the servant in 53:2 who is a root out of dry ground (שרש מארץ ציה)? The servant poem wonders who can imagine the servant's generation (53:8), yet affirms that he will see offspring (53:10). Similarly, under certain conditions (sabbath keeping, choosing what God desires, holding fast to God's covenant), God promises in 56:5 to give those eunuchs in God's house[41] a name better than sons and daughters.[42]

A eunuch as the servant fits with some of the vocabulary of the servant poem. His appearance is disfigured (משחת) beyond that of a man (איש), leading him to be despised and rejected. This term for disfigurement is used in Leviticus 22:24–5, where an animal whose testicles have been bruised, crushed (דכא), torn, or cut is referred to as having deformities (משחתם) and is thus unacceptable as an offering to the Lord. The intense language of illness and affliction in the servant poem matches the eunuch's experience, particularly being crushed (דכא; 53:5, 10), and cut off from the land of the living (53:8). Deuteronomy 23:2 (E 23:1) specifically excludes any man wounded by crushing (דכא) or cutting the genitals from entering the assembly of the Lord.[43] Such would be the situation of the eunuchs in Isaiah 39:7 and 56:3–5. The cutting language of slaughter and shearers (53:7) is especially appropriate for the eunuch's affliction. An Israelite eunuch in a Babylonian court might also make kings shut their mouths (52:14) and have his grave (metaphorical or otherwise) with the wicked rich (53:9). Heavily veiled reference, even metaphorically, to a sexually damaged male servant would also parallel the allusions to woman-Zion's sexual defilement.

Suffering Today: Engaging Metaphors

While the vision of a eunuch may continue to trouble contemporary hearers,[44] it serves primarily as a spark to our imaginations, to help us consider the poem's sufferer as real and actual. The particular identity of the servant seems intentionally ambiguous. As is the case in lament psalms and thanksgiving hymns, the anonymity of the servant, the speakers, and the "many" allows the poem's readers in all ages to contemplate visions of suffering and horror in our own times. We may recognize ourselves as the silent sufferer or as the speakers whose sins have occasioned the suffering. We are invited in these roles respectively to be confident in our ultimate exaltation and to reflect on our relationship with God and our treatment of our neighbors.

The poem continues to convict those who speak ourselves in the poem's "we" with the recognition that others suffer in part because of our sins: a homeless person, a battered woman, an AIDS victim, the disabled, abused children, refugees, the hungry, and groups targeted for genocide. Whether by our active involvement as perpetrators of their torture, by our conspiracies of silence about the realities of their lives and deaths, or by our passive complicity in systems that ignore or exploit them, others are wounded because of our transgressions. As in the poem, there is often no beauty to make these people attractive to us (53:2). They may even be disfigured by their illness or suffering, startling us but also causing them or us to hide our faces (53:3). The silence of many of these sufferers and their pouring out of their lives even to death may not attract our attention, yet some of these sufferers intercede for us as transgressors (53:12). The poem compels those of us who view such anguish rather than suffering it, not only to ponder our relationship with God, but to take action, so that the Lord's purpose might prosper through the servant's suffering (53:10). It convicts us, compelling us at last, in the book's opening words, to give ear to God's instruction (1:10) and to respond appropriately – not with sacrifices (1:11) or with prayers, ritual, and ceremonies (1:13–15), but by washing our crime-stained hands, learning to do good, and devoting ourselves to justice (1:16–17).

As I hope my discussion above has shown, the Zion poems and the servant songs offer engaging metaphors, moving both God and listeners to ongoing relationship. Yet the overwhelming recent scholarly attention to the servant songs has largely eclipsed focus on Zion or on the relationship of the two motifs. A few scholars have attended to both. John Sawyer observes the following similarities between Zion and the servant.[45] Both are elaborated over many chapters and have ambiguous identity. Both are concerned with offspring, suffer humiliation and affliction, are ultimately vindicated, and affect nations. Both have supernatural endings, with the suffering being deemed out of proportion to their guilt. Finally, both Zion and the servant serve in some sense as heralds of good news. Tod Linafelt also addresses the relationship between Zion and the servant in his study of speech and silence in the servant passages. He notes a "movement from a silent community in the first passage to a community beginning to regain its power for speech in the final passage."[46] He sees Zion's speaking in 49:14 (which he refers to as Israel's speaking) as a sign of despair, as signal that the people have not heard the prophet's speaking to them.[47] While laments may voice despair, Zion's cries also challenge and move God. Thus, they may not be signs of the prophet's failure but of his success in moving the people to speech – at least in the form of accusation and perhaps anger at God.

Reflection on Zion and the servant offers two modes of doing theology to ancient and modern readers. David Blumenthal has described doing theology as "an act of inter-pretation, of standing between the text-tradition, God, and the reader or believer."[48] He further proposes four criteria for doing this: that interpreters (1) "always speak the truth"; (2) "deal with the texts"; (3) "cannot reject God"; and (4) that "plurivocity . . . is normative."[49] Feminist biblical scholarship contributes to this doing of theology. It helps us deal with all the texts by lifting up the female metaphors in prophetic literature, and it insists that we speak the truth even if that may lead to labeling God as an abuser. While some feminists reject this abusive God rejecting God is precisely why the Israelites suffer in Isaiah.[50]

The plurivocity of the Isaiah texts themselves provides an appropriate interpretation, a standing between that can function in our time as it may once have done in Israel. The Zion and servant texts both function in relation to God and to the people. Zion's laments and the servant's silent suffering both move God, effecting an irreversible change toward everlasting love. The city's speeches and the vision of the sufferer also address those who hear their poems, providing avenues of continued approach to God in the midst of suffering: challenging lament and anguished endurance. Both metaphors engage us, wracking our own minds and bodies with suffering. The plurivocity of the texts consists not only in the multiple effects of the Zion and servant poems individually, but in the ways they work together. Whether we see ourselves as abandoned and forlorn, as obediently accepting suffering, or as sinfully complicitous in causing it, together these poems convince us finally that God is ultimately *for us*.

The Zion and servant metaphors still grip us theologically. They urge our ongoing wrestling with them and with God for meaning and they *do* things to us. We experience the abuse, abandonment, and anger. We suffer the rejection and anguish and recoil at the horror and offense. And *if* God gets through again in our reading, hearing, and studying of these poems, we know also the vindication and God's everlasting, lavish love.

Notes

1 My reading is based primarily on the Masoretic text. Because of its difficulty and the differences in ancient versions, scholars have proposed various emendations. On these text-critical matters, see the commentaries: James Muilenburg, "Isaiah: Introduction and Exegesis," in *The Interpreter's Bible*, ed. G. A. Buttrick (Nashville: Abingdon Press, 1956) 5: 381–773; John L. McKenzie, *Second Isaiah* (AB 20; Garden City: Doubleday, 1968); Claus Westermann, *Isaiah 40–66: A Commentary*, trans. David M. G. Stalker (OTL: Philadelphia: Westminster, 1969); H. L. Ginsberg, *The Book of Isaiah* (Philadelphia: Jewish Publication Society, 1973); R. N. Whybray, *Isaiah 40–66* (NCB; London: Oliphants, 1975); Richard Clifford, *Fair Spoken and Persuading: An Interpretation of Second Isaiah* (Ramsey, N. J.: Paulist Press, 1984). See also A[nthony] Gelston, "Isaiah 52:13–53:12: An Eclectic Text and a Supplementary Note on the Hebrew Manuscript Kennicott 96," *Journal of Semitic Studies* 35 (1990): 187–211.

2 Bernhard Duhm, *Das Buch Jesaia* (Göttingen: Vandenhoeck & Ruprecht, 1892); Christopher R. North, *The Suffering Servant in Deutero-Isaiah: An Historical and Critical Study*, 2nd edn. (Oxford: Oxford University Press, 1956); Colin G. Kruse, "The Servant Songs: Interpretive Trends Since C. R. North," *Studia Biblica et Theologica* 8 (1978): 3–27; and Peter Wilcox and David Paton-Williams, "The Servant Songs in Deutero-Isaiah," *JSOT* 42 (1988): 79–102.

3 There is considerable scholarly discussion on the personification of cities as females. See A. Fitzgerald, "The Mythological Background for the Presentation of Jerusalem as a Queen and False Worship as Adultery in the OT," *CBO* 34 (1972): 403–16 and "*Btwlt* and *Bt* as Titles for Capital Cities," *CBO* 37 (1975): 167–83; Elaine R. Follis, "The Holy City as Daughter," in *Directions in Biblical Hebrew Poetry*, ed. Elaine R. Follis (JSOTS up 40; Sheffield: JSOT Press, 1987), pp. 173–84; Mark E. Biddle, "The Figure of Lady Jerusalem: Identification, Deification and Personification of Cities in the Ancient Near East," in *The Biblical Canon in Comparative Perspective: Scripture in Context IV*, ed. K. Lawson Younger, Jr., W. W. Hallo, and B. F. Batto (Lewiston: Edwin Mellen, 1991), pp. 173–94; Tikva Frymer-Kensky, *In the Wake of the Goddess: Women, Culture, and the*

Biblical Transformation of Pagan Myth (New York: Free Press, 1992); F. W. Dobbs-Allsopp, *Weep, O Daughter of Zion: A Study of the City-Lament Genre in the Hebrew Bible* (BibOr 44; Rome: Pontifical Biblical Institute, 1993), and "The Syntagma of *bat* followed by a Geographical Name in the Hebrew Bible: A Reconsideration of Its Meaning and Grammar," *CBQ* 53 (1995): 451–70; and Peggy L. Day, "The Personification of Cities as Female in the Hebrew Bible: The Thesis of Aloysius Fitzgerald, F.S.C.," in *Reading From This Place: Social Location and Biblical Interpretation in Global Perspective*, ed. Fernando F. Segovia and Mary Ann Tolbert (Minneapolis: Fortress, 1995), 2: 283–302. While Fitzgerald contends that the city-woman metaphor in the Hebrew Bible (HB) originates from a pattern in Western Semitic culture of capital cities being personified as goddesses married to patron gods, Frymer-Kensky and Day challenge his conclusion as based on assumption rather than evidence. Dobbs-Allsopp observes that the city-woman in the HB often functions similarly to the weeping goddesses in ancient Near Eastern city laments.

4 Barbara Bakke Kaiser, "Poet as 'Female Impersonator': The Image of Daughter Zion as Speaker in Biblical Poems of Suffering," *JR* 67 (1987): 164–82.

5 Ibid., pp. 178–9.

6 These three phases occur respectively in Jer. 4:16–17, 18, and 19–26; see ibid., p. 170.

7 Ibid., p. 174.

8 For a more complete listing see David J. Clark, "Sex-Related Imagery in the Prophets," *The Bible Translator* 33 (1982): 409–13.

9 For a graphic translation and analysis of the sexual innuendo in Ezekiel 16 and 23, see Julie Galambush, *Jerusalem in the Book of Ezekiel: The City as Yahweh's Wife* (SBLDS no. 130; Atlanta: Scholars Press, 1992).

10 T. Drorah Setel, "Prophets and Pornography: Female Sexual Imagery in Hosea," in *Feminist Interpretation of the Bible*, ed. Letty M. Russell (Philadelphia: Westminster, 1985), pp. 86–95. More recently, see the following essays in *A Feminist Companion to the Latter Prophets*, ed. Athalya Brenner (Feminist Companion to the Bible, 8; Sheffield: Academic Press, 1995): Athalya Brenner, "On Prophetic Propaganda and the Politics of 'Love': The Case of Jeremiah," pp. 256–74; and Fokkelien van Dijk-Hemmes, "The Metaphorization of Woman in Prophetic Speech: An Analysis of Ezekiel 23," 244–55. In this volume, Robert Carroll is not convinced, due to unbalanced use of feminist scholarship on pornography, that "pornographic" is an appropriate designation; see his "Desire under the Terebinths: On Pornographic Representation in the Prophets – A Response," pp. 275–307.

11 In the prophetic literature, Isa. 13:16, Zech. 14:2, and Lam. 5:11 include the rapes of real women as part of war's destruction. See Susan Brooks Thistlethwaite, "'You May Enjoy the Spoil of Your Enemies': Rape as a Biblical Metaphor for War," in *Women, War, and Metaphor: Language and Society in the Study of the Hebrew Bible*, ed. Claudia V. Camp and Carole R. Fontaine (Semeia 61; Atlanta: Scholars Press, 1993), pp. 59–75; and Pamela Gordon and Harold C. Washington, "Rape as Military Metaphor in the Hebrew Bible," in *A Feminist Companion to the Latter Prophets*, pp. 308–25.

12 Mary Joan Winn Leith, "Verse and Reverse: The Transformation of the Woman, Israel in Hosea 1–3," in *Gender and Difference in Ancient Israel*, ed. Peggy L. Day (Minneapolis: Augsburg Fortress, 1989), pp. 95–108. See also F. Rachel Magdalene, "Ancient Near Eastern Treaty-Curses and the Ultimate Texts of Terror: A Study of the Language of

Divine Sexual Abuse in the Prophetic Corpus," in *A Feminist Companion to the Latter Prophets*, pp. 326–52.

13 Phyllis Bird, "'To Play the Harlot': An Inquiry into an Old Testament Metaphor," in *Gender and Difference in Ancient Israel*, p. 89.

14 Most feminist discussion has centered around the marriage metaphor in Hosea. See Renita Weems, "Gomer: Victim of Violence or Victim of Metaphor?" in *Interpretation for Liberation*, ed. Katie Geneva Cannon and Elisabeth Schüssler Fiorenza (Semeia 47; Atlanta: Scholars Press, 1989), pp. 87–101; Fokkelien van Dijk-Hemmes, "The Imagination of Power and the Power of Imagination: An Intertextual Analysis of Two Biblical Love Songs: The Song of Songs and Hosea 2," *JSOT* 44 (1989): 75–88; and both feminist and masculist interpretations of Hosea in several essays in *A Feminist Companion to the Latter Prophets*. On the marriage metaphor more broadly, see Tikva Frymer-Kensky, *In the Wake of the Goddess* and Renita J. Weems, *Battered Love: Marriage, Sex, and Violence in the Hebrew Prophets* (OBT; Minneapolis: Fortress, 1995).

15 On the cycle of abuse see Lenore Walker, *The Battered Woman* (New York: Harper & Row, 1979). For abuse in relation to biblical interpretation and theology, see Susan Brooks Thistlethwaite, "Every Two Minutes: Battered Women and Feminist Interpretation," in *Feminist Interpretation of the Bible*, pp. 96–107; and Joy M. K. Bussert, *Battered Women: From a Theology of Suffering to an Ethic of Empowerment* (New York: LCA Division for Mission in North America, 1986). for discussion of abuse in relation to Hosea, see Gale A. Yee, "Hosea," in *The Women's Bible Commentary*, ed. Carol A. Newsom and Sharon H. Ringe (Louisville: Westminster/John Knox, 1992), pp. 195–202; Weems, "Gomer"; and Naomi Graetz, "God is to Israel as Husband is to Wife: The Metaphoric Battering of Hosea's Wife," in *A Feminist companion to the Latter Prophets*, pp. 126–45.

16 Setel, "Prophets and Pornography," p. 95; Magdalene, "Treaty-Curses," p. 349. For other responses to teaching and proclaiming troubling prophetic texts, see Katheryn Pfisterer Darr, "Ezekiel's Justifications of God: Teaching Troubling Texts," *JSOT* 55 (1992): 97–117 and Richard Nysse, "Keeping Company with Nahum: Reading the Oracles against the Nations as Scripture," *Word & World* 15 (1995): 412–19.

17 For a detailed review of the Zion passages and analysis of critical issues pertaining to each, see Kathryn Pfisterer Darr, *Isaiah's Vision and the Family of God*. Literary Currents in Biblical Interpretation (Louisville: Westminster/John Knox, 1994).

18 Magdalene, "Treaty-Curses," p. 333. The movement in Isa. 47:6 and discussion of Babylon in the book as a whole show that God is not the rapist. God gave up God's people to Babylon. God's judgement is thus mediated. It is Babylon who goes too far, showing the people no mercy, and thus meriting her own debasement. The analogy of a mother colluding in or even somewhat helplessly standing aside while knowing about the sexual abuse of her daughter comes, unbidden, to mind.

19 Rather than signalling distrust, continued conversation with God in laments may also be a sign of ongoing faith in the deity.

20 Terence E. Fretheim notes that God's questions show openness to human views and indicate that "the people have a role to play in determining what God's final answer to his own questions will be." *The Suffering of God: An Old Testament Perspective* (OBT; Philadelphia: Fortress, 1984), p. 123.

21 Isa. 40:2. Note that Shechem also "speaks tenderly" (עַל-לֵב) to Dinah after raping her in Gen. 34:3.

22 The comment in 54:1 that "the children of the wife forlorn shall outnumber those of the espoused" reminds readers of the battle between beloved Rachel and hated Leah for children and perhaps of the more recent love triangle between God, Babylon, and Zion, where Babylon presumed that she alone (47:8–10) would always be the mistress (47:7) and not become a widow or know loss of children (47:8).

23 In view of the recently experienced Assyrian "flood" in Isa. 8:7–8, Zion may reasonably wonder at how comforting this promise is.

24 While feminists have discussed the theological implications of suffering generally, I am not aware of detailed feminist analyses of the Isaiah 53 text.

25 Joanne Carlson Brown and Rebecca Parker, "For God So Loved the World?" in *Christianity, Patriarchy, and Abuse: A Feminist Critique*, ed. Joanne Carlson Brown and Carole R. Bohn (Cleveland: Pilgrim, 1989), pp. 2, 23, 26. Also on suffering and Christology see Rita Nakashima Brock, *Journeys by Heart: A Christology of Erotic Power* (New York: Crossroad, 1988). For analysis and critique of feminist claims about atonement theory, see Leanne Van Dyk, "Do Theories of Atonement Foster Abuse?" *Dialog* 35 (1996): 21–5 and Thelma Megill-Cobbler, "A Feminist Rethinking of Punishment Imagery in Atonement," *Dialog* 35 (1996): 14–20. On the relationship of suffering and redemption, see also Jane Strohl, "Suffering as Redemptive: A Comparison of Christian Experience in the Sixteenth and Twentieth Centuries," in *Revisioning the Past: Prospects in Historical Theology*, ed. Mary Potter Engel and Walter E. Wyman, Jr. (Minneapolis: Fortress, 1992), pp. 95–112.

26 Commentators note the piling up of torturous terms in the poem: disfigured (משחת) 52:14; smitten (נגע) 53:4, 8; struck down (מכה) 53:4; afflicted (ענה) 53:4, 7; pierced (חלל) 53:5; crush (דכא) 53:5, 10; let strike (פגע) 53:6, 12; oppressed (נגש) 53:7; slaughter (טבח) 53:7; shearers (גזז) 53:7; cut off (גזר) 53:8; pain (מכאב) 53:3, 4; disease (חלי) 53:3, 4, 10; chastisement (מוסר) 53:5; bruises (חברה) 53:5; trouble (עמל) 53:11.

27 While many commentators presume them, others argue that the poem does not support vicarious suffering or substitutionary atonement (which need not be equated). Assuming vicarious suffering are: Clifford, *Fair Spoken and Persuading*, pp. 178–81; Fretheim, *Suffering of God*, pp. 139, 164 Abraham J. Heschel, *The Prophets* (New York: Harper & Row, 1962), 1: 151; Baruch Levine, "René Girard on Job: The Question of the Scapegoat," in *René Girard and Biblical Studies*, ed. Andrew J. McKenna (Semeia 33; Decatur, GA: Scholars Press, 1985), pp. 128, 131; Tod Linafelt, "Speech and Silence in the Servant Passages: Towards a Final-Form Reading of the Book of Isaiah" (see chapter 14 of this book, p. 208) Patrick D. Miller, *They Cried to the Lord: The Form and Theology of Biblical Prayer* (Minneapolis: Fortress, 1994), p. 266; and Gerhard von Rad, *Old Testament Theology*, trans. D. M. G. Stalker (New York: Harper & Row, 1965), 2: 256–7. On 14 of 31 Jewish authors viewing exilic Israel's suffering as vicarious see Joel E. Rembaum, "The Development of a Jewish Exegetical Tradition Regarding Isaiah 53," *HTR* 75 (1982); 301. For English translations of many of these Jewish interpretations, see Samuel R. Driver and Adolf Neubauer, trans., *The "Suffering Servant" of Isaiah According to the Jewish Interpreters* (New York: Hermon, 1969). On the vicarious suffering of this blemished servant constituting a radical desacralization of sacrifice see Westermann, *Isaiah 40–66*, pp. 263, 268.

Against vicarious suffering in the poem, see John J. Collins, "The Suffering Servant: Scapegoat or Example?" *Proceedings of the Irish Biblical Association* 4 (1980): 62; J.

Severino Croatto, "Exegesis of Second Isaiah from the Perspective of the Oppressed: Paths for Reflection," in *Reading From This Place*, 2: 234; Francis Landy, "The Construction of the Subject and the Symbolic Order: A Reading of the Last Three Suffering Servant Songs," in *Among the Prophets: Language, Image and Structure in the Prophetic Writings*, ed. Philip R. Davies and David J. A. Clines (JSOT Sup no. 144; Sheffield: Sheffield Academic Press, 1993), p. 61; Harry M. Orlinsky, "The So-Called 'Servant of the Lord' and 'Suffering Servant' in Second Isaiah," in *Studies on the Second Part of the Book of Isaiah* (VTSupp 14; Leiden: Brill, 1967), pp. 17–74; and R. N. Whybray, *Thanksgiving for a Liberated Prophet: An Interpretation of Isaiah Chapter 53* (JSOTSup 4; Sheffield: JSOT, 1978), pp. 29–76.

28 Of course the accusations need not be true. God can be falsely blamed for suffering. Fretheim notes, instead, that God experiences the suffering of the prophet in this poem, *Suffering of God*, p. 165. Paul D. Hanson concurs: *Isaiah 40–66* (IBC; Louisville: Westminster/John Knox Press, 1995), p. 160.

29 For example, while the agent inflicting the beatings of God's rebel children in Isa. 1:5–6 is not specified, the parallelism in Isa. 9:12 (E 9:13) suggests that the one who struck the people is the Lord of Hosts. The people's refrain "Yet his anger has not turned back and his arm is outstretched still" may pick up this image of God continuing to beat them (E Isa. 5:25; 9:12, 17, 21; 10:4). Jer. 2:30 describes God as smiting the people in order to correct them. The image of God striking repeated blows is particularly forceful in Lam. 3:1–4. While this is all metaphorical language (no bolts from heaven) and the destruction is in every case historically mediated by the enemies of Israel and Judah, this poetry attributes the infliction of suffering to God.

30 God's opening complaint is that the children God brought up do not *know*, do not understand (Isa. 1:3). In Second Isaiah, God makes deserts blossom so that the people will see and *know* (41:20). God chooses Israel as God's servant so that they may *know* and believe/trust God (43:10). God gives the people treasures of darkness so that they may *know* that the God of Israel summons them (45:3). Though the people have not acknowledged God, God will strengthen them so that people will *know* that there is none besides God (45:5–6; cf. 49:23; 52:6; 60:16).

31 God regularly offers reassurance, "do not fear" (40:9; 41:10, 13, 14; 43:1, 5; 44:2, 8; 51:7; 54:4) and urges trust (40:27–31), and in Isa. 41:21 and 43:26 God invites people to submit their case or argue with God.

32 Brown and Parker, "For God So Loved the World?" want to "do away with the atonement," p. 26. They neglect Lutheran discussions of atonement, which reverse the direction, moving from God to humans rather than human to God. Traditional theories before Luther tried to figure out how humans can be made right for God, with God as the object. Luther, instead, considers how God as subject creates a people who love and trust God. Gerhard O. Forde discusses this reversal of direction in his essays on "The Work of Christ," in *Christian Dogmatics*, ed. Carl E. Braaten and Robert W. Jenson (Philadelphia: Fortress, 1984), 2: 5–99. His discussion of the offense of the cross, the actual nature of God's wrath, and God getting through were helpful in shaping my discussion of Isaiah 53.

33 Brown and Parker, ibid, pp. 13–21, describe these aspects of the modern and post-modern critical tradition as the "suffering God" and the "necessity of suffering" atonement theories. They reject these theories also because they seem to suggest that suffering should be understood positively – as something to emulate.

34 For discussion of the emphasis on seeing in Isa 52:13–53:12, see David J. A. Clines, *I, He, We, and They: A Literary Approach to Isaiah 53* (JSOT Sup no. 1; Sheffield: JSOT, 1976), pp. 40–44. On seeing and the prophets generally, see Fretheim, *Suffering of God*, pp. 84–86, 149–66.

35 This reward can lead to the problem of suffering being seen as an example to be emulated. If the righteous servant suffers and is rewarded, then perhaps you or I should suffer silently and passively as well, in the hope of our ultimate vindication. It may be that the poem should offer some hope to those righteous among us whose suffering is so great that even a silent scream to God is impossible. Yet the point of the poem is not the embrace of suffering. In contrast to New Testament exhortations to endure suffering righteously (e.g. Matt. 5:11–12; Heb. 12:2–13; 1 Pet. 2:19–23; 3:17–18; 4:19), the HB does not commend suffering.

36 Jack Miles, *God: A Biography* (New York: Alfred A. Knopf, 1995), pp. 250–1. The effect on God is so astounding that Miles claims that God, until this point in his history, "has not loved" (p. 233), and that Israel's sufferings lead God toward love p. (249). Miles seems to ignore God's passionate love for Israel/Ephraim in Hosea.

37 Weems, *Battered Love*, pp. 26, 71.

38 For a discussion of different types of suffering and God's involvement in them, see Elizabeth A. Johnson, *She Who Is: The Mystery of God in Feminist Theological Discourse* (New York: Crossword, 1992), pp. 246–72.

39 The servant as eunuch is not included among proposals catalogued by North and others.

40 A. Kirk Grayson studies eunuchs in ancient and modern civilizations: "Eunuchs in Power: Their Role in the Assyrian Bureaucracy," in *Vom Alten Orient zum Alten Testament: Festschrift fur Wolfram Freiherrn von Soden zum 85. Geburtstag am 19. Juni 1993*, ed. Manfried Dietrich and Oswald Loretz (Alter Orient und Altes Testament, no. 240; Neukirchen-Vluyn: Neukirchener Verlag, 1995), pp. 85–98. While acknowledging lack of definitive evidence, Grayson is convinced that eunuchs played a significant role in Babylonian society. A Middle Assyrian law presents what may be a striking parallel to Zion as an adulterous woman: the penalty for an adulterous man is that the wronged husband would turn him into a eunuch.

41 בית perhaps here referring to descendants, as with David in 2 Sam. 7:11.

42 Frederick J. Gaiser observes in his study of the eunuch passages in Isaiah that God in Isa. 56:1–8 speaks a new work on eunuchs precisely to demonstrate that Babylon can't win theologically by cutting off the offspring of Israel (p. 287); see "A New Word on Homosexuality? Isaiah 56:1–8 as Case Study," *Word & World* 14 (1994): 280–93.

43 The similar restrictions on priests in Lev. 21:16–23 use different vocabulary.

44 Grayson notes the marked scholarly avoidance of the subject of eunuchs in ancient and modern civilizations: "Eunuchs in Power," p. 85.

45 J. F. A. Sawyer, "Daughter of Zion and Servant of the Lord in Isaiah: A Comparison," *JSOT* 44 (1989): 89–107. For other examinations of Zion and the servant, see Knud Jeppesen, "Mother Zion, Father Servant: A Reading of Isaiah 49–55," in *Of Prophets' Visions and the Wisdom of the Sages: Essays in Honour of R. Norman Whybray on his Seventieth Birthday*, ed. Heather A. McKay and David J. A. Clines (JSOTSup no. 162; Sheffield: Sheffield Academic Press, 1993), pp. 109–25; and L. E. Wilshire, "The Servant City: A New Interpretation of 'The servant of the Lord' in the servant Songs of Deutero-Isaiah," *JBL* 94 (1975): 356–67 and "Jerusalem as the 'Servant City' in Isaiah

40–66: Reflections in the Light of Further Study of the Cuneiform Tradition," in *The Bible in the Light of Cuneiform Literature: Scripture in Context III*, ed. W. W. Hallo, B. W. Jones, and G. L. Mattingly (Lewiston: Edwin Mellen, 1990), pp. 231–55.

46 Linafelt, "Speech and Silence" (see chapter 14 of this book, p. 207).

47 Ibid., p. 207.

48 David R. Blumenthal, *Facing the Abusing God: A Theology of Protest* (Louisville: Westminster/John Knox, 1993), p. 237.

49 Ibid., pp. 237–9.

50 It may be prudent here to distinguish between the God portrayed in the biblical texts, who may sometimes merit the label "abuser," from the God who is. While biblical texts certainly embody human perceptions of the nature of God, insofar as scripture also reveals God's nature, feminists may need to study and live with a more ambiguous God. In the words of Judith Plaskow, "[U]nless the God who speaks to the feminist experiences of empowerment and connection can also speak to the frightening, destructive, and divisive aspects of our lives, a whole side of existence will be severed from the feminist account of the sacred." See her "Facing the Ambiguity of God," *Tikkun* 6/5 (1991): 70.

Matthew 5–7

Selections from John Chrysostom's Homilies on Matthew

Translated and introduced by Robin Darling Young

Introduction

John Chrysostom, priest of Antioch and later Archbishop of Constantinople, the "goldenmouth," remains one of the most influential biblical interpreters in the history of the Christian intellectual tradition. Famous as an orator in the late fourth century, his sermons once written down became standard liturgical fare in the eastern Churches, and were translated from Greek into the oriental Christian languages. They continued to influence scholarly commentators in the Greek and Latin Churches, including Thomas Aquinas. In early modern and modern times, they have been highly esteemed for another reason – apparently literal and sober interpretations of biblical texts, they avoided the now-suspect, allegedly "spiritualizing" readings associated with the Alexandrian exegetes, most notably, of course, Origen. When in the early twentieth century the historical-critical interpretation of scripture began to be prized exclusively, and particularly among scholars, John Chrysostom and the other "historical" exegetes of the early Church seemed more creditable than the "allegorizers."

A mere glance at the text below will serve to show that John Chrysostom is no critical, scientific interpreter – at least by modern standards. John thought that through the text of the Bible, and particularly that of the gospels and Pauline epistles, the Holy Spirit spoke directly to his congregation, and to all Christian congregations of whatever time. Although, as Homily One on

Matthew makes clear, it is preferable to have the Holy Spirit incised directly upon the heart rather than written in letters on a page, the Christian is supposed to hear each word as being spoken directly to him or to her as a disciple. What was needed was an interpreter of the gospel in the line of the apostle Paul, the prophets and the saints – and this was John's own role.

Therefore, when the reader wants to enter into the world of John's interpretation, it is advisable to read his words aloud, as they would first have been heard in the Golden Church of Antioch in the year 390. John worked slowly through the text, word by word, using a method taught him by his monastic teacher and applying to each *lexis* comparisons to other biblical texts drawn from his thorough knowledge of the whole scripture, won by heart during his monastic youth. So should the modern reader hear, word by word, the inquisitiveness, the tension, and the repetitiveness of this ancient priest's investigation of a gospel he had already meditated upon and made his own. For the goal of interpretation, as the reader will hear, was not information to be possessed by the reader, but transformation of the hearer. The hearer was to become, instead of a habitual lawbreaker, an obedient philosopher and citizen in the Christian *politeuma*, or society, which was forming inside the city limits of Antioch and other cities of the Roman world.

Chrysostom, by his display of investigation and meditation, tries to exhort and persuade, and to prepare his hearer for a conversion to a life of Christian self-discipline closely modeled on the monastic life he had known – a life of virtue in which the scripture could be more and more deeply appropriated, and in which, finally, the Christian could gain *theoria*, or visual contemplation, of God. No one could do this without virtue; but neither was it possible without holding the Nicene faith which had been much embattled among the hostile parties which contested for the Church of fourth-century Antioch. Hence Chrysostom spent the second and third of his sermons on Matthew discussing the "generation of Christ," i.e. the Incarnation of the second person of the Trinity, *homoousios* with the Father. However, not only Arians and Anomoeans were the opponents envisaged in these sermons; Chrysostom was aware that contemporary Gnostics, the Manichaeans so successful in fourth-century Syria and elsewhere, taught a kind of determinism which undermined Christian moral teaching just as it contradicted orthodox cosmology and theology. His opposition to Manichaeism doubtless sharpened his emphasis upon the legal aspect of the Gospel of Matthew, in which Christ appears (following the Gospel itself) as a second lawgiver, establishing a superior set of commandments upon the foundation of the Old Testament's law and its giver, Moses. With the assistance of grace, Christians could be gradually re-formed according to their image, Christ, and obey the new laws he gave. Chrysostom has become infamous for another set of opponents against whom his homilies are aimed, namely the Jews of Antioch. A strong and admired community in northern

Syria, the Jews apparently made credible claims to superior antiquity, to stronger cohesion, and to more veracity of biblical interpretation. Chrysostom's own sermons attest to their attraction for local Christians; here he makes an indirect case against Jewish interpretation by showing how the Old Testament and its law are incomplete without the New which it already anticipated – by now an ancient claim among Christians.

For despite Chrysostom's apparent attention to the historical level of scripture, in fact he was just as committed as any "Alexandrian" interpreter to a typological interpretation, in which the marks of Christ were inscribed deeply in the writings of Moses and the prophets. The gospel was the antitype, the confirmation and replacement, of the Old Covenant. What distinguishes Chrysostom from other kinds of exegetes is his approach. Here he can be seen as a member of a distinct "school," the most notable members of which were the monk-teacher Diodore of Antioch, later Bishop of Tarsus, and Theodore, his monastic comrade and schoolmate, later Bishop of Mopsuestia. Although most of the work of the first, prolific author is lost, and much of the work of the second survives in Syriac or Latin translation alone, each can readily be seen to be interpreters of John's ilk. In their (now-fragmentary) commentaries on the Psalms, each tries to establish the authorship of the Psalms, the mentality and intentions of the author, the overall aim of the book, and the modes of expression (figures of speech, metaphors, concrete references) consciously deployed by the author. They approach the text by considering the composition of each sentence, and consider why the sentence might not have been written in a *different* way – the significance of a choice not exercised. Finally, but not least importantly, Diodore and Theodore consider the ethical level of the text – not only what the reader should do, but the mental framework within which he or she should hear the scripture in order to be able to carry out its instructions.

The Antiochene approach to biblical interpretation, which employed what later exegetes would call typology, tropology, and anagogy, was made widely popular by Chrysostom, who emulated his teachers but had the opportunity, since he occupied the most important pulpits in two capital cities, to extend their approach throughout much wider portions of the Bible. After Chrysostom, two exegetes, Nestorius, controversial Archbishop of Constantinople 429–433, and Theodoret, Bishop of Cyrus in northwest Syria, continued the Antiochene approach. It also spread to the Syriac-speaking Church of eastern Syria and Mesopotamia when the works of Diodore and Theodore were adopted as centerpieces of the curriculum of the "School of the Persians" in early fifth-century Edessa, later moved to Nisibis in Persian-controlled northern Meso-potamia. Through translations of their works, Syrians and Armenians learned to follow their methods, adhering to the narrative, typological, and ethical aspects of the text.

Chrysostom preached a series of 90 homilies on the Gospel of Matthew in Antioch in 390. They comprise the first sustained commentary on that Gospel in the early Church, and seem to have taken the entire year to deliver. In 391 he delivered homilies on John before beginning a continuous series of sermons on the Pauline epistles. In the series on Matthew, Chrysostom highlights three main points: that Christ is the second person of the Trinity, that Christians should interiorize his words just as his disciples did, and that in consequence they should practice the same mercy with respect to the poor of the city as Christ and his apostles did for the crowds they encountered. In the "makarisms" of Matthew 5, Christ was laying down the foundations for a "new *politeia*" of citizens who would display just those characteristics he indicated by the terms "poor in spirit," "humble," "peacemakers," etc. The selection below, taken from the fifteenth sermon on Matthew, is particularly interesting because it discusses a virtue much scorned in the ancient world – humility. In a city where the traditional Roman institutions of the theater, the horse races, and the Olympic games were prized, Chrysostom proposed that a typical attitude of the urban citizen, mental pride, *aponoia*, led to the devil's fall, and to mankind's. It itself had to be broken up in the heart of the Christian citizen by humility (*tapeinophrosyne*, literally, humility of mind) and mourning, the sorrow (*penthos*) made famous in the biographies of monks whose lives were to form a new model for Christians. In doing so, Christians would not only be more inclined to care for their poor, but they would also be preparing themselves to inherit the earth.

The following is a translation of the text in *Patrologiae Graecae* (vol. 57 ed J. P. Migne, 1860).

John Chrysostom. Homily 15 on the Gospel of Matthew

Matthew 5:1, 2

And Jesus, seeing the crowds, went up upon the mountain, and when he sat down, his disciples came to him. And he opened his mouth and taught them, saying, "Blessed are the poor in spirit, for theirs is the kingdom of the heavens."

See the one without ambition or boasting! For he did not lead the crowds about with him, but when he had to heal, he went around everywhere, visiting their cities and fields. When the crowd increased, he sat down in one spot. And he does not do so in a city or in the middle of a forum, but on a mountain and in a desert, teaching us to do nothing for the sake of show, and to separate ourselves from our daily cares, and most of all whenever it is necessary to philosophize and to hold a conversation about the actions we must take.

When he had gone up and "sat down, the disciples approached." Do you perceive their progress in virtue, and how all at once they became better? For on the one hand, a multitude were spectators of wonders, but these ones even longed to hear were spectators of wonders, but these ones even longed to hear some great and high matter. This it was that inclined him to teach, and caused him to begin these discourses. For not only did he heal bodies, but he also set souls aright; and he changed from care of the former to therapy for the latter, at the same time varying his assistance, and mixing with the teaching of his discourses the demonstration from works, and blocking up the shameless heretics' mouths. On their account he showed care for both substances [*ousiai*], demonstrating that he is Creator of all parts of life. Therefore he was distributing a share of his great care to each substance, now amending that one, now this one.

This he did at that time. For "he opened his mouth and taught them." And why is the saying attached that, "He opened his mouth"? In order that you might also learn that he taught while silent, not only speaking, but sometimes opening his mouth, sometimes emitting his voice from his works. When you hear that "he taught them," do not think only that he spoke to his disciples, but understand (he taught) all through those ones. Since the crowd was common, made up of those creeping on the earth, he instituted the chorus of disciples and made discourses to them. In his dialogue with them he provided for the rest, still very far from his sayings, preparing the teaching of his philosophy to be unburdensome. Of which both Luke said, speaking in riddles, "He directed his words to them" (Luke 6:20), and Matthew made clear the very same thing when he wrote, "His disciples approached him, and he taught them" (Matt. 28:20). Thus also the others were likely to be more eagerly devoted than if he had extended (his discourse) towards all.

Therefore whence did he begin, and what sort of foundations has he established for us of his new *politeia*? Let us listen to his words with acuity; for although it was spoken to those ones, it was written for all who came after them. Therefore although speaking publicly he considered his disciples, he does not limit his sayings to them, but undividedly offers his blessings to all. For he did not say, "Blessed are you, if you should become poor," but "Blessed are the poor." And even if he did speak to them, the words of his advice would still be general. For when he said, "I am with you always unto the end of the age" (Matt. 28:20), he did not speak to them alone, but through them to the whole inhabited world. And when he blessed them as being persecuted and hunted down and suffering intolerable afflictions, he plaited a crown not for them alone, but for all those bringing to a successful issue the same activities.

However, in order that this become even clearer, and that you might learn that the sayings have great affinity for you and for all human nature, if someone will pay attention, listen to how he begins these wonderful words: "Blessed are the poor in spirit, for theirs is the kingdom of the heavens." What is the [expression] "poor in spirit"? The humble and contrite in mind. Herein he called "spirit" the soul and the intention (*proairesis*). For since there are many humble people, not willingly but constrained under necessity, leaving aside those ones (because there is no praise here) he blesses those first who intentionally humbled and cast themselves down.

But for what reason did he not say, "the humble," but "the poor"? Because this is more than that. Herein he speaks of those cowering and quaking at the injunctions of God, whom also God, through his prophet Isaiah, approved greatly and said, "Upon whom will I look, but to him who is humble and peaceable, and trembles at my words?" (Isa. 66:2 LXX).

And there are many ways of humility – one is humble moderately, another entirely excessively. This is the humility the blessed prophet praises, sketching out for us a mind not simply cast down, but completely broken in pieces, when he says, "The sacrifice for God is a contrite spirit; a heart contrite and humble God will not despise" (Ps. 50:17 LXX). And the three boys offer this to God instead of a great sacrifice, saying, "Nevertheless in a contrite soul and a spirit of humility may we be accepted" (Dan. 3:39 LXX). Now Christ blesses this, too.

For since the greatest of evils, and those destroying the whole world, came in out of arrogance of mind (for the devil, not being such a one before this, thus became "devil" [which Paul also clearly said in this, "Lest being conceited he should fall into the judgement of the devil" (1 Tim. 3:6); and the first man, puffed up by the devil with these hopes, had his neck laid bare and became mortal, for expecting to become God, he also lost what he possessed, and God reproaching him and satirizing his mindlessness said, "Behold, Adam has become as one of us" (Gen. 3:22); and each of those coming after these things ran aground on impiety, fantasizing equality with God) – since, then, this was the acropolis of evils, and the root and source of all wickedness, God, preparing a medicine suitable for the disease, like some strong and safe foundation laid down this first law. With this established beneath, the builder lays down all the other [laws] in safety. But when this [humility] is removed, even though the citizen of the Christian life (*politeuomenos*) should draw near to the heavens, all is dragged down easily, and is brought back to a bitter end. Even if you have collected fasting, prayer, almsgiving, temperance, and whatsoever kind of good, without humility, all waste away and are demolished.

This very thing came about in the case of the Pharisee. For even after his arrival at the summit, "he went down" (Luke 18:14), having lost everything since he did not have the mother of the virtues. For just as arrogance of mind is the fountain of every evil, humility is the source of all philosophy. Hence he begins here, too, uprooting false pretension from the soul of his hearers.

"And what is this to his disciples," one asks, "who were thoroughly humble? For they had no occasion for arrogance of mind, being fishermen, and poor, and obscure, and ignorant." Even though these things did not apply to his disciples, they were said to those present at that time, and those who after them were to receive them, in order that they should not despise [the disciples]. But, rather, also towards the disciples! For even if it were not [applicable] then, but later they needed this assistance, after signs and wonders, after the honor of the entire world, and their freedom of speech towards God. For neither wealth, nor power, nor a kingdom itself could exalt them as what they themselves possessed. Anyway, it was natural to them that, even before the signs, then they might be exalted, seeing the crowd and the audience surrounding their teacher, to suffer some human [affection]. Therefore he immediately overthrew their presumption.

And he does not introduce his sayings in an arrangement of exhortation and commandments, but in the arrangement of a blessing, making his word less heavy, and to all opening the amphitheater of his teaching. For he did not say, this one and that one, all who do these things are blessed. Whether you are a slave, a poor man, a beggar, an alien, or a simpleton, there is no obstacle to your becoming blessed, if you will live according to this virtue.

Having begun where the need was greatest, he proceeds to another commandment seeming to be opposed to the judgement of the entire world. For all those reckoning themselves when joyful, to be enviable, he blesses others instead of them – those in dejection, poverty, mourning, miserable. The latter he calls blessed, not the former, saying, "Blessed are they who mourn." Yet all call them miserable. Therefore he worked signs beforehand, in order that he might be credible in his lawgiving. And here as well again he indicated not merely mourners, but all who do this for their sins, since that other kind is entirely forbidden, which bewails anything in (earthly) life. Paul also made this very thing clear when he said "The grief of the world works death, but that according to God accomplishes repentance to salvation, not to be repented" (2 Cor. 7:10).

These then also he blesses here whose sorrow is of that kind; but not merely did he indicate those sorrowing, but those strenuously sorrowing. Therefore he did not say, those who sorrow, but "those who mourn." For

245

even this commandment is a teacher of all philosophy. For if those who
sorrow for children, or wife, or any kin gone away, have no love for
advantage or bodily things during that time of grief, if they do not aim
at glory, are not stirred up by insults, if they are not held captive by envy,
of by any other passion are assaulted – how much more will those
mourning their sins, as worthily mourning, display a better philosophy
than this?

Next, what is the contest-prize for these ones? He says, "For they will
be comforted." Where will they be comforted, tell me? Both here, and
there. For since the order was exceedingly heavy and galling, he promised
to give that thing which would most of all lighten it. Thus if you will be
comforted, mourn. And do not consider this saying to be an enigma.
When God comforts, though a myriad of sufferings approach like
snowflakes, you will be entirely above them. For God always gives
rewards much greater than our works; he has done so here, showing the
mourning blessed, not according to the worth of the deed, but according
to his own love of mankind (*philanthropia*). For those who mourn mourn
for errors, and to them it is sufficient to gain forgiveness and a legal
defense (*apologia*). But since he is very much a lover of man, he does not
choose just the removal of punishments, nor does he establish an antidote
for the removal of sins, but he even calls blessed, and abundantly gives
much consolation. He tells us to mourn not only for our own sins, but
for those errors of others. Similar were the souls of the saints; similar were
the souls of Moses, Paul, and David; all these mourned often the evils
of others.

"Blessed are the gentle, for they will inherit the earth." What kind of
earth, tell me? Some say an intellectual earth (*noete ge*). But this is not
so. Nowhere in the scripture do we discover any mention of an
"intellectual earth." But what, then, is the [meaning of the] expression?
It indicates a sensible contest-prize, just as with Paul. For he says, "Honor
your father and your mother"; he added, "thus you will be long-lasting
upon the earth" (Eph. 6:2). And he himself again, to the thief: "Today
you will be with me in Paradise" (Luke 22:43). For not only does he move
us forward by means of the coming good things, but also by present
things, for the benefit of the more dense among his hearers, and before
those seeking things to come. Therefore also further on he said, "Be
agreed with your enemy" (Matt. 5:25). Then he appoints the contest-
prize of such philosophy, and said, "Lest at any time the enemy deliver
you to the judge, and the judge to the officer (Matt. 5:25)." Do you see
how he frightens us? By the sensible things, by the things occurring right
at our feet! And again, "Whoever shall say to his brother, 'Raka [you fool]'
is in danger of the council" (Matt. 5:22).

And Paul, too, sets down sensible contest-prizes extensively, and exhorts by means of present things, as when he talks about virginity. For saying nothing there about the heavens, he endorses it from things present, saying, "because of the present distress," and "I spare you," and "I wish you to be without cares" (1 Cor. 7:26, 28, 32).

Thus also Christ has mingled the sensible with the spiritual. For since the gentle person is reckoned to lose entirely his own, he promises the opposite, saying No, but this is the one possessing his own in safety, not rash or boastful, while the other sort of man often loses his patrimony and his own soul. And elsewhere since in the Old Testament the prophet said constantly, "The gentle shall inherit the earth" (Ps. 36:11 LXX), he weaves in as a pattern into his speech expressions familiar to them, so as not to employ speech entirely foreign.

And he says this, not to limit the rewards to present things, but joining them with the other kind [of gifts]. For in saying something spiritual he does not exclude the present life, nor in promising something from this life does he limit [his promise] to this. For he said, "Seek the kingdom of God, and all these things will be added to you" (Matt. 6:33) and "Whoever has left houses or brothers, shall receive a hundredfold in this world, and in the future will inherit everlasting life."

Further reading

Chase, Frederic Henry. *Chrysostom: A Study in the History of Biblical Interpretation*. Cambridge: Cambridge University Press, 1887.

Hill, Robert. *"On Looking Again at Synkatabasis," Prudentia* 13 (1981): 3–11.

——*"Akribeia*: A Principle of Chrysostom's Exegesis," *Colloquium* 14 (1981): 32–6.

——*Saint John Chrysostom: Homilies on Genesis 1–17*. Washington, D.C.: Catholic University Press, 1986.

Kaczynski, Reiner. *Das Wort Gottes in Liturgie und Alltag der Gemeinden des Johannes Chrysostomus*. Freiburg: Hesden, 1974.

Kelly, J. N. D. *Goldenmouth. The Story of John Chrysostom, Ascetic, Preacher, Bishop*. Ithaca, N.Y.: Cornell University Press, 1985.

Selections from Martin Luther's
Sermons on the Sermon on the Mount

Translated and introduced by Mark S. Burrows

There are two sorts of knowledge: first, that of names; and second, that of the subject matter [res] itself. To one who has no knowledge of the subject matter, the knowledge of the names will be of no help . ... Grammar alone does not give us this meaning [sententia] . . .; this comes from our knowledge of sacred things [rerum sacrarum cognitio]. . . . Take care above all that you have a firm knowledge of the subject matter; after that it will be easy to learn the grammar. To err in matters of grammar is to commit a venial sin, but to sin in the subject matter is a mortal sin. Furthermore, I consider this knowledge of the subject matter [notitia rerum] nothing other than a knowledge of the New Testament, for when this is well known it clarifies the entire scripture of the Old Testament.[1]

Introduction

The act of reading scripture was for Martin Luther a deliberately theological task. It required a proper theological viewpoint, one that arose from an engagement with the true "subject" (*res*) of scripture, the God who promises salvation. As he went on to say, "grammar is indeed necessary and what it says is true; it should not, however, rule the subject matter [*res*] but ought itself to serve it."[2] Such a theologically engaged reading of scripture might well appear to modern readers, at least those following a thoroughly critical approach to ancient texts such as scripture, as an illegitimate method. Skeptics of a premodern reading such as Luther's might well ask whether "the meaning" should not, rather, arise from an understanding of the grammar, cultural-historical context, literary form found in biblical texts, and so forth. To such questions, Luther's adamant rejoinder is his insistence that "Scripture is God's witness to himself."[3] Thus the "proper" reading of scripture could not be a simply literary or historical examination, even if this were construed as the critical prolegomenon for a subsequent theological interpretation or for preaching.[4]

Thomas Aquinas had voiced this premise in an earlier age, insisting that "the duty of every good interpreter is to consider not the words but their [proper] sense,"[5] and by this he meant the text's theological intention. With Aquinas, Luther would have recoiled at the modern critical attempt to read scripture without theological prejudice.[6] The question Luther posed along with earlier monastic and scholastic readers of scripture was not whether but how to grasp the theological *sensus* of the text, how to crack the "husk" of the "letter" in order to discern its proper "spirit." As he argued:

> The divine words [of scripture] are solely and entirely the first principles of the Christian [*Christianorum prima principia*], while human words are the derivative consequences from these. It is thus our task to relate our words back to these; ours must be tested by these. And thus these words should be for all people that which they know above all else. It is not that these should be examined by us, but that we should be judged by them.[7]

Scripture was a treasury of divine meaning, and as such functioned as God's way of "reading" and interpreting the world. One must read the Bible, according to Luther, expecting an encounter with God which would never be "without fruit."[8]

Luther's interpretative method did not deviate significantly in formal terms from late medieval patterns of interpretation. The reformer ascribed to the premise unquestioned in the patristic and medieval commentaries that scripture was a unity, but he stood among the *moderni* in insisting that its coherence lay not in the spiritual meanings of its "four fold sense" but in the *sensus litteralis* as this witnessed to Christ.[9] But this interest should not be confused with what a modern exegete might mean by "history," nor was the "clarity" of scripture (*claritas scripturae*) of which Luther spoke in his early debate with Erasmus to be understood as an explicit dimension of the *text* as such.[10] Luther lacked his counterpart's humanist confidence that grammatical study alone could discern the meaning of a biblical passage. Here, we begin to discern the pressure of what one historian has called Luther's "crisis of vocabulary," his attempt to reconstruct the exegetical task in terms of "a new technical vocabulary, new theological categories, and a new relation of Christian doctrines to one another."[11] In this blending of "old" form and "new" method, Luther stood in continuity with medieval exegetes who read scripture as a theological "sourcebook," but beyond this shared assumption the originality of Luther's mind begins to emerge: the "clarity" of the biblical text was to be discerned in the very "grammar" of scripture, but discerning this was a *theological* and not simply a *philological* task. The grammar of scripture was itself *verbum Dei*, a witness to the divine promise of salvation, since in the "letter" of history one could discern God's saving actions in the world. A properly grammatical reading – or the *grammatica theologia*[12] to recall his usage – was necessarily theological, engaged as it was in the text's *res*.

This is not to suggest that Luther's intention as an exegete was to undermine serious textual scholarship or resist applying the most rigorous linguistic tools of the day.[13] But these were at best "servants" and not the master for the biblical reader. Beyond the exacting work of grasping the text as such, Luther identified the exegete's task as twofold: first, that of proper listening to the living Word of God (*verbum Dei*) as one heard this in and through the biblical "words" (*verba*); second, and as a consequence, that of proper speaking or preaching.[14] In explaining how this "listening" was to transpire, Luther borrowed an image that echoed the ancient monastic practice of *lectio divina*,[15] the slow and meditative reading of scripture, insisting that we must "chew" the gospel (*evangelium ruminabimus*).[16] But he meant something different from the pondering of texts in a meditative style. His interest was not in the manner of reading but in the apprehension of the proper subject matter – viz., the gospel which promised a saving encounter with the living Word of God.

This emphasis locates the center of Luther's hermeneutic and establishes the texture of his actual exegetical practice in a soteriological schema, grounded in what he understood as the center of Paul's theology.[17] Thus, in interpreting the verse from the Beatitudes, "You are the salt of the earth . . ." (Matt. 5:13), he commented:

> The real salt is the proper interpretation of the scripture, which rebukes the whole world and lets nothing stand but the simple faith in Christ. It is all over and of no help if one teaches or rebukes in any other manner, since in this case both the teaching and the life, both the master and the student are rejected and condemned before God. In other words, where this article concerning Christ is not held – viz., that we are justified and made holy only through him, and without him all things are damned – there can be no defense or restraint, no measure or limit of all heresy and error, of all sects and factions, but everyone will begin to discover something for themselves and disseminate it abroad.[18]

This "article of faith" functioned for Luther as the heart of scripture: "If you take Christ out of the scriptures," he insisted, "what more [*quid amplius*] remains for you to find in them?"[19] Scripture was the seat upon which Christ, the *Dominus scripturae*[20] or "sovereign" of the Bible, was enthroned. "Christ is the Lord, and not the servant," he contended; "he is the Lord of the Sabbath, of the law, and of all else. And since scripture must be understood not against but through Christ, so we must rely upon Christ rather than scripture.[21] In other words, the methodological principle "scripture alone" was itself second-ary to Luther's fundamental principle, "Christ alone." Or, to echo the language more familiar in his writing, the Word of God is the heart of scripture. Beyond the bounds of the encounter with this Word, scripture remained for Luther a closed book.

Luther's christological principle alone, however, explains only one side of the manner in which the Christian was to "read" scripture. The subjective side of this encounter Luther described as the "experience" of faith. "Faith alone [*fides sola*]," he insisted, provided "the saving and efficacious use of the Word of God."[22] It was by faith that one grasped – or, more to the point, was grasped by – the word of divine promise through the "hearing" of the gospel.[23] But faith was not identical with catechetical or merely "historical" knowledge, even while it presumed such knowledge.[24] It was itself the expression of a salvific relationship, the experience of "grace alone" (*sola gratia*), by which we find that Christ's alien righteousness stands where ours fails (justification). This relationship is itself "the gospel" (*das Evangelium*), the means by which Luther himself came to an "existential understanding" of scripture[25] and the shaping horizon for his hermeneutic.

This is a crucial point: Luther's vocation as a theologian and reformer took shape on the basis of the discoveries he made when reading scripture. His exegesis was theological but it was also self-consciously subjective and "contextual," in the sense that Luther expected to find in scripture guidance in facing contemporary questions and crises of his day.[26] As he once put it, "You must keep your eye on the word that applies to you."[27] His grammatical exposition of biblical texts, in other words, was never devoid of an attentiveness to the existential predicament he faced. "God first gives us the Word in order to enlighten us," he contended, "and then offers us the Holy Spirit who works by igniting faith within us."[28] Christ alone, grace alone, and by faith alone: these three stand as the pillars upon which Luther erected the structure of his theological reading of scripture.

In practicing his profession as *doctor in biblia*,[29] Luther would today be called a "biblical theologian" because of his overriding interest in the theological exposition of scripture.[30] His interest was the practice of preaching and not the method of reading, an approach governed by several clear principles. First, Luther assumed that scripture was itself a unified narrative whose coherence was to be found in a christological reading. Second, and as a consequence of this, he insisted that scripture interpreted itself and was not reliant upon external authorities.[31] Third, he insisted that the "subject matter" – *verbum Dei* heard in and through the "words" – had preeminence over grammar, just as the spirit and gospel took precedence over the letter and the law.[32] And, finally, he emphasized the role of the promise from God's side and of faith from ours in grounding what he called "a saving and efficacious use of the Word of God."[33]

Finally, then, a brief word about the passage selected from Luther's writings before us. In interpreting the Sermon on the Mount, Luther assumed that these were "the first dear words that the Lord Christ preached," and he points out in the opening pages of his commentary that the written form of this preaching is a great gain for Christians, but its written form presents a particular problem for Christians: "But now since it is so common that everyone has it written in a book and can read it every day, no one thinks of it as anything special or precious. Yes, we grow sated and neglect it, as if it had been spoken by some shoemaker rather than the high majesty of heaven."[34] But these instructions were not meant to guide Christians in their life in what he called the "earthly kingdom"; rather, this sermon and Christ's teachings more generally were "intended to teach how we are to come to that other [i.e. heavenly] life."[35] It was to awaken his auditors and readers to the evangelical claims of the gospel that Luther preached this sermon series.

In explaining the proper audience for such scripture, he identified the "pure of heart" (Matt. 5:8) as those persons who "watch and consider what God says and in the place of their own thoughts depend upon the Word of God."[36] This is a central theme that resounds throughout this treatise: Christians attain a purity of life and a righteousness before God not because of outward religious profession (for example, as monks who sought perfection by fulfilling the *consilia evangelii*[37]) but on account of the Word of God which they come to hold inwardly in their heart through faith. Again, Luther:

> The word of faith toward God ... purifies the heart, and the word of understanding ... teaches [them] what [they] are to do toward [their] neighbor ... Everything depends upon God's word.[38]

The text included in this section is taken from a commentary first published in 1532, based upon a series of sermons Luther preached on Wednesdays, from 1530 to 1532, on the Sermon on the Mount from Matthew's Gospel.[39] The translation, with minor editorial changes, is taken from *Luther's works*, vol. 21, *The Sermon on the Mount (Sermons) and The Magnificat*, translated and edited by J. Pelikan (St Louis: Concordia Press, 1956), pp. 139–45, and is reprinted, with minor editorial changes, by permission of the publisher.

Martin Luther: Selections from Sermons on the Sermon on the Mount

(Matt. 6:5) *And when you pray, you must not be like the hypocrites; for they love to stand and pray in the synagogues and at the street corners, that they may be seen by others. Truly, I say to you, they have their reward.*
(6:6) *But when you pray, go into your room and shut the door and pray to*

your Father who is in secret; and your Father who sees in secret will reward you.

. . . [I]n instructing [Christians] how to pray correctly, Christ begins by showing them how they should go about it: they are not supposed to stand and pray publicly on the streets, but they should pray at home, in their own room, alone, in secret. This means that, above all, they should rid themselves of the false motive of praying for the sake of appearance or reputation or anything of that sort. It does not mean that prayer on the street or in public is prohibited; for Christians are not bound to any particular place and may pray anywhere, whether they are on the street or in the field or in church. All it means is that this must not be done out of regard for other people, as a means of getting glory or profit. In the same way Christ does not forbid the blowing of a trumpet or the ringing of a bell at almsgiving for its own sake, but denounces the addition of a false motivation when he says: "In order to be seen by others."

Nor is it a necessary part of this commandment that you have to go into a room and lock yourself in. Still, it is a good idea for you to be alone when you intend to pray, so that you can pour out your prayer to God in a free and uninhibited manner, using words and gestures that you would not use if you were in human company. Although it is true that prayer can take place in the heart without any words or gestures, yet such things help in stirring up and enkindling the spirit even more; but in addition, the praying should continue in the heart almost without interruption. As we have said, Christians always have the Spirit of supplication with them, and their hearts are continually sending forth sighs and petitions to God, regardless of whether they happen to be eating or drinking or working. For our entire life is devoted to spreading the name of God, God's glory and kingdom, so that whatever else we may do has to be subordinated to this.

Nevertheless, I say, outward prayer must also go on, both individual prayer and corporate prayer. In the morning and in the evening, at table and whenever we have time, we all should speak a benediction or the "Our Father" or the Creed or a psalm. And in assemblies the Word of God should be employed and thanks and petitions voiced to God for our general needs. This must necessarily be done in public, with a special time and place set aside for such assemblies. Such prayer is a special thing and a powerful defense against the devil and his assaults. For in it, all Christendom combines its forces with one accord; and the harder it prays, the more effective it is and the sooner it is heard. At the present time, for example, it is of real benefit as a defense and a barrier against the many tricks which the devil might otherwise perpetrate through members of his body. Thus it is certain that whatever still stands and endures, whether it is in the spiritual or in the secular realm, is being preserved through prayer . . . The component parts and the characteristics which every real prayer has to possess . . . are as follows: first, the urging of God's commandment, who has strictly required us to pray; second, God's promise which declares that God will hear us; third, an examination of our own need and misery, which burden lies so heavily on our shoulders that we have to carry it to God immediately and pour it out before God, in accordance with the divine order and commandment; fourth, true faith, based on this word and promise of God, praying with the certainty and confidence that God will hear and help us – and all these things in the name of Christ, through whom our prayer is acceptable to the Father and for whose sake he gives us every grace and every good.

Christ indicates this by using one word when he says: "Pray to your Father who is in secret"; and later on makes it even more explicit when he says: "Our Father, who art in heaven." For this is the same as teaching that our prayer should be addressed to God as our gracious and friendly father, not as a tyrant or an angry judge. Now, none of us can do this unless we have a word of God which says that God wants to have us call him "Father" and that as a father has promised to hear us and help us. To do this, we must also have such a faith in our hearts and a happy courage to call God our father, praying on the basis of a heart confidence, relying upon the certainty that the prayer will be heard, and then waiting for help. . . .

Learn, therefore, that there can be no real prayer without this faith. But do you feel weak and fearful? Your flesh and blood is always putting obstacles in the way of faith, as if you were not worthy enough or ready enough or earnest enough to pray. Or do you doubt that God has heard you, since you are a sinner? Then hold on to the Word and say: "Though I am sinful and unworthy, still I have the commandment of God, telling me to pray, and God's promise to hear me graciously, not on account of my worthiness but on account of the Lord Christ." In this way you can chase away the thoughts and doubts, and you can cheerfully kneel down to pray. You need not consider whether you are worthy or unworthy; all you need to consider is your need and God's Word on which he tells you to build. This is especially so because God has set before you the manner of praying and put into your mouth the words you are to use when you pray, as follows here. Thus you may joyfully send up these prayers through Christ and put them into his bosom, so that through his own merit he may bring them before the Father.

(Matt. 6:7) *And in praying do not heap up empty phrases as the Gentiles do; for they think that they will be heard for their many words.*

(6:8)   *Do not be like them, for your Father knows what you need before you ask him.*

(6:9)   *Pray, then, like this: Our Father, who art in heaven, hallowed be thy name.*

(6:10)   *Thy kingdom come, thy will be done, on earth as it is in heaven.*

(6:11)   *Give us this day our daily bread;*

(6:12)   *And forgive us our debts, as we also have forgiven our debtors.*

(6:13)   *And lead us not into temptation, but deliver us from evil. For thine is the kingdom, and the power, and the glory, forever. Amen.*

Earlier, Christ had denounced their false motivation in prayer, namely, the fact that they sought their own glory and profit among people even in a work which was aimed at God alone, calling upon God and asking for God's help in our need and temptation. Now, Christ goes on to denounce the false manner of their prayers, that is, the fact that they supposed praying meant using many words and babbling. Christ calls it the manner of the Gentiles, a reckless and worthless prattle, the sort of thing that would come from people who supposed that they would not be heard otherwise. For he saw very well that this would develop and that the same sort of abuse would continue in Christendom that existed among them already in those days: that prayer would become a mere work, to be judged on the basis of its size and length, as though this made it a precious accomplishment; and that instead of true prayer there would be mere jabbering and babbling, which did not belong to the experience of the heart. As we can see, this is what happened to the inmates of the monasteries and the cloisters and to our whole clergy, whose way of life seems to have involved no other work than beating themselves and wearing themselves out every day with so many hours [of prayer], as well as singing and reading their canonical hours at night. The more of this they could do, the holier and greater an act of worship did it seem. Yet amid all this, there was not a single one who spoke a genuine prayer from the heart; but they were all laboring under the gentile delusion that prayer meant making both God and oneself tired with yelling and mumuring, as though God neither could nor would listen any other way. And all they achieved by this was a useless waste of time; like asses, they simply punished themselves with their praying.

For this reason, they themselves have said that there is no harder work than prayer. And of course, this is true if the aim is to turn prayer into a work or a chore which the body is forced to undertake, reading or singing for so many hours in a row. Therefore any day laborer would prefer to work at threshing for an entire day to just moving his mouth for two or three hours in a row or starting straight at a book.

255

In short, their prayers have not been the sighs or petitions of their hearts, but merely the slave labor of their mouths or their tongues. Even though monks may have been reading or muttering their canonical times for forty years, they have not prayed from their heart for a single hour during all those years. They never think of this as an opportunity to present a need to God; all they think of is their own obligation to do this, and God's to pay attention to all this trouble and toil.

But the Christian's prayer is easy, and it does not cause hard work. For it proceeds in faith on the basis of the promise of God, and it presents its need from the heart. Faith quickly gets through telling what it wants; indeed, it does so with a sigh that the heart utters and that words can neither attain nor express. As Paul says (Rom. 8:26), "the Spirit prays." And because Christians know that God has heard their cry they have no need of such everlasting twaddle. That is how the saints prayed in the scriptures, like Elijah, Elisha, David, and others – with brief but strong and powerful words. This is evident in the Psalter, where there is hardly a single psalm that has a prayer more than five or six verses long. Therefore the ancient church fathers have said correctly that many long prayers are not the way. They recommend short, fervent prayers, where one sighs toward heaven with a word or two, as is often quite possible in the midst of reading, writing, or doing some other task.

But the others, who make it nothing but a work of drudgery, can never pray with gladness or with devotion. They are glad when they are finally through with their babbling. And so it must be. Where there is no faith and no feeling of need in a petition, there the heart cannot be involved either. But where the heart is not involved and the body has to do all the work, there it becomes difficult drudgery. This is evident even in physical work. How difficult and dreary it is for the person who is doing something unwillingly! But on the other hand, if the heart is cheerful and willing, then it does not even notice the work. So it is here, too: those who are serious in their intentions and take pleasure in prayer neither know nor feel any toil and trouble; they simply look at their need, and they have finished singing or praying the words before they have a chance to turn around. In other words, prayers ought to be brief, frequent, and intense. For God does not ask how much and how long you have prayed, but how good the prayer is and whether it proceeds from the heart. . . .

But you may say, "Since God knows and sees all our needs better than we do ourselves, why should we bring our petitions and present our needs, instead of giving these to us without our petitioning? After all, God freely gives the whole world so much good every day, like the sun, the rain, crops and money, body and life, for which no one asks or thanks God. God knows that no one can get along for a single day without light, food, and drink. Then why does God tell us to ask for these things?"

The reason God commands it is, of course, not in order to have us make our prayers as instruction concerning what God ought to give us, but in order to have us acknowledge and confess that God is already bestowing many blessings upon us and can and will give us still more. By our praying, therefore, we are instructing ourselves more than God. It makes me turn around so that I do not proceed as do the ungodly, neither acknowledging this nor thanking God for it. When my heart is turned to God and awakened this way, then I shall praise God, thank God, take refuge with God in my need, and expect help from God. As a consequence of all this, I learn more and more to acknowledge God's character. Because I seek and knock at God's door (Matt. 7:7), God takes pleasure in giving me ever more generous gifts. You see, that is how genuine petitioners proceed. They are not like those other useless babblers, who prattle a great deal but who never recognize all this. They know that what they have is a gift of God, and from their heart they say: "Lord, I know that of myself I can neither produce nor preserve a piece of my daily bread; nor can I defend myself against any kind of need or misfortune. Therefore, I shall look to you for it and request it from you, since you command me this way and promise to give it to me, you who anticipate my every thought and sympathize with my every need."

You see, a prayer that acknowledges this truly pleases God. It is the truest, highest, and most precious worship which we can render to God, for it gives God the glory that is due. The others do not do this. Like pigs, they grab all the gifts of God and devour them. They take over one country or city or house after another. They never consider whether they should be paying attention to God. Meanwhile, they lay claim to holiness, with their many loud tones and noises in church. But a Christian heart is one that learns from the Word of God that everything we have is from God and nothing is from ourselves. Such a heart accepts all this in faith and practices it, learning to look to God for everything and to expect it from God. In this way praying teaches us to recognize who we are and who God is, and to learn what we need and where we are to look for it and find it. The result of this is an excellent, perfect, and sensible person, one who can maintain the right relationship to all things.

Notes

1 Martin Luther, *Vorlesungen über 1. Mose von 1535–1545*, in *D. Martin Luthers Werke.*

Kritische Gesamtausgabe, vol. 42 (Weimar, 1906), pp. 596, 11. 16–18; 600, 11. 23–7; all further references to this edition cited as "WA" (Weimar Ausgabe), followed by volume number, pagination, and line (s). Translations in this introduction are mine, unless otherwise cited. The standard English translation of this treatise is in *Lectures on Genesis*, in *Luther's Works*, vol. 3 (St Louis: Concordia Press, 1961), pp. 67, 72–3; all further references to this text cited as "LW," followed by volume number and pagination.

2 "Grammatica quidem necessaria est et vera, sed ea non debet regere res, sed servire rebus." WA 42: 599, 7–8; in LW 3: 70–1. He went on to argue that scripture promised a "utility for teaching," echoing 2 Tim. 3:16, and offered something more than the "futility" of mere grammar. The play on words is deliberate and intended for emphasis: "Sic scriptura, ut Paulus inquit, ad docendum est utilis: non est futilis grammatica . . ." See WA 42: 598, 17–18.

3 *Die drei Symbola oder Bekenntnis des Glaubens Christi*; in WA 50: 282, 7. All translations from citations noted by German or Latin title are mine, unless otherwise noted.

4 Gerhard Ebeling emphasizes this point when he concedes the point that modern biblical scholars might well discount Luther's persistent tendency of applying the schema of Pauline theology to interpret the Old Testament and gospels. But he goes on to clarify the integrity of Luther's exegetical method, noting that "Luther, als ein Mensch vor Erwachen des neuzeitlichen historischen Bewusstseins, [betrieb] Schriftauslegung nicht als eine aufs Historische beschränkte theologische Spezialdisziplin, die einer Ergänzung durch dogmatische Theologie bedurft hätte. Der gesamte theologische Denk- und Urteilsvorgang war hier in die Exegese des Textes hineingenommen." "Luther und die Bibel," in *Lutherstudien*, vol. 1 (Tübingen: J. C. B. Mohr, 1971), p. 296.

5 "Officium est enim boni interpretis non considerare verba, sed sensum." *Super Evangelium S. Matthaei Lectura*, ed. P. Raphaelis Cai, O.P. (Turin, Rome, 1951), p. 358.

6 In the writings òf Hans-Georg Gadamer, and particularly his *Truth and Method* (ET, New York: Continuum, 1986), we find a cogent apology of a "prejudiced" or tradition-oriented reading. In expanding on the Heideggerian notion of a "hermeneutical circle," Gadamer speaks of the necessity of a "fusion of horizons" – viz., that of the (ancient) text, and that of the contemporary reader. The relationship to Luther is anything but accidental; indeed, Gadamer prefaces the section dealing with this theme, entitled "The Extension of the Question of Truth to Understanding in the Human Sciences," with a quotation from Luther: "Qui non intelligit res, non potest ex verbis sensum elicere." This passage, which Gadamer cites without reference, echoes the thrust of Luther's argument about grammar and *res* in the *Lectures on Genesis*, cited earlier in this introduction.

7 See *Assertio omnium articulorum M. Lutheri per bullam Leonis X* (1520), in WA 7: 98, 4– 6. Cited in Friedrich Gogarten, *Luthers Theologie* (Tübingen, 1967), p. 228. See also below, n. 32; and, for a detailed discussion of Luther's argument in this treatise, see Karl-Heinz zur Mühlen, *Nos Extra Nos. Luthers Theologie zwischen Mystik und Scholastik* (Tübingen: J. C. B. Mohr, 1972), pp. 232–5.

8 Thus, for example, in WA 42: 598, 5: "Verbum Dei nunquam est sine fructu."

9 This trend dominated the Parisian university setting, a loose trajectory that included Nicholas of Lyra, Pierre d'Ailly, Jean Gerson, Nicolas of Cleémanges, and others. Henri du Lubac traces this development, under the rubric "Décadence," into the fifteenth century; see his *Exégèse médiévale. Les quatre sens de l'écriture* (Paris, 1964), II: 369–91.

A more sympathetic treatment can be found in G. R. Evans, *The Language and Logic of the Bible: The Road to Reformation* (Cambridge: CUP, 1985), esp. chap. 7. For discussion of Gerson on this point, see my treatment in *"De Consolatione Theologiae" (1418): The Consolation of a Biblical and Reforming Theology for a Disordered Age* (Tübingen: J. C. B. Mohr, 1991), esp. pp. 103–25. See also Karlfried Froehlich, "'Always to Keep the Literal Sense in Holy Scripture Means to Kill One's Soul': The State of Biblical Hermeneutics as the Beginning of the Fifteenth Century," in *Literary Uses of Typology from the Late Middle Ages to the Present*, ed. E. Miner (Princeton: Princeton University Press, 1977), pp. 20–48.

10 Here, zur Mühlen, *Nos Extra Nos*, pp. 235–43. See also R. Hermann, *Von der Klarheit der Heiligen Schrift* (Berlin, 1958); Friedrich Beisser, *Claritas Scripturae bei Martin Luther* (Göttingen: Vandenhoeck and Ruprecht, 1966); and E. Wolf, "über 'Klarheit der Heiligen Schrift' nach Luthers *De servo arbitrio*," *ThLZ* 92 (1967): 721–30.

11 See Gordon Rupp, "A Crisis of Vocabulary," in *The Righteousness of God. Luther Studies* (New York, 1953), p. 83.

12 On this usage, see Siegfried Raeder, *Grammatica Theologia: Studien zu Luthers Operationes in Psalmos* (Tübingen: J. C. B. Mohr, 1977).

13 See, for example, his caveat in WA 42: 597, 28–9: "Non autem accipienda haec eo modo sunt, quasi grammatices studium damnem, quod omnino necessarium est: sed nisi cum grammatica etiam ipsas res discas, nunquam fies bonus Doctor."

14 On this point, see Scott Hendrix, "Law and Gospel in Luther's Hermeneutic," *Interpretation* 37 (1983): 240–52. As he here argues, "for Luther proper preaching is the solution to the problem of interpretation. Unless the interpretation issues in proper preaching, the interpretation has gone awry. That is the *Sitz im Leben* of the proper distinction between 'law' and 'gospel' in Luther's 'hermeneutics.' " Ibid., p. 241.

15 See Jean Leclercq, *The Love of Learning and the Desire for God*, trans. by Catharine Misrahi (New York: Fordham University Press, 1961), pp. 90–5.

16 "In cor non accipimus verbum: per aurem intrat, per alteram egreditur. Sed ut faciamus et de verbo ad verbum, ut munda animalia illus kauen, Evangelium ruminabimus." "Predigt an 15. Sonntag nach Trinitatis" (4 September 1524), in WA 15: 676, 9.

17 The phrase is borrowed from Ebeling who concedes the point to biblical scholars who read scripture with a modern historical consciousness. "Eine andere Frage freilich ist es," he concedes, "ob Luther in engem Verständnis historischer Exegese ein Recht dazu hat, etwa bei alttestamentlichen oder Evangelientexten Schemata paulinischer Theologie zur Interpretation heranzuziehen. Das ist sicher zu verneinen." *Lutherstudien*, vol. 1, p. 296; see also n. 4 above.

18 *Wochenpredigten über Matth. 5–7 (1530/2)*, in WA 32: 348, 2–11.

19 "Tolle Christum e scripturis, quid amplius in illis invenies?" *De servo arbitrio (On the Bondage of the Will)*, in WA 18: 606, 28–9.

20 *In epistolam S. Pauli ad Galatas Commentarius* (1535) (*Galatians Commentary of 1535*), in WA 40/1: 421, 458. See also Paul Althaus, *The Ethics of Martin Luther*, trans. Robert Schultz (Philadelphia: Fortress, 1965), pp. 79–81.

21 *Thesen de fide* (1535) (*Theses concerning Faith*), in WA 39/1: 47, 1. This principle had radical implications for Luther, leading the reformer to argue that "if the text of scripture is opposed to [his] gospel-centered interpretation . . ., his interpretation becomes gospel-centered criticism of scripture." See Althaus, ibid., p. 81.

22 *Fides enim sola est salutaris et efficax usus verbi Dei.* From *Tractatus de libertate Christiana* (1520) (*On Christian Liberty*), in WA 7: 51, 17.

23 The allusion to Rom. 10:17, "faith comes by hearing," was a familiar theme in early Protestant apologetics; for a detailed discussion of Luther on this, see Ernst Bizer, *Fides ex auditu. Eine Untersuchung über die Entdeckung der Gerechtigkeit Gottes durch Martin Luther* (Neukirchen: Neukirchener Verlag, 1958).

24 For a detailed discussion of this point, see my "Jean Gerson on the 'Traditioned Sense' of Scripture as an Argument for an Ecclesial Hermeneutic," in *Biblical Hermeneutics in Historical Perspective*, ed. M. S. Burrows and P. Rorem (Grand Rapids, MI: Eerdmans, 1991), pp. 152–3, n. 1. See further Luther's remark concerning the character of faithful preaching, in his sermon "In die Adnunciationis Marie" (23 March 1521), in WA 9: 630, 19–27: "In preaching, it is not enough only to report on what is 'historical' – i.e., how something happened. Rather, it is necessary to speak as the angel spoke [to Mary]: 'You will conceive . . .', so that everyone who hears the gospel receives it for themselves just as [Mary] received it, so that they too might say, 'It happened to me according to your word.' One must preach so that one is preaching to us, in order that we might receive Christ and He might be born and rule in us. . . . But this means that preaching should follow the *usus verbi*, and not only the *historia* or news, so that one might learn how to use the gospel and how it helps us and makes us holy."

25 On this point, see D. Walther von Loewenich, *Luther als Ausleger der Synoptiker* (München: List, 1954), pp. 83–8. He elaborates this point in suggesting that "Luther hat seine Erfahrung in und an der Schrift gewonnen, aber ohne diese Erfahrung kann die Schrift in ihrem eigentlichen Sinn nicht verstanden werden. Darum kann ein bloss historisches Verständnis der Schrift niemals genügen; es erhebt sich für Luther die Forderung existenziellen Verstehens." Ibid., p. 83.

26 Scott Hendrix points out that in Luther's treatment of biblical texts, the word "today" (*hodie*, or *heute*) occurs with frequency and decisive emphasis. See "Luther Against the Background of the History of Biblical Interpretation," *Interpretation* 37 (1983): 237.

27 "Du musst auff das wort sehen, das dich betrifft, das zu dyr geredt wird. Es ist zweyerley wort ynn der geschrifft: das erst gehet mich nicht an, betrifft mich nicht, das ander betrifft mich, und auff das selbig, das mich angehet, mag ichs könlich wagen und als auff eynen starcken felsen verlassen, trifft es mich nicht, so soll ich still stehen." *Unterrichtung, wie sich die Christen in Mosen sollen schicken* (27 August 1525), in WA 16: 385, 13–14. See further Karl Holl, "Luther's Bedeutung für den Fortschritt der Auslegungskunst," in *Gesammelte Aufsätze zur Kirchengeschichte. Luther* (Tübingen: J. C. B. Mohr, 1927), vol. 1, p. 549.

28 "In die Adnunciationis Marie" (23 March 1521), in WA 9: 632, 32.

29 Luther often reminded his readers of this vocational identity; see, for example, WA 31/1: 212, 6–13.

30 On this point, see Jaroslav Pelikan, *Luther the Expositor. Introduction to the Reformer's Exegetical Writings*, the Companion Volume to Luther's Works (St Louis: Concordia Press, 1959), pp. 46–7.

31 See further Walter Mostert, "*Scriptura sacra sui ipsius interpres*. Bemerkungen zum Verständnis der Heiligen Schrift durch Luther," *Lutherjahrbuch* 46 (1979): 60–96. See also Althaus, *Ethics*, pp. 76–8.

32 Luther's earliest attempts to discern the hermeneutical question led him to distinguish

the letter from the spirit, an approach reflecting an ancient understanding based upon the Pauline text from 2 Cor. 3. But in the course of his own exegetical work he came to a different view: viz., how the received "word" of scripture became Word, the gospel with its promise of forgiveness. For a careful discussion of this development, see Ebeling, *Lutherstudien*, vol. 1, p. 298.

33 See above, n. 25.

34 LW 21: 10; see WA 31: 305, 9–11, 22–5.

35 LW 21: 9; WA 31: 304, 27–32. For a discussion of the so-called "two kingdoms" theory which lies at the heart of Luther's argument regarding the intended purpose of the Sermon on the Mount, see Rupp, "Luther and Government," in *The Righteousness of God*, pp. 286–309; cf. also Althaus, *Ethics*, pp. 43–82.

36 WA 32: 325, 33–5; in LW 3: 34.

37 See, for example, WA 32: 300, 5–6: "Daher haben sie [i.e. monks] die zwelff Consilia Evangelii ertichtet, zwelff guter rat im Evangelio, die man halten müge wer da wolle, so er etwas fur und uber andern Christen höhers und volkomers sein wil, haben also nicht allein ausser dem glauben inn das werck Christliche seligkeit ja auch die volkomenheit gesetzt, sondern auch die selben werck frey gemacht." Cf. LW 3: 4.

38 LW 3: 34; WA 31: 326, 15–19.

39 For detailed discussion of the circumstances surrounding the preaching of these sermons and the eventual publication of these as a commentary, see P. Pietsch, "Einleitung: Wochenpredigten über Matth. 5–7," in WA 32: lxxv–lxxviii, and a detailed account of the various editions by O. Brenner, "Ausgaben," ibid., lxxviii–lxxxv. A shorter, and largely derivative, discussion is found in J. Pelikan, "Introduction," to LW, vol. 21, pp. xvii–xxi.

Further reading

Ebeling, Gerhard. *Evangelische Evangelienauslegung*. München, 1942.

—— *Lutherstudien*, vol. 1. Tübingen: J. C. B. Mohr, 1971.

Evans, G. R. *The Language and Logic of the Bible: The Road to Reformation*. Cambridge: Cambridge University Press, 1985.

Loewenich, D. Walther von. *Luther als Ausleger der Synoptiker*. München: List, 1954.

Pelikan, Jaroslav. *Luther the Expositor*. Saint Louis: Concordia Press, 1959. (Companion volume to *Luther's Works*.)

Righteousness from the Inside:
The Transformative Spirituality of
the Sermon on the Mount

Brian K. Blount

Introduction: A Sociolinguistic Inquiry

> I wish to propose that we try to understand the religious significance of Jesus' words hand in hand with the conferring of gracious human dignity to the poor. Spirituality then will inevitably be understood as a dynamic call to dehumanized people to assert their God-given right to be human beings. This is a spirituality for combat.[1]

Shun Govender is writing about the Sermon on the Mount from the perspective of a South African black. It is his contention that the ethics of the Sermon can neither be proclaimed nor taught in the pressurized vacuum of a historical critical or literary analysis that throttles the contributions context and perspective make to the determination of meaning. Although obedience, love, patience, humility, forgiveness, faith, righteousness, and the many other well-known Sermon expectations may ring philosophically true, they will nonetheless be practically meaningless and perhaps even socially oppressive if their Matthean exegesis is divorced from the Matthean and contemporary socio-historical context.

The language of a written text is saturated with meaning potential. Just as individual words conjure up a plethora of conceptual references, and conceptual references are elucidated by a host of individually distinct words, so the combination of words and conceptual references in the complex structure of textual and ideational patterns that make up a written text plays host to a variety of meaning possibilities. Simply put, texts do not harbor a single meaning possibility which can be uncovered by scientific endeavor the way a petrified Jurassic fossil is unearthed from a nondescript desert floor by the erudite skill of an experienced paleontologist. Instead, texts harbor meaning possibilities, meaning potential.[2] We will soon see, even in such a brief study, that the Sermon on the Mount is filled with such meaning potential. Sociolinguistic theory contends that this potential is accessed contextually; the sociolinguistic location of a reader influences the perspective from which he or she approaches a text to such a degree that the reader accesses as "meaning" that part of the potentiality that is most applicable to his or her social and linguistic context.[3]

Though constraints of space prevent the explicit consideration of the Sermon from a contemporary perspective, we do intend to consider fully the first half of Govender's challenge. Therefore, once we have considered the meaning potential of the Sermon, the next step in our sociolinguistic inquiry will be a summary reconstruction of the Matthean location. Having determined the location we will be in a better position to determine the perspective from which the Matthean community read and interpreted the material we now know as the Sermon on the Mount.[4] In other words, we will be in a better position to hypothesize which slice of the meaning potential the community would have accessed as "meaning."[5]

In a situation where struggle for survival is the primary life concern radical alterations in the patterns of life and living are demanded. For Matthew those alterations are theologically determined and christologically executed. God initiates the radical alteration by moving personally to be in the midst of the people (1:23) in the guise of his son, Jesus, who will usher in the kingdom his ministry has already initiated (cf. 4:23–5; 9:35–8; 11:1). This radical life-transforming act generates in the believer an inner disposition toward God, a spirituality, which in turn provokes the living response of an equally radical righteousness. That living response is laid out, not idealistically but realistically, in the Sermon on the Mount. The "blessed" reality is that the living response will itself become part of the divine life transformation that models collective life in God's radical kingdom. This is why believers should "live" the expectations of the Sermon, not simply because they are mandated, that is to say, law, but because they are the proper transforming response to the theologically determined transformation that God has already christologically set in motion. This is how Matthew's community would have accessed the meaning potentiality of the Sermon's textual and ideational clues.

The Potential for Meaning

While the verb μετανοέω, repent, is not used in the Sermon it acts as a strategic preface for it. Both John the Baptist (3:2) and Jesus (4:17) initiate their ministries with the call to repent in the face of the coming kingdom. The verb has the potential for both negative and positive determination. The negative implications begin at 3:2 and 3:7–12, with John who wields his kingdom-motivated repentance like a sword forged to slice away scurrilous behavior. John envisions a kingdom come with wrath and vengeance. His listeners, designated by the hostile epithet, "brood of vipers," are warned to flee the furor by discontinuing inappropriate conduct.[6] Though it is not his primary use of the concept, the negativity of repentance also finds its way into Jesus' vocabulary. At 11:20, 21 and 12:41, his use of the terminology specifies a turning away from improper behavior.

The positive implications for repentance center exclusively on Jesus. Unlike John, Jesus, following his 4:17 proclamation, calls for the positive action of "following" (4:18–22) rather than the negative action of avoidance. This tonal transformation is all the more striking considering that Matthew has Jesus mimic John's proclamation verbatim. Though the words are the same, the message is strikingly unique. Here the potentiality of a key symbol, βασιλεία (kingdom) comes into play. Because they maintain different sensibilities about the kingdom, Jesus and John envision different understandings of how humans are to respond to it. To be sure, etymologically, repentance involves a turning back to God from an improper direction. This turning back is the transformation that makes one righteous in God's sight, and therefore a proleptic citizen of the kingdom. But Matthew opens up the potentiality for conceptual meaning. Jesus primarily expects a positive manifestation of the kingdom as a salvific gift from God (cf. 4:23–5) rather than as an indignant act of judgement. The positive gift solicits a positive response of righteousness which is concerned less with the termination of evil behavior than it is with the motivation and continuation of "following" discipleship behavior (Matt. 5–7) that is so radically positive as to be termed "perfect" (5:48).

Matthew's use of this kingdom terminology is decidedly Jewish; he prefers the rabbinic appellation, βασιλεία των ούρανῶν.[7] Knecht et al. point out that the term is also theologically driven. Whenever he uses it, Matthew connects it directly to the initiatory actions of God. It is God who both establishes the kingdom and draws it near.[8]

There are also strong christological implications. This kingdom that is theologically induced is christologically executed. Matthew's key summary statements, 4:23–5 and 9:35–8, make it clear that the kingdom is directly related to the ministry of Jesus and his disciples. Knecht et al. also point out that

Matthew uses βασιλεία in hendiadys with a host of synonymous expressions like παλιγγενεσία, δόξα, ζωή, γνῶσις, and δικαιοσύνη.[9] Each use opens up a new possibility for the meaning potential of βασιλεία. What is common to each synonymous use is the soteriological component we have already discussed. The kingdom represents God's salvific action on behalf of humankind, and that soteriological relationship is conceptualized in unique ways by Matthew's attribution of the different synonyms. δικαιοσύνη, righteousness, is significant for our purposes because Matthew pairs the term with βασιλεία four of the seven times he uses it. Three of those pairings are in the Sermon on the Mount. δικαιοσύνη can certainly be God's gift of saving activity since Matthew connects it conceptually to the kingdom. However, its prolific use in a Sermon[10] which is heavily nuanced by its connection to repentance as positive acts of radically responsive discipleship suggests the possibility, even before we evaluate it, that it may just as provocatively refer to the kind of human action that is necessary for entrance into the gift that is the kingdom.[11]

μακάριος, blessed, also has a significant range of meaning potential. It is now commonly recognized that beatitudes, formulaic expressions initiated with μακάριος (macarisms), are of two forms, wisdom (cf. Ps. 1) and apocalyptic (cf. Dan. 12:12–13). The 44 New Testament beatitudes are most often found in the latter mode. Both types recognize that the person who seeks to do God's will is blessed. In that sense it has both indicative and imperative potential. G. Bertram and F. Hauck acknowledge the indicative implications when they observe, "The special feature of the group μακάριος, μακαρίζειν, μακαρισμός, in the NT is that it refers overwhelmingly to the distinctive religious joy which accrues to man from his share in the salvation of the kingdom of God."[12] In this sense μακάριος is a state of being that describes the participant in the kingdom. There are also clear indications, however, that μακάριος formulations have an imperative sense. As the Daniel 12:12–13 citation demonstrates, the person who performs a particular activity is considered blessed and is subsequently rewarded. By envisioning a proleptic reward the macarism encourages what is considered positive, "salvific" behavior.

The point of biblical macarisms may become clearer when we realize that most advertisements in today's media are, at bottom, secular beatitudes. The TV iconography of the retired home-run hitter enjoying a cool, sparkling mug of a certain beer is, at heart, a macarism. The message of the commercial might be paraphrased: "Happy are those who drink 'Old ——'! They not only quench their thirst. They also place themselves in the company of the likes of this all time great." Those ads are wisdom macarisms – at least they purport to be. Like most biblical beatitudes, the point of the secular macarism is to get you to do something.[13]

The reward component suggests a comparative nature. In the indicative mode secular blessings are relegated to a position inferior to the joys associated with the kingdom. In the imperative, it is clear that while some behaviors are considered μακάριος others are not. No wonder, then, that Luke's Sermon on the Plain balances the celebration of "blessed" behavior against the kind of behavior worthy of "woes."

The combination of the verb περισσεύω and the adjective πλεῖον in 5:20 also demands a consideration of meaning potential. When Matthew calls for a righteousness greater than that of the scribes and Pharisees it is not immediately clear whether he means a quantitative or qualitative comparison. His adjectival use of πολύς in a comparative form suggests both qualitative (6:25; 12:41, 42) and quantitative (20:10; 21:36) uses. Indeed, Willi Marxsen argues quite correctly that a determination here will have powerful implications for one's interpretation of the Matthean agenda. If a quantitative use, as he notes, it means that the scribes and Pharisees do little and members of the Matthean community must do more, which means that the ethic of the Matthean Jesus would not be qualitatively distinct from that of the scribes and Pharisees. However, a qualitative determination would suggest that Matthew's Jesus was talking about a different kind of ethical expectation, not just more of the same, but a different ethic. Marxsen argues for the quantitative and therefore dismisses Matthew's ethic as nothing really new.[14] The question is whether his accessing of the meaning potential does justice to the way Matthew's community would have accessed it.

τέλειος also has considerable meaning potential. Gerhard Delling notes that in the Hellenistic sense, which would certainly apply to Matthew, it implies totality or completeness.[15] As such it might very well, particularly applied in relationship to God, as in 5:48, suggest an indicative state of existence. One must, in other words, exist as God exists, in a state of complete wholeness. But there is also the implication of conduct, again, precisely because the term is connected with God. Delling points out that when the rich young man asks at 19:16 what he must do in order to achieve eternal life, he is speaking in the context of doing good deeds. Jesus' response also directs the reader's attention to the proper conduct of the commandments. When the young man responds that he has performed this conduct and asks what more he should do, Jesus responds with the language of perfection (19:21–2). To be perfect he must perform actions which are very similar to the mandates of the Sermon on the Mount, mandates which conclude with the call to follow. In other words, the language of perfection can just as easily involve the concept of imperative activity.

φαρῖσαιος, Pharisee, is the final term we shall consider. Though it certainly demands more, we are only able to give it cursory attention here. A reader of Matthew's text gets a clearly negative picture of the Pharisees. A follower's righteousness must better than theirs (5:20) because theirs is a cultic-based form that cares primarily about ritual performance.[16] This happens because they believe that righteousness is an exterior concept, that it begins and ends with a visible action (Matt. 23). They miss the point that righteousness begins from the inside, from a recognition of God's gift, and the gratitude that results from that recognition which in turn initiates a response that intends what God's gift intends, human transformation, mercy, rather than cultic performance, sacrifice (9:13; 12:7).

Though this negative presentation is clearly Matthew's intent, historians accurately point out that Matthean readers would have recognized a broader potentiality, much of it positive, to the meaning of the term Pharisee. The Pharisees were themselves reform-oriented. It was their intention to interpret the Torah by way of the Oral Law so that it maintained contemporary usefulness despite the continually changing life circumstances of its people. Thus, while it is certainly true that the Pharisees wanted persons to obey the law carefully as a way of being righteous before God, "By no means did [they] intend to make fulfillment of the law more difficult; their interpretation in fact wanted to make fulfillment possible – for the sake of the rule of God!"[17] It is also just as certain that had the Pharisees of Jesus's time wanted to impose their views upon all of Jewish society, they would have had neither the power nor the numbers to do so. Judaism of the time was multiform, as it continued to be during the time in which Matthew wrote, even if during this later time a pharisaic form of Judaism, the rabbinate, was becoming the most representative and influential type of formative Judaism.

For the Matthean readers, then, the term Pharisee would have inspired a range of meaning possibilities, some positive, some negative, some of them as a group struggling for representation even though Matthew's portrait suggests a group that was representative of Jewish political and social power.[18]

The Matthean Social Location

The language and style of the Matthean text give every indication that the community to whom Matthew was writing was Jewish in its background and orientation.[19] We are talking about a community that would access the meaning potentiality of the Sermon on the Mount from a decidedly Jewish perspective.

> For me Jesus is less the founder of Christianity than the instigator of a Christian way of life that has its great manifesto in the Sermon on the Mount: a Christian way of life that at bottom amounts to a Jewish way of life.[20]

We really don't know what this means, however, until we connect this Jewish

267

perspective to the sociological circumstance that prevailed in the post-CE 70 period in which Matthew was writing. CE 70, of course, marks the date of Jerusalem's destruction and the razing of the Temple by the Roman forces. It is the critical turning point of Jewish life which must be considered in any sociolinguistic evaluation of material written from a Jewish orientation. Harrington argues quite convincingly that there were three primary reactions to the destruction in the Jewish community: apocalyptic, the forming rabbinate, and Jewish Christianity.[21] Each of these reactions presumed for themselves the crucial soteriological role of interpreting the Torah as the source of ethical guidance for human life in the wake of the Temple's loss. Each, in other words, attempted to become the primary and proper interpreter of God's word, law, and intent for the ethical existence of the people of God. It is no wonder that in such a highly charged social circumstance, given such a critical self-imposed mandate, these communities would enter into conflict with one another. A war for the interpretative leadership of the people of God had begun.

A. Overman points out that the war was being fought on a multiplicity of fronts. He notes that formative Judaism, which would ultimately develop into pharisaic, rabbinic Judaism, was only one of several movements struggling to gain influence and control. One of its primary competitors was that brand of Judaism represented in the Matthean community and designated by Harrington as Jewish Christianity. It is no wonder, then, that when the Matthean community began to interpret the Torah, and develop ethical ways of living as a result of that interpretation, they would weigh their conclusions against those of their chief interpretative rival, pharisaic Judaism.

> I believe what the reader encounters in Matthew's Gospel is a Jewish community, which claims to follow Jesus the Messiah, discovering that they are now different from what is emerging as the dominant form of Judaism in their setting. The defensive posture of the Gospel and strident attacks on the Jewish authorities represented in Matthew by "the scribes and Pharisees," comprise all the emotion and tension of a family falling apart.[22]

In other words, Matthew was writing to and for a community in the midst of a *sectarian* interpretative war.[23] One of the principal interpretative concerns of these sectarian communities was the proper interpretation of the Torah. "The claims and disputes of these communities usually centered on the law and the proper understanding and interpretation of it. The law emerged as both the common ground and the battleground between the competing factions and communities during this period."[24] The stakes were high; the person who properly understood the Torah and lived by its demands did righteousness. And since righteousness garners the reward that is entrance into the kingdom of heaven it becomes of critical importance that a follower have the proper interpretative direction and that he or she follow it. It is from this shared sociolinguistic perspective that Matthew and his reading community approached the interpretative project he called Gospel.

If Overman is correct, and I believe that he is, this sectarian "interpretative difference of opinion" would have had dramatic social consequences. As Overman sees it, the descendants of the Matthean community would eventually come to be called Christians and be seen as a socio-religious entity distinct from Judaism. At the time of Matthew's writing, however, it appears that they were Jews who harbored dangerous opinions about the Torah, and who felt that their Jesus-directed interpretation of it was the only way for one to be recognized as righteous. "Like many of their contemporaries and competitors, however, they understood themselves as the 'true Israel' and set themselves over against those they believed to be the false covenant people and false leaders who would lead the people astray."[25] This kind of exclusive claim to interpretative Torah strategy, in their sectarian social scenario, would have drawn hostile rhetorical and, as 5:10–12 indicates, social fire. In other words, their identity as Jesus followers led them to a unique and confrontational interpretative position within an already combustible Jewish theological location. It is unremarkable that in such a climate such an interpretative strategy would have led to the kind of persecution the final beatitudes perceived. The Matthean community felt itself "marginalized" because of its identity-driven interpretation and understanding of the Torah, but felt that its interpretation was so vital for the prospect of human entrance into the kingdom of heaven that, in spite of the conflict it generated, they must continue to proclaim it. Because in his time of writing pharisaic, rabbinic Judaism was emerging as the predominant Jewish voice, Matthew expressed both the interpretative rivalry and the "oppressive" climate it fostered by his handling of the character type he labels Pharisee.

A Sociolinguistic Conclusion: Accessing Meaning

How, we must now ask, in Matthew's Jewish location, would the Sermon on the Mount have been interpreted? The Torah was the single Jewish soteriological institution to survive the Roman destruction; it therefore became the religious center of focus. In this environment no one could address the topic of salvation without addressing the law. It is no wonder that 5:17–20, with its emphasis on the interminable necessity of the law and the importance of observing it, operates as the Sermon's thematic proposition. Repentance must be more than a conceptual turning back; it must also have a positive, functional identification with the law. This is why Matthew locates the concept narratively with his Sermon on the Mount. But the Torah is action-oriented; it is performance-based. The question, then, might well be phrased, how is one to do the Torah in such a way that one does the righteousness necessary for salvation? In the Matthean community, given the sectarian nature of its existence, the question must also be a comparative one. That is to say, *whose* interpretation of the Torah must one follow to do the righteousness necessary for salvation? The answer, of course, is Jesus' interpretation as it has been handed down to the Matthean community. The Sermon functions to tell the reader how he or she can "do" the law in this proper way, what he or she must do, so that the proper, that is to say, "better," kind of righteousness, the kind that is rewarded with the kingdom, can be achieved.

Jesus' "Beatitudes" should be seen from this contextual angle; they should be read imperatively. They are the first step in the "doing" of a repentance that is functionally tied to the Torah. In other words, Matthew's readers would have understood the Beatitudes to be demands for specific kinds of behavior rather than declarative statements about theoretical realities. Those who perform in the expected way are blessed by God, are esteemed worthy of the divine joy of the kingdom, whereas those who do not, presumably those led by pharisaic traditions, are not. Indeed, the last two Beatitudes proclaim that those who do the actions so prescribed here, because these actions follow the interpretative lead of Jesus and therefore override the interpretative guidelines of the Pharisees, will be persecuted, presumably by the pharisaic leadership. Given their context, the Matthean reader would understand this persecution to have had a sectarian base.

These are apocalyptic beatitudes. The reward for those who become what the macarisms celebrate will be the kingdom of heaven. And since it is better righteousness that allows for such entrance (5:20), it makes sense that the Beatitudes initiate the description of that better righteousness. Be poor in spirit! Mourn![26] Be meek! Hunger and thirst for righteousness! Be merciful! Be pure in heart! Be peacemakers! This is the kind of repentance that sets the community apart (5:16), that is the beginning of a better righteousness that makes entrance into the kingdom possible.

To be sure, as many critics have argued, Matthew had a decidedly internal orientation. He appears on the surface to be spiritualizing the Beatitudes that Luke's apparently more faithful representation from Q showed to be socially oriented. I would argue instead that the internalization is part of Matthew's social program, not an attempt to eliminate it.[27] Just because righteousness comes from the inside does not mean it stays there. It is, as Matthew's Sermon projects it, an individual orientation that presumes a socially transformative result. For example, Matthew presents these apocalyptic beatitudes as demands for present action that imitates the kingdom–oriented action of Jesus (4:23–25). They will therefore, though they prefigure realities of the kingdom, live themselves out physically and socially in the life of the community. Meekness, purity of heart, poverty of spirit are imperatives to be initiated as works (5:16; 7:24–7) of better righteousness. And as *works* of better righteousness they function to help distinguish Matthew's Jewish community from the surrounding Jewish communities. As the members of the community *do* this righteousness the community transforms itself into the image of this righteousness. Such a distinction can only be realized if these Beatitudes have a living, *working* reality which demonstrates that this community has been transformed by its Torah interpretation in a way that others have not. These Beatitudes, in other words, realize a practical, social benefit.

Simultaneously, they demand that followers of this Torah interpretation act their righteousness from an internal orientation. This would be another distinction which makes their righteousness "better." A reading from the Matthean context would suggest that the evangelist's words encourage an inner orientation towards doing righteousness precisely because it would set his community apart; their righteousness is internally rather than externally motivated (6:1–18; ch. 23). Matthew 5:21–48 will bring out this emphasis and its relationship to the Torah quite specifically. I would argue that a Matthean reader would already sense it in reading the opening Beatitudes.

The imperative nature of the final three major sections of the Sermon is more apparent. So is the fact that there is an intention to set the righteousness derived from Jesus's Torah interpretation apart from the righteousness of the pharisaic community. There is no clearer indication of this than the antitheses of 5:21–48, which pointedly demonstrate what the better righteousness is. It is Torah activity that goes beyond a "pharisaic" external obedience, and enters a radical realm where God's original intent of the law is fulfilled (5:17).[28] And, as with the Beatitudes, it is clear that this "better" righteousness is internally driven (5:22, 28, 43–4). It is the performance of this kind of righteousness that makes one perfect, as the heavenly Father is perfect (5:48). Perfection, then, would be accessed not as a state of being, but as the "blessed" active existence that derives from an engagement of radical activity that is internally driven and realizes divine rather than human legal intent. This kind of Torah enactment will transform the Matthean community so that it becomes physically distinct from any other, particularly its chief, pharisaic rival. It is a "better" righteousness that has a potent social consequence; it creates a "better" community of faith.

The discussion of the "better" righteousness in 6:1–18 has a similar focus. Once again a negative comparison is drawn with the chief rival interpretative community,[29] and once again the "better" righteousness (6:1) draws its reward from God.[30] Just as "better" righteousness in 5:20 was defined by 5:21–48, so the "better" righteousness of 6:1 is defined by the references to piety in 6:2–18. Whereas "they" give alms, pray, and fast for external appreciation and demonstration, Matthean readers understand that they are to operate from an internal motivation that seeks divine rather than human approval. The actions are still necessary, and no doubt their effects will be as socially demonstrable, but the motivation behind them has shifted dramatically.

The miscellaneous imperatives of 6:19–7:27 continue the emphasis of stressing the ethical demands that make up this better righteousness. And even though there are not as many direct references to the ethical impotence of a rival interpretative community, continuation of the epithet "hypocrite" suggests a survival of the negative comparison, as does the demand to enter by the narrow gate, which implies others who seek less harrowing entry points.[31] Nowhere is this comparative contrast more inclusive of gentiles who may have been associated with the Matthean community than at 7:21–3 where a righteousness born of a pharisaic-like cultic reverence and prophetic enthusiasm is condemned as a "lesser" form that fails to "do" the imperatives demanded by Jesus' Torah interpretation. The text finishes with a flourish that clearly focuses on a righteousness that is anchored in activity, a doing that follows the guidelines of Jesus' Torah interpretation.

What becomes clear from this sociolinguistic evaluation is that better righteousness would have been understood in the Matthean Jewish context as activity, not God's gift, but human ethical behavior. This behavior is not simply quantitatively better than that of rival Jewish communities because it comprises more activity; indeed, we see time and time again that the activity expected is the same activity already being performed in rival communities.[32] And, as we saw earlier, the Matthean community would have been aware that historically the Pharisaic community was also reform-oriented and concentrated on trying to make the actions of "righteousness" apply to contemporary and changing life circumstances. The Pharisees, too, were interpreting the Torah and issuing similar imperative demands in the light of their interpretation. Matthean righteousness is instead qualitatively "better" because it operates from an internal orientation and has in sight the radical goal of realizing God's original intent in and for the life of community when God originally gave the gift of the Torah.

In Matthew's context, then, the Sermon would be seen as a positive way to respond to the call to repentance as the doing of good actions. God's doing is a good thing, a gracious gift of offering acceptance into ("a bringing near of") the kingdom; we are to respond with positive acts of righteousness. So one level of the better righteousness is the better kind of response to the nearness of the kingdom, not avoidance strategies, but engagement strategies, actions of discipleship, positive acts of discipleship that transform one and one's community, and prepare one for the coming kingdom. Thus the ethics of the Sermon: do this, be this, be perfect, do more righteousness. The doing establishes the context of repentance, which is the prerequisite for the kingdom. One is not transformed for the coming of the kingdom through avoidance strategies, but through the use of engagement strategies. So here we are talking about doing *acts* of righteousness to transform one's self and, as we have said, one's community, to be ready for the kingdom. The subsequently transformed community models the kingdom's collective reality just as Jesus' transforming acts model the kingdom's in breaking power.

This language of response must be taken quite seriously, for with it lies the final, and perhaps most crucial characteristic that the Matthean community would have understood to separate their "better" righteousness from rival forms of it. To be sure, responsive ethics were nothing new in a Jewish context. As Harrington points out,

> For Jews the Torah was (and is) the revelation of God's will, a kind of divine blueprint for action. It is a gift and privilege to Israel, not a burden. Acting upon the Torah is the privileged way of responding to the Creator God who has entered into covenant relationship with Israel. It presupposes the prior manifestation of God's love.[33]

Given this contextual realization, Matthew's argument with the Pharisees would only make real sense if the community were to understand that the Pharisees had stopped seeing righteousness as a response because they had externalized, "legalized," the Torah. His readers in this Jewish context would thus understand him to be calling them back to where they began just as Jesus' fulfillment of the law was a call back to God's original intent, to a place where deeds of righteousness were understood to be an internally motivated response to divine activity and not simply an external compliance with religious legislation.

It is, then, righteousness that begins with God; it is theologically driven. This is what makes it radical. The focus is always on what God is doing. The Pharisees' problem is that obedience has ceased to be secondary and has become primary (Matt. 23). It is this reality that makes Matthean Sermon ethics qualitatively different from those of the Pharisaic leadership; it is not a legalism that requires external commitment to human legislation, but, rather, an internal orientation of gratitude that motivates visible acts of righteousness. It is therefore appropriate that the Sermon begin with an internally oriented demand that one become poor in spirit. The intent is not to deemphasize the physical poor, but, in this sectarian environment, to focus on the proper attitude of response to God as opposed to the more pharisaic self-congratulatory pose that comes from external legal observance.[34]

This righteousness is also qualitatively different because it is christologically executed. In the Matthean sectarian environment this is a critical distinction. Jesus is seen as the primary interpreter of God's will and intent as revealed through the Torah.[35] Indeed, he not only teaches the righteousness that is necessary for kingdom acceptance, he models it. At 3:15, when he submits to baptism it is not as a negative act of repentance, a turning away, but as a positive act of obedience to the will of God. Baptism still retains its connection with

273

repentance in this sense, but as a positive action of righteousness. Jesus is modeling a "better" kind of righteousness, positive repentance.[36] He also proleptically models the reward for this righteousness through his teaching and healing ministry. His itinerant life of obedience to God's will is itself a life of fulfilling righteousness that is simultaneously a manifestation of God's kingdom which will and already is dramatically transforming human existence at both the individual and communal levels. It not only heals individual brokenness, it transforms whole communities like the one to which Matthew is now writing.

Perfection, then, is not a static reality that can be humanly achieved; it is an action-oriented adjective that is divinely energized. The proper response, that is to say, the "perfect" imperative response, to the radical, God-driven, Christ-executed gift of the kingdom must be equally radical. This is why the ethics demanded in the sermon are as radical in nature as they are. Jesus, therefore, does not hold this ethic as an idealistic yardstick, but holds it literally as a transforming response to God's transformative act.[37] Followers are expected in this Jewish environment to live it. Indeed, it is expected that they could live it if they are motivated from an internal attitude of gratitude for God's radical action. G. Theissen's *Social Reality and the Early Christians* provides assistance at just this point.[38] Theissen makes the provocative case that radical ethics like these posited in the sermon were actually lived within the community of believers who followed Jesus. In fact, in the experience of readers in the Matthean community, such a radically oriented community of believers following the travel plans and dictates of an itinerant teacher would not have been unusual. The Hellenistic world was filled with Cynic, Stoic and other such communities observing the radical lifestyle of their teacher.[39] Theissen argues that it would be such a community that would have been responsible for not only orally recording Jesus' words, but for passing them along as tradition.[40] In no other community would they have made sense, since in no other would they have been seen to be realizable goals. But in a radical community of believers following an itinerant teacher like the Jesus presented in the gospel accounts, the demands made sense because the demands were actually being lived.[41] Jesus' call for a radical, living response to the gift of God's kingdom drawn near was being followed in the community of believers following him. The ultimate consequence of this following was the representation of the healing reality of the kingdom (4:23–5; 9:35–8).

Theissen also makes the point that in later urban communities like those of Paul, and we should add, this one of Matthew's, such demands made less social sense and therefore were traditionally passed along, if they were passed along at all, as ideals rather than realistic ethical goals. No wonder, then, that Paul's letters relay little evidence of such radical ethical demands. But Matthew does include them for his community. Given the probable Pauline-like urban make-up of his community we must ask why. How might he have expected his reading community to read this Sermon within their context? I would suggest that context is the key point. Matthew's community was more urban, but it remained a community without a real social home, it remained a community under fire. The fire was of a different type, it was sectarian-based, but it caused problems of living that were as dramatic as those faced by the wandering Jesus community. Indeed, in many ways they were, themselves, though a located community, without roots. They were a community under fire socially precisely because of their make-up theologically. This indeed is the critical observation. As Overman suggests, they were in an interpretative war to decide which community best interpreted God's law, and it appears from the tone of the Gospel that they were losing. In this context of sectarian struggle for survival the community needed to identify itself, it needed to mark its distinctive interpretative boundaries and hold to them in order to survive. It needed to demonstrate that it was the one community that correctly fulfilled God's Torah demands for righteousness, and because of that singularity was the only community capable of representing the healing (transformative) reality of the kingdom. Such a claim would only be borne out if their righteousness stood apart from the righteousness of the pharisaic community which already demanded, quantitatively, a great deal of legal observance from those who wished to be deemed righteous. That is to say, since quantitatively it would be difficult to do more than the Pharisees were already doing, the righteousness practiced in their community would need to stand qualitatively apart. To do this, the Matthean community would have to imitate the traditional Jesus community and its radical obedience. These radical Jesus demands would not only actually have to be lived, they would have to demonstrate the proper orientation of grateful response to God's own radical work as already initiated through Jesus, and imply the same transformative potentiality. This implication is derived from the narrative placement of 4:23–5 just before the Sermon, and by the ultimate suggestion in 28:16–20 that this community is the one which must fulfill the prophetic mandate of being a light to the gentile nations. In fact, it is only this christological awareness that makes possible the fulfillment of such radical imperatives. "Jesus *is* the authority of the Sermon on the Mount. Without him it would only be a merely utopian philosophy, but with him it becomes a message of promise and a demand from God who speaks in and through Jesus."[42]

Such a radical presentation would inaugurate a radical social transformation. In the end, then, it would, this call to better righteousness in the Sermon on the Mount, be a social invitation. To see it as such means that the burden can never be on some individuals to live up to the Sermon demands while others take advantage of them because they do (as in being meek and forgiving). Instead, the community as a whole must "do" the Sermon's expectations of righteousness.

275

Such observance would cause a communal transformation by way of individual transformations; the Matthean community would thus become an alternate social existence that claimed to model the communal reality and transformative power of the kingdom. The reward for those who participated in its imperative call would be the "blessed," proleptic inclusion into that reality. Only in this way would the community be able to demonstrate to its sectarian disputant communities and those undecided Jews who were seeking a community that Jesus's interpretation of the Torah created the community marked by the kind of righteousness that God's law had originally intended. It would be in this way that the community would be able to demonstrate *visibly* its claim that it was indeed the community that fulfilled the Torah, and therefore held the right to interpret it through the teachings of its Christ.

This would be the only way Matthew's community could win the sectarian war of interpretation in which it was engaged. The strategic goal of demonstrating that his community was the only one that fulfilled and therefore properly interpreted the Torah demanded the tactical moves of a communal transformation. It was therefore to this performative end that individual spirituality in the Sermon on the Mount would have to be directed. A sociolinguistic assessment which reads Matthew's concern for spirituality "out of" rather than "into" his context therefore concludes that Matthew's first community would have understood that his spirituality had social, communal implications. From this perspective meekness, purity of heart, poverty of spirit, turning the other cheek, forgiveness, prayer, love . . . are all imperatives designed to transform at the communal as well as the individual level.

Performance Spirituality

Our sociolinguistic conclusion is that Matthew's community would have accessed the textual and ideational signals in the Sermon so as to comprehend a spirituality for transformation. Our final question is, how will this spirituality for transformation be meaningfully accessed in a contemporary setting? The answer, of course, is that it will depend dramatically on the setting itself. While Govender considered the sermon from the perspective of South African blacks, I would like to close by considering it briefly from the perspective of African Americans. Particularly, I would like to view it through the lens of an African-American hermeneutic that Theophus Smith calls conjurational spirituality.[43] Smith argues that the Bible has been a transformative tool for African Americans. I have been arguing that the material that makes up the Sermon on the Mount was, similarly, a transformative tool for the Matthean community. Specifically, for the African-American community, the Bible has been and remains "a book of ritual prescriptions for reenvisioning and, therein, transforming history and culture."[44] Biblical interpretation from a Euro-American perspective is combined with African magical folk practices like conjure to develop an interpretative strategy that not only brings the Bible to life for African Americans, but transforms that life with healing vision and power.

Particularly useful for our purposes is Smith's contention that conjure is a system of signs and symbols which are used to foster understanding of the world. From that understanding, the conjuror hopes also to establish control, particularly transformative control. Smith traces this conjure tradition through the work of historical African-American figures like Zora Neale Hurston, Howard Thurman, W. E. B. DuBois, and Martin Luther King, Jr. He argues that each of these figures, and most African-American Christian leaders, have used the typological symbols in the Bible mimetically. They have, for example, acted out the Mosaic image of liberation or the Jesus image of triumph over victimization. In other words, they have performed the language of the Bible typologically in order to conjure cultural transformation.

Take, for example, Smith's analysis of the Exodus typology in African-American hands. He notes that African Americans have perceived their reality through the lens of the Israelites in Egyptian bondage. Leaders of the people imitate, through both their rhetoric and performances, key Israelite figures (e.g. King's mountaintop speech) who assisted God in the liberation of the people. In this way the exodus of the Hebrew slaves becomes a "mundane reality in contemporary terms." Biblical figures thus become part of a conjure strategy. Smith calls the process a conjurational spirituality.

What is even more exciting than the figurative parallelism and mimetic performance, however, is the conjurational expectation which comes with the performance, that God could be invoked to initiate the powerful typology of Exodus in the contemporary life of the people. "From this perspective I propose the hypothesis that black North American experience features a development from designating or 'summoning' God in workship, to an intention to conjure God for freedom."[45] Human actions (as, for example, King's mimetic Moses performance) could, in this way, conjure the presence of God for the purpose of establishing a new cultural reality. Smith is careful to observe that the actions do not create God, but instead "collectively create the phenomenal conditions conducive to their subjective apprehension of the divine."[46]

> Henceforth more than a minority of believers and converts would be convinced of the possibility that through prayer and expectation, through *acts* of obedience, and *righteousness*, black folk could inherit divine promises of prosperity and freedom.[47]

I would argue that, given this hermeneutical perspective, actions of righteousness like meekness, purity of heart, love, forgiveness, prayer, motivated from the interior by a spirituality that makes them a better righteousness, can be understood to be actions that "conjure" God. It is in this way that the imperatives in the Sermon on the Mount come sociolinguistically alive. Textual and ideational potentiality allow for this kind of exciting meaning access. Since the purpose of conjure is cultural transformation, it is easy to see how the spirituality of the Sermon can be understood as a social and cultural transformative strategy.

African Americans viewing the "works" demands of the Sermon from this hermeneutical perspective would not be surprised at the emphasis on performance. Indeed, from this perspective, transformative spirituality *depends* upon performance.

> As we have seen throughout this study, concrete practices and embodied performances are crucial for conjurational and other ritual practices in African American religious traditions. The performative element is indispensable (a *conditio sine qua non*) for shamanic operations generally, and for the conjurational and shamanic aspects of black social prophetism in particular.[48]

Doing the imperatives of the sermon becomes a performative strategy, a conjure act, which induces, summons, and conjures the divine for the realization of an emancipatory future.[49] Acts of righteousness remain unimportant in and of themselves. One does not do the imperatives because they are law, but because the actions create something powerfully unique, a "blessed" reality, a transformed community which stands apart from all others because, through its fulfillment of the sermon imperatives, it mimics the transforming reality of the kingdom. In this contemporary, "sectarian" world, the community would therefore be seen to be a unique community that provides access to (conjures) the kingdom of God. Finally, because what is to be conjured is so radical, the conjure acts themselves must be radical. The Sermon expectations in this way, one would think, would remain literal expectations, not for individual achievement, but for communal transformation.

Notes

1 Shun Govender, "The Sermon on the Mount and the Question of Ethics," in *Hammering Swords Into Ploughshares: Essays in Honor of Archbishop Mpilo Desmond Tutu*, ed. Buti Tlhagule and Itumeleng Mosala (Grand Rapids: Eerdmans Publishing, 1976), pp. 173–84 at p. 181.

2 For an in-depth and more critical discussion of the semasiological and onamosiological reality which establishes the potentiality of text meaning cf. Brian K. Blount, "The

Problem of Meaning," in his *Cultural Interpretation: Reorienting New Testament Criticism* (Minneapolis: Augsburg/Fortress Press, 1995). pp. 89–92.

3 Cf. Ralph Fasold, *The Sociolinguistics of Language* (Cambridge, Mass: Basil Blackwell, 1990), p. 52: "A possible consequence of this would be that speakers of different languages could stand side by side and experience precisely the same event and yet understand it in profoundly different ways . . . Furthermore, each would find it difficult or impossible to understand the event from the other's perspective."

4 It is, of course, appropriate to be concerned about a circular process of argumentation at just this point. Much of one's evidence for establishing the community's location comes from material in the text itself, material which is then used to help interpret the text. While this is always a problem with textual analysis there are ways to lessen the impact of such circularity. Other source materials can be researched which augment the picture garnered from textual evidence. Once one establishes the time in which Matthew wrote one can then utilize other sources, religious and secular, to determine what traits characterized the temporal and social location and subsequently use this evidence in tandem with evidence garnered from the text itself.

5 Cf. M. A. K. Halliday, *Language as a Social Semiotic: The Social Interpretation of Language and Meaning* (London: Edward Arnold, 1978), p. 32. Halliday notes that all language functions in contexts of situation and culture, and is relatable to those contexts. The question is not what peculiarities of vocabulary, or grammar or pronunciation, can be directly accounted for by reference to the situation. It is *which* kinds of situational factors determine *which* kinds of selection in the linguistic system. His notion of register is thus a form of prediction: given that we know the linguistic situation and social context of language, we can predict a great deal about the language meaning that will occur, with reasonable probability of being right.

6 The verb φεύγω, flee, is used seven times by Matthew at 2:13; 3:7; 8:33; 10:23; 23:33; 24:16; 26:56. In each case it involves the determination to escape a negative condition of wrath and destruction by the movement away from a source problem, whether that problem be in the form of a hostile person or inappropriate behavior.

7 Cf. Hermann Klein Knecht, Gerhard Von Rad, Karl Kuhn, and K. L. Schmidt, "Βασιλεύς, βασιλεία . . .," *TDNT* 1: 581–9. Knecht et al. note that while Matthew also uses the term βασιλεία τού θεού five times (12:28; 21:31; 21:43; 6:33; 19:24 (the last two citations do have some text-critical concerns) his clear preference is for the Jewish form of the virtually interchangeable appellations.

8 Ibid., p. 582.

9 Cf. Ibid., p. 583.

10 Of Matthew's seven uses of δικαιοσύνη, five are found in the Sermon on the Mount.

11 Indeed, the possibilities for meaning are broad. Quell and Schrenk point out that δικαιοσύνη is almost always used in the New Testament as the right conduct of humans that is pleasing to God and leads to an evaluation of uprightness (righteousness) before God. (Gottfried Quell and Gottleb Schrenk, δίκη, δίκαιος, δικαιοσύνη . . .," *TDNT* 2: 198.) John Reumann, appealing to arguments by J. P. Meier, points out, however, that δικαιοσύνη can also, particularly in Paul and the Old Testament, refer to the saving activity of God. Thus, since there is this dual possibility, one should withhold judgement about the particular use of the term until each individual citation has been evaluated. (Cf. John Reumann, *Righteousness in the New Testament* (Philadelphia: Fortress Press,

1982) pp. 125–6. Indeed, Meier argues that this dual use can be seen in Matthew. He contends that while the citations at 5:10, 20, and 6:1 refer to human ethical activity, the citations at 5:6; 6:33 and possibly 21:32 refer to God's saving activity. Cf. John P. Meier, *The Vision of Matthew: Christ, Church and Morality in the First Gospel* (New York: Paulist Press, 1979) p. 225.) Reumann follows Meier in arguing that while the citations at 5:10, 20 and 6:1 deal with human moral conduct, 5:6 and 6:33 refer to God's saving activity. His stand on 21:32 is less clear as he argues that John came in the way of righteousness so that his conduct imitates the divine gift of God. What is clear, however, is that Reumann recognizes that Matthew is working with a term of broad potential. However, his inability to sense a focus from Matthew results in a lack of focus in his own conclusion. Quoting Conzelmann, he concludes (p. 135) that" Matthew sees the kingdom as the gift and righteousness as the response." This conclusion appears to disregard his earlier contention that righteousness is also the gift so that it is not separate from the kingdom even though it must also be the response to the kingdom. His conclusion appears to suggest that righteousness not only has broad meaning potential but that it means completely different things for a single author and his audience. I would argue, however, that for Matthew's audience it has one clear meaning focus, that one part of the meaning potential as accessed from their particular contextual perspective.

12 G. Bertram and F. Hauck, "μακάριος . . . ," *TDNT* 4–366.

13 Dennis Hamm, *The Beatitudes in Context: What Luke and Matthew Meant* (Wilmington, DE: Michael Glazier, 1990), p. 12.

14 Willi Marxsen, *New Testament Foundations For Christian Ethics*, trans. by O. C. Dean, Jr. (Minneapolis: Fortress Press, 1989), pp. 237–8.

15 Gerhard Delling, "τελος, τελέω, . . . τέλειος . . .," *TDNT* 8: 49–88.

16 Cf. 9:11; 12:2, 14; 15:1, 12; 23:23, 25–39.

17 Helmut Koester, *Introduction To The New Testament* (Berlin: Walter DeGruyter, 1982), p. 242.

18 Cf. Rudolf Meyer and Konrad Weiss,"φαρισαῖος," *TDNT* 9 (19xx): 11–49.

19 This position, like the probable urban locale of Matthew's text and its post-CE70 dating, has been documented by so many researchers that we need not spend a great deal of time on it here. While there are a very few scholars (cf. Meier, Vision of Matthew p. 18) who believe that Matthew was a Gentile, the vast majority believe that Matthew's style and language presumptions betray a strong Jewish heritage. As Eduard Schweizer notes, "The Jewish background is plain": *The Good News According to Matthew*, trans. by David E. Green (Atlanta: John Knox Press, 1975) p. 16. The Gospel is written in a rabbinic style of *pesher* interpretation which fits the period of CE 85–90, when Matthew is thought to have been written. In fact Stendahl points out that Matthew's use of the formula quotations presupposes a rather advanced form of Hebrew exegesis. (Cf. Krister Stendahl, *The School of St Matthew: And Its Use of the Old Testament* (Philadelphia: Fortress, 1968) p. xiii.) Ernst von Dobschütz is so convinced that he refers to Matthew as a Christianized rabbi who operates in the Talmudic tradition to the point of boredom: "Matthew as Rabbi and Catechist," *The Interpretation of Matthew*, ed. Graham Stanton (Philadelphia: Fortress Press, 1983) pp. 24–5. There are other structural clues. The text assumes a continued observance of the sabbath (12:1–14; 24:20). Matt. 23:2–3 supports a continued observance of the authority of Pharisaic teaching. Principal themes like the kingdom of heaven and righteousness, and christological titles (Son of David, Son of

Man, Son of God, etc.) all have rich Jewish backgrounds. And as 10:5–6 makes clear, the primary mission field is Israel. (Cf. Daniel S. Harrington, *The Gospel of Matthew* (Collegeville, MN: The Liturgical Press), pp. 8–9.

The language in the Sermon on the Mount bears the same rabbinic stamp. References to the kingdom of heaven, the Father who is in heaven, the argued interpolation of 5:18, 19, and the extensive comparisons to Jewish *halakah* all indicate that the ethical conduct expected in the Sermon is decidedly Jewish in its formulation and expression. (For more extended discussions on the comparisons of individual Sermon precepts with Jewish rabbinic teachings of *halakah*, cf. Eduard Lohse, *Theological Ethics of the New Testament*, trans. by M. Eugene Boring (Minneapolis: Fortress, 1991) pp. 67–8, and Jack Dean Kingsbury, *Matthew: Structure, Christology, Kingdom* (Minneapolis: Fortress, 1975), p. 3 for discussion of halakic similarity to the Golden Rule.)

20 Pinchas Lapide, *The Sermon on the Mount: Utopia or Program For Action?*, trans. by Arlene Swidler (Maryknoll: Orbis Press, 1986), p. 7.

21 Cf. Harrington, *The Gospel of Matthew*, pp. 12–16. Harrington argues that apocalyptic writers like 4 Ezra and 2 Baruch were asked the question, "How could this happen to God's people?" The answer lay in the reality of the two ages. In the present age, evil triumphs. In the final age, God's people will be vindicated. Until that time God's people must live patiently by the Torah. It is therefore critical that the Torah be interpreted accurately. The Jewish Christian response was similar. Followers of this Jewish persuasion agreed with the apocalyptists as to why the tragedy of 70 occurred and the answer of the two ages, and the need to be faithful to the end. The difference was the belief in Jesus as the Son of Man, the messenger of God who represented God's kingdom and interpretative power, who would usher in this new age. Living by the Torah suddenly took on a new look. Not the Torah, but Jesus' interpretation of the Torah became the source of guidance for present living. The rabbinate also staked everything on the interpretation of the Torah. However, it was their Oral Law that was understood to be the valid interpretative mechanism.

22 J. Andrew Overman, *Matthew's Gospel and Formative Judaism: The Social World of the Matthean Community* (Minneapolis: Fortress, 1990), p. 4.

23 Overman's (ibid.) reconstruction is particularly helpful and persuasive at this point. He traces five critical aspects of Judaism during the period of 165 BCE to CE 100, and each suggests that Judaism of the time was multifaceted, and that its many sectarian components (e.g., Qumran, Pharisees, Sadducees, the communities responsible for literature such as 4 Ezra, 2 Baruch and Psalms of Solomon) battled with one another regarding the efficacy of their interpretative strategies and conclusions. He presents five aspects which characterize Jewish groups of the period: fragmentation and factionalism, a language of sectarianism, hostility towards Jewish leadership, centrality of the Law, and a concern for the future of God's covenant people. In each case he demonstrates how the Matthean text has language representative of each aspect. It is this and other evidence which leads him to the conclusion that the Matthean community was one of many sectarian Jewish communities vying for interpretative control in the latter half of the first century CE.

24 Overman, ibid., p. 24.

25 Ibid., p. 5.

26 Mourning appears to be an odd imperative command. However, Hamm, *The Beatitudes*

in Context (cf. pp. 85–86), connects the mourning Beatitude with the controversy about fasting in the wake of being separated from Jesus the bridegroom at 9:14–17. "Against this background, Matthew's second beatitude takes on new life. For those who respond appropriately to the gospel of the kingdom of heaven, those who know their need for God's saving intervention in Jesus are 'happy mourners,' for not only can they anticipate God's final comforting when the kingdom of heaven is fully established; even now in their share in the life of the messianic community, like the finder of the buried treasure selling all he has 'in his joy,' they perform the 'mourning' gesture of fasting in joy" (p. 86). Hamm's full discussion of the Beatitudes elucidates the imperative possibilities for each of them.

27 Cf. R. David Kaylor, *Jesus the Prophet: His Vision of the Kingdom on Earth* (Louisville: Westminster/John Knox, 1994), pp. 93–113. "For Matthew, it is not merely those who are poor, hungry, mourning, and persecuted who will receive blessing; it is those who combine those objective situations with ethical qualities: the 'poor in spirit' (= humble), the meek, the merciful, the pure in heart, those who hunger and thirst for righteousness. This emphasis on quality, both interior and exterior, makes God's promises for the future more rational and acceptable: God is for the pious who are presently suffering because the world sets itself against God and the community of God's people" (p. 95).

28 Cf. Gerhard Delling, "πλήρης, πληρόω . . .," *TDNT* 6: 283–311, at 294: "Jesus does not merely a will maintain them [the law and prophets]. As he sees it, His task is to actualise the will of God made known in the OT. He has come in order that God's Word may be completely fulfilled, in order that the full measure appointed by God Himself may be reached in Him."

29 Cf. Harrington, *The Gospel of Matthew*, p. 97: "In their Matthean context these teachings about true and false piety would have been taken as criticism of the rival Jews who controlled 'their synagogues,' the 'synagogues of the hypocrites.' "

30 The discussion for the three pious activities follows a parallel form: (1) Whenever you do a thing that is righteous: alms, v. 2; prayer, v. 5; fasting, v. 16; (2) don't to it as hypocrites only so that others can see it, v. 2, 5, 16; (3) their reward has already been received, v. 2, 5, 16; (4) do it without show so no one can see, v. 3, 4, 6, 17; and (5) God will reward you, v. 4, 6, 17.

31 Cf. Harrington, *The Gospel of Matthew*, pp. 109–10. Harrington points out that 6:19–7:29 is crafted like a wisdom book. The earlier part, 6:19–7:12 has strong rabbinic parallels and would have been familiar to Jewish readers. So does the second half, 7:13–29, which breaks humanity into two kinds of people, those who do God's will and those who do not. Harrington notes that this commonplace wisdom division is also found in the Qumran *Manual of Discipline* or *Community Rule*. As in Matthew, the comparison there is not between Jew and Gentile, but between Jews who accept the proper interpretation of the Torah, in Matthew's case Jesus', and those who do not. Once again we find that "The texts make better sense when taken as part of a struggle between the Mother community and its Jewish rivals" (p. 110).

32. Harrington, ibid., p. 91 particularly points out that the ethics demanded by Jesus in the sermon have conspicuous parallels with Jewish ethics: "The biblical text in each case is the starting point, and one can find early Jewish rabbis who agree with Jesus at almost every point."

33 Ibid.

34 Cf. Knecht et al., "βασιλεία," p. 589: "To try to bring in the kingdom of God is human presumption, self-righteous Pharisaism and refined Zealotism."

35 Introductory texts on the Gospel of Matthew point out that the evangelist presents Jesus as the authoritative interpreter of God's law. In his introduction to the New Testament, for example, Luke T. Johnson argues that Jesus not only teaches the Torah, but is so integrally connected with God's will for the people that he embodies, personifies and fulfills the meaning and intent of the Torah. As Johnson points out, "One form of messianic expectation within Judaism looked for the Messiah to interpret Torah definitively": *The Writings of the New Testament: An Interpretation* (Philadelphia: Fortress, 1986), p. 185. For Matthew, Jesus fulfills this role. And his primary offering of Torah interpretation occurs in the Sermon on the Mount. Indeed, it is because he so authoritatively interprets the Torah that he need not appeal to the traditions of the elders before ruling on a legal question, but can say with utter integrity and authority, "But I say." It is no wonder that Johnson can conclude, ibid., p. 190, "In Matthew's Gospel, Jesus is teacher of Torah, fulfillment of Torah, and the very personification of Torah."

36 Cf. Jack Dean Kingsbury, *Matthew As Story* (Philadelphia: Fortress, 1986), pp. 9–10. Kingsbury notes from his literary critical standpoint that Jesus' character is endowed with a key trait of obedience (3:15; 4:1–11; 26:36–46). All other characters are judged against Jesus, particularly as to how they stand in relationship to Jesus' obedience. To approach Jesus' obedience is to gain positive story stature.

37 For a discussion of the various ways in which the sermon has been interpreted, cf. Carl G. Vaught, *The Sermon on the Mount: A Theological Interpretation* (Albany: SUNY, 1986), pp. ix–xiv. Vaught appeals to the three classic types presented already by Joachim Jeremias: (1) perfectionist conception, (2) impossible ideal, (3) interim ethic. Cf. also Joachim Jeremias, *The Sermon on the Mount*, trans. by Norman Perrin (Philadelphia: Fortress, 1963), pp. 1–12.

38 Gerd Theissen, *Social Reality and the Early Christians: Theology, Ethics, and the World of the New Testament*, trans. by Margaret Kohl (Minneapolis: Fortress, 1992), pp. 35–46.

39 Cf. ibid., p. 41. Theissen appeals particularly to the Cynic Epictetus.

40 Ibid., p. 36: "Their ethical radicalism makes Jesus' sayings absolutely impracticable as a regulative for everyday behavior. So we are faced all the more inescapably with the question: Who passed on sayings like these by word of mouth over a period of thirty years and more? Who took them seriously?" "But in general we may assume heuristically, or as a working hypothesis, that the sayings of Jesus were practiced in some form or other. If they had been notoriously disregarded, they would hardly have survived over a period of one or two generations" (Ibid., pp. 36–7). Theissen, ibid., p. 45, points to Didache 11 as an example of believers expected to follow the Lord's way of life (τρόπους κυρίου, Did. 11: 8).

41 Cf. Matthew 4:18–22; 8:18–22; 10:34–8; 16:24–8; 19:27. In each case the language of following is used and the narration presents the reader with the circumstance of followers who imitate Jesus' radical kingdom responsive lifestyle.

42 Hermann Hendrickx, *The Sermon on the Mount* (London: Geoffrey Chapman, 1984), p. 182.

43 Cf. Theophus Smith, *Conjuring Culture: Biblical Formations of Black America* (New York

and Oxford: Oxford University Press, 1994). Indeed, Smith argues that it is *the* hermeneutical approach that African Americans bring to biblical interpretation.

44 Ibid., p. 3.
45 Ibid., p. 58.
46 Ibid., p. 122.
47 Ibid., p. 55 (emphasis mine).
48 Ibid., p. 172.
49 Ibid., p. 59.

Selections from
The Cost of Discipleship

Dietrich Bonhoeffer

14 The Hidden Righteousness

*Take heed that ye do not your righteousness before men, to be seen of them:
else ye have no reward with your Father which is in heaven. When therefore
thou doest alms sound not a trumpet before thee, as the hypocrites do in the
synagogues and in the streets, that they may have glory of men. Verily I say
unto you, They have received their reward. But when thou doest alms, let not
thy left hand know what thy right hand doeth: that thine alms may be in secret:
and thy Father which seeth in secret shall recompense thee. (Matt. 6:1–4)*

In Matthew 5 we were told how the disciple community is essentially visible
in character, and how its visibility culminates in the περισσόν. We saw that the
hall-mark of Christianity is our separation from the world, our transcendence
of its standards, and our extraordinariness. The next chapter takes up the theme
of the περισσόν, and lays bare its ambiguity. How easy it would be for the
disciples to misinterpret it! We can well imagine them saying: "Now we must
set to work and build the kingdom of heaven on earth" – and in so doing they
would ignore and perhaps even overthrow the established order of things. They
might adopt an attitude of indifference to this present age, like the enthusiasts,
and try to realize the extraordinary quality of the age to come in a visible
institution. Their ideal would then be to withdraw radically and uncompromisingly from the world and by means of force to set up a Christian order more
compatible with their following of Christ and more in accordance with his

extraordinary demand. There was an obvious temptation to mistake Christ's work for a commendation of a new, however novel, free, and inspiring, pattern for pious living. How eagerly would the religious embrace a life of poverty, truthfulness and suffering, if only they might thereby satisfy their yearning not only to believe, but to see with their own eyes! One might have been prepared to move the distinctions between the two a little, so that a pious pattern of life and obedience towards God's Word might come a little closer together, so that in the end you could really not tell one from the other. After all, they could argue, they were doing it all for the supreme cause, the realization of the "extraordinary."

Others on the other hand would be waiting to hear what Jesus had to say about the "extraordinary," only to pounce upon him with all their fury. Here at last, they would say, the fanatic, the enthusiastic revolutionary has come out in his true colors. Now we know he wants to turn the whole world upside down and bids his disciples leave the world and build a new one. Is *this* obedience to the word of the Old Testament? Is it not, rather, the most glaring example of self-righteousness? Does not Jesus know that all he demands is bound to come to grief because of the world's sin? Does he not know the manifest laws of God given so that sin might be banished? Does it not prove him a victim of spiritual pride, always the first sign of fanaticism? No, they would say, genuine obedience and humility are only to be found in the ordinary, the commonplace, and the hidden. Had Jesus urged his disciples to return to their own kith and kin, back to duty and calling, back to the obedience of the law as the scribes expounded it, they would then have known that he was devout, humble, and obedient. He would then have given his disciples an inspiring incentive to deeper devotion and stricter obedience. He would have taught what the scribes knew already, what they would gladly have heard him emphasize in his preaching, namely that true devotion and righteousness consist not merely in outward behavior, but in the disposition of the heart, and conversely not only in the disposition of the heart, but also in concrete action. That would have been just the kind of "better righteousness" the people needed, and one which nobody could have gainsaid. But now Jesus had lost his chance. He had stepped forth not as a humble teacher, but as an arrogant fanatic. Fanatics of course have always known the secret of kindling the enthusiasm of men, especially the noblest and best of them. Did not the doctors of the law know that for all its nobility the heart of man still spoke with the voice of the flesh? Did they now know themselves what power even pious flesh could have over a man? The "extraordinary" was simply the spontaneous work of devotion and piety. It was the assertion of human freedom against unreflecting obedience to the command of God, the illegitimate self-justification of man, which the law does not permit; the lawless self-sanctification which the law was bound to condemn; free service to God as opposed to bounden duty, the destruction of the Church of God, the denial of faith, blasphemy against the law and against God himself. . . . If the law had its way Jesus would be put to death for teaching the "extraordinary."

And how does Jesus answer these objections? He says: "Take heed that ye do not your righteousness before men, to be seen of them." The call to the "extraordinary" is the inevitable risk men must take when they follow Christ. And therefore Jesus warns us to take heed. He calls a halt to the innocent spontaneous joy we get from making our Christianity visible. He calls us to reflect on what we are doing.

The disciples are told that they can possess the "extraordinary" only so long as they are reflective: they must beware how they use it, and never fulfill it simply for its own sake, or for the sake of ostentation. The better righteousness of the disciples must have a motive which lies beyond itself. Of course it has to be visible, but they must take care that it does not become visible simply for the sake of becoming visible. There are of course proper grounds for insisting on the visible nature of Christian discipleship, but the visibility is never an end in itself; and if it becomes so we have lost sight of our primary aim, which is to follow Jesus. And, having once done that, we should never be able to carry on again where we had left off; we should have to begin all over again at the beginning. And that would bring it home to us that we were no true disciples. We are therefore confronted with a paradox. Our activity must be visible, but never be done for the sake of making it visible. "Let your light so shine before men" (5:16) and yet: Take care that you hide it! There is a pointed contrast between chapters 5 and 6. That which is visible must also be hidden. The awareness on which Jesus insists is intended to prevent us from reflecting on our extraordinary position. We have to take heed that we do not take heed of our own righteousness. Otherwise the "extraordinary" which we achieve will not be that which comes from following Christ, but that which springs from our own will and desire.

How is this paradox to be resolved? The first question to ask is: From whom are we to hide the visibility of our discipleship? Certainly not from other men, for we are told to let them see our light. No. We are to hide it from *ourselves*. Our task is simply to keep on following, looking only to our Leader who goes on before, taking no notice of ourselves or of what we are doing. We must be unaware of our own righteousness, and see it only insofar as we look unto Jesus; then it will seem not extraordinary, but quite ordinary and natural. Thus we hide the visible from ourselves in obedience to the word of Jesus. If the "extraordinary" were important for its own sake, we should, like fanatics, be relying on our own fleshly strength and power, whereas the disciple of Jesus acts simply in obedience to his Lord. That is, he regards the "extraordinary" as the natural fruit of obedience. According to the word of Jesus it cannot be otherwise: the Christian is a light unto the world, not because of any quality of his own, but only because he follows Christ and looks solely to him. But precisely because the Christian life is of its very nature extraordinary, it is at the same time ordinary, natural, and *hidden*. If not, it is not the Christian life at all, it is not obedience to the will of Jesus Christ.

Second, we have to ask how the visible and the invisible aspects of discipleship can be combined, and how the same life can be both visible and hidden. To answer this question, all we need to do is to go back to Matthew 5, where the extraordinary and the visible are defined as the cross of Christ beneath which the disciples stand. The cross is at once the necessary, the hidden, and the visible – it is the "extraordinary."

Third, we have to ask how the contradiction between the fifth and the sixth chapters is to be resolved. The answer lies in the meaning of discipleship. It means an exclusive adherence to him, and that implies, first, that the disciple looks only to his Lord and follows him. If he looked only at the extraordinary quality of the Christian life, he would no longer be following Christ. For the disciple this extraordinary quality consists solely in the will of the Lord, and when he seeks to do that will he knows that there is no other alternative, and that what he does is the only natural thing to do.

All that the follower of Jesus has to do is to make sure that his obedience, following, and love are entirely spontaneous and unpremeditated. If you do good, you must not let your left hand know what your right hand is doing, you must be quite unconscious of it. Otherwise you are simply displaying your own virtue, and not that which has its source in Jesus Christ; Christ's virtue, the virtue of discipleship, can only be accomplished so long as you are entirely unconscious of what you are doing. The genuine work of love is always a hidden work. Take heed therefore that you know it not, for only so is it the goodness of God. If we want to know our own goodness or love, it has already ceased to be love. We must be unaware even of our love for our enemies. After all, when we love them they are no longer our enemies. This voluntary blindness in the Christian (which is really sight illuminated by Christ) is his certainty, and the fact that his life is hidden from his sight is the ground of his assurance.

Thus hiddenness has its counterpart in manifestation. For there is nothing hidden that shall not be revealed. For our God is a God unto whom all hearts are open, and from whom no secrets are hid. God will show us the hidden and make it visible. Manifestation is the appointed reward for hiddenness, and the only question is where we shall receive it and who will give it us. If we want publicity in the eyes of men we have our reward. In other words, it is immaterial whether the publicity we want is the grosser kind, which all can see, or the more subtle variety which we can only see ourselves. If the left hand knows what the right hand is doing, if we become conscious of our hidden virtue, we are forging our own reward, instead of that which God had intended to give us in his own good time. But if we are content to carry on with our life hidden from our eyes, we shall receive our reward openly from God. But what kind of love is this that is so unaware of itself that it can be hidden until the day of judgement? The answer is obvious. Because love is hidden it cannot be a visible virtue or a habit which can be acquired. Take heed, it says, that you do not exchange true love for an amiable virtuousness, a human "quality." Genuine love is always self-forgetful in the true sense of the word. But if we are to have it, our old man must die with all his virtues and qualities, and this can only be done where the disciple forgets self and clings solely to Christ. When Jesus said: "Let not thy left hand know what thy right hand doeth," he was sounding the death-knell of the old man. Once again, who can live a life which combines Matthew 5 and 6? Only those who have died after the old man through Christ, and are given a new life by following him and having fellowship with him. Love, in the sense of spontaneous, unreflective action, spells the death of the old man. For man recovers his true nature in the righteousness of Christ and in his fellow man. The love of Christ crucified, which delivers our old man to death, is the love which lives in those who follow him. "I live; yet no longer I, but Christ liveth in me" (Gal. 2:20). Henceforth the Christian finds himself only in Christ and in his brethren.

15 The Hiddenness of Prayer

And when ye pray, ye shall not be as the hypocrites: for they love to stand and pray in the synagogues and in the corners of the streets, that they may be seen of men. Verily I say unto you, They have received their reward. But thou, when thou prayest, enter into thine inner chamber, and having shut thy door, pray to thy Father which is in secret, and thy Father which seeth in secret shall recompense thee. And in praying use not vain repetitions, as the Gentiles do: for they think that they shall be heard for their much speaking. Be not therefore like unto them: for your Father knoweth what things ye hath need of, before ye ask him. (Matt. 6:5–8)

Jesus teaches his disciples to pray. What does this mean? It means that prayer is by no means an obvious or natural activity. It is the expression of a universal human instinct, but that does not justify it in the sight of God. Even where prayer is cultivated with discipline and perseverance it can still be profitless and void of God's blessing. The disciples are permitted to pray because Jesus tells them they may – and he knows the Father. He promises that God will hear them. That is to say, the disciples pray only because they are followers of Christ and have fellowship with him. Only those who, like them, adhere to Jesus have access to the Father through him. All Christian prayer is directed to God through a Mediator, and not even prayer affords direct access to the Father. Only through Jesus Christ can we find the Father in prayer. Christian prayer presupposes faith, that is, adherence to Christ. He is the one and only Mediator of our prayers. We pray at his command, and to that word Christian prayer is always bound.

We pray to God because we believe in him through Jesus Christ; that is to say, our prayer can never be an entreaty to God, for we have no need to come before him in that way. We are privileged to know that he knows our needs before we ask him. This is what gives Christian prayer its boundless confidence and its joyous certainty. It matters little what form of prayer we adopt or how many words we use; what matters is the faith which lays hold on God and touches the heart of the Father who knew us long before we came to him.

Genuine prayer is never "good works," an exercise or a pious attitude, but it is always the prayer of a child to a Father. Hence it is never given to self-display, whether before God, ourselves, or other people. If God were ignorant of our needs, we should have to think out beforehand *how* we should tell him about them, *what* we should tell him, and whether we should tell him or not. Thus faith, which is the mainspring of Christian prayer, excludes all reflection and premeditation.

Prayer is the supreme instance of the hidden character of the Christian life. It is the antithesis of self-display. When men pray, they have ceased to know themselves, and know only God whom they call upon. Prayer does not aim at any direct effect on the world; it is addressed to God alone, and is therefore the perfect example of undemonstrative action.

Of course there is a danger even here. Prayer of this kind can seek self-display, it can seek to bring to light that which is hidden. This may happen in public prayer, which sometimes (though not often nowadays) degenerates into an empty noise. But there is no difference; it is even more pernicious if I turn myself into a spectator of my own prayer performance, if I am giving a show for my own benefit. I may enjoy myself just like a pleased spectator or I may catch myself praying and feel strange and ashamed. The publicity of the marketplace affords only a more naive form than the publicity which I am providing for myself. I can lay on a very nice show for myself even in the privacy of my own room. That is the extent to which we can distort the word of Jesus. The publicity which I am looking for is then provided by the fact that I am the one who at the same time prays and looks on. I am listening to my own prayer and thus I am answering my own prayer. Not being content to wait for God to answer our prayer and show us in his own time that he has heard us, we provide our own answer. We take note that we have prayed suitably well, and this substitutes the satisfaction of answered prayer. We have our reward. Since we have heard ourselves, God will not hear us. Having contrived our own reward of publicity, we cannot expect God to reward us any further.

Where is the innermost chamber Jesus is thinking of where I can hide, if I cannot be sure of myself? How can I lock it so well that no audience spoils the anonymity of prayer and thus robs me of the reward of hidden prayer? How are we to be protected from ourselves, and our own premeditations? How are we to drive out reflection by reflecting? The only way is by mortifying our own wills which are always obtruding themselves. And the only way to do this is by letting Christ alone reign in our hearts, by surrendering our wills completely to him, by living in fellowship with Jesus and by following him. Then we can pray that his will may be done, the will of him who knows our needs before we ask. Only then is our prayer certain, strong, and pure. And then prayer is really and truly *petition*. The child asks of the Father whom he knows. Thus the essence of Christian prayer is not general adoration, but definite, concrete petition. The right way to approach God is to stretch out our hands and ask of One who we know has the heart of a Father.

True prayer is done in secret, but this does not rule out the fellowship of prayer altogether, however clearly we may be aware of its dangers. In the last resort it is immaterial whether we pray in the open street or in the secrecy of our chambers, whether briefly or lengthily, in the Litany of the Church, or with the sigh of one who knows not what he should pray for. True prayer does not depend on either the individual or the whole body of the faithful, but solely upon the knowledge that our heavenly Father knows our needs. That makes God the sole object of our prayers, and frees us from a false confidence in our own prayerful efforts.

> After this manner therefore pray ye: Our Father which art in heaven, Hallowed be thy name. Thy kingdom come. Thy will be done, as in heaven, so on earth. Give us this day our daily bread. And forgive us our debts, as we also have forgiven our debtors. And bring us not into temptation, but deliver us from the evil one. For if ye forgive not men their trespasses, neither will your Father forgive your trespasses. (Matt. 6:9–15)

Jesus told his disciples not only *how* to pray, but also *what* to pray. The Lord's Prayer is not merely the pattern prayer, it is the way Christians *must* pray. If they pray this prayer, God will certainly hear them. The Lord's Prayer is the quintessence of prayer. A disciple's prayer is founded on and circumscribed by it. Once again Jesus does not leave his disciples in ignorance; he teaches them the Lord's Prayer and so leads them to a clear understanding of prayer.

"Our Father which art in heaven." The disciples call upon the heavenly Father as a corporate body, they call upon a Father who already knows his children's needs. The call of Jesus binds them into a brotherhood. In Jesus they have apprehended the loving-kindness of the Father. In the name of the Son of God they are privileged to call God Father. They are on earth, and their

Father is in heaven, He looks down on them from above, and they lift up their eyes to him.

"Hallowed be thy name." God's name of Father, as it has been revealed to the disciples in Jesus Christ, shall be kept holy among them. In this name the whole content of the gospel is embraced. May God protect his holy gospel from being obscured and profaned by false doctrine and unholiness of living, and may he ever make known his holy name to the disciples in Jesus Christ. May he enable all preachers to proclaim the pure gospel of saving grace, defend us against the tempters, and convert the enemies of his name!

"Thy kingdom come." In Jesus Christ his followers have witnessed the kingdom of God breaking in on earth. They have seen Satan crushed and the powers of the world, sin, and death broken. The kingdom of God is still exposed to suffering and strife. The little flock has a share in that tribulation. They stand under the sovereignty of God in the new righteousness, but in the midst of persecution. God grant that the kingdom of Jesus Christ may grow in his Church on earth, God hasten the end of the kingdoms of this world, and establish his own kingdom in power and glory!

"Thy will be done, as in heaven, so on earth." In fellowship with Jesus his followers have surrendered their own wills completely to God's, and so they pray that God's will may be done throughout the world. No creature on earth shall defy him. But the evil will is still alive even in the followers of Christ, it still seeks to cut them off from fellowship with him; and that is why they must also pray that the will of God may prevail more and more in their hearts every day and break down all defiance. In the end the whole world must bow before that will, worshipping and giving thanks in joy and tribulation. Heaven and earth shall be subject to God.

God's name, God's kingdom, God's will must be the primary object of Christian prayer. Of course it is not as if God needed our prayers, but they are the means by which the disciples become partakers in the heavenly treasure for which they pray. Furthermore, God uses their prayers to hasten the coming of the End.

"Give us this day our daily bread." As long as the disciples are on earth, they should not be ashamed to pray for their bodily needs. He who created men on earth will keep and preserve their bodies. It is not God's will that his creation should be despised. The disciples are told to ask for bread not only for themselves but for all men on the earth, for all men are their brethren. The disciples realize that while it is a fruit of the earth, bread really comes down from above as the gift of God alone. That is why they have to ask for it before they take it. And since it is the bread of God, it is new every day. They do not ask to lay up a store for the future, but are satisfied with what God gives them day by day. Through that bread their lives are spared a little longer, that they may enjoy life in fellowship with Jesus, praising and thanking him for his loving-kindness. This petition is a test of their faith, for it shows whether they believe that all things work together for good to them that love God.

"Forgive us our debts, as we also forgive our debtors." Every day Christ's followers must acknowledge and bewail their guilt. Living as they do in fellowship with him, they ought to be sinless, but in practice their life is marred daily with all manner of unbelief, sloth in prayer, lack of bodily discipline, self-indulgence of every kind, envy, hatred, and ambition. No wonder that they must pray daily for God's forgiveness. But God will only forgive them if they forgive one another with readiness and brotherly affection. Thus they bring all their guilt before God and pray as a body for forgiveness. God forgive not merely *me my* debts, but *us ours*.

"Lead us not into temptation." Many and diverse are the temptations which beset the Christian. Satan attacks him on every side, if haply he might cause him to fall. Sometimes the attack takes the form of a false sense of security, and sometimes of ungodly doubt. But the disciple is conscious of his weakness, and does not expose himself unnecessarily to temptation in order to test the strength of his faith. Christians ask God not to put their puny faith to the test, but to preserve them in the hour of temptation.

"But deliver us from evil." The last petition is for deliverance from evil and for the inheritance of the kingdom of Heaven. It is a prayer for a holy death and for the deliverance of the Church in the day of judgement.

"For thine is the kingdom . . ." The disciples are renewed in their assurance that the kingdom is God's by their fellowship in *Jesus Christ, on whom depends the fulfilment of all their prayers*. In him God's name is hallowed, his kingdom comes and his will is done. For his sake the disciples are preserved in body and receive forgiveness of sin, in his strength they are preserved in all times of temptation, in his power they are delivered and brought to eternal life. His is the kingdom and the power and the glory for ever and ever in the unity of the Father. That is the assurance the disciples have.

As a summing up Jesus emphasizes once more that everything depends on forgiveness of sin, of which the disciples may only partake within the fellowship of sinners.

The Sermon on the Mount as Radical Pastoral Care

Richard Lischer

Early in the *Church Dogmatics* Karl Barth asserts that the task of theology is to assess the relationship of the Church's distinctive talk about God with the Church's being.[1] How do doctrinal and liturgical formulas square with the life of the Church, and how faithful is the Church to the various charters which have shaped its identity and purpose? The Sermon on the Mount is one such charter. Yet for many reasons, not the least of which is its alleged impracticability, the Sermon is usually ignored by practical theology or isolated from its churchly context and admired for the grandeur of its moral or psychological truths.

Contemporary Christians, however much they may admire the Sermon on the Mount, want even more to *use* it or to know if it is usable in the congregation. Most Christians are convinced that the Sermon cannot regulate a secular society, and many doubt its viability in the bureaucracy and political intrigues of the denomination. Yet what of the congregation, the empirical community of Jesus Christ which often lives in tension with both society and Church bureaucracy? One would suspect that the congregation enjoys a more intimate relationship with the Sermon on the Mount, for the congregation derives its identity, tasks, and sustenance from the scriptures and the sacraments as they are expounded and celebrated in its midst. May we not reasonably expect to find that the Sermon is not merely *applicable* to the Church but is, as Barth put it, expressive of the "being" of the Christian congregation? The congregation is, in fact, the most appropriate theater for this, Jesus' greatest teaching.

One finds little published support for such a claim. The Church has directly

294

appropriated little of the Sermon on the Mount into its polity and ritual, and only a few contemporary works in practical theology, ministry, pastoral care, and preaching comment on the Sermon. It is another essay to say why this is true. Instead, I will sketch a few characteristics of the congregation in order to confirm and promote the organic relationship that continues to exist between the Sermon on the Mount and the life and ministry of the contemporary congregation.

The Sermon as a Church Document

The Sermon on the Mount is set in the most ecclesially oriented of the gospels. No other gospel is so shaped by the Church's thought or designed for its use as Matthew's. For this reason it has exercised a uniquely normative influence in the later Church. In Matthew alone the congregation is the *ekklēsia* (Matt. 16:18), which is the *qᶜhal Yahweh* of Old Testament–Jewish expectations.[2] Matthew's Gospel does not rely on a hierarchy of pastoral offices to make Jesus present to the Church. Quite the opposite is true (Matt. 20:25–8). Because Jesus is still the pastor in this Church, in the midst of his people (Matt. 18:12, 20), his congregation offers the richest possibilities for fellowship, service, discipleship, and suffering. Matthew does not delineate gradations of "church," with the greatest of these residing somewhere beyond the local congregation; nor does he feed modern idealizations of "community" by glossing over the sins of his own group.

Matthew's congregation has its problems,[3] and those problems appear to revolve around the "being" of the Church in the physical absence of Jesus. What is the nature of the Church? The question of the temple tax in 17:24–7 apparently reflects the unresolved issue of the Church's distinctive identity amidst the conflicting currents of popular piety, Judaism, and Paulinism. Matthew's community is also torn by the more banal disputes that perennially divide congregations: moral laxity, legalism, bad preaching, factionalism, ignorance, and wealth. Who may belong to the Church? Like any pastor, the Evangelist is concerned with the quality of relationships within the congregation, with offenses and restoration; yet the Sermon breathes a different spirit than later manuals of Church discipline. Matthew agonizes over the mixed nature of the community, but the Sermon pleads for reconciliation and makes no provision for expelling sinners and heretics. What is the mission of the Church? Even the Gospel's perception of the Church's mission is not without ambiguity. Matthew begins and ends with delegations from and toward the nations; yet it portrays a teacher whose concern is only momentarily deflected from the lost sheep of the house of Israel. The radicality of the "you have heard . . . but I say to you" construction is balanced by respect for the law, which Jesus has come to interpret and fulfill, not to relax or abolish (Matt. 5:17). The members of this community will take the law seriously in their dealings with one another. If the Sermon on the Mount is a catechism, as some have characterized it,[4] it is not so much a doctrinal summary as a guide to pastoral care for those who are endeavoring to live in God's new congregation. In sum, the Gospel renders typical Christians struggling to be faithful in what one writer calls "the climate of ordinary Christianity,"[5] a major feature of which I take to be the intense and conflicted life of the local congregation.

That there appears to be a movement of audience from "the disciples" in 5:1 to "the crowds" in 7:28 does not suggest an attempt to generalize something so peculiar as a church's catechism. If the disciples represent the "typical" Christian and the crowd the potential disciple, then the audience of the Sermon has merely shifted from the initiated to those who have overheard the teaching and must now decide if they are ready to commit themselves to the One who makes such a blessed and difficult life possible.

The Eschatological Community

The Sermon on the Mount is difficult in many ways: difficult to *try*, as in love for one's enemy or uncoerced generosity, difficult to *do*, as in non-resistance or total sexual purity, but even more difficult to *conceptualize* as a framework for Christian existence. The framework larger than any of the precepts or prohibitions within it is the eschatology of the Sermon. The Rule of God provides more comprehensive auspices for the Christian life than even the most thoroughgoing principle of nonviolence, for the latter is ultimately a response to the former, a courageous way of bringing oneself or one's group into alignment with the hidden but real dynamic of God's governance in the world. Whereas morality – if we are to believe Reinhold Niebuhr – suffers in collision with institutions but proves workable in the individual, eschatology in anything but its crassest varieties of futurism meets with incomprehension at all levels: institutions, communities, groups, and individuals. It is the eschatology of the Sermon, not its morality, that confounds contemporary Christians.

The eschatology of the Sermon begins with the Beatitudes but underlies the entire discourse. The Beatitudes characterize those who have been called by God.[6] They are less a roll-call of kingdom-virtues than an affirmation of the eschatological blessedness which is already enjoyed by those who are followers of Jesus Christ. The Beatitudes are not a strategy or exhortation to blessedness but an indicative with the force of a promise. So sure is the reality of the kingdom which has been inaugurated by Jesus that his followers already have what the kingdom promises.

The promise of the Beatitudes serves as preface to what Robert Tannehill calls "focal instances" or imaginative examples of life in the kingdom.[7] In Matthew 5 Jesus repeatedly cites a command, radically deepens its significance, and provides an imagistic amplification of his teaching. Not only shall we not kill, we shall not be angry. This is what that looks like: If you bring your gift to the altar and there remember a broken relationship, leave your gift and first be reconciled (Matt. 5:21–4). The focal instance is as concrete and realistic as everyday life; yet it is extreme and shocking when compared with ordinary behavior. The focal instance is not a cut-and-dried law, like the legislation on divorce found in 5:31–2 and in the other gospels, from which deductions may be drawn. Rather, it operates metaphorically, producing an imaginative shock to the moral imagination and enabling the hearer to see his or her own life in a radically new way.[8] That the Beatitudes should produce a metaphoric effect is not surprising, for metaphor, with its multiple and contradictory layers of meaning, is the unit of expressive language most suited to the *is/is not/will be* tension characteristic of eschatology in general and the Beatitudes in particular.

When the Beatitudes are reduced to virtues or the maxims of positive thinking, the rest of the Sermon is lost as well. Then the sayings about purity, love generosity, piety, and all the others can no longer be understood as representative portraits of the new community's daily life of discipleship. Rather, they become new rules, and as rules they eventually produce the predictable forms of ethical activism, anguish, or security – depending on the species of self-deception at work in the hearer. So the reconciliation urged upon litigants as they rush to court (Matt. 5:26–7) "makes sense" to Christians, for everyone knows that people who go to the same church or live in the same neighborhood ought to get along. But why should the Teacher be crucified for reinforcing what everyone already knows? What if reconciliation and the other behaviors advocated by the Sermon are not "rules" in the sense of new and more stringent laws, but are, rather, ingredient to the Rule of God? In this New Rule we do not do the law, but what the law ordains is fulfilled *in* us (cf. Rom. 8:4). We reconcile with our neighbor, not because we feel better afterward, but because the court we are rushing toward belongs to God. We seek reconciliation, not merely as an individualistic response to a command, but because the End toward which we journey will be characterized by the reconciliation already effected in Jesus Christ. Our ethical behavior, what we *do* now, is a down payment on the perfect peace, harmony, love, purity, and worship that will characterize the End.

How perverse it is to claim that the Sermon can only be done by individuals. It is precisely as individuals cut off from the community that we are bound to fail. For the Sermon portrays a dyadic constellation of relationships – a kind of radicalized *Canterbury Tales* – within the pilgrim community. Because the pilgrims have experienced by faith the assurance of their destination, they are encouraged by its promise and guided by its rubrics.

297

Eschatology and ethics have always had to do with each other,[9] but what is their relationship? In an important work published nearly fifty years ago, Amos Wilder asserted that eschatology serves as a sanction for Jesus's ethical teaching. It is, he said, the symbolic "overtone" of the ethical element that lends motive and significance to Jesus' message of this worldly redemption. Wilder's study grades the levels of the sanctions beginning with the lowest or "formal" sanctions, which are predictions of rewards and punishments (e.g. Matt. 5:25–6). These sanctions are ultimately based on self-interest, for the rewards and punishments not only stretch into eternity but impinge upon the present messianic times. The highest or "essential" sanctions derive from the nature, character, or glory of God ("You, therefore, must be perfect, as your heavenly Father is perfect," Matt. 5:48; cf. Matt. 5:16).[10] We might question the priority of ethics above eschatology in Wilder's interpretation or suggest that he inflates the distinction between the formal aspects of literary eschatology and the essential character of the God who makes promises. Yet Wilder's inventory of sanctions is a reminder that the Church too often employs the biblical representations of formal sanctions, which feed upon self-interest, but ignores essential sanctions in the nature of God and God's kingdom.

The result is the suffocating atmosphere of moralism in many Protestant churches. Moralism is comfortable with lists of virtues or suitable causes, the pursuit of which will stave off unhappiness and issue into present or future satisfactions. "The Be-Happy Attitudes," to cite a current bestseller, promise the reader a sense of personal fulfillment. We are inoculating the world with a mild form of Christianity, E. Stanley Jones said, so that it is now all but immune to the real thing. The aim of any such inoculation is security: not security in Christ but security from Christ and his terrible freedom.[11]

Because the Church has overlooked the promise of eschatology, it is left with the baffling residue of commands which will not work in the world but whose performance is ominously tied to eternal salvation (cf. Matt. 7:24–7). As a compromise, preachers continue to lash their listeners with the "principles" of the Sermon, avoiding embarrassing specifics like the word on divorce, and concentrating on viable issues such as peace and prayer. Recovering the individual injunctions without appropriating the eschatological-communal-evangelical complex summarized by the word "gospel" (Matt. 4:23) is like trying to build the ship in the bottle. It never works. Our only hope of living as the community of the Sermon is to acknowledge that we do not retaliate, hate, curse, lust, divorce, swear, brag, preen, worry, or backbite because it is not in the nature of our God or our destination that we should be such people. When we as individuals fail in these instances, we do not snatch up cheap forgiveness, but we do remember that the *ekklēsia* is larger than the sum of our individual failures and that it is pointed in a direction that will carry us away from them.

How does one combine eschatology and ethics in the local congregation? The question sounds ridiculous because we know that the problem is of a different order from "How can we involve the youth?" or "How can we improve our music?" One way, of course, *the* Protestant way, is to preach the Sermon on the Mount as an indication of the community's effort to live out its own identity. This is to set the Sermon into the larger framework of God's present and coming kingdom. Root out the moralism that urges an attitude or task but offers no resources in God for its attainment.

Since moralism is not limited to preachers but pervades all strata of congregational life from the board of trustees to the children's Sunday school class, let the entire congregation become an incubator of the promise and the demand of the Sermon. For example, is there a gospel-based method of making a church budget that will exemplify the congregation's mission without being "anxious about tomorrow"? In my first parish my predecessor had quietly refused his salary until the congregation met its mission commitments. By the time I arrived, a small, rural congregation, easily stereotyped as "ingrown,' was giving away well over half its income every year. Are there ways in which the congregation can refuse to try to serve God and mammon, perhaps by offering both coat and cloak to a floundering sister church? In such focal instances the congregation's enactment of the Sermon will not only teach its members how to live as faithful disciples, but the congregation itself will become, without self-advertisement, what Jesus says it is: "the light of the world" (Matt. 5:14).

Pastoral Care and Conversation

It is somewhat puzzling that Matthew's rendering of the new congregation in the Sermon on the Mount should be ignored by contemporary studies of pastoral care and conversation. If the Sermon presents a series of case studies of daily life in the kingdom, why does the Sermon appear only in a few scattered footnotes in the literature of pastoral care? Over the past few decades pastoral care has focused on individual counseling with little attention given to the corporate dimensions of moral guidance, cure of souls, and the formation of the congregation. Yet even when the Sermon on the Mount was governed by an equally individualistic hermeneutic, there seems to have been little communication between the privatized demands of the Sermon and the personal liberations wrought through pastoral counseling, no doubt because the Sermon shakes the therapeutic foundations upon which pastoral counseling is based.

Every year I lead a seminar in our university's medical center on the topic of psychiatry and the Christian faith. The discussion inevitably touches on those elements of Christianity which the psychiatrists consider most toxic to the mental health of their patients. It occurs to me that most of their examples

299

are drawn from the Sermon on the Mount. They have patients who want to be perfect, who feel guilty about anger and embarrassed by lust, people who actually believe that Big Brother God knows what they are thinking. "I grew up in a Lutheran home" (an ominous opening statement), "and I never heard anything healthy about human nature, nothing about recreated humanity in Christ, but only don't do this or don't do that." The Sermon is one more example of "the rules," only in this case the rules run counter to our essential humanity. The Sermon's tone violates the moral neutrality necessary for self-acceptance and change. Its obsession with purity gives free reign to the tyranny of the super-ego. The main objection to its message is that those who take it too seriously move away from the median ranges of mental health, our culture's translation of *salvus*. Far from a set of helpful guidelines for living the happy life, the Beatitudes detail the disjunction of blessedness from happiness, and salvation from health. In a society that celebrates "the narcissism of similarity" the Sermon disappoints repeatedly.[12] What someone said of the characters in the stories of Flannery O'Conner applies to the adherents of the Sermon: "You shall know the truth, and the truth shall make you odd." The psychiatrists have a point. Theirs is no small indictment to bring against a religious program that so thoroughly disaccommodates its adherents for a well-balanced life in a technological and therapeutic society.

Before we can recover the Sermon on the Mount for pastoral care, we need to retrieve pastoral care from pastoral counseling and pastoral counseling from its reliance on formal rather than essential sanctions for its work. In some theories of pastoral care, the Bible is merely a "resource" for counseling, so long as it is interpreted according to reputable psychotherapeutic principles.[13] The Church is a "context" for pastoral care, and more than a few pastoral counselors cite the physical location of their office in a church building as reason enough for omitting the explicit language of God from the counseling session.[14] In much of modern pastoral care God has become a "fiction" or a formal symbolization – in Wilder's terms, the overtone which lends significance to the therapeutic task. The essential sanction for pastoral care has become human nature as it is explicated by various psychological theories. God and Church are too often appended to studies in pastoral care the way "last things" was tacked on to the end of dogmatics books.

Several pastoral theologians are leading the retrieval of the communal and moral dimensions of the Church's rich tradition of pastoral care.[15] There is now growing criticism of pastoral counseling's uncritical adoption of psychological models and techniques. William Clebsch and Charles Jaekle have noted, "In our time, the weakness of reconciling as a function of pastoral care is obvious. There is no place in the structure and rhythm of the life of modern congregations where a serious discussion concerning the state of one's soul is expected."[16] Don Browning reminds us of the "system of practical moral rationality" that characterized the communities of Judaism. Although the methods of the scribes and the Pharisees were criticized and transcended by Jesus, his Church's pastoral care presupposes the tradition of moral casuistry and cannot be understood apart from it.[17] Browning's attention to the original moral context and method of pastoral care is an important contribution. But Browning does not say where pastoral care finds its normative meanings so that the Church can become the "community of moral discourse, inquiry, and action" he wants it to be. Nor does he say which values are normative or by what criteria they might be judged normative.[18]

Attention to the Sermon on the Mount will create the atmosphere for moral inquiry, but only the type of moral inquiry sanctioned by the holiness of God. Browning's analysis of the moral context of pastoral care does not rely on the primary language of the Christian symbols and thereby perpetuates the notion that the reality of God, perhaps veiled as the process of moral inquiry or the inherent goodness of community, has a legitimate functional equivalent within the Church.

Thus our quest for pastoral or congregational uses for the Sermon on the Mount leads to a fundamental conclusion. The Sermon's authority is sanctioned by the essential nature of God and is delivered by the only One capable of mediating that holiness. Jesus says repeatedly, ". . . but I say to you." When for whatever reason we cannot bring the reality, immediacy, and authority of *God* to articulation in our pastoral care, counseling, and conversation, our continued reference to the Sermon on the Mount lapses into sentimentality.

For many the word "pastoral" does suggest a situational relaxation of the Church's dogma. The "pastoral" approach is accommodating. It appears to suspend the demands of the Christian faith and to substitute for them the more widely accepted values of decency and acceptance. Indeed, this misconception of "pastoral" has obscured for many the pastoral tendencies of the Gospel of Matthew and the Sermon on the Mount. The Sermon is a pastoral care document, not in the sense that it sentimentalizes the promise and demands of the kingdom, but in the sense that it applies them in concrete situations. It presupposes an intensity of community life far removed from the anonymity, mobility, and amorphous values of what Robert Bellah and others calls "the lifestyle enclave."[19] What often passes for "tolerance" in the modern congregation is in reality excommunication through indifference. "Tolerance" cares so little for the other that it will not endure the pain of confrontation and reconciliation. The Sermon delivers a form of pastoral care many contemporary Christians would politely decline.

Yet the care is genuine. The Sermon recognizes the demands the community's members constantly place upon one another and realistically appraises the daily opportunities for failure and faithfulness in the Christian community. The Sermon wants to show that the demands of the kingdom can work even in difficult situations. It makes provisions for degrees of anger in Matthew 5:21–6; it permits an exception to the absolute prohibition of divorce (5:22) – a pastoral concession to reality easily overlooked in our society; it offers the Lord's Prayer as an alternative to the complicated demands of conventional piety.[20] The Sermon takes our humanness seriously.

The second misconception of pastoral care is that it is private care exercised by the professional minister or pastor. Matthew is not yet aware of this subtle form of clericalism. The Sermon seems strangely bereft of a pastor; yet what it offers can best be characterized as radical pastoral care, radical because it is an expression of God's holiness and because its chief actor is not a chosen professional but the people themselves. In the Sermon it is the whole organism that functions in obedience to the kingdom.

For the congregation wishing to live by the Sermon the most helpful suggestion may have less to do with the Sermon's individual features and more to do with its framework or grid for ministry. Many congregations have an extensive structure of boards and committees, ranging from the Board of Properties to the Pastor – Parish Relations Committee, but no systematic mechanism for engaging members in pastoral care or for delivering pastoral care in the congregation or the community. That is the pastor's business. Most congregations operate with a "trickle down" theory of pastoral care. Were a congregation to adopt the Sermon on the Mount's model of pastoral care based on Christians' radical responsibility for one another – as it is derived from Jesus' mediation of God's holiness – the congregation's life and ministry would change dramatically. One of the pastor's most important tasks would be the equipping of "pastors" for the care of the sick, conflict resolution, education, ethical deliberations, prayer, and evangelization. Those appointed for such work might not be the most influential or powerful members in the congregation, but those with the spiritual maturity and gifts requisite to the pastoral tasks. This view of pastoral care reflects the Sermon's rational but not legalistic framework for ministry. Pastoral care in this sense can no longer be separated from "administration," but now, instead of training Christians to be committees, the Church will train them to be pastors, those who care for their brothers and sisters in the stress and conflict of daily life.

Liturgical Life

Yet any congregation may stumble over the Sermon on the Mount precisely because it does reflect "a system of practical moral *rationality*" which seems alien to a religious culture that has grown weary of rationalism and is turning to narrative expressions of its faith and identity. We claim our identity as members of God's new congregation less by deliberating the provisions of the Sermon, especially where they are unamplified by focal instances, than by telling and retelling the community's formative stories. We do not embrace the admonition concerning the laying up of treasures (Matt. 6:19–21) as readily as its narrative expression in the parable of the Rich Fool (Luke 12:16–21). We seem to learn less about God and mammon from Matthew 5:24 than from the parable of the Shrewd Steward in Luke 16:1–13. The admonition on the forgoing of oaths in Matthew 5:24 means little to us until we see what that can look like in the story of Jesus' silence before Caiaphas (Matt. 26:57–64; cf. 27:11–14) and Peter's perjury in the courtyard (Matt. 26:69–75). The story means even more to us as we sit in the shadows of Lenten vespers, hear the passion read, and experience the futility of oath-taking in a world that is filled with lies.

How can the congregation integrate the Sermon on the Mount into the story of its own pilgrimage? That integration takes place in the liturgy. Liturgical actions themselves are often misconceived as special ceremonies which are unrelated to the rest of life. Yet baptism is not an episode of private initiation but an action involving the entire Church and one that will be recalled and renewed daily. Confession is not a formula for personal remorse but a moment in the ongoing mutual admonition and absolution of the brothers and sisters. Preaching is not a virtuoso performance but the language of the Church as it engages in the laborious reversal of Babel and the formation of a new people. Eucharist is not a postscript to preaching but the symbol and reality of the transformation of all things through the death and resurrection of Jesus. Doxology is not a hymn to be sung but a life to be lived. In the liturgy the Sermon on the Mount imparts its character to the formation of God's people. It is the lyrics to the Church's song.

In most lectionaries a substantial part of the Sermon on the Mount is read during the Epiphany season. In the Sermon on the Mount the glory of God begins to shine in the face of Jesus as he manifests the holiness and authority of the Father. That glory will move, as it were, from mountain to mountain in the Gospel of Matthew: from the Sermon on the Mount to the Mount of Transfiguration (Matt. 17) where his place above Moses is reiterated, to the Mount of Olives (Matt. 21:1; 24:3), to Golgotha, and finally to the Galilean mountain for the culmination of his epiphany (Matt. 28:16–17). In the church year the Sermon takes its place as one of a series of stations in the journey. The Church also reads Jesus' words on ostentatious piety (Matt. 6:1–6, 16–21) on Ash Wednesday and the Beatitudes on All Saints' Day, when future and realized aspects of eschatology are fused as on no other festival day.

In the Church's worship the Sermon's Lord's Prayer is a part of every service. It is the eschatological prayer of the new community, of the community now committed to live by the promise of the kingdom. Aside from this prayer, little of the Sermon has gained direct access to the liturgy. Indirectly, however, its emphasis on holiness, obedience, and sanctification is everywhere. In the Lutheran service of Holy Baptism, for example, the minister charges the parents:

> You should, therefore, faithfully bring them [the children] to the services of God's house, and teach them the Lord's Prayer, the Creed, and the Ten Commandments. As they grow in years, you should place in their hands the Holy Scriptures and provide for their instruction in the Christian faith, that, living in the covenant of their Baptism and in communion with the church, they may lead godly lives until the day of Jesus Christ.[21]

This liturgy presupposes the kind of community that was nurtured by the Sermon on the Mount. It presupposes an ordered and intense process of formation directed by those who are mature in faith, for the purpose of godly thought and behavior. Such formation is the result of God's covenant of grace which is actualized in the Church through baptism. Its end is not personal happiness or fulfillment but "the day of Jesus Christ," which is the same End for which the Sermon on the Mount was given to the Church.

There can be no fitting *conclusion* to the study of a living eschatological document. The Sermon belongs to the pilgrim Church. The Church is not the context for the Sermon but its agent. Therefore no individual has ever captured its definitive meaning, for as the expression of God's radical pastoral care, the Sermon on the Mount can only be "interpreted" as communities of Christians attempt to live it.

Notes

1 Karl Barth, *Church Dogmatics*, trans. by G. W. Bromiley (Edinburgh: T. & T. Clark, 1975), vol. I, 1, p. 4.

2 Günther Bornkamm et al., *Tradition and Interpretation in Matthew*, trans. by Percy Scott (Philadelphia: Westminster, 1963), p. 38.

3 The Matthian community's problems are outlined by W. D. Davies in *The Setting of the Sermon on the Mount* (Cambridge: Cambridge University Press, 1964), pp. 316 and passim; Jack Dean Kingsbury, *Matthew*. Proclamation Commentaries (Philadelphia: Fortress, 1977), pp. 91–3; William G. Thompson, *Matthew's Advice to a Divided Community*, *AnBib* 44, pp. 258–9; Hans Dieter Betz, *Essays on the Sermon on the Mount*, trans. by L. L. Welborn (Philadelphia: Fortress, 1985), pp. 20–2; and Bornkamm et al., ibid., p. 22.

4 Bornkamm et al., ibid., p. 27, and Joachim Jeremias, *The Sermon on the Mount*, trans.

by Norman Perrin (Philadelphia: Fortress, 1963), p. 23. The radical nature of the teaching in Q prompts Davies, ibid., p. 386, to remind us that this is not a catechism in the sense of elementary instruction.

5 James P. Martin, "The Church in Matthew," *Interpretation* 29 (1975): 41, n. On the disciples as "typical" Christians in Matthew, see Edward Schillebeeckx, *Ministry*, trans. by John Bowden (New York: Crossroad Publishing, 1981), p. 22.

6 Dietrich Bonhoeffer, *The Cost of Discipleship*, trans. by R. H. Fuller (New York: Macmillan, 1963), p. 119, n., writes: "neither privation nor renunciation, spiritual or political, is justified except by the call and promise of Jesus, who alone makes blessed those whom he calls, and who is in his person the sole ground of their beatitude."

7 Robert C. Tannehill, "The 'Focal Instance' as a Form of New Testament Speech: A Study of Matthew 5:39*b*–42," *The Journal of Religion* 50 (1970): 380.

8 Ibid., pp. 381–3. Jeremias, *The Sermon on the Mount*, p. 31, paraphrases the Sermon as follows: "And now you should know that this is what life is like when you belong to the new aeon of God." Barth, *Dogmatics*, vol. II, 2, p. 688, interprets the dictates of the Sermon on marriage, swearing, anger, etc., to be "incidental and only by way of illustration," for "it has always proved impossible to construct a picture of the Christian life from these directions." On the other hand, Robert Grant, "The Sermon on the Mount in Early Christianity," *Semeia* 12 (1978): 219, reminds us that the earliest Christians received the Sermon "literally as commands to be obeyed."

9 Davies, *Setting of the Sermon*, pp. 424–5 (emphasis removed), writes: "They may seem uneasily yoked but the conjunction to which we refer should not be unexpected because, in the Jewish hope for the future, eschatology was never divorced from the ethical, the Messianic King was to be also a teacher or interpreter of the Law: the Messiah could be like Moses."

10 Amos N. Wilder, *Eschatology and Ethics in the Teaching of Jesus* (New York: Harper and Row, 1939), pp. 47 and 57ff.

11 Richard Lischer, *A Theology of Preaching* (Nashville: Abingdon Press, 1981), p. 64. George Buttrick, "Is It the Golden Rule?" In *The Twentieth Century Pulpit*, ed. James W. Cox (Nashville: Abingdon Press, 1978), pp. 30–5, directly addresses the problem of moralism in his sermon on Matt. 7:12.

12 See Robert Bellah et al., *Habits of the Heart* (New York: Harper and Row, 1985), p. 72.

13 For a summary of the relation of biblical study and pastoral conseling see Donald Capps, *Biblical Approaches to Pastoral Counseling* (Philadelphia: Westminster, 1981), pp. 18–46.

14 See "The Church as Context," in E. Brooks Holifield, *A History of Pastoral Care in America* (Nashville: Abingdon Press, 1983), pp. 342–8.

15 E. g. William H. Willimon, *Worship as Pastoral Care* (Nashville: Abingdon Press, 1979); William B. Oglesby, Jr., *Biblical Themes for Pastoral Care* (Nashville: Abingdon Press, 1980); Thomas C. Oden, *Pastoral Theology* (San Francisco: Harper and Row, 1983); John Patton, *Pastoral Counseling, A Ministry of the Church* (Nashville: Abingdon Press, 1983); Gerald L. Borchert and Andrew D. Lester, eds, *Spiritual Dimensions of Pastoral Care* (Philadelphia: Westminster, 1985).

16 William A. Clebsch and Charles R. Jaekle, *Pastoral Care in Historical Perspective* (New York: Jason Aronson, 1964, 1983), pp. 65–6.

17 Don S. Browning, *The Moral Context of Pastoral Care* (Philadelphia: Westminster, 1976), pp. 122–5.

18 Ibid., pp. 95–100. "The minister is interested primarily in building a moral universe and facilitating right conduct in a community of persons" (p. 99).
19 Bellah et al., *Habits of the Heart*, pp. 71ff.
20 Davies, *Setting of the Sermon*, pp. 387–99, compares the pastoral qualities of M, as opposed to Q, to the Gemera or commentary on the Talmud.
21 *The Lutheran Book of Worship* (Minneapolis: Augsburg Publishing; Philadelphia: Board of Publication, Lutheran Church in America, 1978), p. 121.

Romans 9–11

Selections from Augustine's *Propositions from the Epistle to the Romans* and *To Simplician – on Various Questions*

Introduced by Peter Gorday

During the years CE 394–7 Augustine of Hippo developed his exegetical understanding of Paul's Letter to the Romans. In the emergence of Augustine's mature theology this period was critical, for it is bounded by his writing of the latter portion of the work *On Free Will* at one end and the composition of the *Confessions* at the other. Further, this is the period of his most active rebuttal of the theological claims made by the Manichaean sect. Central features of Augustine's exposition of Romans from this time have dominated the exegesis of the letter down to the present, particularly his focus on salvation as an entirely unmerited gift from God as well as the allied contention that original sin has rendered human nature impotent in obtaining salvation. Augustine's further, and later, contentions about the nature of God's inscrutable will in electing some, and not others, for salvation have been more problematic and controversial in theology as well as exegesis.

The selections printed here are portions of Augustine's exegesis of Romans 9 and, much more briefly (for he did not comment on it at length) Romans 11. Augustine brings to the text a puzzle that preoccupied the middle-platonic philosophy of the period: how could one make a convincing case for the reality of a rational, benign divine governance of the world and at the same time continue to believe in human responsibility for the outcome of historical events?

A further form of the question inquired into the compatibility of divine governance with the existence of genuine (and not just seeming) moral evil. In order to answer these questions Augustine sought for a rational principle in the actions of God, as these are evidenced in scripture, and for a way to affirm human free will in the face of the fatalism and determinism offered by his Manichaean opponents and then, somewhat later, in the face of the legalism represented in the teachings of the Donatist sect. God must be truly sovereign, human beings must be truly free, and salvation must be truly gratuitous. Augustine's challenge was to understand, with the help of the Letter to the Romans, how salvation happens for sinful human beings, why it happens in *this way* and no other, and, indeed, why it happens at all. The answers that he believed he heard to these questions took the form of the efficacious call, humankind as the "mass of damnation," and the divine equity of mercy and justice.

Augustine inherited an exegetical tradition, though there is great debate as to exactly what it was and how well he really knew it. In this tradition, where exegetes approached the text with much the same questions that troubled Augustine, certain biblical texts functioned as prime sources of difficulty. One of these was Romans 9:11–13, where God chooses, before their birth, Jacob over Esau to be the object of blessing. When the question was asked on what basis God could make such a decision, exegetes prior to Augustine appealed to the notion of foreseen merits, that God had already foreseen the meritorious deeds that Jacob would perform and was rewarding him in advance. Through such a device the rationality of God could be preserved, as well as the importance of free will, and thus just deserts, for human beings. Augustine already saw, however, as the first selection below from the *Propositions from the Epistle to the Romans* of 394 shows, that such a view contradicts Paul's contention that salvation is not God's response to human "works" (earlier Greek exegetes got round the problem by claiming that a good deed done out of reverence toward God is not a "work"). The solution, according to Augustine at this time, is to argue that it is a person's character, ultimately the faith held by that person, that merits salvation, this view being consistent with Paul's leading contention in Romans that salvation is by faith and not by works. At this point Augustine had moved to a modification of the older view, in that he still clung to the importance of divine foreknowledge in order to preserve divine rationality, but he had limited the human contribution to salvation by insisting on faith alone as that which is foreseen. As an exegete Augustine was searching for logical progression in Paul's thought, as if the Apostle's thought moved in the manner of a platonic dialogue through the interlinked internal unfolding of ideas. What distinguishes Augustine at this point is the rigor of his pursuit of the thought-train, for in the *Propositions* he noted at the end of Romans 9:11 Paul's emphasis on the "call" as the source of election, but then dropped it until returning to the text in the work *To Simplician – on Various Questions*, a portion of which is reprinted below. In this work of 396–7 he argued that the call is the key: now in no sense does God foresee something meritorious on the part of Jacob, since it is purely by virtue of a gratuitous, merciful call that he is saved. Notice, however, that even at this point where Augustine had begun to press for an interpretation in which any notion of foreseen merit is discarded he is still constrained by other texts that come to mind. His use of Matthew 22:14 allowed him to distinguish between those who are called and those who are called efficaciously, only these latter being able to receive salvation since only they are ready for the gift. In this way human free will is preserved and required for salvation, though it is not by virtue of any human "doing" that this salvation comes.

Indeed, what had happened for Augustine between the writing of the earlier work on Romans and the later composition addressed to Simplician was that he had completed his study *On Free Will*. In the latter part of this work he moved toward his understanding of inherited sin and its power over human acting. Beginning with the disobedience of Adam and Eve the human condition has been marked by a state of penal bondage to mortality, ignorance and difficulty such that the ability to overcome sin and do God's will is now impossible. Free will itself continues to exist, for human beings can still choose the good, but now they can no longer *do* it – God's help has become indispensable. In Augustine's terminology, free will still exists, but as a result of Adam's sin freedom has been lost. As a matter of the exegesis of Romans, this movement in Augustine's thought was reflected in his increased attention to the nature of human helplessness and the way this plight is portrayed in the treatment of the hardening of Pharaoh's heart in Romans 9:16– 18 and the notion of the "lump" in 9:21. In the *Propositions* Pharaoh's heart is hardened by God because he deserves to be punished after he refuses to free the Israelites, while the Israelites are saved because they are ready to hear God's call and to obey. Implied is the idea that God already finds human beings in varying states of readiness, such that the "lump" of 9:21 can refer only to those "unspiritual" persons who are obtuse to divine wisdom. By the time he set out his thought in the work addressed to Simplician he had come to different conclusions such that the plain sense of 9:16 must be honored: since it is *God's mercy* that determines salvation, and not human exertion, the contrasting destinies of Pharaoh and the Israelites must be the result of divine decision alone. By implication again Pharaoh and the Israelites are in the same boat with regard to the human condition, namely that of sinners unable to do the good. A logical conclusion follows to the effect that, since all have died in Adam, all belong to the same "lump," which now can be seen to be a "mass of damnation." When God comes to humankind in Christ, all are equal. All carping, therefore, against God for having chosen only some for salvation must give way to the recognition that the condemnation of all is perfectly just, while the salvation of even a portion of the race is due completely to unmerited divine mercy. In a different kind of a way from the logic of foreseen merits God is now seen to be rational: it is the balance of justice and mercy in divine action that makes sense of things, though the choice of *this particular* person rather than another will always be inscrutable.

Having brought, then, certain questions to the text of Romans, Augustine gradually worked out answers that satisfied his need to construe the text as a logically compelling, tightly knit argument. That he took some of his insights from various sources, such as the earlier Roman exegete called in later tradition "Ambrosiaster" or the Donatist writer Tyconius (particularly this latter in this typological method of relating Old Testament to New Testament), seems certain. Probably, however, it was the very tendency of the Pauline text to push him towards an increasingly refined historical perspective that was decisive. The more he studied Paul, the less able he was to use imported notions like that of foreseen merits as a way of getting around difficulties. He came to see that the Letter to the Romans depends for its coherence on some sense that the human condition and God's action with regard to that condition are the result of an unfolding in which contingencies are central. In other words, there is an interplay, a drama of becoming with its twists and turns, such that God's eternal purposes really do come to pass, but only in a way that is responsive to the limitations and shortcomings of human nature. This perspective is suggested in the final section of the *Propositions* printed below, where Augustine in commenting on Romans 11:11 tried to incorporate the Jewish rejection of the gospel into this unfolding of salvation: he does this in his own way, namely by claiming that the fall of the Jews can serve as a lesson in humility for the Gentiles. What Augustine did not see, something perceived more clearly by Origen before him, was that the Jewish refusal of faith in Christ would remain a counterpoint to the Church, a kind of loyal opposition within the same household, so that the history of salvation can move forward to that time when "all Israel will be saved" (Rom. 11:25). Augustine's success, therefore, is that he moved the interpretation of Romans 9–11 in the direction of a real salvation-history. His failure, from a modern perspective, is that he was not historical enough.

The following is the translation found in *Augustine on Romans: Propositions from the Epistle to the Romans, Unfinished Commentary on the Epistle to the Romans*, trans. Paula Fredriksen Landes, Society of Biblical Literature Texts and Translations 23, Early Christian Literature Series 6 (Chico, CA: Scholars Press, 1982) and *To Simplician – On Various Questions* in *Augustine's Earlier Writings*, trans. J. Burleigh (Philadelphia: Westminster Press, 1953).

Augustine, Propositions from the Epistle to the Romans, 60–62 and 80

60 "For when they were not yet born, nor had they done anything either good or evil, in order that the purpose of God's election might continue, not because of works but because of his call, she was told, 'the elder will serve the younger,' as it is written, 'Jacob I loved, but Esau I hated' " (9:11–13). (2) This moves some people to think that the apostle Paul had done away with the freedom of the will, by which we earn the esteem of God by the great good of piety, or offend him by the evil of impiety. (3) For, these people say, God loved the one and hated the other before either was even born and could have done either good or evil. (4) But we answer that God did this by foreknowledge, by which he knows the character even of the unborn. But no one should say, "Therefore God chose the works of the man he loved, although these works did not exist, because he foreknew what they would be." If God elected works, why does the Apostle say that election is not according to works? (5) For this very reason, then, one should understand that we are able to do good works through love, and we have love through the gift of the Holy Spirit, as the Apostle himself says: (6) "For the love of God has been poured into our hearts by the Holy Spirit, which has been given to us" (5:5). Therefore no one should glory in his works as though they were his own, for he does them by the gift of God, since this love itself works good in him. (7) What then has God elected? For if he gives the Holy Spirit, through whom love works good, to whomever he wishes, how does he choose the Spirit's recipient? (8) If he does not choose according to merit, it is not election, for all are equal prior to merit, and no choice can be made between absolutely equal things. (9) But since he gives the Holy Spirit only to believers, God indeed does not choose works, which he himself bestows, for he gives the Spirit freely so that through love we might do good, but rather he chooses faith. (10) For unless each one believes in him and perseveres in his willingness to receive, he does not receive the gift of God, that is, the Holy Spirit, whose pouring forth of love enables him to do good. (11) Therefore God did not elect anyone's works (which God himself will grant) by foreknowledge, but rather by foreknowledge he chose faith, so that he chooses precisely him whom he foreknew would believe in him; and to him he gives the Holy Spirit, so that by doing good works he will as well attain eternal life. (12) For the same Apostle says: "It is the same God who *works* all things in all" (1 Cor. 12:6). Nowhere is it said, "God *believes* all things to all" (cf. 1 Cor. 13:7). Belief is our work, but good deeds are his who gives the Holy Spirit to believers. (13)

This argument was used against certain Jews who, once they believed in Christ, both gloried in the works they did before receiving grace and claimed that they had merited this same grace of the Gospel by their own previous good works, though only the person who has already received grace can do good works. (14) Moreover, the nature of grace is such that the call precedes merit, reaching the sinner when he had deserved only damnation. (15) But if he follows God's call of his own free will, he will merit also the Holy Spirit, through whom he can do good works. And remaining in the Spirit – no less also by free will – he will also merit life eternal, which cannot be marred by any flaw.

61 "I will have mercy on whom I will have had mercy, and I will show him compassion on whom I will have had compassion" (9:11–15).[1] Here Paul shows that there is no iniquity with God, as certain people can say when they hear "Before they were born, Jacob I loved, but Esau I hated." (2) "I will have mercy," he says, "on whom I will have had mercy." God was merciful to us the first time when he called us while we were still sinners. (3) "On whom I will have had mercy," he says, "so that I called him," and *still* "I will have mercy on him" yet again once the man has believed. Yet how does God have mercy this second time? He gives to the believing seeker the Holy Spirit. (4) Now, having given the Spirit, God will then give compassion to those to whom he has already been compassionate. That is, he will make the believer compassionate, so that he can do good works through love. (5) Hence let no one dare to credit himself when he acts compassionately, since God gave him this love through the Holy Spirit, without which no one can be compassionate. (6) Therefore God did not elect those doing good works, but those who believed, with the result that he enabled them to do good works. (7) It is we who believe and will, but he who gives to those believing and willing the ability to do good works through the Holy Spirit, through which the love of God is poured forth in our hearts, thus making us compassionate.

62 "Therefore it depends not on man's willing or running, but on God's mercy" (9:15). Paul does not take away the freedom of the will, but says our will does not suffice unless God helps us, making us merciful so that we can do good works through the gift of the Holy Spirit, as he had just said above, (2) "I will have mercy on whom I will have had mercy, and I will show him compassion on whom I will have had compassion." (3) For neither can we will unless we are called, nor after our calling, once we have willed, is our will and our running sufficient unless God both gives strength to our running and leads where he calls. (4) Therefore, clearly, we do good deeds not by our own willing or running but by the mercy of God, although our will (which alone can do nothing) is also present. (5) And this relates to Pharaoh's punishment, where Scripture says: "I have raised you up for this purpose, to show my power in you, so that my name might be proclaimed in all the earth" (9:17). And thus we read in Exodus that (6) Pharaoh's heart was hardened, so that he remained unmoved even by clear signs (cf. Exod. 10:1). Thus Pharaoh's disobedience to God's commands came as a punishment. (7) And no one can say that this hardness of heart befell Pharaoh undeservedly: it was the penalty of the just judgment of God punishing his unbelief. (8) Nor should one think that Pharaoh did not obey because he could not because his heart had been hardened. Rather, he had merited his hardness of heart by his prior infidelity. (9) For as with the chosen (not works but faith initiating merit so that through the gift of God they do good), so with the condemned: infidelity and impiety initiate their meriting their penalty. Thus because of the punishment itself they do evil, as the same Apostle says above: (10) "And since they did not see fit to acknowledge God, God handed-them over to a base mind so that they did unseemly things" (1:28). (11) Wherefore the Apostle concludes: "Therefore he has mercy on whom he will and hardens whom he will" (9:18). (12) On whom he has mercy, he causes him to do good, and whom he hardens, he leaves to doing evil. But that mercy was given to the preceding merit of faith, and that hardening to preceding impiety, (13) so that we work both good deeds through the gift of God and evil through his chastisement. Nevertheless, man's free will remains, whether for belief in God so that mercy follows, or for impiety followed by punishment. (14) Having delivered this conclusion, Paul introduces a question as if from an opponent: "You say to me, 'Why does he even now find fault? For who resists his will?' " (9:19). (15) He responds to this question sensibly, so that we might understand that only to spiritual and not to earthly men are these difficult issues made clear, issues like the first merits of faith and impiety, the way God in his foreknowledge elects those who will believe and condemns the unbelieving, (16) neither electing nor condemning because of works, but granting to the faith of the one group the ability to do good works, and hardening the impiety of the other by deserting them, so that they do evil. (17) This understanding, as I have said, is given only to spiritual men and is far removed from the wisdom of the flesh. And thus Paul refutes his interlocutor, that he might understand that one should first put away the man of clay in order to deserve to investigate these things by the spirit. (18) And so Paul says, "Who are you, O man, to answer back to God? Does that which is molded say to its molder, 'Why have you made me thus?' Does the potter not have power over the clay, to make out of the same lump a vessel for honor, and another for shame?" (9:20–1). (19) As long as you are a molded thing, says Paul, and you are like this lump of clay, not yet led to spiritual things so that as a spiritual being you might judge all things and be judged by no one, it behooves you to restrain yourself from this sort of inquiry and not to answer back to God. (20) For, appropriately, every one desiring to know God's counsel should first be received into his friendship, a possibility only for spiritual men already bearing the image of the heavenly man. For "then," says the Lord, "I will call you not servants but friends. For everything that I have heard from my father I have made known to you" (John 15:15). (21) For as long as you are a potter's vessel, you must first be broken by that iron rod of which it was said: (22) "You will govern them with an iron rod, and you will break them as if they were a potter's vessel" (Ps. 2:9). Then, with the outer man destroyed and the inner man renewed, you might be able, rooted and established in love, to understand the length and breadth and height and depth, to know even the overpowering knowledge of the love of God (Eph. 3:18). (23) So now since from the same lump of clay God has made some vessels for honorable use and some for dishonorable, it is not for you to discuss, whoever you are who still lives according to this lump, that is, who is wise by earthly senses and fleshly wisdom.

70   "So I say, have they sinned so as to fall? By no means! But by their trespass salvation has come to the Gentiles" (11:11). Paul does not say that the Jews have not fallen, but that their fall was not in vain, since it profited the Gentiles by salvation. (2) Thus they did not sin so as to fall, that is, only to fall as a punishment, but so that this fall itself would be profitable to the Gentiles for salvation. (3) Thereafter he even begins to praise the Jewish people for this fall of unfaithfulness, so that the Gentiles might not be proud, since this fall of the Jews was so precious for their salvation. Rather, the Gentiles ought to take heed all the more lest, when they grow proud, they likewise fall.

Augustine, To Simplician – on Various Questions Book I, ii, 7, 10, 13, 15–16

7   But the question is whether faith merits a man's justification, whether the merits of faith do not precede the mercy of God; or whether, in fact, faith itself is to be numbered among the gifts of grace. Notice that in this passage when he said, "Not of works," he did not say, "but of faith it was said to her, The elder shall serve the younger." No, he said, "but of him that calleth." No one believes who is not called. God calls in his mercy,

and not as rewarding the merits of faith. The merits of faith follow his calling rather than precede it. "How shall they believe whom they have not heard? And how shall they hear without a preacher?" (Rom. 10:14). Unless, therefore, the mercy of God in calling precedes, no one can even believe, and so begin to be justified and to receive power to do good works. So grace comes before all merits. Christ died for the ungodly. The younger received the promise that the elder should serve him from him that calleth and not from any meritorious works of his own. So the Scripture "Jacob have I loved" is true, but it was of God who called and not of Jacob's righteous works.

10 This is all right, but why was this mercy withheld from Esau, so that he was not called and had not faith inspired in him when called, and was not by faith made compassionate so that he might do good works? Was it because he was unwilling? If Jacob had faith because he willed it, then God did not give him faith as a free gift, but Jacob gave it to himself, and so had something which he did not receive. Or can no one believe unless he wills, or will unless he is called, and can no one be called unless God by calling him also gives him faith? For no one can believe unless he is called, although none can believe against his will. "How shall they believe whom they have not heard? And how shall they hear without a preacher?" No one, therefore, believes who has not been called, but not all believe who have been called. "For many are called but few are chosen" (Matt. 22:14). The chosen are those who have not despised him who calls, but have believed and followed him. There is no doubt that they believed willingly. What then of what follows? "So then it is not of him that willeth, nor of him that runneth, but of God that hath mercy." Does it mean that we cannot even will unless we are called, and that our willing is of no avail unless God give us aid to perform it? We must both will and run. It would not be said in vain, "On earth peace to men of good will" (Luke 2:14). And, "Even so run that ye may attain" (1 Cor. 9:24). But it is not of him that willeth, nor of him that runneth, but of God that hath mercy, that we obtain what we wish and reach what we desire. Esau, then, was unwilling and did not run. Had he been willing and had he run, he would have obtained the help of God who by calling him would have given him the power both to will and to run, had he not been reprobate by despising the calling. There are two different things that God gives us, the power to will and the thing that we actually will. The power to will he has willed should be both his and ours, his because he calls us, ours because we follow when called. But what we actually will he alone gives, i.e., the power to do right and to live happily for ever. But Esau was not yet born and consequently could

be neither willing nor unwilling in all these matters. Why was he rejected when he was still in the womb? We come back to that difficulty, troubled not only by the obscurity of the question but also by our own abundant repetition.

13   But if that calling is the effectual cause of the good will so that every one who is called follows it, how will it be true that "Many are called but few are chosen"? If this is true, and consequently not everyone who is called obeys the call, but has it in the power of his will not to obey, it could be said correctly that it is not of God who hath mercy, but of the man who willeth and runneth, for the mercy of him that calleth is not sufficient unless the obedience of him who is called follows. Possibly those who are called in this way, and do not consent, might be able to direct their wills towards faith if they were called in another way; so that it would be true that "Many are called but few are chosen." Many, that is to say, are called in one way, but all are not affected in the same way; and those only follow the calling who are found fit to receive it. It would be no less true that "it is not of him that willeth, nor of him that runneth, but of God that hath mercy." For God calls in a way that is suited to those who follow his calling. The call comes also to others; but because it is such that they cannot be moved by it and are not fitted to receive it, they can be said to be called but not chosen. And again it would not be true that it is not of God who hath mercy but of man who willeth and runneth. For the effectiveness of God's mercy cannot be in the power of man to frustrate, if he will have none of it. If God wills to have mercy on men, he will call them in a way that is suited to them, so that they will be moved to understand and to follow. It is true, therefore, that many are called but few chosen. Those are chosen who are effectually [*congruenter*] called. Those who are not effectually called and do not obey their calling are not chosen, for although they were called they did not follow. Again it is true that "it is not of him that willeth, nor of him that runneth, but of God that hath mercy." For, although he calls many, he has mercy on those whom he calls in a way suited to them so that they may follow. But it is false to say that "it is not of God who hath mercy but of man who willeth and runneth," because God has mercy on no man in vain. He calls the man on whom he has mercy in the way that he knows will suit him, so that he will not refuse the call.

15   But why do we ask such a question? The apostle himself goes on, "The Scripture saith unto Pharaoh, For this very purpose did I raise thee up, that I might show in thee my power, and that my name might be published abroad in all the earth." The apostle adds this as an example

to prove what he had said above, that "it is not of him that willeth, nor of him that runneth, but of God that hath mercy." As if some one had said to him, What is the source of this doctrine of yours? His reply is "The Scripture saith unto Pharaoh" etc. Thus he shows that it is not of him that willeth but of God that hath mercy. And he concludes with these words: "So then he hath mercy on whom he will, and whom he will he hardeneth." Earlier he had not stated both of these truths. He said: "It is not of him that willeth, nor of him that runneth, but of God that hath mercy"; but he did not say "It is not of him that is unwilling, nor of him that contemneth, but of God who causeth the hardening of the heart." So by putting both sides – he hath mercy on whom he will hath mercy, and whom he will he hardeneth – we are given to understand that the new statement agrees with the former one, viz., the hardening which God causes is an unwillingness to be merciful. We must not think that anything is imposed by God whereby a man is made worse, but only that he provides nothing whereby a man is made better. But if there be no distinction of merits who would not break out into the objection which the apostle brings against himself? "Thou wilt say then unto me, Why doth he still find fault? For who withstandeth his will?" God often finds fault with men because they will not believe and live righteously, as is apparent from many passages of Scripture. Hence faithful people who do the will of God are said to walk blamelessly, because Scripture finds no fault with them. But he says, "Why does he find fault? Who withstandeth his will" though "he hath mercy on whom he will and whom he will he hardeneth." Let us look at what was said above and let it direct our interpretation as the Lord himself gives us aid.

16   The apostle said a little before, "What shall we say, then? Is there unrighteousness with God? God forbid." Let this truth, then, be fixed and unmovable in a mind soberly pious and stable in faith, that there is no unrighteousness with God. Let us also believe most firmly and tenaciously that God has mercy on whom he will and that whom he will he hardeneth, that is, he has or has not mercy on whom he will. Let us believe that this belongs to a certain hidden equity that cannot be searched out by any human standard of measurement, though its effects are to be observed in human affairs and earthly arrangements. Unless we had stamped upon these human affairs certain traces of supernal justice our weak minds would never look up to or long for the holy and pure ground and source of spiritual precepts. "Blessed are they who hunger and thirst after righteousness, for they shall be filled." In the drought of our mortal condition in this life it would be a case of being burnt up rather than of merely thirsting, did not some gentle breath of justice from on high scatter

showers upon us. Human society is knit together by transactions of giving and receiving, and things are given and received sometimes as debts, sometimes not. No one can be charged with unrighteousness who exacts what is owing to him. Nor certainly can he be charged with unrighteousness who is prepared to give up what is owing to him. This decision does not lie with those who are debtors but with the creditor. This image or, as I said, trace of equity is stamped on the business transactions of men by the Supreme Equity. Now all men are a mass of sin, since, as the apostle says, "In Adam all die" (1 Cor. 15:22), and to Adam the entire human race traces the origin of its sin against God. Sinful humanity must pay a debt of punishment to the supreme divine justice. Whether that debt is exacted or remitted there is no unrighteousness. It would be a mark of pride if the debtors claimed to decide to whom the debt should be remitted and from whom it should be exacted; just as those who were hired to work in the vineyard were unjustly indignant when as much was given to the others as was duly paid to themselves (Matt. 20:11ff). So the apostle represses the impudent questioner. "O man, who art thou that repliest against God?" A man so speaks back to God when he is displeased that God finds fault with sinners, as if God compelled any man to sin when he simply does not bestow his justifying mercy on some sinners, and for that reason is said to harden some sinners; not because he drives them to sin but because he does not have mercy upon them. He decides who are not to be offered mercy by a standard of equity which is most secret and far removed from human powers of understanding. "Inscrutable are his judgments, and his ways past finding out" (Rom. 11:33). He justly finds fault with sinners because he does not compel them to sin. Justly also he has mercy on some that they may have this calling, to be heartily penitent when God finds fault with sinners, and to turn to his grace. He finds fault, therefore, both justly and mercifully.

Note

1 Augustine's exegesis demands strict attention to Latin sequence of tenses.

Further Reading

Brown, Peter. *Augustine of Hippo*. Los Angeles and Berkeley: University of California Press, 1967. Especially ch. 15, "The Lost Future."

Gorday, Peter J. *Principles of Patristic Exegesis: Romans 9–11 in Origen, John Chrysostom and Augustine*. New York and Toronto: Edwin Mellen Press, 1983. Chapter on Augustine. For the larger exegetical perspective within Augustine's treatment of Romans and within earlier patristic exegesis of Romans.

Landes, Paula Fredriksen. *Augustine on Romans: Propositions from the Epistle to the Romans, Unfinished Commentary on the Epistle to the Romans*. Text and Translation by Paula Fredriksen Landes. Society of Biblical Literature Texts and Translations 23, Early Christian Literature Series 6. Chico, CA: Scholars Press, 1982. For general introduction.

TeSelle, Eugene. *Augustine the Theologian*. New York: Herder and Herder, 1970. Especially ch. 3: "On Sin and Grace." For theological context and perspective.

Selections from Thomas Aquinas's *Commentary on Romans*

Translated and introduced by Eugene F. Rogers, Jr.

A Theologian of the Bible

Thomas Aquinas, the most influential theologian of the Middle Ages, was born in 1224 in Aquino, Italy, now Roccasecca, between Rome and Naples. At the age of 18 or so, he joined a new order of mendicant friars, the Dominicans, or Order of Preachers. (Its founder, Dominic, had been dead for only some twenty years.) His family seems to have regarded the order, for its newness, fervor, and eschewal of worldly goods, in the way some modern Americans might regard an evangelical cult; in 1244 they imprisoned him in their own castle until early 1246. The Dominicans devoted themselves to a revival of the gospel by preaching; hence "the Order of Preachers." Throughout his life Thomas devoted himself to the Bible. His title at the University of Paris, where he taught from 1256 to 1259 and again from 1269 to 1272, was *magister in sacris paginis*, master of the sacred pages, or professor of Bible. He never lectured on theology, but on Job, Psalms, Lamentations, Isaiah, Matthew, John, Romans, 1 and 2 Corinthians, Galatians, Ephesians, Philippians, Colossians, 1 and 2 Thessalonians, 1 and 2 Timothy, Titus, Philemon, and Hebrews. In the selection that follows, Thomas regularly offers a veritable catena of biblical verses in support of his interpretations. In the beginning of the selection, ellipses mark places where many of those quotations have been omitted, but toward the end they have been left in.

Thomas's special calling as a Dominican was to integrate the newly ascendent philosophy of Aristotle into biblical Christian thought. He had encountered it at the secular University of Naples in 1239; he become the greatest pupil of the

320

Aristotelian master Albertus Magnus at Cologne around 1246; in maturity he had some of Aristotle's works translated directly from Greek into Latin (rather than through Arabic). Thomas became the foremost Aristotle scholar of his age. Besides the books of the Bible, he also commented on most of the books of Aristotle. Ironically, it is as an Aristotelian philosopher that Thomas is perhaps best known. His Aristotelian-inspired Five Ways, or arguments in support of the proposition "God exists," are his most frequently studied passage – without much consciousness, if any, that Thomas is turning the proofs to a theological · purpose, illustrating that the Apostle Paul is correct to say that "the things of God are known from the things God has made" (*Summa Theologiae*, I.2.2) and that the existence of God is proved first of all from God's own say-so, "I am" (*ST*, I.2.3.). In the Romans commentary, where the first of those warrants is at home, Thomas causes the knowledge of God from the things that are made to be part and parcel of a narrative in which "salvation is from the Jews."[1] Contrary to popular belief, Thomas sees that proofs for the existence of God do not serve, in the context of God's history with the Jews, to praise human knowledge, but to increase Gentile guilt – so that God might have mercy upon all. In the passages presented here we see how Thomas follows Paul to derive salvation from God's history with the Jews for both Jews and Gentiles, with certain complications of the plot.

Although Thomas's best-known works, the *Summa contra Gentiles* and the *Summa Theologiae*, are admired for their clear and comprehensive character, for their use of Aristotle and their intellectual rigor, it is not often noted how those works fit into Thomas's vocation to promote the Bible. The systematic works consist of thousands of disputed questions on which Thomas presents arguments from both sides, supplies his own resolution, and answers the opposing views. To naive readers they look like philosophical disputes. In fact, however, *they arise from commentary on scripture*. They simply place in thematic order the disputes that arise from rival traditions of interpreting the texts on which Thomas lectures. Alasdair MacIntyre puts it this way:

> In the reading of texts there is a movement both towards apprehending what the text says and towards apprehending that of which the text speaks. Because obscurities, discrepancies, and inconsistencies were found both within and between texts obstacles to those movements were identified. So the development of a tradition of commentary and interpretation was required, a tradition which took as its models the commentaries on scripture of Augustine and Jerome.
>
> Within that tradition there were elaborated large agreements in interpretation, so that the onus placed upon dissenting interpretations became progressively more difficult to discharge. But there developed also against this background of agreement a set of more or less systematically disputed and debated issues in which problems of perhaps apparent, perhaps real disagreement within the texts commented upon were multiplied by problems of real disagreement between rival

commentators and interpreters. So certain issues emerged as *quaestiones*, the formulation and discussion of which became in time incorporated into the methods of formal teaching, supplementing exegetical exposition by affording opportunity for what became increasingly stylized forms of disputation.[2]

Some of the same disputed questions arise *ad hoc* in the passage presented here. Thomas will introduce a plausible rival view with the word *videtur*, "it would seem," cite a counter-authority with the phrase *sed contra*, "on the other hand," and resolve the dispute with the phrase *dicendum quod*, "it must be said that . . ." (for example, #844 and ##924–6).

It was in the midst of work on the *Summa Theologiae* that Thomas himself lectured on Romans for the second and last time, whence we have our text. He died in 1274 at the age of only 49, having written so many thousands of pages that rumors circulated claiming he could dictate to three secretaries at a time. His biblical Aristotelianism proved such a shock for his contemporaries that in 1277 some propositions from his works were condemned at Oxford. But by 1323 his fortunes had turned and he was beatified. At the Council of Trent his *Summa* lay on the altar next to the Bible it interpreted, and in 1879 the encyclical *Aeterni Patris* of Pope Leo XIII made him the chief witness to Catholic teaching.

A Theologian of Election

The prologue to Thomas's commentary on Paul's epistles begins not as a modern commentary might – with a discussion of hermeneutics – but with a discussion of election. The commentary is radically theological from its opening words. Thomas introduces Paul not as a particular sort of thinker whom readers ought therefore to understand and interpret in a certain way – Thomas introduces Paul as God's chosen instrument, "a vessel of election" (Acts 9:15, in *Prologus* to Paul's epistles ##1–14). In that description God's eternal predestination and Paul's this-worldly vocation become two sides of the same coin. Paul was elected "to carry the name of Christ" (#3), among other ways in letters. The subject of *all* of Paul's teaching, according to Thomas, is "the grace of Christ" (#11). And the subject of Romans in particular is the grace of Christ not as in Christ or in the Church, but as such (*secundum se*, #11).

In the commentary on 1:16b, which according to Thomas's plan sets up the entire theological exposition of the letter, he makes a threefold programmatic statement: "the power of gospel grace [*evangelicae gratiae*] is for the salvation of all human beings . . . is necessary for their salvation . . . is effective or sufficient" (at 1:18, #109). The phrase "gospel grace" is very important. It indicates first of all that the nature-grace way of dividing up theology, characteristic of later Catholic theology, and of most accounts of Thomas himself, and the law-gospel way of doing theology, characteristic of Protestant thought, especially Luther, have yet to come apart.[3] Second, and more important for this purpose, it shortly introduces the notion of God's plan for human beings, and and that part of God's history with them covered by the epistle to the Romans. Thomas defines "Gospel" as "good news" *(bona annuntiatio)*, and it is good news of something quite specific: friendship with God as the human good: "For in [the gospel] is announced the joining [coniunctio], joining, especially in friendship or marriage] of the human being to God, which is the good of the human being" (#23). The joining is at once the joining of divine and human natures in Christ (the incarnation), and more important for the present purpose, the joining together in a divine-human polity or community *(communitas)*, which is the human end, variously described as friendship *(amicitia)* with God, the "republic" *(res publica)* or "homeland" *(patria)* with God that human beings will enjoy in heaven. Aquinas's varied metaphors for corporate community with God (to which "city of God," "kingdom," and "Jerusalem" should be added) are important because they are foreshadowed in that community with God that the nation of Israel has and into which the Gentiles are incorporated. So in the passages to follow "Gentileness," as opposed to Jewishness, depends precisely on lacking corporate community with God (#851).

Such remarks provide an avenue into evaluating Thomas's attitude toward Jews contemporary with him.

Thomas lived in a time just before persecution of many minority groups in Europe would increase, including gypsies, lepers, gay people, and Jews.[4] It is a matter of dispute how much influence Thomas had in exacerbating or moderating that trend.[5] Although the Romans commentary has until lately been rarely cited because not yet translated, it offers Thomas's most sustained reflection on the theological relation of Jews and Gentiles.[6]

Consider a threefold distinction in the way God relates to human beings, implicit in Christian thought generally (for example in the Creeds) and in Thomas (under the rubrics of nature, grace, and glory). God relates to human beings as Creator, Redeemer, and Consummator. (These relationships are not the same as the persons of the Trinity, since all three persons create, redeem, and consummate.) Redemption is defined by its starting point: it is *from* sin. Consummation is defined by its ending point: it is *for* friendship or community with God. Redemption is a remedy, but consummation is a goal. The Hebrew Bible may be read in terms of either theme. In terms of the order of consummation, it supplies God's promises of good things for a community – land, descendants, a polity (whether of patriarchs, judges, or kings), and a place for God to live among God's people (ark, tabernacle, temple). Israel anticipates the community with God that the blessed will enjoy when God consummates their desire.[7] When Aquinas concerns himself with the form of community with

God, he is working in the order of consummation. The good news of the gospel, as we have seen, is of a joining of God with human beings, not only in the incarnation, but also in community. And at 10:19, commenting on Paul's question, "Did not Israel know God," Thomas actually defines "Gentileness" as a lack of peoplehood, or of true polity, since they lack the community with God enjoyed by Israel (#851). In the order of consummation, the God-ordered community enjoyed by Israel is something Gentiles are saved *for*. When consummation is the main plot and redemption the subplot, the constancy of God's promises to Abraham predominates in the evaluation of contemporary Jews.

When redemption is the main plot and consummation the subplot, on the other hand, the accusations of the prophets against Israel predominate. And in the order of redemption, Christian thinkers, including Thomas, have even sometimes seemed or tended to identify contemporary Jews with the God-alienated sinfulness recorded by the prophets, and render God's history with Israel, rather than sin, as something Christians are saved *from*.[8] Thomas follows Paul, and a long tradition of Christian commentators, to call the Jews "enemies of Christ" (11:28a, #922). The phrase "killers of Christ" does not appear in this commentary,[9] and the "enemies of Christ" trope gets taken back as soon as it is applied (11:28b–29, ##923–7). The root trouble, for Thomas, remains: that the covenant with Abraham and the promises to Israel, while they establish a community with God that the Gentiles lack, nevertheless fail to procure the forgiveness of sins (11:27, #920, quoting Heb. 10:4) that Christian Gentiles now possess. The order of consummation is positive but not remedial. Thus a resource and a puzzle: the covenant with Abraham does not take away sins, yet it is a guarantee of election (##923, 927).

Although Paul requires him to make sense of the phrase "enemies of Christ," his attention to the order of consummation allows Thomas to erect a logical roadblock against many of the bad consequences of that description. (The effectiveness of the roadblock is another question.) Thus the current existence of the Jews is God-willed (#916), and violence against Jews is specifically ruled out (#919). Indeed, attempts to convert Jews before the end of the world anticipate God's plan and will prove largely futile (#919). For then " 'all Israel will be saved,' not individually, as now, but all universally" (11:26, #916).

The Vulgate of Romans 11:29, "The gifts and the calling of God are without penitence," provides Thomas with a special opportunity to elevate the order of consummation over the order of redemption in the case of the Jews. The Latin introduces a fruitful ambiguity into the predicate of that verse. Thomas interprets *"sine poenitentia"* to mean either without penitence (on the part of the Jews) or without regret (on the part of God). In English it is God's promises that are "irrevocable." But in Latin, it is not only God's promises that are irrevocable, since God makes them "without regret," but their fulfillment requires specifically and textually *no repentance on the part of the Jews* (#927). Not only, therefore, are Christians not to expect or require repentance from the Jews, but as Gentiles most Christians are also to recognize a signal difference between themselves and the Jews, namely that God requires repentance to accompany the participation of Gentiles in the salvation in Christ, but Jews participate in the salvation in Christ in a more mysterious way, both already and not yet.[10]

For under conditions of sin, the promise of salvation gets separated from its cause. Bruce Marshall describes it this way: the separation "does imply a distinction between what visibly guarantees Jewish election (descent from Abraham) and what ultimately and mysteriously causes it (Jesus' death and resurrection); for most Jews, Paul seems to say, there is at this point a divinely willed disharmony between the order of knowing and the order of being which will only be overcome at the end of time (cf. Rom. 11:25–27)."[11]

The passage that follows opens as Thomas is still struggling with that divinely willed disharmony, and he comes to his most articulate statement near its end, when he finds the sacraments of penance and baptism unnecessary for Jews. At the eschaton, consummation will overwhelm redemption.

Paragraphing numbering, and scriptural citations follow *Super Epistolas S. Pauli lectura*, 8th edn, revised by Raphael Cai (Turin and Rome: Marietti, 1953).

The Commentary

Chapter 9, lectio II, v. 9:13

763. It is furthermore to be considered in these words of the Apostle [about God's love], that he posits in God three things pertaining to the saints [love, choice, and predestination] . . . which are indeed really the same in God, but differ according to their rationale [that is, as human beings understand them]. For the love [*dilectio*] of God itself is defined as God's wishing good for someone absolutely; whereas *election* [*electio*, or choice] is defined as God's bringing forward or exposing someone over another by the good that God wishes for that one; while *predestination* is defined as God's *leading* [*dirigit*] a human being into that good which God wishes for him or her, by loving and electing. And therefore according to its rationale predestination follows love, as also the will for some end naturally precedes leading people toward that end.

Choice and love, furthermore, are ordered differently in God from in the human being. In the human being choice precedes love, for the will of a human being is moved to loving by the good that he or she perceives in the thing loved, for reason of which good he or she pre-elects or pre-chooses that thing over another and invests his or her love in the pre-elected thing. But the will of God is the cause of all good that is in a created thing, and therefore the good by which one creature is set before another by way of election is a consequence of the will of God for the good of that one, and that pertains to the rationale of love. Thus it is not that God loves human beings for the sake of anything good that God chooses in them, but rather that God loves them, setting them before others by electing [to some end].

Chapter 9, lectio V, v. 9:24

796. After the Apostle shows that the grace of God is given to human beings out of the divine election, through which human beings are called to grace [the household of God], here he shows that that election or vocation [note equivalence: election is not something otherworldly and vocation something this-worldly, but they are two aspects of God's one design] pertains not only to the Jews . . . but also to the nations [*Gentes*].

Chapter 10, lectio I, v. 10:1

813. After the Apostle shows how, through the election of the grace of God the Gentiles have been called to faith and also some from among the Jews – the greater part of the people of the Jews having been offended and scandalized – here he treats specially of the stumbling of the Jews.

And about that he makes three points.

First he displays the cause of their stumbling, which he had covered above, from which their stumbling is shown to be deserving of compassion [*miserandus*].

Second he shows that their stumbling is not universal, where he says in chapter II, "I say therefore, By no means!"

Third he shows that their slip is neither without benefit [*inutile*] nor unable to be made good [*irreparabile*], where he says "I say therefore, By no means!"

825. Nor is it unfitting if what Moses said about the command of the law, the Apostle attributes to Christ: for Christ is the Word of God, in which are all the commands of God.

829. When Paul says "the Lord Jesus," it refers to the incarnation. And when "Christ" follows, it clearly refers to the resurrection.

Lectio II

837. Now there is a twofold hearing: one is internal, by which someone

hearkens to the revealing God . . . whereas the other sort of hearing is that by which someone hears a human being speaking externally. . . . Now the first hearing does not pertain generally to all, but pertains properly to the grace of prophecy, which is a freely given charism [*gratia gratis data*]. . . . For external hearing is a certain experience in the hearer, which cannot be without the action of a speaker. Whence even the Lord commanded the disciples, according to the end of Matthew [28:19]: "Go into the whole world, preach the gospel to every creature."

But preachers do not have those things that are of faith from themselves, but from God. . . . And therefore the Apostle . . . adds "But how could they have been preaching, if they had not been sent?" as if he should have said it unworthily. Jer. 23:21: "I did not send [the prophets], but they ran."

838.   Now people are sent by God in two ways.

In one way immediately by God through internal inspiration . . .

In another way people are sent by God through the mediating authority of prelates, who act in God's place . . .

844.   Then when he says "Therefore faith comes by hearing," and so on, he infers the conclusion from the foregoing, saying: Since people do not believe unless they have heard, faith comes by hearing. Ps. 17:45 [18:44]: "As soon as their ear heard of me they obeyed me."

But on the other hand it seems to be that faith is a virtue divinely infused. Phil. 1:29: "It has been granted to you that you should believe in him."

It is therefore to be said that for faith two things are required: of which one is the inclination of the heart toward believing, and that is not by hearing, but by the gift of grace; whereas the other is the determination of things to be believed, and that is by hearing. And therefore Cornelius, who had a heart inclined toward believing, needed for Peter to be sent to him, who determined for him what was to be believed.

From this therefore what Paul had said [v. 14]: "How are they to hear without a preacher? And how can they preach, unless they are sent," he concludes "For hearing," namely of believers, is "through the word" of preachers, which is "the word of Christ," either because it is about Christ,

1 Cor. 1:23: "We preach Christ Jesus," or because it is by Christ that they have what they have been sent 1 Cor. 11:23: "For what I received from the Lord I delivered also to you."

[At 10:19, Paul quotes Deot 32:21, "I will lead you into jealousy of a non-people, a foolish people, I will send you into wrath." Thomas takes this as an occasion to investigate *gentilitas*, gentleness or peoplehood. Here we see him philosophizing out of biblical categories.]

851.   Here a twofold distinction is to be observed.

First now with respect to the gentleness [*gentilitas*] which he calls a non-people, as if not worthy to be called a people, for the reason that it had not been integrated into the worship of the one God. Ecclesiasticus (Sirach) 50:27: "The second nation I hate is not a people." Now he calls the same people a foolish people, and if in some way it is able to be called a people since it is unified and governed by human law, it is nevertheless called foolish, as if deprived of true wisdom, which consists in the recognition and worship of God. – Ephesians 4: 17ff: "As the nations also walk in the vanity of their own sense, having their understanding obscured in darkness, alienated from the way of God." And so this refers to gentleness as the state before conversion.

These two characterizations [no people, foolish people] can also be attributed to gentleness after conversion, which is called no people, that is, not living as Gentiles [*non gentiliter vivens*], as the Apostle says in the same place [Eph. 4:17]: "Now you will no longer walk as the nations do." Converted gentleness is also called a foolish people according to the opinion of unbelievers. 1 Cor. 3:18: "If anyone among you seems to be wise in this age, let him become foolish in order to be wise."

852.   A second difference is to be observed with respect to the fact that, on the one hand, he mentions jealousy, or envy, by which the Jews envied the converted Gentiles, Gal. 4:17: "They emulate you, but not well." On the other hand, he mentions wrath, by which they are angered against them. Ps. 36:12: "The sinner will observe the just, and he will hiss," and so on.

And those two things belong together, since wrath is caused by jealousy. Whence it says in Job 5:2: "Vexation kills the fool, and jealousy slays the simple."

God is therefore said to induce envy and to make angry, not indeed causing malice in them but withdrawing grace, or rather bringing about the conversion of the nations, whence the Jews take an occasion of anger and jealousy. . . .

854.   Now in these words [Paul] first designates the conversion of the nations, saying, "I am discovered by nations not seeking me." And therefore their conversion is shown to have been apart from the merit and intention of the gentiles . . .

Second he shows the cause and manner of their conversion.

Now he shows the cause, since it was not brought about by chance that they found what they were not seeking, but by the grace of the one who wanted to appear to them. . . . Titus 2:11: "The grace of the savior of our God appeared to all human beings."

Then he shows the manner, since Christ did not appear to the nations in the riddles and figures of the law but in plain truth . . .

855. Second he shows that Isaiah predicted the incredulity of the Jews, saying, "To Israel on the other hand," that is, against Israel, "he says," Isa. 65:2: "I held out my hands all day long to a people not believing but contradicting me." Here our text has it thus: "I held out my hands all day long to an unbelieving people, who walk in not a good way following their own thoughts, a people who provoke me to anger."

856. Now since he says "I held out my hands," it can be understood in one way of the stretching out of the hands of Christ on the cross, which stretching out is indeed said to have lasted on the cross all day long, that is, for the principal part of the entire day, namely from the sixth hour until evening (Matt. 27:45). And although he was stretching out his hands on the cross, the sun was obscured, stones shook, the temple was opened, the Jews nevertheless persisted in their unbelief, blaspheming him, as it says in Matt. 28:39ff. Whence [Paul] adds "to a people not believing, but contradicting me." . . .

857. In another way, he can be referring to the stretching out of the hands of God in doing miracles . . .

858. In a third way it can be understood of the stretching out of the hands of God for exhibiting benefits to the people . . .

Lectio IV

912. After the Apostle has lead the Gentiles into a recognition of the divine judgments, in which the divine goodness and severity is manifested [9:22, n. 903], here he expounds what appears to him about these things, as it were not sufficiently considered in the foregoing. And

first he puts forward what has been done;

second, he proves it, where he says [11:26b, n. 917], "As it is written," and so on;

third he assigns a reason, where he says [11:30, n. 930], "Just as," and so on.

913. On the first point he makes three points.

First he states his intention, saying, Therefore I lead you to consider the goodness and the severity of God, "For I do not want you, brothers and sisters, to be ignorant of this mystery," for you are not able to grasp every mystery. For that is of the perfect, to whom the Lord says in Luke 8:10: "To you it has been given to know the mysteries of the kingdom of God." – Wisdom 6:24 [22]: "I will hide no secrets [*sacramenta*] from you." But ignorance of this mystery would be damnable for you. 1 Cor. 14:38: "Anyone who is ignorant of this is to be ignored."

914. Second he assigns a reason for his intention, "So that you may not be wise to yourselves," that is, not presuming on your own sense in

condemning others, preferring yourselves to them. – Below, 12:16: "Do not be wise in your own eyes." Isa. 5:21: "Woe to those who are wise in your own eyes, and shrewed in your own sight!"

915.   Third he asserts what he intends.

First indeed with respect to the particular stumbling of the Jews, when he says, "Because a blindness has come upon Israel," not universally but in some part, as has been shown above. Isa. 6:10: "Make the heart of this people blind."

Second he names the limit of this blindness, saying "until the fullness of the nations should come in," to faith, that is, not only certain ones particularly from among the nations, as are now being converted, but, either in whole or in the greater part, the church should be established in all nations. Ps. 23 [24]:1: "The earth is the Lord's and the fullness thereof."

Now it says that the Gentiles will enter converted to faith, as if from the external and visible things which they used to venerate, to something spiritual, even the divine will. Ps. 99 [100]:2: "Enter into his presence in exultation."

916.   And it is to be noted that this adverb "until" can designate the cause of the blinding of the Jews. For it is for this reason God permitted them to be blinded, in order that the fullness of the nations should come in, as is plain from what has been said above.

It can also designate a limit, since namely the blindness of the Jews will last up to then, until such time as the fullness of the nations shall enter into faith. And it accords with this what he says below about the future relief of the Jews, when he says "and then," namely when the fullness of the nations shall enter, "all Israel will be saved," not individually [*particulariter*], as now, but all universally. Hos. 1:7: "I will save them in the Lord their God." Micah at the end [7:19]: "He will turn and have compassion on us."

917.   Then when he says "As it is written," and so on, he proves what he has said about the future salvation of the Jews. And

first he proves this by authority;

second by reason, where he says [11:28, n. 921], "According to my gospel," and so on.

918.   He says therefore first of all: I say that all Israel will be saved, as it is written in Isa. 56:20 [*sic*; 59:20–1], where our text has it like this: "A redeemer will come out of Zion, and to those who return to Jacob, this is my covenant with them, says the Lord." But the Apostle quotes here according to the text of the Septuagint and touches on three words written there.

First the advent of the Savior, whom he says "will come," God namely humanified [*humanatus*] to save us, "from Zion," that is, from among the people of the Jews, which is signified by Zion, which was the mount of Jerusalem, which was the chief city of Judah. Whence it says in Zechariah 9:9: "Rejoice greatly, O daughter of Zion! Shout aloud, O daughter of Jerusalem! Lo, your king comes to you," and so on. John 4:22: "Salvation is from the Jews."

Or he says that he comes from Zion not because he is born there but because from there his teaching will go out into the whole world by this means, that the Apostles in the upper room in Zion would receive the Holy Spirit. Isa. 2:3: "For out of Zion shall go forth a law." [Aquinas describes grace as a "new law," written on the hearts of believers by the Holy Spirit (*Summa Theologiae*, I–II.106.1.]

919.   Second he names the salvation through Christ offered for the Jews [*Iudaeis oblatum*], saying "who will deliver and avert impiety from Jacob." And a delivery can refer to a liberation from punishment. Ps. 114 [116]:8: "He will deliver my soul from death." But since he says "he will avert impiety from Jacob," it can refer to liberation from guilt. Ps. 13 [14]:7: "The Lord will avert captivity from his people."

Or both can refer to liberation from guilt, but he says "who will deliver," on account of a few, who are now converted with difficulty, as it were with a kind of violence. Amos 3:12: "As the shepherd delivers from the mouth of the lion two legs, or a piece of an ear, so shall the children of Israel be rescued." Yet he says "he will avert impiety from Jacob," to show the ease of conversion of the Jews at the end of the world. At the end of Micah [7:18]: "Who is a God like you, pardoning iniquity and passing over the transgression of the remnant of your possession?"

920.   Third he shows the mode of salvation, when he says "and this covenant," namely a new one, will be "with them from me, when I take away their sins." For the old covenant did not take away sins, since, as it says in Heb. 10:4: "It is impossible for the blood of bulls and goats to take away sins." And therefore, on account of the imperfection of the old covenant, a new covenant was promised to them. Jer. 31:31: "I will make a new covenant with the house of Israel and the house of Judah." That one will indeed have efficacy for remission of sins through the blood of Christ. Matt. 26:28: "This is my blood of the new convenant, which is poured out for many for the forgiveness of sins." At the end of Micah [7:19]: "He will put down our iniquities, and cast all our sins into the depths of the sea."

921.   Then, when he says, "According to my gospel," and so on, he proves his assertion by reason. And

first he adduces the proof;

second he answers an objection, where he says "For [the gifts and the calling of God are] without penitence [English: are irrevocable]."

922. He says first that since their sins have been taken away and since they have sins afterwards, it is evident that they are enemies of Christ. "According to the gospel they are indeed enemies," that is, with respect to what pertains to the teaching of the gospel, which they impugn, "for you," that is, it turns out to your advantage, as has been said above. Whence it says in Luke 19:27: "But as for those enemies of mine who did not want me to be king over me [*sic*; them], bring them here and slaughter them before me." John 15:24: "But now they have seen and hated both me and my father."

Or he says "according to the gospel, because their enmity gains an advantage for the gospel, the preaching of which is spread out everywhere on occasion of that enmity – Col. 1:5ff: "In the word of the truth, the gospel, which belongs to you, as it is also in the entire world, it bears fruit and grows."

923. But they are "most beloved [*charissimi*]" of God "on account of their ancestors," and that "as regards election," since namely on account of the favor [*gratiam*] of the ancestors, [God] elected their seed. Deut. 4:37: "He loved your ancestors, and elected their seed after them."

Which is not to be so understood as if the merits shown by the ancestors should have been the cause of the eternal election of the descendants, but that God from eternity elected gratis both ancestors and descendants, yet in this order, that the descendants would attain to salvation on account of their ancestors, not as if the merit of the ancestors should suffice for the salvation of the descendants, but by a certain abundance of divine grace and mercy – this is what he is saying – which is shown to the ancestors in such a way that on account of the promises made to them even their descendants will be saved.

Or it is to be understood that "as regards election," that is, with respect to the elect from among that people, as was said above, election is attained. Now if they are most beloved of the Lord, it is rational that they will be saved by God, according to the famous passage at Isa. 64:4: "No eye has seen any God besides you, who works for those who [wait for you]."

924. Then when he says "For [the gifts and the calling of God] are without penitence," and so on, he excludes an objection.

For someone could object, and say that even if the Jews had formerly been most beloved on account of their ancestors, the enmity that they exercised against the gospel still prohibits them from being saved in the future. But this the Apostle asserts to be false, saying "for they are without penitence," namely the "gifts and calling of God," as if he should say, that God should give something to certain ones, or call certain ones, this is "without penitence," since God does not repent of this, according to the famous passage in 1 Kings [1 Sam.] 15:29: "The champion of Israel will not be sparing, nor will he be deflected in penitence." [NRSV: "The Glory of Israel will not recant or change his mind."] Ps. 109:5 [110:4]: "The Lord has sworn and will not change his mind."

925. But that appears to be false. For God says in Gen. 6:6: "I repent that I made humankind." And Jer. 18:9ff: "I may declare concerning a nation or a kingdom, that I will build up or plant it, but if it does evil in my sight, I will do penitence about the good that I have declared that I would do for it."

But it is to be said that God is said to become angry not on account of this, that any *commotion* of anger should exist in him, but because the sense of "anger" extends itself as far as the effect of punishment, so that he is sometimes said to repent, not as if the alteration of repentence existed in him, but because the word "anger" accommodates itself to the sense of penitence when God changes what he had been doing.

926. But as for that, it seems that the gifts and the calling are not without penitence, since divinely conceded gifts are frequently lost, according to the famous verse Matt. 25:28: "So take the talent from him, and give it to the one with the ten talents." For even the calling of God sometimes seems to be changed, as it is written in Matt. 22:14, "Many are called, but few are chosen."

But it is to be said that a gift is here to be taken as a promise, which is made according to God's foreknowledge or predestination. Now calling is used here as election, since on account of the certitude of each, what God promises, he already in some way grants: and those whom he elects, he already in some way calls. And still the temporal gift of God itself and the temporal calling is not disturbed by a change in God, as if he were penitent, but by a change in the human being who rejects God's grace, according to the famous Heb. 12:15: "Watch lest anyone lose [*desit*] the grace of God."

927. What is said here can also be understood otherwise, that we should say that the gifts of God which are given in baptism and the calling by which the baptized one is called to grace, are without penitence on the part of the human being baptized, which is indeed implied here, lest anyone despair of the future salvation of the Jews on this account, that they are not seen to repent of their sin.

But against this which is said, there is what Peter says in Acts 2:38: "Repent, and be baptized every one of you."

But it is to be said that penitence is twofold, internal and external. Now the internal consists in contrition of the heart, by which one sorrows over past sins, and such penitence is required from one baptized, as Augustine says in the book *De poenitentia*: No judgment constituted of one's will,

333

can begin a new life, unless that one should repent of the old life, unless he or she comes to baptism false.

But external penance [*poenitentia*] consists in the external satisfaction which is not required from someone baptized, since through baptismal grace the human being is liberated not only from guilt but also from the entire penalty by virtue of the passion of Christ, who made satisfaction for the sins of all, as has been said above at 6:3: "All of us who have been baptized into Christ Jesus, have been baptized into his death." Hence it says in Titus 3:5ff: "Through the water of rebirth and renewal by the Holy Spirit, whom he poured out on us abundantly."

928.   But since the keys of the Church [i.e. the sacrament of penance or reconciliation] and all other sacraments operate in virtue of the passion of Christ, it seems by similar reasoning that all other sacraments liberate the human being from guilt and from the whole penalty.

But it is to be said that the passion of Christ operates in baptism by way of a certain generation, which requires that the human being die completely to his or her prior life, in order that he or she accept the new life. And therefore the entire charge of the penalty is taken away, which applies to the former, prior life. But in other sacraments the power [*virtus*] of the passion of Christ works by way of healing as in penance. Now healing does not require that all infirmity be taken away at once. And the same reasoning goes for other sacraments.

929.   But when the confession of sinners pertains to external penance, it can be inquired whether a confession of sins is required from the baptized one; and it seems so. For it says in Matt. 3:6 that people were being baptized by John confessing their sins.

But it is to be said that the baptism of John was a baptism of penance, since namely in receiving that baptism they declared themselves in a certain way as going to accept penance for their sin, and therefore it was fitting that they confess, according to the way penance for their sins was established. But the baptism of Christ is a baptism of remission of all sins, so that any satisfaction no longer remains to the baptized one for previous sins, for which reasons no necessity obtains for oral confession. For as to that, confession is necessary in the sacrament of penance, in order that the priest, by the power of the keys, may fittingly loose or bind the penitent.

930.   Then when he says "Just as you were once," and so on, he assigns the reason for the future salvation of the Jews after their unbelief. And

first he makes a comparison of the salvation of each people;

second he shows the cause of that similarity, where he says [11:32, n. 932], "For God has imprisoned," and so on.

931. Therefore he says first of all: Thus I say that all Israel will be saved, although now they are enemies. For "just as you also," Gentiles, "once did not believe God." Eph. 2:12: "You were at that time without God in this world"; "but you have now received mercy." Below, 15:9: "The nations might honor God for his mercy." Hos. 2:23: "I will have mercy on the one who was without mercy." And this "because of their disobedience," which was namely the occasion of your salvation, as has been said above.

"So also they," that is the Jews, "have now," namely in the time of grace, "not believed," namely in Christ. John 8:43: "Why do you not believe me?" And this is why he adds "by the mercy shown to you," that is, in the grace of Christ, through whom you have reached mercy. Titus 3:5: "He saved us according to his mercy." Or "not believed," as by that they attained the mercy shown to you. Or "not believed," which turned out to be the occasion of your mercy, "in order that they too might" sometime "receive mercy." Isa. 14:1: "The Lord will have mercy on Jacob."

932. Then when he says, "For God has imprisoned," and so on, he assigns a reason for the comparison, since namely God wanted his mercy to have an occasion for all. And this is why he adds "For God imprisoned," that is, permitted to be imprisoned, "all," that is, every group of human beings, Jews as well as Greeks, "in unbelief," as in a certain chain of error. Wisd. 17:7 [*sic*; 21]: "All were tied together in a chain of darkness." "So that he may be merciful to all," that is that in every group of human beings his mercy might have an occasion. – Wisd. 11:24 [23]: "You are merciful to all, Lord." Which is not indeed to be extended to demons according to the error of Origen, nor even with respect to all human beings one by one, but to all groups of human beings. [The difference to be noted between Aquinas and moderns here is not so much that Aquinas is not universalist, as that Aquinas is not individualist. Salvation retains a corporate aspect.] For this distribution is made by groups of individuals and not by individuals of groups. Therefore God wants all to be saved by his mercy, in order that they by humbled by that and ascribe their salvation not themselves but to God. Hos. 13:9: "Your destruction is in you, Israel; your help is only from me." Above, 3:19: "So that every mouth may be silenced, and the whole world may become subject to God."

Notes

1 John 4:22, quoted at *In Romanos* 1: 16b (#101) and here at v. 11:26 (#918). For more on the first, see Eugene F. Rogers, Jr., *Thomas Aquinas and Karl Barth* (Notre Dame, Ind.: U. of Notre Dame Press, 1995), pp. 110–11; for more on the second, and on the frequency with which Thomas adduces the verse, see Steven C. Boguslawski, *Aquinas on Romans 9–11*, Ph.D. dissertation, Yale University, 1996.

2 Alasdair MacIntyre, *Three Rival Versions of Moral Enquiry: Encyclopaedia, Genealogy, and Tradition* (Notre Dame, 1990), pp. 84–5.

3 See Rogers, *Aquinas and Barth*, p. 108.

4 R. I. Moore, *The Formation of a Persecuting Society: 1100–1250* (New York and London: Basil Blackwell; 1987).

5 Thus Jeremy Cohen, in *The Friars and the Jews* (Ithaca, N.Y.: Cornell University Press, 1982) argues that much blame belongs on the Dominicans. John Y.B. Hood, in *Aquinas and the Jews* (Philadelphia: University of Pennsylvania Press, 1995), argues that Thomas offered neither any new purchase for anti-Semitism, nor many new resources for resistance. Boguslawski, in *Aquinas on Romans 9–11*, argues that resources for resisting the persecution of the Jews are available in the Romans Commentary.

6 Hood, for example, cites it only piecemeal. But the gap is being quickly remedied. Large portions of the commentary on Romans 1 appear in Rogers, *Aquinas and Barth*. For a more complete and critical translation of the commentary on Romans 9–11, superseding this one, see Boguslawski, ibid. Boguslawski is also preparing a translation of Thomas's entire Romans commentary.

7 I owe the threefold distinction order of creation, order of redemption, order of consummation to David Kelsey. For this application to Christian theologies of the Jews, see Kendall Soulen, *The God of Israel and Christian Theology* (Philadelphia: Fortress, 1996), esp. chaps 2 and 5.

8 See Soulen, ibid., chaps 1 and 5. Soulen argues that the Christian desire to be saved from God's history with the world in Israel is a special case of heretical forms of Christianity that have sought salvation from the world (rather than from sin). For an argument that the Church must apply the accusations of the prophets to itself rather than to Israel, see George Lindbeck, "The Story-Shaped Church: Critical Exegesis and Theological Interpretation," in Garrett Green, ed., *Scriptural Authority and Narrative Interpretation* (Philadelphia: Fortress, 1987), pp. 161–78.

9 Compare Thomas's treatment at *ST* III.47.5 of the assertion, attributed to the council of Ephesis, that the Jews knowingly crucified God, with Hood's analysis, *Aquinas and the Jews*, pp. 62–76, and Jeremy Cohen, "The Jews as the Killers of Christ in the Latin Tradition from Augustine to the Friars," *Traditio* 39 (1983): 1–27. The body of the article answers the question "whether the prosecutors of Christ recognized him" in the negative, and the notion that "the Jews crucifying Christ recognized him to be the Son of God" appears in an objection (that is, does not represent Thomas's own view). The response to the objection, while insufficient and even chilling by modern lights, is not best interpreted as Thomas's *endorsement* of the idea, but his explanation of how the traditionally received assertion can be *understood*. Thomas has trouble on theological grounds with the claim that any human being could recognize Jesus as the Son of God

without the intervention of sanctifying grace (see III.47.5 *ad* 2; that goes for doubting Thomas, too; II–II.1.4). One might say that by the time Thomas returns to the statement at the end of the reply to the third objection at III.47.5 *ad* 3, he has effectively, if all too subtly, *deconstructed* it. Vatican II (*Nostra aetate* 4 and *Lumen gentium* 16) condemns such statements. For a (complex) modern argument that in killing Jews the *Nazis* were killing God, see Karl Barth, *Dogmatics in Outline*, trans. G. T. Thomson (London: SCM Press, 1949), pp. 72–81.

10 For a related discussion on how Thomas accepts and qualifies the claim that circumcision confers the same grace as baptism, *ST* III.70.4, see Richard Shenk, "Covenant Initiation: Thomas Aquinas and Richard Kilwardby on the Sacrament of Circumcision," in Carlos-Josaphat Pinto de Oliveira, ed., *Ordo sapientiae et amoris: Image et message de saint Thomas d'Aquin . . . hommage au Professeur Jean-Pierre Torell* (Fribourg, Switzerland: Editions Universitaires Fribourg Suisse, 1993), pp. 555–93.

11 Bruce Marshall, "The Jewish People and Christian Theology," in *The Cambridge Companion to Christian Doctrine* (New York: Cambridge University Press, 1996).

Further reading

Boguslawaski, Steven C. *Aquinas' Commentary on Romans 9–11*. Ph.D. Dissertation in preparation at Yale University. Boguslawski is also preparing a translation of Aquinas's commentary on Romans as a whole.

Chenu, Marie-Dominic. *Toward Understanding St Thomas* Trans. A. M. Landry and D. Hughes. Chicago: University of Chicago Press, 1964.

Davies, Brian. *The Thought of Thomas Aquinas*. New York and Oxford: Clarendon Press, 1992.

Hood, John Y. B. *Aquinas and the Jews*. Philadelphia: University of Pennsylvania Press, 1995.

Marshall, Bruce. "Christian Theology and the Jewish People." In *Cambridge Companion to Christian Doctrine*. New York: Cambridge University Press, 1996.

Pesch, Otto Hermann. "Paul as Professor of Theology: The Image of the Apostle in St. Thomas's Theology." *The Thomist* 38 (1974): 584–605.

Rogers, Eugene F., Jr., *Thomas Aquinas and Karl Barth: Sacred Doctrine and the Natural Knowledge of God* (Notre Dame, Ind.: Notre Dame University Press, 1995). This book contains chapters on Aquinas's prologue to the Pauline epistles and on Aquinas's commentary on Romans 1.

——"The Virtues of an Interpreter Presuppose and Perfect Hermeneutics: The Case of Thomas Aquinas." *The Journal of Religion* 76 (January 1996).

Weisheipl, James A. *Friar Thomas D'Aquino*. Washington, D.C.: Catholic University Press, 1974.

Romans 10: 4 and the "End" of the Law

Paul W. Meyer

Paul defined the relationship of Christianity with Judaism and in this way gave it a structure which was never subsequently modified in spite of Marcion's attempts to do so, and so far as can be seen could never be called in question without shaking the very foundations of Christianity.

I

Maurice Goguel used these words a third of a century ago to comment on the historical significance of the Apostle Paul for Christian origins.[1] One will of course not hear them today quite as Goguel wrote them. He described the cause for which Paul struggled as "Christian universalism freed from all ritualism." When he varied this terminology to say that Paul "cut the gospel free from the chains with which Judaism was in danger of strangling it,"[2] he was skirting close to that equation of Judaism with "ritualism" which has become unacceptable today on grounds both historical and theological. And what he meant by "universalism" seems to have been a capacity on the part of the early Christian movement to adapt to its future in Greek culture rather than any fruition of its legacy from its Jewish past. Today one will be more inclined to argue that it was Paul's view of the relation of Israel to the Gentiles that gave to his doctrine of justification its characteristic structure and shape.[3] Or, as I would prefer, one might argue a similar case with respect to Paul's Christology: that he so defined the meaning of Jesus as the Christ for the new movement as to clarify for it at the same time its relation to the Judaism from which it emerged and so contributed to its identity; or that it was Paul's definition of the relation of Christianity to Judaism that gave his peculiar signature to his exposition of the meaning of Christ for the Church. But all these are but variations that confirm the truth of Goguel's remark, not as an axiom settled for all time but as a

338

heuristic proposition to be tested as one continues to explore the absolutely fundamental place occupied in Paul's letters by the matter of Christianity's relation to Judaism. Goguel rightly saw that in one way or another this theme, and the problem of the right interpretation of it, lies at "the very foundations of Christianity."

Nowhere are these themes more incontestably intertwined than in Romans 9–11, which is at the same time the one place in Paul's letters where the historical horizons of his theology become most apparent, where he grapples most directly with the question whether God's purposes and judgements are sustained in the history of his people or whether that history shows God's word instead to have failed (9:6). Here we come, in other words, as close as Paul himself will allow us, to the question of God's control over the course of human events or lack thereof, in appearance and in reality. Yet, just because of the presence of those other themes that run through the rest of Romans – justification and the righteousness of God, the meaning of Christ, and the relation of Jew and Greek, of Israel and the Church – these chapters do not yield to being isolated from their epistolary and historical context and treated as if they constituted an independent treatise upon "salvation history" or were the composition of a "theology of history."[4] Their most adequate interpretation is likely to continue to be located in full-length interpretations of the letter, i.e. in commentaries on Romans.[5] For in these the interpreter will remain to some extent accountable, if not in practice then at least in principle, to the combinations and conjunctions, the ordering and disposition, the arrangements and sequences of thought that were Paul's own at the time of his writing. This will not preclude the selection of some discrete aspect, even some minute detail, for separate discussion. But it will serve as a reminder of that constant reciprocal bearing of the whole upon the part and of the minute part upon the understanding of the whole.

II

One verse in which these problems of interpretation come to a head is Romans 10:4: *telos gar nomou christos eis dikaiosunēn panti tō pisteuonti*. This is variously translated as "For Christ is the end of the law, that every one who has faith may be justified" (RSV); "For Christ ends the law and brings righteousness for everyone who has faith" (*NEB*); "But now the Law has come to an end with Christ, and everyone who has faith may be justified" (*JB*); "For Christ, by realizing righteousness for every believer, proves to be the end of the law" (C. K. Barrett).[6]

The passage is a well-known, not to say notorious, crux primarily because of the lexical possibilities available for *telos* ("end"). Here they are mainly two:

"termination" (as in Luke 1:33) or final state or "outcome." In this latter sense the word may, depending on context, refer to a "goal" intended in advance (1 Tim. 1:5) or to a "consequence" or outcome reached quite apart from any deliberate intent on the part of the one who reaches it (Rom. 6:21–2).[7] In the alternative translations just quoted *telos* is uniformly rendered by "end" not simply because the translators have chosen the first of these options but also because it preserves some of the ambivalence of the Greek term. It will be noted that no such uniformity marks the very diverse treatments given the prepositional phrase at the end of the verse.[8] The RSV rewords it with a purpose clause. The *NEB* and *JB* appear to think rather of result, though for the *JB* this result is clearly potential, a resulting possibility. Barrett treats the phrase as an expression of purpose or goal in his discussion, but he translates it as a modal parallel to the main clause as though it were a participial construction in Greek.[9]

Given these difficulties in the verse as it stands, it is no surprise that the major grounds for preferring one interpretation over another are taken from the context or related considerations. The crucial decisions are made elsewhere and this part of Paul's text is in fact and in practice understood within and from a wider whole. We need briefly to examine this context before we consider just how some of these decisions are made.

There is first of all the context preceding 10:4 and the issue where the present unit of Paul's argument may properly be said to begin. Romans 10:1, inasmuch as it makes a personal affirmation of Paul's concern for Israel and his identification with her, seems at first sight to be quite parallel to 9:1–5 and so also to be making a fresh start. If that is the case, 9:30–3, beginning as it does with the rhetorical question "What shall we say, then?," is a brief aside or interlude. But Paul does not this time follow the question by formulating a conclusion that might have been drawn from his own preceding argument only then to repudiate such a conclusion as wrong ("God forbid") and to go on to correct it, as he does in 9:14 and often. The "conclusion" here is supplied by Paul as a legitimate one that needs only further explanation and elaboration, which the next question and its reply in 9:32 proceed to furnish. Moreover, this "conclusion" does not clearly and easily follow from the preceding argument at all, and Paul's explanation of it is clearly continued in 10:2–3. It turns out that the personal asseveration does not then open a new argument but is evoked by Paul's own statement about Israel in 9:32, "They have stumbled over the stumbling stone." Thus many commentators take 9:30 to be the beginning of a major section that runs through 10:21.[10]

The opening sentences of this section in 9:30–1 are on any reading of Paul's argument a remarkable statement. By skillful rhetorical use of "antithetical parallelism"[11] they underscore the presence of a historical paradox crying out to be made in some measure intelligible. It is important for just that reason not "to rewrite Paul's sentence for him according to our own notions of what he ought to have said."[12] What Paul writes is: "Gentiles, who did not pursue righteousness, (nonetheless) achieved righteousness, to be sure one that comes from faith; but Israel on the other hand, while (or though) pursuing a law of righteousness, did not attain to law." By very wide agreement among commentators, the language is unmistakably that of the race-course: achievement and attainment here are matters of catching up with the pursued quarry or rival or arriving at the aimed-for goal. The tripping of the next verse merely sustains the figure. "A law of righteousness"[13] must in this context have reference to a law that holds out the promise of righteousness in return for the effort given in its observance and pursuit. The paradox is not devoid of irony, but the irony lies in the unforeseen, in the reversal of normal expectations, and these in turn are formulated from what would have to be characterized as a Jewish rather than a Gentile perspective. The foil is provided by Gentiles who are not only indefinite (the article is absent) but also unidentified except by the trait of their non-pursuit of righteousness, just as in 2:14 they are identified simply (but twice in one verse) by their non-possession of the Torah. Of these it is said that they have achieved the *un*-sought-for goal, just as in 2:14 it was said of them that they do occasionally on their own (*physei*) and without the promptings of the Torah what it requires. To be sure, Paul adds, the righteousness these Gentiles have achieved is the sort that comes from faith. It could hardly be otherwise; their achievement of this un-sought-for goal is "apart from law," to echo 3:21. Against such a background it is then said of Israel (with what is now a modal rather than an adjectival participle) that either in spite of or alongside that very pursuit that distinguishes Jew from Gentile, of a divine instruction that Israel alone is distinguished for having and that holds out the promise of righteousness, her goal remains unattained – not the goal of the promised righteousness, it should be noted, but even more drastically the goal of the prior divine instruction. It is the Torah itself that has inexplicably become the unattained goal, the destination not reached. One is compelled by such assertions to resort to the term dialectic in order to designate adequately not only the rhetoric operative here but the very notion of Torah which it conveys as well. Israel does not "have" this Torah so much as she pursues it. Israel is distinguished from the Gentiles by the pursuit of it – and distinguished from the Gentiles at the same time by the odd fact that her pursuit, unlike theirs, remains without consummation.

Normal expectations straightforwardly fulfilled are like the proverbial dead men; at least they ask no questions and demand no replies. But this unforeseen reversal is of another order. No sooner has Paul formulated it than he proceeds to try to make it intelligible with a new question and answer in verse 32. But the most remarkable feature of the new verse is the simple fact that it is there at all. For by being there it shows that while verses 30–1 document the ironical reversal, in themselves they offer no word of resolution or explanation. The modal participle in verse 31 cannot be translated "because of pursuing a law of righteousness;" like the adjectival participle in verse 30, to which it corresponds, it is part of the puzzle and not its solution. The historical paradox is not caused by Israel's pursuit of the law.[14] Rather, Paul goes on, it is due in the first instance to a misunderstanding,[15] a false assumption with which the pursuit was undertaken. "Why? Because not deriving from faith, but as if derived from works" (*hoti ouk ek pisteōs all' hōs ex ergōn*). The severe elliptical brevity of the explanation strips it down to its one basic essential, misunderstanding, but there is little doubt about Paul's meaning.[16]

Returning to the imagery of running pursuit in verse 32b, Paul supplements this first accounting with the flat assertion, in language taken from Isaiah, "They have stumbled against the stone of stumbling." By at once expressly identifying the scriptural source of this language with his usual formula "just as it is written" and offering the well-known and oft-discussed composite quotation from Isaven 8:14 and 28:16 ("Behold I am laying a stone in Zion ...") Paul takes the significant further step of implying that this unexpected outcome was no merely subjective vagary but was rooted in God's deliberate intent. If this seems to complicate Paul's explanation by reintroducing from chapter 9 the tension between divine purpose and instigation on the one hand and human response and accountability on the other, that is no more and no less than what is involved anyway in the mere appropriation of LXX terminology for "a stone of stumbling" and "a rock of offense."[17] The traditional language about such a stone combines the elements of an unavoidable obstruction and an avoidable encounter with it. Indeed the double form of the citation confirms this tension by setting alongside the offense the alternative possibility of believing trust, and assigning this equal sanction in the divine utterance. In the end, Paul's "explanation" is hardly less complex than the baffling and unexpected double reversal it was called forth to illuminate, and it is neither jarring nor surprising that the first verse of chapter 10 should consist, as we have seen, of a renewed asseveration by the apostle of his deep concern for his people and their salvation in the presence of this confounding God, both his and theirs.

It will be noted that we have left unspecified the matter of the application of the composite quotation from Isaiah. What did Paul have in mind as the stone which has been placed by God in Zion and which has confronted Israel with the alternatives of believing or stumbling? The line of thought Paul has been pursuing and the race-course imagery with which he has been working – in short, the context read on its own terms – suggests that the Torah is the rock placed by God in Zion. There is nothing in the antecedent context, in the whole of chapter 9 or all of Romans before it, to suggest anything else. Yet all seem to have missed Paul's intent; no commentary on Romans known to me departs from the unanimous opinion that for Paul this stone is Christ. There is no more striking example in the Pauline letters of a crucial exegetical decision made on grounds extrinsic to the text itself. The reason usually given for the latter interpretation is that Paul is drawing upon a tradition of early Christian use of these texts from Isaiah 8:14 and 28:16 which had already sufficiently established the identification of Christ as the stone so that Paul could take it for granted. Yet this argument has come under increasing attack and has, I think, been decisively undermined.[18] Otherwise, one must in order to sustain this interpretation simply read Paul as anticipating here his mention of Christ in 10:4. But this remains mere conjecture unless one makes additional assumptions: that Paul's view of Jewish reaction to the preaching of the cross (1 Cor. 1:23) was already so generalized, so polarized, and so fixed, and his own thinking so exclusively christological, that it was impossible for him to think that God would cause his people a theological and religious difficulty in any other way; or that *telos* in 10:4 means "abolishment," so that the cause of offense to the Jew is not the messianic claim of the Christians as such or the preaching of the cross but the fact that the Jew cannot accept God's abolishment of his Torah. The first assumption is refuted by chapter 9; the second falls by its own circularity. Except in the total absence of any alternatives, i.e. unless one is reduced to looking ahead because one cannot make sense of an unintelligible passage, Romans 10:4 has little evidential value for the meaning of 9:33.

If Paul makes a "new start" in 10:2–3,[19] it is a renewed attempt to shed light on just the state of affairs with which he began in 9:30–1, another try at reducing what obstinately remains a very intricate explanation to a more manageable dimension. He has no new subject in mind. This is clear from the fact that in verse 3 he returns to the same verbal form (aorist third person plural) he used in 9:32; the same event or sequence of events is in view. Righteousness and justification, i.e. the question who may stand in God's presence and on what grounds, is still at stake as it was in 9:30–1. And though Paul has shifted the categories from pursuit and the failure of attainment to obedience and disobedience, the same reversal is being described. Now the foil is a deposition by Paul on behalf of his people: what distinguishes them is "zeal for God," nothing else than that eager and devoted commitment to the service of God and to living in accordance with his will and claim which elsewhere Paul alleged without apology or dissimulation to be his own proud legacy from his Jewish past (Phil. 3:6). But now against that background there is the same baffling and unexpected outcome: "they did not submit to God's righteousness" (v. 3). There is even something of the same dialectic as in 9:30–1, only without the complicating presence of the Gentiles it comes out much more straightforwardly: obedience, real and genuine in both its intention and its fervor, has turned out as disobedience. Why? Again the explanatory middle link in verses

2b and 3a has two sides: a passive one in a failure of recognition *(epignōsis)*,[20] a knowledge of God's righteousness that has aborted *(agnoein)*;[21] and a more active side in a contrary search to establish "one's own" righteousness.

Kuss[22] points out an important detail in the grammar of the verses we have been following, one to which we have tried to hold. Verse 2, 3, 4 (and 5 as well) all begin with the conjunction *gar* ("for"). Verse 2 gives the grounds for (i.e. explains) Paul's statement of involved concern by characterizing his people both positively and negatively; verse 3 in turn explains verse 2 by elaborating on both aspects of the analysis. Verse 4 next explains verse 3; but how? If verse 4 makes Christ God's termination of the Torah, it can "explain" as disobedience only continued adherence to law, the "zeal" of verse 2 and the pursuit of 9:32; but these are not in themselves perverse for Paul. If verse 4 makes Christ the termination of the Torah, it can "explain" then not the main clause of verse 3 but only its subordinate participle ("seeking to establish their own"), and then only on the secondary premise that there is no way for the Jew to live by the Torah without seeking to establish his own righteousness. But then Paul could have spared himself all the dialectic of 9:30–10:3, just as he could have spared himself the defense of the law's holiness in 7:7–12. So to read 10:4 is to compel Paul into a simplistic antinomian position and to make unintelligible his present intricate argument. It also requires one arbitrarily to fill in an ellipsis in the verse (cf. n. 8 above): "Christ is the end of the law *(as a means to)* righteousness . . ." In fact, however, Paul nowhere suggests that the way to obedience to God for the Israelite lies in abandoning the Torah. If, on the other hand, verse 4 makes the crediting of righteousness to everyone who believes and trusts God the goal and intent of the Torah, it explains directly and straightforwardly, without any need for supplementation by the reader out of his own baggage, why the failure to acknowledge God's righteousness and the attempt to establish one's own are an act of disobedience and defiance.

Paul's new explanation is no more simple than his earlier one. But the reader, no longer merely baffled, finds himself instead coming out into the clear on familiar Pauline terrain. In the first place, the language has become reminiscent of Philippians 3:9 and the paradigmatic way Paul writes of himself there, contrasting two kinds of righteousness: one which belongs to God or comes from God as his gift and can only be recognized and acknowledged in faith, and the other which human beings strive to establish out of their own resources. But more significant than this echo of Philippians 3:9 are those other passages from earlier parts of Paul's argument in Romans that now enter into and shape the recognition process. For to understand God's righteousness, to "attain to" it in faith (9:30), means also to submit to it, to acknowledge God as the one who defines righteousness as well as good and evil, truth and falsehood (3:4); it is to recognize his prerogative as well as his claim (3:6); it is to add to the knowledge of him the recognition of him as God with praise and thanksgiving

(1:21); it is to believe after the manner of Abraham, trusting him to carry through what he has promised (4:21).

Indeed the coalescing of Paul's experience with his perception of his people and of his analysis of his people's experience with his own penetrates to a still deeper level. He gives here no hint whatsoever that in Israel's past the Torah was identified mistakenly, or was of demonic origin, or was corrupted in its transmission. There is no suggestion that her knowledge of God was unreal or ever diverted into idolatry and the worship of false gods. There is no indication that her zeal was half-hearted or cold, that it did not spring from genuine commitment. Yet, in spite of all that, a Torah given and "pursued" but not reached; a knowledge of God aborted in non-recognition; a zeal for God that has turned into disobedience. Where do we find ourselves if not back in Romans 7, at the heart of Paul's own experience with God's holy Torah and with the transcendent (*kath' hyperbolēn*, 7:13) capacity of sin to pervert his deepest commitment to it? "The very commandment which promised life proved to be death to me" (7:10). "I do not understand what I bring about; for it is not what I intend or desire that I put into practice, but the very thing I want to avoid" (7:15).

It was after all not only Paul's discovery of the *iustificatio impii*, of God's vindication of the sinner, in the death of Jesus (and hence of the irreconcilable contradiction between that death and justification through the law, Gal. 2:21), but also, and perhaps for himself personally more importantly, this experience, interpreted in the light of the cross, of the power of sin to convert even his delight in the Torah into captivity (7:22–3) that raised to the level of an axiom in Paul's mind the conviction that no person's standing before God could be secured by observance of the law (Gal. 2:16; 3:11; Rom. 3:20, 28; 4:5; 11:16). Even more: in Romans 7 the holiness of God's Torah was so far beyond dispute for him that even this perverse use made of it by the power of sin to trick and to kill had to be seen as serving the divine purpose, namely to manifest the incalculable dimensions of that power. This point is made twice in 7:13, with two independent purpose clauses. (Unfortunately, the *RSV* here reduces the impact of these clauses by bringing them together and fusing them into one; worse, the *NEB* turns them into matter-of-fact result clauses, eliminating the divine purpose entirely; worst of all, the *JB* makes one a result clause but in keeping the other a purpose construction turns it into a reflexive and assigns the intent to sin itself.) Of course this simply develops a move already made in 5:21, where another purpose clause assigned a deliberate and ultimately redemptive design to the "increase" of sin by the law. The result is the most idiosyncratic feature of Paul's view of the law, the claim that, far from preserving its adherent from sin, it compounds sin.[23] Curiously, this feature has not infrequently been taken to show how far removed Paul had become from his Jewish roots; on the contrary, it shows how unshakable his attachment to the Torah as God's and as gift really was.[24] And now – something completely missed in the conventional equation of the "stone" with Christ – just this peculiar but unmistakable signature of Pauline reflection and experience reappears in his backward look over Israel's corporate history when the law is identified as the "stone of stumbling" (9:32).

There is, to be sure, a difference. In Romans 7, speaking personally and for himself, Paul can thank God for a deliverance he has found in Jesus Christ. In Romans 10 and 11, speaking in solidarity with Israel, his thought can only come to rest in the future of God's irrevocable calling (11:26, 29). But the difference in no way impugns the impartiality of God, who has treated all on the same terms and can be counted on to do so in the future (10:12–13; cf. 2:6–11; 4:11–12; 9:11, 16; and 11:28–32). The end result in the case of those who are "in Christ Jesus" (8:1, 2) has been that God has done what the law could not do to bring about the fulfillment of the law's just requirement (8:4), a new obedience to God and a submission to his will free of that hostility of the flesh that perverts obedience into the securing of a person's own righteousness (8:7–9). Paul does not yet say what the end result will be for Israel, but one can see that it too will be by faith (10:11; 11:23), and by calling upon the Lord, as scripture says (10:13). In any case, that kind of righteousness which belongs to faith and to trust in the God of Abraham, and which Paul now sees from his Christian perspective to have been God's intent all along (4:11–12, 23–4; 9:33b; Gal. 3:8), will be for Israel as it is for himself the Torah arrived at, the knowledge of God made authentic in recognition and thanksgiving, the performance and zeal that deserve the name of obedience, the not-so-obvious Jewish identity and circumcision that receive their praise and recognition from God and not from human beings (2:28–9). "For the intent and goal of the law, to lead to righteousness for everyone who believes, is (nothing different from) Christ."

With that we are back where we started. Before we leave Romans 10:4 we should note that in the next verse Paul goes on, with a new causal sentence, to demonstrate that the grounds for such an affirmation as he has just made are in turn to be found by turning to scripture (10:5–13). With that a new stage is reached which we cannot follow here, although it is of very great significance for understanding the methods, intentions, and assumptions of Paul's exegesis.[25]

One point, however, needs to be recognized and accounted for: 10:5–6 is widely used as evidence to show that in verse 4 Paul uses *telos* in the sense of "abolition." The argument is essentially that the contrast these verses draws between "the righteousness which is based on the law" and "the righteousness based on faith" is so sharp and the resulting confrontation between the Moses who "writes" in verse 5 and a personified faith-righteousness that "speaks" in verse 6 so uncompromising that "law" and "Christ" in verse 4 can only be mutually exclusive and Christ can in Paul's mind only mean the termination of the Torah.[26] We have examined enough of the context of 10:4 to see that such an argument seriously dislocates the polarity from the place where Paul places it, and does this in such a way as to alter crucially Paul's view of the law. The two kinds of righteousness in verses 5–6 are indeed opposites, as irreconcilable as obedience and disobedience, as "submitting to God's righteousness" and "seeking to establish one's own" in verse 3. They repeat the contrast between "from faith" and "from works" in 9:32. There is no compromise between an election "by grace" and one "by works" (11:6), between what depends "on the God who calls" and what "on works" (9:12), between what comes "as a gift" and what "as one's due" (4:4). But the law does not belong on the side of this polarity that is alien to God or opposed to God. When it is found to function there, it does so as a consequence of a fundamental and tragic misunderstanding (9:32), or as an instrument of human disobedience and failure to recognize God and his righteousness (10:3), or as an opportunity seized by the demonic power of sin (7:11) for its own nourishment. But even when it is found to function in these ways, it has not been torn out of God's hand and it does not cease to be his holy instrument, for ultimately it does not contradict even then but advances, however indirectly, the carrying out of God's purpose (Rom. 5:20–1; 7:13; 11:32; Gal. 3:21–2; 24). To make such a claim is not to deny the presence of evil, the power of sin, the tragedy of the distortion of the divine intent in the name of religion. It is, rather, precisely to take all these with utmost seriousness, yet not absolutely, to claim in them and beyond them the ultimate manifestation of God's righteousness, his impartial goodness, and his sovereignty. Of course this is for Paul the Christian to read history in a pattern or meaning derived from the crucifixion of Jesus. But it is also for Paul the Jewish Christian to trace in the movements of history the sovereignty of the God of Abraham, Isaac, and Jacob, the God of Moses, the Judge and Comforter of the Exile, who is also the Father of the Crucified.

III

If such reflections and conclusions as these can claim significant warrant in Paul's own text, it is very difficult to avoid reflecting on the reasons why they are not only not very widely held but also in some quarters, and in the commentary literature generally, firmly opposed, sometimes vehemently. The issue is significant enough to merit a brief postscript.

One matter that we have not mentioned but that has special bearing upon the interpretation of 9:30–10:4 is its relation to 9:1–29. What is the nature of the transition between the body of chapter 9 and 9:30–3? On its face this is a very simple question: how is chapter 10 related to chapter 9? But answering it is one of the major decisions facing the interpreter of Romans 9–11. For, as Dahl has pointed out,[27] through most of its history the interpretation of these chapters has been dominated by the problem of theodicy. More specifically, in the wake of Augustine's preoccupation with the issue of the freedom of the will, Romans 9–11 has been read as a discussion of divine predestination and human responsibility. On the assumption that what primarily troubles Paul in these chapters is his own Jewish people's rejection of the proclamation of Jesus as the Messiah, the three chapters are read as three different and rather unrelated, not to say logically incompatible, attempts to explain and understand this *contemporary* turn of events, this "disobedience of Israel":[28] in 9, by attributing it to God's absolute sovereignty and freedom to elect and to reject (divine determinism); in 10, by attributing it to the Jews' own responsible refusal of the Christ (human freedom); and in 11, by describing it as a temporary expedient that makes possible the inclusion of the Gentiles in God's redemptive purpose and that therefore, frustrating God's sovereignty in appearance only, actually contributes to the salvation of "all Israel" (11:26) and the ultimate victory of God's purpose (not so much in spite of human resistance as in and through it, not wiping it out so much as using it). On such reading of course the transition from chapter 9 to chapter 10 (at 9:30) is abrupt.[29] The discontinuity is as sharp as the contradiction between determinism and freedom. If there is logical coherence here, it would have to be something like the coherence of "thesis" and "antithesis" on the way to "synthesis." But it is questionable whether Paul's argument moves through the stages of this popular but simple and vulgarized schema somehow left to religious language by Hegel. In any case, such reading of these chapters has had the effect through a large part of the history of the exegesis of Romans of isolating these chapters from the rest of the epistle and of creating unnecessary obstacles in the understanding of particular sections.

It is to be sure beyond doubt that the negative reaction of Jews to the Christian kerygma, especially in its contrast to the reception accorded by Gentiles, is one of the things on Paul's mind. It is no accident that Paul's use in 11:8 of language from Deuteronomy 29:3 and Isaiah 29:10 is very close in meaning ("*eine Sinnparallele*")[30] to the text from Isaiah 6:9–11 imbedded in the evangelists' reflections on Jewish response to the gospel (Matt. 13:14–15; Mark 4:12; Luke 8:10; John 12:40; Acts 28:26–7). But the issue in chapter 9 does not begin there, as a matter of "the disobedience of Israel." For Paul – the Jew – this discussion begins in 9:6 with the matter of the consistency and reliability of God's word. This is not a new issue in the text of Romans. It is, rather, a peice of unfinished business left over from a previous stage in the argument, specifically from 3:1–4, just as 6:1–7:6 deals with an issue abruptly turned aside by the apostle and left unresolved in 3:5–8.[31] There, after bluntly pressing the point of God's impartiality, before which Jew and Greek stand on an equal footing, Paul had himself given expression to the question he most naturally expected from a Jew: "What then is the point of being a Jew?" (3:1). His answer, too brief to be anything but a pointer, had been to say that that issue and the matter of God's faithfulness and truth stand or fall together, and to suggest with a quotation from Psalms 51:4 that the real issue in justification is *God*'s being "justified," i.e. acknowledged as true, even if every human being turns out to be a liar. Clearly Romans 9 pursues that matter first. But that means – and this is the point that bears on our discussion – that what occupies Paul is God's faithfulness over the long past and the consistency of his dealings with his people over past and present. As 9:11 and 16 clearly show, Paul is aware of the extent to which his own descriptions of justification "apart from law" depend for their credibility on the case that he can make for this faithfulness and consistency on God's part. It is not at all merely a matter of a contemporary turn of events. It is a matter of surveying and reviewing (without a chronological retelling) essential features of Israel's past from his Christian perspective, just as he had been driven earlier to review (without autobiographical sequence) certain aspects of his individual past as a paradigm of human existence under the Torah (chap. 7).

Thus what we meet in Romans 9:30–10:4 is not an apostate Jew accusing his kinsmen of disobeying God because they have not been won over to his new interpretation of God's righteousness, or of persisting in an anachronism because they cannot accept God's putative termination of his Torah, or of being so attached to Moses that they have been unable to follow the living God in his new revelations of himself in unexpected ways.[32] Rather, we encounter a Jewish Christian whose new religious identity depends on continuity with his old; who must, for his own sake and the sake of those who have made the move with him, as well as for the sake of the right understanding of his gospel on the part of Gentile Christians (11:13), undertake such a review. Just as he had pressed the matter of God's consistency in the problematic of descent from Abraham in chapter 9, so now in chapter 10 he had to pursue God's faithfulness in the dialectic of obedience and disobedience (including Gentile obedience and Jewish disobedience), of Jewish devotion to the Torah and Jewish failure to attain to the Torah, of the problem of a defiance of God in the midst of the greatest possible human zeal for God, in order to be able to discover in his own kerygma the presence of his Jewish God and an answer to the question about that God's intentions in the giving of the Torah.

But these are not the only reasons why an interpretation of Romans 10:4 such as we have suggested here has not commended itself. At once the most vehement attack against all translations of *telos* in 10:4 as "goal" and the most eloquent defense of its rendering as "termination" has been made by Käsemann in his superb commentary.[33] There is much in his argument with which one must agree. This applies especially to his polemic against a Christian moralizing, "pedagogical" interpretation of the law in its relation to Christ that derives from a false translation of *paidagōgos* in Galatians 3:24 as "tutor" rather than "custodian." Such an interpretation makes of both the Jewish Torah and Israel's history a preparatory schooling for Christian truth, a halfway step on the liberal road of progressive religious development climaxing in Christian piety. Such triumphalism among Christians is not only the soil on which a patronizing view of Judaism grows (and worse, where Christendom dominates, a questioning of the Jew's right to existence); it is irreconcilable with Paul's understanding of justification. For Paul the problem with *homo religiosus*, the religious human being, is not that he has been on the right track, only has not exerted himself sufficiently (Paul could then never have formulated the paradox of 9:30–1). Rather, human religious striving and "progress" have made more acute a fundamental problematic in man's relation to God, and God's gift of the Torah has deepened that crisis just where it has been obeyed (Gal. 3:19–24). Here one can only agree with Käsemann.

The problem appears to me to lie elsewhere. Käsemann is quite ready to characterize Paul's understanding of the Jewish Torah in 9:30–1 as "dialectical,"[34] and reminds his readers that "Paul was a Jew, and remained one even as a Christian, in that he still allowed the Torah to be the kernel of the Old Testament."[35] Yet, when he comes to 10:4 he insists upon a unilateral and undialectical view of the Torah that prohibits *telos* from meaning anything other than "termination." The reason is that "law and gospel mutually exclude one another in an entirely undialectical way;"[36] Christ and the Torah of Moses stand in the same kind of contrary relationship as Christ and Adam in 5:12–21, the one belonging to the new aeon and the other to the old.[37] In short, Käsemann's interpretation of Romans 10:4 rests on the premise that the Jewish Torah, the Mosaic law, belongs for Paul to the old aeon that must come, that has come, to an end in Christ. This is a kind of ultimate example of the way in which the understanding of 10:4 depends on decisions that one has made elsewhere.

What is it that casts this dark Manichaean shadow across the pages of Paul and of his commentators? Is this the flaw in an apocalyptic reading of Paul, that it proves impotent to deliver us wholly from our Protestant habit of reading Paul through the eyes of Luther? In any case, this premise does not stand up under scrutiny in the light of such passages as are usually adduced in its support, especially 5:20; 7:1–6; 8:2–4.

We have already alluded to the problem produced by the mislocation of the genuine Pauline polarity in relation to the Jewish Torah.[38] And we have also pointed out that the phrasing of Romans 8:2 ("the law of sin and death") is not to be understood apart from the dialectic of Romans 7 which it summarizes in shorthand from, in which God's holy law is described as having been used by sin in order to produce death.[39] Romans 8:3–4 shows that the counterpart in verse 2 ("the law of the Spirit of life in Christ Jesus") is the same divine Torah brought to fulfillment through the life-giving power which it was itself unable to provide but which belongs to the Spirit. The contraries are sin and righteousness, death and life. Law and Spirit, however, are not related as such opposites but as powerlessness and life-giving power.

The case is similar in Romans 7:1–6. The first three verses are not unclear. In Paul's illustration, living with another man before her husband's death brings upon the woman the label and mark of an adulteress, the "scarlet letter." The very same action after the husband's death brings no such consequence. The law is not annulled by the husband's death, but the power of the law to *condemn* is broken – just the point that is resumed in 8:1 ("There is therefore now no condemnation for those who are in Christ Jesus"). That Paul wishes precisely to avoid suggesting that the law is no longer in effect is shown when he writes (literally translated): "she is annulled *(katērgētai)* from the law of the husband;" the Greek language is being strained to the breaking point to avoid the natural use of this verb, to avoid saying "the law of the husband has been cancelled." The whole purpose of 7:7–12 is to make clear that Paul wants no one to conclude that the Mosaic law is to be equated with the power of sin and to insist instead that as God's holy, righteous and good commandment it is not evil or demonic.

Finally there is the much more complex matter of the law in Romans 5:12–21. One thing is clear: in verses 20–21 the law intrudes itself as "the factor which disturbs the analogy in [the] contrast between Adam and Christ."[40] It functions for Paul on *both* sides of the divide between Adam and Christ, to make of death on the one hand not merely an inexorable fate inherited by all as a result of Adam's trespass alone but a condemnation deserved by the trespasses of all (v. 13), and to make life on the other hand not merely a neutral consequence inherited by all as a result of Christ's obedience but a gift that has its character most of all in being undeserved and gracious. That is why it deepens the trespass in order to deepen all the more the ensuing grace, to show that death is the symptom and result of sin's rule and power, but just as surely to show that life in Christ is the symptom and sign of the rule of God's undeserved grace. The law defines for both the old and the new their character; it does not stand unambiguously on the side of the old.

One might very well ask what the consequences would be of a consistent Christian interpretation that insists on identifying the Mosaic Torah with the old aeon. What would that mean for the Christian's relationship to Judaism, to the Hebrew scriptures, to the God of Moses? That consequence might not be as reprehensible as that other paternalizing view of Judaism as a lower order of religious commitment and behavior on its way to Christianity, but it surely would miss by an even wider mark Paul's deep engagement with the Judaism from which he came and to which he remained profoundly tied. To miss that engagement and so to abandon the structure which Paul gave to Christianity

351

because of it would be, as Goguel observed in the passage referred to at the beginning of this essay, "to shake the very foundations of Christianity."

Notes

1 *The Birth of Christianity* (London: Allen & Unwin, 1953; French original, Paris: Payot, 1946), p. 195.

2 Ibid., pp. 195 and 194.

3 N. A. Dahl, *Studies in Paul* (Minneapolis: Augsburg, 1977), p. 156; cf. p. 148.

4 For the necessity and at the same time the problematic of using such modern terms in connection with Paul, the essential discussion for the present is E. Käsemann's essay, "Justification and Salvation History in the Epistle to the Romans," *Perspectives on Paul* (Philadelphia: Fortress, 1971), pp. 60–78.

5 To the full commentary treatment by Käsemann, *An die Römer* (Tübingen: Mohr, 1973), pp. 241–308, there must now be added the even longer discussion by O. Kuss, *Der Römerbrief*, Dritte Lieferung (Regensburg: Verlag Friedrich Pustet, pp. 1978), pp. 662–935; cf. pp. 667–8 for a select bibliography of earlier special treatments of Romans 9–11. This literature is just now seeing an explosive growth; other major commentaries on Romans 9–11 in the context of the whole letter are being prepared for such series as ICC, Hermeneia, AB and EKKNT.

6 *A Commentary on the Epistle to the Romans* (New York: Harper & Row, 1957), p. 195.

7 Cf. *BAG*, 819. It should be noted that if one sets aside the more specialized meanings *telos* may have as "tax, duty" (Rom. 13:7) or in stereotyped adverbial prepositional phrases such as *heōs telous* (2 Cor. 1:13) or *eis telos* (1 Thess. 2:16), all occurrences in the undisputed Pauline letters apart from Rom. 10:4 fall into the second group (end as "outcome," "conclusion"). This preponderance of meaning is especially clear in 1 Cor. 15:24; 2 Cor. 3:13; 11:15; Phil. 3:19. In these letters the word never means simply end as "cessation"; such a meaning is to be found in the whole of the traditional Pauline corpus only in Heb 7:3. These proportions clearly conform to the general picture of Greek usage provided by *LSJ*, 1772–4.

8 All do connect the dative participle with the prepositional phrase rather than with the main clause. To construe it in the latter way ("in the judgement of every believer Christ has become the end of the law [as a way] to righteousness") might appear plausible in terms of classical usage (R. Kühner and B. Gerth, *Ausführliche Grammatik der griechischen Sprache*, Satzlehre, 1. Teil, 4. Aufl. (Leverkusen, 1955), 1. 421), but internal reasons are strongly against it. (a) Paul's use of the dative alone is never so purely "subjective"; cf. 1 Cor. 1:18, the nearest parallel I can find. (b) The frequent close association of *pisteuein/ pistis* with *dikaioun/dikaiosynē* throughout Paul's letters and in this context in 9:30; 10:6 speaks against separating them here. And (c) the need to supply the words in parentheses in order to yield some sense shows how awkward such a construal is.

9 *Romans*, p. 197. Cf. p. 198: "He puts an end to the law, not by destroying all that the law stood for but by realizing it." Such a strained modal translation is the price he seems to believe himself compelled to pay for the choice of a final meaning for *telos*. It is,

however, not a necessary price. Leenhardt (*L'Epitre de Saint Paul aux Romains* (Neuchatel: Delachaux & Niestlé, 1957), p. 151) translates easily with a purpose clause: "Christ est cependant but et terme de la loi, pour mettre quiconque croit au bénéfice de ce jugement de grâce." This shows, too, that in the other direction a natural final translation of the prepositional phrase (as purpose or result) does not require in its wake interpreting *telos* as "termination," as in RSV, *NEB*, and *JB*.

10 So Käsemann, *Römer*, pp. 264–5; Kuss, *Römerbrief*, pp. 740–8. Dahl, *Studies*, p. 147, calls 9:30–3 a "provisional summary" that "functions as a transition to the following section," but significantly he goes on to say that what it summarizes is not the preceding argument of chap. 9 but "Paul's view of the contemporary situation." Romans 10:1–3 seems to him to make a new start because "only at this point does Paul explain what prompts the sorrow and anguish about which he spoke in 9:1–3" and Dahl finds that explanation in v. 3. But v. 3 is nothing else than Paul's interpretation of 9:32. For Dahl both verses have to do with the Jews' rejection of Jesus as Messiah, so even on his terms 9:30–3 functions as a "transition" mainly by introducing new elements for the next stage of Paul's argument (cf. p. 143, n. 24).

11 Käsemann, *Römer*, p. 265.

12 C. E. B. Cranfield, "Some Notes on Romans 9:30–33," *Jesus und Paulus: Festschrift für Werner Georg Kümmel* (Göttingen: Vandenhoeck & Ruprecht, 1975), p. 36. A good example of such re-writing is found in H. Lietzmann, *An die Römer* (Tübingen: Mohr, 1971), p. 94, but others abound in the commentary literature on these verses as already in the manuscript variants and conjectural emendations to the text.

13 *nomos dikaiōsynēs* is a *hapax legomenon* in the NT; in the LXX it occurs only once (Wisd. 2:11) and then clearly *in malam partem*.

14 On this detail Cranfield is quite correct ("Notes," p. 39). But to go on, as he does, triumphantly to declare "fundamental agreement" between Paul and Jesus on the law is a sharp abridgement of Paul's complex reflections on the law and can only result in caricature. There is nothing in the tradition of Jesus' teaching to compare with Rom. 5:20; 7:13; or Gal. 3:21–2.

15 H. J. Schoeps, who in his very instructive book on Paul's theology climaxes his discussion of Paul's treatment of the law with a whole section on the fundamental Pauline misunderstanding of the Torah, never once mentions this verse of Romans (*Paul: The Theology of the Apostle in the Light of Jewish Religious History* (London: Lutterworth, 1961)).

16 Both Käsemann (*Römer*, p. 265) and Kuss (*Römerbrief*, p. 745) refer to L. Radermacher's discussion of the expressly Greek nuancing of the verse (*Neutestamentliche Grammatik* (Tübingen: Mohr, 1925), p. 26) in the absence of any mention of it in *BDF*. There can be little doubt, in view of Paul's common use of these contrasting prepositional phrases, that the governing word intended but only implied is either the substantive "righteousness" or a cognate verbal form such as "being justified."

17 Cf. G. Stählin, "*skandalon k.t.l.*," *TWNT* 7 (1964): 341–2. The parallel *proskomma* adds the further nuance of "being taken unawares."

18 John E. Toews, *The Law in Paul's Letter to the Romans: A Study of Romans 9:30–10:13* (Dissertation, Northwestern University, 1977). One central argument of this dissertation, that Rom. 9:33 is not a messianic stone testimonium, was presented by Toews in a paper on "Romans 9:33 and the Testimonia Hypothesis" to the Pauline Epistles Section

of the Society of Biblical Literature meeting in New Orleans on November 20, 1978. In this paper he showed that the Christian Christological use of Isa. 8:14 everywhere else presupposes the use of Ps. 118:22, just what is absent in Rom. 9:33. For a general view of the state of the discussion on the so-called "testimonia," cf. J. A. Fitzmyer, " '4Q Testimonia' and the New Testament," in his *Essays on the Semitic Background of the New Testament* (Missoula: Scholars' Press, 1974), pp. 59–89. Klyne R. Snodgrass ("I Peter II. 1–10: Its Formation and Literary Affinities," *NTS* 24 (1977–78): 97–106) shows that the connection of Isa. 8:14 and 28:16 was made already in Jewish tradition, and that the *ep' autō* of Rom. 9:33 is not the result of Christian interpolation; this means that this phrase cannot be taken as evidence for a Christological application by Paul.

19 Dahl, *Studies*, p. 147.

20 *epignōsis* occurs in the undisputed Pauline letters here and Rom. 1:28; 3:20; Phil. 1:9; and Philem. 6. The contexts always show the presence of the connotation "recognition" or "acknowledgement" (e.g. in Phil. 1:9 the parallel term is *aisthēsis*).

21 Cf. R. Bultmann, *"agnoeō," TWNT* 1 (1949): 116–17.

22 *Römerbrief*, p. 748.

23 There is a remarkable biblical precedent for Paul's view in Ezek. 20:25, where concern with the holiness of God himself yields a unique reflection on the statutes and ordinances that, intended for life (vv. 11, 13, 21), lead to death. The concrete allusion is to Exod. 22:28 and the enigma of a divine judgement operating in the command itself (W. Zimmerli, *Ezechiel* 1 (Neukirchen: Neukirchener Verlag, 1969), p. 449: "Die paulinische Erkenntnis vom Wesen des Gesetzes [Rö 5, 20; 7,13; Gal 3, 19] ist hier in einer eigentümlich begrenzten Formulierung von ferne zu ahnen").

24 Schoeps (*Paul*, p. 182), after remarking on the precedents in Jewish tradition for the claim that the law brings knowledge of sin, goes on to say that no Jew can follow Paul when he concludes from this that the law is a law unto death, and then refers to Rom. 8:2–3 and Gal. 3:21. But even the Jew Paul does not draw such a conclusion in the verses referred to. In Rom. 8:2 the phrase "the law of sin and death" is a shorthand summation of Paul's account in 7:7–12 of (God's) law used by sin to produce death; v. 4 goes on to refer to what God has done to turn this state of affairs around in order that "the just requirement of the law might be fulfilled." Gal. 3:21 voices Paul's conviction that the law is powerless to make alive, but that is not yet to say that the *law* (in distinction from the *letter*, 2 Cor. 3:6) kills; the very next verse explicitly makes the function of "scripture," to "consign all things to sin," subservient to the execution of the promise. The negative effects of the law are for Paul always *pen*ultimate.

25 Cf. M. J. Suggs, " 'The Word is Near You'; Romans 10:6–10 within the Purpose of the Letter," *Christian History and Interpretation: Studies Presented to John Knox* (Cambridge: University Press, 1967), pp. 289–312.

26 E.g. Käsemann, *Römer*, p. 272; on the other side, F. Flückiger, "Christus, des Gesetzes telos," *TZ* 11 (1955): 155–6.

27 *Studies*, pp. 142–3.

28 The phrase occurs, for instance, in the opening sentence of Cranfield, "Notes," p. 34. Its use here, where Cranfield is summarizing 9:6–29, illustrates the problem we are addressing. How does one come on careful reading of Romans 9 to speak at all about "Israel's disobedience," especially in the light of v. 11? What must such an interpreter be bringing with him, and whence?

29 Dahl himself (*Studies*, p. 148) sees 10:4–21 to be an important digression, in some ways logically prior to chap. 9.

30 Kuss, *Römerbrief*, p. 791.

31 Cf. Dahl, *Studies*, p. 139. I owe my initial recognition of this feature of Romans and its significance to the valuable little commentary by E. Gaugler, *Der Brief an die Römer*, 2 vols. (Zürich: Zwingli-Verlag, 1945–52), 1. 71.

32 The language used here echoes that used by Kuss, *Römerbrief*, p. 741. It is very doubtful that we should read Romans 10 as an attack ("*Generalangriff*") on Judaism at all, as Kuss does (p. 753).

33 *Römer*, pp. 269–71; cf. also "The Spirit and the Letter," *Perspectives on Paul* (Philadelphia: Fortress, 1971), pp. 138–66.

34 *Römer*, p. 265; *Perspectives*, p. 159.

35 *Perspectives*, p. 154.

36 *Römer*, p. 269.

37 Ibid., p. 270.

38 See p. 346 above.

39 See n. 24 above.

40 Dahl, *Studies*, p. 91.

Divine Initiative and
Human Response

E. Elizabeth Johnson

Romans 9–11[1] begins and ends with the praise of God who is "above all" (9:5) and from whom, through whom, and to whom are "all things" (11:36), and the passage is structured by a series of three rhetorical questions, each of which is followed by further questions that develop the theme or meet potential objections:

1	9:6	God's word has not failed [has it?][2]
	9:14	There is no injustice with God, is there?
	9:19	Why then does God still find fault?
2	9:30–2	Why did the Gentiles who did not pursue righteousness receive it while Jews who pursued the law did not attain it?
	10:14–15	How are they to call upon one whom they have not believed?
	10:18	They have heard, have they not?
	10:19	Israel has understood, has it not?
3	11:1	God has not rejected his people, has he?
	11:11	Israel has not stumbled so as to fall, has it?

There is widespread assumption among interpreters that the three primary questions asked in 9:6, 9:30, and 11:1 are synonymous, that each is a different way of asking why the Jewish majority is not Christian. The problem addressed in 9:6–29 then becomes whether or not God's word of election to Israel has been abrogated; in 9:30–10:21, the question concerns why Israel's election has in fact been rescinded; and in 11:1–27, Paul considers whether or not God might have rejected Israel permanently. So long as all three questions are understood to address the same phenomenon – Jewish unbelief – then the chapters represent three mutually exclusive answers to the same question: part of ethnic Israel's exclusion from the elect is a function of God's sovereign freedom to redefine community boundaries (9:6–29); Israel is nevertheless responsible for its own fate because it refuses to convert to Christianity (9:30–10:21); but despite God's elective freedom and Israel's culpability, God will nevertheless save all Israel (11:1–32). Paul's two incompatible convictions, that God saves all through faith in Christ alone and that God will save Israel, thus drive him to the "desperate expedient" of trying on theological hats until he finds one that fits him, unfortunately neglecting to discard the unsuitable ones once he finds it and leaving the reader to surmise that the last of the three is the hat which "really" fits.[3]

There is reason to suppose that the single problem of Jewish unbelief prompts Roman 9–11, although in the final analysis it is insufficient. Paul indeed returns at 9:1 to the unanswered questions raised at Romans 3:1–8. The advantage of the Jew is defined only partly by the claim in 3:2 that circumcision identifies Jews as recipients of divine oracles. There exists also the very real danger, given Paul's claim that circumcision has no necessary relationship to legal obedience, that God will be attacked with the same slanderous charge (that good ends might be pursued by evil means) that is leveled at Paul himself (3:8). God's covenant faithfulness to Israel is jeopardized if Israel has no faithful relationship with God (cf. "their faithlessness"; 3:3; 11:20, 23). This perspective on Romans 9–11 – that it is simply the delayed conclusion to 3:1–8 – then gives the passage the character of theodicy, an attempt to rescue God's covenant integrity from accusations of caprice or malice. The problem with this view of the chapters as no more than the delayed conclusion to 3:1–8 is that it ignores everything else that is accomplished between 3:9 and 8:39, a point to which we shall return.

The assumption that all three major sections of Romans 9–11 address the same reality of Jewish unbelief relies on a backward reading of the passage, taking the pruning of branches because of faithlessness in 11:20 to be the single source of Paul's anxiety that his non-Christian kinfolk will be cursed (9:3). When he responds to such a possibility with the claim that God's word has in fact not collapsed because not all from Israel are Israel (9:6),[4] commentators then assume that the whole of 9:6–29 constitutes a tortured redefinition of "Israel" in non-ethnic (that is, Christian) terms. If, on the other hand, one refrains from knowing ahead of time that Paul will divide Israel into the "elect" and the "rest" in 10:7, then 9:6–29 does not necessarily redefine Israel at all. It describes instead the consistency of redemptive election as divinely rather than humanly initiated. Although the pathos of 9:1–5 alerts the reader to the potential for Israel's separation from God, Paul does not explicitly raise that possibility until 9:31 and 11:1, and the argumentative function of 9:6–29 is therefore much more penultimate than is often claimed.

The assumption that all three questions (in 9:6, 9:30–1, and 11:1) are synonymous also ignores the fact that the question asked in 9:30–1 explicitly names *two* phenomena as problematic: the arrival of Gentiles at "righteousness" and the failure of Israel to arrive at "the law of righteousness." Not only do most Jews not embrace Paul's gospel, but Gentiles who never sought salvation have unexpectedly stumbled onto it. Both realities – Jewish unbelief and Gentile belief – are under consideration in Romans 10, which calls into question the claim that Israel's election is alone at stake in the argument of chapters 9–11.

Finally, the first eight chapters which bring Paul to Romans 9:1 raise more problems than the incomplete discussion in 3:1–8 of Jewish advantage. From the statement of his theme in 1:16–17, Paul has repeatedly made two parallel claims: that God is utterly impartial, dealing with Jew and Gentile on precisely the same terms, and that God is also abidingly faithful to Israel. The gospel is the power of salvation "to everyone who believes," without regard to ethnic identity or religious behavior, and it is also "to the Jew first" (1:16). Paul explicitly asserts God's impartiality five times in the letter (1:16; 2:11; 3:9, 22; 10:12), and names Jew and Gentile side by side no fewer than nine times (1:16; 2:9–10; 3:9, 29; 9:24, 30–1; 10:12; 11:25; 15:10). Throughout the first four chapters, God judges Jews and Gentiles alike to be under the power of sin and similarly justified by faith. Specifically at 3:29–30, he asks, "Or is God the God of the Jews alone? Is he not the God of the Gentiles also? Yes, of Gentiles also, since God is one."[5]

God's impartiality can never be construed as reneging on God's promises to Israel, however, which is why Paul avers at 11:29 that God's gifts and election are irrevocable, and this, too, has marked the argument of the letter from the start. The other half of the affirmation in 1:16 about God's impartial treatment of Jew and Gentile highlights God's enduring covenant faithfulness: "to the Jew first and also to the Greek." Five times he reiterates Jewish priority and advantage (1:16; 2:9–10; 3:1–2; 9:1–5; and 11:13–16). Although he constantly puts Jew and Gentile on the same footing before God, he also continues to maintain the distinctive identities of the two groups. Even as he mentions Jew and Gentile together nine times, he mentions Jews alone four times (2:17, 28–9; 3:1, 29) and Gentiles alone thirteen times (1:5, 13; 2:14, 24; 4:17; 11:11, 13; 15:9–12, 16, 18, 27; 16:4, [26]). Jews are justified "from faith" and Gentiles "through faith" (3:30); Abraham is the ancestor of all who follow in his faithful footsteps, both circumcised and uncircumcised believers (4:11–12); matters of food and drink or calendrical observance remain properly within ethnic boundaries, and although those boundaries are not allowed to divide the Church in any final sense, neither are they obliterated (14:1–15:13). Christ demonstrates God's truthfulness "in order to confirm the promises given to

[Israel], and in order that the Gentiles might glorify God" (15:8–9). Paul preserves the relative uniqueness of both Israel and the Gentiles as well as God's historic promises to Israel, even as he disallows all claims to preferred status before God.

This balanced tension between God's faithfulness and impartiality is what brings Paul to the dilemma he faces head-on in Romans 9–11: if God deals with all impartially yet remains faithful to Israel, why is the Church full of Gentiles and Jews are staying away in droves? The danger is twofold: either God has ceased to keep promises to Israel and thus cannot be trusted to keep promises to the Church, or God has become partial to Gentiles, since it is they who believe Paul's gospel, in which case God is neither impartial nor faithful. To say that Paul believes that God is both impartial and faithful is but another way to name E. P. Sanders's distinction between Paul's convictions about Christological exclusivism and covenantal nomism,[6] but it deliberately frames the distinction in terms of God rather than of human communities or entrance requirements.

To speak as Paul does of two natures or impulses or even characters of God is remarkably common, although his precise formulation of the relationship between impartiality and faithfulness in Romans is distinctly his own. The Bible itself refuses to allow God's universal sovereignty to compromise God's particular relationship to Israel or to permit God's covenant faithfulness to be restricted by nationalism (Deut. 10:17; Isa. 19:19–25; cf. 45:20–5).[7] Second-temple Judaism consistently honors the two "powers" of God, and the rabbis discuss God's two "measures" as ways of describing God's character.[8] What is most characteristic of Jews, though, as E. P. Sanders points out, is that, for them, God's merciful nature always outweighs divine wrath.[9] In Romans, on the other hand, Paul maintains the tension between divine impartiality and faithfulness to Israel without allowing one to overcome the other. Just as divine goodness, forbearance, and long-suffering serve the purposes of God's wrath at 2:4–5, so love parallels hate at 9:13, and mercy stands beside hardening at 9:18, wrath beside glory at 9:23, and goodness beside severity at 11:22. The gospel is God's power, the revelation of God's righteousness, precisely because it is both "to everyone" and "to the Jew first" (1:16).

It is this balanced tension that drives not only chapters 9–11 but the entire argument of Romans, and that contributes to the notorious difficulty of the epistle's interpretation. Paul most clearly reiterates the dynamic equilibrium between God's impartiality and faithfulness with which he began in 1:16–17 at the conclusion of chapter 11.

A1 On the one hand, as regards the gospel, they are enemies for your sake,
B1 but on the other hand, as regards election, they are beloved for the sake of the ancestors,

C1 because the gifts and election of God are irrevocable.

A2 Just as you were once disobedient to God, but now you have received mercy because of their disobedience,

B2 so they are now disobedient because of your having received mercy, in order that they also might receive mercy,

C2 because God has shut up all to disobedience in order to have mercy on all (11:28–32).

The two C lines which interpret the A and B lines set God's faithfulness to Israel and God's impartial treatment of all side by side without resolving the tension. This means that God's impartiality cannot nullify God's covenant promises to Israel, but neither can God's faithfulness be construed as loyalty which can somehow be manipulated by human behavior or identity. God's mercy is just and God's justice is merciful. The argument is advanced in three related stages.

The supreme confidence in the trustworthiness of God's love which Paul expresses in 8:31–9 is followed by a remarkable shift in tone at 9:1 that has tended to suggest more of a break than is there. Nothing can separate us from God's love, not even Paul's great sorrow and unceasing anguish for his kinfolk (9:3), precisely because (as he will argue for three chapters) God's word has not collapsed (9:6). The same word that assures the Apostle that believers can reliably hope in God also assures that "all Israel will be saved" (11:26).

Three sets of parallel assertions structure the first step in the argument:[10]

1 Ancestry is determined by God's promise rather than by human descent (vv. 6–9).
Election is based on God's call rather than on human works (vv. 10–13).
2 God's call is not arbitrary, but serves the purposes of divine wrath and mercy – e.g., Pharaoh (vv. 14–18).
God's call is not arbitrary, but serves the purposes of divine wrath and mercy – e.g., a potter's vessels (vv. 19–23).
3 Both Jews and Gentiles have been called in the same way (v. 24):
God mercifully calls Gentiles (vv. 25–6); and
God mercifully calls Israel (vv. 27–9).

The first two assertions outline aspects of common Jewish election theology: God's election is independent of human identity or behavior. Ishmael's genetic relationship to Abraham and Esau's moral superiority to Jacob are irrelevant to their ultimate roles in the people of God: Ishmael was Abraham's firstborn, but Isaac was his heir; God determined to love Jacob before either he or Esau had done anything at all – and it is Jacob who is the scoundrel. Even Pharaoh, whom everyone knows to be the very embodiment of malice toward Israel, is finally a useful tool in God's hands, a means of proclaiming God's power and name, just as clay pots perform their intended functions in the hands of their creator. All four illustrations – Isaac, Jacob, Pharaoh, and the clay pots – are designed to make the same point: that God elects on the basis of and for the sake of God's own mercy, power, and glory, rather than because of human identity or behavior. The subject of election is "not the one who wills nor the one who runs but the God who has mercy" (9:16).

The question in chapter 9, then, concerns not who is in the family and who is out, but who is in charge and to what purposes. The issue is the consistency and reliability of God's election. Prior to 9:24, there is nothing particularly "Christian" in Paul's reasoning. His employment of Isaac, Jacob, Pharaoh and the clay pots as parallel images uses biblical language and thought to say what Jews often say: that God alone initiates a saving relationship with the world. With the claim that God calls "not only from among Jews but also from among Gentiles" at verse 24, however, Paul does add a new aspect to the otherwise conventional picture he has painted, and proceeds to redefine God's people (but *not* Israel) by including believing Gentiles rather than excluding unbelieving Jews. There is no question that 11:17–24 raises the potential for such exclusion, but it is important to say that this is not in view in chapter 9.

The string of biblical proofs Paul offers in verses 25–9 supports his claim that God's self-revelation is to be found most compellingly not in the fact of an elect people, but in its being elected solely by God's mercy, apart from human claims or actions. Hosea's description of God who loves the unloved and creates a people out of no people (9:25–6) recalls the earlier descriptions of the God who justifies, raises the dead, and creates *ex nihilo* (4:5, 17). And although the emphatic "concerning Israel" that introduces Isaiah 10:22 suggests that Hosea 2:25 and 2:1 are to be applied to God's call of Gentiles, in a very real sense the words from Hosea are equivalent to Isaiah's description of Israel as rescued solely by divine mercy. Both passages highlight God's creative and redemptive action in contrast to human worth. Those who are by nature unloved un-people become God's beloved people against all odds; those who grow as numerous "as the sand of the sea" are nevertheless rescued by God's swift and sure salvation of the remnant rather than by their numbers or strength. Both these realities are encompassed by Isaiah's prophecy that, apart from God's merciful sparing of "seed" (which recalls Abraham's "seed" in 9:7) no one would survive. Although he reads verses 6–24 as excluding Jews, Richard Hays's sense of the function of verses 27–9 is on target: "Indeed, if we remember that Paul is adducing prooftexts in support of his claim that God has called vessels of mercy from among Jews and Gentiles alike (Rom. 9:24), it makes much better sense to read the Isaiah prophecy as a positive word of hope rather than as a word of condemnation."[11]

The word "remnant" from Isaiah 10:22 in verse 27 inevitably calls Romans 11:5 ("a remnant according to the election of grace") to the minds of interpreters, and wrenches attention away from God's mercy to the individual identities and confessional stances of human beings, but here again a backward reading tends to cloud interpretation of Romans 9. The movement of the argument since 9:24 has been to enlarge rather than reduce the people of God who are created by unmerited and unmanipulated mercy, so there is no reason to suppose that the direction of Paul's thought reverses itself here. The gratuitous "only" inexplicably retained by the NRSV in verse 27 to qualify "a remnant" is indicative of the widespread assumption that 9:6–29 answers the question of 11:1 rather than the question of 9:6. Isaiah 10:22 and 1:9 function for Paul to compare Israel favorably with the rest of the world by pointing to God's continual rescue of the people. Without God's preemptive mercy, Israel's peculiar relationship to the Lord of Hosts would indeed have been lost many times over and Israel would have fared no better than Sodom and Gomorrah. This means that in chapter 9 Paul is looking at God's *past* faithfulness to Israel rather than predicting the future. That issue will remain for chapter 11, where the image of the remnant will no longer suffice for the whole, and instead all Israel will be saved.

Paul's provisional conclusion, then, is that God's redemptive word of election (cf. λόγος, "word", 9:6, 28) has not collapsed with the inclusion of Gentiles because that inclusion has been accomplished on precisely the same terms as God's call of Israel. The call comes only at God's initiative, independent of human right or worth. God's impartial treatment of Jews and Gentiles is therefore a demonstration of God's faithfulness to Israel rather than an abrogation of it.

Such an affirmation raises yet another question, however, in view of the contemporary ethnic imbalance in the Church. If God consistently calls impartially and also keeps faith with Israel, then why have Gentiles reached the finish-line and left Israel in the dust? The answer is that God has rigged the race-course. Just as 9:16 explicitly precludes running as a means to attain God's mercy, so at 9:30 the image of a foot race functions to underscore divine sovereignty. Astonishingly, it is those who do not run who are the winners in this race. Paul's combination of Isaiah 28:16 and 8:14 identifies the very foundation stone of God's righteousness as the cause of offense. Paul Meyer notes that "v. 33 must count as the most remarkable of Paul's OT quotations because of what it attributes to God: placing in the midst of his people a base of security that is at the same time an obstacle over which they will stumble."[12]

The zeal of the runners (10:2) is ironically the source of their undoing. They stumble, Paul says, because they pursue the goal "as if from works" rather than "from faith" (9:32), which means that they seek to establish their own righteousness rather than submitting to God's righteousness (10:3). James Dunn has demonstrated that the language of zeal in Jewish contexts consistently refers to "a dedicated defence of Israel's distinctiveness."[13] To establish one's own righteousness is not simply to grasp after God's righteousness by individual legal perfection, which is neither what Jews do nor what Paul accuses them of doing. To establish one's own righteousness is, rather, to misunderstand the nature of righteousness, to consider it a human possession rather than divine, to be ignorant (10:3) of its impartiality as well as its faithfulness, to construe God's faithfulness *as* partiality.

The shift from the relatively passive image of stumbling over an obstacle to the more active image of refusing to submit to God's righteousness introduces an element of human responsibility into what has heretofore been an argument solely about God's power. Even Israel's failure to submit to God's righteousness and seeking to establish its own, however, is within God's design as Paul attributes its cause to the gospel proclamation. God's tripping of Israel is designed not to shame (9:33) but to save (10:1), because the very stone which causes stumbling is the rock which saves, "the word of faith which we preach" (10:8). The string of γάρ ("for") clauses in verses 2, 3, 4, and 5 explains Israel's unenlightened zeal as ignorance of God's righteousness, which righteousness is in turn identified as "Christ the end of the law" and is interpreted by the exegesis of Deuteronomy 30:12–14 in Romans 10:6–8. The elaborate explanatory pesher on Deuteronomy 30 is deeply indebted to Baruch's exegesis of the passage (Baruch 3:29), and thus predicates of the gospel what Baruch says of God's wisdom: that it is near to all without distinction (10:12). That Paul's exegesis explains what he means by saying "Christ [is] the end of the law for righteousness to everyone who believes" in 10:4 can be seen in the fact that each element of that claim is addressed and expanded in 10:5–13:[14]

end of the law	for Moses writes of the righteousness from the law – Leviticus 18:5 (Rom. 10:5)
Christ	but the righteousness from faith – Deuteronomy 30:12–14 (Rom. 10:6–8)
	if you confess . . . and believe (10:9)
for righteousness	for righteousness . . . for salvation (10:10)
to everyone who believes	it is believed (10:10); everyone who believes (10:11); everyone who calls on the name (10:12–13).

The law itself, Paul says, guards against a misconstrual of God's righteousness as Israel's possession alone. In the first place, Deuteronomy 9:4 ("do not say in your heart") warns against the human attempt to do what God has already done by bringing Christ down from heaven and raising him from the dead. In the second place, by identifying the apostolic proclamation ("the word of faith which we preach") with the wisdom of God, as Baruch does the Torah in Baruch 3:29–30, Paul claims that the gospel is the goal of God's law, near to all and alone able to make righteous.

Hays finds Robert Badenas's argument that "the end of the law" in 10:4 is its "destination"[15] so compelling that he says, "The burden of proof [now] lies strongly on any interpreter who reads τέλος ['end'] as 'termination'."[16] Although I concur with his judgement, it is clear that the case is not yet universally persuasive. Even if the longstanding division between Lutheran and Calvinist readings of τέλος were to be resolved in Calvin's favor, however, the traditional identification of the "stone of stumbling" in 9:33 with "Christ" in 10:4 would derail interpretation. The so-called "stone passages" in Romans 9:33 (Isa. 28:16; 8:14) do not carry the christological freight later Christian interpreters like Mark, Matthew, and 1 Peter place on them, since Paul does not include Psalms 118:22 as the others do.[17] Interpretes nonetheless assume that what trips up Israel in Romans is the person of Jesus, not only because the "stone" vocabulary is sometimes christological elsewhere in early Christianity, but also because the dividing line between Christians and Jews is so often solely christological.

Paul's explanation in 10:5–17 makes clear that it is not the person of Christ but what God has accomplished which brings the law to its intended purpose of making righteous. "Christ" (10:4), "the word of faith" (10:8), and "the word of Christ" (10:17) are parallel ways of referring to the gospel,[18] the proclamation of God's righteousness which includes but is not limited to the person of Christ. The stone of stumbling which ultimately saves all who trust in it is the proclamation of God's righteousness in Christian preaching. This theocentric definition of the gospel which resists a reduction of it to christology is in keeping with the rest of Romans in general and chapters 9–11 in particular, where numerous interpreters have noted the remarkable paucity of language about Jesus.[19]

Because the gospel is near to all without distinction, it bears witness to God's impartiality, but the fact that Israel has stumbled over it suggests that the gospel does not bear witness to God's faithfulness. The second half of chapter 10 therefore addresses this potential weakness in Paul's argument by asking the rhetorical questions of 10:14–15 which set up a causal chain of calling upon God's name, believing, hearing, preaching, and being sent. The worldwide proclamation of the gospel (v. 18) has resulted not in faith but in jealousy and anger. Paul's interpretation of Deuteronomy 32:21 by means of Isaiah 65:2 ("I will make you jealous of a non-nation, I will make you angry at a foolish nation . . .") reiterates the point of 9:30–3 by pointing to God's use of Gentiles to provoke Israel to jealousy. Although they have heard and understood the gospel (10:18–19) they have not believed, and this too is by God's design.

It is fair to ask in what sense the combined citation of Deuteronomy 32:21 and Isaiah 65:1–2 is an answer to the question about Israel's understanding. The Bible verses do not describe human resistance to God or human response to God's words but speak instead of God's action: the psalmist's depiction of the creation in praise of God (Ps. 18:5 LXX) again gives Paul the language to describe Christian proclamation as universally. accessible. Then in Deuteronomy 32:21 Moses predicts what in fact has taken place in Israel's encounter with the gospel. The worldwide proclamation has resulted in the unexpected finding of God by Gentiles. But far from sealing Israel's guilt, as is so often claimed, the universal preaching of the gospel serves to confirm God's faithfulness to Israel. It is not to Gentiles only that the word has been sent, but to Israel as well, which scripture confirms. Paul rearranges the words of Isaiah 65:2, shifting "all day long" to the beginning, to highlight God's *continual* reaching out to Israel.

The third stage of the argument arises from the claim that God's abiding mercy to Israel is in no way compromised by God's self-revelation to Gentiles. The question "God has not rejected his people, has he?" is answered with Paul's second use of "remnant" language (the first, in 9:27, is borrowed from Isaiah). Although the Apostle himself is an illustration of the contemporary "remnant according to the election of grace" (11:5), he emphasizes the rescue of that remnant for God's own sake by adding "for myself" to the citation from 1 Kings 19:18. Believers like Paul are the current evidence ("at the present time") that God has not transferred loyalty from Israel to the Gentiles. But unlike the traditional uses of the theme by the prophets, Paul does not allow the remnant to suffice for the whole, as will become clear in 11:11–27. For all that he holds unbelieving Israel accountable for its disobedience and contrary behavior toward the gospel in 10:21, he refuses to take credit for his own status before God in 11:6. Paul has "heard" and "known" the same gospel he says Israel has "heard" and "known" in 10:18–21. The difference is that God has called Paul but not all Israel – at least not yet. Paul will not allow human willing or running – or even believing – to manipulate God's favor. Paul's being part of the remnant is by grace alone (11:6). The division of the runners into winners ("the elect") and losers ("the rest") in 11:7 reprises the metaphor of 9:16, 30–2 within Israel. But this time, God hardens rather than trips some of the contestants by blinding, deafening, and bowing them down.

The result of such hardening, of course, is that some runners do after all stumble, but in 11:11–12 Paul addresses the temporary nature of the stumbling and its evangelical function. He reiterates what Deuteronomy 32:21 and Isaiah 65:1 predicted for him earlier at 10:19–21, that the purpose for Israel's stumbling/hardening is to allow for the Gentile mission. Just as the supposedly stronger runners in 9:30–3 are tripped up and the non-participants have become the surprise winners, so Israel's misstep means salvation and wealth for the Gentiles in 11:11–12, and Paul glorifies his Gentile mission in 11:13–16 because it in turn serves Israel's salvation. Sanders asks incredulously, "Does [Paul] really think that jealousy will succeed where Peter failed?"[20] The answer is, Yes, he apparently does, although the sharp distinction between the two forces an alternative Paul would not recognize. He thinks Israel's salvation is God's doing rather than his or Peter's, and the worldwide proclamation of the gospel in 10:18–21 encompasses the missions to both circumcised and uncircumcised (cf. Gal. 2:7–8).

Paul shares with several of his Jewish and Christian contemporaries a conviction that Israel's repentance and faithfulness to God will inaugurate the eschaton.[21] Israel's immediate positive response to the gospel could have initiated the judgement and left the Gentile world under a death sentence. Only by God's gracious restraint of Israel are the Gentiles successfully evangelized, and that without compromising the priority of the Jewish mission. The "rest" or "part" of Israel who wait for the "fullness" of the Gentiles to enter God's salvation are, like Pharaoh in 9:17 (Exod. 9:16), the means of demonstrating God's power and name. Terence L. Donaldson draws a helpful distinction between "delay" and "displacement" here.[22] Rather than replacing Israel as God's elect, Gentile Christians step in line ahead of part of Israel. The metaphor of the olive tree in vv. 17–24 envisions branches broken off and regrafted after the inclusion of wild shoots, provided they do not persist in unbelief.

To raise the possibility that some might culpably persist in unbelief (11:17–24) after the assurance that God is responsible for that unbelief (11:7–16) sharpens the tension between divine and human initiative which has been building from the start of this argument. On the one hand, God has held back part of Israel from responding to the gospel to make room for the Gentiles; on the other hand, branches have been broken off because of faithlessness and can be regrafted only if they do not persist in faithlessness. Put in such dichotomous terms, this is the "Catch-22" that Sanders and Räisänen claim dooms Paul's argument to inconsistency, his simultaneous irreconcilable convictions that God saves those who believe in Jesus only and that God saves all Israel with or without faith in Jesus. To pose the problem this absolutely, however, is finally anachronistic.

> This false dilemma pits "faith in Jesus" against the faith of Abraham who trusted in the God who gives life to the dead, where Paul aligns the two. It pits the "Father of Jesus Christ" against the God of Abraham, where Paul aligns the two. It pits Christianity against Judaism in Paul's own breast, . . . where Paul aligns the two.[23]

The mystery revealed in 11:25–6 discloses God's wise plan to save the whole world, restoring the ethnic balance in the Church and maintaining both God's impartiality and God's faithfulness to Israel. The interdependence between Israel and the Gentiles has been hinted at already at 9:30–1 and 10:18–21 and described rather explicitly in 11:11–24. Even the picture in chapter 9 of God who uses unexpected means and inappropriate people to accomplish the goals of elective mercy prefigures this description of the way "God's word has not collapsed" (9:6).

The tension Paul maintains in Romans 9–11 between God's impartiality and faithfulness results in a refinement of each as traditionally understood. Because he allows neither to overwhelm the other, divine faithfulness never becomes blind loyalty nor does divine impartiality obliterate God's eternal promises. He refashions the priority of Israel into an interdependent relationship with the Gentiles that moves far beyond what any of his contemporaries affirm. Israel's privileges are real and irrevocable, but some of them (adoption, glory, worship, and promises) are granted also to Gentiles. Israel's redemptive relationship with God is both first and last chronologically, before and after the Gentiles' inclusion. Paul's substitution of ἐκ for ἕνεκεν ("from" for "on behalf of") when he quotes Isaiah 59:20 at Romans 11:26 is crucial here. The redeemer comes from Zion to establish God's covenant with the whole world, including but not limited to Jacob. God will indeed banish impiety and forgive the sin of Israel, even as the Gentiles. The universal mercy of God as Paul describes it necessarily modifies the traditional self-understanding of Israel as having favored standing with God and the traditional function of the law as protection from sin, but both these points are argued in Romans well before chapters 9–11.

This mutual modification by divine faithfulness and impartiality of each other results in a much more subtle balance in Paul's argument between God's sovereignty and human accountability than is sometimes acknowledged. As substantially as God's power figures in this argument, and thus seems to lessen the weight of human responsibility, Romans 9–11 has a hortatory purpose: to forbid Gentile boasting over Israel's apparent rejection and to urge the Church to remain faithful. The warning in 11:21–2 cuts both ways: God's kindness and severity are for Israel and the Gentiles alike.

The extent to which unbelieving Israel remains in unbelief and Christian Gentiles remain in God's kindness is a matter of human response which is itself empowered by God's grace, much as the Roman Christians have become "obedient from the heart" to the saving gospel to which God has handed them over (6:17). This tension between determinism and voluntarism, between divine initiative and human response, is finally truer to religious experience than is either one alone. A contemporary confession of faith puts it this way: "In all these things [repentance and faith] we are responsible for our decisions. But after we have trusted and repented we recognize that the Spirit enabled us to hear and act."[24] To locate one's experience in this theological context accomplishes more than to explain one's inclusion in the elect and to justify the exclusion of others. It is also to make a particular claim about God. To affirm human responsibility this way, without in any sense limiting divine sovereignty, is to say that God's engagement with the world is intimate, complex, and subtle, neither overpowering the creation with holiness nor relinquishing holiness to accommodate human frailty.

The subtlety and complexity of this situation – that God alone hardens and has mercy and that human beings also participate in the maintenance of their own citizenship among God's people – are difficult to overestimate. Paul's failure to share the later Church's expectation of a mass Jewish conversion at the parousia is a function of his unshakeable confidence in God's power to save the world rather than any neatly worked-out logical or chronological scheme for holding competing convictions together. Paul believes that nothing – neither Jewish unbelief no Gentile presumption – will be able to thwart God's redemptive purpose, but his apostolic commission also underscorés the urgent necessity of preaching and hearing the gospel. This does not mean he is incoherent in Romans 9–11 or that he stubbornly refuses to give up Jewish faith for Christian, but somehow holds them both. In Paul's mind, the two are the same because his faith is first and finally in God.

In Paul we are dealing with a man who simply has not yet learned enough Church history to understand the differences between Christianity and Judaism, much less to recognize the distinction between two religious communities. Paul's place at the center of the canon inevitably tempts us to read his letters through the lenses of the evangelists, his own theological descendants, and the apologists, and to forget that he stands historically prior to them all. By the end of the first century, Christians are nearly unanimous in their desire to shake the dust of the Jewish mission from their feet, but Paul does not yet share their frustration, if indeed he would ever have shared it. The person of Jesus is consistently the focus of debate between those other early Christians and their Jewish neighbors, and they draw emphatically christological lines in the sand. Paul does not. Yes, the Christ is from Israel and the redeemer comes from Zion (Rom. 9:5; 11:26); Israel's salvation is without question achieved by means of Christ's death and resurrection, as is the redemption of the whole world. But for Paul those affirmations are of a piece with his claim that Abraham trusted the God who justifies the ungodly, raises the dead, and creates out of nothing, and is thus the rightful ancestor of all who believe (4:5, 17, 24).

It is not only Pauls chronological primacy which determines his distinctive perspective. Paul is a qualitatively different sort of Christian from Matthew or John or the writer of Hebrews or Justin Martyr, whose attitudes toward non-Christian Israel are finally far more influential in Church history. Paul's experience of Christ crucified and raised never replaces the one God of Israel as the source and object of his faith, but is, rather, incorporated into it in ways that most of his successors are unable to manage.

Paul says the righteousness of God is God's power to save precisely because it both judges and redeems the world's unrighteousness. This can be true only if God remains utterly impartial and also keeps promises. The hymn Paul quotes in Romans 11:33–6 in praise of God's wisdom is borrowed from the very synagogue which has shaped his knowledge and experience of God,[25] to affirm the continuity of God's saving mercy that is always trustworthy but never predicatable.

The radical newness of the gospel poses a challenge not only to Israel's eternal destiny, but more importantly to God's trustworthiness and the reliability of Paul's gospel. In the transforming present of the Christ event as Paul preaches it there lurks the danger that God's past was fruitless and the consequent risk that God's future will similarly disappoint. The Apostle responds in Romans 9–11 by calling the Bible as a witness to God's consistently innovative actions throughout history. Paul reframes the threat to God's integrity and thus disarms it without relaxing the necessary balance between the constitutive qualities of God's righteousness: impartiality and faithfulness.

Notes

1 This essay is adapted from "Romans 9–11: The Faithfulness and Impartiality of God," in *Pauline Theology*: Vol. III: *Romans*, ed. David Hay and Elizabeth Johnson (Minneapolis: Fortress, 1995), pp. 211–39, which gives a fuller account of scholarly discussion of these issues.

2 Although 9:6 is not put in the grammatical form of a question, "it is not as though" denies one possible answer to a question much like that posed in 3:3 ("does their faithlessness nullify God's faithfulness?").

3 E. P. Sanders, *Paul, the Law, and the Jewish People* (Philadelphia: Fortress, 1983), pp. 195–8.

4 Mary Ann Getty points out that Romans 9 contradicts Romans 11 only if Paul's thesis is stated not in 9:6a, "God's word has not collapsed," but in 9:6b, "not all Israel is Israel" ("Paul and the Salvation of Israel: A Perspective on Romans 9–11," *CBQ* 50 (1988): 465).

5 Although Jouette Bassler, *Divine Impartiality: Paul and a Theological Axiom* (Chico: Scholars' Press, 1982) shows that Jewish affirmations of God's impartiality are never absolute, but are qualified to one extent or another by convictions about God's particular relationship with Israel, she labels the tension between divine impartiality and faithfulness in Romans 9–11 a "logical problem" (p. 187).

6 Sanders, *Paul, the Law*, p. 198.

7 Bassler, *Divine Impartiality*, pp. 9–13.

8 E. P. Sanders, *Paul and Palestinian Judaism* (Philadelphia: Fortress, 1977), pp. 117–47.

9 Ibid., p. 124.

10 Johnson, *The Function of Apocalyptic and Wisdom Traditions in Romans 9–11* (Atlanta: Scholars' Press, 1989), pp. 147–48.

11 *Echoes of Scripture in the Letters of Paul* (New Haven/London: Yale University Press, 1989), p. 68.

12 "Romans," *HBC* (1988): 1157.

13 *The Partings of the Ways* (London/Philadelphia: SCM/Trinity, 1991), p. 121.

14 Johnson, *Romans 9–11*, p. 156.

15 *Christ the End of the Law* (Sheffield: JSOT Press, 1985).

16 *Echoes of Scripture*, p. 208, n. 83.

17 Paul W. Meyer, "Romans 10:4 and the 'End' of the Law," in *The Divine Helmsman*, ed. James L. Crenshaw and Samuel Sandmel (New York: Ktav, 1980), pp. 59–78 (and see chapter 24 of this book).

18 Johnson, *Romans 9–11*, p. 158.

19 Krister Stendahl, *Paul Among Jews and Gentiles and Other Essays* (Philadelphia: Fortress, 1976), pp. 3–7.

20 Sanders, *Paul, the Law*, p. 198.

21 Dale C. Allison, "The Background of Romans 11:11–15 in Apocalyptic and Rabbinic Literature," *Studia Biblica et a Theologica* 10 (1980): 229–34.

22 Donaldson, " 'Riches for the Gentiles'," *JBL* 112 (1993): 92–8.

23 Paul Meyer, "A Response" to Heikki Räisänen, "Romans 9–11 and the History of Early Christian Religion," 1992 SBL Annual meeting; typescript, pp. 7–8.

24 *A Declaration of Faith* (Presbyterian Church US, 1977) V. 3. 36–8.

25 Johnson, *Romans 9–11*, pp. 164–74.

Figure and Ground in the
Interpretation of Romans 9–11

Neil Elliott

1 The Legacy of F. C. Baur

Significant advances in the interpretation of Romans, and indeed of Paul's thought, have gone hand in hand with shifts in the perception of Romans 9–11. A century and a half ago Ferdinand Christian Baur challenged the "purely dogmatic" reading of Romans, which treated chapters 1–8 as a more or less self-contained "compendium of Pauline dogma" and relegated chapters 9–11 to the status of an incidental "corollary." In contrast, Baur held up the latter chapters as the "center and pith" of the letter in which Paul sought to answer the question, "how it is to be explained, that so great a portion of the Jewish people, who for ages had been the chosen people of God and the recipients of all kinds of Divine promises, had really no participation in the salvation bestowed by Christ; whilst, on the contrary, the Gentiles adopted the position left vacant by the people of God?"

The source of that question Baur located in the "direct opposition" Paul faced among Jewish Christians in Rome, who held to "the theocratic supremacy of the Jewish nation, the absolute precedence which it claimed to possess over all other nations, and of which it now saw itself about to be irretrievably deprived by the Pauline universalism." At stake in the whole of the letter, on Baur's reading, was nothing less than "the great cause of dispute between Judaism and Paulinism." The anguish Paul expressed for his fellow Jews in 9:1–5 informed the composition not only chapters 9–11 but also chapters 1–8, where Baur saw Paul striving to disentangle "confiding in the fidelity and truth of God," which Paul affirmed, from "Jewish exclusiveness," which he rejected.

The letter thus constituted, in Baur's words, "the most radical and thorough-going refutation of Judaism and Jewish Christianity."[1]

Baur's general insight into the occasional character of Romans is widely accepted today.[2] Moreover, his posing the problem of Paul's theology in terms of a tension between Jewish ethnocentrism, that is, an ideology of national or covenantal privilege, and "inclusivity" or "universalism," is currently the ascendant paradigm in Pauline studies, put forward by James D. G. Dunn and others as an alternative to the still influential "Lutheran" reading and dubbed "the New Perspective on Paul."[3] To be sure, few interpreters today are willing to oppose "Pauline universalism" to "Jewish ethnocentrism" as categorically as did Baur. It is recognized, in the first place, that Judaism contemporary with Paul held *both* "universalistic" and "particularistic" impulses in tension,[4] and second, that Paul's argument in Romans involves what J. Christiaan Beker has called a dialectical *"interaction between* Israel's particularity and the universality of the gospel for the Gentiles."[5] But the force Baur's paradigm continues to exert may be seen, to take one notable example in talmudic scholar Daniel Boyarin's recent book *A Radical Jew.* Despite his insistence that Judaism in Paul's day was not characterized by "exclusiveness in the sense that it excludes, in principle, anyone," Boyarin nevertheless interprets Paul as motivated by the tension within his ancestral religion between "narrow ethnocentrism and universal monotheism."[6]

Modern interpreters also increasingly accept Baur's contention that Romans 9–11 represent the "climax" of Paul's argument in the letter.[7] This does not mean that there is unanimity about Paul's purpose in these chapters, of course. But it is significant that Heikki Räisänen could recently declare a consensus among interpreters that Paul's "real concern" in Romans 9–11 "is the question of the *trustworthiness of God* as regards his promises to Israel." The question arises because of "Israel's being anathema," which presents "a personal difficulty" for the Apostle. Räisänen himself argues, echoing Baur, that Paul here is confronting "the worries of Jewish Christians about the implications of his gospel."[8] Just as significantly, however, a number of other commentators find the thrust of Paul's argument directed primarily against *Gentile* Christians, a theme to which we will return below.

Interpreters also disagree about the coherence of the argument Paul mounts in these chapters. Some find inconsistencies or contradictions between chapters 9 to 10, which they see as an apology (or apologies) for God's rejection of Israel, and chapter 11, where the ultimate salvation of "all Israel" is announced.[9] Older views, according to which these contradictions resulted from the unfortunate remnants of Paul's own ethnic chauvinism (C. H. Dodd, F. W. Beare),[10] are echoed in more recent assessments of the Apostle's "desperate" and logically incoherent attempts to articulate contradictory feelings about his people (E. P. Sanders, H. Räisänen).[11] Räisänen sees here "two sharply diverging solutions" to the treatment of Israel: "that empirical Israel is not elected but hardened and damned in advance to reprobation (9:6–29), and that empirical Israel – or most of it – will be saved because of God's loyalty to his promises and to the election of the people (11:11–36)."[12]

Without resorting to the expedient of labeling Paul an incoherent thinker, other interpreters have accounted for what they see as the Apostle's mixed message concerning Israel by postulating that in Romans 9–11 Paul addresses *two* audiences, one Jewish-Christian and the other Gentile-Christian, within a mixed congregation in Rome. Thus, while he recognizes that in Romans 11:13–25 Paul warns Gentile Christians against arrogance, J. Christiaan Beker argues that "the main body of the letter," including chapters 9–11, "confronts Judaism," containing a "radical polemic" against "the Jewish doctrine of election." Paul rejects "Jewish superiority" (in chapters 9–10) and "Gentile pride" (in chapter 11) alike, in a letter directed to "the Jewish-Christian and Gentile-Christian conflict in Rome."[13] Similarly, Francis Watson finds the arguments of Romans 9–10 and 11 to be contradictory on the level of theology, but intelligible on the level of social consequence. Regarding most of the letter, including chapters 9 and 10, as Paul's setting "his view of the salvation of the Gentiles *in polemical opposition to* the Jewish theology of the convenant," Watson concludes that even "Rom. 11 must therefore have some message for the Jewish Christians."[14] Both Beker and Watson thus propose a "mixed" audience as a way of explaining what W. G. Kümmel described as the "double character" of Romans, i.e. the presence of "Jewish themes" within a letter explicitly addressed to Gentile Christians.[15]

2 Toward A Reversal of Perspective

Chapters 9–11 have continued to attract attention as a significant part of the letter, even as some scholars have considered them logically incoherent and contradictory and held in question their relationship to the rest of the letter. In contrast to the interpretations just reviewed, however, other recent readings of the letter have emphasized, in the first place, the argumentative integrity of chapters 9–11, and second, their coherence within a letter that is explicitly addressed to *Gentile* Christians in Rome.

The argumentative coherence of these chapters may be perceived in the series of rhetorical questions running through them:[16]

1   9:6   God's word has not failed [has it?][2]
     9:14   There is no injustice with God, is there?
     9:19   Why then does God still find fault?
2   9:30–2   Why did the Gentiles who did not pursue righteousness receive it

> while Jews who pursued the law did not attain it?
> 10:14–15 How are they to call upon one whom they have not believed?
> 10:18 They have heard, have they not?
> 10:19 Israel has understood, has it not?
> 3 11:1 God has not rejected his people, has he?
> 11:11 Israel has not stumbled so as to fall, has it?

Further, the *logical* coherence of these chapters may be recognized once we surrender the assumption that these questions are all motivated by an attempt at theodicy, i.e. explaining or defending God's rejection of (most of) Israel. On that assumption, chapter 11 might seem quite superfluous.[17] But E. Elizabeth Johnson has shown that the focus in chapters 9 and 10 is not an attempt to account theologically for "Jewish unbelief." It is, rather, Paul's insistence, *despite* Jewish unbelief, that God's ultimate redemptive purposes (the theme that brackets these chapters: see 8:18–39 and 11:25–36) will prevail. Similarly, Stanley K. Stowers attributes the failure of interpreters like Räisänen and Sanders to perceive the logical integrity of 9–11 to their presumption that 9 and 10 concern God's rejection of Israel. To the contrary, Romans 11 "treats the view that God has rejected Israel as a misunderstanding to be corrected," a *false* conclusion that the reader might have drawn from 9–10. Stowers paraphrases the three chapters, "Yes, God's way of acting is X and Israel is Y, while the Gentiles are X, *but do not conclude Z,* " that is, that God has rejected Israel.[18]

With regard to Romans 9, Johnson refutes the widespread assumption that "the whole of 9:6–29 constitutes a tortured redefinition of 'Israel' in non-ethnic (that is, Christian) terms."[19] Thus, it is *not* Paul's intention in 9:6–31 to create a table of oppositions that effectively aligns non-Christian Jews with Israel's biblical enemies:[20]

"Abraham's true descendants" vs. Abraham's other children (9:7);
"the children of the promise" vs. "the children of flesh" (9:8);
Jacob the beloved vs. Esau the hated (9:13);
(the redeemed Hebrew slaves) vs. Pharaoh (9:17);
"vessels of mercy" vs. "vessels of wrath" (9:22–4);
"my people" vs. "not my people" (9:25–6);
Gentile Christians vs. non-Christian Israel (9:30–1).

The Apostle's theme is, rather, the sovereignty of God: in Johnson's phrase, "not who is in the family and who is out, but who is in charge and to what purposes."[21] Paul stresses the sovereignty of God's promise to Abraham; of God's electing Isaac rather than Esau "before they had been born or had done anything good or bad" (9:11–12); of the hardening of Pharaoh's heart (God "has mercy on whomever he chooses, and he hardens the heart of whomever he chooses," 9:18); of the potter's rights over the clay (9:21).

Again, the point of Paul's contrasting "vessels of mercy" and "vessels of wrath" is not the contrasting fates, glory for the first and destruction for the latter, but precisely God's freedom in "enduring with much patience" the vessels of wrath *rather than condemning them* (9:22). His point is *not* a divine dynamic of discrimination and separation, some "principle of selection" operating throughout Israel's history, as if he meant to equip his readers to identify the "elect" and the "damned" with the Jewish-Christian remnant and the vast non-Christian majority of Jews. Instead, Paul's concern is to stress God's power and freedom in creating a people out of nothing (the citation from Hosea in 9:25–6). He returns to that theme again in chapter 11, now specifying that God's life-creative power will mean the ultimate salvation of (empirical) Israel: "what will their acceptance mean but life from the dead?" (11:15).

Similarly, Paul declares God's freedom in constantly acting to preserve a remnant (the citations from Isaiah in 9:27, 29), then returns in chapter 11 to specify that *in the present* he himself is a member of the "remnant chosen by grace" (11:1–5), i.e. Jewish Christians. The point is not that Israel has survived *in part*, through the remnant (as the wholly gratuitous insertion of "only" at 9:27 in the RSV and NRSV implies),[22] but that the remnant's survival is evidence of God's sovereign redemptive action, *which guarantees the salvation of the whole*. Note that in 11:4 Paul stresses not Elijah's mournful protest as a survivor, "I alone am left," but the divine rebuke, "I have kept for myself seven thousand." The lesson for the reader is that God's redeeming purposes transcend what can be seen and measured at present.[23] Seen in this light, the assurance in 11:26 that "all Israel will be saved" is no surprise, but "a neat deduction from the logic of divine purpose and human instruments in chapter 9."[24]

The *dual* aspects of the problem addressed in these chapters – not only the "unbelief" of Israel, but the surprising belief of so many Gentiles as well[25] – are alike attributed to God's freedom, as 9:30–10:21 makes clear. Yes, Israel has stumbled, allowing the Gentiles to surpass them, but only because "God has rigged the race-course": Paul's purpose in the metaphor is "to underscore divine sovereignty."[26] The point of the metaphor is not to inquire after the nature of Israel's "fault," despite the abundance of Christian theological commentary on that problem. As Stowers declares, since God has "tripped" one of the runners, it is "silly or perverse to ask, 'How could Israel have run the race so as to have won?' " It is *God* who has caused Israel to stumble, "in order to provide opportunity for the gentiles and show that he is a just God":

> God's answer is to bring Israel to a sudden awakening by tripping her in the race and allowing the gentile runner to fly past her toward the goal. The shocking

realization that she has been passed by "ungodly gentiles" will fill her heart with a competitive zeal to catch the leader. As a result, both will end the race running well.[27]

The redemption of all Israel, explicitly announced in 11:26, is thus prepared for throughout chapters 9–10 by Paul's emphasis upon God's sheer sovereignty in election. Far from being a disingenuous and desperate last-ditch attempt to salvage some shred of hope for his people (Heikki Räisänen), Paul's insistence that he evangelizes Gentiles in order to make his people jealous "and thus save some of them" (11:11, 13) reflects his understanding of God's purposes toward Israel in scripture (see 10:19, citing Deut. 32:21). Instead of subordinating the solemn assurance of Israel's salvation as an unreflective emotional outburst "tacked on" to the "real" argument of chapters 9 and 10, we should recognize chapter 11 as the rhetorical climax toward which chapters 9 and 10 build, and beside which they are *"penultimate"* (E. Elizabeth Johnson) or *"parenthetical"* (Richard B. Hays). In Hay's words, "while Rom. 9:6–29 and 11:1–32 affirm the unshakable efficacy of God's word and God's elective will, Rom. 9:30–10:21 pauses in midcourse to describe how Israel has *temporarily* swerved off the track during an *anomalous* interval preceding the consummation of God's plan."[28]

The words I have italicized mark a shift in interpretive weighting. To the extent Romans 11 is taken seriously as genuinely expressing Paul's convictions, even forming the argumentative climax of this section of the letter, Romans 9 and 10 are no longer read as the Apostle's "last words" on the fate of Israel. The perception of contradictions across these chapters begins to disappear, just as the question being framed changes from "does God's rejection of Israel impugn God's integrity?" to "have God's redemptive purposes failed?" But this perceptive shift of figure and ground in Romans 9–11 points toward a renewed appreciation of the letter as a whole.

3 Reimagining Romans

New insights into the argumentative coherence of chapters 9–11 suggest a single, coherent audience for that argument as well.[29] In contrast to views of a "mixed" audience for these chapters (see above) – in which Paul is seen as turning from a defense of his message against *Jewish* objections (chapters 9, 10) to take a rather incidental sidewipe at *Gentile*-Christian arrogance as well (chapter 11) – several interpreters have vigorously challenged the assumption that Jewish Christians need to be imported to explain these chapters at all. "The admonition in 11:13–32 is not gratuitous," Stowers insists: "even the fundamental structure of 9–11 forms a warning to Gentiles."[30]

Stowers's close attention to rhetorical patterns throughout Romans includes the observation that the relationship of chapter 11 to chapter 9 and 10 mirrors the rhetorical structure of 1:18–2:16. "The design of both 1:18–32 and 9:6–10:21 invites the proud Gentile believer to arrogantly laud the condemnation of those other people who are sinful." Just as in 2:1–5 Paul indicts the *Gentile* reader for judging others and presuming on God's mercy while doing the same things,[31] so the discussion of Israel's "stumbling" in chapters 9 and 10 "baits the trap" for the Gentile Christian. "Chapter 1:11–16 makes the Gentile reader aware of the presumption of his arrogant and hasty conclusions; 11:17–32 describes and addresses his conceit. . . . Here we have the warning given in 2:1–5 except the letter now explicitly reveals the object of Gentile superiority: Jews who have in some sense rejected Jesus Christ or the plan to which Jesus Christ is central." The irony of Stowers's "rereading" is startling: "Generations of Christian readers have taken the apostle's bait without ever feeling the spring of the trap."[32]

But more must be said. Following the original impulse of Johannes Munck, a number of scholars, including William S. Campbell, Lloyd Gaston, John Gager, Peter Tomson, and Stanley K. Stowers, have insisted on reading the whole of Romans as directed to the audience explicitly identified in its opening and closing lines, i.e. Gentile Christians in Rome (see 1:6, 13, 15 and 15:14–16).[33] "One of my principles in reading the letter will be to take the explicit audience in the text literally unless strong reasons arise for subverting the encoded audience," Stowers declares. "Because Paul begins by explicitly describing his readers as Gentiles . . . even if I suspect that Paul 'knew in his head' that Jews or Jewish believers would read the letter, I must still account for the audience in the text, asking why he would describe his readers as Gentiles."[34] The so-called "double character" of the letter (W. G. Kümmel) cannot justify the "erasure" of the Gentile-Christian audience or the importation of an implicit Jewish or Jewish-Christian audience. Romans 9–11 show a "double character" simply because Paul "speaks to Gentiles about Jews."[35]

Indeed, the principle put forward by Stowers shifts the burden of proof onto the conventional reading, which must postulate a Jewish-Christian target for the letter's discussion of "Jewish questions." For his part, Stowers describes the conventional erasure of the letter's inscribed audience as "a hermeneutical move that facilitates reading the letter as canonical scripture of the orthodox catholic church," addressed to "an essentially undifferentiated universal audience," "universal" being assumed to mean *non-Jewish*.[36] Lloyd Gaston concurs: "Why letters specifically addressed to Gentiles should have been understood as opposing Judaism is not hard to explain. It developed as part of the displacement theory, whereby the early church thought it could claim its own legitimacy only by denying that of Judaism."[37]

Whatever the reasons behind the conventional assumption that "Jewish themes" within the letter require that Romans is "confronting Judaism" (J. C.

Beker), careful rhetorical-critical examination of patterns of argumentation throughout the letter has yielded a provocative alternative view. The letter to the Romans *in its entirety* is addressed as a paraenetic appeal to Gentile Christians in the imperial capital, encouraging them to resist a nascent Christian anti-Judaism that may already be at work among them. Important elements of this alternative interpretation include the following observations:

1　Gentile Christians are specifically and emphatically identified as the letter's addressees; Paul links his purpose in writing to the Roman Church directly to his apostolate to Gentiles (1:5–6, 13, 15; 15:14–16).[38]

2　The letter has a specifically paraenetic purpose, the "sanctification of the offering of the Gentiles" (15:16). The Gentile Christians of Rome can preserve the sanctity of this offering not only through their prayers (15:30–2) but through their positive response to Paul's appeal *in the letter itself* (15:14–15).[39]

3　The deep structure of the letter mediates a fundamental contrast between the human depravity and injustice pictured in 1:18–32 and the "true worship" demanded in 12:1–2, as Victor Paul Furnish observed almost thirty years ago:[40]

suppressing the truth (1:18) vs. refusing conformity to this age (12:1)
senseless minds (adokimos nous, 1:28) vs. renewed minds (anakainosis tou noos, 12:2)
dishonored bodies (atimazein somata, 1:24) vs. bodies presented as a holy sacrifice (12:1)
false worship (sebazesthai, latreia, 1:25) vs. "spiritual worship" (logike latreia, 12:1)
indecent conduct (ta me kathekonta, 1:28) vs. God's will (to thelema tou theou, 12:2).

Further, Furnish observes that the contrast between depravity and lack of self-control (chapter 1) and the present call for holiness (chapter 12) is possible because of Christian baptism (chapter 6): indeed "the appeals made already in chapter 6," in the context of baptism, "are simply being recapitulated and reemphasized" in chapter 12. In this regard the letter mirrors what Rudolf Bultmann described as the "once – but now" scheme of early Christian preaching and paraenesis.[41]

4　Far from being an "indictment" of the Jew or a "demolition of Jewish privilege" (Ernst Käsemann), the apostrophe to "the Jew" in Romans 2 relies upon the ancient rhetorical technique of teaching through a stylized dialogue.[42] The lessons learned, in the following chapters, through the dialogue with a Jewish interlocutor – about divine impartiality and the equal accountability of Jew and Gentile before God's justice – are brought out for the benefit of the Gentile, for it is the Gentile Christian who risks presuming on God's grace *in*

Christ ("doing evil that good may come" (3:8) = "continuing in sin that grace may abound" (6:1, 15).[43] The attack on "judging" in 2:1–6 is specifically echoed in the warnings against presumption in chapter 11 and against judging one's brother in chapters 14–15, that is, in warnings addressed to Gentile Christians.[44]

5   Against older interpretations that related Romans 9:1–5 to chapter 3 as something of an "afterthought," Paul's response to Jewish "objections" to his gospel, attention to rhetorical characteristics shows that these verses begin the climax of Paul's argument in the letter. Nils Dahl observed features in chapters 9–11 characteristic of Paul's letter openings (personal address to *adelphoi*, oathlike assurances and intercessions, references to Paul's apostolic vocation); Stowers notes that here for the first time Paul speaks with a "bold and forceful" *Jewish* persona.[45] The effect of Paul's declaration of anguish is, however personal, also a powerful rhetorical strategy by which the Apostle seeks to evoke a sympathetic response from his Gentile audience.[46]

6   Equally significant is the dramatic juxtaposition of chapter 8 and 9:1–5. Verbal and thematic echoes across the artificial chapter division show that Paul is *not* turning to a new and unrelated subject in chapter 9, nor is he giving rein to unreflected feeling. This is a rhetorical *tour de force* in which Paul catches up the solemn and joyous confidence of those who know, by the Spirit's inner testimony, that they are "the children of God" (8:14–17), and redirects it toward those to whom "the sonship" (hyiothesia) rightfully belongs (9:4). Though no power in the universe "can separate us from the love of God" (8:35–9), the Apostle would gladly "cut himself off" from Christ "for the sake of my own people" (9:3). The same Spirit that "bears witness [symmartyrein] with our spirit that we are children of God" (8:16) now "bears witness" in his conscience (*symmartyrein*) as he expresses his heartfelt anguish for his kindred (9:1).

It is crucial here to recognize the rhetorical movement from the premises Paul shares with his audience to the position he wants them to adopt.[47] "We know" by the Spirit's testimony that "we are children of God" (8:15–17); "we know" that the whole creation groans in labor pains (8:22); "we know" that God works in all things for good for the elect (8:28). From all this "*we*" must conclude that "if God is for us who can be against us?" (8:31). In contrast, Paul speaks personally, intimately, to contrast "present sufferings" with the glory "about to be revealed" (8:18); to contrast "what is seen" with "what is hoped for" (8:23–5); to contrast the forces arrayed against the elect – "hardship, distress, persecution, famine, nakedness, peril, sword," even wholesale slaughter at the hands of enemies (as the citation from Israel's scripture attests) – with the unwavering love of God (8:35–9). It is Paul who feels deep anguish for his fellow Israelites (9:1–4), who prays for them fervently (10:1), who stands before the Romans as proof that God has not abandoned the covenant people (11:1–2).

Finally and climactically, it is Paul, the apostle to the Gentiles, who addresses the Gentiles of Rome to announce to them that they are but an instrument of God's design to save Israel (11:13–15). And it is Paul who, claiming the inner testimony of the Holy Spirit (9:1) whose purposes are fathomed only by God (8:27), now reveals as an apocalyptic "mystery" (11:25) the Spirit's purpose, known to the Roman congregation only in the inarticulate groans of charismatic utterance (8:23, 26–7): the apparent hardening of Israel is only temporary, and is the wholly unpredictable way God has chosen to *save* Israel (11:26).[48]

7   Paul's warning against Gentile-Christian boasting (11:13–32) sets the immediate backdrop for his more general exhortations to "sober self-estimation" (12:3), care for the poor (12:16), and mutual love (13:8). These in turn give way to more specific instructions in 14:1–15:6 that "the strong" defer to those "weak on account of faith," that is, that Gentile Christians honor the sensibilities of their Jewish neighbors in matters of food observance. At length the chorus of praise in which the voices of Israel and the nations blend (15:9–12) echoes Paul's own doxology to the "depths of the riches and wisdom and knowledge of God" (11:33–6). *The argument of 9–11 is integrally related to the exhortation of 12–15, suggesting that the Gentile-Christian boast against which Paul warns in 11 is the immediate target of the more prosaic paraenesis that follows.*

The cumulative effect of these observations is a radically new understanding of the Letter to the Romans. Far from being a "compendium of Christian doctrine," as the Reformers thought, or (in more recent views) a theological "position paper" drafted to garner Church support for the law-free Pauline mission, Romans comes to be seen as an urgent paraenetic letter, as are all of Paul's other letters, directed toward securing the eschatological sanctity of the "offering of the Gentiles" (15:14–16) by opposing the nascent anti-Jewish "boast" among elements of the Gentile Christian community in Rome. The premises Paul shares with his audience include the perception that Israel has "stumbled," that is, that a majority of Jews have not accepted the Christian message. As Daniel Fraikin contends, this perception has by the time Paul writes Romans become a "theological fact" within Gentile Christianity,[49] inviting the sort of speculations that would become a full-blown Christian supersessionism a generation later.

In Romans, Paul is already combatting the theological infection of Christian anti-Judaism.[50] It is of utmost importance to understand Paul's rhetorical strategy here correctly. He does not contest the data, by arguing for example that there is a yet-untapped "market" for the Christian gospel among receptive Jews. Contrary to some modern interpreters, he *neither accepts the option of seeing the Jewish-Christian "remnant" as God's final answer on Israel, nor does he simply* assert Israel's privilege out of personal feeling, in contradiction to his own stated *theological convictions*. Rather, Paul argues forcefully that the Gentile Christians of Rome enjoy their standing before God through God's grace, not through their own inherent merit (chapters 1–8). Since God's purposes retain their own integrity, the present standing which the Gentiles enjoy no more exhausts God's mercy than the present standing of the majority of Israel exhausts God's justice. Understood correctly (that is, from Paul's viewpoint), the confidence the Roman converts enjoy in the Spirit (8:12–39) – no doubt one spring of their own theological boast *against* Israel – is itself the clearest proof that God's purposes toward Israel, indeed toward all creation, cannot be thwarted.

4 An Apocalyptic Theology of Liberation

In an earlier work I have suggested that the immediate context for Romans was a virulent anti-Jewish sentiment in the imperial capital, clearly attested in literary sources a few decades after Paul but surely present already in the environment of the Roman congregations in the wake of the unrest under Claudius (*c.*49) and the "war," as Claudius termed it, in Alexandria.[51] When Paul urges the Romans to refuse conformity to the mentality of "this world" (12:2), he means, at least in part, resisting the subtle coercion of anti-Jewish sentiment in the imperial capital, especially as it has begun to metastasize in the emerging supersessionism of the Gentile Christian movement (the "boast" of 11:13–26).

Is Paul's own apocalyptic answer in Romans 11 better than that emerging Gentile-Christian supersessionism?

Writing as a "Jewish cultural critic," Daniel Boyarin has revived F. C. Baur's opposition of Pauline universalism to Jewish particularism by means of an analysis of what he considers the allegorical structure of Paul's thought. For Paul, Boyarin writes, "the physical, fleshly signs of the Torah, of historical Judaism, are re-interpreted as symbols of that which Paul takes to be universal requirements and possibilities for humanity."[52] Citing the work of William S. Campbell, Boyarin is "convinced that the main point of Paul's argument [in Romans 11] is precisely to persuade Gentile Christians of the invalidity of a certain notion of supersession . . . to the effect that God has rejected the Jews *tout court* and that the new Israel is entirely Gentile Christians." He argues, however, that "from a Jewish perspective [Paul's] theology is nevertheless supersessionist." Although "Paul's doctrine is *not anti-Judaic*! It does not ascribe any inherent fault to Israel, Jews, or Judaism that led them to be replaced, superseded by Christianity, except for the very refusal to be transformed," Boyarin contends that Paul's "spiritualized and philosophical Judaism" effectively "deprives Jewish ethnicity and concrete historical memory of value by replacing these embodied signs with spiritual signifiers."[53]

> There is no more role for Israel as such in its concrete sense – except always for the promise of Romans 9–11 that in the end it will not be abandoned but redeemed by coming to faith in Christ. .... Israel has no more role to play in history. .... If the only value and promise afforded the Jews, even in Romans 11, is that in the end they will see the error of their ways, one cannot claim that there is a role for Jewish existence in Paul. It has been transcended by that which was its spiritual, allegorical referent always and forever: faith in Jesus Christ and the community of the faithful in which there is no Jew or Greek.[54]

Boyarin detects "the peculiar logic of supersession" even in Romans 11:16–24, where Paul reminds Gentile Christians that they have been "grafted" onto the olive tree of Israel:

> What we must remember as we read these verses, clearly intended as a stirring call to Gentile Christians not to despise Jews, is that the Jewish root which supports them has been continued solely in the Jewish Christians. .... *Because* Israel has not been superseded, therefore most Jews have been superseded. .... Precisely *because* the signifier Israel is and remains central for Paul, it has been transformed in its signification into another meaning, an allegory for which the referent is the new community of the faithful Christians, including both those faithful Jews (as a privileged part) and the faithful Gentiles but excluding the Jews who do not accept Christ.[55]

Boyarin acknowledges that "Surely, those left behind will in the end be gathered into this community of faith, so God's honesty has not been impugned, but for the moment at least, Jews who have not accepted Christ are simply left by the wayside." For such Jews, the "salvation" promised in Romans 11:26 is "a bitter gospel not a sweet one, because it is conditional precisely on abandoning that to which we hold so dearly, our separate cultural, religious identity, our own fleshy and historical practice, our existence according to the flesh, our Law, our difference. Paul has simply allegorized our difference quite out of existence."[56]

I dispute Boyarin's contention that "there is no more role for Israel" in Paul's thought. In light of Paul's conviction that the risen Jesus is the Messiah whose return is imminent, it is of course correct that he could not imagine the existence over centuries of Israel "in its concrete sense," by which Boyarin refers to "Jewish ethnicity and historical memory" separate from Christianity. But that is the result of Paul's apocalyptic expectation, *not* his supposed allegorizing of Israel. Precisely in Romans, Jewish existence has *not* been "transcended" for Paul by "the community of the faithful in which there is no Jew or Greek." The point of Romans 9–11 is instead to remind that very community of the eschatological significance of Israel "in its concrete sense."

Were it true that for Paul "the Jewish root . . . has been continued solely in the Jewish Christians," Romans 11 would simply not have been necessary. Boyarin regards the "branches lopped off" in 11:16–4 as "at best vestiges, at worst simply dead" in Paul's estimation.[57] But the central point of Paul's metaphor is that *God's purposes for Israel continue not only in the preservation of a "remnant" of Jewish Christians but also precisely in the continued existence of these "dead" branches*, which God can not only restore to life (11:15) but regraft into their native stock (11:23–24). In other words, I contend (against Boyarin) that "Israel" for Paul includes the "living" tree, with its ingrafted Gentile branches, *and* the "dead" branches, "those Jews who remain faithful to the ancestral faith and practice and who do not accept Jesus as the Messiah."[58] Paul's distinction between the "wild" olive branches (i.e. the Gentiles) and the "cultivated" tree and its native branches (i.e. the Jews) is precisely an insistence upon the significance of Jewish difference, "Jewish ethnicity and historical memory." The branches, *even lopped off*, remain holy (11:16). Precisely as they stand now as disobedient "enemies of God" (11:28, 30), they are nevertheless "beloved as regards election, for the sake of their ancestors, for the gifts and the calling of God are irrevocable" (11:28–9).

Boyarin has fused the traditional reading of Romans 9 ("Israel" vs. "true Israel," "children of the flesh" vs. "children of promise") with the allegorical logic of Galatians 3–4. But whatever the import of the allegoresis in Galatians for its Gentile-Christian audience,[59] Romans is directed *against* the very pseudo-universalism of the "church of Jews and Gentiles" that has distorted Paul's legacy since the writing of Ephensians.[60] Paul's fervent hope is *not* that his kindred according to the flesh will merge with the Church – that "Jews, during the course of the present age, will come to Christian faith and so be grafted back in," in "a steady flow of Jews into the church" (N. T. Wright), thus "renouncing their 'difference' and becoming the same and one with the grafted Israel of Gentile and Jewish believers in Christ" (Boyarin).[61] Rather, he hopes for nothing less than an eschatological miracle: that the entourage of Gentile converts he will lead in train to Jerusalem (Rom. 15:25–32; 1 Cor. 16:1–4) will so astound his Judaean brethren that they will spontaneously recognize the fulfillment of Second Isaiah's promises regarding the messianic age. The "offering of the Gentiles" (*he prosphora ton ethnon*, Rom. 15:16) is "the occasion that, according to Paul, will coincide with the salvation of all of Israel, as that event which according to Rom. 11:25–7 demonstrates the ingathering of the Gentiles."[62]

To be sure, Paul's hopes were doubly disappointed: by the catastrophic reception he received in Jerusalem and its aftermath, described (however flamboyantly) in Acts 21–28, and by the non-return of the Messiah. More to the point, the eschatological significance he held out for "Jewish difference" was swallowed up for subsequent Christian theology, not by his own allegorizing, but by history. As Boyarin himself puts it with regard to Romans 11:

> For the moment at least, Jews who have not accepted Christ are simply left by the wayside. *Precisely, however, as that moment stretched into millennia,* this doctrine became inevitably one of supersession even without – indeed, as it may have stood against – the sectarian formulation and violence of a community such as the one that later would produce John's gospel.[63]

The apocalyptic coordinates of Paul's thought are crucial at this point, and must not be collapsed into allegory (against Boyarin).[64] It is in "the glory about to be revealed to us," the liberation of all creation from "its bondage to decay," and "the freedom of the glory of the children of God" (8:19–23), that Paul hopes for Jews *as Jews* and Gentiles *as Gentiles* to be united: thus his vision of the chorus of Gentiles voices joining with Israel (15:9–12).[65] Being "left by the wayside" was, indeed, "the fate of the Jews in Christian history," as Boyarin declares.[66] In retrospect – looking back, for example, from the position of an Augustine – it is certainly true that "Paul had (almost against his will) sown the seeds for a Christian discourse that would completely deprive Jewish ethnic, cultural specificity of any positive value and indeed turn it into a 'curse' in the eyes of Gentile Christians.[67] But that process took place in a historical context that the Apostle himself could not have imagined, and it took place against the current of Paul's thought in Romans 11.

Instead of characterizing Paul as "the fountainhead of western universalism,"[68] I envision him in Romans with his metaphorical finger in the dike, holding back the mounting pressure of a universalism that would flood Gentile Christianity within a generation. Though it is not Boyarin's intention, I hear echoes of Paul in his own appeal for a "stubborn hanging on to ethnic, cultural specificity but in a context of deeply felt and enacted human solidarity."[69] I would agree with J. Christiaan Beker's declaration that "the primary task of the Christian toward Judaism is to safeguard the peace of the Jew in the world," not only as a fundamental human imperative and an observance of the Sixth Commandment, but as a response to Paul's message in Romans.[70]

But there is more here than an affirmation of Jewish difference on the part of an Israelite awaiting the redemption of Jewish and Gentile bodies. The Letter to the Romans is an assault against a false theology of privilege on the part of a triumphant Christian majority that vaunts to have supplanted its progenitors and the dispossessed in its midst.[71] Especially in a day in which the poorest and most vulnerable of our neighbors, in our own nation and around the globe – the hungry, the indigent, those driven from their homes and lands by poverty and war – are systematically deprived of the economic and political means of life by people of privilege acting in the name of "Christianity," Paul's message may be heard today as "a theology of and for the world in its pain and longing for justice" (N. T. Wright). If – in contrast to the traditional Christian appropriation of Paul – the message of Romans is recognized as "the very antithesis of all Christian triumphalism or imperialism," it may flower in a genuine theology of liberation, of the Spirit-inspired yearning and perseverance toward the "freeing of creation from its bondage to decay" and "the freedom of the glory of the children of God," the "redemption of our bodies" (Rom. 8:19–23).[72] For Christians, the Pauline gospel requires the renunciation of supersessionist claims over-against Judaism in the name of "universalism"; for Christians of the First World, it also means relinquishing the ideology of privilege over-against the mass of the world's poor. In Beker's apt phrase, "As Christians, we do not come to perfection without the unredeemed creation, to which our 'bodies' bear witness."[73] As Paul put it more succinctly in Romans (12:16), Christians may learn to "make your way in the company of the poor."

Notes

1 Ferdinand Christian Baur, *Paul: His Life and Works*, vol. 1, 2nd edn, trans. by E. Zeller (London: Williams & Norgate, 1873), chapter 3; see also J. Christiaan Beker, *Paul the Apostle: The Triumph of God in Life and Thought* (Philadelphia: Fortress, 1980), chapter 5.

2 On the occasion and purpose of Romans see, for example, the essays in Karl P. Donfried, ed., *The Romans Debate*, revised edn (Peabody: Hendrickson Publishers, 1991).

3 James D. G. Dunn, "The New Perspective on Paul," *Bulletin of the John Rylands Library* 65 (1983): 95–122. Daniel Boyarin recognizes the affinity between the "New Perspective" and Baur's synthesis (*A Radical Jew: Paul and the Politics of Identity* (Berkeley, Los Angeles, London: University of California Press, 1994), pp. 10–11 and passim).

4 Alan Segal, "Universalism in Judaism and Christianity," in *Paul in His Hellenistic Context*, ed. Troels Engberg-Pedersen (Minneapolis: Fortress, 1995), pp. 1–29; Boyarin, ibid., chapter 1.

5 J. Christiaan Beker, "The Faithfulness of God and the Priority of Israel in Paul's Letter to the Romans," in *The Romans Debate*, p. 330 (emphasis added). Similarly Bruce W. Longenecker speaks of Paul's "dynamic awareness of the process whereby God works in history with a particular people [= Israel] for the salvation of humanity" (*Eschatology and the Covenant: A Comparison of 4 Ezra and Romans 1–11* (JSNTSup57; Sheffield: JSOT Press, 1991), p. 265.

6 Boyarin, *A Radical Jew*, pp. 52, 54. Boyarin acknowledges the similarity of his interpretation to Baur's, noting, however, that "where I am generously critical [of Paul], Baur waxed panegyrical": he objects in particular to Baur's characterization of Judaism as "a lower state of religious consciousness" (p. 11).

7 So, for example, Krister Stendahl, *Paul among Jews and Gentiles* (Philadelphia: Fortress, 1976), p. 4; William S. Campbell, *Paul's Gospel in an Intercultural Context: Jew and*

Gentile in the Letter to the Romans, Studies in the Intercultural History of Christianity 69 (Frankfurt am Main: Peter Lang, 1991), p. 43; N. T. Wright, *The Climax of the Covenant: Christ and the Law in Pauline Theology* (London and Minneapolis: T. & T. Clark and Fortress, 1991), p. 234. Stanley K. Stowers, *A Rereading of Romans: Justice, Jews, and Gentiles* (New Haven: Yale University Press, 1994), p. 293; Beker, *Paul the Apostle*, p. 87.

8 Heikki Räisänen, "Paul, God, and Israel: Romans 9–11 in Recent Research," in *The Social World of Formative Christianity and Judaism: Essays in Tribute to Howard Clark Kee*, ed. Jacob Neusner et al. (Philadelphia: Fortress, 1988), pp. 178, 181.

9 Francis Watson, *Paul, Judaism, and the Gentiles: A Sociological Approach*, SNTS Monograph Series 56 (Cambridge and New York: Cambridge University Press, 1986), pp. 168–74. Räisänen declares that in Rom. 11, "God has not rejected his people . . . Instead, Paul has rejected the thrust of his argument begun in 9:6" ("Paul, God, and Israel," p. 189).

10 C. H. Dodd found here "the emotional interest in national hopes which [Paul's] estrangement from his nation had not destroyed" (*The Epistle of St Paul to the Romans* (New York: Harper & Row, 1932), p. 151); F. W. Beare saw the apostle "attempting to salvage some remnant of racial privilege for the historic Israel . . . in spite of his own fundamental position" (*St Paul and His Letters* (Nashville: Abingdon Press, 1962), p. 97).

11 "What is interesting is how far Paul was from denying anything that he held deeply, even when he could not maintain all his convictions at once without both anguish and finally a lack of logic" (E. P. Sanders, *Paul, the Law, and the Jewish People* (Philadelphia: Fortress, 1983), p. 199); Räisänen considers this the most persuasive solution to these chapters ("Paul, God, and Israel," p. 196).

12 Räisänen, "Paul, God, and Israel," p. 192.

13 Beker, *Paul the Apostle*, pp. 75, 77, 86–8, 92.

14 Watson, *Paul, Judaism, and the Gentiles*, pp. 170–1.

15 W. G. Kümmel, *Introduction to the New Testament*, trans. H. C. Kee, rev. ed. (Nashville: Abingdon, 1975), p. 309; Beker, *Paul the Apostle*, pp. 75–6; Campbell, *Paul's Gospel in an Intercultural Context*, p. 53; on the letter's "double character" as a rhetorical-critical problem, see Neil Elliott, *The Rhetoric of Romans: Argumentative Constraint and Strategy and Paul's Dialogue with Judaism* (JSNTSup 45; Sheffield: JSOT Press, 1990), pp. 11–43.

16 E. Elizabeth Johnson, "Divine Initiative and Human Response," chapter 25 of this book, p. 356.

17 At 9:29 "the reader hardly feels that the treatise should go on. Nothing seems to be lacking; there is no need for a continuation" (Räisänen, "Paul, God, and Israel," p. 184).

18 Johnson, "Divine Initiative," p. 359; Stowers, *A Rereading of Romans*, p. 298.

19 Johnson, ibid., p. 357.

20 Against Räisänen, "Paul, God, and Israel," p. 182; Richard Hays, *Echoes of Scripture in the Letters of Paul* (New Haven: Yale University Press, 1989), p. 67.

21 Johnson, "Divine Initiative," p. 361; see also Elliott, *The Rhetoric of Romans*, pp. 263–9.

22 Elliott, *The Rhetoric of Romans*, p. 266, n. 2; Hays, *Echoes of Scripture*, p. 68.

23 Elliott, *The Rhetoric of Romans*, pp. 263–5.

24 Stowers, *A Rereading of Romans*, p. 301.

25 Johnson, "Divine Initiative," p. 362.
26 Ibid., p. 362.
27 Stowers, *A Rereading of Romans*, pp. 305, 316.
28 Johnson, "Divine Initiative," p. 365; Hays, *Echoes of Scripture*, p. 75.
29 Stowers distinguishes the encoded or inscribed audience of a text from the empirical audience, which in the case of Romans is no longer accessible to us (*A Rereading of Romans*, pp. 21-9).
30 Ibid., p. 298.
31 One of the most important aspects of Stowers's work on diatribal forms in Romans is his demonstration that Rom 2:1-5 is *not* a rhetorical "trap" set for *the Jew*, contrary to the near ubiquitous reading. "It is anachronistic and completely unwarranted to think that Paul has only the Jew in mind in 2:1-5 or that he characterizes the typical Jew" (*The Diatribe and Paul's Letter to the Romans* (Chico: Scholar's Press, 1981), p. 112). See also Elliott, *The Rhetoric of Romans*, pp. 119-127, and Stowers, *A Rereading of Romans*, pp. 100-9. One great disappointment in Boyarin's *A Radical Jew* is that he has not taken an analysis like Stowers's into account but relies instead on the conventional reading (pp. 86-95); ironically, since just that reading has served so well the Lutheran dogmatics Boyarin hopes to discredit (p. 11)!
32 Stowers, *A Rereading of Romans*, p. 299. Another irony: despite his insistence that "the whole letter, even 9-11, directs itself toward gentile readers" (p. 287) and despite his critique of conventional efforts to "import" Jewish Christians into the audience of Romans (pp. 22-33), Stowers himself feels compelled to make an occasional claim that Paul "also opposes Jews who would attempt to redeem gentiles by teaching them parts of the law" (p. 286; see also pp. 36, 300), without any exegetical substantiation.
33 Johannes Munck, *Paul and the Salvation of Mankind*, trans. Frank Clarke (Atlanta: John Knox Press, 1959), pp. 200-1; Campbell's important essays since 1972 are gathered in *Paul's Gospel in an Intercultural Context*; Lloyd Gaston, *Paul and the Torah* (Vancouver: University of British Columbia Press, 1987); John Gager, *The Origins of Anti-Semitism: Attitudes toward Judaism in Pagan and Christian Antiquity* (New York: Oxford University Press, 1985); Elliott, *The Rhetoric of Romans*; Stowers, *A Rereading of Romans*; and Peter Tomson, *Paul and the Jewish Law: Halakha in the Letters of the Apostle to the Gentiles* (Assen: Van Gorcum; Philadelphia: Fortress, 1990).
34 Stowers, *A Rereading of Romans*, p. 30.
35 Ibid., p. 33; Campbell, *Paul's Gospel in an Intercultural Context*, p. 54.
36 Stowers, ibid., pp. 26, 33; on the *false* universalism of most Christian interpretation of Paul see Boyarin, *A Radical Jew*, passim.
37 Gaston, *Paul and the Torah*, p. 8.
38 Elliott, *The Rhetoric of Romans*, pp. 69-86.
39 Ibid., pp. 86-93.
40 Victor Paul Furnish, *Theology and Ethics in Paul* (Nashville: Abingdon, 1968), pp. 99-106; Elliott, *The Rhetoric of Romans*, pp. 97-8.
41 Furnish, *Theology and Ethics in Paul*, pp. 105-6; Rudolf Bultmann, *Theology of the New Testament*, vol. 1 (New York: Charles Scribner's Sons, 1955), pp. 72-3, 105-6; Elliott, *The Rhetoric of Romans*, pp. 69-70, 277-8. On "self-control" as the thematic key to Romans see Stowers, *A Rereading of Romans*, chapter 2.
42 Ernst Käsemann, *Commentary on Romans*, trans. G. W. Bromiley (Grand Rapids:

Eerdmans, 1980), p. 78. See Stowers, *The Diatribe and Paul's Letter to the Romans*, pp. 106–15; Elliott, *The Rhetoric of Romans*, pp. 119–27.

43 Campbell, *Paul's Gospel in an Intercultural Context*, pp. 25–42.

44 Wayne A. Meeks, "Judgment and the Brother: Romans 14:1–15:13," in *Tradition and Interpretation in the New Testament: Essays in Honor of E. Earle Ellis*, ed. G. F. Hawthorne and O. Betz (Grand Rapids: Eerdmans, 1987), especially pp. 290–2.

45 Nils Dahl, "The Future of Israel," in *Studies in Paul* (Minneapolis: Augsburg, 1977), pp. 139–42; Elliott, *The Rhetoric of Romans*, p. 257; Stowers, *A Rereading of Romans*, pp. 289–91.

46 Elliott, *The Rhetoric of Romans*, pp. 258–63.

47 "From start to finish, analysis of argumentation is concerned with what is supposed to be accepted by the hearers. . . . When a speaker selects and puts forward the premises that are to serve as foundation for his [*sic*] argument, he relies on his hearers' adherence to the propositions from which he will start" (Chaim Perelman and L. Olbrechts-Tyteca, *The New Rhetoric: A Treatise on Argumentation*, trans. John Wilkinson and Purcell Weaver (Notre Dame: University of Notre Dame Press, 1969), p. 65).

48 On the apocalyptic background of the term see R. E. Brown, "The Semitic Background of the NT *mysterion*," *Biblica* 39 (1958): 218–40; Beker, *Paul the Apostle*, p. 334; on the charismatic experience behind Romans 8, Käsemann, *Commentary*, pp. 229–52.

49 The phrase is borrowed from Daniel Fraikin, "The Rhetorical Function of the Jews in Romans," in P. Richardson and D. Granskou, eds., *Anti-Judaism in Early Christianity*, Vol. 1: *Paul and the Gospels* (Waterloo: Wilfrid Laurier, 1986), pp. 91–106.

50 Elliott, *The Rhetoric of Romans*, pp. 271–75, 279–83; and *Liberating Paul: The Justice of God and the Politics of the Apostle* (Maryknoll: Orbis, 1994), pp. 214–16; compare Stowers, *A Rereading of Romans*, p. 36; Campbell, *Paul's Gospel in an Intercultural Context*, passim.

51 Elliott, *Liberating Paul*, pp. 215–16; John Gager, *The Origins of Anti-Semitism* (New York: Oxford University Press, 1984), pp. 63–88.

52 Boyarin, *A Radical Jew*, pp. 7–8.

53 Ibid., pp. 25, 202, 205.

54 Ibid., p. 151.

55 Ibid., pp. 201–2.

56 Ibid., pp. 203, 152.

57 Ibid., p. 204.

58 Ibid., p. 202.

59 Boyarin takes Galatians as the hermeneutical key to Paul's thought (ibid., p. 4). Unfortunately he does not proceed exegetically or rhetorical-critically, but constructs an allegorical scheme from Galatians 3–4 that is presented as the structure of Paul's thought (chaps. 3–5). One result is the lack of a clear picture of the *purpose* of Galatians. We are told at one point that "Paul's theme in Galatians is his dissent from the notion that one particular people could ever be the children of God to the exclusion of other peoples," a notion Boyarin attributes to Jewish Christianity (p. 23). Yet he at last admits that "Paul's opponents [in Galatians] are not actually Jewish Christians," but Gentiles who "do not keep the Law, nor do they intend that their converts will keep the Law – they are essentially in agreement with Paul – but they cave in to pressure from the conservative wing of the Jerusalem church" (p. 116). Rather than substantiate this scenario through the text, however, Boyarin returns on the next page to generalizations about Paul's "Jewish-Christian opponents".

60 Beker, *Paul the Apostle*, pp. 334–5.
61 Wright, *The Climax of the Covenant*, pp. 248–9; Boyarin, *A Radical Jew*, p. 204.
62 Beker, *Paul the Apostle*, p. 379, n. 65, following Johannes Munck, *Christ and Israel: An Interpretation of Romans 9–11*, trans. Ingeborg Nixon (Philadelphia: Fortress, 1967); idem, *Paul and the Salvation of Mankind*, pp. 301–8; and Dieter Georgi, *Die Geschichte der Kollekte des Paulus für Jerusalem* (Hamburg-Bergstet: Reich, 1965).
63 Boyarin, *A Radical Jew*, p. 203 (emphasis added).
64 Ibid., pp. 35–6.
65 Beker, *Paul the Apostle*, pp. 345–6.
66 Boyarin, *A Radical Jew*, p. 206.
67 Ibid., p. 229.
68 Ibid.
69 Ibid., p. 257
70 Beker, *Paul the Apostle*, pp. 338–9.
71 For further discussion see Elliott, *Liberating Paul*, pp. 214–26.
72 Wright, *The Climax of the Covenant*, p. 256.
73 Beker, *Paul the Apostle*, p. 364.

Index

2452605

CPSIA information can be obtained
at www.ICGtesting.com
Printed in the USA
BVHW042000190919
558962BV00017B/138/P

DATE DUE
